Introduction to infant development

Introduction to infant development

SECOND EDITION

Edited by

Alan Slater
University of Exeter, UK

Michael Lewis
University of Medicine and Dentistry of New Jersey

OXFORD
UNIVERSITY PRESS

OXFORD

UNIVERSITY PRESS

Great Clarendon Street, Oxford OX2 6DP

Oxford University Press is a department of the University of Oxford.
It furthers the University's objective of excellence in research, scholarship,
and education by publishing worldwide in

Oxford New York

Auckland Cape Town Dar es Salaam Hong Kong Karachi
Kuala Lumpur Madrid Melbourne Mexico City Nairobi
New Delhi Shanghai Taipei Toronto

With offices in

Argentina Austria Brazil Chile Czech Republic France Greece
Guatemala Hungary Italy Japan Poland Portugal Singapore
South Korea Switzerland Thailand Turkey Ukraine Vietnam

Oxford is a registered trade mark of Oxford University Press
in the UK and in certain other countries

Published in the United States
by Oxford University Press Inc., New York

British Library Cataloguing in Publication Data
Data available

Library of Congress Cataloging in Publication Data
Data available

Typeset by Laserwords Private Limited, Chennai, India
Printed in Great Britain
on acid-free paper by
Ashford Colour Press Ltd, Gosport, Hampshire

ISBN 978–0–19–928305–7

10 9 8 7 6 5 4 3 2 1

To Theresa, Adam and Sam, for inspiration and memories (AS)
To Suzanne, whose intelligence and support makes all things possible (ML)

Preface

Infancy is the time of life during which enormous changes take place—the helpless newborn seems almost a different creature from the active, inquisitive 2-year-old. Although accounts of infant development date back many centuries, the scientific study of infancy really began in the 1960s when ways of investigating early development were found, and it is true to say that the study of infant development is a truly modern science.

Our aim in producing this textbook is to offer a representative, comprehensive and completely up to date, 'state of the art' account of infant development. We appreciated that this needed to be an edited book rather than one written by the two editors, since one can be an expert in a couple of fields of study, but not all! By making it an edited book that fulfilled our aims of a comprehensive textbook we first decided the areas that needed covering, specified in some detail the topics for each chapter, and then invited the world's leading experts to write the chapters. Our invitations were received with enthusiasm, and we have been extremely gratified at the ways in which our authors have responded to our suggestions, and we are confident that the book reads well and coherently as a whole.

In preparing the second edition we have taken guidance from reviewers and added new chapters to give more complete coverage, and the authors of chapters that were in the first edition have made their contributions completely up to date. New chapters are: 4, Motor development: How infants get into the act; 6, The development of intelligence in infancy; 8, Perception and knowledge of the world; 9, Memory development; 10, Language development: From speech perception to first words; 16, Early intervention research, services and policies; 17, Culture and infancy; 18, Health, nutrition, and atypical development.

The book is organized into five parts, each concerned with different aspects of development and each containing two or more chapters. Here are brief comments on each part.

Part 1—History and Methods. In order to see how our current knowledge of infancy has developed the student needs to be aware of the history of infancy research, and of the several methods that have been developed since the 1960s to explore development in preverbal infants. These are described in Chapters 1 and 2.

Part 2—The Foundations of Development. The development of the infant has a starting point, and in Chapter 3 we have an account of biological and psychological development from conception to birth. In order to act upon, learn about, and communicate with the world the infant has to have functioning motor (action) and sensory systems. We know that many important motor and sensory developments take place in the womb, and Chapters 4 and 5 continue the story of their development after birth.

Part 3—Cognitive Development. Cognition refers to our ability to reason and to make sense of the world, and the study of cognitive development is a major area of research. In Chapter 6 we have an overview of major theories of infant cognitive development, followed in Chapter 7 by an account of infants' ability to categorize objects and people—without the ability to categorize, the world would be an impossibly complex place. In Chapter 8 infants' growing understanding and knowledge of the world, and Chapter 9 describes the development of memory. What has become clear is that an understanding of speech begins in the womb, and by the time infants produce their first word, around a year from birth, they have a detailed understanding of speech sounds and words. These developments, and the child's first words, are the focus of Chapter 10.

Part 4—Social Development. The infant is born into a complex social world. Much of its early development is learning about that world by engaging in social interaction and with communication with others. One of the most important social stimuli for infants (and adults!) is the human face, and Chapter 11 gives an account of how infants perceive faces. If we observe newborn infants we see a rather narrow range of emotional behavior—they display pleasure, distress, and interest. By 3 years of age these same children display a wide range of emotions. Development takes place within the social network that surrounds the infant, and the story of social and emotional development is discussed in Chapters 12 and 13. All humans and even nonhuman primates play. Chapter 14 describes the changing nature and purpose of play throughout infancy.

A major theme throughout Part 4 is that social development can only be understood in relation to developments in children's verbal and cognitive abilities. This theme is emphasized in Chapter 15: young infants communicate by acts like crying, but the cry of the newborn is certainly not an *intentional* communication; by the end of the first year the infant is able to communicate intentions through symbolic gestures and words, and can read the intentions of others through their social signals.

Part 5—Early Interventions, Culture, Nutrition, and Health. Not all infants are born into an ideal world, able to fulfill their potential. This sad fact alerts us to many social concerns—how can we (parents, communities and governments) improve the life course of children in adverse circumstances or at risk for developmental delay? These important issues are discussed in Chapter 16. Chapter 17 describes the effects that differing cultural backgrounds have on infant development, and Chapter 18 illustrates the intertwining of nutrition and health in fostering normal development in infancy, and demonstrates how problems that impact these two factors, along with other circumstances, may move an infant toward atypical development.

The text is designed for a broad range of readers, and in particular those with little previous exposure to psychology. The comprehensive coverage and emphasis on core topics on infant development make it an appropriate text for introductory students. We owe enormous thanks to our authors, and to Oxford University Press who have encouraged us from the start, and have been patient with the delays.

Alan Slater and Michael Lewis

May 2006

Contents

Part 3   Cognitive Development

Part 4   Social Development

Part 5   Early Interventions, Culture, Nutrition, and Health

List of Contributors

Karen E. Adolph — Department of Psychology, New York University, New York, USA

Margaret Bendersky — Institute for the Study of Child Development, University of Medicine and Dentistry of New Jersey, Robert Wood Johnson Medical School, New Brunswick, New Jersey, USA

Marc H. Bornstein — Child and Family Research, National Institute of Child Health and Human Development, Bethesda, Maryland, USA

J. Gavin Bremner — Department of Psychology, University of Lancaster, Lancaster, UK

Ila Deshmukh — Eliot-Pearson Department of Child Development, Tufts University, Medford, Maryland, USA

M. Ann Easterbrooks — Eliot-Pearson Department of Child Development, Tufts University, Medford, Maryland, USA

Anne Fernald — Department of Psychology, Centre for Infant Studies, Stanford University, California, USA

Tiffany Field — Touch Research Institute, Department of Paediatrics, University of Miami, Florida, USA

Peter Hepper — Wellcome Trust Fetal Behaviour Research Centre, School of Psychology, Queen's University of Belfast, Belfast, Northern Ireland

Jane S. Herbert — Department of Psychology, University of Sheffield, Sheffield, UK

Maria Hernandez-Reif — Touch Research Institute, Department of Paediatrics, University of Miami, Florida, USA

George J. Hollich — Department of Psychological Sciences, Purdue University, West Lafayette, Indiana, USA

Derek M. Houston — Department of Otolaryngology Head and Neck Surgery, DeVault Otologic Research Laboratory, Indiana University School of Medicine, Indianapolis, Indiana, USA

Vikram K. Jaswal — Department of Psychology, University of Virginia Charlottesville, Virginia, USA

Amy S. Joh   Department of Psychology, New York University, New
                                    York, USA

Scott P. Johnson   Department of Psychology, New York University, New
                                    York, USA

Judith H. Langlois   Department of Psychology, University of Texas at Austin,
                                    Texas, USA

Robin Gaines Lanzi   Georgetown University Center on Health and Education,
                                    Washington, DC, USA

Michael Lewis   Institute for the Study of Child Development, University
                                    of Medicine and Dentistry of New Jersey, Robert Wood
                                    Johnson Medical School, New Brunswick, New
                                    Jersey, USA

Jayanthi Mistry   Eliot-Pearson Department of Child Development, Tufts
                                    University, Medford, Maryland, USA

Olivier Pascalis   Department of Psychology, University of Sheffield,
                                    Sheffield, UK

Paul C. Quinn   Department of Psychology, University of Delaware,
                                    Newark, USA

Craig T. Ramey   Georgetown University Center on Health and Education,
                                    Washington, DC, USA

Sharon Landesman Ramey   Georgetown University Center on Health and Education,
                                    Washington, DC, USA

Jennifer L. Ramsey-Rennels   Department of Psychology, University of Nevada Las
                                    Vegas, College of Liberal Arts, Las Vegas, Nevada, USA

Alan Slater   School of Psychology, University of Exeter, Devon, UK

Margaret W. Sullivan   Institute for the Study of Child Development, University
                                    of Medicine and Dentistry of New Jersey, Robert Wood
                                    Johnson Medical School, New Brunswick, New
                                    Jersey, USA

Catherine S. Tamis-LeMonda   New York University, Steinhardt School of Education,
                                    Applied Psychology, New York, USA

John Worobey   Department of Nutritional Sciences, Rutgers University,
                                    New Brunswick, New Jersey, USA

PART ONE

History and Methods

CHAPTER ONE

A brief history of infancy research

MICHAEL LEWIS and ALAN SLATER

Our earliest memories

There are two interesting and apparently simple questions to which everyone will have an answer. The questions are 'What is the earliest thing you are sure you can remember?' and 'How old were you?' If you ask a group of people these questions, perhaps a class of students, you find that the age of the earliest memory is around 3 years 4 months, and that there are some interesting trends—the age of earliest memory increases over birth order (firstborns have the earliest memories), females have earlier ones than males, and, curiously, it is earlier for Caucasian than Asian children (Mullen, 1994). Interestingly, children aged 6–9 years have earlier first memories (about 3 years) than older children and adults: the 3-year-olds 'are able to verbally retrieve memories from a period of their lives to which they later have little or no verbal access' (Peterson et al., 2005).

Here is one of the earliest memories recounted by the great infant and child psychologist, Jean Piaget:

... one of my earliest memories would date ... from my second year. I can still see, most clearly, the following scene. I was sitting in my pram [stroller], which my nurse was pushing in the Champs Elysée, when a man tried to kidnap me. I was held in by the strap fastened round me while my nurse bravely tried to stand between me and the thief. She received various scratches, and I can still see them vaguely on her face. Then a crowd gathered, a policeman with a short cloak and a white baton came up and the man took to his heels. I can still see the whole scene, and can even place it near the tube station. (Cited in Sants & Barnes, 1985)

Notice the vividness and clarity of this dramatic incident. The remarkable thing about it is that it never happened! Piaget believed this until he was around 15, at which time the truth was told to him—his nurse had simply made up the story, for which she received a reward (a watch) and the gratitude of his parents—and much later she confessed! It turns out that many early (and later) memories bear only a slight resemblance to the truth—memory plays tricks and often what we think we remember is actually an inaccurate recollection of something which (as in Piaget's case) may never have happened.

These considerations tell us two things. One is that it is pointless to study infant development by asking adults and children to think back to their infancy, because we can't remember it! The other is that when people do give accounts of early memories we can't trust them because they may not be a true record of what happened. Neither can we trust parents' reports of their infant's development. For example, mothers will give very unreliable accounts of developments which, at the time, were of great importance–'When did your baby first take solid foods?'–'When did he/she first start to walk?'

Baby diaries

From what has been said so far, it is clear that in order to begin to study infant development we cannot rely on memory, whether this is our own early memories, or others' memories of their infant's development. The first scientific attempts to record infant development are known as **baby diaries** (or sometimes **baby biographies**) in which someone close to the infant (mother, father, or guardian) make detailed written observations of aspects of the child's development from birth to 2 or 3 years of age.

These diaries are notable for at least two main reasons: (1) they give us an insight into child-rearing practices and theories at different ages, and (2) they give insights into important aspects of infant development. Here we will give accounts taken from four baby diaries to illustrate these themes.

The seventeenth century—King Louis XIII of France

In 1601 Louis the Dauphin (the title given to the oldest son of the king of France) was born to King Henri IV of France. The king's physician, Dr. Jean Héroard, began a lengthy journal which continued until Héroard's death in 1628. Louis became King Louis XIII in 1609 and died in 1643. During infancy Héroard recorded Louis' play with peers, temper tantrums, nightmares, the beginnings of language development, and discipline. Louis was not weaned until he was 2 (being breastfed by wet nurses) and for the first 9 months he was swaddled—that is, his body was tightly wrapped—in the belief that this would make his limbs strong. Henri IV wrote to Louis' governess insisting that he be whipped regularly:

I command you to whip him every time that he is willful or naughty, knowing by my own experience that nothing else did me so much good. (Wallace, Franklin & Keegan, 1994, p. 4)

Fortunately, Louis managed to make it to 2 years old before he received his first whipping, and presumably as a 9-year-old king was able to tell them to stop! It is worth noting that Dr. Héroard was against this practice and recommended that instead we teach children 'rather by the way of gentleness and patience than by harshness.'

In these short extracts we have an example of child-rearing practices (early swaddling) and of 'folk theories' of parental practices—kindness or harshness. We will comment on the first of these in the next few extracts, and on the second a little later.

The eighteenth century—Dietrich Tiedmann

The German philosopher Dietrich Tiedmann kept a diary of his son's development from his birth in 1781. This detailed record is often referred to as the first scientific diary, but we will focus here only on one set of observations. Like the future Louis XIII 180 years earlier, this child was swaddled in order to prevent free movement of the limbs, and Tiedmann recorded of his 19-day-old son that:

If now for short periods his hands were released from their swathings, he beat and scratched himself painfully . . .
(Wallace *et al.*, 1994, p. 5)

Fortunately for the infant, a fairly short period without being swaddled reduced the number of such 'self-beatings.' The practice of swaddling infants, which has been around for thousands of years, was intended to strengthen the limbs by preventing too much wasteful and uncoordinated movement, but, as we have seen, when released from their wrappings infants are liable to harm themselves unintentionally. Why might this be the case? One clue came from a study by Melzack and Scott (1957). They reared puppies in an environment intended to remove any unpleasant experiences—there were no hard edges, no steps, and if they fell over they experienced no harm. A very interesting effect was observed when the puppies were exposed to a noxious stimulus in the form of a lighted candle. What happened then was that the puppies, who were naturally curious, put their noses in the flame, yelped, and gave other signs of distress, but they didn't take their noses out of the flame!

As we now understand it, what was happening was this. The puppies, just like the infant Louis and Tiedmann's son, have learned that their movements—in the infants' case muscle movements of the arms—have no negative consequences, and the longer your environment tells you this, the more ingrained the learning. When you then find out that your own movement can lead to painful consequences, it takes a while to unlearn old habits. We know that this is a general principle throughout development. For example, when infants first begin to crawl, around 9 months of age, they have a tendency to fall down stairs and get into dangerous situations, simply because they don't know the possible consequences of their actions.

The nineteenth century—Charles Darwin

Charles Darwin (1809–1882) is widely regarded as the greatest naturalist of the nineteenth century, and his powers of observation were sharpened by his 5-year round-the-world voyage on the *H.M.S. Beagle* (from December 1831 to October 1836). Not long after his return, on 29 January 1839, he married his cousin Emma. Their first child, William Erasmus Darwin (nicknamed Doddy) was born on 27 December 1839. Shortly afterward Darwin began a diary record to detail his son's early development, but this account was not published until 1877, by which time he and Emma had had another nine children, five boys and four girls: thus Darwin was able to compare his eldest child with his others. We will give three extracts from this account in order to illustrate some of the strengths and weaknesses of such biographies.

Seeing

With respect to vision,—his eyes were fixed on a candle as early as the 9th day, and up to the 45th day nothing else seemed thus to fix them; but on the 49th day his attention was attracted by a brightly coloured tassel . . .

Hearing

Although so sensitive to sound in a general way, he was not able even when 124 days easily to recognize whence a sound proceeded, so as to direct his eyes to the source.

Anger

When two years and three months old, he became a great adept at throwing books or sticks, etc., at anyone who offended him; and so it was with some of my other sons. On the other hand, I could never see a trace of such an aptitude in my infant daughters; and *this makes me think that a tendency to throw objects is inherited by boys* (italics added).

Despite the fact that Darwin was one of the finest observers of natural behavior who has ever lived, we now know that his account of the development of vision and hearing is wrong. As is described in Chapter 5, we know from careful experimentation that although vision at birth is poor it is sufficient for the infant to begin learning about the visual world: for instance, within hours of birth infants show some preference to look at their mother's face when hers is shown paired with that of a female stranger. We also know that newborn infants can localize sounds at birth, an ability that Darwin was unable to detect in his son, even at 124 days (4 months).

Darwin assumed that children brought up in the absence of physical punishment will display less antisocial behavior in later life. We can compare this view with those of King Henri IV and Dr. Jean Héroard, mentioned earlier. Henri IV, in demanding that his son Louis be whipped regularly, was expressing the belief embodied in the expression 'Spare the rod and spoil the child'—the belief that the failure to use harsh physical punishment carries with it the possibility, if not the certainty, that the child will grow up to be disobedient, and his/her very soul may be at risk. This belief has been prevalent in views of child-rearing. Here is part of a letter from Susanna Wesley (a woman of strong religious beliefs) to her son John Wesley (the founder of the religious movement known as Methodism) about how to rear children, written in 1728:

Let him have nothing he cries for; absolutely nothing, great or small; else you undo your own work ... make him do as he is bid, if you whip him ten times running to effect it. Let none persuade you it is cruelty to do this; it is cruelty not to do it. Break his will now, and his soul will live, and he will probably bless you to all eternity (cited in Sants & Barnes, 1985, p. 24).

Charles Darwin and Jean Héroard were of the opposite persuasion, perhaps captured in the expression 'like begets like'—that children should be reared with gentleness and patience and the absence of physical punishment. The findings from many years of research have shown that Darwin and Héroard were right: that is, the use of punishment is not a good way of changing behavior, and children disciplined with the use of physical punishment are more likely to misbehave and become aggressive. Of interest, even today, is the controversy in child-rearing with most experts agreeing that reasoning is the best parenting practice, while a few still argue that it is more important to control children's behavior and teach them to obey their parents' wishes. Here is an extract from the famous poem 'If a child lives' by Dorothy Lawe Holt which expresses this view—the complete poem can be found at *www.scrapbook.com/poems/doc/1559/14.html*

If a child lives with criticism she learns to condemn
If a child lives with hostility he learns to fight
BUT
If a child lives with approval she learns to like herself
If a child lives with acceptance and friendship he learns to find love in the world

The twentieth century—Jean Piaget

We have already referred to Piaget, and an account of his views on infant development is given in Chapter 6. Jean Piaget (1896–1980) was born in Neuchâtel, Switzerland, and his first publication—an account of an albino sparrow—appeared when he was aged 11. This short paper marked the beginnings of a brilliant scientific career, during which he published over 60 books and several hundred articles, most of them on child development.

He began his exploration of infant development by making very detailed records of the development of his own three children, Jacqueline, Lucienne, and Laurent. But Piaget was not content simply with observing his infants' development. He would note an interesting behavior and then, in order to understand it better, he varied the task to note any changes in the infant's response. This technique, which is a combination of observation and loosely structured experimentation, is known as the **clinical method**. Here is a brief extract (Piaget, 1954, pp. 177–178) to illustrate the procedure. Piaget is observing his son Laurent (aged 6 months 22 days) when reaching for objects:

Laurent tries to grasp a box of matches. When he is at the point of reaching it I place it on a book; he immediately withdraws his hand, then grasps the book itself. He remains puzzled until the box slides and thanks to this accident he dissociates it from its support.

Piaget's reasonable interpretation of this observation is that when one object is on top of, and hence touching, another object, his infant did not realize that there were two objects. In fact, it was not until he was 10 months old that Laurent

immediately grasps matchboxes, erasers, etc., placed on a notebook or my hand; he therefore readily dissociates the object from the support. (p. 178)

Piaget's observations and experiments enabled him to develop a theoretical account of the development of reasoning and thinking that is still influential, and he was one of the first to begin systematic experimentation of infants' development.

Coming of age: towards the present day

In the last 50 years there have been enormous advances in our understanding of infant development. In the past, theories and speculations about infants had come from those who had strong views but no evidence, and from the many baby biographies which really began the systematic study of infant development. There are some drawbacks to baby biographies. For example, the biographers may have biases which lead them to note anecdotes supporting their own theories, so that their observations may be unsystematic and biased. However, there are many strengths of such accounts: (1) the biographer can give a detailed account of subtle changes in behavior because of his/her intimate knowledge of the child; (2) the observations can lead to the production of theories of child development, which can then be given a more systematic (often experimental) test.

The proper understanding of infants awaited the development of research methods that could reveal the nature of the perceptual, cognitive, and social abilities of creatures who, by definition, are unable to speak. Many of these research methods are described in detail in the next chapter, so we will give just a few illustrations here, from investigators who told us that the worlds of infants could be explored and that it revealed a fascinating world of change and development.

The first studies: social development

The scientific interest in infancy can be traced from several important events which all occurred around the 1950s and 1960s. To begin with, the psychoanalytic tradition started by Sigmund Freud extended into research with children, even very young ones. Wolf's work with infants raised without their mothers in hospitals and orphanages gave rise to the ideas of 'hospitalism' and 'anaclitic depression,' both of which describe infants' depression brought about by the absence of their mothers (Wolf & Wolff, 1947). A bit later, John Bowlby, a British psychoanalyst, working for the World Health Organization, wrote a 1951 monograph, which continued the psychoanalytic tradition, now called **object relation theory**, and said that the mother was the most important person in the infant's life and that her absence constituted a significant loss for her infant. At the same time, there were any number of other scientists working with infants who believed that the effects of the loss of the mother were due to the general loss of all positive stimulation, and that if this was supplied by others, it would not lead to failure to thrive (see Leon Yarrow's 1961 excellent review of this work). The argument continued in the 1960s with the classic work by Sally Provence and Rose Lipton (1962) on orphans in institutions which concluded that the loss of the mother mainly affected infants' development because there were not enough consistent caregivers to satisfy the social and emotional needs of the infant.

This argument in regard to the social and emotional needs of the infant lead to a series of volumes published under the editorship of another English psychologist, Brian Foss, who edited four excellent volumes on infants' social and emotional development. Among these reports is the work of the American psychologist Harry Harlow and his wife Margaret, who published widely on nonhuman primates (Harlow & Harlow, 1965). The Harlows' work gave an important boost to the argument that biological forces dictated the importance of the mother (not the father) in the infant's life. The Harlows' work, as reviewed in Chapter 13, involved isolating infant macaque monkeys and letting them live alone, away from other infants and their mothers. They found and reported the same phenomenon that Wolf had observed in hospitalized infants, namely that these monkeys failed to thrive when separated from their mothers. Indeed, when they were raised alone, they showed severe problems in their social and emotional development. They failed to mate properly when they were sexually mature and, when they did give birth, these motherless mothers were abusive and uncaring, often killing their infants. From this, Harlow argued that mothers are biologically important for their infant's development.

There were several problems with these studies, the most important of which was that the infant monkeys were not only raised without their mothers, they were raised in social isolation. Alone in a cage, they could not see other monkeys nor make physical contact with them. Were the results of Harlow's studies the result of not being with their mothers or, as has been claimed, being without proper stimulation? As it turns out, for the most part, raising these infants with other infants without mothers at all takes care of the problem. Even Harlow thought that the peer system was equal to that of the mother (Harlow, 1969). As for the mothering of the motherless mothers, it also turns out that with the birth of each new infant, these mothers got better and better at raising their young. This suggests that these mothers, raised without mothers, could do the job if they got some experience.

In the study of infant social development, Michael Lewis, in Chapter 13, has argued that this controversy can be handled by considering the infant as being born into a social network and that the child's evolutionary task is to adapt to that larger network, which includes mother, father, siblings, and peers. If only the mother is present, her absence is highly destructive to the infant's development, but if there are others present, then the infant has the ability to adapt (Lewis & Takahashi, 2005).

As you can see, this argument anticipated the contemporary arguments on the risks of infant daycare (i.e., care away from the home, with a child minder or a preschool nursery provision). The results are in, and they show that if infants receive good infant care, they thrive as well as mother-reared infants (NICHD, 1997).

This work of the 1950s and 1960s has relevance for our own times and represents, long before the work on perceptual and cognitive development, that the study of infants was well on its way.

The next studies: attentional and cognitive development

William James, in his book *The principles of psychology* (1890), talked about two different kinds of attention, one passive and one active. In passive attention, the infant is drawn toward an object or sound because the stimulus pulls the child; for example, a loud noise automatically causes the child to hear the sound and to jump with startle. It was the other kind of attention, the active one, that was of more interest for him and has mostly occupied the work of others since his classical work.

Active attention involves the infant's interests and association and the child attends because of these associations. An infant will look longer at the face of his mother than a stranger because the mother is associated with the infant's care and the satisfaction of his/her needs. It is this type of attention that has been the chief concern of infant researchers, although as you can see in Chapter 5 by Alan Slater, Tiffany Field, and Maria Hernandez-Reif, infants' sensory capacities have also been studied by using attentional processes.

Although Darwin had observed infants in the late nineteenth century, and there were early studies of infants' social behavior, infants' perceptual and learning abilities were not studied. This is also because of William James' belief that infants, and certainly newborns, could not see or hear and could not learn; in fact, he called the infant's world a 'blooming, buzzing confusion.'

This state of affairs lasted until the late 1950s and early 1960s, when Robert Fantz (1958, 1964) conducted a series of studies using a very simple technique. He presented an infant with two pictures—one an all-gray pattern and one a striped pattern. Looking at the infant's face from a peephole, he could see the reflection on the infant's pupil, and could tell which picture the infant was looking at. Fantz found that infants preferred to look at the more complex picture, whether it was on the left or right side. This told him that the infants could see, and that they preferred to look at the more complex picture. These findings excited the research community and they quickly realized that infants had many perceptual capacities: that they could see, hear, and smell, and that they had preferences. It also indicated that many of these capacities were present at birth and did not have to be learned. That they were inborn and innate meant that part of Piaget's theory about the role of learning was wrong and needed to be revised.

Tom Bower was one of the first to demonstrate that training and conditioning procedures could be used with young infants in order to explore their visual worlds. In an early experiment (1966), he trained (conditioned) infants to turn their heads whenever they saw a cube of a particular size—if they turned their heads when the cube was there, a hidden experimenter suddenly appeared and 'peek-a-booed' at the infant (she smiled and nodded, tickled the baby's tummy, and then disappeared from view). Once the babies were conditioned, they were shown either the same cube at a different distance, or a larger cube that was farther away. Would the babies recognize the same-size cube despite the change of distance? It turned out that they did—they turned their heads when this cube was shown (expecting the reinforcing adult), but not when the different-sized cube was shown. This was an experiment on what is called **size constancy**—appreciating that an object is the same size despite changes to its distance from the infant. Size constancy has even been shown in newborn infants (see Chapter 5) and variations on this conditioning procedure are much used in exploring infant development.

At about the same time Fantz was publishing his studies, researchers were studying other attentional processes. Lewis and colleagues (1963) and

Kagan and Lewis (1965) were exploring attentional processes, looking at whether the child was looking at visual information, and studying their physiological responses. Changes in heart rate—how many heartbeats per minute—was shown to be related to looking. Infants who looked intently at a picture slowed their heart rates. From these studies of looking patterns and physiological responses, researchers were now able to study infants' abilities in several areas of development (Lewis, Kagan & Kalafat, 1966; Lewis, Kagan, Kalafat & Campbell, 1966). The use of heart rate also allowed for the study of the infant's auditory processing, since infants do not reliably turn their heads while listening.

The Russian researcher Sokolov (1963), a student of Pavlov's work, was interested in one particular aspect of attention. He wanted to know what would happen if you looked at the same picture over and over again and what would happen if you changed the picture. He found that for adults, seeing the same picture led to increasing boredom and, therefore, a decrease in looking at the picture. However, when the picture was changed, adults renewed their interest and again looked a lot. This procedure was used by Lewis, and led to a published monograph about infant attention (Lewis, Goldberg & Campbell, 1969). Lewis found, as had Fantz, that as infants got older, they showed faster disinterest (habituated faster) than younger infants. He also showed that infants who were born with birth difficulties showed slower habituation than normal infants, and finally, and most interestingly, he found that the speed of habituation was related to the IQ of preschool children. This last was particularly important, since infant IQ tests were not very good at predicting subsequent IQ. These findings and more, using different techniques and measures, were explored by a large number of early infant researchers including Robert McCall, Leslie Cohen, and Jeffrey Fagan. Of even more interest was the understanding that rate of habituation and recovery could be used as measures of other aspects of infant development.

Emotional development

The emotional development of infants was one of the most recent areas of infant studies to receive much attention. By 1983, when Michael Lewis published the first volume on emotional development, he reported that between 1933 and 1979 on average only 7% of the pages of the leading textbooks were devoted to emotional development. Since the mid 1980s, the research on emotional development has blossomed, although there were earlier works that led the field (Lewis & Rosenblum, 1974, *The origins of fear*, for example). In 1979, the U.S. Social Science Research Council started a discussion group called SAD which stood for Social Affective Development, the outcome of which was published in a book on the measurement of emotion (Izard, 1982).

In fact, it was the ability to measure emotion that led to its burgeoning development. Charles Darwin is often considered to be the leader of the study of emotions, since in 1872 he published a book called *The expression of emotions in man and animals*. In it, he described emotions as sets of action patterns which had significance because these behaviors were adaptive. For example, anger was an action pattern of facial and bodily behaviors designed to overcome an obstacle to a desired goal. Darwin also described two classes of emotions, those that emerged early which were for him the primary emotions and those which required the development of cognitions, which he called the self-conscious emotions. His descriptions of the action patterns was further developed by Sylvia Tomkins (1962; 1963), in a set of books which lead directly to elaborate measurement systems developed by Paul Ekman (Ekman & Friesen, 1978) and Cal Izard (1983). These measurement systems, utilizing the movements of the facial muscles, notably those around the eyes and mouth, gave researchers a way to reliably measure such emotions as fear, anger, sadness, joy, and disgust (see Lewis, Chapter 12). Having a measurement system that everyone would agree on led to the growth of the research on emotions, allowing the direct measurement of their expressions rather than relying on self-report, a procedure impossible in infants!

Lewis and Michalson, in *Children's emotions and moods* (1983), were the first to articulate a theory about emotional development. In it, the two classes of emotion that Darwin discussed, the primary emotions and the self-conscious emotions, were linked in a developmental model which showed for the first time the interface between the emotions and their development, and their dependency upon the growth of cognitive skills, most notably the development of the self as cognitive representation. This research was an outgrowth of Lewis's earlier research on the development of consciousness. Borrowing the idea of self-recognition in minors from Gordon Gallup's (1977) work with chimpanzees, Lewis and his colleagues developed techniques for measuring self-recognition which they argued was really a measure of consciousness or the idea that 'that's **me**, in the mirror.' By applying rouge to an infant's nose and standing (or sitting) them in front of the mirror, they found that somewhere between 15 and 24 months, infants can recognize themselves by touching their noses, not the mirror image (Lewis & Brooks-Gunn, 1979). This ability, along with the growth of personal pronouns, like 'me' or 'mine' and the onset of pretend play, represent the origins of consciousness.

It was the onset of consciousness that allowed for the development of the self-conscious emotions, notably embarrassment, pride, shame, and guilt, most of these emerging by 3 years of age. Thus, the work of Darwin and his observation of his son's own development of moral sense at the age of 3 years of age, was confirmed 100 years later by using the research teachings developed during this time. Chapter 12 on emotional development describes this in some detail.

Current developments

Over the last 20 years or so two other interrelated strands of research, connectionist modelling and neuroscience, have assumed increasing importance in our understanding of infant development. We give the briefest of introductions to them here.

Connectionism

Connectionism is a modern theoretical approach, which developed from information processing and uses computer programs to test models of development. It combines biological and computational knowledge. Computers are programmed to simulate the action of the brain and nerve cells (neurons). The programs often create so-called artificial **neural networks** and, although there is an enormous number of such networks in existence, they all have three things in common:

- First, the network is given some initial constraints or guides to learning. This is typically a starting point that represents innate abilities or a particular level of development.
- Second, the network is given an **input** that represents the experiences a child might have.
- Third, the neural network acts on the input in order to produce an **output**, which should resemble the sort of learning seen in real life.

Through the construction of such models, connectionists (advocates of connectionism) hope to gain insights into the way in which learning and development take place in the real world, and how the physiological processes taking place in the brain result in a given behavior, or in changes of behavior. Connectionist models have been applied to many areas of infant development, e.g., perception, attention, learning, memory, early language, problem-solving, and reasoning. As an example, O'Toole *et al.* (1991) created a connectionist model of face perception which was trained with a number of faces from a given race and found that it produced an 'other race' effect such that it was better able to discriminate between faces from that race. This would predict a similar effect that has recently been found with Caucasian and Chinese infants (Kelly *et al.*, in press a). These authors found that by 3 months of age infants prefer to look at adult faces from their own race (i.e., Caucasian infants preferred to look at Caucasian faces and Chinese infants preferred to look at Chinese faces) whereas newborn infants of both races showed no preferences. Many researchers see connectionism as one of the best ways of modeling human cognition and cognitive development. With respect to infant development, such models enable us to clarify the starting point of particular aspects of development, and how higher levels of cognitive or mental functioning emerge from lower levels of functioning.

Neuroscience

Increases in our understanding of the human brain and its development increasingly enable researchers to link brain development with social, motor, language, and cognitive development. Clearly, the brain is involved in all behavior and all development, and there are known to be very many functions, from memory to motor development, whose development is associated with particular (i.e., localized) brain areas. Accordingly, the researcher's task is to see how the growth and development of different brain areas have an effect on development. We will give just one example, concerning the origins and development of face perception. **Prosopagnosia** is a curious disorder in which those with the condition have great difficulty in perceiving and recognizing faces; they may not recognize even very familiar faces including family members and friends. It is usually an acquired disorder, resulting from brain injury later in life, perhaps as a result of a stroke, and it can leave object recognition relatively intact, implying a neural dissociation between face and object perception. In an intriguing paper Farah, Rabinowitz, Quinn and Liu (2000) describe an individual case study:

Adam sustained brain damage at one day of age as a result of meningitis, and one area of the brain that was lesioned (i.e., destroyed) was the fusiform gyrus, a structure in the temporal lobe, which is known to be associated with face perception in adults. When Adam was tested at 16 years of age he displayed the classic symptoms of prosopagnosia, which suggests that the neural substrate for face perception is present at birth and that other neural structures cannot 'take over' if this area is damaged, even as young as one day from birth.

Studies like these are increasing our understanding of how brain development affects and allows development to take place, and the extent to which brain areas are specialized or localized for particular psychological functions.

Key issues in infancy research

A number of key issues have dominated research into infant development and you will encounter these as you read the chapters of the book. Here we describe three related issues: the nature/nurture debate; stability vs. change; are infants active or passive in their development?

The nature/nurture debate

We are all a product of the interaction of two broad factors: **nature**—our inheritance or genetic factors, and **nurture**—environmental influences or our upbringing. It is important to note that without both factors no development could occur! For example, it has been argued that humans are genetically predisposed to acquire language, but which language we acquire is determined by the language(s) we hear and learn (Chapter 10). We will see many examples of the nature/nurture issue in this book. As examples: do infants have to learn to see? (Chapter 5); is motor development caused by maturation (a term which means development that reflects genetic influences and not environmental ones) or is it influenced by the environment? (Chapter 4); are infants born with an innate knowledge of the human face? (Chapter 11). The nature/nurture issue arises in all aspects of development, even the development of the fetus (Chapter 3).

Stability vs. change

Infancy can be characterized by its rapid change—the 2-year-old is so very different from the newborn baby in almost every characteristic. Change is an important part of development. Piaget argued for an orderly sequence of change; all infants go through the same sequence of stages. In some sense then, human infants develop in the same manner.

The question of stability and change is one of the most discussed topics in development. The question has to do with whether differences between infants remain the same—i.e., they are stable—or do differences between infants change? Is the infant who first sits up the same infant who first walks? Does the infant who shows more fear of strangers at 8 months remain the same infant who is fearful of new situations when she is 2 years old?

This question continues to be asked, since it has important social policy implications. For example, some believe that what infants are like in the first 2 or 3 years will tell us what they will be like when they are adults. Because they believe in stability, they feel that the more they do for the infant, the better will be the adult. Social policy is designed to make the first years as good as possible and so the most money should be spent early, since later it is too late. Such a view fits well with the psychoanalytic view, except that Freud argued that the first 6 years were important whereas John Bowlby (1969) and Mary Ainsworth and colleagues (Ainsworth, Blehar, Waters & Wall, 1978) have argued that it is the first year, where the infant forms its attachment to the mother, that is the most important. Their concept is what Lewis in his book, *Altering fate: Why the past does not predict the future* (1997), calls the **inoculation theory**. When you inoculate the baby against diseases, it is forever safe from them. So, too, it is with the early relationship with the mother. A good mother–infant relationship or attachment forever protects the infant. On the other hand, psychoanalysts also believed that people could change; that is, the purpose of therapy was to allow us to separate out the early bad experiences from future experiences.

The view of change, rather than stability, is an optimistic one, meaning that if infants have a bad childhood, they are not doomed, but can change. The research that follows children over long periods of time is called **longitudinal**

research. Most of the longitudinal studies that have been done show only a little stability over age. In fact, as the distance between ages increases, the stability decreases. The idea of stability rests on the notion that forms and functions, once developed, cannot easily be changed by the environment in which the child lives. The idea of change rests on the notion that environments have profound effects on children and that if the environment changes, so, too, does the child. An environment approach is often contrasted with the more biological view, since it is often assumed that if it is biological, it is fixed. The most recent brain research, however, now sees the brain as continuously changing with the creation of new connections between neurons. Gerry Edelman, a Nobel laureate, has argued for something he calls **neural Darwinism**, which means for him that neurons are connected, grown, and maintained as a function of the kind of intellectual activities the infant is engaged in. Increasingly, then, the idea of change as a function of the environment rather than stability seems to best characterize many of the infant's capacities.

Is the infant passive or active in development?

What has become clear is that the infant and the child are active in shaping their own development. That is, they are not simply dependent on others and moulded in any direction that parents and environmental influences dictate, but actively involved in learning and making sense of their worlds. Their development of consciousness, this idea of 'me,' facilitates this growth and change. Perhaps, this is nowhere better seen than in the examples of the 'terrible twos'—the time where infancy ends. Up until the age of 2, infants generally do what their caregivers tell them to do. However, somewhere around 2, infants start to say 'no.' The infant has now started to develop a sense of itself; it is no longer just part of the mother or father, but is now a separate self with its own needs and wants. What appears to be a problem turns out to be an important marker in the infant's development.

SUMMARY

A comprehensive picture of infant development is emerging as researchers use a variety of observational and experimental procedures to explore different aspects of development. The systematic study of infant development began with the early baby biographies or diaries, and the experimental study of development really began with Piaget's observations and experiments. In the last half century more and more techniques have been developed to help us understand how infants sense, feel, and know, and it is to these that we turn next.

CHAPTER TWO

Basic methods in infant research

MARGARET BENDERSKY and MARGARET W. SULLIVAN

Introduction and overview

In just 3 years, infants change from being totally dependent creatures to active children who understand much about their immediate social and physical world. Because infants cannot tell us directly what they know and feel, researchers must devise ways to discover these answers. Many of the techniques used to study infants were developed in the last half of the twentieth century. Better recording equipment; electronic control and automation of stimulation; more accurate, automated measurement; and of course, the computer, put new and more sophisticated tools into the hands of scientists. This chapter surveys some of the innovative methods for answering questions about how and why infants behave the way they do. It is impossible to review all of the methods currently in use for studying young infants in these few pages, so we have concentrated on the most widely used methods. The chapter begins by describing the three general methods used in infancy: naturalistic observation, developmental assessment, and experimental designs. Discussion of some of the specific procedures used in infant research then follows, organized by major questions about infant development. We will highlight those methods that have become 'classics' and that have spanned the various areas of infant research.

How do researchers figure out what nonverbal infants know and feel?

Even if you have limited experience with infants, you probably have many questions about how infants change from helpless, naive creatures to 'real' people. They are likely to be some of the same questions that researchers have asked over the years: for example, are infants born with different personalities? The answers to such questions are not at all simple or obvious.

As you will see from the chapters in this book, many continue to generate active research and sometimes controversial findings.

The methods of study that researchers choose will depend, in part, on the particular question of interest. Researchers may choose to observe the everyday, spontaneous behavior of infants, interfering as little as possible with the setting and participants. This method, used in the baby diaries described in Chapter 1, is called **naturalistic observation**. Alternatively, researchers may choose to measure the progress infants are making toward attaining specific milestones. They may compare an infant's progress to the average age when developmental milestones are reached based on large representative samples of infants using **standardized developmental tests**, questionnaires, or scales developed for this purpose. Or, they may use **experimental designs** developed to observe infant behaviors under controlled conditions that the researcher manipulates. There are two basic forms of experimental methods. In one, researchers randomly assign infants to conditions that differ from each other in one critical way. The research question is answered by comparing infants in these conditions, known as **experimental** and **control** conditions. For example, to study how a mother's presence affects her infant's response to strangers, infants are randomly assigned either to have their mothers present (experimental) or not (control) when a stranger approaches. The critical difference is mother's presence. Systematic differences can be attributed to whether or not the mother was there when the stranger approached.

In the other common experimental method, groups of infants are identified for study on the basis of some characteristic of interest and the responses of this target group are compared to a similar group without the characteristic. For example, infants born prematurely would be compared to full-term infants under the same controlled conditions.

Whatever their approach, researchers always try to obtain information that is accurate, objective, and can be replicated. Reliability, validity, and generalizability of findings are three standards that mark good research methods. **Reliability** refers to whether the same behaviors will be observed if the study is repeated. Usually this is addressed by having a second observer record the same behavior. Do two observers agree, for example, that a baby played with a particular toy for the same amount of time? Seem simple? Consider this case: The baby pauses for 2 seconds and then resumes play. Is this counted as one continuous play period or two? Researchers make their decisions based on the questions they are asking, and determining whether such fine distinctions can be coded reliably. The observations are considered to be reliable only if the inter-rater agreement is high, usually at least 80%. The observations also must be **valid**, or relevant to the research question posed. To insure validity, researchers often will use behaviors shown to be relevant in previous work. Or, alternatively, they may figure out several ways to measure the same underlying behavior. For example, (1) beginning to cry when a stranger approaches, (2) looking at mother anxiously, and (3) avoiding the stranger, are all behaviors that should measure wariness—fearful behavior infants often display after about 7 months of age. Finally, the best studies generate knowledge about infant behavior that can be extended beyond the specific context of the study. That is, the new finding explains behavior under many conditions or for infants in general, not the particular groups of infants who were studied. This is called **generalizability of findings**. As we describe techniques researchers have used to obtain answers to some of the questions listed, keep in mind that each has met acceptable standards of reliability, validity, and generalizability.

Relation to later chapters

Many of the procedures and methods in this chapter will be cited again in later chapters because they have been used to test theories and hypotheses about various aspects of infant behavior from sensory capacity to conceptual knowledge, from memory to emotion. First encountering basic descriptions of these methods here will enhance your understanding of specific findings and lead to a better appreciation of how researchers go about answering the major questions of our field. We have organized the research questions into major areas of psychological functioning such as sensory capacity, mental abilities, and socio-emotional behavior, although some questions fall into more than one area.

Sensory capacities

Sensation is the basis for taking in the world. Most of us have the full range of senses—seeing, hearing, feeling, tasting, touching. Unlike many other mammalian species, most of our senses are functional at birth, although some refinement occurs as a result of maturation of the nervous system and exposure to environmental stimulation. It is important to find out if newborns have the basic sensory capacities and are developing properly, because if not, their further mental (cognitive) and emotional development may be compromised. Some methods can detect responses to stimuli presented in one or more sensory domains to even very young infants.

Do young infants see and hear the things we do?

Tracking

One of the earliest signs that an infant can see and hear is tracking behavior. Normally, newborns will turn their eyes and heads in the direction of an interesting sound or sight, especially a human voice or face. Tracking is used to determine an infant's early visual integrity. Similarly, a startle is a normal reaction to an unexpected loud noise. A reduction in movement and head turning indicate the ability to hear softer sounds. Recently, the technology for tracking eye movements has entered the twenty-first century with the availability of automated systems (Aslin & McMurray, 2004).

A behavioral instrument often used to measure tracking ability is the **Neonatal Behavioral Assessment Scale** (NBAS; Brazelton, 1984). The examiner attempts to elicit the best performance by bringing the infants through a careful progression of states designed to arouse and then calm them. The NBAS has six orientation items to measure the infant's attention and tracking of inanimate stimuli and the examiner's voice and face. A failure to orient to any of these stimuli indicates that a newborn may have a serious vision or hearing problem.

Habituation

One of the most often used experimental methods to examine infants' perceptual abilities is based on the principle of **habituation**. Infants prefer to pay attention to novel sights, sounds, smells, and temperatures rather than familiar ones. This principle has been used in assessment by presenting the same stimulus repeatedly (familiarization) to see if the infant stops paying attention to it. Then a novel stimulus is introduced. If the infant has habituated to the familiarized stimulus, the novel stimulus will re-engage their attention (Sokolov, 1963; Colombo, 2000). This procedure can easily be used to test sensory abilities by varying specific characteristics of the familiar and novel stimuli, for example the shape of a visual stimulus, its movement, or different speech sounds.

High-amplitude sucking

A reliable measure of a young infant's attention to sound is called **high-amplitude sucking**. Young infants can control the rate and pressure at which they suck, and will suck even if they are not obtaining food. Infants are given a nonnutritive nipple to suck that is connected to a pressure transducer. When the sucking pressure reaches a predetermined level, a stimulus goes on. This has been used in habituation procedures to determine if infants can tell the difference between two sounds. A sound goes on when the infant sucks sufficiently strongly. Once the sucking pressure declines, it is assumed that the infant has habituated to the redundant stimulus. If infants start sucking strongly again when a new sound is introduced, researchers know that they are able to tell the two sounds apart. For example, if we were interested in knowing if infants can distinguish between two similar speech segments, one ('Hello, Baby!') would be used as the familiarization stimulus and the other ('Hi, Sweetie!') as the novel. If the infants habituate to 'Hello, Baby!' and then increase sucking pressure when 'Hi, Sweetie!' is presented, it indicates that they can distinguish these two samples of speech. The procedure can be used to determine whether and at what age infants are capable of hearing the distinction (see Chapter 10 for a detailed account of speech perception in infancy).

Preference paradigms

The preference paradigm is based on an infant's tendency to attend to the more complex of two novel stimuli. In preferential looking procedures, the infant is shown two targets side by side (see Figure 2.1). An observer who cannot see the stimulus makes a judgement as to which target the infant is looking at. To study visual acuity the young infant is presented with one stimulus that contains black vertical stripes that have specific widths corresponding to a level of visual acuity, and another target that is a uniform gray. If infants can distinguish the stripes, they will prefer to look at that more complex target. If not, both targets will look gray, and there will be no preference over a series of trials (Teller, 1979).

Conditioned head turning

Conditioned head turning is used to assess hearing thresholds and auditory discrimination in young infants. A sound is presented through a speaker away from the infant's gaze. If the infant turns toward the sound, an animated toy beside the speaker is activated to reward the head-turn response (see Figure 2.2). The volume of the sound is varied systematically and an estimate of the hearing threshold is obtained by comparing head turns toward the speaker in the presence vs. the absence of the sound. This procedure can

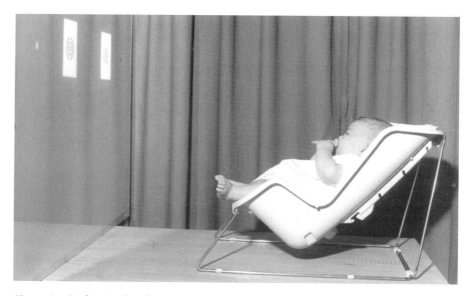

Figure 2.1 In the visual preference procedure the infant is shown two targets side by side and an unseen observer records which the baby looks at.

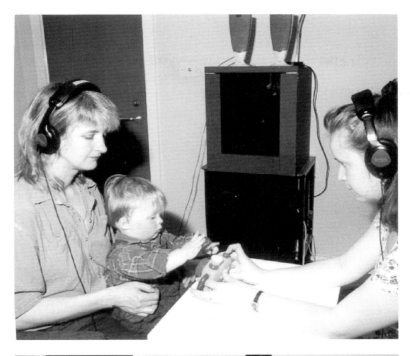

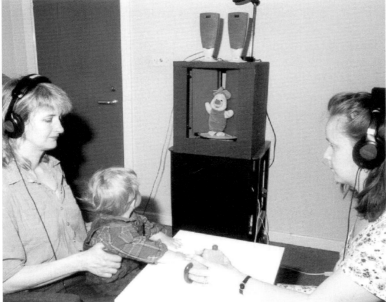

Figure 2.2 An infant performing in the conditioned head-turn procedure. The top picture was taken when the reinforcer (a bouncing toy) was not activated, and the bottom picture when it was.

also be used to find if infants can detect a change in sounds, e.g., from one rhyming sound to another (Hayes *et al.*, 2001).

Cognition and learning

Sensory capacities have to do with an infant's ability to take in the stimulation afforded by the world, while cognition has to do with how the infant makes sense of those sensations. Cognition is therefore about what infants learn, think, and remember. Methods used to measure cognition and learning, include standardized instruments and ingenious experimental procedures.

Can you tell how smart an infant is?

Standardized assessment

The **Bayley Scales of Infant Development** (BSID; Bayley, 1993, 2005) have the longest history of use in infant assessment and are the most widely used tools for assessing the general cognitive level of infants. The BSID presents test items arranged in a developmental sequence. The children's responses to these tasks determine their developmental level. The BSID has a set of items tapping mental capacity that is summarized by the Mental Development Index (MDI), and a motor skill set summarized by the Psychomotor Development Index (PDI). These scores are like IQ scores, where 100 designates average performance for age, with a range of 50–150. It is these norms for the MDI and PDI that make this assessment instrument so popular. The most recent revision (BSID-III; 2005) has test items appropriate for ages 1–42 months. This test has five subtests which are intended to measure development, and to identify deficits or delayed development, in five major areas of development: cognitive, language, motor, adaptive behavior, and socio-emotional. Most of the items have specified administration procedures and require standard materials. Examples include determining if the infant turns to the sound of a bell, how many cubes can be stacked, and if all pegs can be put in a board within a certain amount of time.

MDI scores are often used to provide information about developmental level or as a measure of the effects of intervention. For example, the BSID has been used to assess the general impact of prenatal drug exposure on cognitive development, as well as the effects of early intervention programs (Lewis & Sullivan, 1994; Colombo *et al.*, 2004).

Rate of habituation

Standardized instruments such as the BSID have not been found to predict later outcomes from early infancy very well. Other methods, designed to tap basic processes of learning and memory, may do a better job. For example, Colombo and colleagues (2004) showed that older infants needed less looking time to habituate to repeated trials of a visual display than younger infants over the age range 3–9 months. Furthermore, shorter looking time to habituation was associated with better performance on the Bayley mental and motor scales. The rate of habituation is considered an indication of brain integrity and fundamental cognitive competence.

What do infants learn and remember?

Besides habituation, two types of conditioning procedures often are used to explore what young infants learn and remember. Infants learn early in life that certain environmental events are associated with their behavior. **Classical conditioning** examines how infants learn associations between environmental signals or cues. **Contingency (operant) methods** study how infants learn that their actions have consequences. Learning procedures have particular appeal for researchers. Unlike habituation and preference paradigms which essentially measure passive behavior, conditioning procedures inform researchers how infants act on what they know.

Classical conditioning

Even very young infants learn signals or environmental cues that are related to events important to them. For example, in the first weeks of life they learn the many auditory, olfactory, and sensory cues that predict being fed. This form of learning, classical conditioning, is based on the principle that repeated pairings of one stimulus with another allow the infant to learn that one event predicts the occurrence of the other. Researchers know that the infant has learned an association when they respond to the previously novel cue. For example, newborn infants will turn toward the breast and begin rooting when the cheek is stroked (rooting reflex). Noirot & Algeria (1983) preceded the touch of an infant's cheek by the taped sound of the mother's voice. After several pairings of voice and touch, newborns anticipated the touch: cued by their mother's voice alone, they began to root! Another procedure, using a reflexive eyeblink to a puff of air, assesses responses to sounds or light changes (Herbert *et al.*, 2004). Classical conditioning methods such as these show the types of stimulus information the youngest infants learn, how rapidly they learn, and how long they remember.

Expectancy violation

More complex procedures can be used to assess older infants' prediction of events in the world. Because infants will readily watch and track moving objects, their visual and facial responses when an object deviates from a path are good ways to infer what they expected to happen. Typically they are shown an event, for example, an object appearing in different locations successively. The same action sequence is then repeated several times, so that they can learn to predict the object's location. On the test trial, the object's appearance in the expected location is delayed. Monitoring eye movements determines whether the infants anticipated the next location, indicating that they understood the sequence and were able to predict the object's next appearance (Wentworth *et al.*, 2001).

Contingency or operant learning

A major developmental task is understanding that certain behaviors have consequences. Infants use many responses to explore, or operate on the environment, including vocalizing, touching, banging, etc. The relation between these behaviors (called **operants**) and the consequences they produce is called a **contingency**. Contingency methods assess whether operant behavior increases when it is followed by a rewarding consequence. For example, infants were taught to pull a ribbon to see a slide of a baby and hear children singing (Lewis *et al.*, 2004). The infants were placed in the apparatus shown in Figure 2.3. The spontaneous level of pulling was recorded but not rewarded in any way (**baseline**). During the next phase (**contingency**), pulls were followed immediately by 3 seconds of the slides and music. For many infants from about 8 weeks on, this contingency results in increased pulling as well as increased smiling as the infant learns that arm action turns on an interesting

Figure 2.3 An infant in a contingency learning apparatus. A ribbon connected to an elastic wrist band worn by the infant triggers a slide to appear (not shown), accompanied by pleasant music.

event. In the next 2-minute phase, pulling no longer turned on the pleasant stimulus. This period of nonreward is called **extinction** because it ultimately leads to reduction of the learned response. However, infants learned that their pulling results in reward and their initial response to extinction was to respond somewhat more (Sullivan *et al.*, 1992). Increased response during this phase may reflect mild frustration because it is accompanied by negative facial expressions and increased heart rate (Lewis *et al.*, 2004). Through procedures such as this researchers can focus on what is learned, how long it takes infants to 'make the connection', and whether certain groups of infants learn more rapidly than others, as well as the emotional and physiological correlates of learning.

Imitation

Imitation is another way that infants learn how to act in the world. It is more common after about 6 months, although some have reported imitation of certain facial actions in newborns (Meltzoff & Moore, 1983). Researchers are interested in what behaviors infants will imitate (e.g., facial actions, sounds, or gestures) and who (or what) they will imitate at a given age. Facial expressions, familiar and novel gestures, and actions on objects, such as talking on the telephone, have been modeled by live or televised people, and even objects. Imitation shows what infants regard as interesting or important behavior, as well as their ability to perceive and process similarities between their own actions and those of others. There remains much controversy about the nature and brain processes involved in neonatal imitation. The question of whether neonatal imitation requires a social model, and the minimum stimulus features required to stimulate matching, is not yet well known. In older infants, researchers have found that from about 9 months infants will look and smile more at an adult who imitates their own actions than one who plays with the same toys but not exactly as the infants do (Agnetta & Rochat, 2004).

Mandler and McDonough (1998) have used procedures capitalizing on older infant's ability to imitate in their study of early concepts. By studying whether infants will generalize imitation to novel objects, they are able to assess how nonverbal toddlers (11–15 months) categorize their world. Researchers model simple events such as putting a toy dog to bed. Then they give the toddler the bed and a choice between two perceptually similar objects, such as a toy bird and an airplane, encouraging them to imitate the action previously observed. If the child puts the bird but not the plane in the bed, it is inferred that the child understands what sleeps and what does not. In this way, the child's conceptual understanding about animals, vehicles, furniture, plants, etc. can be studied.

In studies of **delayed imitation,** several days or weeks may pass between an infant's initial exposure to a novel modeled action and a test (Bauer & Hertsgaard, 1993). The focus of these studies is to see how long infants are able to remember the novel action, and the level of prompting needed to recall the behavior. Imitation has also been used to study the development of early communicative gestures (e.g., waving bye-bye, pointing) and vocalizations (Poulson *et al.*, 1991).

Memory

Habituation, imitation, and conditioning procedures are used to study memory. When using habituation, a particular stimulus is repeatedly shown to an infant, and then is presented again on the memory test after a delay as brief as several minutes or as long as several days. The response on the memory test lets infants answer the question 'Have you seen this before?' If the infant pays a lot of attention to the old, repeatedly presented, stimulus, effectively treating it as 'novel,' then researchers infer that infants do not recognize that they have seen it before. The amount of time between the habituation and memory trials is varied to see how long infants of different ages remember (Martin, 1975).

When memory is tested using contingency learning procedures, the time between initial learning of the contingency and the memory test is varied. For example, infants learn to jiggle colorful mobiles hung above their cribs by means of a ribbon attached to one ankle (see Figure 2.4). They are then tested after days or weeks with either a dissimilar or an identical mobile to see if they will attempt to jiggle it (Grecco *et al.*, 1990). The research shows that infants initially remember exact details about the mobile for at least 4 days. After that the specific mobile appears to be forgotten, but infants still remember that mobiles are for jiggling for at least 2 weeks. Cue procedures have been used to show that infants who appear to have forgotten previously learned responses can be reminded effectively by simply re-exposing them briefly to the contingent stimulus (Rovee-Collier *et al.*, 2000). Such simple reminders (**reactivation**), as well as the opportunity to briefly rehearse the contingent response (**reinstatement**), allow infants to maintain learned information for periods of a month or more.

When using deferred imitation to assess memory, infants as young as 6 months might watch an experimenter remove a mitten from a hand-puppet, shake it to ring a bell hidden inside, and replace the mitten. Several studies now show that infants this age can remember this unusual action with the puppet for periods of 1–14 days (Hayne *et al.*, 2000).

Socio-emotional behavior

How do infants learn to interact with others?

Most studies of early social behavior focus on mother–infant interaction. Until the infant is about 6 months of age, most social contact takes place

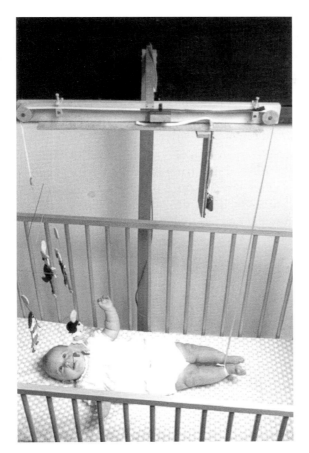

Figure 2.4 The ankle ribbon attached to the baby's foot causes the mobile to jiggle about when she kicks her legs. Photo by Rachel Cooper.

face-to-face during play or caregiving with a limited set of caregivers (see Chapter 12). The procedures used to measure these interactive behaviors have remained fairly constant.

Many studies of mother–infant interaction are observations in naturalistic settings such as the home or in settings designed to be home-like, such as a laboratory playroom. Typically the mother and infant are observed while playing or during feeding. The interaction is coded as it occurs, or is videotaped and later coded for a variety of mother and infant behaviors of interest. Coding schemes vary, depending on the focus of the study. Two aspects of the interaction may be coded, whether specific behaviors occur and their order, i.e., was the behavior an initiation or a response to behavior of the other member of the dyad (Bendersky & Lewis, 1986)? More complex methods of analyzing response patterns, such as conditional probability, and sequential analysis also may be used (Lewis & Freedle, 1973; Bakeman &

Gottman, 1989). Another common approach is to have observers rate the dyad on more global categories of behavior, for example maternal emotional expression (Forman *et al.*, 2003). Several more structured procedures have become fruitful methods for studying particular aspects of mother–infant interaction. These procedures examine how infants react when their mother's usual pattern of responding changes.

Still-face procedure

Think of a mother playing with her young infant. Mothers usually assume an animated style, coaxing the baby to interact by using exaggerated facial and verbal expressions. At very early ages infants come to expect this sort of reciprocal social behavior from their mothers. The still-face procedure was designed to see how infants react when this expectation is violated (Adamson & Frick, 2003). The mother is first asked to play with her infant briefly as she normally would at home, and then to assume an expressionless, unresponsive facial expression. After a few minutes of this still-face period, she is told to resume face-to-face play. Both mother and infant are videotaped and observers code vocalizations, facial expressions, direction of gaze, and head and body position of the two participants. Typically, when the mother assumes the unresponsive still face the infant attempts to get her to respond by smiling and vocalizing. When these behaviors that usually engage the mother fail, the infant withdraws and turns away. Turning away is one way for young infants to regulate their emotional arousal. Infants quickly resume play when their mothers re-engage following the still-face period. This procedure is used to explore normal parent–infant interaction, as well as deviations due to high-risk conditions affecting the infant, such as being exposed prenatally to drugs of abuse, or conditions affecting the mother, such as depression (Field, 1984; Bendersky & Lewis, 1998). This classic procedure continues to prompt new questions, methodologies, and applications (Muir & Lee, 2003; Tronick, 2003).

Desynchronized interaction

Several other ingenious experiments have 'uncoupled' infant and maternal behavior to examine the importance of the contingent quality of maternal interactions. In one such study (Bigelow & DeCoste, 2003), mothers responded to their infants via closed-circuit video for a brief period. This allowed the infants to 'interact' with their mothers shown 'live' on TV. The mothers' behavior was taped during this period. The baby then viewed the videotaped mother on the monitor, but maternal behavior was no longer tied to what the infant did—the two were 'out of sync.' This procedure elegantly controls the level and distribution of maternal stimulation. Since the infant views its own mother, the stimulation is exactly the same in both phases. However, the responsivity or contingent quality of the social interaction for the infant has been lost. Studies tend to agree that infants detect this disruption in maternal contingency rather quickly and become upset.

Attachment

Strange situation

Some time after 6 months, most infants develop a strong emotional attachment to the primary caregiver, usually their mother. One of the most influential procedures used to study the development, the quality, and outcomes related to this first emotional relationship is the **Strange Situation** (Ainsworth *et al.*, 1978). This paradigm shows that although the infant is able to move freely about the environment, the mother serves as a 'secure' base that the infant will seek when stressed (Bowlby, 1982). The procedure comprises increasingly stressful episodes in which a stranger interacts with the infant in the mother's presence and alone; the infant's behavior during the separation and reunion allows researchers to classify the mother–child relationship into different attachment types (Ainsworth *et al.*, 1978; Main & Solomon, 1990). Major issues in the latest studies are determining the process through which attachment develops, the relative contribution of specific maternal and infant behaviors to the classification, and the stability over time of the attachment classification.

Social referencing

Social referencing procedures are designed to present the infant with a potentially distressing ambiguous situation, allowing researchers to study whether infants use maternal behavior and signals to regulate their behavior. Social referencing occurs when the infant attends to and then behaves in a manner consistent with mother's message. The approach of a stranger, originally designed to study fearfulness, has been adapted to study social referencing because it mimics a common dilemma in the lives of infants: should they accept the stranger as a friend? When the stranger enters the room, the mother interacts either positively, negatively, or not at all. Subsequently, the stranger interacts with the infant, offering a toy in some studies, or picking the child up in others. At about 1 year of age, the infant will respond positively to a stranger when the mother's reaction to the stranger is positive (Striano & Rochat, 2000). The results for negative reactions are more mixed. It also is not yet clear if infants pick up cues simply from observation of the mother–stranger interaction or require more direct socio-emotional cues from their mother to accept the stranger's overtures.

Other studies have used potentially frightening situations to study whether infants use maternal cues to guide their behavior. The visual cliff, originally designed to study depth perception (see Chapter 5), was adapted to study infants' monitoring of maternal facial expressions (Sorce *et al.*, 1985). Infants were placed on a raised glass surface in which the visual pattern beneath the glass made it appear that there was a deep drop-off in the surface just ahead. Their mothers, positioned on the opposite side, tried to coax the infants across the 'chasm.' Infants were more likely to cross the cliff when mothers looked happy, and less likely to cross when mothers looked fearful (Feinman *et al.*, 1992).

Joint attention

The ability to coordinate attention with a social partner is called **joint attention** and is considered a major developmental milestone usually attained in the 9–12-month period. It is one of the bases of language and social competence (Vaughan *et al.*, 2003). Following the gaze, head turns, or pointing of a social partner, as well as initiating pointing, showing, or alternating gaze between an interesting object or event and the social partner, have been considered measurable instances of joint attention in infants. Even newborns have been shown to follow the direction of gaze more often than not (Farroni *et al.*, 2004). Joint attention is usually studied by naturalistic observation during problem-solving or play (Vaughan *et al.*, 2003).

How do infants react to stressful events?

There are two ways in which all people, including infants, react to stress. Our behavior changes, and we have internal, bodily changes as well. Researchers examine both stress response systems to understand how infants react to stress and how quickly they return to a calmer state.

Behavioral stress reactivity and regulation

Adults may be able to mask their stress levels and not show too much outward reaction, for example when getting an inoculation, but infants usually cannot. Infants will show different levels of distress in response to a painful event and will also calm down at different rates. These two aspects of response are called **reactivity** and **regulation**. Reactivity refers to the initial behavioral or physiological response to a stressful event. Regulation refers to the time that it takes the response to return to pre-stress levels. Both of these aspects are important to understanding individual differences in stress response. In one series of studies infants are videotaped during and following inoculations. The intensity of crying and fretting, as well as facial expressions, are coded from the tapes (Lewis & Ramsay, 1995). The initial reaction and the return to calm do not necessarily go together. Intensely negative reactions, as well as difficulty calming in stressful situations, have widespread implications for social interactions and learning (Lewis & Ramsay, 2002).

Physiological responses

Think of how you feel when you are in the middle of a big exam and time is running out. Your body will react to this kind of stressful situation, first with a rush of epinephrine (adrenaline), the 'fight or flight' hormone, that makes your heart pound and your hands sweat. About half an hour later you are still in an agitated state because the level of another more long-acting stress hormone, cortisol, has risen. Changes in levels of these stress hormones, as well as heart rate changes, can be used to study infant reactions to stress.

Cortisol is a hormone released by the adrenal glands in response to stress. It is easily extracted from saliva and has become a popular measure of the physiological stress response because it is easy to collect from subjects of all ages. Typically, cortisol has been collected during painful medical procedures such as circumcision (Gunnar, 1989) and inoculation (Lewis & Ramsay, 1995). A baseline level is obtained in advance and a post-stimulation level after the procedure. The post-stimulation sample is usually obtained about 20 minutes after the painful procedure, because that is when cortisol reactivity is at its peak. The mouths of infants are swabbed with cotton pads to absorb saliva that is then squeezed into test tubes and assayed for cortisol. Obtaining successive samples after the reactivity peak allows for measurement of regulation, i.e., the onset of recovery toward baseline (Ramsay & Lewis, 2003). Reactivity as well as regulation measures have been associated with behavioral inhibition (Schmidt *et al.*, 1997), other temperamental qualities (Gunnar *et al.*, 1997), and insecure attachment (Hertsgaard *et al.*, 1995).

Heart-rate changes

Heart rate and its variability are other measures of emotional response that are relatively easily measured. Heart-rate variability is considered more reflective of brain activity than other measures of heart-rate change and has been used frequently as a measure of physiological self-regulatory capacity (Bornstein & Suess, 2000). In order to measure heart rate, a small number of sensors are placed on the infant's chest and a count of heart rate is obtained. These data are processed to obtain the desired cardiac baseline, reactivity, and regulation measures. Some studies have been interested in resting measures (e.g., Fox & Porges, 1985); others have examined changes in response to stimulation (e.g., Bornstein & Suess, 2000). Both resting and reactivity measures have been shown to predict cognitive and socio-emotional competence (Porges *et al.*, 1996).

Relation between measures

Behavioral responses and physiological reaction to the same event are not necessarily related. Lewis *et al.* (1993), for example, found that infants fell into four groups in their reactions to inoculation: (1) 'cry babies' had low physiological reactions, but took a long time to quiet; (2) 'stoics' had high physiological reactions, but quieted quickly; (3) 'high reactors' had both strong physiological reactions and took a long time to calm; (4) and finally, 'low reactors' had neither strong physiological nor behavioral responses. These findings suggest that behavioral and physiological stress reactions have different meanings, and are likely to relate to development in different ways.

How do infants express emotion?

Infants express emotion by crying and vocalizing, by their body posture, and by their facial expressions. Parents no doubt make use of all of these cues in attempting to figure out what their infants are feeling.

Facial expressions

Researchers have been particularly interested in facial expressions as a way of understanding how emotions are organized early in life and develop (see Chapter 12). Infants make a variety of facial expressions that can be scored by observing the muscle movements in the brow, eye/cheek, and mouth regions of the face (Izard, 1995). For example, pretend for a moment that you are surprised. How did your face change? Probably, you raised and arched your brows, your eyes widened and your jaw dropped—the typical surprised expression. Now, pretend to express anger and notice the contrast. Your brows are now lowered and drawn together; your eyes narrowed, and your mouth, if open, was wide and squared, and if closed, your lips and teeth were strongly compressed, chin drawn up. All components of basic emotions that adults express (enjoyment, surprise, anger, fear, sadness, and disgust) are observable in infants from the opening weeks of life. However, infants do not always make the facial expressions that adults expect in a given situation and they may show several different emotions in rapid succession (Bennett *et al.*, 2002). These observations have triggered a lively debate on the meaning of the various expressions, particularly the negative ones. Researchers have developed situations designed to produce such emotions as disgust (tasting of sour and bitter solutions, Rosenstein & Oster, 1988) and anger (arm restraint, Stenberg & Campos, 1990; blocked contingencies, Lewis *et al.*, 1990). Some of the newest work in measuring emotion has added physiological measures such as heart rate, cortisol, and electroencephalography (EEG) to the study of infant facial expression (Lewis *et al.*, 2004).

Are infants born with different personalities?

Most of us would agree that adults have different personalities. Some people are easily excited, others are easy-going; some seem to be eternal optimists, whereas others seem to see only the dark side of a situation. The key is that people seem to behave in similar ways, no matter what the circumstances. Thus, personality is thought of as a 'trait,' or an unchanging characteristic. Are we born that way, or do our environments contribute to the development of our personalities? The term **personality** is generally reserved for adults. In infants and children, the concept most closely related to personality is **temperament**. Definitions vary, but there is general agreement that temperamental differences appear relatively early in life and seem independent of social experience, cognitive ability, or learning. These differences in temperament interact with later family and other environmental experience; are relatively enduring, and contribute to behavior across a variety of situations (Rothbart & Bates, 1998). The intensity of emotions, thresholds to react to environmental stimuli, and the ease with which an infant calms down, are important emotional and self-regulatory components of temperament. It is easy to understand how powerful a contributor temperament is to developing social interactions. Difficult temperament, i.e., low threshold to react, intense negative reactions, poor adaptability to new situations, and difficulty in calming, presents a particular challenge to caregivers.

Parent reports

The most widely used method of measuring temperament is standardized parent questionnaires. The starting point for most of these is the nine dimensions of temperament derived from extensive parent interviews done as part of the New York Longitudinal Study (Thomas *et al.*, 1963). These dimensions are used to characterize infants as difficult, easy, or slow to warm up. Several questionnaires have been derived from these dimensions (Bates *et al.*, 1979; Carey, 1970). The **Infant Behavior Questionnaire** (IBQ, Rothbart, 1981), designed to measure six dimensions of temperament in infants under 1 year of age, has a broader conceptual base than the others and is widely used. Rothbart used not only the Thomas *et al.* perspective, but also those of perceptual-cognitive, neurophysiological, genetic, interactional, and adult temperament work. There are temperament questionnaires for older infants as well (Fullard *et al.*, 1984; Goldsmith, 1996).

In these questionnaires the parent is asked to rate how much a statement about a child's behavior applies. For example, 'Before falling asleep at night during the last week, how often did the baby show no fussing or crying?' (in the IBQ choices range from 'never' to 'always'). There are many questions worded in different ways on these instruments that ask about the same underlying temperament dimension across various situations in order to obtain a reliable report from the parent.

Despite the popularity of parent reports of temperament, these instruments tend to have relatively poor validity, test–retest, and inter-rater reliability. Moreover, responses reflect what the mother thinks about the infant's temperament. Observational procedures have been developed which provide greater objectivity.

Observational methods

Reactions to unfamiliar stimuli are an important method for studying certain aspects of temperament, especially behavioral inhibition. Brightly colored toys, tape recordings of voices, and unpleasant odors have been used in young infants; interactions with unfamiliar adults, being shown frightening toys, and being encouraged to participate in novel activities have been used in the second year of life (Calkins *et al.*, 1996; Forman *et al.*, 2003). These procedures indicate to what extent infants exhibit the temperamental quality of being withdrawn and inhibited.

When and how do infants develop a sense of themselves as individuals?

Infants' ability to know and think about themselves develops between 1 and 2 years of age (Bertenthal & Fischer, 1978; Lewis & Brooks-Gunn, 1979). Its appearance has important implications for socio-emotional behavior, as well as motivation and personality development. In a classic series of studies, Lewis and Brooks-Gunn (1979) established that visual recognition of the self emerges by 18 months. In the most widely known of their procedures (the **mirror rouge task**) infants are first placed before a mirror and their responses are recorded. Next, the mother surreptitiously puts a dot of rouge on her child's nose. After a short interval the infant is placed again in front of the mirror. Infants who look in the mirror and then touch their noses are classified as showing self-directed behavior. This type of behavior never occurs before 15 months of age and increases dramatically between 18 and 24 months.

Infants who were classified as showing self-recognition in the mirror rouge task were more likely to show embarrassment as toddlers (Lewis *et al.*, 1989). Embarrassment is elicited by procedures that call the children's attention to the fact that they are being observed by others, such as being pointed at. Greater physiological reactivity to stress and less soothability in infants is also related to earlier self-recognition (Lewis & Ramsay, 1997). These findings suggest that self-recognition is related to other aspects of the child's social and emotional life.

SUMMARY

This chapter has highlighted some of the more commonly used methods for studying what young infants know and feel. As you can see, researchers have devised many creative ways to do this. Some methods, such as habituation, preference for novelty, and operant conditioning, have been used to study a myriad of phenomena, from basic perceptual abilities to sophisticated concept formation and memory. Social interactive methods including imitation, naturalistic parent–infant interactions, and paradigms in which expected maternal behavior is violated (e.g., still face, Strange Situation) inform us about early cognitive as well as social functioning. Methods are often combined in order to manipulate psychological variables in quasi-experimental situations and to see if evidence from different response modalities converges or adds to our understanding of the phenomena being studied. New procedures based on advances in technology such as magnetic resonance imaging (MRI), electroencephalography (EEG), and the ability to map or localize brain activity in relation to ongoing behavior are being developed. The questions posed to organize this chapter, as well as many new ones prompted by ongoing work, will challenge the next generation of researchers to find ways of understanding why and how infants behave the way they do.

PART TWO

The Foundations of Development

CHAPTER THREE

Prenatal development

PETER HEPPER

Introduction

The prenatal period is one of the most fascinating, yet least well understood, stages of our development. Its end is marked by a beginning; the birth of a newborn baby. In most societies the newborn is given an age of zero, as if to imply that nothing of importance has occurred before this. But, as I shall demonstrate, the prenatal period is important for our development.

The prenatal period encompasses the most rapid phase of development of our lives, beginning as a single cell and ending as a newborn baby emerging into the world. For many years the period was viewed as simply one of growth and maturation, a time during which the body and organs were formed—in this context the term **maturation** refers to those aspects of development that are primarily under genetic control. Thus, development during this time was considered as proceeding largely under genetic control and immune to external influences. However, as technology has advanced and scientists have become more sophisticated in examining the fetus, it has become apparent that development during this time is far from a simple question of genetically determined growth. Environmental agents may adversely affect the development of the fetus, and moreover the environment may determine the functional capacity of the organs of the body. The actions and reactions of the baby will shape its own development.

This chapter provides an introduction to prenatal development and how this acts as a foundation on which all subsequent development builds. It examines the physical development of the individual before birth and explores the impact of the environment on development. It discusses the behavior of the fetus and how this may be important for future development. The processes initiating birth and the reflexes of the newborn infant are discussed.

Key issues

Three key related issues have dominated discussion of the prenatal period.

- **The nature/nurture debate.** How much is development during this period determined by genes and how much by the environment? Traditionally, the prenatal period has been viewed as largely under the control of genes which direct the physical growth of the individual. However, environmental influences contribute more to development than previously thought. Development during this period is an interaction between genes and environment.

- **Is development continuous or discontinuous?** For many years the event of birth was considered a new beginning, ignoring events before as having any meaning for future development. However, this view is now changing. As progress has been made in understanding the abilities of the newborn, the question of when newborn abilities begin has been raised. It is logically possible, although unlikely, that at the moment of birth the behavioral, sensory, and learning abilities of the newborn are suddenly switched on. More plausible is that these abilities have their origins in the prenatal period, implying a continuity of development across the birth period.

- **The function of fetal behavior.** The question that has been raised as studies have begun to unravel the behavioral abilities of the fetus is: why does the fetus exhibit the behavior and reactions that it does? Are they a by-product of its maturation, or do they serve a function?

These issues will be discussed as the prenatal development of the fetus is described.

Physical development

The prenatal period, beginning at conception and ending at birth, is divided into three stages: the **conceptual or germinal period**, the **embryonic period**, and the **fetal period** (Moore & Persaud, 2003).

The germinal period

The germinal period begins with the fertilization of the egg by the sperm and concludes with the establishment of the pregnancy, approximately 2 weeks later. At ovulation a mature egg is released from the ovary and enters the fallopian tube. Sperm travel up the tube to meet the egg, and fertilization takes place in the fallopian tube. The fertilized egg (the **zygote**, a single cell) now begins to divide. The first division to produce two cells takes place

24–36 hours after fertilization. The cells divide, first to form a ball of cells (the **morula**) and then, with the formation of a cavity within the morula, the **blastocyst**. The cells, in the course of dividing, travel down the fallopian tube and enter the womb where the blastocyst implants itself into the wall of the uterus (5–6 days after fertilization). During the next 5–7 days the blastocyst establishes a primitive placenta and circulation, thus ensuring the supply of nutrients and oxygen essential for continued development. Two weeks after fertilization, pregnancy is established. As well as developing a placenta the blastocyst must also ensure pregnancy continues, and it secretes hormones: first, to prevent menstruation and thus stop the shedding of the uterine lining and consequent loss of the pregnancy; and, second, to prevent the mother's immune system from attacking the embryo or fetus.

The embryonic period

The **embryonic period** begins during the middle of the second week and concludes at the end of the eighth week, at which time the physical appearance of the embryo is clearly human (see Figure 3.1). It is during this time that all the major organs of the body begin to form. It is a time of specialization where cells divide and differentiate to form specific organs, e.g., the heart and lungs. One of the mysteries of development is how cells 'know' to become a heart or lung cell, given that they are all identical at the start of the differentiation process. The local environment of surrounding cells and chemical messages is undoubtedly important, but exactly how one cell becomes a toenail, another

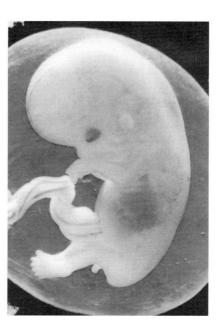

Figure 3.1 9 week fetus (from Nilsson *et al.*, 1977).

a hair, is unknown. During this period the individual is called an **embryo**. The heart, although only two-chambered, begins to beat and blood is circulated around the embryo by the end of the third week. This enables the removal of waste and the acquisition of nutrients. As all the body's organs begin to form during this period, it is considered the most critical stage of development.

The fetal period

The **fetal period** follows from the end of the embryonic period, beginning at 9 weeks and ending with the onset of labor and birth of the baby. The individual is referred to as a **fetus** during this period. The period is marked by the continued development and differentiation of structures that emerged during the embryonic period. Basic structures that were laid down in the embryonic period are refined and grow to their final form. Very few new structures appear. Particularly noticeable is the rapid rate of growth during the third and fourth month, with the fetus growing from about 2.5 cm (1 inch) at 8 weeks to 13–15 cm (5–6 inches) at 16 weeks. It is during this period that the origins of motor, sensory, and learning behavior are to be found (see later).

Principles that guide development

Three major principles seem to guide development:

- Development proceeds in a **cephalocaudal** direction (from head to foot). That is, at any specific time structures nearer the head are more developed than those near the toes.
- Development proceeds from the **basic to the more specialized**. Thus, organs do not initially appear as a miniature version of their final form but first develop their basic characteristics, and detail is added as development proceeds. For example, the heart is initially a two-chambered structure and its final four-chambered form develops later.
- Development proceeds **in order of importance**. Thus, it begins with the 'more important' organs for survival and the less important ones develop later. Thus, the brain and heart are amongst the first organs to develop.

Brain development

The brain begins its development at 18 days after fertilization. It is one of the slowest organs to develop, with development continuing for many years after birth. The relative proportion of brain to body decreases as development proceeds; the brain comprises some 25% of body weight in the 9-week fetus, 10% in the newborn, and only 2% in the adult.

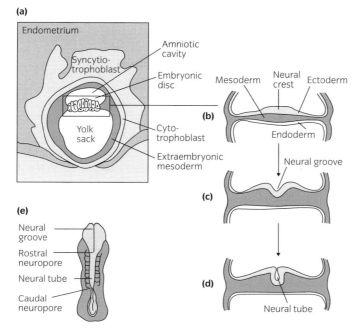

Figure 3.2 Formation of the neural tube (adapted from Moore, 1988) (a) Approximately 9 days. The blastocyst has nearly fully implanted itself into the endometrium. The embryonic disc forms between the primary yolk sac and amniotic cavity. The individual develops from the cells of the embryonic disc. Initially formed as a layer of 2 cells thick, the embryonic disc undergoes a process of **gastrulation**. This begins at the end of the first week and continues to the third week by which time three layers of cells, the primary germ layers, are formed: the ectoderm, mesoderm, and endoderm. (b)–(d) Around 16–18 days cells in the ectoderm thicken to form the neural plate (b), a groove appears in the neural plate around 18 days (c), and begins to close over forming the neural tube (d). The walls of the neural tube will thicken and form the neuroepithelium from which all the cells of the brain, neurones, glia develop. (e) View of the embryo and closure of the neural tube in embryo around 22 days. Closure of the tube begins in the middle and moves to each end. The neural tube is fully closed by the end of the fourth week. Failure to close properly may lead to defects such as spina bifida.

The brain develops from a layer of cells from the embryonic disc, the neural plate (see Figure 3.2). This plate folds to form the neural tube, which closes, beginning in the middle and progressing to each end. **Neural tube defects**, e.g., spina bifida or anencephaly, arise as a result of the failure of the neural tube to close properly. The neural tube has closed by the fourth week and the walls begin to thicken (Müller & O'Rahilly, 2004). The walls of the neural tube contain progenitor cells which will give rise to the neurons and glia cells of the brain.

The development of the brain may be considered at two levels. First, at the gross level considering how the neural tube develops to form the main structures of the brain, hindbrain, midbrain, and forebrain. Second, at the

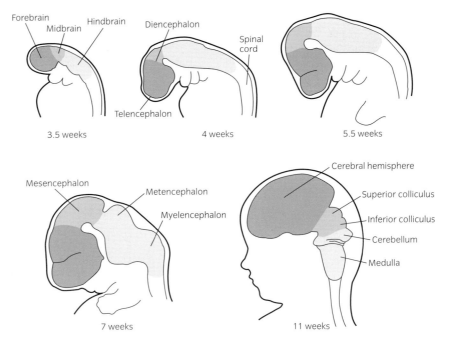

Figure 3.3 Development of the brain (adapted from Carlson, 1994). The brain begins its development following the closure of the neural tube. The rostral end, destined to become the brain enlarges to form three swellings, the forebrain, the midbrain and the hindbrain. During the fourth week the forebrain further subdivides into the diencephalon and telencephalon. Towards the end of the fourth week the hindbrain divides into the metencephalon and myelencephalon. By the fifth week this 5 part structure of the brain is clearly visible. Although much more complexity is added as the brain develops, this basic 5 part organization remains throughout the rest of life. By the 11th week the telencephalon has greatly developed and covered the dienecephalon to form the cerebral hemispheres. Although initially smooth in appearance, future development will see a massive increase in the surface area of the cerebral hemispheres which become folded and assume their adult-like appearance with many grooves (sulci) and convolutions (gyri).

micro level examining how the complex organization of cells within the brain is achieved.

At the gross level (see Figure 3.3) the hindbrain, the midbrain, and the forebrain are formed during the fourth week as one end of the neural tube expands to form three primary vesicles (Müller & O'Rahilly, 2004). The forebrain further subdivides during the fifth week into the telencephalon and diencephalon. The telencephalon gives rise to the neocortex (cerebral cortices). The hindbrain and brain stem develop first, followed by the midbrain and later the cerebral cortices (Mai & Ashwell, 2004), development of which continues after birth. This probably reflects the need for basic biological functions, controlled by the hindbrain and forebrain, to be operational at birth, e.g., breathing and digestion. The cerebral cortices involved in mental processing (often called the gray matter) develop later, a process that continues well into postnatal life

At the micro level, all the neurons we will ever possess have been generated by the end of the second trimester (Caviness *et al.*, 1996). Between the 10th and 26th weeks cells are produced at an extremely rapid rate; up to 250 000 cells are produced each minute. The adult brain contains an estimated 100 billion cells. Initially there is massive overproduction of cells, and part of the development of the brain includes natural cell death. Although mainly occurring after birth this cell death (pruning or apoptosis) is a key element of the developmental process, removing neurons that have not made connections or have made inappropriate connections. It is estimated that up to 50–70% of brain cells initially produced are pruned in the postnatal period. Although development is often seen as an additive process, the development of the brain involves cell death as a central element in its ontogenesis (Oppenheim, 1991).

The cellular development of the brain comprises three main stages:

- **Proliferation**, the production of nerve cells, is completed by the end of the second trimester.
- The **migration** of cells. Cells are formed from progenitor cells in the wall of the neural tube and move from here to their final location. Other cells, the radial glia cells, are produced alongside the neurons and serve as guides forming pathways along which the nerve cells migrate to their final position (Hatten, 1999). Migration takes place between the fourth and ninth months of gestation.
- The final stage involves myelinization and synaptogenesis. **Myelinization** is the process whereby the nerve cell is insulated from other cells by the development of a fatty sheath, myelin, around it. This greatly enhances the transmission of nerve impulses along the nerve. **Synaptogenesis** is the process by which nerve cells communicate with each other or with end organs, e.g., muscles to enable the transmission of neural impulses across the brain and from the brain to other organs and vice versa. These latter processes continue for some time after birth.

The development of the brain is a highly complex process in which timing of events is crucial to ensure that development proceeds normally (Mai & Ashwell, 2004). Numerous factors control the organization of neural development, with it being largely under genetic control. Some of the genes involved are now known (e.g., des Portes *et al.*, 1998), but our understanding of the processes that enable the progenitor cells in the neural tube to form the most highly complex organ in our body—the brain—are poorly understood.

Environmental influences on development

Prenatal physical development appears to proceed largely under instruction and direction from the individual's genes. However, this does not mean that it is immune to external influences that may alter the course of development. Environmental factors may influence the individual's ontogenesis and indeed may be crucial for establishing the functional capabilities of the various organs of the body.

Teratogens

The clearest example of environmental influence is presented by those substances which exert an adverse influence on development, teratogens. Initially it was thought that while developing within the womb the fetus was safe from external influences that could harm its development. However, it is now appreciated that the developing individual is at risk from environmental influences even in the womb (Kalter, 2003). The study of adverse consequences of exposure to environmental agents is termed **teratology**. It should be noted that teratogenic effects are not only caused by substances extra to the embryonic or fetal environment, e.g., alcohol through maternal drinking, but also by deficiencies of substances, e.g., vitamin and other dietary deficiencies such as malnutrition, (see Chapter 18) which may also lead to adverse development, as we discuss below.

The first agent to be identified as a teratogen was rubella (the medical term for German measles) when it was noticed that children born to women who had German measles during their pregnancy often suffered eye anomalies (Gregg, 1942). However, not until the thalidomide tragedy in the 1950s and 1960s was it finally accepted that environmental agents could severely affect the individual's development. (Thalidomide was a supposedly safe tranquillizer/sedative which was taken by mothers during pregnancy and resulted, most noticeably, in the birth of children with severe limb abnormalities.)

The effects of teratogens may range from spontaneous abortion of the fetus, major and minor structural defects, or growth retardation through to developmental retardation and behavioral disorders. Some effects are readily apparent at birth, e.g., the major structural anomalies resulting from exposure to thalidomide, whereas others, e.g., behavioral anomalies arising from exposure to alcohol, may not become apparent until later life.

One crucial factor determining the impact of any teratogen is the time of exposure. Generally speaking, exposure during the embryonic period, i.e., the period of **organogenesis** (when the major organs of the body begin to form), results in major impairments and malformations, whereas exposure during the fetal period (from about 9 weeks from conception) results in growth impairments and delay. Many organs have specific periods, often just 2–3 days, during which they are especially susceptible, and exposure to teratogens at this time will have major effects on their formation; outside these times the effects will be more limited. For example, a crucial period for development of the arms is 27–30 days, and exposure to thalidomide at this time resulted in malformation of the arms. At other times the severity of the drug's effect on the arms was reduced or nonexistent.

Many substances have been identified as having harmful effects on the fetus (see Table 3.1). The length of the period during which the brain is developing makes it particularly vulnerable to the effects of teratogenic agents. Substances may result in abnormalities in brain development in the

Table 3.1 Teratogens and some of their main effects. Duration and timing of exposure play a key role in determining the extent of any effect

Type of teratogen		Adverse effects
Prescription drugs	Thalidomide (sedative)	Arm and leg malformation
	Warfarin (anticoagulant)	Mental retardation, microcephaly (abnormally small head)
	Trimethadione (anticonvulsant)	Developmental delay, 'V'-shaped eyebrows, cleft lip and/or palate
	Tetracycline (antibiotic)	Tooth malformations
Substances of abuse	Heroin	Fetal/newborn addiction, slower growth
	Cocaine	Growth retardation; possible long-term behavioral effects
	Solvents	Microcephaly
Social drugs	Alcohol	Fetal alcohol syndrome, fetal alcohol effects
	Smoking	Spontaneous abortion, growth retardation
	Caffeine	Few human studies. High doses induce abnormalities in animals.
Disease	Rubella	Cataracts, deafness, heart defects
	Herpes simplex	Microcephaly, microophthalmia (abnormally small or absent eyes, associated with blindness)
	Varicella (chickenpox)	Muscle atrophy, mental retardation
Radiation		Cell death, chromosome injury, mental and growth retardation. Depends on dose and timing of exposure
Maternal	Altered metabolism (e.g. diabetes)	Increased birth weight, increased risk of congenital abnormalities
	Stress/anxiety	Evidence pointing to effects on birthweight, behavioral development

absence of major physical structural abnormalities. These effects are much more difficult to detect, as they may only become apparent years after birth.

Many teratogens are freely taken by mothers, e.g., alcohol and the products of cigarette smoking. Exposure to large amounts of alcohol may result in **fetal alcohol syndrome**, the symptoms of which include a small head, an abnormal facial appearance, growth retardation, learning disabilities, and behavioral disorders. At lower doses the individual may manifest **fetal alcohol effects**, where facial appearance may be normal but learning and behavioral problems are present in later life (Abel, 1989). Alcohol exhibits what is called a **dose-dependent effect**; the greater the exposure, the greater the effect on the fetus. It appears that even small amounts of alcohol may exert an effect on the developing individual (e.g., Hepper *et al.*, 2005).

Teratogenic effects are not simply the result of environmental exposure. In many cases the effect(s) is a result of an interaction between the individual's genes and the environmental agent. For example, not all women who drink the same amount of alcohol during pregnancy will have babies with identical syndromes. Some will be more affected than others, depending on the interaction between the environment and the individual's genes.

Consideration is also being given to the potential 'teratogenic' influence of maternal psychological state during pregnancy and its influence on the fetus and longer-term outcome. Maternal anxiety or depression influences the behavior of the fetus and newborn infant. Moreover stress or anxiety in pregnancy has been linked to lower temperament ratings at 4–8 months after birth (Austin *et al.*, 2005) and higher levels of behavioral and emotional problems at 81 months of age (O'Connor *et al.*, 2003).

Fetal origins hypothesis

Postnatal health may be influenced by prenatal factors; this is the **fetal origins hypothesis** (Gluckman & Hanson, 2005). This hypothesis argues that the environment experienced during the individual's prenatal life 'programs' the functional capacity of the individual's organs, and this has a subsequent effect on the individual's health.

When the fetus experiences a poor nutritional environment it develops its body functions to cope with this. The environment experienced prenatally is the one that it expects to continue experiencing, and hence its body develops to cope with it—a **predictive adaptive response** (Gluckman & Hanson, 2005). When the fetus experiences poor nutritional status this changes its rate of growth and the fetus develops according to its current environment. Resources may be redistributed away from body organs to spare the brain and this influences the development of these organs, e.g., the liver (the organ responsible for regulating cholesterol levels). Decreased body size in babies is associated with increased cholesterol levels when they become adults. These low-birthweight babies when born experience a normal nutritional status, but one for which their organs are not programmed and cannot deal with, hence the increase in cholesterol levels when they become adults.

A number of functions may be programmed in the womb, including blood pressure, insulin response to glucose, and cholesterol metabolism. In situations of poor nutrition these may be programmed incorrectly and possibly lead to subsequent health problems. Although the extent of prenatal programming is debated, evidence suggests poor prenatal conditions have long-term effects resulting from the mismatch between the prenatal environment in which the organs were developed and the postnatal environment in which they must function. The prenatal environment may thus determine the functional capacity of various organs for the rest of life.

Behavior of the fetus

The behavior of the human fetus has aroused much speculation, but only in recent years has it been the subject of scientific study. Views of the behavior of the fetus have ranged from the fetus as a miniature human with all its abilities, to the fetus as an unresponsive passive organism. As science has examined the prenatal period, a picture of an active fetus is emerging: a fetus which exists in an environment of stimulation and reacts to it. The following sections review evidence pertaining to fetal movement, fetal sensory abilities, and fetal learning.

Fetal movements

The advent of ultrasound technology (see Figure 3.4) has provided clinicians and scientists with a window through which to watch the behavior of the fetus.

Mothers feel their fetus move from around 18–20 weeks of gestation (a time known as the **quickening**), although there is much individual variation in the maternal perception of movements. Using ultrasound, however, fetal movements are observed to emerge much earlier, at 8 weeks (Prechtl, 1988).

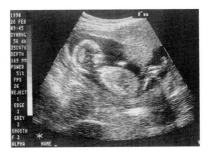

Figure 3.4 Ultrasound image of human fetus at 16 weeks.

Table 3.2 Gestational age at which behaviors are first observed in the fetus (from de Vries *et al.*, 1985)

Behavior	Gestational age (weeks)
Just discernible movement	7
Startle	8
General movement	8
Hiccup	9
Isolated arm movement	9
Isolated leg movement	9
Isolated head retroflexion[a]	9
Isolated head rotation	9–10
Isolated head anteflexion[b]	10
Fetal breathing movements	10
Arm twitch	10
Leg twitch	10
Hand–face contact	10
Stretch	10
Rotation of fetus	10
Jaw movement	10–11
Yawn	11
Finger movement	12
Sucking and swallowing	12
Clonic movement arm or leg[c]	13
Rooting	14
Eye movements	16

[a]retroflexion = head bends backwards; [b]anteflexion = head bends downwards; [c]clonic = short spasmodic movements.

These slow movements originate in nerve impulses from the spinal cord, and may result in passive movements of the arms and legs. Over the next few weeks a variety of different movements emerge (see Table 3.2) and by 20 weeks most of the movements the fetus will produce are present in its behavioral repertoire (Prechtl, 1988).

Behavioral states in the fetus

The fetus remains active throughout its time in the womb, but as it develops its movements become concentrated into periods of activity and periods of inactivity (James *et al.*, 1995). Towards the end of pregnancy, behavioral states have been observed in the fetus. Behavioral states are defined as recognizable and well-defined associations of variables, which are stable over time and with clear transitions between each. Four behavioral states have been identified in the fetus, based on the observation of behavioral states in the newborn (Prechtl, 1974). Behavioral states are observed from 36 weeks of gestational age (Nijhuis *et al.*, 1982) and it has been argued that their emergence represents a greater degree of integration within the various parts of the central nervous system. The four states that have been defined, using the variables of heart rate pattern, the presence or absence of eye movements, and the presence or absence of body movements, are:

- **State 1F: Quiet sleep**. The fetus exhibits occasional startles, no eye movements, and a stable fetal heart rate. This occurrence of state increases from about 15% at 36 weeks of gestation to 32% at 38 weeks and 38% at term.

- **State 2F: Active sleep**. This state is characterized by frequent and periodic gross body movements, eye movements are present and the fetal heart rate shows frequent accelerations in association with movement. This is the most commonly occurring state, being observed around 42–48% of time in the fetus.

- **State 3F: Quiet awake**. No gross body movements are observed, eye movements are present, and the fetal heart rate shows no accelerations and has a wider oscillation bandwidth than in state 1F. This is a rare state to observe, as it occurs only briefly. In fact its occurrence is usually represented by number of occurrences rather than as a percentage of time.

- **State 4F: Active awake**. In this state the fetus exhibits continual activity, eye movements are present, the fetal heart rate is unstable, and tachycardia (increased pulse rate) is present. This state occurs about 6–7% of the time between 36 and 38 weeks of gestation increasing to 9% just before birth, around 40 weeks of gestation.

Fetal senses

All the senses adults have operate to some degree in the fetus (with the possible exception of vision; see below). However, in order for them to operate a requirement is that stimulation penetrates the womb to be received by the fetus's sensory receptors. As we shall see, the fetal environment is one of ever-changing stimuli which the fetus can detect and respond to.

Hearing

The fetus responds to sound from 22–24 weeks by exhibiting a change in its movement (Shahidullah & Hepper, 1993). The fetus's response is influenced by the frequency, intensity, and duration of the sound presented (Hepper & Shahidullah, 1994). For example, louder intensities elicit a greater response.

The fetus's hearing begins in the low-frequency part (250 Hz, 500 Hz) of the adult hearing range (20–20 000 Hz) and as it develops the range of frequencies it responds to increases (Hepper & Shahidullah, 1994). As well as simply responding to sounds the fetus is able to discriminate between different sounds, e.g., spoken words such as 'babi' and 'biba' (Lecanuet et al., 1987).

The environment of the fetus is quite noisy. Sounds from the mother's heartbeat, blood flow, and digestive system will permeate the fetal environment (Querleu et al., 1988). All the sounds you or I hear can also penetrate the mother's womb and stimulate the fetus's hearing. However, sounds from the external environment are attenuated by the mother's skin and other tissues. High-pitched sounds over 2000 Hz are attenuated by as much as 40 dB and thus are probably not experienced by the fetus (Querleu et al., 1989). To make them audible to the fetus would require a sound level that would damage the hearing of the mother! Interestingly, there is little attenuation around 125–250 Hz, the fundamental frequency of the human voice. Thus, the mother talking and other speech sounds in the environment will be readily heard by the fetus.

Chemosensation

The senses of smell and taste are difficult to separate in the womb as the amniotic fluid bathes both receptor types and may stimulate both sensory systems. For this reason the fetal responses to smell and taste are usually considered under the same heading, **chemosensation**.

The fetus is able to discriminate between sweet and noxious substances added to the amniotic fluid. Fetuses increase their swallowing when a sweet substance (sugar) is added to the amniotic fluid by injection but decrease it when a noxious substance (iodinated poppy seed) is added. Newborns show a preference for the odor of their mother compared to that of another woman and orient to their own amniotic fluid, further suggesting experience of odors/tastes in the womb (Schaal et al., 2004).

The fetus swallows amniotic fluid from around 12 weeks of gestation, so substances that diffuse into the fluid, e.g., from the mother's diet, will be experienced by the fetus (Schaal et al., 2004). Moreover, as the mother's diet changes so will the stimulation received by the fetus.

Somatosensory stimuli

Pain

The question of whether the fetus feels pain is at the center of many scientific and political debates. Answering this question is made more difficult by the fact that pain is a subjective phenomenon and can be difficult to examine. Pain responses have been observed in the premature infant from around 24–26 weeks, and neural pathways for pain are formed around 26 weeks of gestation (Fitzgerald, 1993). Behavioral reactions to possibly painful stimuli, e.g., if the fetus is touched by the needle during amniocentesis (a test for chromosome abnormalities in the fetus), or following fetal scalp blood sampling (to assess fetal status during labor) have been observed. Biochemical stress responses to needle punctures during blood transfusions have been observed from 23 weeks of gestation. These, however, are all indirect measures of pain experience and there is still a debate as to whether the fetus feels pain.

Temperature

Anecdotal reports suggest that mothers feel more fetal movements as they take a hot bath. However, in the normal course of pregnancy the temperature of the mother's womb is regulated and maintained so there will be little variation for the fetus to experience.

Touch

Touch is the first sense of the fetus to develop at around 8 weeks. If the fetus's lips or cheeks are touched at 8–9 weeks, it responds by moving its head away from the touch (Hooker, 1952). Later in pregnancy this response changes, and during the second trimester the fetus now moves towards the touch. By 14 weeks of gestation most of the body, excluding the back and top of the head, is responsive to touch. The fetus's arms will make contact with its face from about 13 weeks of gestation, providing a source of stimulation. For twins and other multiple pregnancies, there will be much tactile stimulation from other womb partners.

Vision

Vision is the sense least likely to be stimulated during the normal course of pregnancy (Hepper, 1992). At best the fetus may experience some general change in illumination. When tested under experimental conditions the fetus exhibits a change in heart rate or movement when a bright light is flashed on the mother's abdomen from around 26 weeks of gestation, demonstrating that the visual system is operating to a certain extent.

Fetal learning

The ability of the fetus to learn is perhaps the most fascinating of all fetal abilities, because learning is often seen as the pinnacle of adult achievement. The ability to learn also has implications for the functioning of other abilities, e.g., it requires a sensory system able to detect and discriminate stimuli and a memory system able to store information.

Habituation

The presentation of a loud, discrete sound initially elicits a large reaction (change in heart rate or movement) in the fetus but as this sound is repeated the fetus's response wanes and eventually disappears—this waning of response is termed **habituation.** The fetus habituates to auditory stimuli from around 22–24 weeks of gestation, and female fetuses have been observed to habituate faster than male fetuses at any particular gestational age, a finding which may indicate that female fetuses are developmentally more advanced than male fetuses (Hepper & Leader, 1996).

Exposure learning

Most studies examining fetal learning have studied whether the newborn responds differently to sounds it has been exposed to before birth compared to sounds it has not been exposed to (Hepper, 1996).

Mother's voice Newborns prefer their mother's voice to that of an unfamiliar woman (DeCasper & Fifer, 1980). Some very elegant experiments were performed to reveal this remarkable ability. These studies used the newborns' ability to suck. Newborns sucked on a dummy in the absence of any stimulation to establish a baseline sucking rate. Once this was established the newborn was given two choices: if it sucked faster than the baseline it received the sound of its mother's voice through headphones, whereas if it sucked slower it received the voice of an unfamiliar woman. Newborns sucked faster to hear their mother's voice. If the contingencies were reversed and sucking slower led to hearing the mother's voice, newborns sucked slower. What is clear is that this ability to recognize the mother's voice is acquired before birth (Fifer & Moon 1989).

Music Newborns prefer music they have heard prenatally compared to that which they have never heard. Interestingly, this preference can be observed at 36 weeks of gestation but not 30 weeks of gestation, which may indicate that learning of familiar sounds or tunes occurs after 30 weeks (Hepper, 1991).

Functions of behavior

The fetus exhibits a complex and varied behavioral repertoire. But why does the fetus exhibit these behaviors? There are a number of possible reasons.

Practicing for life outside the womb

One key role for prenatal behavior is to practice behaviors that will be essential for survival after birth; fetal breathing movements are an example of this. These movements are observed from 9–10 weeks of gestation (de Vries *et al.*, 1985). Although there is no air in the womb these movements, motion of the diaphragm and rib cage, would result in breathing after birth and hence are termed **fetal breathing movements.** At 30 weeks of gestation these movements occur around 30% of the time (Patrick *et al.*, 1980). Later in pregnancy fetal breathing movements increase during periods of fetal activity. Practicing before birth ensures the neural pathways responsible for breathing are fully mature, thus ensuring a fully operational system when required, at the moment of birth

Ontogenetic adaptations

Although fetal behavior research currently emphasizes the continuity of development, it should not be forgotten that the embryo and fetus exist in a very different environment from that to be experienced after birth. It may thus be expected that the fetus would exhibit behavior designed to ensure its survival in the womb, and such behaviors are termed **ontogenetic adaptations**—that is, adaptations to its life in the womb. Although the concept of ontogenetic adaptations is well accepted, fetal adaptations to life in the womb have been little studied. Some reflexes may be important for the process of birth and labor. An example of these is the kicking movements that appear near the end of pregnancy. These reposition the head of the fetus so that it is in the position for safe delivery (**vertex presentation**).

Recognition of mother

The learning abilities of the fetus may be crucial for its survival and development in the first weeks after birth, by enabling it to recognize its mother and begin the process of attachment and exploration. Many studies have demonstrated the ability of the newborn infant to recognize its mother by auditory and odor cues, an ability acquired prenatally (DeCasper & Fifer, 1980; Porter & Winberg, 1999). The mother is a crucial figure for the newborn's survival. In terms of recognizing items in its environment the newborn is a blank canvas, and has to learn what objects are in its environment as it develops. It makes good sense to provide one object, and a very important one at that, that the individual may recognize at birth. Prenatal learning may serve to ensure that the newborn recognizes its mother at birth.

Breast-feeding

Prenatal learning may also be important for the establishment of breast-feeding. The same processes that flavor the mother's breast milk also flavor the amniotic fluid (Schaal *et al.*, 2004). The fetus may learn about the flavor of the amniotic fluid while in the womb, and when placed to the breast for the first time it recognizes a familiar flavor and sucks readily. Successful breast-feeding is crucial for the newborn's survival (see Chapter 18), and prenatal learning may ensure the successful establishment of breast-feeding (Hepper, 1996).

Developing physical form and developing the brain

The behavior of the fetus is important for shaping the development of its body. The movements of the fetus are important for its structural development. The formation of the body's joints and the development of muscle and muscle tone all rely on the fetus moving its limbs during development. Joints do not form properly when their movements are restricted (Moessinger, 1988). The behavior of the fetus may also influence the long-term development of the brain. Sensory experiences may shape the development of its sensory system. It is well established that visual experience after birth shapes the development of the visual system (Blakemore and Cooper, 1970), as we shall see in Chapter 5. For those senses active and stimulated before birth, e.g., audition, stimulation may influence the development of these sensory systems. The potential for experiential factors to influence the development of the brain is great.

Birth and labor

For most of pregnancy the aim of mother and baby is to keep the baby within the womb until it is sufficiently mature to survive outside. Once this time is reached, however, the fetus can leave its uterine environment for life in the postnatal world.

Preparation for birth

The activity of the uterine muscles is inhibited during pregnancy by the hormone progesterone (the hormone found in the ovaries which helps to maintain pregnancy). However, the muscles of the uterus are not completely inactive. During pregnancy mothers often feel a tightening of the uterus at regular intervals, known as **Braxton Hicks contractions**. These contractions play an important role in preparing the uterus for delivery by developing its muscle tone. These are different from the contractions that are felt during labor, which are shorter in duration and occur every few minutes, increasing in frequency and intensity as labor progresses.

As the time of birth approaches the fetus's brain signals for more production of new chemicals, e.g., adrenocorticotrophin (ACTH) and cortisol. These chemicals act to convert progesterone to estrogen. Estrogen, in contrast to progesterone, promotes muscle activity in the uterus. The inhibitory control exercised over the muscles from the beginning of pregnancy is removed and mothers may feel a 'tightening' in their uterus and may experience contractions in the days leading up to delivery.

These changes also stimulate the breast to prepare for the production of milk—a process completed when the baby begins to suck.

Labor and birth

Birth and labor involve a constant interaction between the baby and mother. For example, as the fetus's head presses against the cervix, this stimulates the mother's pituitary gland to release oxytocin. This in turn stimulates the muscles of the uterus to contract, forcing the fetus's head into the cervix and continuing the cycle of contraction. Moreover, oxytocin also stimulates the release of prostaglandins which increase the strength of uterine muscle contractions. This process continually escalates during labor, contractions becoming more forceful, and eventually resulting in the birth of the baby.

Exactly what determines the onset of labor is unknown. However, somehow the fetus 'knows' when it is ready to be born and it initiates a series of processes that culminate in its birth. The actual birth process is divided into three stages.

- The **first stage**, usually the longest, begins with uterine contractions, each maybe lasting up to a minute, occurring every 15–20 minutes. As this stage progresses, the contractions become more frequent and more intense. These contractions enable the mother's cervix to expand and stretch and enable the baby to move from the womb to the birth canal. At the end of the first stage the cervix has dilated to about 9 cm (3.5 inches). The length of this stage generally decreases after the mother's first baby, but there is huge variability between individual mothers in the duration of this stage of pregnancy. In first pregnancies it may last 8–24 hours.

- Once the baby's head passes through the cervix and into the birth canal, the **second stage** of labor has begun. Mothers bear down at the time of contractions in an effort to push the baby from their body. It culminates when the baby is born, free from the birth canal but attached to the mother by the umbilical cord and placenta.

- The **third stage** is the afterbirth, and here contractions expel the placenta.

Survival after birth

Two important changes need to take place after birth, as a result of the umbilical cord being cut and the baby having to survive on its own. First, the baby must now breathe for him or herself. The previous 25 weeks spent practicing breathing movements now reap benefits as the baby starts breathing and obtaining oxygen through its own actions. The second adaptation involves a change from the fetal pattern of blood circulation to the adult pattern of circulation. This is triggered by the fact that the baby now oxygenates its blood from the lungs and not the placenta. Perhaps the most important change is the closure of the foramen ovale which prevents the blood, now deoxygenated blood, flowing from the right atrium to the left atrium of the heart. These changes in blood flow occur over the first few days and weeks after birth (Moore & Persaud, 2003).

Reflexes

The newborn baby's motor repertoire consists mainly of reflexes, which are involuntary movements elicited in response to stimulation, e.g., touch, light, change in position (see Table 3.3). These motor behaviors are controlled by neural structures below the level of the cortex. These reflexes are present at birth and disappear in the months after birth.

The normal exhibition and disappearance of these reflexes is an important indicator of the functioning and integrity of the baby's brain. Reflexes that persist beyond the time when they usually disappear, or are weaker than

Table 3.3 Some of the baby's reflexes

Reflex	Description	Developmental time course
Rooting	Touch the side of the mouth or cheek and the baby turns towards touch	Birth to 4–5 months
Sucking	Touch the mouth or lips and the baby begins to suck	Birth to 4–6 months
Grasping	When the baby's palms are touched the baby grasps the object	Birth to 4 months
Moro	In response to a sudden loud sound or 'dropping' the baby suddenly the baby startles, throws its head back and arms and legs stretch out and then rapidly brings them back to the centre of the body	Birth to 4–6 months
Babinski	Stroke the bottom of the foot and the toes fan out and then curl	Birth to 9–12 months.
Swimming	When the baby is placed in water it holds its breath and makes swimming movements with arms and legs	Birth to 4–6 months
Stepping	If the baby is held above a surface and its feet allowed to touch the surface, it begins to show walking movements	Birth to 3–4 months
Labyrinthine	When the baby is placed on its back it extends its arms and legs, or when placed on its stomach it flexes its arms and legs	Birth to 4 months

normal, may be indicative of underlying neural impairment such as cerebral palsy.

Reflexes are important for the survival of the newborn infant and also serve as the basic building blocks on which future motor development is based. Some reflexes are essential for survival, e.g., breathing, swallowing. To enable breast-feeding the newborn infant has a rooting and sucking reflex. Touch on the side of the mouth or cheek stimulates the newborn to turn towards the touch, to locate the nipple. This is **rooting**. Once it is located, another reflex initiated by stimulation on the mouth or lips, **sucking**, enables the newborn to grasp the nipple and stimulate it to produce milk and thus obtain nutrients essential for growth. Rooting and sucking disappear at about 4–6 months, to be replaced by voluntary eating behavior. Some reflexes remain throughout life, e.g., blinking and yawning. In the normal course of events reflexes may disappear or become incorporated into more voluntary gross and fine motor movements—for example, the grasping reflex of the infant.

Newborn senses

As has been discussed, all of the individual's senses are functional to a certain extent in the womb and the baby's arrival into the world makes little difference in its abilities, but rather marks a difference in the quality of sensation the individual is exposed to. The biggest change is in the visual stimuli experienced by the baby. Other than a diffuse orange glow the visual system of the fetus will be unstimulated during pregnancy, yet from birth the newborn is exposed to the same visual stimuli as adults. However, of all the senses the visual sense is least well developed. The newborn has poor visual accommodation and an underdeveloped pupillary reflex. Visual accommodation is the process whereby small muscles attached to the lens change the shape of the lens, thus bringing objects at different distances from the eye into focus. The newborn infant has limited visual accommodation and can see objects most clearly about 20–50 cm (7–20 inches) away from its eye—an excellent distance for viewing the mother's face when feeding. The pupillary reflex controls the amount of light entering the eye and after birth this ability is poor, further inhibiting the ability of the baby to focus. Both processes develop rapidly and, along with the development of other crucial processes for accurate vision—eye movements, tracking, scanning—enable the infant's vision to improve with age.

Audition, chemosensation, and various somatosensory senses have been operating since before birth and continue their development after birth to provide the baby with information about its new environment.

SUMMARY

The prenatal period is a crucial period of development of our lives. It is the formative period for all our body organs and plays a role in establishing their functional capacity. The potential exists for severe disruption to the normal developmental process from environmental agents. However for the vast majority of pregnancies the environment exerts a positive effect, shaping the individual's development. The fetus is an active participant in its own development. Its behavior is important for progressing normal development within the womb and for its life in the postnatal world. It is the foundation on which all future development after birth is built.

CHAPTER FOUR

Motor development: how infants get into the act

KAREN E. ADOLPH and AMY S. JOH

Overview: motor actions and psychological function

Motor development is truly amazing. In their first year of life, infants acquire the ability to direct their eyes at targets, support their bodies against gravity, grasp and manipulate objects, and locomote across the room. One reason why these accomplishments appear so amazing is that motor actions are directly observable. Whereas we must infer developments in perception and cognition on the basis of infants' overt behaviors, development in motor skills require no inferential leap from observable behavior to underlying competence. When infants turn their head to gaze up at a parent's smiling face, stretch out an arm to reach for an attractive toy, and maintain balance while toddling across the room, the overt motor performance is direct evidence of their developing skill.

Perhaps not so readily apparent are the links between motor skills and other psychological functions. Motor actions are not merely a matter of muscles and biomechanics. Perception and cognition are integral to the real-time control of movement (Adolph & Berger, 2005, in press; Bertenthal & Clifton, 1998; Gibson & Pick, 2000). Perception informs infants about which movements to do and how to execute them to suit the constraints of the current situation. Perceptual information guides infants' eyes, hands, and bodies toward the target, and perceptual systems provide feedback about the consequences of the movement. Cognition—learning, thinking, remembering, and means–ends problem-solving—helps infants to discover new solutions for challenging motor problems and to avoid repeating mistakes that they have tried in the past. Action, in turn, provides new information for perceptual systems and new grist for cognition. Every movement points both backward and forward, generating information about the consequences of the prior movement and specifying which movements to do next.

Motor skills are also linked with developmental changes in perception and cognition. As Piaget (1952) and Gibson (1988) pointed out, the acquisition of new motor skills provides infants with new sources of information about the world. The development of **eye–head control** provides infants with opportunities to learn about events and the location of objects and surfaces. **Looking** is probably the most pervasive mode of access to information about things at a distance. The development of **manual skills** invites a new world of learning about objects and surfaces. Once infants can reach, grasp, and manipulate objects, they can bring things to their eyes and mouth for additional exploration and see what objects look like from multiple angles. Once they can stretch out an arm to explore a surface, they can discover what things feel like and whether surfaces can support their weight. The development of independent **locomotion** allows infants to learn about places and the objects and surfaces that populate various locations. Now, infants can position their own bodies to see what is around the corner or under the table, exert change on the environment by fetching and carrying objects, and assert new forms of emotional independence by leaving their caregivers to explore on their own (Figure 4.1).

Perhaps most amazing are the deeper psychological implications of basic motor skills. Integral to the seemingly simple acts of looking, reaching, and walking are what E. Gibson (Gibson, 1997; Gibson & Pick, 2000) eloquently termed the **hallmarks of psychological development**. Motor actions involve **agency** (knowledge of a distinct self who can effect change on the environment), **prospectivity** (gearing actions to the future), **behavioral flexibility** (adapting behaviors to variable and novel circumstances), and **means–ends problem-solving** (finding new ways to achieve one's goals). Although these psychological achievements are central to every domain of development, Gibson's hallmarks are perhaps best illustrated in the motor domain where researchers can directly observe psychology in action.

The chapter is divided into three sections, each representing an action system that infants master in the first year of life: eye–head control, manual skills, and locomotion. Typically, infants acquire these action systems in sequence, so that development proceeds from head to toe and the earlier developing action system serves as a building block for the later developing one. Developments in postural control underlie the entire progression because looking, reaching, and locomotion can only emerge from a stable postural base (see changing postures in Figure 4.1). In each section of the chapter, we illustrate the importance of motor development by highlighting the reciprocal relationship between motor actions and psychological development. Drawing on examples from classic and recent research, we focus on the facilitative effects of motor development. We show how infants' emerging motor skills expand the scope of their effective environment and thereby enlarge and enrich their psychological world. A pervasive theme is the central role of motor experience in facilitating developmental change. We also illustrate

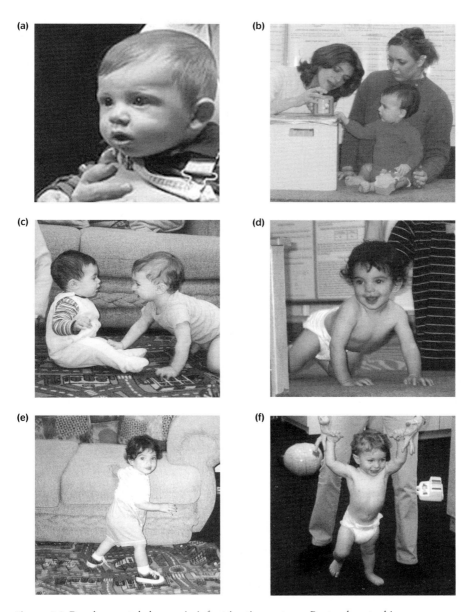

Figure 4.1 Developmental changes in infants' action systems. Postural control is a prerequisite for each new skill. (a) Eye-head control allows visual exploration by looking. (b) Sitting and reaching provide new means for interacting with objects. (c, d) Sitting and crawling give infants new vantage points and new access to varied locations. (e, f) Cruising (moving sideways along furniture) and walking provide a higher vantage point and different ways of interacting with objects, people, and places (pictures courtesy of Karen Adolph).

the flip side of the developmental story: how the hallmarks of psychological growth are expressed in the context of motor action.

Eye–head control

For many years, developmental researchers have treated infants' eyes as a perceptual system rather than an action system. Part of this traditional view stems from several decades of reliance on infants' looking time as a dependent measure: Most studies of perceptual and cognitive development with infants use preferential looking, habituation, and violation of expectation paradigms. Indeed, many recent studies have juxtaposed looking with **action-based measures** such as reaching (Munakata, McClelland, Johnson & Siegler, 1997, p. 704) and **active object search** (Keen, 2003, p. 79), as if the eyes are perceptual whereas the arms are motor. However, looking is no more passive than reaching. Although looking may serve as a convenient window into perceptual and conceptual processes, it is a motor action (Adolph & Berger, in press). Infants must move their eyes and heads to look at the displays (rather than at the ceiling or their bellies and feet) and looking-time measures depend on how long infants aim their eyes in the various directions. Eye-tracking studies make this point very clearly because the traces provide a record of infants' eye movements. The single data point that results from a looking-time study is actually a summary of dozens of exploratory eye movements.

Looking is not only an exploratory system. It is also a performatory action system that infants can use to respond to and initiate changes in the external environment, in this case, the social environment (Gibson, 1988). Indeed, looking is one of infants' first means for social interaction and one of the first signs of agency. Through looking behaviors, infants begin to gain a sense of a distinct self with intentions and powers that can act on the world. In normal face-to-face interactions between infants and caregivers, both social partners initiate and respond to each other's eye movements, facial expressions, vocalizations, and gentle touches. When the social contingencies are broken, for example, by a caregiver presenting a still face rather than a reciprocally moving and interacting one, infants stop directing their gaze at their partner, stop smiling, and may become distressed (Gusella, Muir & Tronick, 1988).

Like all action systems, eye–head coordination develops. At first, looking is mostly opportunistic. Young infants have difficulty focusing visual attention on interesting objects and events because they lack the muscle strength to hold their heads up against gravity and they lack the coordination to turn their heads in unison with their eyes (Daniel & Lee, 1990). Newborns can turn their heads from side to side while resting on their stomachs or backs, but they cannot lift their heads off the floor for extended periods of time (Bly, 1994). When they are held upright, their large heads loll. By 2–3 weeks after birth, infants' muscles have become strong enough to lift their chins from the floor while prone. By 5–10 weeks, infants can lift their heads and chest from the floor. By 3 months, infants can hold their heads steady while propping themselves on their arms in a prone position and when held upright on their parents' laps (Bly, 1994). Now, infants need not wait for objects to fall into their line of sight. Instead, they can control where they are looking.

Smooth pursuit is an especially complex type of eye movement. To move their gaze at the same speed as an object, infants must control their eye movements prospectively. They must anticipate and predict where the object will be next. At 1 month of age, infants can smoothly follow a moving object with their eyes for short periods of time, but only if the conditions are just right (Aslin, 1981; Rosander & von Hofsten, 2000; von Hofsten & Rosander, 1996). For example, objects must be large and move slowly along a predictable path (von Hofsten & Rosander, 1997). Moreover, infants' heads must be held in place by a caregiver's hands or supported by cushions because infants do not have sufficient control to manage their heads on their own. Smooth pursuit improves rapidly over the next few months, so that looking at moving objects shows longer periods of smooth pursuit and shorter periods of corrective jerky **saccades** (Figure 4.2A). With practice, infants become better able to follow smaller, faster objects (Phillips, Finoccio, Ong & Fuchs, 1997; Richards & Holley, 1999; Rosander & von Hofsten, 2002).

Prospectivity in looking requires not just improvements in smooth pursuit and head control, but also coordination between eye and head movements. While following a moving object, sometimes the head may move too slowly and the eyes may need to compensate. Initially, eye and head movements are not well coordinated (von Hofsten, 2004; von Hofsten & Rosander, 1997). Weeks after infants can track moving objects smoothly with their eyes, they begin to make large tracking movements with their heads. However, initially their heads lag so far behind the target that they must put their eyes ahead of the target to keep it in view. As a consequence of their poor eye–head coordination, infants show a decrease in tracking precision. By 4–5 months, they can move their eyes and heads together to follow objects smoothly (Rosander & von Hofsten, 2004).

Experience moving the eyes and head to track objects facilitates infants' object knowledge. When a moving object disappears behind an occluder (imagine a ball moving behind a square screen), infants must possess a rudimentary knowledge of objects to understand that the object continues to exist and to anticipate when it will reappear on the far side. Normally, 6-month-olds exhibit more anticipatory eye movements than 4-month-olds while tracking an object as it moves behind an occluder, and the older infants' eye movements are faster. However, only 2 minutes of experience tracking an object moving on an unoccluded trajectory was sufficient to boost 4-month-olds' performance to that of 6-month-olds when tested with the object moving behind an occluder (Johnson, Amso & Slemner, 2003).

Even at the same age, the ability to keep the eyes on a moving target predicts infants' level of object knowledge (Johnson, Slemmer & Amso,

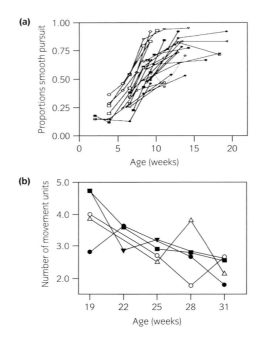

Figure 4.2 Developmental improvements in looking, reaching, and locomotion.
(a) Improvements in smooth pursuit, the ability to smoothly track moving objects with the eyes, from 3 to 20 weeks. Curves show developmental trajectories of individual infants. Adapted from von Hofsten, C. (2004). An action perspective on motor development. *Trends in Cognitive Sciences, 8*, 266–272, with permission from Elsevier, copyright © (2004).
(b) Improvements in reaching from 19 to 31 weeks of age. Fewer movement units imply fewer corrections and straighter reaching paths. Curves show developmental trajectories of individual infants. Adapted from von Hofsten, C. (1991). Structuring of early reaching movements: A longitudinal study. *Journal of Motor Behavior, 23*, 280–292, with permission of the Helen Dwight Reid Educational Foundation. Published by Heldref Publications, 1319 18th Street, NW, Washington, DC 20036–1802. www.heldref.org. Copyright © (1991).
(c) Improvements in crawling proficiency (indexed by velocity) over weeks of experience. Solid curve represents infants who crawled on their bellies prior to crawling on hands and knees. Dashed curve represents infants who skipped the belly crawling period. Adapted from Adolph, K. E., Vereijken, B. & Denny, M. A. (1998). Learning to crawl. *Child Development, 69*, 1299–1312, with permission from Blackwell Publishing. (d) Improvements in walking proficiency over weeks of experience (indexed by step length). Each symbol represents one infant's data. Adapted from Adolph, K. E., Vereijken, B. & Shrout, P. E. (2003). What changes in infant walking and why. *Child Development, 74*, 475–497, with permission from Blackwell Publishing.

(c)

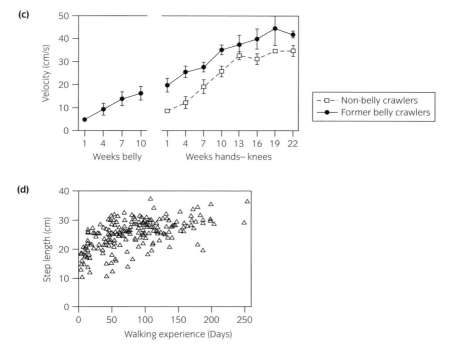

(d)

Figure 4.2 continued.

2004). At 3 months of age, some infants spontaneously watched the visible ends of a rod as it moved back and forth behind an occluder during an initial familiarization period. Other infants directed more of their eye movements toward the occluder or the background. Thus, the former group showed higher levels of visual object exploration. They were also more likely to show increased looking times at test displays of two end bits of rods, suggesting that they had perceived that the rod was complete as they tracked its trajectory during familiarization. The latter group, who had looked at the occluder rather than the moving object, were more likely to show increased looking to a test display of the complete rod, suggesting that they had failed to detect object unity during the initial familiarization period.

Given the powerful facilitative effects of only 2 minutes of experience moving their eyes in a laboratory looking task, the benefits of everyday experiences with looking must be enormous. By some estimates, 2-month-old infants have logged more than 200 hours of visual experience and have made over 2.5 million eye movements (Johnson *et al.*, 2003)! By 3.5 months, infants have executed between 3 and 6 million eye movements as they scan, track, and explore their visual surrounds (Haith, Hazan & Goodman, 1988). Developing motor skill with eyes and head presents infants with increasing opportunities to learn by looking.

Manual skills

Many misconceptions about motor development stem from our vernacular. We talk of 'fetuses kicking' and 'infants reaching' because we don't have common expressions to describe the spontaneous flails, wiggles, twitches, arches, thrashes, and so on that characterize so many of infants' early limb movements. Most fetal 'kicks' felt by mothers are really spontaneous movements of arms, head, trunk—and legs—against the uterine wall because the fetus cannot fully extend its body parts in the tight space of the womb. Most of infants' early 'reaches' are really spontaneous arm extensions with no ability or intent to grasp an object. Spontaneous motility is one of the pervasive features of early motor development. Movements begin at 6 weeks of gestation, from the instant that fetuses acquire rudimentary muscles and neural circuitry (Moore & Persaud, 1998). Fetuses and infants spend vast amounts of time in motion.

The earliest examples of infants' manual behaviors occur before birth. Fetuses flail their arms, wiggle their fingers, form a fist, and suck their thumbs (Prechtl, 1985, 1986). Manual exploration also begins prenatally. Approximately 2/3 of fetal hand movements are directed toward objects and surfaces—the umbilical cord, the uterine wall, and their own faces and bodies (Sparling, van Tol & Chescheir, 1999). Spontaneous arm movements continue after birth and persist in high frequency throughout the first year (Thelen, 1979). Infants bang their arms and hands against surfaces, flap their arms up and down, bend and straighten their elbows, rotate their hands in circles, and wave their fingers.

Spontaneous manual activity can quickly become goal-directed when harnessed by the appropriate experimental arrangement. For example, 2- to 8-month-olds increased the frequency of their arm flails when the movements activated an engaging slide show (Lewis, Alessandri & Sullivan, 1990). The shift from spontaneous to instrumental activity reflects a sense of agency. Infants' facial expressions were neutral as they flailed their arms spontaneously during baseline activity. Their expressions showed interest, joy, and surprise as they explored the contingency between their arm movements and the slide show and then worked to maintain the reinforcement. Their expressions conveyed anger when the contingency was broken in an extinction period and infants showed interest and joy—but not surprise—when the contingency was reinstated. The facial expressions of yoked controls tended toward neutral across conditions, suggesting that it was the sense of control—their own power over the environment—that was reinforcing, not simply the slide show.

The development of reaching depends on postural control (Bertenthal & von Hofsten, 1998). The problem is not sufficient strength to lift the arms; the impediment to reaching is sufficient strength and control to support the rest of the body as the arms lift or swing (Adolph & Berger, 2005). Infants cannot engage in manual activities while their heads loll or their trunks collapse; they cannot reach when their arms are needed to support their bodies. Thus, when left to their own powers, infants' first goal-directed reaches appear at about 4 months while lying on their backs, at 5 months while lying on their stomachs propped on one arm, and at 6–8 months while sitting with their legs outstretched in a 'V' (Bly, 1994; Rochat, 1992). Around the time infants begin to sit independently, they also begin to show coordinated manual and visual exploration: They finger objects and rotate them in front of their faces, alternate between mouthing and looking, and transfer objects from one hand to the other (Rochat, 1989). Better sitting abilities predict more sophisticated behaviors such as leaning forward to grab objects, using both right and left hands interchangeably, and retrieving objects across a wider range of space (Rochat & Goubet, 1995).

However, with the right kind of external postural support, even newborns can extend their arms in the general direction of a target (Amiel-Tison & Grenier, 1986; von Hofsten, 1982, 1984; von Hofsten & Ronnqvist, 1993). In the most popular paradigms, infants are strapped high around the chest to a slightly reclined board with their heads propped upright by tiny side cushions, or are supported on their parents' laps with the adults' hands holding up their torsos (Figure 4.3). While supported, infants begin reaching for stationary objects between 12 and 18 weeks of age (Berthier & Keen, 2006; Clifton, Muir, Ashmead & Clarkson, 1993) and for moving objects at around 18 weeks (von Hofsten, 1979, 1980). Usually, infants' first supported reaches end with object contact rather than capturing the object in their grasp.

As with the eye–head system, reaching and grasping show developmental improvements in prospective control. Initially, infants' reaching movements

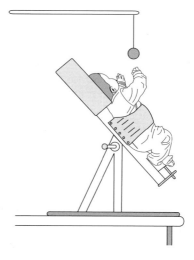

Figure 4.3 Typical experimental set-up to test reaching in young infants. The reclining seat and head cushions provide external postural support for infants who cannot yet sit independently. The chest strap leaves infants' hands free for reaching objects. Adapted from von Hofsten, C. (1982). Eye–hand coordination in the newborn. *Developmental Psychology, 18*, 450–461, with permission from APA.

are jerky and composed of several corrections as infants guide their hands toward the goal. Reaching becomes progressively smoother and straighter until, at approximately 31 weeks of age, infants' reaches resemble the adult form: a large movement to bring the hand to the vicinity of the target and a second smaller movement for the grasp (von Hofsten, 1991) (Figure 4.2b). Toward the end of the first year, prospective control of reaching is sufficiently well developed for infants to catch objects moving at different speeds (van Hof, van der Kamp, Caljouw & Savelsbergh, 2005) and to catch moving objects as they emerge from behind an occluder (van der Meer, van der Weel & Lee, 1994).

Prospective control of grasping develops during the same time period. Infants' first grasps are little more than accidental swipes, but by 5 months of age, infants change their grip configuration to match the size and shape of target objects (Newell, Scully, McDonald & Baillargeon, 1989). By 7.5 months, they preform the orientation of their hands to match the orientation of a target dowel (Witherington, 2005). By 9 months, they open their hands to match an object's size and start closing it in anticipation of contacting the object (von Hofsten & Ronnqvist, 1988). By 10 months, their grasps are so accurate that they can pincer-grip small objects between their thumb and fingers (Gesell, 1952).

New opportunities for learning abound after infants solve the problem of postural control and free up their hands for exploration. They can discover a new world of objects, surfaces, and the relations between them. For example, 6- to 10-month-old infants explored a wooden cube by scratching and picking it and a sponge cube by squeezing it (Bourgeois, Khawar, Neal & Lockman, 2005). They used rubbing, picking, pressing, and slapping movements differentially to explore rigid, spongy, net, and liquid tabletop surfaces. Most interesting, infants related the objects to the surfaces differentially with their exploratory movements. They rubbed the cubes against the rigid tabletop, pressed the cubes into the spongy tabletop, and banged the wooden cube against the rigid and net tabletops. The 10-month-olds' actions were the most discriminating.

Exploration is intrinsically rewarding. The ability to learn through manual manipulation makes infants eager for more interactions with objects and surfaces. For example, a clever manipulation—sticky Velcro mittens—allowed 3-month-olds to reach, grasp, and manipulate Velcro-covered toys (Needham, Barrett & Peterman, 2002). With their transformed manual skills, these normally floundering infants picked up objects and brought them to their eyes and mouths for exploration. After practicing 10 minutes a day for 2 weeks, infants looked at objects, swatted them, mouthed them, and exhibited more alternations between looking and mouthing than a control group of infants without manual motor experience. Motor experience also facilitates intermodal perception of objects. At 5.5 months of age, some infants have poor object manipulation skills (like a typical 3-month-old without sticky mittens) and others have quite developed skills. Infants with more highly developed object-manipulation skills looked differentially at displays of single- and multiple-impact object events (a spoon banging against a bowl vs. marbles rattling around a glass jar) depending on whether the sound from a central loudspeaker matched the event (Eppler, 1995). Poorly skilled infants looked equally at both displays.

The ability to manipulate objects, explore surfaces, and relate objects to surfaces lays the groundwork for improvements in cognitive function; most notably, the means–ends reasoning involved in **tool use** (Lockman, 2000; Willatts, 1999). Using a tool requires infants to carry out a series of steps. First, they must notice a discrepancy between what they can do and their goal. Second, they must find a new means to resolve the discrepancy by incorporating an external object or environmental support into their action plan. Finally, they must enact the appropriate behaviors to implement the tool and achieve their goal (Berger & Adolph, 2003).

One example of means–ends problem-solving is infants' ability to extend the limits of their reach by using nearby sticks, hooks, and rakes to drag the desired object closer (Bates, Carlson-Luden & Bretherton, 1980; Brown, 1990; Chen & Siegler, 2000; Leeuwen, Smitsman & Leeuwen, 1994). A more familiar example is how infants use a spoon to feed themselves (McCarty, Clifton & Collard, 1999, 2001). At 9 months of age, infants recognize the spoon as a tool, but they do not plan their reaching actions appropriately. Thus, they may grab a spoon by the bowl end instead of the handle end or grasp the handle palm up and then awkwardly rotate their hand to eat the food. By 18 months, their means–ends skills are so developed that they know exactly which end of the spoon to grab and they configure their grip most efficiently palm down. By 24 months, infants show behavioral flexibility in their tool use: they modify their grip to eat from a spoon with a bent handle (Steenbergen, van der Kamp, Smitsman & Carson, 1997).

Locomotion

Locomotion is the most outwardly dramatic of infants' emerging action systems. Parents herald infants' first walking steps as the transition from infancy to childhood and celebrate the occasion with the same joy and gravity as infants' first words. Parents might be less likely to recognize, however, the protracted period of locomotor development that precedes their infants' first steps, and less likely to appreciate the psychological concomitants and consequences of independent mobility (see Adolph & Berger, 2005, in press; Bertenthal & Clifton, 1998; Campos, Anderson, Barbu-Roth, Hubbard, Hertenstein & Witherington, 2000; Gibson & Schmuckler, 1989).

The view that locomotor development is a series of orderly stages is simply wrong. Each infant can exhibit an individual trajectory of locomotor achievements. Typically, the ability to move the whole body begins in the first 6 months of life as infants roll from their bellies onto their backs, pivot in circles while prone, hoist themselves to a sitting position and flop back onto their bellies, and so on (Bly, 1994). Many infants discover idiosyncratic ways of translating their bodies through space: bum-shuffling in a sitting position, crabbing on their backs, and log rolling. Some infants begin crawling with their bellies on the floor for part of each crawling cycle (Adolph, Vereijken & Denny, 1998). Before acquiring a hands-and-knees gait, they may 'combat crawl' using their arms for propulsion and dragging their legs behind, 'inchworm crawl' by alternately pushing their chest off the floor then springing forward onto their bellies, or 'swim' using all four limbs at once. Other infants skip the belly-crawling period and proceed straight to hands and knees (or hands and feet) at approximately 8 months of age. Still other infants never crawl; their first successful mobility is in an upright position.

Improvements in locomotor skill are experience dependent. For example, with each week of experience, infants' crawling becomes faster and their movements become larger. Experience is a better predictor of crawling skill than infants' age or body dimensions. In fact, infants who belly crawled are more proficient in their first weeks on hands and knees than infants who never belly crawled (Figure 4.2c), despite the fact that former belly crawlers and sole hands-and-knees crawlers are the same age, on average, when they begin crawling on hands and knees and their bodies are the same size (Adolph *et al.*, 1998). Similarly, experience pivoting, rocking on hands and knees, and other precursory prone movements facilitate improvements in the speed and size of hands-and-knees crawling movements, despite differences between the earlier and later developing movements in the patterns of inter-limb coordination and the body parts used for support and propulsion.

At approximately 7–13 months of age, infants pull themselves to a standing position and begin cruising; they move sideways in an upright position while holding onto the wall or furniture for support (Bly, 1994; Frankenburg & Dodds, 1967). Around their first birthday, they begin taking independent walking steps (Bly, 1994). Note, however, that the normal age range for walking onset is wide—11–15 months (Frankenburg & Dodds, 1967). As with crawling, improvements in walking are experience driven. At first, infants' balance is so precarious that their steps are tiny and their legs are splayed wide and toes pointed outward for extra stability; their cadence is choppy because they keep both legs on the floor for as long a time as possible and one leg in the air for as short a time as possible (Bril & Breniere, 1989, 1993). Over the first few months of walking, step length increases, step width and external rotation decrease, the percentage of the gait cycle spent with both feet on the floor decreases, and the percentage of the gait cycle spent with one foot in the air increases (Figure 4.2d). Walking experience is a stronger predictor of improvements in infants' walking skill than their age or body dimensions (Adolph, Vereijken & Shrout, 2003).

What might infants experience while rolling, pivoting, crawling, and walking that facilitates improvements in locomotor proficiency? Or, for that matter, what might infants experience during balance and locomotion that provides them with new opportunities for learning? One thing is clear: experience is not a forced march or rote repetition. Under the most optimal conditions, while traveling over the smooth path of a laboratory floor, infants start and stop at will and their crawling and walking steps are highly variable from cycle to cycle (Adolph *et al.*, 1998; Adolph *et al.*, 2003).

Home diaries, step counter devices, and video tracking methods show that the quantity and variety of infants' locomotor experience is truly staggering. Crawling and walking infants spend approximately half of their waking day on the floor engaged in balance and locomotion (5–6 hours of activity out of 12 hours awake). During most of the time that infants are free to locomote, they do not. Nonetheless, in short bursts of locomotor activity, crawlers manage to take 1028–3198 crawling steps/day and cover a daily distance of 60.4–187.8 m (66–206 yards)—about the length of two football fields (Adolph, 2002). In 16 minutes of free indoor play—during most of which time they are stationary—walking infants average 586 steps and 3–4 falls. By extrapolation, walkers average 13 185 steps and 90 falls a day and travel a daily distance of 39 football fields (Garciaguirre & Adolph, 2006). Every day, infants crawl or walk through nearly every room in their homes and travel over 6–12 different ground surfaces (Adolph, 2002; Garciaguirre & Adolph, 2006).

One consequence of experience with balance and locomotion is a new source of information about the self. As infants sit, stand, crawl, or walk, their body sways around its base of support. Each swaying movement generates a flow of optic information that specifies the direction and speed of the movement—the self in motion. When necessary, infants can use this information to produce a compensatory postural sway in the opposite direction.

Researchers can test infants' ability to use visual information for self motion in a 'moving room,' a life-size enclosure that rolls back and forth along a track (Lee & Lishman, 1975; Lishman & Lee, 1973). Infants sit, stand, or walk as the room moves around them. Room movement in one direction creates optic flow that simulates a postural sway in the same direction. To compensate, infants sway in the opposite direction. New walkers sway so forcefully that they stagger and fall, but older children and adults show less dramatic postural responses (Schmuckler, 1997; Stoffregen, Schmuckler & Gibson, 1987; Wann, Mon-Williams & Rushton, 1998). Locomotor experience serves to differentiate peripheral optic flow from the side walls from radial flow from the front wall. For example, pre-crawling 8-month-olds swayed in response to both side and front wall movement, but 8-month-olds with crawling experience showed adult-like responses by swaying primarily after movement of the side walls (Higgins, Campos & Kermoian, 1996). In adults, the two types of optic flow structure serve different functions: peripheral flow for balance and radial flow for steering (e.g., Stoffregen, 1986; Warren, Kay & Yilmaz, 1996). In a continuously oscillating room, older, more experienced infants timed their swaying movements more closely to the room movements than did younger, less experienced infants (Barela, Godoi, Freitas & Polastri, 2000; Bertenthal, Rose & Bai, 1997; Delorme, Frigon & Lagace, 1989).

A second consequence of experience with balance and locomotion is increased behavioral flexibility. Experience facilitates infants' ability to cope with novel, variable, and challenging tasks. In the most famous paradigm, infants are tested at the edge of an apparent drop-off on a **visual cliff** (e.g., Gibson & Walk, 1960) (Figure 4.4a). Infants begin on a narrow board looking down into an abyss 90 cm (3 feet) deep, while parents at the far side encourage them to cross (the entire apparatus is covered with glass to ensure the infants' safety). In a frequently cited study, locomotor experience predicted adaptive avoidance responses (Bertenthal, Campos & Barrett, 1984; Campos, Hiatt, Ramsay, Henderson & Svejda, 1978). At the very same age at testing (7.5 months), infants with 6 weeks of crawling experience, on average, were likely to avoid the apparent drop-off, but infants with 2 weeks of crawling experience, on average, were likely to cross. However, the role of experience in avoiding the deep side of the visual cliff has been hotly debated (Bertenthal & Campos, 1984; Rader, Bausano & Richards, 1980; Richards & Rader, 1981). Moreover, the visual cliff has several methodological limitations (Adolph & Berger, in press). The size of the drop-off is fixed, so researchers cannot test the precision of infants' responses or ask whether infants scale their motor decisions to the size of the challenge. The safety glass presents mixed messages: The visual cliff looks dangerous, but feels safe. In fact, because infants quickly learn that the apparatus is perfectly safe (albeit creepy), avoidance attenuates and they can only be tested in one or two trials (Campos et al., 1978; Eppler, Satterwhite, Wendt & Bruce, 1997).

One way to address the methodological problems with the visual cliff is to test infants on a real cliff with adjustable dimensions. Adolph (2000) constructed such a device, a **veritable cliff** (Figures 4.4b, c). In this case, the apparatus challenged infants with gaps in the surface of support, varying in 2-cm increments from 0 to 90 cm (36 inches). The largest gap width had dimensions equivalent to that on the standard visual cliff. In lieu of the safety glass, an experimenter rescued infants if they began to fall into the precipice. Because infants could be tested over dozens of trials, psychophysical methods determined the accuracy of their responses.

On the gaps apparatus, experience maintaining balance and locomotion predicted infants' level of behavioral flexibility (Adolph, 2000). However,

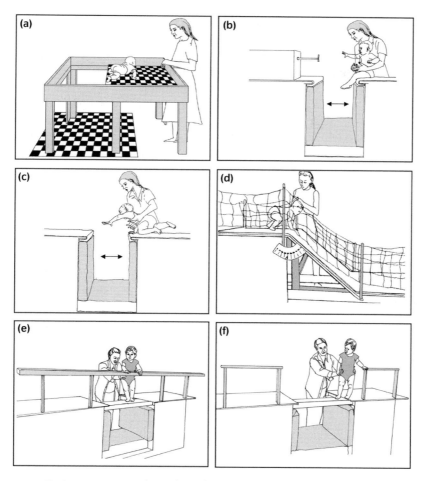

Figure 4.4 Various experimental paradigms for testing infants' response to novel locomotor challenges: (a) The visual cliff. Parent (shown) coaxes infant from far side of glass table. Adapted from Walk, R. D. & Gibson, E. J. (1961). A comparative and analytical study of visual depth perception. *Psychological Monographs: General and Applied, 75*(15, Whole No. 519). (b–c) Adjustable gap in the floor to test infants in sitting and crawling postures, respectively. Experimenter (shown) follows alongside infants to ensure their safety. Parents (not shown) encourage infants from the far side of the gap. Reprinted from Adolph, K. E. (2000). Specificity of learning: Why infants fall over a veritable cliff. *Psychological Science, 11*, 290–295, with permission from Blackwell Publishing. (d) Adjustable sloping walkway to test infants in crawling and walking postures. Experimenter (shown) follows alongside infants to ensure their safety. Parents (not shown) encourage infants from the far side of the slope. Reprinted from Adolph, K. E. (1997). Learning in the development of infant locomotion. *Monographs of the Society for Research in Child Development, 62*(3, Serial No. 251), with permission from Blackwell Publishing. (e, f) Bridges with and without handrails. Experimenter (shown) follows alongside infants to ensure their safety. Parents (not shown) encourage infants from the far side of the precipice. Reprinted from Berger, S. E. & Adolph, K. E. (2003). Infants use handrails as tools in a locomotor task, *Developmental Psychology, 39*, 594–605, with permission from APA.

learning did not transfer from an earlier developing action system to a later developing one. Each infant was tested in two postures, an experienced sitting posture (15 weeks of sitting experience, on average) and a less familiar crawling posture (6 weeks of crawling experience, on average). In both postures, their task was to lean across the gap to retrieve a toy on the far side. In their more experienced sitting posture, infants closely matched their motor decisions to the actual probability of falling: They attempted safe gaps and avoided risky ones. In their less familiar crawling posture, the same infants showed poorly adapted decisions: they attempted impossibly risky gaps on trial after trial, including the widest 90-cm (36-inch) gap.

A similar pattern of results holds for other action systems and other tasks. For example, in both cross-sectional and longitudinal studies, experienced crawling and walking infants showed finely adapted motor decisions for descending shallow and steep slopes (varying in $2°$ increments from $0°$ to $90°$) (Figure 4.4d). They attempted safe slopes but slid down or avoided risky ones (Adolph, 1995, 1997). Infants could even update their risk assessment after experimental manipulation of their body dimensions with a lead-loaded vest (Adolph & Avolio, 2000). They correctly attempted to walk down steeper slopes on trials when their vests were filled with feather weights and shallower slopes on trials when their vests were loaded with lead. However, in their first weeks of crawling and walking, infants' decisions were poorly adapted and they attempted slopes far beyond their capabilities. When tested week after week, the same infants who could discern the limits of their abilities as crawlers plunged headlong down risky slopes as new walkers (Adolph, 1997). In sum, experience promoted flexibility for the practiced action system but not for the newly acquired one.

Learning from locomotor experience typically requires more than one exposure, even when the experience seems highly salient. For example, learning from falling is not automatic or immediate. When 15-month-olds fell head first into a 'surprise' foam pit, they required several trials before they learned that the particular patch of ground would not support their weight (Joh & Adolph, 2006) (Figure 4.5). The foam pit was situated in the middle of an otherwise solid walkway. Although the deformable area was distinctly marked by salient visual cues (a bumpy surface with rounded edges, a colored and patterned cloth covering, prominent landmarks around the laboratory), on their first trial, all participants walked straight into the foam pit and fell. Surprisingly, infants continued to fall into the foam pit on subsequent trials (7 trials, on average) before selecting an alternative method of locomotion or avoiding the risky area. A quarter of the 15-month-olds never learned, and fell on 16 test trials. Only 11% of the infants learned after their first exposure. The number of 1-trial learners increased with age. By 39 months, 50% of children learned in 1 trial and nearly all adults showed 1-trial learning. Perhaps falling is so commonplace for younger children that they do not link the visible appearance of the ground surface with the consequence of loss of balance.

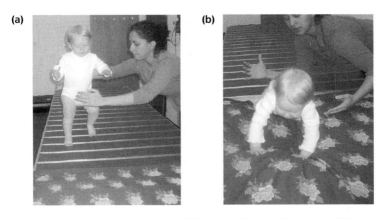

Figure 4.5 Apparatus to test learning from falling. (a) Infant walking over solid platform toward foam pit and (b) falling headlong into the foam cushions (pictures courtesy of Amy Joh).

A third consequence of locomotor experience is the opportunity to discover new means for achieving end goals. Although means–ends problem-solving is typically studied in manual tasks, in locomotor tasks new means can involve motor actions with the whole body. In Köhler's (1925) classic studies, chimps retrieved a banana hanging from the ceiling by stacking boxes on top of each other, seriating pedestals, or using a pole to vault themselves toward the ceiling. Human infants were initially not as clever as the adult chimps and tried vainly to obtain the lure (food or an attractive toy) by merely reaching toward it without using the boxes or pedestals as a means to an end (McGraw, 1935). After weeks of training, infants learned that the various pedestals and boxes could be arranged systematically to allow access to the lure.

In a more recent example of whole-body problem-solving, 16-month-old infants used handrails to augment their balance while crossing narrow and wide bridges (Berger & Adolph, 2003) (Figures 4.4e, f). The bridges (12–72 cm, 5–28 inches) spanned a deep precipice between two platforms. On some trials a wooden handrail was available and on others it was not. When bridges were wide enough to permit safe passage, infants ran straight across without noticing the handrail. When bridges were impossibly narrow, infants remained on the starting platform regardless of whether the handrail was present. But on bridges of intermediate widths, infants crossed only when the handrail was available and not when the handrail was absent. Moreover, infants took the material composition of the handrail into account when evaluating its use as a tool to extend their abilities. They crossed intermediate bridges more often with a solid wooden handrail than with a wobbly foam one (Berger, Adolph & Lobo, 2005).

SUMMARY

The amazing parade of new motor skills in infants' first year of life illustrates more than a triumph of muscles over gravity. Motor skill acquisition involves perception, cognition, and vast amounts of learning. Motor skills facilitate developments in other psychological domains because the ability to move the various parts of the body provides infants with new opportunities for learning. Motor skills are unique in psychological development because movements are directly visible. Motor actions share with achievements in other domains the central hallmarks of psychological development. What is unique to motor skill acquisition is the opportunity for researchers, parents, and teachers to directly observe these hallmarks in action: displays of agency and infants' discovery of a sense of self, examples of behavioral flexibility and infants' ability to adapt their behaviors to changing circumstances, and invention of new means as infants acquire new ways to achieve their goals.

CHAPTER FIVE

The development of the senses

ALAN SLATER, TIFFANY FIELD, and MARIA HERNANDEZ-REIF

Theories, questions, and methods

In order to start making sense of the world the infant has to perceive it, and for this reason the study of perceptual development is one of the major research areas in infancy research. Two main questions have interested investigators:

- What can infants perceive at and before birth?
- How do these abilities change over the first few months from birth, and what is the role of maturation and learning in their development?

These questions appear important for several reasons. One, as we have already noted, is because without functioning sensory and perceptual systems the infant would be unable to make contact with the world. Another relates to the age-old nature/nurture issue: do infants have to learn to perceive, or do they perceive in an adult-like fashion soon after birth?

Perhaps because the young infant appears to be so helpless, early theories emphasized an **empiricist** view of perceptual development, that infants perceive very poorly and that experience is vital for the development of the senses. The opposing **nativist** view would hold that perceptual development continues according to a timetable set out by an individual's genes. We noted in Chapter 1 that Charles Darwin suggested that hearing and vision were not really functional until a few weeks after birth. The famous developmental psychologist Jean Piaget (whose views are discussed in more detail in Chapters 6 and 8), writing about vision, claimed that 'perception of light exists from birth, and reflexes to light (such as pupil constriction to bright light, blinking), but all the rest (perception of forms, sizes, positions, distances, prominence, etc.) is acquired through the combination of reflex activity with higher activities' (1953, p. 62).

For Piaget (and perhaps for Darwin) experience was all, and the newborn baby could hardly be said to perceive anything. However, the last 50 years of research have shown that Piaget and Darwin were wrong—although experience is of great importance, infants display considerable perceptual competence at a surprisingly early age, and as we will describe here even the newborn baby perceives an organized and structured world.

Relation to earlier chapters

If you have read the earlier chapters you will know that each of them makes reference to the senses. In Chapter 3 it was noted that all of the senses (with the exception of vision) are functioning in the fetus, so that birth represents a time of change, but not a beginning. Since infants cannot tell us what they perceive, studies of infant perception need procedures that do not rely on language. Advances in research techniques now allow investigators to make use of a variety of responses, which help us to investigate babies' perceptual worlds. These include looking, sucking, startle responses, head turning and tracking, changes in facial expression, and physiological indices such as changes of heart and respiration rate and changes of brain electrical activity. These measures are described in Chapters 2 and 3. However, in order to avoid the reader constantly shifting between chapters, we will make this chapter as self-contained as possible, but refer the reader to other chapters where these are relevant.

Chapter overview

All of the senses provide important information and in this chapter we will review our current understanding in this order: touch (which includes touch discrimination, temperature and pain); taste; smell; hearing; vision; posture and balance; and cross-modal integration (a modality is an individual sense domain, such as touch or vision) A focus of the chapter will be the sensory capacities of the newborn baby—at birth the infant enters a new world, one that they will experience for the rest of their life.

Touch

Touch sensitivity

The sense of touch is the first to develop in the womb, and the sensory cortex is the most developed at birth. In evolution, virtually every animal's sense of touch is the first to develop. Touch begins to develop at around 8 weeks from conception and as early as 3 months the fetus will turn towards a tactile stimulus, much like a rooting reflex (see Chapter 3). A newborn baby can discriminate between fine brush hairs of different diameters, and will respond to electrical stimuli and puffs of air (see Jacklin *et al.*, 1981, for a review). Recent research into touch sensitivity suggests that even newborns are able to discriminate between stimuli using their hands and mouths. In one study, the stimuli were nipples that differed in texture, being either smooth or 'nubby.' Newborns were given the opportunity to suck on one and then the other nipple texture across six trials. They sucked three times longer on the smooth than on the nubby-textured nipple, suggesting they prefer to suck on smooth nipples (Hernandez-Reif, *et al.*, 2000). In another study, newborns were given little tubes filled with cotton or with pellets, which made the tubes light (cotton) or heavy (pellets). When newborns were given one of these tubes they explored it with their hands. This exploration gradually lessened (i.e., the infants habituated), but there was a recovery of attention when the other tube was presented, suggesting that as early as the newborn period, babies can detect weight changes in objects (Hernandez-Reif *et al.*, 2001).

Temperature

A related sense is the sense of temperature. This was recently investigated in newborn infants by Hernandez-Reif and her colleagues (2003, 2004) in two experiments. In one experiment, they presented newborn infants with tiny tubes of either warm or cold water to explore by hand. Over trials they habituated to one temperature and then recovered their attention when the other temperature was presented. In the other experiment, the newborns sucked on alternating cold and warm nipples. The cold nipple stimulated greater sucking, as the newborns sucked more on all trials after sucking on the cold nipple. In any event, the findings from these two studies suggest that from mouthing or handling objects, newborn infants can differentiate cold from warm objects.

Pain

Still a third type of touch sense is the sense of pain. Neural pathways for pain are present by around 26 weeks from conception, and there is no doubt that the newborn infant feels pain. Most painful stimuli make contact with the skin, and painful stimuli elicit a significant stress response from newborn infants. Pain has been measured in infants by changes in facial expressions, and also by physiological measures such as heart rate. One way of inducing pain in the newborn infant (unintentionally!) is by a heel-stick procedure—this is a routine blood test to check for any abnormalities. This is clearly a painful stimulus in that it typically produces facial grimacing, heart-rate changes, and crying.

In adults, pain can often be alleviated by touching—this is why we rub a bumped 'funny bone' or 'crazy bone.' There is a physiological reason for this—the tactile receptors that experience the touch transmit information quicker than pain receptors, so the brain gets the rubbing or tactile information before the pain message, and the first message blocks out the second! In infants it turns out that the stress from a painful heel-stick can be alleviated by a variety of stimuli, which include sucking, white noise (noise that is 'random,' like that on a TV screen with no signal), the sounds of the maternal heartbeat, a sucrose solution to suck, and the presentation of odors such as milk and lavender. Thus, tactile stimuli, sounds, and odors all act to alleviate the stress responses caused by pain.

Although the sense of pain is well developed even in the newborn infant, there is evidence that this sense develops with age: Wolf (1996) found that older infants gave more stress responses to a heel-stick than younger ones. But it is certainly not the case, as some have claimed, that newborn infants don't feel pain.

Taste

In Chapter 3 we saw that even the fetus discriminates between sweet and noxious substances, and the sense of taste is well developed in the newborn infant, perhaps because of the significant experience with taste in the womb. The amniotic fluid contains many different tastes, including sweet, sour, salt, and bitter, and thus provides the newborn with significant prenatal experience. The newborn (like the fetus) will show a preference for sweet solutions by sucking more vigorously. In several studies newborn infants have been observed making distinct facial expressions when they tasted different sweet, sour, and bitter solutions, and these facial expressions were very similar to the expressions of adults who tasted the same solutions—typically, a smile occurs in response to sweet substances, puckered lips to sour, and disgust expressions to bitter (e.g., Rosenstein & Oster, 1997). Figure 5.1 shows an infant's reaction to sweet and to sour solutions.

Despite the newborn infant's fine sensitivity to different tastes, there is still a lot to learn (preferences for hot, spicy foods take years to acquire!). At birth, the infant has food preferences and dislikes which affect its food intake. But even in the first few days and weeks from birth infants develop preferences for tastes to which they are exposed, and by around 3 months they become more active and accepting of new tastes (the introduction of solid foods usually comes around this time, or a little later). Early infancy is the time of development that the psychoanalyst Sigmund Freud called the 'oral stage'—for the first year from birth the infant sucks just about any suckable object, which, fortunately, often includes food! The young infant will often watch other people feeding with great interest and in the first year a range of foods will come to form the basis of the infant's diet. Thereafter, new foods will be less readily accepted and in older infants and children the taste for new foods will depend on exposure and also cognitive factors, but

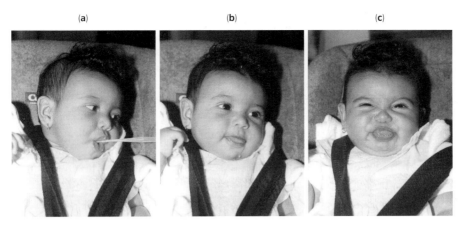

Figure 5.1 An infant being given a sweet solution (a), and the reaction (b). The response to a sour solution (c).

the development of food phobias—the hatred of certain foods—does not usually appear until after 2 years of age (Harris, 1997).

During infancy there is a gradual shift in the importance of internal (**intrinsic**) and external (**extrinsic**) factors in food preferences and intake. Early infancy is intrinsically hunger-driven (the baby cries to be fed when hungry), and this is gradually replaced by extrinsic factors—parental and cultural conventions on meal times and appropriate foods for certain times of day (Harris, 1997).

Smell

From about 9 or 10 weeks from conception the fetus breathes—that is, inhales and exhales amniotic fluid. This gives the fetus a range of experiences with odors, and the sense of smell is well developed by birth. In much the same way that they show preferences for tastes, newborns show by their faces that they have very clear odor preferences and aversions. Steiner (1979) spearheaded research into odor preferences by presenting newborns with fruit odors which elicited positive facial expressions and fishy/rotten egg odors which elicited disgust expressions. Several studies have demonstrated highly developed odor perception in newborn infants—they will turn their heads toward a pleasant smell and away from an unpleasant one, and will show discrimination between subtle smells as measured by habituation procedures. In the latter studies the infants are presented with one odor (such as anise oil) on a cotton bud under the nose. This produces changes to respiration rates which soon habituate (respiration rates return to normal). When a new odor (such as asafetida) is then presented the respiration changes occur again, which is a clear indication that the infants discriminate between the odors.

A much more sophisticated olfactory discrimination is that between the mother's breast pads and those of an unfamiliar nursing mother; even newborns will show a preference for their mother's breast pad (Cernack & Porter, 1985). To some extent, the chemical profile of breast secretions overlaps with that of amniotic fluid, which may help to explain infants rapidly learning their mother's unique scent.

In a recent study in the second author's laboratory we added lavender to the bath oil of newborn infants. The infants who received the lavender spent more time in deep sleep and less time fussing than those who did not. In a similar manner, some newborns showed more positive/approach behaviors (measured through brainwave patterns) when lavender and rosemary aromas were introduced into the room air (Fernandez *et al.*, 2004)—aromatherapy works, even with newborn infants!

Hearing—sound, voices, and speech

Once again, auditory perception begins in the womb. As was noted in Chapter 3 the fetus responds to sounds as early as 22–24 weeks, and although the womb is a noisy place it is a good conductor of sounds so that external sounds will penetrate the womb and stimulate the fetus's auditory system. Sounds that carry particularly well are those of the human voice—to paraphrase a well-known developmental psychologist, Annette Karmiloff-Smith—'When two heavily pregnant mothers-to-be are talking there are four people listening to the conversation.'

Basic auditory abilities—hearing and localizing sounds

The newborn infant's ability to hear low-frequency sounds—particularly those in the range of speech—is close to that of adults, though it is possible that sensitivity to higher-pitched sounds undergoes development during infancy. It is also clear that newborn infants can localize sounds. This was first suggested by Wertheimer (1961) who reported that his newborn daughter, only 10 minutes old, would turn her head in the direction of a click (from a toy cricket) that was sounded to either her left or right ear. This finding was confirmed by Muir in several publications (e.g., Muir, Humphrey & Humphrey, 1999). In their experiments newborn infants were tested in complete darkness (to avoid visual distractions) and they presented a rhythmic, rattle sound for a few seconds to one ear at a time, over several trials, and on 88% of these trials the babies turned their heads in the direction of the sound.

Auditory preferences at birth

In a classic study (described in more detail in Chapter 3) newborns were given the opportunity to hear either their mother's voice, or a female stranger's voice (the stranger was another newborn baby's mother). They could select which voice they heard by varying the way they sucked on a pacifier (dummy), and they preferred to listen to their mother's voice. What is clear is that this preference for the mother's voice develops before birth. This was demonstrated by DeCasper and Spence (1986) who conducted a study in which one group of pregnant women read the Dr. Seuss story *The cat in the hat* to their unborn babies, and another group read a version in which the words 'cat' and 'hat' were replaced by 'dog' and 'fog.' Soon after birth the newborns showed a preference for the version of the story that had been read to them while still in the womb.

Perception of speech

In addition to learning about their mother's voice, normally hearing infants learn some of the characteristics of their native language before they are born. As an example, even the spoken expressions of emotion are most preferred in the language to which infants have been exposed in the womb (Mastropieri & Turkewicz, 1999). In this study newborn infants were presented with a range of emotional speech expressions—happy, sad, angry, and neutral—in both their native language and a foreign language. What they found was that the newborns were more likely to open their eyes to happy speech patterns than to the other emotions. More interestingly, an increase in eye opening was observed only when the infants listened to happy speech sounds when spoken by speakers of the native language—infants born to Spanish-speaking mothers showed more eye-opening in response to the presentation of a happy vocal expression in Spanish, and newborns of English-speaking mothers showed more eye-opening to the happy expression in English.

If you were to read accounts of language development written as recently as 20 or 30 years ago you would likely read that language begins around 1 year of age—the time that babies utter their first meaningful word—and that language devices are 'switched on' around that time, perhaps because of some internal biological and genetically determined time clock. Recent research indicates that this is far from the truth—that speech and language perception begins even in the womb. The infant is born with the capacity to discriminate between all the speech sounds used in all the world's languages, but by the end of the first year something remarkable has happened—babies around the world have lost some of this ability and have become exquisitely attuned to their native language(s)—in Janet Werker's (1989) expression they have become **native listeners**. The development of speech perception and the transition to spoken language is described in Chapter 10.

Visual perception

All the senses provide important information, but it is clear that humans have evolved to rely heavily on vision at all ages—in adults it has been estimated that more than half of the brain deals in some way with the processing of visual information (Sereno *et al.*, 1995). This alerts us to the fact that what appears effortless—seeing—is actually extraordinarily complex. In this section we will discuss the development of visual abilities in infants—from basic issues to do with how well the infant sees the world through an understanding of the complex visual worlds of people and objects.

Basic visual abilities

Vision is unique amongst the senses in that there is no opportunity for it to be used before birth. Although the fetus might be presented with enough visual input to discriminate light from dark, a proper visual world, of shapes, people, and objects, awaits its arrival into the outside world. It is, then, no surprise to find that vision is perhaps the least developed of the senses at birth. In this chapter we review research on some aspects of vision which use looking as a means of testing for perceptual and cognitive abilities; however, it must be remembered that looking, and eye–head control, is a developing action system and its development is described in Chapter 4.

One simple way of getting at the ability to discriminate detail (known as **visual acuity**) is to use the visual preference method (described in Chapter 2) in which pairs of stimuli are shown to the babies. If they look longer at ('prefer') one of the two we have clear evidence of visual discrimination. The infant is shown a pattern of black-and-white stripes alongside a gray patch, and the smallest stripe width that is looked at in preference to the gray gives an estimate of acuity. (This is the equivalent, for infant testing, of the acuity estimates an optician or optometrist obtains by getting patients to read smaller and smaller letters from an eye chart.) Measured in this way, acuity in the newborn baby is some 10–30 times poorer than that of adults (Figure 11.1 shows a picture of a face as it might look to a newborn).

A newborn's level of acuity, curiously, is about the same as that of an adult cat—so that if newborns could move about they probably wouldn't bump into things! The cat, like the infant, does not need the fine acuity needed to read small print, and for the cat, as for the infant, movement and change in the visual world are particularly attention-getting. Infant acuity reaches adult levels some time after about 6 months, but may not reach full adult acuity until around 3 years. It is worth noting, though, that the poorer acuity of the young infant does not really constitute any disadvantage—infants see perfectly well at near distances, which is where the things happen that are of most interest in their developing world.

Many other visual abilities are poor at birth and improve to near-adult levels by 6 months (Slater & Oates, 2005). For example, sensitivity to subtle variations in contrast shows rapid improvement in early infancy. Color vision also improves rapidly, and by a few months from birth is probably like that of adults. Other abilities that are present in weak form at birth include the ability to focus on objects at different distances (known as **visual accommodation**), and precise control over eye movements—these, too, develop rapidly in early infancy. Depth perception also develops rapidly in early infancy. An early demonstration of depth perception used the **visual cliff** (also discussed in Chapters 2, 4, and 8). This was first described by Gibson and Walk (1960), and consists of a central platform with a solid surface on one side and what seems a deep drop on the other. On both sides there is a strong sheet of glass so that the infant is in no danger of falling, but when infants can crawl (usually 6 months or later) they will typically refuse to venture on to the side with the apparently deep drop (Figure 5.2). This experiment tells us that depth perception is present in the second half of the first year. However, more recent research has demonstrated that some aspects of depth perception are present at birth, but others develop later, for example **binocular vision**. Binocular vision refers to the fact that we have two eyes and because they are spatially separated by a few centimeters they provide slightly different images of any scene we look at. The brain is able to fuse these two images so that we see one scene and not two, and it uses the variations between the two images to provide a powerful cue to depth (this is known as **stereopsis**). This ability comes in around 3 or 4 months.

An organized visual world

Although newborn infants' vision is much poorer than ours, their visual world is highly organized. An experiment on **size constancy** serves to illustrate this: size constancy refers to the fact that we perceive an object as being the same size despite changes in its distance from us, and hence changes to its retinal image size. In this experiment we (Slater *et al.*, 1990) showed newborn infants (2 days old) a single object—either a small or a large cube, which, over trials, was shown at different distances from the eyes. Figure 5.3 shows a baby being tested. On subsequent test trials the babies looked more (i.e., gave what is called a 'novelty preference') at a different-sized cube than to the same-sized one, even though the two cubes were at different distances in order to make their retinal sizes the same. This finding demonstrates that size constancy is an organizing feature of perception that is present at birth. Note that this procedure is dependent on the infants learning about the characteristics of the stimulus shown in the early 'familiarization' trials, and also on the infants subsequently preferring to look at novel stimuli on the later test trials. This procedure is therefore a variation on the habituation procedures discussed in Chapter 2.

Figure 5.2 Ten-month-old Liam being enticed across the deep side of the visual cliff! Photograph from Joe Campos's lab by Amy Smith.

The human face is one of the most complex visual stimuli encountered by the infant: it moves, it is three-dimensional, it has areas of both high and low contrast; also it contains features that change (when talking, when changing expression, when looking at or away from the baby), but which are in an invariant relationship (the eyes are always above the mouth, etc.). It seems likely that the newborn infant enters the world with some inborn knowledge, or representation of the face. Perhaps the clearest evidence that

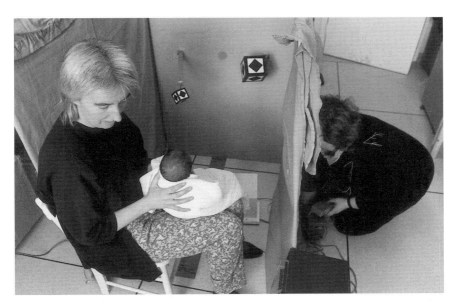

Figure 5.3 A newborn baby being tested in a size constancy experiment.

faces are special for infants is the finding that newborn infants, only minutes from birth, will imitate a range of facial expressions that they see an adult produce. Apparently, this was first discovered by one of Piaget's students, Olga Maratos, who reported to him that if she stuck out her tongue to a young baby, the baby would respond by sticking its tongue out to her. (This goes against Piaget's views on imitation—according to his theory it should not appear until the second year.) Apparently, when Piaget was informed of these findings he sucked contemplatively on his pipe for a few moments, and then commented 'How rude'!

Neonatal facial imitation indicates that the baby can match what it sees to some inbuilt knowledge of its own face, and can then use this match to produce the same facial gesture (which might be tongue protrusion, mouth opening, furrowing of the brow, or other gesture) which the infant, of course, cannot see. This is clear evidence of an inborn ability and raises the question of why infants imitate. An intriguing idea is that babies imitate as a form of social interaction and as a way of learning about people's identity (Meltzoff 2004).

The infant learns about faces soon after birth: several groups of researchers have reported that infants as young as 12 hours from birth will spend more time looking at their mother's face when she is shown paired with a stranger's face (e.g., Bushnell, 2003, and see Figure 5.4), but they will only learn her face if they hear her voice! (Sai, 2005). By 3 months of age infants have learned which of several familiar voices goes with which face (Slater *et al.*, 2003), that female faces are in a different category from male faces (see Chapter 7)

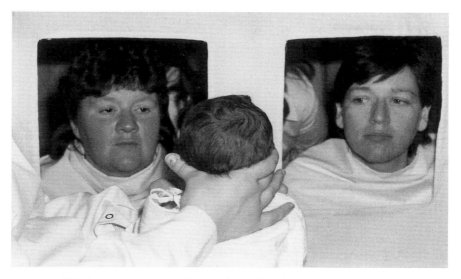

Figure 5.4 Which one is mother? Only a few hours from birth infants prefer to look at their mother's face.

and they can discriminate between faces of their own race and those of other races (Kelly *et al.*, in press b). Before the end of the first year a **perceptual narrowing** effect, similar to that which occurs in speech perception, is found in face perception: 9-month-olds easily discriminate between different human faces, but find it difficult to discriminate between monkey faces (Pascalis *et al.*, 2002).

The topic of infant face perception has probably generated more research than any other single topic, and raises questions about possible innate or inborn abilities, recognizing people, facial expressions, judgements of attractiveness, and the role of faces and people in social development. These important and intriguing issues are taken up and described in detail by Jennifer Ramsey and Judith Langlois in Chapter 11.

The infant's world of objects

At birth infants can discriminate between a variety of shapes, including people, and their visual world is structured and organized by mechanisms such as size constancy, but they have a long way to go before they fully comprehend the world of objects. As we look around us, most of the objects we see are partly occluded by objects that lie in front of them—a book occludes that part of the table it is lying on, a tree occludes part of the horizon, and so on. Babies begin to realize that partly occluded objects are whole, or complete, behind an occluder from about 2 months of age (Figure 5.5). By around 5 or 6 months infants are beginning to understand that two objects that are touching are two, not one. By 6 or 8 months they

Are these two objects shaped ...

... like this? ...

... or like this?

Figure 5.5 Understanding occlusion.

have learned about support and about gravity—that an object hanging off the end of a table should fall, that ball-bearings will travel further when rolled down a longer rather than a shorter ramp, that cup handles will fall if not attached to the cup. They learn about the relative importance or reliability of different types of information from experience, so that their experiences and actions on the world of objects help shape up their understanding of physical laws. In this respect they are becoming 'budding intuitive physicists, capable of detecting, interpreting and predicting physical outcomes' (Baillargeon, 1993, p. 311).

But a proper understanding of the physical world is hard won, and even at the end of infancy it is incomplete. In an experiment to test toddlers' understanding of solidity and support described by Hood, Carey, and Prasada (2000), 2-year-olds were tested in a situation in which a ball was dropped from a height into a box. The children knew that in the middle of the box there was a shelf, and older children appreciated that the ball could not fall through the shelf. The 2-year-olds had different ideas, and when asked to fetch the ball they persisted in searching on the floor, below the shelf! In another experiment, also by Bruce Hood (1995) even older children—2- to 4 1/2-year olds—were given a task in which the goal was to find a toy ball that was dropped through an opaque tube (Figure 5.6). As is apparent from the figure, if the ball is dropped into the tube at the top right it will land in the box at the bottom left. But in this task almost all the younger toddlers and some of the older children persisted in searching in the box immediately beneath the dropping point—for them, gravity rules!

Posture and balance

We have a tendency to think that we have only five senses—touch, taste, smell, hearing, and vision—but a couple of simple demonstrations convinces us otherwise: (1) stand on one leg and close your eyes; (2) with your eyes closed touch the tip of your nose with your right hand. Note that touch,

(a)

(b)

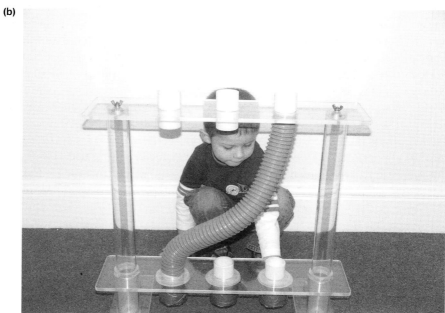

Figure 5.6 Gravity rules. Even when toddlers see a ball dropped into the tube (a) they will search for it immediately below the dropping point (b). Pictures by Bruce Hood.

taste, smell, hearing, and seeing contributed little to these tasks, but in the first instance you didn't fall over, and in the second you touched your nose effortlessly! Your ability to do these sorts of tasks relies upon two senses—the sense of bodily posture and balance, which is controlled by the semi-circular canals in the inner ear (this is known as the **vestibular system**), and feedback from the nerves throughout our bodies telling us where our body parts are (known as **kinesthetic feedback**).

These two senses begin their development in the womb (even the fetus has been known to move its hand so that it can suck its thumb!) and they are constantly developing throughout infancy and later life. Here we will give two examples, one from infant reaching, the other from the so-called 'moving room' to illustrate both their importance in infancy, and how they interact with other senses.

Infant reaching

Thelen and Spencer (1998) followed the same four infants from 3 weeks to 1 year (a **longitudinal study**) in order to explore the development of successful reaching. What they found was that this development followed a clear sequence. First, the infants acquired stable control over the head several weeks before the onset of reaching, then there was a reorganization of muscle patterns so that the infants could stabilize the head and shoulder. These developments gave the infants a stable base from which to reach, and successful reaching followed. This is an indication that infants need a stable posture before they can attain the goal of reaching successfully, and of course visually directed reaching (which first appears around 4–5 months) needs good vision and also the kinesthetic (arm position) information to guide the hand. It is true to say that all motor developments in infancy (and indeed throughout life) are dependent on both vestibular (balance) and kinesthetic (body position) information.

The moving room

You will almost certainly have had an experience like this. You are sitting in a train in a station and there is another train on the next track. This train then starts moving, but for a moment or two you are convinced that it is your train that is moving. This impression can be so strong in some individuals that if they are standing up they will lurch forwards (or backwards, depending on the direction of the other train's movement) to compensate—that is, they make inappropriate postural controls. Infants will do this too. In ongoing experiments by Joe Campos at the University of California at Berkeley, infants and toddlers are tested for posture control in a 'moving room' (see Figure 5.7). This is a small room placed in a larger room and consists simply of three walls—front and two sides—which are on castors so that they can

Figure 5.7 Infant being tested in the moving room. Photograph from Joe Campos's lab by Amy Smith.

move independently of the floor (which doesn't move). Older infants (15- to 34-month-olds) have been tested standing up facing the front wall and then the room moves, either towards or away from the infants. The results were clear—when the room moved towards the infant, the baby fell over backwards, and if the room moved away the baby fell forwards (the floor was soft!). Younger babies, from birth onwards, have been tested in the moving room sitting in an infant chair, and for all infants there are appropriate head and postural control movements when the room moves (i.e., head movements backward when the room moves toward the infant, and forward when it moves back).

Overview

These two examples tell us that the posture and bodily position senses are developing in the fetus, and help to guide the infant's behavior from birth. These senses also interact with other senses, particularly the sense of vision and motor development. With each new motor development—for instance, from sitting to crawling—infants need to readjust their posture and body senses to make the next 'step forward.'

Coordination between the senses

The American psychologist William James (brother of the novelist Henry James) is rightly considered to be the 'father of modern psychology.' His two-volume work *The principles of psychology*, which appeared in 1890, set the scene for future psychological research, and in it is one of the most memorable (and much quoted) sentences that have been written about infants:

The baby, assailed by eyes, ears, nose, skin and entrails at once, feels it all as one great blooming, buzzing confusion. (Vol. 1, p. 488)

This is the first expression of what is known as **infantile synesthesia**. The term **synesthesia** means the inability to distinguish between the information coming from the different senses, and what James was claiming is that young infants are bombarded with stimulation to all the senses (which they are!) and that they cannot discriminate between them—that is, they confuse the information from the different senses. A simple set of tests convinces us that James was wrong: if a pleasant substance is sucked then sucking will increase; if a light is too bright the infant will close its eyes; if a finger is placed in the baby palm the baby will grasp it; if an unpleasant smell is presented the baby will wrinkle its nose in disgust. That is, the infant's response to sensory stimulation is highly specific and appropriate to the modality stimulated.

However, James alerted us to the importance of intersensory information, and there is no doubt that the baby's world would be very confusing if they could not integrate the information from the different senses. We will describe two experiments, both with newborn infants, which suggest that infants can indeed integrate and coordinate information coming from different senses, and that there are inborn, unlearned rules which guide this learning. A study on intermodal correspondence was by Streri and Gentaz (2004). In this study newborns were given an object to touch (either a small cylinder or a prism) by placing it in one hand. The babies were prevented from seeing the object and then on test trials they were shown pictures of the two objects side by side. On these trials they looked longer at the novel object that they hadn't previously touched and manipulated—a demonstration that they could visually recognize the shape they had previously touched.

A rather different experiment, also with newborn infants, but this time using sight–sound pairings and with a focus on intermodal coordination, was carried out in the first author's laboratory (Slater *et al.*, 1999). In this we familiarized 2-day-olds to two different, simple visual stimuli (a red vertical line and a green diagonal line) where each was accompanied by its 'own' sound. There were two different experimental conditions—in one the sound was presented for the whole time that the visual stimulus was shown, irrespective of whether the baby looked at the visual stimulus or not, and in the other the sound was presented only when the baby looked (it turned off automatically when the baby looked away, and turned on when they looked again). In this latter instance the presentation of each sound–sight pair was synchronized in that the baby either had both together or none at all. The results were clear—the babies only learned the sight–sound combinations when their on/off presentation was synchronized.

The first of these two experiments tells us that newborn infants have an innate ability to extract shape information from both tactual and visual modalities, and can transfer this across modalities. The second tells us that newborns can learn about auditory–visual events, but that this learning is guided by the same rules that apply throughout life—only associate stimuli from different modalities if there is information (such as synchrony) that specifies that they genuinely belong together. We can see how these 'rules' or guides work naturally in the real world—we would only associate a voice with a person if we see their lips move, we would only associate a sound with a particular animal if it comes from the same place. In technical terms the information that specifies that information from one modality is linked with that from another is called **intersensory redundancy**, that is, the information from the two (or more) modalities provide similar, or linking information, and when this is available the infant learns more quickly about the characteristics of people and of objects. Lorraine Bahrick and her colleagues (e.g., Bahrick, 2004) suggest that redundant information is extremely important in infants and children learning the names for objects—the synchronous presentation of the word and the object it names assists the child in learning the arbitrary word–object associations.

SUMMARY

In order to make contact with the world you have to be aware of it. This obvious statement, with which we began the chapter, tells us the senses are vitally important in order for the infant to develop. We can make a distinction between **sensation**, **perception**, and **cognition**. By sensation is meant the ability to register information. We have seen that all of the senses, other than vision, function in the fetus, and vision is clearly functioning from birth. At a slightly higher level, the term perception means acting on the sensory information in order to begin to make sense of it—so that localizing a sounding object, or visual size constancy would be considered acts of perception. At the next level up the infant (or the perceiver in general) comprehends the perceived information—to learn about people, to classify information, to make sense of the world of objects and space, to comprehend speech. All of this is known as cognition, and it is to important aspects of cognitive development that we turn in the next chapters.

PART THREE

Cognitive Development

CHAPTER SIX

The development of intelligence in infancy

SCOTT P. JOHNSON and ALAN SLATER

Introduction

Cognition is a term referring to mental abilities—thinking, memory, problem-solving, categorization, reasoning, language development, and so on. In Chapters 7–10 we focus on specific aspects of cognitive development, and in this chapter we give an account of broad theoretical approaches to the development of intelligence in infancy.

Infancy is a period during which a great deal of intellectual development takes place, and much of it can be seen as falling within four major approaches.

- One of the most influential theorists to develop a theory of cognitive development was Jean Piaget (1896–1980), whose **Piagetian approach**, involving six stages of **sensorimotor** development, is described in the next section.

- The **nativist approach** argues that some forms of knowledge are innate, or present in very early infancy, and form a core around which more mature cognitive functioning will develop.

- The **information processing approach** attempts to understand the reasoning processes used by infants and the ways in which the processing of information changes over time.

- The fourth broad way of looking at cognitive development is the **psychometric approach** which involves testing infants to measure their current level of development, and to predict subsequent cognitive development.

These major approaches take quite different views on cognitive development, stressing different aspects of intellectual functioning and how it changes or remains constant over time. The views therefore complement each other and often shed light on different aspects of development. A point worth emphasizing, and which has been mentioned in other chapters, is that all areas of development impact on each other, so that advances in cognition influence developments in all other areas of development. We will now examine each of the four approaches in turn.

Piagetian approach

Piaget (1937/1954) proposed a theory of infant cognitive development organized around four broad themes: object, space, time, and causality (cf. Kant, 1767/1934). Knowledge in these domains developed in tandem, and they were thought to be highly interdependent. The principal goal of Piagetian theory was to explain **objectification**, the knowledge of the self and external objects as distinct and separate entities, persisting across time and space, and following common-sense causal rules. Objectification is a major cognitive achievement that takes place during the first 2 years, roughly, of postnatal development in most children, which Piaget termed the **sensorimotor** period. During this time, the child's thinking is manifest in overt actions. Objectification stems from the recognition of one's body as an independent object and one's movements as movements of objects through space, analogous to movements of other objects. This, in turn, happens via development and coordination of **schemes**, or action repertoires.

The sensorimotor stages

Piaget suggested that sensorimotor intelligence emerges in six stages, each based on the infant's acquisition of novel schemes and scheme combinations. All ages provided here are approximate.

Stage 1: modification of reflexes (birth to 1 month)

In this stage, termed **modification of reflexes**, the infant engages in reflexive behavior repeatedly in response to stimulation; gradually the reflexes are adjusted to meet the requirements of different circumstances. For example, reflexive sucking behaviors can be modified via actions of the tongue, lips, and swallowing, depending on what is placed in the mouth.

Stage 2: primary circular reactions (1–4 months)

This stage sees the emergence of **primary circular reactions**. A circular reaction is simply a scheme that is repeated; a primary circular reaction is one that is repeated simply because it is interesting in and of itself, and often provides an opportunity to explore the world. In stage 2, for example, sucking becomes a scheme (rather than a reflex) as a means of exploring the environment.

Stage 3: secondary circular reactions (4–8 months)

In this stage, **secondary circular reactions** are first seen, which Piaget described as 'discovering procedures for making interesting events last.' A secondary circular reaction refers to an activation of schemes to produce an event in the world, not simply for the pleasure of activating the scheme. Production of schemes now results in a specific desired outcome: shaking a rattle in order to hear the sound, hitting a ball to make it roll, or kicking one's feet to see them move. Also in stage 3, schemes are beginning to be organized: in the rattle example, looking, grasping, and shaking schemes are used in a coordinated fashion.

Stage 4: coordination of secondary schemes (8–12 months)

Secondary circular reactions now become coordinated and intentional, a means to an end. This implies a goal, and a plan to reach the goal. For example, the child might push aside daddy's hand to obtain a toy being covered: this is **means–end** behavior where one behavior (pushing the hand) is the means to the end (obtaining the toy). Earlier, pushing the hand might have been interesting enough by itself (and it still might be), but in this case the desired goal is one step removed from this action.

Stage 5: tertiary circular reactions (12–18 months)

In this stage, the child begins to produce behaviors that signal novelty and exploration, or **tertiary circular reactions**. This means combining secondary circular reactions, in a purely exploratory fashion, deliberate trial and error exploration of objects: dropping a toy from the high chair in different ways, to see what happens, or pulling a blanket on which a desired toy rests, to see if that will result in obtaining the toy.

Stage 6: the beginnings of thought—mental representations (18–24 months)

Finally, at the end of the sensorimotor period during stage 6, the child invents **new means via mental representation**: trying out different combinations of actions mentally, and anticipating the consequences without necessarily engaging in overt behaviors.

The development of spatial and object concepts

Piaget proposed as well that the development of spatial concepts and object concepts, leading to objectification, were organized into six stages corresponding to the six stages of general cognitive development just described (Piaget, 1936/1952). Initially (during stages 1 and 2), infants exhibited a kind of recognition memory, for example, seeking the mother's breast after losing contact shortly after birth, and within several months, continuing to look in the direction of a person's exit from the room. These behaviors were not systematic, however, and they were considered more passive than active. For Piaget, active search schemes, initiated by the child, were a critical feature of object concepts, both as evidence for their development, and as a mechanism by which development occurs.

More active search behavior emerges after 4 months, marking the onset of objectification during stage 3. Piaget outlined five examples, in roughly chronological order (i.e., the order in which they could be elicited across stage 3). The first was **visual accommodation to rapid movements**, when an infant responds to a dropped object by looking down toward the floor, behavior that becomes more systematic when the infant herself drops the object. A second behavior, **interrupted prehension**, refers to the infant's attempts to re-acquire an object that was dropped or taken from her hand if it is out of sight briefly and within easy reach. (There is no search if the object is fully hidden.) **Deferred circular reactions** describes the child's gestures when interrupted during object-oriented play activity, resuming the game after some delay (involving memory of object, actions, and context). **Reconstruction of an invisible whole from a visible fraction** occurs when, for example, the child retrieves an object from a cover when only a part of the object was visible. Finally, the infant engages in **removal of obstacles preventing perception**, as when she pulls away a cover from her face during peekaboo, or retrieves a fully hidden toy from beneath a blanket. This behavior marks the transition to stage 4.

During stage 4, the infant will often search actively for a fully hidden object. Search may not be systematic, however, when the object is hidden first at a single location followed by (successful) search, and then hidden in another location, as the infant watches. Here, the infant often tries to find the obstacle at the first location visited by the object, even though she saw it hidden subsequently somewhere else. This response has come to be known as the **A-not-B error**, or the **stage 4 error** (discussed in greater detail in Chapter 8). The transition to full objectification is completed across the next two stages as the infant first solves the problem of multiple visible displacements, searching at the last location visited by the object (stage 5), and then multiple invisible displacements (stage 6). For Piaget, systematic search revealed a decoupling of the object from the action, and knowledge of the infant's body itself as merely one object among many, and brought into an **allocentric system** of spatially organized objects and events. By 'allocentric' is meant that the infant can judge spatial organization with reference to the external world: for example, if an older infant sees a toy being hidden in a location to her left on a small table, and the infant is then moved to the opposite side of the table, she will then reach to her right in order to (correctly) retrieve the object. The younger infant is likely to judge spatial organization **egocentrically** (with respect to her own body), and in this task will reach (incorrectly) to her left even though she has been moved through 180°.

Overview

Piagetian theory enjoys strong support for many of the kinds of behavior that Piaget described, such as the many replications of the A-not-B error that have been reported. Indeed, in addition to his enormous theoretical contribution Piaget left us a legacy of hundreds of experiments and experimental paradigms which continue to influence and dominate current work on cognitive development. Nevertheless, some researchers have questioned whether cognitive development is as heavily dependent on manual experience, and whether infant cognition is purely sensorimotor. Also controversial is the idea that early concepts of objects and people are subjective, not objective, and a function of the child's own behavior. In the following section we review evidence for alternate views of infant cognition that claim a more sophisticated foundation for intellectual development from an early age.

Nativist approach

A central tenet of nativist theory is that a limited number of early-emerging kinds of knowledge form a central core around which more diverse, mature cognitive capacities are later elaborated. That is, some kinds of knowledge are **innate**. Philosophical discussions of innateness are ancient; historically, these discussions have centered on the extent to which knowledge must necessarily be rooted in, or is independent of, postnatal experience. Plato and Descartes, for example, proposed that some ideas were innate because they were elicited in the absence of any direct tutoring or instruction, or were unobservable in the world, and thus unlearnable (e.g., concepts of geometry or God).

Innate object knowledge

More recently, theories of innate object knowledge have arisen: concepts of objects as obeying physical constraints, such as persistence and solidity across occlusion. Three arguments have been mounted for these hypothesized innate object concepts. First, evidence of object knowledge can be observed in very young infants, perhaps too early to have derived from postnatal learning. Second, infants' detection of apparent violations of physical constraints has been proposed to arise from experience with **contrastive evidence**, opportunities to observe objects behaving in a manner consistent or inconsistent with a particular concept (Baillargeon, 1994). If this proposal is correct, then a concept of persistence across occlusion must be innate, because it cannot have been acquired from observing contrastive evidence: only very rarely are there observable events in the real world in which an object goes out of existence (the obvious examples are a soap bubble or a balloon bursting). Third, there is evidence from nonhuman animals and anatomical specialization in humans for commonality of cognitive function across species (such as working memory for small numbers of objects), and commonality of cortical structure across individual humans (such as Broca's area which deals with speech production, Wernicke's area which deals with language comprehension, and the fusiform face area which deals with face perception), suggesting an inevitability of certain concepts that are 'programmed' via evolutionary pressure (Dehaene, 1997).

There is evidence from a variety of laboratories and experimental settings for infants' representations of objects as solid bodies that are spatio-temporally coherent and persistent, representations that appear to be functional by 4 months after birth. Nevertheless, unequivocal evidence for **innate** object concepts (arising in the absence of experience) has not yet been reported. Moreover, findings from experiments on infants' perception of partly occluded objects, reviewed in brief next, cast doubt on the likelihood that object concepts are innate.

Perception of partly occluded objects

Kellman and Spelke (1983) devised a task to examine the perceptual equivalence of two identical forms, one of which was partially occluded; this paradigm exploits the tendency of infants to look longer at a novel visual stimulus than at a familiar one. After exposure to a partly occluded rod, 4-month-old infants looked longer at two rod parts than at a complete object (see Figure 6.1), implying a representation of unity in the original, partly occluded stimulus. When newborn infants were tested in a similar procedure, however, they responded to a partly occluded object display solely on the basis of its visible parts, failing to perceive completion behind the occluder (Slater, Morison *et al.*, 1990). Johnson and Aslin (1995) found that under some conditions, 2-month-olds would perceive object unity, as when the occluder is made narrow and the distance of perceptual interpolation is thereby reduced, relative to a display in which older infants are able to achieve perceptual completion. A parallel pattern of responses was reported by Johnson, Bremner *et al.* (2003), Johnson (2004), and Bremner *et al.* (2005) in experiments examining perception of object persistence when fully occluded (i.e., an object moving back and forth, becoming completely hidden behind an occluder for a short time before re-emerging). Four-month-olds perceived object persistence only when the object was out of sight for a very brief interval; when it was out of sight for a more extended duration, the infants appeared to perceive only the visible segments of the object trajectory, failing to perceive persistence (see Figure 6.2). In other words, they behaved similarly to newborns viewing a partly occluded object, responding on the basis of what is directly visible only. Six-month-olds seemed to perceive persistence even under the longer occlusion duration.

Habituation display

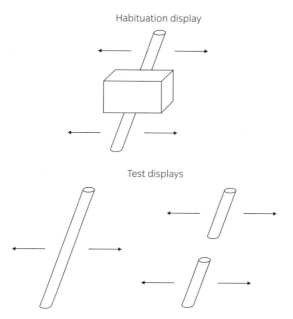

Test displays

Figure 6.1 Infants are first habituated (top) to a rod that moves back and forth behind an occluder, and on test trials are shown a complete rod and two rod pieces (bottom). Four-month-old infants look longer at the two rod pieces, a novelty preference that indicates that they had seen a complete rod on the habituation trials. Newborn infants, however, look longer at the complete rod, suggesting they had seen two rod pieces during habituation.

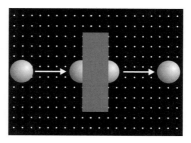

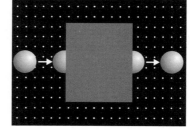

Figure 6.2 When 4-month-olds are shown a ball moving behind a narrow occluder (top), so that it is out of sight for a very short period of time, they see it as one object moving on a continuous trajectory. However, when the occluder is wider (bottom) they see it as two separate objects.

Consider these results in the light of the claims for innateness outlined previously. All evidence to date indicates that perception of occlusion is not available in humans at birth, and without perception of occlusion a functional object concept, and understanding of an object as a whole, is impossible since infants would usually see only fragments of the whole object. How the change occurs toward perception of objects as unified and persistent is unknown at present, but it may well be dependent on postnatal experiences.

A comparison of empiricist and nativist views: innate social knowledge?

In addition to theories of innate **object** knowledge, theories of innate **social** knowledge have also emerged, and in this section we compare two different theoretical views, those of Piaget and Meltzoff and Moore, on the nature and development of infant imitation, particularly of adults' facial gestures. For Piaget the capacity for imitation develops gradually as infancy progresses. For the first 8–10 months there are behaviors that can be interpreted as imitation, but this is often illusory: if a model (i.e., an adult) imitates a sound or a gesture the infant is producing, the infant is likely to continue making the sound or gesture, but this may be simply repeating her own actions rather than reproducing or imitating another's actions. According to the Piagetian account, infants in this age range are unable to imitate actions that require them to use parts of their body that they cannot see, such as tongue protrusion or mouth opening. Around 8–10 months the first 'true' imitation emerges, and for the first time the infant becomes able to produce imitative gestures that she cannot see, such as the movement of her lips. A little later the infant becomes able to imitate novel gestures: an example that Piaget gave was imitation of movements of the forefinger.

Later still, around 18–24 months, the capacity for **deferred imitation** emerges. Piaget gave this example from his daughter Jacqueline, when she was aged 1 year 4 months:

At 1;4 Jacqueline had a visit from a little boy of 1;6 whom she used to see from time to time, and who, in the course of the afternoon got into a temper tantrum. He screamed as he tried to get out of his playpen and pushed it backward, stamping his feet. Jacqueline stood watching him in amazement, never having witnessed such a scene before. The next day she herself screamed in her playpen and tried to move it, stamping her foot lightly several times in succession.

(Piaget, 1951, p. 63)

What has developed? In this example his daughter reproduced the event some time after it had happened. Therefore, she must have internalized the action at the time of its occurrence and retained a **representation** of the event so that it could be evoked and acted on at a later time.

We can see that Piaget's account suggested that the capacity for imitation develops slowly over infancy and it progresses concurrently with other aspects of development. The ability to imitate **novel** actions (i.e., those not already in the infant's repertoire) does not appear until around 9 months, around the time that the infant becomes able to imitate actions (such as movements of the lips or tongue protrusion) where she cannot see the imitative actions on herself. The capacity for representation appears towards the end of infancy, around 18 months, or a little earlier, bringing with it the capacity for deferred imitation.

A different account, suggesting that representation is the starting point and not the end point of infancy, has been put forward by Meltzoff and Moore (1977) and elaborated by Meltzoff (2004). Meltzoff and Moore (1977) have proposed an early-developing system in infants for recognizing and responding to other people, a system that is expressed behaviorally in imitative gestures. That is, under some circumstances, infants have been reported to imitate certain facial and manual gestures produced by adults, particularly tongue protrusion and mouth opening (see Figure 6.3).

Some authors (e.g., Anisfeld *et al.*, 2001), have reported failures to replicate imitation of facial gestures in newborn infants, but others have reported successful replications, even in infants within an hour from birth, where the experimenter's face was the first they saw (Reissland, 1988). Imitation by newborn infants seems a remarkable achievement, given that such imitation

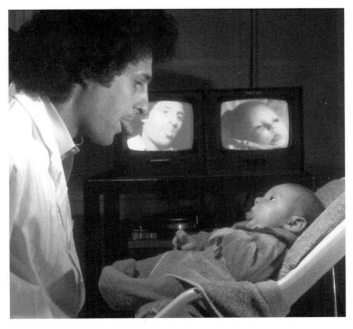

Figure 6.3 An infant imitating an adult's tongue protrusion. Photo from Andrew Meltzoff.

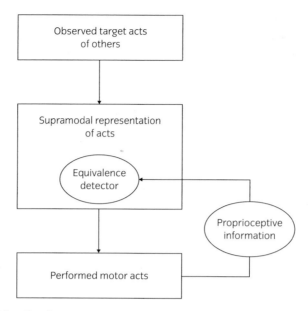

Figure 6.4 Meltzoff and Moore's active intermodal matching model of infant imitation. The infant sees the target act, such as tongue protrusion, and is able to represent the act. She then attempts to imitate the act and the equivalence detector informs her how accurate she is, and through proprioceptive feedback she is able to match her behavior more and more closely to the target act.

occurs without the infant being able to see her own face. How might newborn infants be able to do this? Meltzoff and Moore suggest that it is done by a process of **active intermodal matching**, which is illustrated in Figure 6.4. In this model the infant is able to match her behavior (e.g., tongue protrusion or mouth opening) with the behavior observed from the adult model, because the infant is able to detect **proprioceptive feedback**, which is information about the movement of its own (unseen) facial movements, and match this information to its own imitative behavior. Imitation of the appropriate facial gesture emerges rapidly within a session as the equivalence detector enables the infant to match its own behavior more and more closely with that of the adult model. Meltzoff and Moore (2002) have also reported evidence of deferred imitation in 6-week-old infants. In this study the infants saw an adult producing a gesture (either mouth opening or tongue protrusion) and 24 hours later they saw the same adult, this time presenting a passive face. The infants then produced (i.e., imitated) the gesture they had seen the day before.

The finding of imitation in very young infants suggests that infants are born with a fairly detailed representation of the human face (Meltzoff, 2004) and supports the view that 'newborns begin life with some grasp of people' (Meltzoff, 1995). An intriguing view put forward by Meltzoff and Moore is that infants imitate as a form of social interaction and as a way of learning about people. These views suggest that infants are born with some sort of innate 'template' or representation of the human face that is part of a genetic preparedness for discriminating between people and for bonding with caregivers.

Comparing nativist and empiricist views

As we have seen above, nativist views argue for innate knowledge, i.e., knowledge that the infant is born with and which helps to guide subsequent learning. Empiricist views, on the contrary, argue that the infant is born with little or no knowledge of the physical and social world and knowledge about the world is constructed from the infant's actions and experiences, and emerges over time. Piaget's account of cognitive development is often referred to as a **constructivist** account in that he argued that knowledge was constructed from the infant's experience and actions on the world. We will see in the next section that information-processing approaches typically offer a constructivist view of development.

Information-processing account

Rather than presuppose an unchanging, innate core of cognitive capacities, information-processing theorists posit a set of sensory, perceptual, and (non-conceptual) cognitive processes that are constant across development, such as auditory and visual perception, memory, attention, and categorization (Cohen, Chaput & Cashon, 2002). On this view, knowledge is constructed from the function of these more primitive mechanisms over time, and learning. With development, infants become able to integrate the lower-level units of information into a more complex, higher-level unit, these higher-level units serve as the components for even more complex units, and so on. Concepts are thus formed incrementally rather than being provided innately.

Experiments that examine infants' perception of causality provide evidence for this approach, and studies on this topic that also demonstrate the dynamic shifting between processing lower- and higher-level components of events were reported by Cohen and Amsel (1998) and Cohen and Oakes (1993). Infants 4–10 months of age were shown videos of an object moving into the vicinity of a second object. If objects make contact in such events, and the second object moves away abruptly, adults report a **causal** relation between the two: a **launching event**. Launching is not perceived, however, if there is no contact between the two objects, or if there is a delay between contact and launch (see Figure 6.5). The likelihood of perception of causality at any particular age is a function of the complexity of the events. For example, 6.5-month-olds responded to causality, and not merely the movements of

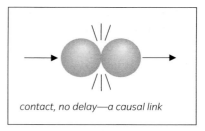

contact, no delay—a causal link

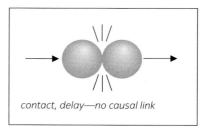

no contact, no delay—no causal link

Figure 6.5 Perception of causality. If adults see a display where one object makes contact with another and the second then moves away without a delay (top—a launching event) they typically report that the first object *caused* the second to move. However, if the second object moves without any contact with the first (middle), or if the second object moves some time after the first has made contact (bottom), there is no perception of a causal link between the movements of the two objects.

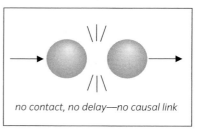

contact, delay—no causal link

the individual components of the event, if the objects were simple shapes. If more complex objects participate in such events, infants at this age provide no evidence of causality perception. Ten-month-olds perceive causality in displays with more intricate objects, yet fail when objects change from trial to trial but a causal relation is maintained. Presumably, the infants were compelled to process the events under these circumstances at a perceptual, rather than a conceptual level, due to increased constraints presented by the added complexity of the stimuli.

Important progress has been made in understanding developmental mechanisms underlying causality perception in infants by using **connectionist** models, which are computer programs designed to learn from experience. Connectionist models take as input similar kinds of information as do human observers, coded in terms of input to which a computer can respond, and provide as output a prediction about the next in a series of events. Cohen *et al.* (2002) modeled development of causality perception and found that it can be explained with a combination of sensitivity to the temporal and spatial aspects of the event, in accord with the stipulations of information-processing approaches, rather than by supposing an innately determined 'concept' of causality. In other words, causality was constructed from a combination of perceptual sensitivities, memory, and experience. Connectionist models have been used to examine a variety of aspects of cognitive development (see Mareschal, 2002).

Psychometric approach

The **psychometric approach** attempts to measure various aspects of individuals to understand how development takes place, and also to compare the development of individuals with those of a comparable group of people—this is the measurement of individual differences.

Bayley Scales of Infant Development (BSID)

The most frequently used test of infant development is the Bayley Scales of Infant and Toddler Development. Nancy Bayley published the California First Year Mental Scale in 1933, and this included measures of both motor and mental development. It later became the Bayley scales, and the third edition (Bayley-III) appeared in 2005. This test is described in more detail in Chapter 2.

We can ask whether scores on this test predict later IQ, and the answer is that infants' scores on the tests generally do not, although as a measure of overall development the Bayley scales are clearly good. Given that standardized tests of infant cognitive development generally do not predict later development or, by themselves, detect infants at risk of delayed development, the search has been on for alternative measures that might do this, and in this search visual habituation and dishabituation are seen as among the main contenders.

Habituation and dishabituation as measures of cognitive development

Habituation to a visual stimulus, and subsequent recovery of attention to a novel stimulus (dishabituation), as discussed in Chapter 2, is considered an indication of brain integrity and cognitive competence, and rate or speed of habituation, and amount of recovery of attention to a novel stimulus are considered a measure of speed and amount of information processing.

We know that these measures show individual differences between infants, and there have been many studies which report a modest predictive correlation between measures of habituation and dishabituation in infancy and later IQ. In a recent evaluation and analysis of dozens of these studies (known as a **meta-analysis**) Kavsek (2004) suggested that the average correlation between infant habituation/dishabituation and measures of intelligence in later life is .37 and concluded that 'the predictive validity of habituation/dishabituation is substantial and stable up until adolescence' (p. 369). Bornstein *et al.* (2006), similarly, suggested that 'Infants who habituate efficiently are infants who scan and pick up information economically, assimilate that information quickly, or construct memories more easily and faithfully than other infants. Children who successfully solve the perceptual, language, abstract reasoning, and memory tasks that are included in children's intelligence tests do likewise' (p. 157).

Integrating the four approaches

Although the four approaches that we have described might seem quite disparate, their basic aim is the same, that is, to come to an understanding of the ways in which intellectual and cognitive abilities develop and can be measured in infancy. The approaches are also interrelated and draw upon each other. For example, measuring habituation/dishabituation may be seen in the context of the information-processing approach since it clearly involves the infant in taking in information; information-processing methods are used to test concepts that Piaget first drew our attention to; Piagetian tasks, such as object permanence are often incorporated into tests of infant development, such as the Bayley scales. Nevertheless, having different approaches to the growth of intelligence adds to the richness and variety of our developing understanding of infant development, and tells us that intelligence shows both continuities and discontinuities in development.

The effects of early experiences on the development of intelligence

Several authors have discussed the relative contributions of genetic and environmental factors on cognitive development in infancy, and it has often been claimed that, except for extreme deprivation, mental development in infancy follows a genetically predetermined, species-typical growth path, known as a **creod**, a term derived from the Greek words for 'necessity' and 'a path.' Those who adopted this view argued that intervention studies that are aimed at infants from disadvantaged backgrounds, and are at risk for developmental retardation, should begin after the first year or so, since development before this age is genetically determined and not at risk from environmental deprivation: thus, Ramey *et al.* (1984, p. 1923) suggested that 'intervention programs for initially healthy children might be more beneficial during early childhood than during infancy'; 9 years later much the same conclusion was reached by Brooks-Gunn *et al.* (1993, p. 746) who offered the view that 'early infant intelligence is canalized ... rendering it relatively impervious to intervention.' (Development that is **canalized** refers to that which is genetically programmed and kept within narrow boundaries even in the presence of disturbing or deprived environments.)

Research over the last 15 years or so, however, has shown that this view is mistaken. Michael Rutter and colleagues (1998) have followed up over 100 Romanian children who were adopted into the United Kingdom after living in conditions that were characterized by extreme neglect, being reared in orphanages where they received little care, stimulation, or attention, with few toys or objects to play with. Half of these children were below the third percentile in body size, head circumference, and levels of developmental function. However, if they arrived in the UK before 6 months of age they made a remarkable recovery and had caught up and reached normal developmental levels in cognitive functioning. Those who entered the UK at a later age showed a degree of developmental catch-up compared with their level of functioning at the time of entry, but on average, this improvement was not complete. In this study, the strongest predictor of cognitive status at age 4 years was the age of entry to the UK. A later study of the same children (Beckett *et al.*, 2002) also found other disturbances, such as a difficulty in chewing and swallowing solid foods at age 6 years, whose prevalence was also related to the amount of time the children had spent in severe deprivation. This is a clear indication that deprivation affects many aspects of development and is rarely confined to cognitive development. These findings, by themselves, argue for early intervention, at least in cases of severe deprivation.

Begun in the 1960s, the **Head Start** program in the United States was one of the first large-scale attempts to support the view that the earlier the intervention, the greater the likelihood of positive results. Early intervention programs are reviewed in Chapter 16.

SUMMARY

Over the last 100 years we have made great inroads into an understanding of the development of intelligence and cognitive abilities in infancy. Before Piaget, whose work on infants and children began in the 1920s, developmental psychology barely existed. Piaget's work demonstrated that the child was an active contributor to his or her own development, and he was the first to demonstrate that major aspects of cognitive development were present and developing in infancy and could be investigated. Piaget's work continues to influence research (e.g., see Chapter 8) and his impact has been and continues to be enormous: Flavell (1996) wrote an assessment of Piaget's contribution, entitled 'Piaget's legacy,' and quotes an anonymous reviewer of his article — 'The impact of Piaget on developmental psychology is ... too monumental to embrace,' to which Flavell simply adds the words 'I agree.'

We also considered the nativist approach, which argues that infants are born with evolutionarily/genetically provided innate knowledge of the cognitive and/or social world and that this knowledge forms a core around which more mature cognitive functioning will develop.

Information-processing approaches view the human mind as a complex system through which information flows. There is not a single information-processing theory, but most approaches along these lines suggest that there are three components to cognitive activity. First, information is taken in from the world and encoded into some meaningful form. Next, a number of internal processes such as memory, recognition, problem-solving strategies work on the information, so that finally individuals are able to change their cognitive structures and knowledge in order to act on the information. As development continues, increasingly improved ways of acting on the world emerge in infancy.

Finally, we considered the psychometric approach, which attempts to measure cognitive development in individual infants in order to compare their development with that of other infants.

Clearly, each of the four approaches makes an important and interrelated contribution to our understanding of infant cognitive development. We now know that development in infancy is rapid and that infants begin learning from before birth. The findings from early intervention and deprivation studies emphasize the importance of development, and of environmental influences, throughout infancy and childhood.

CHAPTER SEVEN

Categorization

PAUL C. QUINN

Introduction

In this chapter we focus upon an important aspect of mental development, **categorization**, which addresses a fundamental question about human knowledge: how is it stored and manipulated? Over time and with experience, members of the human species accumulate a great wealth of information about the world. An internal record of such knowledge is presumed to be compiled in long-term memory (see Chapter 9). Cognitive scientists are interested in describing how this memory is structured. Consider a system of memory storage resembling a large basket of laundry, freshly washed, and just removed from the dryer. Searching for a particular item of clothing within such a basket would take time and effort because the items of clothing have been thrown together in a random arrangement. Imagine instead a memory system resembling a chest of drawers in which the clothing items from the laundry basket are neatly stored with particular kinds of clothing (i.e., shirts, trousers, socks) placed in different drawers. Finding a specific article of clothing within a storage system organized by categories of clothing would be fast and easily accomplished.

Because human cognitive processes like the recognition and retrieval of information from memory are, in most instances, also fast and easily accomplished, many cognitive scientists believe that our memory is structured according to the 'chest of drawers' model rather than the 'laundry basket' model, with information about various kinds of objects and their relations represented in particular locations within the storage system. The basic unit of organization and storage within a 'chest of drawers' type of memory system has been called a **concept** or **category representation**—terms which refer to a mental representation for similar or like entities. Concepts are believed to underlie our ability to **categorize**, that is, to respond to discriminably different entities from a common class as members of the same category.

Thus, as an example, there are many varieties of dogs, but we treat them all as belonging to the same category of 'dog,' despite the many perceptual differences between the different varieties.

To give my students a concrete metaphor for thinking about concepts, I tell them to think about file folders. We use file folders to organize information into various meaningful groupings, and we may have mental files or category representations to hold information about various object **classes**. By developing a storage system in which information about related instances (e.g., cats) is stored in the same **basic** file, and information from related **basic** files (e.g., dogs) is nested in larger **global** or **superordinate** 'higher up' files (e.g., mammal or animal), we enable intellectual functioning to be mediated or handled by a cognitive system in which objects are related to each other through a set of interconnected concepts.

With concepts, we gain the ability to respond with familiarity to an indefinitely large number of examples from multiple categories, which will include instances never before encountered (Murphy, 2002). Each day we may be presented with novel stimuli—new faces, new furry, four-legged creatures that meow, and new, shiny objects that move on rubber discs. Yet, we do not respond to these entities as if we are unfamiliar with them. Rather, we think to ourselves or even say out loud, 'This is a person. That is a cat. There is a car.' In other words, concepts allow us to respond to the novel as if it is familiar, thereby freeing finite **cognitive resources** to assist with higher-order mental activities such as problem-solving and decision-making. If we did not possess concepts, then our memory would consist of a large number of unrelated instances, and intellectual development would be slow going, because much of our experience would consist of learning to respond anew to the many novel entities we encounter every day.

Concepts also help make mental life more tractable and manageable by simplifying the diversity of the natural environment. In particular, concepts reduce the inherent variation of the physical continua around us into cognitively manageable proportions, that is, smaller chunks. For example, although there are 7 000 000 discriminable shades of color, most languages collapse color experience into a dozen or so basic categories (Bruner, Goodnow & Austin, 1956). Likewise, our cognitive system parses or sorts the orientation continuum, which can be from $0°$ to $360°$, into three basic categories: vertical, horizontal, and slanted (Quinn & Bomba, 1986; Quinn, 2004d). Imagine how much more complex early cognitive development would be if we had to learn to map 7 000 000 color terms onto 7 000 000 color experiences! And consider the cognitive load placed on the storage and search components of a memory system that represented each degree of orientation as a distinct entity. The processing of continuous information is thus simplified by concepts that represent **category-level** (i.e., summary) information, rather than **exemplar-specific** details (i.e., details about each individual instance or member of a category).

Overall, the processes of categorization, and the concepts that underlie them, permit organized storage, the capability of responding equivalently to an indefinitely large number of instances from multiple categories, and the reduction of physically continuous information into a limited number of separate groupings. Because of the importance of concepts to mental life, and the recognition that they have to begin at some point during development, there has been interest in when and how concepts emerge.

This chapter reviews what is known about the development of categorization in infants. Included in the review are: (1) a brief account of historical views on the development of categorization, (2) a description of the methodologies that have been used to infer categorization in preverbal infants, and (3) a discussion of recent trends in infant categorization—research that centers on the kinds of category representations formed by infants, their timing of emergence during early development, and the processes by which such category representations are generated. Although category formation by infants has been studied for visual and speech stimuli (Quinn & Eimas, 1986), the present chapter focuses on infant categorization abilities in the domain of vision.

Historical views briefly considered

There has been a lingering tradition in developmental psychology to consider the acquisition of concepts to be a relatively late achievement (i.e., of childhood or even early adolescence), dependent on the emergence of naming and language, the receipt of instruction, and the possession of logical reasoning skills. For example, Hull (1920; see also Gauker, 2005) argued that children come to have a concept for dog by associating environmental encounters with different dogs and parental labeling of those dogs as 'dog.' The idea that verbal labels provided a means for acquiring concepts continued into the 1950s with work on **acquired equivalence**—a research program which suggested that items given the same verbal label increased in perceived similarity, whereas items given different verbal labels increased in dissimilarity (e.g., Spiker, 1956; see also more recent work by Balaban & Waxman, 1997; Sloutsky, Lo & Fisher, 2001; Xu, 2005; Yoshida & Smith, 2005). Another perspective, one which emerged from the anthropology literature, argued that children were taught through formal and informal means of tuition to assign objects to categories (Leach, 1964). Also contributing to the late estimate of concept emergence in humans was the classical view of concepts—the idea that concepts were represented by sets of necessary and sufficient features—and the findings that even young children, before the onset of logical reasoning (e.g., age 6 or the beginnings of a new stage in Piaget's theory of development—the concrete operational period, as discussed in Chapter 6), had difficulty maintaining good criteria for grouping a set of objects as members of a particular category (Bruner, Olver & Greenfield, 1966).

Ideas about the ontogenesis, or development, of concepts during infancy and childhood began to change as ideas about how adult concepts were represented began to evolve, particularly through the work of Eleanor Rosch and her collaborators (reviewed in Rosch, 1978). Embracing the **family resemblance** view of concepts originally formulated in the philosophy literature by Wittgenstein (1953), Rosch argued that categorization is highly determined because objects in the perceived world do not appear to human observers as unstructured sets of equally likely occurring attributes. Rather, the world is structured so that object categories are marked or characterized (like family members) by bundles of correlated attributes. For example, objects like birds fall into one grouping because they have feathers, beaks, two legs, and an ability to chirp, whereas dogs are compiled into a separate bin because they have fur, noses, four legs, and the ability to bark. If the Rosch view is correct, then an organism that can detect such correlations and compile them into separate representations is capable of categorization. Thus, by the Rosch view, some of the abilities involved in grouping objects into individuated categories may be present **before** the emergence of language, instruction, and logic. It therefore becomes important to examine the abilities prelinguistic infants may have to categorize their environment, as it may be from these abilities that the complex concepts and categories of the adult will develop.

Categorization in infants

In order to study categorization in preverbal infants, researchers have utilized procedures that were initially used by investigators of an earlier era to study simple perceptual discrimination and memory abilities (Fantz, 1964). These procedures capitalize on the visual selectivity of infants and the fact that infants will look at some stimuli reliably more than they will look at others (Aslin & Fiser, 2005). For example, if a group of infants displays a consistent preference for one stimulus over another, in the sense of looking more at this one, it can safely be inferred that the infants can discriminate between them on some basis.

The preference for looking at novel stimuli (or overall examining preference for novelty, which includes touching in older infants) is a reliable behavior that extends across a variety of stimulus patterns and age groups—from newborns to 18-month-olds—and has proved particularly valuable in providing a methodology for understanding infant cognitive abilities (Mareschal & Quinn, 2001). This preference is the basis for the **familiarization/novelty-preference procedure**. As can be seen in the top panel of Figure 7.1, in order to determine whether infants can discriminate between two visual patterns,

Discrimination using the familiarization–novelty
preference procedure

Familiarization		Novelty preference test	
F	F	F	N

Categorization using the familiarization–novelty
preference procedure

Familiarization		Novelty preference test	
F_1	F_2		
F_3	F_4	F_{n+2}	N
F_n	F_{n+1}		

Figure 7.1 Schematic depiction of the familiarization/novelty-preference procedures used to measure discrimination and categorization abilities of infants.

they can be familiarized with two identical copies of one of the patterns, and subsequently presented with the familiar stimulus paired with the novel stimulus. Greater looking at the novel stimulus, referred to as a preference for the novel stimulus, that cannot be attributed to an *a priori* preference (i.e., a 'natural' or unlearned preference for this stimulus), implies both memory for the familiar stimulus and the ability to discriminate between it and the novel stimulus.

To study categorization in infants, it is necessary to make two modifications in the familiarization/novelty-preference procedure, and these are depicted in the bottom half of Figure 7.1. First, a number of different stimuli (referred to as **category exemplars**), all of which are from the same category, are presented during a series of familiarization trials. Second, during what is called a **novel category preference test**, infants are presented with two novel stimuli, one from the familiar category, and the other from a novel category. If infants generalize their familiarization to the novel instance from the familiar category, and display a preference for the novel instance from the novel category, then it can be inferred that the infants have on some basis grouped together or categorized the instances from the familiar category (including the novel one) and recognized that the novel instance from the novel category does not belong to this grouping (or category representation). Another way of describing this is to say that the infants have formed a category representation of the exemplars presented during familiarization that includes the novel instance of the familiar category, but excludes the novel instance from the novel category.

Considerable care must be taken to insure that the infants are not responding to specific features of individual exemplars (or small sets of exemplars) when performing in a study of category formation. One way of meeting this objective is to pre-select a large number of exemplars to represent each category under investigation. The exemplars should be chosen so as to approximate the variability of the exemplars as they appear in the natural environment. For example, if we want to determine whether infants would form a category representation for cats that excludes dogs and a category representation for dogs that excludes cats, then realistic, photographic exemplars of cats and dogs, representing a variety of breeds, stances, colors, and hair lengths, should be chosen (Quinn, Eimas & Rosenkrantz, 1993). Black-and-white examples are presented in Figure 7.2. Infants in separate experimental groups could be familiarized with a subset of the cats or dogs, randomly selected and different for each infant, and then preference tested with a novel cat and a dog, also randomly selected and different for each infant. The experimental design is depicted in Figure 7.3. By taking these precautions, the investigator increases the validity of the experiment as a study of category formation, one in which the infants must represent category-level information (e.g., features characteristic of the category as a whole), to perform at above-chance levels.

Figure 7.2 Black-and-white examples of the cat and dog stimuli used in Quinn, Eimas, and Rosenkrantz (1993).

Familiarization	Cats		Dogs	
	C_1	C_2	D_1	D_2
	C_3	C_4	D_3	D_4
	•		•	
	•		•	
	•		•	
	C_{11}	C_{12}	D_{11}	D_{12}
Novel category preference test	C_{13-18}	D_{1-18}	D_{13-18}	C_{1-18}

Figure 7.3 Schematic depiction of the experimental design used to assess whether infants can form category representations for cats versus dogs.

It should also be mentioned that claims of category formation by infants require that two further conditions be met. First, it must be shown that the preference for the novel category instance did not occur because of an *a priori*, or pre-existing preference. The category formation study should thus be repeated with a control group of infants, with one important difference: the infants would be presented with only the preference test exemplars and not the familiarization exemplars. In this way, we can obtain a measure of spontaneous preference for the exemplars that appeared on the preference test trials of the category formation study. An inference of category formation is permitted if the novel category preference observed in the experimental group is significantly greater than the spontaneous preference (for the same category) observed in the control group.

Given that categorization is defined as equivalent responding to a set of discriminably different instances, a second condition that must be met for category formation to be inferred is that the infants be shown capable of **within-category** discrimination. If the infants are not able to discriminate between the individual instances from the familiar category, then the category formation study would amount only to a demonstration of **between-category** discrimination, a process that may be considerably simpler than a categorization process that requires grouping of discriminably different instances together.

In order to demonstrate within-category discrimination, each infant in a separate control group is first familiarized with one exemplar from the familiar category and subsequently presented with a preference test pairing the familiar exemplar and a novel exemplar from the same category. The exemplar pairings are randomly chosen and different for each infant in the control group. Positive evidence for discrimination in the form of a novelty preference that is reliably above chance would tell us that infants could discriminate between the different exemplars. This then allows for the conclusion that the infants in the category formation study had grouped together a class of discriminably different entities.

In addition to the familiarization/novelty-preference procedure, at least two other procedures are available for assessing categorization in infants. One is called the **sequential touching procedure**, and has been used with older infants and toddlers in the age range 12–30 months. The sequential touching procedure involves presenting infants with a number of exemplars from two categories simultaneously. The exemplars are small, three-dimensional, toy models which are placed before the infant in a random arrangement. Categorization is inferred if the infant touches exemplars from one category in sequence before touching members of the other category.

A more recently developed procedure for assessing infant categorization is called **generalized imitation** (McDonough & Mandler, 1998). In this procedure, an infant is presented with a small model of a real-world object (similar to the stimuli used in the sequential touching studies) and an experimenter then models an action appropriate for that object (e.g., a dog drinking from a cup). Categorization is inferred if the infant generalizes the action to other members of the same category, but not to members of contrast categories. Like the sequential touching procedure, the generalized imitation procedure has been used with older infants and toddlers in the age range 9–20 months.

What kinds of categories do infants represent?

Through the use of the three procedures described in the preceding section of the chapter—familiarization/novelty, sequential touching, and generalized imitation—infants have been shown capable of representing a variety of categories **at different levels of inclusiveness**. This means that, in the domain of **objects**, infants have been shown to represent exemplars at **global** or **super-ordinate**, e.g., animal, and increasingly more specific (**basic** and **subordinate**) levels of inclusiveness, e.g., cat and Siamese cat (Quinn, 2002, 2004a). In the domain of **space**, infants have been shown to represent concepts for spatial relations such as **above vs. below**, **between**, and **left vs. right**, as well as categories used in particular locations (at specific times), e.g., bathroom or kitchen items (Quinn, 2003a, 2004c; Mandler, Fivush & Reznick, 1987).

Infants have also been shown to form category representations for attributes of objects, including **color, orientation, form**, and **facial expression** (Bornstein, 1984; Quinn & Eimas, 1986; Nelson, 1987). In addition, it is possible to interpret the results of other studies in the infant cognition literature as evidence that infants possess physical concepts such as **support, containment**, and **causality** (Baillargeon & Wang, 2002; Casasola & Cohen, 2002; Cohen & Oakes, 1993; McDonough, Choi & Mandler, 2003). In view of the importance and utility of category representations as discussed in the introductory section of the chapter, it should not be surprising that infants can represent much of their experience at the category level.

Current issues

Researchers have begun to investigate a number of interrelated questions regarding how infants form category representations. Some of these questions are likely to have complex answers.

Information used to form category representations

One question concerns the basis for category formation by infants. It is possible that infants use **perceptual** attributes that can be found in the appearances of static exemplars of the category. For example, infants might form a category representation for mammals that includes instances of novel mammal categories, but excludes instances of furniture, on the basis of the presence or absence of such features as faces, fur, tails, and **curvilinear** vs. **rectilinear** (curved or straight) contours (Quinn, 2002). Alternatively, it is possible that infants may use more complex, **dynamic** attributes such as the fact that animals form a class of self-starters (i.e., being biological organisms they can move by themselves), whereas furniture items form a class of non-self-starters. Some have argued that such dynamic attributes are more conceptual in nature in that they permit the infant to begin to know 'animals' and 'furniture' as distinct 'kinds of things' as opposed to just knowing what the two classes look like (Mandler, 2004).

One strategy that has been used to identify the cue (or cues) that infants may use to form a particular category representation is to demonstrate that infants form the category representation when the cue is present, but do not form the category representation when the cue is absent. Such a strategy has been used to determine how, for example, infants form a category representation for cats that includes novel cats, but excludes dogs, and a category representation for dogs that includes novel dogs, but excludes cats (Quinn & Eimas, 1996a; Quinn, Eimas & Tarr, 2001). Given that the two species of animals have considerable perceptual overlap—both possess facial features, a body torso, four legs, fur, and tail—there is no obvious indicator of category membership.

It is possible that subtle differences, not noticeable upon cursory visual inspection, in one attribute, the pattern of correlation across a number of attributes, or the overall **gestalt** or whole might be used to form the category representations. Interestingly, infants were found to form the category

Figure 7.4 Black-and-white examples of the cat–dog hybrid stimuli used in Spencer, Quinn, Johnson, and Karmiloff-Smith (1997).

representations of cats vs. dogs when the exemplars presented during familiarization and test trials displayed only information from the head region (minus the body region), and did not form the category representations when the exemplars displayed only information from the body region (minus the head region). Infants were also found to form the category representations based on the head region (and not the body region) when presented with whole cats or dogs during familiarization, and preference tested with a pair of hybrid stimuli: a novel cat head on a novel dog body and a novel dog head on a novel cat body (Spencer, Quinn, Johnson & Karmiloff-Smith, 1997). Examples of the hybrid stimuli are shown in Figure 7.4. In this case, the novel category preference was found for the stimuli containing the novel category head. These studies thus suggest that information from the head region provides the infants with a necessary and sufficient basis to form a category representation for cats that excludes dogs, and a category representation for dogs that excludes cats.

Although the above research strategy was successful in demonstrating that head information is used by infants to form category representations for cats vs. dogs, some limitations of the approach should be acknowledged. Given that the stimuli were static photographic exemplars of the categories, we do not know the extent to which infants might rely on head information when categorizing real-world instances of cats and dogs encountered in the natural environment. Real cats and dogs display different movement patterns, and it is possible that such movement patterns might also help indicate category membership. Some evidence already suggests that infants can use motion information to categorize more general categories such as animals and vehicles (Arterberry & Bornstein, 2002).

Another limitation of the studies demonstrating the importance of the head region in categorizing cats and dogs is that we do not know the extent to which infants who are presented with different category contrasts would rely upon the head information. When cats or dogs are contrasted with birds or horses, for example, other cues such as the number of legs or the shape of the body may become important in the formation of exclusive category representations for cats and dogs. In fact, recent evidence indicates that when humans are contrasted with cats, and humans are the familiarization category, cats are actually incorporated into a broadly inclusive category representation for humans (Quinn & Eimas, 1998), and the whole of the stimulus is the basis for this inclusion (i.e., a head adjoined to an elongated body with skeletal appendages; Quinn, 2004b).

These examples suggest that category representations may be anchored by multiple static and dynamic attributes, any one or subset of which may be relied upon or used by infants in a particular context. The task of determining those attributes and identifying the conditions in which they are diagnostic of category membership has begun, and will likely continue for some time, given the cognitive complexity created by the large number of categories, each of which must be differentiated from a large number of contrast categories.

Category formation vs. category possession

Another current issue regarding the category representations of infants is whether they are formed online, i.e., during the course of an experiment (**category formation**), or whether the experiment is simply tapping into category representations that were constructed (presumably on the basis of real-life experience) before the experiment began (**category possession**). One variable to consider in deciding whether a given experiment is demonstrating category formation vs. category possession is the type of experimental task used.

The design of the familiarization/novelty-preference procedure lends itself to an interpretation couched in terms of category formation. Infants are presumed to construct the category representation as more and more exemplars from the familiar category are presented (Mareschal, French & Quinn, 2000). In contrast, in the sequential touching procedure, exemplars from two categories are presented simultaneously, and spontaneous touching behavior is recorded. This procedure would seem to tap category representations formed before the experiment. Another variable to consider is age. With increasing age, infants have more real-world experience, and are thus more likely to tap their own knowledge base, when performing in laboratory experiments. Yet another variable to think about is stimulus class. Infants are likely to experience some stimulus classes with greater frequency than others (e.g., humans vs. nonhuman animals). This additional experience might translate into an increased likelihood of influencing performance in a laboratory categorization task.

Even with task, age, and stimulus class as guidelines, it can often be difficult to determine the precise mixture of perceptual process and knowledge access that is occurring in a particular experiment. Consider, for example, the performance of young infants (2–4 months of age) presented with a mammal vs. furniture contrast in a familiarization/novelty-preference experiment (Quinn, 2002). Given that such young infants are not likely to have observed (at least directly) mammals such as elephants or hippopotamuses, or the particular furniture exemplars to be presented in the task, one might be tempted to say that the participating infants rely largely, if not exclusively, on perceptual processing, and that they are forming the category representation during the course of the familiarization trials. However, parents are known to read to their infants from picture books that may contain pictorial exemplars of animals, and infants are likely to have at least some visual experience with generic furniture items such as chairs and tables. Moreover, even young infants may be able to recognize that mammals like elephants and hippopotamuses are more like other animals (including humans) than furniture items (Quinn, 2005). Thus, even in an experiment that is designed as a study of concept formation, young infants may recruit from a preexisting knowledge base that at least in part determines their preference behavior.

Consider also the performance of older infants (18-month-olds) presented with an animal vs. vehicle contrast in the sequential touching procedure. One would suspect that infants well into their second year of life have encountered a number of animals and vehicles, through either direct or indirect experience (e.g., picture books, television), and that such experience would support the construction of separate category representations for animals and vehicles—representations that could then be used as a basis for successful performance in the experiment. And indeed, this hunch appeared to receive confirmation from the initial experimental findings: older infants spontaneously divided animals and vehicles into separate groupings in the sequential touching procedure (Mandler, Bauer & McDonough, 1991). However, in follow-up experiments, it was demonstrated that if one removes the legs from the (toy!) animals, and the wheels from the vehicles, the differentiation does not occur (Rakison & Butterworth, 1998). If the concepts for animal and vehicle were clearly established before participation in the experiment, then one would have expected the conceptual contrast between animals and vehicles to be maintained despite the perceptual alterations to the exemplars.

This issue of whether experiments conducted with the familiarization/novelty-preference procedure are investigations into category formation or possession has been empirically investigated in two ways. First, in one set of studies, following Rakison and Butterworth (1998), the categorization performance of infants presented with nonhuman animal contrasts (i.e., cat vs. dog) was manipulated by changing the featural characteristics (e.g., specific values of surface attributes such as leg length, nose width, horizontal extent of body torso), although not categorical characteristics of the stimuli, i.e., the exemplars were still clearly recognizable to adults as cats and dogs (French,

Mareschal, Mermillod & Quinn, 2004). If the infants had been tapping into cat and dog representations established before participation in the experiments, responsiveness should not have varied with the featural variations in the category information presented. The fact that infant responsiveness did vary suggests that the categories were being formed during the familiarization experience and that the boundaries could be manipulated depending on the information presented during familiarization.

Second, because a number of studies have investigated whether infants form individuated category representations for nonhuman animals, it is possible to compare the categorization performance of infants who have been exposed to pets at home with those who have not. Quinn (2004a) reported that categorization of cats or dogs at the subordinate level by 6- to 7-month-olds was not influenced by the presence of a pet at home that matched the category contrast presented in the laboratory (i.e., cat or dog). These null results thus fail to support the suggestion that infant categorization of nonhuman animals in the laboratory is assisted by real-world experience with nonhuman animals occurring before the infant's arrival at the laboratory.

Another study conducted with a similar rationale demonstrates that stimulus class (e.g., human vs. nonhuman animal) is an important factor to consider when attempting to tease apart the contributions of previously acquired knowledge vs. online learning to infant categorization performance (Quinn, Yahr, Kuhn, Slater & Pascalis, 2002). This study focused on how infants categorize the gender of human faces. In particular, the familiarization/novelty-preference procedure was used to examine the representation of the gender of human faces by 3- to 4-month-olds. The faces were color photographs of female and male models. The female and male faces had neutral to slightly positive emotional expression, were judged by adult observers to be of comparable attractiveness, and were matched for direction of gaze. Examples are shown in the left half of Figure 7.5. In the first experiment, infants were administered familiarization trials with male or female faces and then given test trials with a novel male face paired with a novel female face. The findings were that infants familiarized with males preferred females, but infants familiarized with females did not prefer males. Interestingly, this asymmetrical pattern of results had also been reported for older infants in the age range 5–12 months by Leinbach and Fagot (1993), suggesting that it is not an isolated finding, and represents instead a phenomenon of a more general nature.

In a second experiment, a possible explanation for the asymmetry, namely, that infants might spontaneously prefer female faces, was explored by presenting a group of 3- to 4-month-olds with a series of preference trials, each of which paired a different male face with a different female face. A mean preference for females was observed. The asymmetry reported in the categorization experiment thus appeared to be the result of a spontaneous

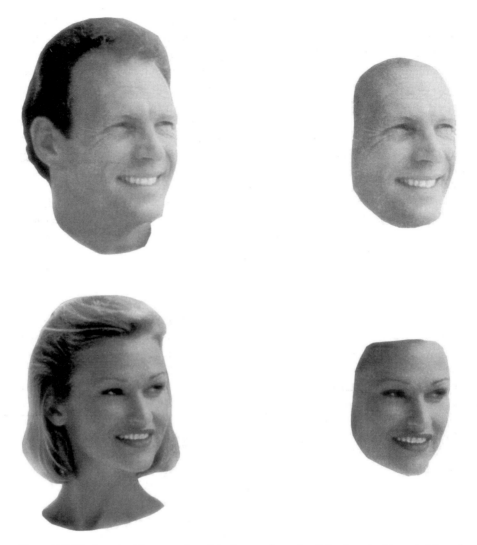

Figure 7.5 Black-and-white examples of the human face stimuli (with and without hair) used in Quinn, Yahr, Kuhn, Slater, and Pascalis (2002).

preference for female faces. This spontaneous preference could have facilitated a novel category preference for females after familiarization with males, and interfered with a novel category preference for males after familiarization with females.

In additional experiments, two lower-level sensory explanations for the spontaneous preference for female faces were assessed. The first inquired into whether the spontaneous preference for female faces might be attributable to higher external contrast information resulting from a greater amount of hair surrounding the internal face region of the stimuli. The experiment assessing spontaneous preference was thus repeated, but in this instance with face stimuli without external hair cues. Examples are shown in the right half of Figure 7.5. Here, the infants still preferred the female faces, indicating that the preference for female faces was not the result of higher external contrast created by a greater amount of hair.

A second inquiry was whether the spontaneous preference for female faces was due to higher contrast of the internal features, possibly resulting from the female models' greater use of cosmetics. The first control experiment with faces without hair was thus repeated, but in this instance, the faces were inverted. The reasoning was that if the female preference was due to higher contrast of the internal features, then the preference should be preserved with the inversion manipulation, because the internal features are present in both upright and inverted faces. The result was that the infants no longer preferred the female faces, suggesting that the spontaneous preference depended on processing of the internal features in their upright orientation.

Given that the evidence did not support either of the sensory explanations for the female face preference displayed by young infants, a cognitive explanation for the preference was investigated. This explanation was based on the idea that infants might prefer female over male faces because of greater familiarity with female faces. It is known that familiarity preferences can be observed in face comparisons, as is evidenced by the finding that young infants will display a spontaneous preference for mother's face over a strange female face, even in the absence of external hair cues (Bartrip, Morton & de Schonen, 2001). In addition, a majority of infants in the first 3 months of life are reared with female primary caregivers, and this was true for all the infants thus far described for the experiments of Quinn *et al.* (2002). These observations led to the hypothesis that infants might generalize their experiences with primary caregivers who are female to female faces more generally (at least when compared with male faces). If this hypothesis is correct, then it should be possible to reverse the gender preference in a sample of infants reared with male primary caregivers. Although far fewer infants are reared primarily by their fathers, Quinn *et al.* (2002) and Quinn (2003b) tested 8 such infants between 3 and 4 months of age. On the spontaneous preference test between upright male and female faces without hair, 7 of the 8 infants preferred the male faces. This outcome is consistent with the idea that infant attention to human stimuli may be biased toward the gender with which the infant has greater experience. More broadly, it provides evidence for the suggestion that representation of humans by infants as assessed in familiarization/novelty-preference procedure is influenced by experiences occurring before their participation in the tasks.

One- vs. two-process frameworks for understanding category representation by infants

A further source of current debate concerns the processes that infants rely on to represent category information. One view has it that the category representations of infants develop gradually through a process of quantitative enrichment (Quinn & Eimas, 1996b, 1997). In this **single-process** view, infants develop a category representation for animal or animal-like entities, for example, by encountering various animals over time, and joining together into a common representation their perceived attributes such as an elongated body shape, skeletal appendages, facial attributes bounded by a head shape, biological movement patterns, and communicative sounds.

The observable static and dynamic attributes that can be detected from the surfaces and trajectories of the exemplars by perceptual input systems can be supplemented by less apparent information regarding biological structures and functions such as 'has a heart' and 'can reproduce' that are usually acquired by means of language. Language in this view serves as an additional input system that can deliver information which further defines representations already established through vision (and other sensory modalities). As Quinn and Eimas (2000) summarize,

a representation like animal that may begin by picking out relatively simple features from seeing and other sensory modalities comes over time to have sufficient knowledge to permit specifying the kind of thing something is through a single continuous and integrative process of enrichment. (p. 57)

An alternative **dual-process** framework for thinking about the category representations of infants begins with the idea that 'seeing is not the same as thinking' (Mandler, 1999). This view embraces the idea that category representations formed on the basis of static perceptual attributes are merely **perceptual schemas** that define what a group of things looks like (i.e., categories based on appearance), but that do not contain the content required to define the meaning of something. True category representations or concepts are formed through the analysis or redescription of continuous perceptual input—a process which produces mental representations called **image schemas** (i.e., categories based on meaning). Image schemas are the forerunners of mature concepts and can be used to separate animals from nonanimals by conceptual primitives or features such as whether the members of the concept are 'self-starters' or 'non-self-starters.' The dual process framework thus suggests that infants possess both perceptual schemas that can be used for **identifying** entities and image schemas that can be used for **conceptualizing** entities—different systems of representation for perception vs. conception that operate in parallel.

Is there an order of emergence for category representations at different levels of inclusiveness?

In the opening section of the chapter, it was noted that category represent-ations may exist at different levels of inclusiveness and form hierarchically organized systems of knowledge representation. Human adults can, for example, represent 'mammal' or 'animal' at a **global** or **superordinate** level of inclusiveness, cat at an **intermediate** or **basic** level of inclusiveness, and Siamese cat at a **specific** or **subordinate** level of inclusiveness. Likewise, in the domain of furniture items, furniture is superordinate, chair is basic, and lawn chair is subordinate.

Investigators have been interested in the order of emergence for category representations at different levels and whether development consists primarily of progressive differentiation of the basic and subordinate levels from the global level (i.e., from the highest to the lowest level), or whether development reflects the grouping of specific subordinate representations into basic, and eventually, global levels (i.e., from the lowest to the highest level).

The conventional wisdom for a number of years was that the basic level was the first to be acquired by children, and that development consisted of grouping together basic-level representations to form the superordinate level, and differentiation of the basic level into separate groupings to form the subordinate level. The evidence supporting the **basic-to-superordinate** part of this claim came from a sorting task in which 3-year-olds were asked to identify which two of three simultaneously presented objects were alike (Rosch, Mervis, Gray, Johnson & Boyes-Braem, 1976). The main result was that children succeeded in the basic-level task involving, for example, two airplanes and a dog, but performed poorly in the superordinate level task involving, for example, an airplane, a car, and a dog. This finding provided the initial basis for the basic-to-superordinate view of early category development.

The data supporting this basic-to-superordinate view have been criticized because of the presence of a confound in the basic-level task (Mandler & Bauer, 1988). In particular, it has been pointed out that the basic-level task could be solved either with basic-level knowledge (i.e., how much the two airplanes are alike), or with superordinate-level knowledge (i.e., how much the two airplanes are different from the dog), or both. The more appropriate test of the basic-to-superordinate view is to determine whether basic-level categories from the same superordinate category (i.e., airplanes vs. cars, dogs vs. cats) can be represented before two contrasting superordinate categories can be represented (i.e., vehicles vs. animals). In a number of subsequent studies conducted in accordance with this experimental design, infants from a variety of age groups, performing in looking, touching, and generalized imitation procedures, have provided evidence of global category representations earlier and more readily than basic-level representations

(Mandler *et al.*, 1991; McDonough & Mandler, 1998; Quinn, 2002). The results of these studies thus support a differentiation-driven, **global-to-basic** view of early category development, and the most recent findings suggest that the full course of category development proceeds from the global to the basic to the subordinate level (Quinn, 2004a).

SUMMARY

Although concept formation has a history of being considered a late acquisition, dependent on the availability of language, logic, and instruction, studies conducted over the last 20 years suggest that preverbal infants are equipped with skills for developing category representations that later come to have conceptual significance. In particular, infants appear to possess core abilities for representing within-category similarity and between-category dissimilarity that may be deployed to form representation for a variety of generic categories. Such representations may serve as perceptual placeholders for the acquisition of knowledge beyond infancy. The discovery of the categorization abilities in infants has been made possible by advances and refinements in methodologies such as the familiarization/novelty-preference, sequential touching, and generalized imitation procedures. Current debates include the nature of the attributes that infants use to represent category information, the mix of on-line learning vs. access of previously acquired knowledge, one- vs. two-process models of category representation, and the order of emergence for category representations at different levels of inclusiveness. Given the importance of category representations for the efficiency and stability of cognition, future research investigations will be likely to continue on each of these fronts.

ACKNOWLEDGEMENTS

Preparation of this chapter was supported by NIH Grants HD-42451 and HD-46526. The author thanks Alan M. Slater for helpful comments on an earlier draft.

CHAPTER EIGHT

Perception and knowledge of the world

J. GAVIN BREMNER

Introduction

As adults, we inhabit physical environments that we understand well. Although objects often go out of sight temporarily behind others as we move or the objects themselves move, we know that these objects continue to exist. And although there are differences in navigational ability, we are generally fairly adept at finding our way around our world and remaining oriented in it as we weave around obstacles to reach a goal. We are also aware of hazards in our environment. For instance, we know at a glance when a vertical drop can be negotiated in a large step or a jump, and when it is so deep as to be a hazard. A question that has fascinated philosophers and more recently developmental psychologists concerns how we come to possess these abilities. Are they innate, or do they have to be learned? The controversy over the origins of knowledge still dominates this area of infancy research, and in this chapter I aim to present a selection of the key studies addressing infants' knowledge of objects and space. As you will see, taken together, the results of these studies do not point to a simple answer. Rather, the picture emerging from current work suggests that important foundations of knowledge are probably innate but that through action in the world infants transform this early knowledge into something much more sophisticated that they can use to guide their actions on objects and movements through their world.

Knowledge of objects

Object search and object permanence

Imagine you are playing with a 6-month-old baby. You take a toy that has her interest, and cover it with a cloth. What would you expect her to do?

Would she remove the cloth and retrieve the object, or would she show no attempt to find it, as if 'out of sight' were 'out of mind'? This is just the sort of activity the famous psychologist Jean Piaget used to reveal the stages infants went through in developing knowledge of the permanence of objects (Piaget, 1954). And what he found was that 6-month-olds showed no attempt to retrieve an object hidden in the way described above. A couple of months later, however, the story had changed; hide an object from an 8-month-old and she would retrieve it readily.

If you had been someone other than Piaget, you might have concluded that, somewhere between the ages of 6 and 8 months, infants developed knowledge that even though an object was out of sight it still existed, in other words, that they had fully achieved knowledge of object permanence. However, Piaget was never satisfied with one test of ability. With 8- and 9-month-olds he complicated the task by introducing a second location and switching where the object was hidden during the task. He found that infants searched almost without error at the first location (A), but that when the object was hidden, before their eyes, at the second location (B) they showed a strong tendency to search back at the original (A) location. This **A-not-B error** persists until about 12 months, when it is followed by errors on tasks involving more complex sequences of object hiding and displacement. Search failure and the A-not-B error are just two of the phenomena on which Piaget based his account of the development of object permanence. According to him, infants are born without any form of knowledge of the world but are equipped with systematic ways of functioning that lead them to construct knowledge, in particular knowledge of object permanence, through their own systematic actions in the world. A key transition takes place between 6 and 8 months when infants begin to search for hidden objects. This marks the first crude representation of the absent object, but as the A-not-B error indicates, it is a very limited representation, limited to a single place where the infant has successfully retrieved the object before.

For many years, this account of development of object permanence was fairly well accepted. The phenomena could readily be replicated, and the interpretation seemed plausible. However, in the 1960s and 1970s researchers began to question whether these object search tasks were the best way to investigate infants' knowledge. For instance, maybe 6-month-olds fail to search because they cannot organize the reach to remove the cover. It turns out that this is not a plausible explanation, because Bower and Wishart (1972) showed that 6-month-olds who failed to retrieve an object hidden under an opaque cup did so successfully when it was hidden under a transparent cup. This result has been replicated for the case of an object behind an opaque or transparent curtain (Shinskey, Bogartz & Poirier, 2000), so clearly the infants can organize the action and it was something about the object's invisibility that led to the problem. Nevertheless, requiring the infant to act might in some way put a load on their cognitive resources such that underlying knowledge was concealed. Considerations of this sort led investigators to seek more subtle measures of infants' knowledge. Later I shall mention some further alternative interpretations of Piaget's phenomena, and in the breaks in reading this you may want to think of some of your own.

Violation of expectation and object permanence

From the mid 1960s right through the 1970s, T. G. R. Bower carried out a series of influential studies of infants' object knowledge. He used tasks that did not require manual search, measuring infants' anticipation of the reappearance of objects moving behind screens (by measuring whether they looked in the place where they should reappear), or surprise (through heart-rate change) when a hidden object failed to reappear once the concealing cover was removed. These measures had their own problems, however, and we had to wait until the 1980s for a methodology to emerge that appeared to be a satisfactory means of measuring object knowledge in young infants. The **violation of expectation technique**, as it has come to be known, is essentially very simple. Usually, infants are first familiarized with an event sequence so that we can be confident that they are cued into what we want to test them on. For instance, they may be repeatedly exposed to an event in which an object moves from left to right, passing behind a screen on the central part of its trajectory. After this, they are presented with two test trials, one that is possible by the rules of mechanics and one that is impossible. For instance, the test events might be identical to the familiarization event but for the addition of a stationary object behind the screen. In both cases the object moves just as before, re-emerging from behind the screen. What makes one test trial possible and the other impossible is whether the second object is placed behind the path of the moving object (possible) or actually in its path (impossible). The rationale in this case is that if infants (1) know that the moving object continues to exist behind the screen, and (2) know that one object cannot move through another, the impossible test trial should be a violation of their expectation based on these two principles. The assumption is that such a violation will surprise them and that for this reason they will look longer at the impossible event. Thus, the dependent measure is very simple: we just measure the amount of time infants spend looking at the two test trials, and if they look significantly longer at the impossible test trial we conclude that they have noted the violation of the principle or principles in question. But we do have to be quite careful to rule out other interpretations. We know that infants look longer at events that are perceptually novel, so studies have to be designed to ensure either that the two test events do not differ in perceptual familiarity, or that the impossible event is actually more familiar than the possible one.

Baillargeon (1986) performed a study very much like the one I outlined above. As Figure 8.1 indicates, the set-up involved a ramp down which

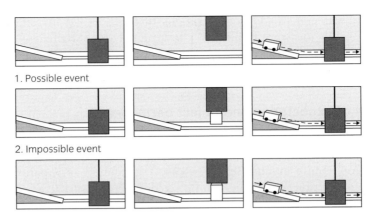

Figure 8.1 The procedure used by Baillargeon (1986) to investigate young infants' object knowledge. The familiarization event is at the top and the two test events are below.

a truck rolled, progressing on to a horizontal section partly hidden by a screen. Before each trial, the screen was lifted, revealing empty space during familiarization, and revealing a stationary object behind or in the path of the moving object in possible and impossible test trials, respectively. The elegance of this study is that once the screen is lowered again, the familiarization and test events are identical: the object rolls down the track, disappears and re-emerges. Thus the only basis for longer looking at the impossible event is knowledge of permanence and of the impenetrability of the object on the track, and hence realization that re-emergence of the object from the screen is impossible. And Baillargeon found that 6- and 8-month-olds looked significantly longer at the impossible test event, a result later replicated with 4-month-olds by Baillargeon and DeVos (1991).

The drawbridge study

Another approach used by Baillargeon, Spelke, and Wasserman (1985) to tackle the same questions is illustrated in Figure 8.2. Infants are familiarized with an event in which a flat rectangle (the drawbridge) is rotated through 180°, from lying flat with its free edge facing the infant, through vertical to lying flat with the free edge away from the infant. Test trials follow in which a cube is placed in the path of the drawbridge, and either the drawbridge rotates until coming to stop in contact with the cube (possible event) or the draw-bridge rotates the full 180° as before (impossible event), apparently moving through the space occupied by the cube (the cube is surreptitiously removed to make this possible). One good feature of this study is that in terms of surface perceptual appearances, the possible event is more novel than the impossible one (the flap rotates through a smaller distance). Thus, opposite predictions arise depending on whether infants are responding in terms of perceptual difference or in terms of violation of expectation. Baillargeon *et al.* (1985)

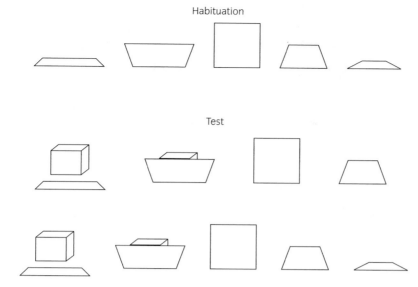

Figure 8.2 The infant's view of the possible and impossible test events in Baillargeon *et al.* (1985).

found that 5-month-olds looked significantly longer at the impossible event, again evidence that young infants understood object permanence (they knew that the cube was still present once hidden by the drawbridge) and the fact that one object could not move through the space occupied by another.

Innate core knowledge

Evidence from these studies and others is used to paint a very different picture from Piaget's regarding infant object knowledge. These investigators claim that infants are born with certain core knowledge in place, including knowledge of permanence of objects (Spelke, Breinlinger, Macomber & Jacobson, 1992). Because of their adherence to the view that these basic forms of knowledge are innate, these accounts tend to be labeled **nativist** (see Chapter 6 for a full account). But this does not mean that all knowledge is assumed to be innate. The nativists also identify developmental changes through which innate core knowledge becomes more refined. For instance, take the case of infants' understanding of **support relationships** (see Figure 8.3). The claim is that for young infants any form of contact (of an above–below nature) between objects is assumed to be sufficient for support. Later on, infants require there to be a certain percentage of the object supported by the one below (Baillargeon, Needham & DeVos, 1992), but they do not take account of whether this support is near enough to the center of gravity to stop the object toppling. Finally, they take account of the point of support relative to the center of gravity (Huettel & Needham, 2000).

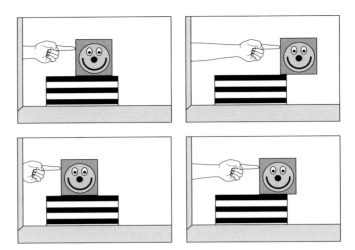

Figure 8.3 Examples of adequate and inadequate support relationships. In the case on the upper right, support is insufficient to prevent the upper object from toppling, whereas in the case on the lower right, the upper object is adequately supported. From Baillargeon *et al.* (1992).

Infants reason about events

Another aspect of the nativist argument is that infants use core knowledge to reason about the events they encounter. The tasks outlined above do not seem to demand that infants reason, but another example makes a stronger case for reasoning. Spelke, Kestenbaum, Simons, and Wein (1995) familiarized 3- and 4-month-old infants with one of the two moving object events illustrated in the top half of Figure 8.4. Each display contained two narrow vertical

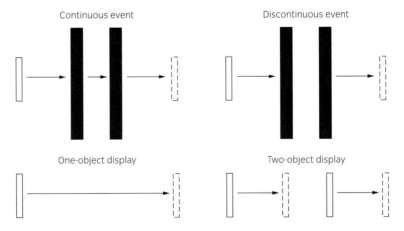

Figure 8.4 Displays presented by Spelke *et al.* (1995). Infants were first familiarized with one of the events in the upper half of the figure, and were tested on the two test events in the lower half of the figure.

screens, and in the **continuous** event an object moved from left to right, disappearing and reappearing from behind each screen in turn and appearing in the gap between the screens during its movement. In the **discontinuous** event the same happened, but no object appeared between the two screens. After familiarization to one of these, infants viewed two test displays with the screens absent, one containing a single object moving from left to right, and one containing two objects, the first moving to the point where the first screen had been and the second starting from the point where the second screen had been. Infants who had been familiarized with the continuous event looked longer at the two-object test and those who had been familiarized with the discontinuous event looked longer at the single-object test. The authors conclude that, on the basis of what they had perceived during familiarization, the infants reasoned that either one or two objects were involved, and looked longer at the test event that did not contain that number of objects.

Alternative accounts of search failure and search errors

On the face of it, these two bodies of data present a conflict. On the one hand, there is well-established evidence that infants do not begin to search for hidden objects until about 6 months, and that even when they do, they make striking search errors when more than one hiding location is involved. On the other hand, the violation of expectation evidence suggests that infants as young as 3–4 months understand object permanence and reason about events. I have already mentioned that we know search failure is not due to an inability to organize the action (Bower & Wishart, 1972; Shinskey *et al.*, 2000). However, maybe the search task imposes an additional load in some other respect.

Memory limitations?

Could search failure at 6 months arise because the memory load is too great and infants simply forget the object is there? This is most unlikely, because search failure occurs even when infants are allowed to search almost immediately, certainly after a delay shorter than the time objects are out of sight in the violation of expectation work. At one time, the A-not-B error seemed a more plausible candidate for explanation in terms of a memory deficit. It was suggested, for instance, that infants are subject to interference between the memory of the object being hidden and retrieved from the A location there and memory for it being hidden in the new location (Harris, 1973). But again this account does not seem to hold up, because it has been shown that infants make this search error even when the object is in clear view at the B location, either under a transparent cover (Butterworth, 1977) or completely uncovered (Bremner & Knowles, 1984). Under these conditions there is no need to hold the new location of the object in memory, and yet errors still occur.

Response perseveration?

Another possibility is that after several searches at the first (A) location, infants form a response habit, a phenomenon referred to as **response perseveration**. Thus, maybe they automatically repeat this response (reaching at the A location) when the object is hidden at the new place B. If this were the case, however, we would expect infants to correct their errors either immediately or on subsequent trials. But although some infants do correct themselves, many continue to make the error for many trials. However, the strongest evidence against the response perseveration account is that infants make the A-not-B error after simply seeing the object hidden and revealed a few times at the first location (Landers, 1971; Butterworth, 1974). Thus they have not established a response habit to the first location, yet they search there on the first opportunity even though the object has been hidden at B.

Different levels of knowledge?

Other explanations of the A-not-B error have been presented, but none is entirely satisfactory and it is hard to avoid the conclusion that search failure at 6 months and search errors from 8 months on reflect a limitation in understanding object permanence. But some other evidence makes the puzzle even greater. Wilcox, Nadel, and Rosser (1996) used a violation-of-expectation methodology (Figure 8.5) to demonstrate that 2.5-month-old infants who saw an object disappear at one location looked longer when it was subsequently retrieved from another location, and Wilcox *et al.* suggest that even very young infants have appropriate expectations about the location of a hidden object, specifically that it should reappear at the place where it disappeared.

Does this mean that the search evidence and violation-of-expectation evidence are irreconcilable? Probably not, because there is a growing view

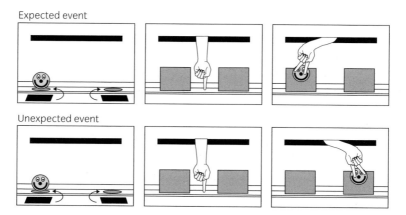

Figure 8.5 The events presented by Wilcox *et al.* (1996). In the expected event, the lion is hidden in one location and, after a delay, is revealed at the same location. In the unexpected event, the lion is hidden in one location and, after a delay, is revealed at the other location.

that the two types of task measure different levels of knowledge. It is possible, for instance, that young infants have a relatively unstructured awareness of object permanence, which is revealed in longer looking at impossible events, but which is not sufficient to guide action sequences. Thus, when faced with the A-not-B task, infants are aware of the continued existence of the object in a particular location, but are simply unable to use that knowledge to guide action (Willatts, 1997; Bremner, 2001).

Infants' spatial awareness

Spatial orientation

Apart from certain situations, such as emerging from an underground station in a strange city, we generally stay quite well oriented in our surroundings as we move through them. The question I tackle in the second half of this chapter is whether infants possess these orientation skills in any measure and also whether there is evidence for development of spatial skills during infancy. Until the age of 8–9 months infants are unable to crawl, so one might assume they had little need to reorient themselves. However, infants are frequently moved around by parents. This often happens in such a way that infants have a better view of their parents than of their surroundings, so reorientation after these moves might pose particular problems. Added to that, one classic view regarding spatial orientation (Held & Hein, 1963) suggests that passive movements of this sort are taken account of much less than active movements executed by the individual. Given these considerations, it is little surprise that investigators have asked questions about infants' spatial skills.

The 'peek-a-boo' paradigm

The commonest method of assessing infants' spatial orientation ability has come to be known as the 'peek-a-boo' paradigm (Figure 8.6). The infant sits within a circular surround and periodically one of the investigators pops up at a particular location. This sort of event fascinates infants, and after a short time they anticipate the peek-a-boo by looking to the relevant location in advance of the event. Once this has happened, they are rotated to a new direction of facing, so that, for instance, the event location which was 30° to their left is now 60° to their right, and the investigator measures the direction of their anticipation. If they take no account of their rotation, they would anticipate by turning to the inappropriate 30° left location, whereas if they took account of it accurately, they would turn to the correct 60° right location. In actual practice, the technique is generally a little more complex than this. Just as in the A-not-B search error, it is possible that infants build up a perseverative response in this looking task. To avoid or reduce this, they

Figure 8.6 The peek-a-boo paradigm used by McKenzie and colleagues. The investigator hides behind the circular barrier and pops up repeatedly at a fixed location. Once the infant consistently anticipates this event with a head turn, s/he is rotated to a new direction of facing and is tested for direction and extent of anticipatory head turn.

are generally given training trials from two directions of facing, and are then tested for anticipation from a third direction of facing.

The picture to emerge from this work is that between 4 and 8 months of age infants show an increasing ability to take account of bodily rotation (Keating, McKenzie & Day, 1986; McKenzie, Day & Ihsen, 1984; Meuwissen & McKenzie, 1987) and, their performance is enhanced by the presence of a distinct visual landmark at the event location. This latter finding is not too surprising, given that such a landmark directly cues the event location. However, Lew, Bremner, and Lefkovitch (2000) showed that by 8 months, infants are capable of making use of the relationship between landmarks, anticipating correctly at a point between two landmarks, and some evidence for this has been obtained even at 6 months (Lew, Foster, Crowther & Green, 2004).

The results of older research at first sight appear to paint a rather more pessimistic picture. Acredolo (1978) trained infants of 6, 11, and 16 months to anticipate an event at one of two laterally placed windows in a rectangular room (Figure 8.7). The cue was the sounding of a centrally placed buzzer, which, during training, was followed by a peek-a-boo appearance of the investigator consistently at one of the windows. On the test trial, the infant was moved around to the opposite side of the room, whereupon the buzzer sounded but no event occurred, and direction of looking was measured. Bremner (1978) used a search task to investigate the same form of infant movement. Infants saw an object hidden in one of two containers to left and

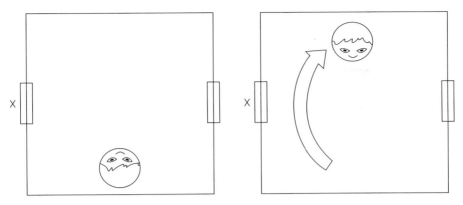

Figure 8.7 The method used by Acredolo (1978) to investigate infants' spatial orientation ability. Infants are trained to anticipate an event at one window (marked x), following which they are relocated at the opposite side of the room and the direction of their anticipatory head turn is measured.

right of the infant's midline, but the infant was rotated to the opposite side of the table before being allowed to search. Acredolo found that 6-month-olds were unable to update their relationship to the target, even if clear landmarks cued its location. Eleven-month-olds, in contrast, updated when landmarks were present, and 18-month-olds updated even without landmarks. In keeping with Acredolo's finding with 11-month-olds, Bremner found that 9-month-olds only updated the target location when strong landmarks in the form of differently colored covers were present. The general finding was that between 9 and 18 months of age infants show reduced reliance on direct landmarks to take account of bodily movements.

A link with crawling?

There is a good reason why success on this form of the task might emerge later. In this case, infants are not simply rotated on their axis; they are also moved bodily to a new location. There is evidence that infants find this sort of composite rotation-plus-displacement particularly hard (Landau & Spelke, 1988). And it is possible that there is a developmental progression here that ties into the infant's developing postural control and crawling ability. Once infants can sit unaided at around 6 months, they develop control of rotational movements of head and trunk—similar rotations to those that occur in the McKenzie peek-a-boo task. A few months later, when they develop the ability to crawl, they gain control over bodily displacement and rotation of the sort used in Acredolo's task. Possibly these abilities emerge as they are needed in relation to new action capabilities.

There is some evidence in support of the idea that crawling enhances spatial orientation. Bertenthal, Campos, and Barrett (1984) showed that infants with more crawling experience performed better on Acredolo's spatial orientation task and Bai and Bertenthal (1992) found that the same held true in Bremner's task involving manual search for a hidden object. But probably crawling experience does not fundamentally change how infants perceive space. Instead, we are probably seeing a change in the way infants organize space and reference objects within it, a change that equips them better to orient in space as they move actively through it. This does not mean that we cannot ask questions about infants' perception of space: it is just that this is a different question, one that I consider in the next section.

Perception of depth and wariness of drops

A fundamental aspect of space is its three-dimensionality. According to Piaget, infants are not initially aware of a three-dimensional world, only gradually constructing this awareness through extending their action further and further into space. Reaching actions organize the third dimension, but only within the space the infant can reach to. Beyond arm's length, objects in space are all understood as if arranged at a fixed distance just beyond reach. And in this respect, the onset of crawling should be important because it radically extends the scope of the infant's activity. However, not all theorists have accepted Piaget's account. An alternative is that infants perceive the third dimension from birth and, as we shall see, much of the evidence supports such a view.

A classic study: the visual cliff

The motivation for this study was the quest for an answer to the question of whether or not infants perceived depth from birth. To tackle this question, Gibson and Walk (1960) devised the apparatus illustrated in Figure 8.8. The **visual cliff**, as mentioned in Chapter 5, consists of a central platform with a very shallow drop to one side and a deep visual drop to the other side. Each side is covered by a strong glass platform. On the shallow side this is immediately above a patterned surface, whereas on the deep side the patterned surface is some feet below. Infants ranging in age from 6 to 14 months were placed on the central platform and attempts were made to get them to crawl across the shallow and 'deep' sides. Of the 27 infants tested, only 3 ventured onto the deep side, whereas all crossed the shallow side.

Gibson and Walk took their results as support for the notion that infants are born perceiving a three-dimensional world. But this is really a highly problematic conclusion. To test the notion that infants are born with an ability, we really need to look for that ability at birth or soon thereafter. And although many investigators manage to carry the argument that an ability is inborn on the basis of evidence from infants 2 or 3 months old, the youngest of these infants were 6 months old, and there is plenty that can develop in 6 months.

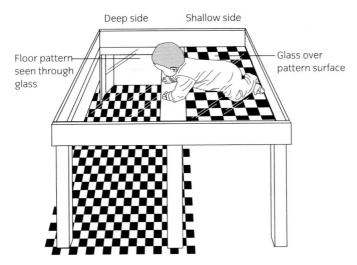

Figure 8.8 The 'visual cliff' used by Gibson and Walk (1960) and others. Infants are placed on the central platform and attempts are made to induce them to crawl over the 'shallow' and 'deep' sides.

Using heart-rate change to measure wariness

Subsequent work paints quite a different picture with regard to the origins of visual cliff avoidance. It has been possible to adapt the visual cliff task to allow testing of pre-crawling infants. Schwartz, Campos, and Baisel (1973) measured infants' heart rate as they were lowered onto the deep and shallow sides of the visual cliff. Taking heart rate on the shallow side as baseline, they found that pre-crawling 5-month-olds showed a deceleration in heart rate on the deep side relative to the shallow side, whereas 9-month-olds showed an increase. Because a decrease in heart rate is generally taken as an indicator of attention and a increase is taken as an indicator of stress or unease, Schwartz *et al.* (1973) concluded that the younger infants perceived the difference between deep and shallow sides but that only the older ones showed wariness of the drop.

Crawling experience and the development of wariness

The suggestion arising from the study above is that crawling experience leads to wariness of drops. Although the idea that the onset of crawling leads to developments in spatial awareness is quite straightforward, investigating such a cause-and-effect relationship link is far from simple. In the study mentioned above the crawling group was older than the immobile group so would be likely to be more advanced cognitively as well as in crawling ability. Svejda and Schmid (1979) surmounted this problem by gathering two groups of infants who differed in whether or not they could crawl but whose average ages were the same. They found that even with age held constant, those infants with crawling experience showed evidence of wariness on the visual cliff, whereas those who were still immobile did not. However, even this study has its problem. Infants who crawl early may do so because they are generally more advanced. This means that simply holding test age constant is no guarantee that all other variables other than crawling ability will be controlled.

This problem can be counteracted by matching the two groups on a range of general ability tests. This is generally what has been done in more recent work, and the finding is still that the crawling group show more wariness on the visual cliff. Additionally, Campos, Hiatt, Ramsay, Henderson, and Svejda (1978) tested newly crawling infants on the crawling version of the visual cliff task, and found that it took some time before they began to avoid the deep side of the cliff. Nearly half of infants with 11 days crawling experience crossed the deep side, whereas less than a quarter did after 41 days experience. Even stronger evidence comes from a study by Campos, Svejda, Bertenthal, Benson, and Schmid (1981) who selected two groups of infants according to whether their parents had provided baby-walkers for them during their fifth month. These two groups were matched for age and general cognitive ability, and subsequently, their responses on the visual cliff were compared. Those given early locomotor experience were more likely than control infants to show wariness on the deep side of the cliff. It is worth noting that the wariness that develops as a result of crawling experiences generalizes to later motor behavior: when crawling infants become newly walking infants they also avoid the deep side! (Witherington *et al.*, 2005).

Depth perception vs. wariness of drops

Just as in the case of development of spatial orientation, the change that occurs as infants gain crawling experience is probably not a change in their basic ability to perceive the third dimension. In fact, there is now good evidence that newborn infants perceive a three-dimensional world. The best example of such evidence concerns the case of size constancy. When we perceive two identical objects at different distances, we perceive them as the same size despite the fact the retinal images they project are different in size (the closer one projects a larger retinal image). This ability involves perceiving the distances of the two objects and computing true size on the basis of distance and retinal image size. Slater, Mattock, and Brown (1990, and see Chapter 5) demonstrated that newborns have size constancy, which implies that they perceive depth. Thus, it appears that Gibson and Walk were right in their view that depth perception was innate, even though the evidence on which they based this was flawed.

If depth perception is innate, what is the nature of the change resulting from crawling experience? To get an answer, we must remind ourselves of the nature of the response on the visual cliff. As indicated above, both pre-crawling and crawling infants show different responses to the deep and shallow sides, so both groups appear to perceive the large drop. The difference is that the crawling infants show wariness of the deep side, both through heart-rate increase and through refusing to crawl across it. So a fair conclusion is that, well before they crawl, infants are perfectly able to perceive the different distances of the two patterned surfaces, but that crawling leads infants to be wary of the large drop.

How could crawling have this effect? There is little mileage in the idea that they learn about drops through painful experience of falling down stairs; parents take elaborate precautions to avoid such events, and they must be a very rare experience. Campos *et al.* (2000) suggest that one factor leading to wariness has to do with learning which sorts of visual experience are normal during crawling. As we move through the world, we experience a flow of visual information around us. As infants accumulate time crawling, they get used to certain kinds of visual flow while they are moving. As they approach a drop, the visual flow suddenly changes a great deal because of the greater distance of surfaces and objects, and this unexpected change triggers a direct emotional response.

Another likely factor here is the way parents respond to the infant's new-found mobility. As indicated above, they take great care to protect infants from the new dangers arising from their mobility, and this includes emotional responses when infants approach danger. We know that infants show the phenomenon of **social referencing** (see Chapter 15), that is, they take cues from parents' emotional responses in deciding how to act in ambiguous or new situations, and it is very likely that in the process they become aware of the emotional significance of dangerous situations, including drops.

SUMMARY

In the first half of this chapter I reviewed evidence indicating that, on the one hand, young infants appear to be aware of the permanence of objects, but that on the other hand, they fail to search for hidden objects, and when they do they make serious errors. In the second half of the chapter, I outlined evidence that young infants perceive space in quite an advanced manner, but that they show developments in the way they organize space and respond to its dangers. There is a common theme emerging from both these bodies of work, namely that very young infants have quite advanced general perception and knowledge of the world, but that their growing ability to act through reaching and later crawling both places new demands on them and leads to restructuring of the early knowledge. Thus, early knowledge of permanence does not initially guide action, and has to be developed through some form of coordination of perception and action. Similarly, young infants perceive their environment as a three-dimensional space, but the way they organize space and react emotionally to dangers follows from the development of action in space, in particular crawling.

Thus, although it appears that Piaget seriously underestimated the state of knowledge of young infants, he was probably right concerning the importance of the infant's active participation in construction of knowledge. However, what they develop in this way is not so much perceptual understanding of the world as knowledge of how to respond and act effectively in it.

CHAPTER NINE

Memory development

JANE S. HERBERT and OLIVIER PASCALIS

Introduction

Infancy is a time of rapid development and unparalleled rates of learning. Arriving in an unfamiliar world, infants need to rapidly develop a knowledge base that allows them to predict and respond to the events occurring in the environment. To achieve this, infants require the ability to maintain and retrieve knowledge about previous experiences. Creating a memory representation for previously experienced events enables infants to develop more complex representations of stimuli that they repeatedly encounter and will help them learn how to respond to other similar stimuli encountered in the future. In this way, infants can benefit from their past experiences rather than having to constantly relearn with each encounter. The question of how memory systems develop and change from birth, allowing infants to remember and learn from their experiences, has been the focus of considerable debate. The purpose of this chapter is to briefly review current theory and experimental data on memory development during infancy and to discuss whether memory systems present in infancy are substantially different from those present later in life.

Childhood amnesia

There is considerable evidence to suggest that early experiences are fundamental to a child's social, emotional, and cognitive development. Surprisingly, however, there is little evidence that we can actually remember any of these formative events. When directly questioned with either free recall procedures (for example, being asked 'what is your earliest memory') or using cued recall of notable events (for example, being asked to provide details about the birth of a younger sibling), most adults report very few memories from before 2 or

3 years of age (for a recent review see Hayne, 2004). The inability to recall early childhood memories was coined **childhood amnesia** by Freud. Although research predominately links this phenomenon to the infancy period, the paucity of adult recall for early events actually extends well into childhood.

Causes of childhood amnesia

Freud originally proposed that childhood amnesia was the result of the active blocking of unacceptable impulses in early childhood. Although this **repression theory** has largely been discredited, researchers have continued to debate the cause of childhood amnesia. Explanations for its source include the development of abilities generally considered to be uniquely human such as a sense of self and language skill, as well as more universal developmental changes such as brain maturation, and we discuss these next.

Development of a sense of self

The decline of childhood amnesia is marked by the onset of autobiographical memory, the ability to verbally recall memories of a personally experienced event. Some researchers have therefore proposed that the development of a self-concept, the child's ability to recognize themselves as an individual and separate from others, is an important factor in allowing the infant to store, maintain, and retrieve memories about themselves (Howe & Courage, 1997). At around 18 months of age, infants begin to react to their image in a mirror in a way that suggests that they have developed visual self-recognition, a major milestone in self-concept. Visual self-recognition is traditionally demonstrated when a distinctive mark is placed on the child's nose and they touch their own face rather than touching the mirror image, indicating their awareness that the mirror image is a reflection of themselves rather than the image of a different person: this has come to be known as the **rouge on the nose test** (see Chapters 2 and 12). However, using a different paradigm, Legerstee *et al.* (1998) have shown that 5-month-old infants prefer to look at a live video of another child than a video of themselves, suggesting recognition of their own face may actually occur early in development. As children become verbally skilled, their language skill also suggests there are changes in their understanding of self vs. other. For example, at approximately 22 months of age children acquire the ability to use personal pronouns such as 'I' and 'me' (de Villiers & de Villiers, 1978).

Language development

The development of language also provides a logical explanation for the inability to recall early memories which were encoded in the absence of language. In support of this idea, Simcock and Hayne (2002) demonstrated that young children are unable to verbally report memories encoded before they shift from being predominately nonverbal to verbal. In their study, 2- to 4-year-olds participated in a unique game with a magic shrinking machine. In this event, children place large toys into a special machine. If the machine is activated correctly, through a short sequence of pulling and turning levers, a much smaller version of the toy will be delivered through the door at the bottom of the machine (see Figure 9.1). Children's memory for this event is assessed 6 or 12 months later through verbal recall for the event sequence, photographic recognition of the toys, and behavioral re-enactment of the

Figure 9.1 A 4-year-old child places a big bottle of bubbles in the top of the magic shrinking machine. After 'activating' the box in the correct sequence, she then opens the door at the bottom and retrieves the now much smaller bottle of bubbles. This event is extremely fun and memorable, and even young children remember the actions for many months. Will preverbal children also be able to verbally report their memories for this unique event in the future?

actions. In no instance during the test session did a child use any word to describe the event that had not been in their vocabulary at the time of the original event. That is, even though children at all ages could remember the event when tested with behavioral measures, there was no evidence of verbal recall for aspects of the event that were encoded behaviorally. Language cues were only effective for retrieving memories encoded with language.

The importance of language in the decline of childhood amnesia has also been linked to children's participation in parent–child conversations about the past (K. Nelson, 1993). The way in which parents talk to their children about past events influences the way in which children report memories when they begin talking about the past (for review see Reese, 2002). For example, parents who provide richly detailed accounts of past experiences appear to highlight the important and interesting details of an event to their children, subsequently altering the way in which children themselves remember and report their autobiographical memories. Katherine Nelson (1993) proposed that children are taught and encouraged to generate narratives during the social discussion of joint memories. Within these interactions, children learn both the way in which to report memories, and what content is considered worthy of subsequent retelling. With the acquisition of language, Nelson claims that children also develop the ability to use another's conversation as a retrieval cue for past events. That is, conversations about the past function as a partial reinstatement of a particular experience allowing children to repeatedly retrieve memories and maintain them over the long term.

Infantile amnesia

Our understanding of the development of memory processing from infancy to early childhood is, however, limited if our explanations are only applicable to understanding the phenomenon of childhood amnesia in humans. In fact a nonhuman analogue of childhood amnesia, **infantile amnesia**, is commonly seen in the animal literature and is defined by more rapid forgetting during infancy than later in life. Campbell and Campbell (1962), for example, examined age-related changes in retention on a conditioned avoidance task with rats aged 18, 23, 38, 54, and 100 days. The rats were conditioned to run out of an area when a buzzer was sounded: if they didn't they got an electric shock, which caused a fear reaction. Retention of fear was shown to vary as a function of age. While 18-day-old rat pups showed no retention of conditioning after 21 days, 100-day-old rats exhibited almost perfect avoidance 42 days after conditioning, the longest retention interval examined. These findings indicate that our explanations for maturational changes in memory processing must be applicable across species. Neurological immaturity is a prime candidate for explaining infantile amnesia because it suggests that the young infant may be unable to store information in an accessible form. Although brain structures such as the hippocampus are present and functioning early in life (see later), it is likely that maturation in the connections between regions occurs across development and alters the ability to appropriately store and subsequently retrieve memory representations (for review see Bachevalier & Vargha-Khardem, 2005). These maturational changes may be responsible, at least in part, for the gradual changes in memory processing that are observed when memory development during infancy and early childhood is studied behaviorally.

Assessing memory in infants

Asking adults to verbally recall their childhood memories can inform us of the age at which language ability became proficient enough to enable us to retrieve and report memories. This technique, however, provides little information about what basic memory abilities are present or evolving before the acquisition of language. A major barrier to experimentally determining how memory processing emerges and changes across development is that infants lack the ability to tell us what they remember. In adults and verbal children we can assess whether they remember the details of an event by simply asking them to declare the content of their memory. That is, an adult can verbally report information about the 'who, what, when, where, and why' of a previous event and this information can be assessed for the amount and accuracy of detail recalled. In infants, memory must be inferred through behavioral change as the result of a specific learning experience.

Procedures for studying memory development

Chapter 2 reviews some of the techniques which are currently available to study cognitive development in infants. Three paradigms in particular have been especially effective for examining the development of memory processing in infancy. These are: (1) habituation and subsequent preferences for novel stimuli (here called the **visual paired comparisons (VPC) task**); (2) **operant conditioning**, and (3) **deferred imitation**. These paradigms can be used to study memory by inserting a delay between the learning and retrieval phases. The precise duration of the delay used, from seconds to months, depends on the task and the age of the infant being tested.

In these types of behavioral paradigms memory is inferred when past experiences influence present behavior. For example, in the deferred imitation task an experimenter demonstrates a series of novel actions and the infant's ability to reproduce those actions is assessed either immediately or after a delay. The performance of infants in these experimental conditions is compared to the performance of infants who have not seen the target actions before the test. This comparison group, also known as a **control condition**, provides a measure of spontaneous infant activity. That is, the control condition provides a baseline level of performance in the absence of the infants having learnt the specific actions that can be performed with the stimuli. In other control conditions infants may see an adult reach out and hold the target objects, or they may see the outcome of manipulating the target objects, but they do not see a demonstration of the target actions. In all of these control conditions, children rarely perform the target actions. Therefore, we can conclude that infants in demonstration conditions who produce the target actions are exhibiting evidence of memory from a specific observational event. Forgetting is inferred when the mean number of actions produced by the demonstration groups is not significantly greater than the mean number of actions produced by the control groups.

Recognition and recall

In the absence of language, these types of behavioral paradigms can be used to assess what an infant can recall and recognize from previous learning experiences. **Recall memory** is a form of information retrieval that occurs in the absence of any cues or prompts to aid the process. Recall memory is measured in tasks such as deferred imitation because, although the target objects are present at the time of memory retrieval, the infant must recall what actions to do with the objects. In contrast, procedures such as the VPC task measure **recognition memory**, a basic form of information retrieval that involves judging whether a stimulus or event has been experienced before. The VPC procedure indexes the infant's level of interest for one stimulus in a pair after one of these stimuli has been learned during a prior familiarization or habituation period. Recognition memory is inferred from the infant's tendency to fixate toward the novel stimulus. Forgetting of the original stimulus is inferred when the fixation times for the familiar and the novel test stimuli are equal.

By combining together findings from tasks thought to tap recognition and recall memory in infancy, we can begin to obtain a more complete picture of memory development. Taken together, research on memory development with behavioral paradigms has revealed that even in infancy a single event can have a long-lasting impact on behavior.

How long are events remembered for in infancy?

Irrespective of the paradigm used to assess memory, systematic changes in the duration of retention are observed. Older infants remember for longer than younger infants. For example, in the operant conditioning tasks designed by Rovee-Collier and her colleagues and described in Chapter 2, 2-month-old infants exhibit retention for 1 day, 9-month-old infants exhibit retention for

6 weeks, and by 18 months of age infants exhibit retention for 13 weeks (e.g., Hartshorn *et al.*, 1998).

Similarly, in deferred imitation tasks there are age-related changes in the duration of retention even when the original level of encoding is equivalent across age. In a recent study (Herbert *et al.*, 2006) a model performed an action with a novel object with 6- and 9-month-old infants. The novel object was either a toy cow or a duck, and the action was to press the button at its base—this caused the cow to make a 'moo' sound and the duck to make a 'quack' sound. Although infants of both ages imitated the action when tested immediately, only the 9-month-olds exhibited imitation after a 24-hour delay (see Figure 9.2). With older infants longer delays between seeing the

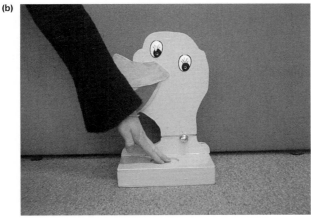

Figure 9.2 Deferred imitation stimuli (a black and white cow and an orange duck) that have been used with 6- and 9-month-old infants to examine how long memories last. In this instance the target behavior to be imitated is pressing the button on the base of the toy, which results in a rewarding sound! Nine-month-olds remember the target behavior after a 24-hour delay, but 6-month-olds have forgotten it.

demonstration and being tested can be tolerated. Thus, in a different deferred imitation task 24-month-old infants exhibited retention after a 3-month delay whereas 18-month-old infants exhibited retention for only 2 weeks (Herbert & Hayne, 2000; see Figure 9.3).

Different techniques give different results

On the basis of our current knowledge about infant memory, it is not yet possible to say for how long an infant of a particular age will remember

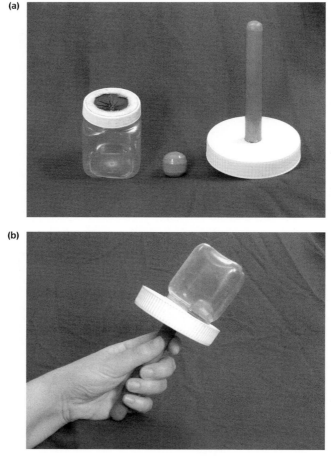

Figure 9.3 In this deferred imitation task, 18- to 30-month-old infants are shown how to make a rattle. There are three target actions: put the ball into the container, put the handle on the top of the container, and shake the handle. Infants can remember how to create the rattle weeks after an adult demonstration of the actions, though the older infants remember the actions for longer. These impressive memory abilities are observed even though the infant does not have the opportunity to copy the actions immediately after she saw them demonstrated.

a specific event. Across procedures there is considerable variation in the events that occur during learning, and at the time of retrieval making it difficult to draw conclusions across paradigms, let alone to real life. For example, when 6-month-old infants are tested in an operant conditioning task they exhibit retention for 2 weeks. These operant conditioning tasks involve 12 minutes of active participation during learning which is spread across 2 days. In contrast, deferred imitation tasks typically involve only a single 60–90 second learning session which is passively observed by the infant. When 6-month-old infants are tested in deferred imitation tasks they usually exhibit retention for only 24 hours. Although we are as yet unable to establish a definitive duration of retention across procedures, these findings highlight the importance of using multiple procedures when assessing memory development. Only by using multiple measures can we be sure that our findings reveal developmental changes in memory processing at a general level rather than paradigm-specific memory changes. The finding that the retention of memories increases systematically across development, irrespective of the paradigm used to access memory, reveals that it is an important developmental progression in memory processing.

Are infant memories more impoverished than adult memories?

It is often assumed that infants' memory representations lack the quality and specific details that are present in memory representations at older ages. This assumption comes at least in part from research on young children's developing ability to verbally recall their memories. As young children learn to talk about past events their verbal reports reveal that memory for **specific** event knowledge emerges out of **generalized** memory reports (Fivush & Hamond, 1990). For example, a 3-year-old might provide general details about cake and presents when asked about a birthday party he had recently attended, but his verbal report would lack any specific details. Perhaps memory representations develop as a general body of knowledge first before specific event details are able to be encoded and retrieved? This account of the development of verbal reports appears, however, to be inconsistent with the development of memory processing during infancy. Behavioral studies reveal that infant memory does not develop in this general-to-specific manner.

Infant memories can be highly specific

From at least 2 months of age, infants' memory representations contain detailed information about the target event and the broader learning environment. For example, 3-month-old infants exhibit retention in Rovee-Collier's mobile conjugate reinforcement task for up to 1 week. However, if more than one novel item is substituted into a five-item test mobile in the mobile conjugate reinforcement task, memory retrieval is disrupted (Hayne *et al.*, 1986). That is, infants not only remember that the target object was a mobile, but they remember exactly what their training mobile looked like. A similar but not identical mobile fails to retrieve the memory. In deferred imitation tasks, changes in the color or form of the target objects between the demonstration and test session, as seen in Figure 9.2, disrupts memory retrieval throughout the infancy period: thus, if young infants were shown the target action with the cow, and later given the duck, then they would fail to show generalization of the target action (pressing the button at the base in order to hear a sound). These findings reveal that unlike early verbal memory reports, which are general rather than specific, infants' memory representations, as assessed by behavioral techniques, are highly specific.

The richly detailed content of young infants' memory representations also extends to the environmental details of where learning has occurred. In operant conditioning, changes to immediate contextual details such as the color and pattern of the liner present around the crib during training, or to the extended environment such as the room in which training occurs, disrupt memory retrieval at 3 months of age (e.g., Hayne *et al.*, 1991). Even a change in the odors present in the room during learning and at retrieval will impair 3-month-old infants' memory performance (Rubin *et al.*, 1998). Similar effects of context are observed in the VPC task, where memory retrieval fails if the color of the background is changed between the habituation and test phase (Robinson & Pascalis, 2004; see Figure 9.4), and in deferred imitation where 6-month-old infants fail to transfer knowledge acquired in one physical location, the laboratory, to a test session in a different location, at home (Hayne *et al.*, 2000). The finding that memory is disrupted by changes to more distant environmental cues such as the room in which learning occurs provides further evidence that infant memory representations are highly detailed and specific.

What causes age-related changes in retention?

Several factors can influence the recognition and recollection of events during infancy. With age, additional cues are available in the environment and may help the infant to recognize something. Infants become better able at generalizing across contexts and changes to the target object with age. Language development has also been suggested to help in remembering events because it provides children with additional cues at the time of learning and for rehearsing and maintaining the memory through conversions. For example, in a case study of one child's crib talk, a 2-year-old was documented to talk

(a)

(b)

(c)

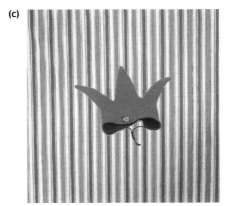

Figure 9.4 An example of the stimuli used in the VPC paradigm to examine the effect of a background change on visual recognition memory. If the color or pattern of the background is changed from familiarization (a) to test [(b) and (c)] infants show no sign of remembering, i.e., they show no novelty preference for (c) when paired with (b).

herself through the events of the day before going to sleep in the evening (K. Nelson, 1989), a practice that is likely to help both with the structuring and future recall of her later memory reports.

Brain development

Multiple events make up a single memory. For example, your memory for sitting your driving test might include specific information about the type of car you drove, what you were asked to do, and what the examiner looked like. You can probably remember details such as the feeling of anxiety beforehand and the sense of relief afterwards (assuming you passed!) You might also be able to recall the smells and sounds you encountered. Hopefully you still remember the comments your examiner made about looking in the rear-view mirror more frequently and you apply that memory to the way you drive now! The diverse range of events that can go into a single memory means that the encoding, storage, and retrieval of memories is a complex phenomenon. Many brain regions are involved, and it is difficult to pinpoint a single area for a particular memory. Structures of the **medial temporal lobe** such as the **hippocampal formation** and the **parahippocampal gyrus**, which are located in the lower middle portion of the brain, are particularly important for storing information over the long term. During infancy, the brain is still going through intensive changes: brain regions are maturing and the connections between the regions are strengthening. Could the development and maturation of structures within the medial temporal lobe account for differences in memory observed between different age groups?

Studies on the development of memory and its neural basis have burgeoned in the last 15 years. A key factor in this advance is that some of the procedures that are used to examine infant memory have also been studied with human adults with damage to the medial temporal lobe and/or animals with brain lesions, providing some confirmation of the brain structures involved in memory processing on these tasks, and strengthening claims that can be made about the type of memory being exhibited. For example, human adults with medial temporal lobe damage fail on age-appropriate tests of deferred imitation (McDonough *et al.*, 1995), indicating that hippocampal memory structures are required for successful memory performance on the deferred imitation task.

Visual recognition memory

One of the most thoroughly researched aspects of memory that can be assessed during the first 2 years of life is visual recognition memory of pictures or events as measured in tasks such as the VPC. The principal neural structures and pathways that allow visual recollection/recognition memory in human and nonhuman primates are shown in Figure 9.5. A lesion

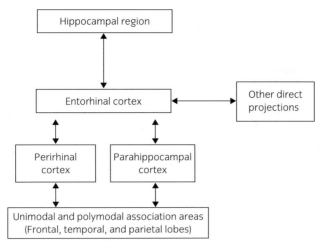

Figure 9.5 A schematic of the principal neural structures and pathways that allow visual recollection/recognition memory in human and nonhuman primates.

in any of these structures during infancy or in adulthood will lead to a range of memory problems such as impairment in showing visual preference when measured with the VPC task. The principal structures involved in visual recognition memory are parts of the medial temporal lobe (rhinal cortices and hippocampal formation). Memory functions involving the medial temporal lobe system are present early in life (C. Nelson, 1995) and improve gradually with further postnatal maturation.

Maturation of brain structures

The age at which each of the brain structures is mature enough to support recognition memory may provide an explanation for memory ability differences observed during the first years of life. It has been thought for years that the hippocampal formation was not mature at birth and that it developed slowly during infancy (Diamond, 1990). However, this assumption was based on anatomical data from rodents, species that are less developed at birth than primates. Recently, Alvarado and Bachevalier (2000) reviewed the development of the medial temporal lobe system in monkeys and showed that at birth the vast majority of cells and connections in the hippocampal formation are in place. Those connections are even functional before birth (Berger *et al.*, 1993). In human infants, Seress *et al.* (2001) studied the development of the hippocampal formation and found that these structures are anatomically more mature than was initially thought at birth, even if it cannot be firmly concluded that they are equally functionally mature.

The maturation of the other structures in the medial temporal lobe is less well documented. The inferior temporal cortical areas are not adult-like until around 12 months of age but are functional before this age. In monkeys, the entorhinal cortex, which is the major source of input of the hippocampal formation, matures after 3 months of age (Lavenex *et al.*, 2004). Age-related changes in the retention and specificity of memory retrieval across the infancy period may therefore reflect the slow maturation of the association areas of the cortex rather than the slow maturation of the hippocampal formation.

However, it is important to highlight that the term 'mature' is sometime used as a synonym of 'adult-like' but it is also used as 'functional.' A cerebral structure can then be labeled as not mature by some authors as its anatomical structure and properties are not adult-like, although it may be functional enough to support some behavior. Visual recognition observed in infants may in fact involve the adult hippocampal network but the way the visual information reaches the hippocampus may be different. It is therefore possible that early episodes can not be remembered well because the visual pathways that were use to create them may not exist any more in adulthood.

Why is retention in experimental studies so short?

There are several limitations to the experimental designs classically used to assess infant memory that need to be considered before concluding on infants' memory abilities. Infant memory researchers are indeed using rather poor stimuli to examine early memory skill. In real life, a stimulus is not unimodal like the still-picture stimuli in the VPC task but is presented in various modalities—vision, audition, olfaction—that will help in encoding and remembering. For example, the mother's face is learned from birth in a multimodal environment. Sai (2005) showed that the voice has to be presented concomitantly with the face to allow the face to be learned as the 'mother.' As discussed earlier (Chapters 3 and 5) we know that newborns recognize the mother's smell and voice from prenatal exposure and that these cues are present when the newborn is learning her mother's face for the first time. The mother's face (a multimodal stimulus, given the usual presence of her voice) can be recognized even after a 15-minute delay during the first week of life (Bushnell, 2003). Will it be the same for a unimodal visual stimulus? Perhaps not. The lack of recognition observed in infants can also reflect the lack of interest in a stimulus and it is necessary to try several paradigms before reaching any strict conclusion on infants' memory abilities. Moreover, in real life stimuli are learnt in a variety of environments and contexts, over extended durations, and in many different situations: a face appears when the child is happy as well as distressed, many times a day, for several minutes, in the bedroom or in a park. It is then possible that infants can learn quickly invariants in their environment with stimuli such as their parents or favorite toy and that the trace of those stimuli is stronger than the ones we are studying in the laboratory.

Learning and memory abilities depend on how they are tested

Finding no recognition or recall of a stimulus in the way we test it should not immediately be taken as evidence of lack of memory. In particular, the limited motor abilities of infants pose special challenges to studying memory. When no evidence of memory is observed it must first be ascertained that this is actually an indication of cognitive limitations and not behavioral limitations. When the memory task requires an infant to reach out and perform an action, such as in the imitation task in Figure 9.2, it is important to first ensure that the physical skills required are within the motor capabilities of the infant. For example, reaching for and grasping an object with one hand develops between 5 and 8 months of age. Therefore we couldn't expect younger infants to exhibit memory on tasks that required them to produce this type of behavior. For infants younger than 6 months, behaviors such as looking, head-turning, or leg-kicking are more appropriate for examining memory.

In some tasks, the expression of memory may also change as the time between learning and testing increases. For example, although a novelty preference in the VPC task is an indication of recognition memory shortly after learning, there is a growing body of research indicating that a familiarity preference (looking at the familiar stimulus) may also be an indicator of memory after longer delays: Bahrick and Pickens (1995) have suggested that infants' looking preferences change from a novelty preference to a null preference and then to a familiarity preference over a period of 1 month following habituation. Other variables such as the emotional salience of the test stimuli may also be important factors to consider in how or if memory will be expressed. For example, Bornstein *et al.*, (2004) have shown that 5-month-old infants who participated in a visual episode involving an emotional component between the infant and an adult (the still-face paradigm described in Chapter 2), exhibit evidence of memory up to 15 months later. No one has shown such long-term memory for a still picture at that age.

What type of long-term memory system do infants have?

Studies with adults distinguish two qualitatively different kinds of long-term memory:

- A **declarative memory** is the memory for events (episodic memories), such as how you celebrated your 18th birthday party, and facts (semantic memories), such as knowing that a robin is a bird.
- A **procedural memory** involves memory for habits and skills such as driving a car.

Many areas of the brain are involved in memory formation and storage, and different areas of the brain carry out different functions. Declarative memory involves the medial temporal lobe structures (i.e., hippocampus and surrounding cortices), whereas procedural memory can survive damage to these structures (for review see Squire, 2004). For example, when an adult has damage to the medial temporal lobe structures he might express that he does not want to shake hands with a researcher but is unable to remember why. As a result of damage to the medial temporal lobe structures, the patient is unable to form and maintain a declarative memory from the previous occasions when that researcher had a sharp tack concealed in his hand. However, the patient still has a procedural memory for these previous occasions and thus knows to avoid shaking hands with this person.

Until recently the general consensus was that performance on tasks sensitive to damage to the hippocampal formation emerged comparatively late in development (Schacter & Moscovitch, 1984). It was assumed that the infant hippocampus was too immature to support declarative memory and that infants, therefore, learned through habits and routines but did not remember specific one-off events. More recently, the view that declarative memory develops later has been challenged. Charles Nelson (1995) has proposed that, in primates, both memory systems are present at birth, although the declarative system may exist in an immature form, referred to as **predeclarative memory**, due to the immaturity of cortical inputs to the hippocampus. As these connections grow, predeclarative memory becomes more like the adult declarative system at approximately 9 months of age in human infants. Unfortunately, there is as yet no evidence concerning the processes underlying this transformation.

It is also important to highlight that it is very difficult to use the term declarative memory with nonverbal infants. Although there is evidence of long-term memory that is detailed and specific in many behavioral paradigms, indicating that infants possess at least basic declarative memory skill early in life, the procedures used to assess infant memory are often very different than those used with children and adults. No instructions are given, and in procedures such as operant conditioning the infant may need to be taught the behavior that can subsequently be used to demonstrate learning and memory. Ideally, we need to develop procedures that can be used in identical ways across the lifespan and use procedures where the neural structures responsible for learning and memory have been well documented. At present, the number of paradigms that meet these requirements remains limited. The nature of infant memory systems in relation to the adult systems remains an important topic for further research.

SUMMARY

Childhood amnesia refers to the phenomenon that adults fail to verbally report memories for events that happened in the first 2 or 3 years of life. Explanations for this phenomenon have included the development of a sense of self, language development, and neurological immaturity. The absence of verbal memory reports from the infancy period has led some people to believe that infants are unable to encode, store, or retrieve memories for unique events. Using behavioral recall and recognition techniques, researchers have begun to tell us a different story about how memory develops. Behavioral measures open up a world of possibilities for uncovering memory abilities before the onset of language. In the first 2 years of life behavioral paradigms have revealed impressive changes in the duration over which memories can be maintained, and demonstrated that, even within the first few months of life, memory representations are richly detailed and specific. The type of memory which is being expressed by infants remains the topic for considerable debate. It is important for researchers to continue to develop appropriate behavioral measures which can accurately assess infants' cognitive abilities, and for researchers to remain curious about the early emergence and changes in memory processing across development. When infants fail on a memory task it is important to ask whether we have tested them in an appropriate manner or whether we have found a cognitive boundary.

CHAPTER TEN

Language development: from speech perception to first words

GEORGE J. HOLLICH and DEREK M. HOUSTON

Introduction

Language is amazingly useful. We use it to talk about things that are not present, to communicate abstract concepts and thoughts in our heads, and even (through writing) to pass on such ideas when we are not physically present. Furthermore, we seem to be the only species that does so in a manner that is so organized, complex, and productive. Language would seem to be the capstone of the human evolutionary experience.

Unfortunately, by some accounts, learning a language ought to be impossible. With enormous acoustic variation between human voices and words, the sheer size of our vocabularies, and the complexity of grammar, infants would seem doomed to failure in their attempts to make sense of it all. Indeed, Gold (1967) argued that to induce the rules of language from the input would take longer than a human lifetime.

Yet, like the bumblebee who goes on flying in spite of the apparent mathematical impossibility of such a feat, children do learn their language—and quickly. Infants utter their first words at around 12 months of age. By 18 months, their productive vocabularies increase rapidly to approximately 50 words and their development surges as they characteristically acquire, on average, 9 new words a day (Carey, 1978). Thus, in just a little less than 2 years, infants go from crying to talking.

For anyone who has tried to learn additional languages later in life, this is an amazing feat. It is made even more impressive given that infants don't have the advantage of being able to use their first language to guess how a new language might work. Furthermore, the task is complicated by the fact that language has many parts. To learn a language, infants must discover the salient sounds and auditory units of their language (a task called **phonology**); they must also learn the meaning for words (a task called **semantics**), and finally, they must learn the rules for how words and different word forms can be combined to express new meanings (a task called **grammar**).

To solve the separate tasks of phonology, semantics, and grammar, infants make use of a wide variety of skills. Infants can use their understanding of how communication works (a skill called **pragmatics**) as well as their understanding of the subtle nonverbal cues that parents use to aid in comprehension. Infants also make use of many perceptual skills that are not specific to language (such as the generalization and categorization abilities covered in Chapter 7). Finally, each episode of successful (and unsuccessful) learning sets the stage for subsequent acquisition. That is, once children have some linguistic knowledge (knowledge about how words work) they use this knowledge to aid them in subsequent acquisition.

In the coming pages, we will cover how infants move from being **universal perceivers,** equally capable of learning any of the world's languages, to being **specialists** in the sounds (phonology), meanings (semantics), and structure (grammar) of their own native tongue, and how infants ultimately move to being **language-learning sophisticates,** able to learn the meaning of words very quickly and understand complicated sentences and questions, even to the point of being able to produce words that they have never actually heard, such as past tenses and plurals.

The universal baby: birth–6 months

Infants come into the world ready to learn any one, or more, of the world's languages. The first 6 months of life is a time of many changes corresponding to infants' growing ability to communicate with the people around them, perceive the sounds of speech, recognize the melody of their native language, and begin to make the first connections between sight and sound.

Early production and social skills

Newborns typically communicate their needs by crying. These cries are reflexive responses to feelings of hunger, sleepiness, or discomfort. During the next few months, young infants start making more intentional vocalizations—first vowel-like cooing sounds and then exploratory sounds such as raspberries and lip smacking and eventually alternations of vowel-like and consonant-like sounds that combine to resemble syllables.

Infants receive and respond to social and affective communication from a very early age. Normal-hearing newborns will respond to sounds with an eye blink or a startle response or by crying, and may also turn their heads in the direction of sounds. Newborns will also react differently based on the affective quality of the caregiver's voice. Also, infants make eye contact with speakers by 2 months of age. (See Part 4 for chapters that more thoroughly describe the socio-emotional development of infants.) These behaviors may help encourage caregivers to communicate more with infants. And it is possible that the emotional information infants derive from speech motivates them to attend more carefully to speech, and encourages language acquisition: another reminder that all aspects of infant development interrelate and do not occur separately from each other.

Early speech perception

In stark contrast to their limited social and productive abilities, infants possess remarkable perceptual abilities at birth, and even before (Chapters 3 and 5). Normal-hearing infants are born with an extremely acute perceptual system. They are able to differentiate many of the speech sounds that distinguish words across all of the world's languages, even when the differences are very subtle.

For example, take the difference between the [p] in **pat** and the [b] in **bat**. Both of those speech sounds are produced with the same articulatory movements (i.e., putting the two lips together and then releasing them and vocalizing). The only difference between the two is that for the [b] there is no or very little time between the release of the lips and the beginning of the vocalization whereas for the [p] there is a short (<100 ms) lag between the release of the lips and the beginning of the vocalization. This meaningful difference between vocal sounds is called a **phonemic contrast.**

In the late 1960s, Peter Eimas and his colleagues tested young infants' discrimination of these two speech sounds (Eimas *et al.*, 1971). They chose this contrast to test because earlier work had shown that adults discriminate those sounds **categorically.** That is, synthesized samples that they heard that had a lag between the release of the lips and the vocalization (**voice onset time, VOT**) of 0–20 ms they heard as [ba] and all examples that had a VOT of 40 ms or greater were heard as [pa]. Adults are unable to discriminate differences that fall within the same category (e.g., a 0 ms VOT vs a 20 ms VOT) but are able to discriminate the same difference when it falls **across** different categories (e.g., a 20 ms VOT vs. a 40 ms VOT). This kind of effect is called **categorical perception.**

Eimas *et al.* tested 2-month-old infants' discrimination of those sounds using the **high-amplitude sucking procedure** (see Figure 10.1). They found that 2-month-olds could detect 20-ms changes in VOT when the changes crossed phoneme boundaries but not when they fell into the same category. These findings showed that very young infants not only can discriminate [b] and [p] but do so categorically, as do adults.

That investigation sparked an enormous amount of research, which has shown that young infants are able to discriminate many different speech sounds. For example, within the first 6 months of life they are able to discriminate [b] and [d], [r] and [l], [m] and [n], [w] and [y], and [b] and [w] (Jusczyk, 1997). There is also evidence that young infants are able to

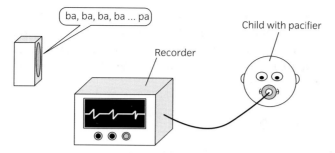

Figure 10.1 High-amplitude sucking procedure. The infant is seated in a car seat and given a pacifier that is connected to a pressure transducer and computer that measures each time the infant produces a hard suck. During a habituation phase, the computer presents a sound (e.g. ba) each time it registers a suck from the infant. At first, infants usually produce sucks at a fast rate, presumably because they are stimulated by the speech sound. After some time, infants typically habituate to the repeating speech sound and decrease their sucking rate. When their sucking rate decreases enough to reach a pre-established 'habituation criterion,' they enter a test phase. During the test phase, infants in a control group are presented with the same sound (e.g. 'ba') while other infants in an experimental group are presented with a novel sound (e.g. 'pa'). If the sucking rate of the experimental group increases more than the sucking rate of the control group during the test phase, it is taken as evidence that infants can detect the change in sounds and respond to them.

discriminate some speech sounds that their adult counterparts cannot. For example, 6- to 8-month-olds in Japanese-speaking environments are able to discriminate [ra] and [la], whereas their adult counterparts have much difficulty.

Findings like these have led to a common view that infants are born as **universal language perceivers**. That is, they are able to discriminate all sounds that could possibly be relevant for any of the world's languages. However, although their speech perception capacities are very acute at birth, much of their speech discrimination abilities are shaped and enhanced by the language(s) that they are exposed to. In the next section we will see how infants' speech discrimination abilities change to fit the language they are exposed to.

Even by birth infants have had some linguistic experience. In the womb the fetus is able to hear some sounds, including the mother's voice. Several investigations have shown that newborns have already learned some characteristics of their mother's speech patterns. DeCasper and Fifer (1980) used another sucking methodology to investigate newborn's preference for their own mother's speech over the speech of another woman. They found that newborns sucked faster in response to their own mother's speech patterns. Using similar methodology, Mehler *et al.* (1988) found that newborns could discriminate between their own language and some foreign languages.

How are newborns able to make such distinctions between their mother's and a stranger's speech or between different languages at birth? Recent investigation has shown that newborns' discrimination for different languages happens when the rhythmic and intonational properties (called **prosody**) of the languages differ substantially (Nazzi *et al.*, 1998). They can even discriminate the languages when the speech is filtered in a way that removes all information except the rhythm and intonation. Importantly, these are the very properties that are available to the fetus in the womb, suggesting that fetuses become sensitive to the rhythmic and intonational properties of their mother's speech and their native language from prenatal experience in the womb.

By 6 months of age, infants' experience with language allows them to recognize well-formed phrases or sentences. Thus, infants show a preference (measured by duration of looking time) for sentences that have pauses inserted **between** clauses to sentences with pauses **within** clauses, even when the speech is similarly filtered. For example, infants preferred passages like 'The cat chased the mouse. [pause] The mouse ran into the hole. [pause] The cheese was...' to passages like 'The cat chased [pause] the mouse. The mouse ran into [pause] the hole. The cheese was....' It is possible that early sensitivities to rhythmic and intonational properties of speech may ultimately contribute to learning about the grammatical organization of speech.

Multimodal perception

Acquiring language requires not only learning about speech sounds, but also being able to connect what one sees with what one hears. There is evidence that infants have the perceptual capacity to relate the two at a very young age. In one study, 2-month-olds were presented with two videos simultaneously—one of a woman producing an [i] sound and one of the same woman producing an [a] sound, with only one of the corresponding two vowels presented at a time. Infants tended to look longer at the matching video for both of the vowels, suggesting that they detected the association between the shape of the articulations and the sounds that they produce (Kuhl & Meltzoff, 1982). The findings that infants are sensitive to the association between auditory and visual aspects of speech are one example of infants' integration of information from multiple sensory modalities when forming percepts about the world. Numerous investigations have shown that young infants are highly sensitive to the events in the world that are conveyed through multiple sensory modalities.

Perhaps the most dramatic evidence of relating what infants hear with what they see comes in the form of early 'word learning.' That is, part of the earliest language acquisition involves learning associations between the sound patterns of words and meaning. Recent investigations have shown that by 6 months of age, infants are already starting to learn the meanings of some very common words. Using the preferential looking paradigm (see

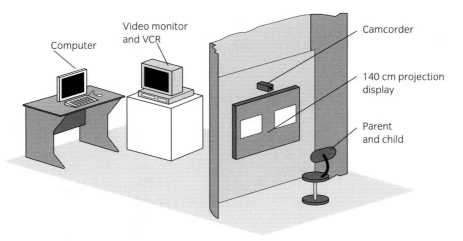

Figure 10.2 The intermodal preferential looking procedure. Children sit in front of a large display with two possible screens to watch. Infants prefer looking at the screen that matches the audio. Thus, a child might see a ball and a book on the screen. If asked to 'look at the book,' infants will look longer at the book, and will look longer at the ball when asked to 'look at the ball.'

Figure 10.2), Tincoff and Jusczyk (1999) presented 6-month-olds with two videos, one of their mother, the other of their father, playing side-by-side simultaneously. They also presented them alternating recordings of a voice saying 'mommy' or 'daddy.' They found that the infants looked more often at the correct video than the other video in response to hearing the words. Of course, it is not known whether or not 6-month-olds know that speech sounds 'mommy' and 'daddy' actually refer to their own mother and father, or if they simply have noticed that those speech sounds and objects are associated (e.g., simply noticing that they tend to hear 'mommy' when mother is present). More advanced, **referential**, word knowledge (knowing that words can 'stand for' objects) is thought to come at a later age, which will be discussed in the final section.

Universal baby summary

Investigations over the past 35 years into the speech perception abilities of infants have begun to uncover the remarkable perceptual capacities that develop even before birth. These early perceptual abilities enable young infants to detect the subtle properties in speech that distinguish words, acquire knowledge about the rhythmic and intonational properties of the ambient language, link speech sounds to the facial articulatory movements that form them, and learn the names of some common objects in their world, such as their own mother and father (Table 10.1).

Table 10.1 Universal baby (birth–6 months). Infants are born with a host of skills that put them in the position to acquire any language that they hear

Type of skill	Skill	Examples
Early production/social	Crying	Cry to communicate hunger, pain, discomfort
	Match emotion	Will match the expression of caregivers
Early speech perception	Categorical perception	Can distinguish between subtle phonemic differences—even those not in the native language
	Detect melody of speech	Distinguish between different languages based on rhythmic properties
Multimodal perception	Face–vowel connection	Can tell difference between faces producing different vowels
	Associative word learning	Can connect frequent sights and sounds, such as 'mommy' to a picture of mom

Native language specialist: 6–12 months

Toward the end of the first year of life, infants begin to exhibit a developing knowledge of, and specialization for, their native language. This specialization includes a new-found ability to babble and understand social cues (see Chapter 15), losing the ability to distinguish some nonnative sounds, and learning to use certain acoustic properties to segment the fluent flowing stream of speech.

Production and developing social skills

Infants make vocalizations from birth but around 6–7 months they typically begin producing an important type of babbling, which is called **canonical** or **reduplicated babbling** and is characterized by repetitions of the same speech sounds, such as 'ga-ga,' 'ma-ma,' 'goo-goo.' The characteristics of early babbling may reflect fundamental constraints of the vocal apparatus. MacNeilage and colleagues (2000) have found that certain consonant–vowel combinations within syllables tend to co-occur as a result of how the tongue is positioned. For example, consonants that are produced with the tongue placed forward in the roof of the mouth tend to co-occur with vowels that are articulated with the front part of the tongue raised (e.g., 'day') whereas consonants that are produced with the back of the tongue placed in the back part of the mouth tend to co-occur with vowels that are articulated with the back part of the tongue raised (e.g., 'go').

Babbling also appears to happen with the hands. Both normal-hearing infants and deaf infants make rhythmic gestures with their hands in a way similar to vocal babbling, and both babble vocally. Thus, some have proposed that both types of babbling are in large part a result of the development of motor skills. However, there is evidence that babbling (both verbal and signed) is influenced by the input to the child. Petitto *et al.* (2004) recently showed that the manual babbling of normal-hearing infants exposed to sign language more closely resembled the rhythmic properties of sign language than the manual babbling of normal-hearing infants exposed only to spoken language. Moreover, when infants around 11 months of age begin producing **variegated babbling**, which is characterized by strings of varying syllables (e.g., 'bagoo'), infants exposed to languages of different rhythms tend to babble in ways that reflect these differences. Taken together, these findings suggest that the language infants are exposed to influences their early vocal productions. We will see below that infants' language-specific early productions mirror some of their perceptual sensitivities to language-specific input.

While infants are producing sounds that reflect what they hear, their communication is also becoming more engaged with the people around them. They become increasingly more sensitive to emotional expression in voices and faces and become more emotionally expressive. Also, infants begin demonstrating an understanding of referential gestures. For example, whereas a 6-month-old will look at a pointing finger, a 9-month-old will look at what the finger is pointing at. At the same time that infants are showing better understanding of communicative intent and producing speech sounds that are beginning to take on the characteristics of their native language, numerous investigations of the speech perception and language skills of infants during the second half of the first year of life suggest that they are learning much about the structure and organization of the speech sounds in the ambient language.

Shaping of the perceptual system

Exposure to a language affects infants' perceptual systems. The most direct evidence of this comes from studies of speech discrimination in older infants. Whereas infants up to around 6–8 months of age are able to discriminate most speech sounds regardless of their relevance to the ambient language, 10- to 12-month-olds lose the ability to discriminate many contrasts that do not signify different words in their native language. For example, Japanese-learning 10- to 12-month-olds do not discriminate the [r] and [l] contrasts discussed above. For some other contrasts, the ability to discriminate improves with age. For example, the ability of infants learning French or English to discriminate a contrast relevant only for English ([d]–[ð]—the 'th' sound in 'the') does not differ, whereas English-speaking adults can discriminate this contrast much better than French-speaking adults (Polka *et al.*, 2001). These findings and others suggest that infants begin life with some general auditory processes that allow them to discriminate many contrasts and then exposure to the ambient language influences their perceptual system and changes what they can and cannot discriminate (see Houston, 2005, for a review).

Some investigators have developed theoretical models to explain sensitivity to nonnative contrasts. Best (1994) proposed the **perceptual assimilation model (PAM)** which posits that discrimination of a contrast depends on whether and how the two speech sounds are categorized into native-language perceptual categories (e.g., the variations of [b] that would be labeled as [b]). If the two sounds fall within one perceptual category, listeners are not likely to discriminate them. If they fall into different perceptual categories, listeners typically will discriminate them. If one or both do not fall into any native categories, then listeners are still likely to discriminate them—though less so than if they fall into different categories. Before infants have formed mature perceptual categories of sound their discrimination of contrasts are likely to be more universal and less like their adult counterparts.

Other investigators have proposed that the distribution of variants of speech sound categories in the input influences how infants perceive and discriminate speech sounds (e.g., Jusczyk, 1997; Kuhl, 1991). For example, Jusczyk (1997) proposed that the distribution of input to infants causes them to develop a perceptual weighting scheme such that acoustic features that are important for distinguishing words in the ambient language receive more attention. Thus, infants lose the ability to discriminate the nonnative speech sounds that differ on features that are not relevant to their language.

Kuhl (1991) has proposed that infants' speech sound categories are influenced by the most common phonemes they hear. That is, by 6 months of age, infants become sensitive to common acoustical values and form perceptual prototypes based on them. These prototypes act like a magnet; indeed, variations of speech sounds surrounding the prototype are perceived as being equivalent to the prototype. Evidence for this effect comes from studies which show that infants are less likely to discriminate between a prototypical sound and a nonprototypical sound than a pair of nonprototypical sounds—even when the two pairs of sounds are acoustically equally dissimilar.

Computations of the ambient language

Much of what infants learn about language appears to occur by them spontaneously picking up on regularities in speech rather than by being explicitly taught. In this way, infants are viewed by many as **statistical learners**—they encode speech sounds and implicitly compute how often sounds occur and their sequences. There are two types of evidence for this

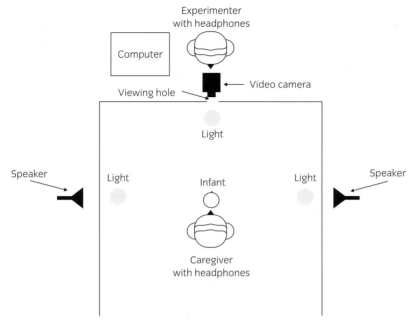

Figure 10.3 Head-turn preference procedure. Infants are seated on their caregiver's lap in a 3-side booth with a light on each side. At the beginning of each trial, the infant's attention is brought to a neutral position by blinking the middle light until the infant looks at it. Then the center light stops and one of the two side-lights begins blinking. When the infant looks to that light a stimulus is presented from behind the light and continues playing until the infant looks away for 2 or more seconds. A difference in looking time to the blinking lights in response to one type of speech stimulus compared to another is taken as evidence that the infant can discriminate the two stimulus types and prefers one over the other.

view. One type of evidence is indirect. Several studies have shown that infants become sensitive to properties of their native language that they would not likely become sensitive to unless they were computing the frequency of occurrence of speech characteristics. For example, there are many more two-syllable words in English that begin with a stressed syllable (e.g., *doc*tor) than with an unstressed syllable (e.g., gui*tar*). Using the head-turn preference procedure (see Figure 10.3), Jusczyk *et al.* (1993) presented 6- and 9-month-olds with lists of both kinds of words. The 6-month-olds showed no preference for either kind of words, whereas 9-month-olds oriented longer to the words that follow the predominant stress pattern of English—i.e., they begin with a stressed syllable.

Similarly, investigators have found that 9-month-old infants but not 6-month-olds orient longer to nonwords made up of phoneme sequences that are more common in their native language (e.g., 'bis') than phoneme sequences that are not common (e.g., 'zeeg'), even if the phonemes themselves were common in the native language (Friederici & Wessels, 1993; Jusczyk *et al.*, 1994). The findings suggest that infants become sensitive to the frequency of occurrence of syllable stress and orderings of phonemes in the ambient language between 6 and 9 months of age. Presumably, they become sensitive to these properties by implicit computations of the speech sounds that they hear.

Another type of statistical learning is infants' sensitivity to the **transitional probabilities** of syllables (e.g., the probability that given syllable X the next syllable will be Y is the transitional probability of XY). To see how this might work, consider a baby whose name, let's say, is Julie. The baby will hear her name on many occasions, but embedded in different speech contexts—'Hello, Julie, how are you?'; 'Don't worry Julie, mommy's here'; 'Where are Julie's socks?' In all these, and countless other sentences, the one constant is the bisyllable 'Julie'—the syllable 'Ju' is always followed by the syllable 'lie' (thus the transitional probability of 'lie' following 'Ju' is close to 1.00).

In a recent study Saffran *et al.*(1996) investigated 8-month-olds' sensitivity to the transitional probabilities of syllables in an artificial language. They presented infants with 12 consonant–vowel (CV) syllables for 2 minutes at a constant rate. The syllables were organized into four three-syllable sequences (e.g., [da][ro][pi]) and the order of the sequences was balanced so that each sequence was followed by and preceded by the other three sequences an equal number of times. Thus, each pair of syllables either had a 1.00 probability of co-occurrence (e.g., [da] was always followed by [ro]) or a .33 probability of co-occurrence ([pi] was followed by three different syllables). After the 2-minute exposure, infants were presented with repetitions of 3-syllable sequences that were either 1.00 probability sequences (e.g., [da][ro][pi]) or .33 probability sequences (e.g., [pi][go][la] or [tu][da][ro]). Infants oriented longer to the. 33 probability sequences, suggesting that they learned something about the transitional probabilities of the syllables.

These findings provide evidence that by 8 months of age, infants' perceptual and cognitive abilities allow them to implicitly encode 'statistical' information about speech sounds and lend support to the idea that their sensitivity to the properties of the language, such as rhythm and phoneme ordering, is a result of implicitly performing statistical computations of the ambient language.

Segmenting words from fluent speech

When we speak, words flow together fluently without any obvious pauses or other markers of where one word ends and the next begins. We can appreciate this when listening to a person speaking an unfamiliar language. It sounds fast, as if there is nothing to distinguish one word from another. But this perceptual effect occurs only because we do not know the words of the language. For infants coming into language for the first time, their impression of the language they are learning may be similar to ours when we hear a foreign language. While speech to infants differs from that used to speak to adults, infant-directed speech is also continuous with no clearly marked word boundaries (van de Weijer, 1998). In order to learn the meanings of words, infants must find (or **segment**) them in fluent speech. But how do they do this before they know many words? Investigations of infant speech segmentation show that infants' sensitivity to the properties of the ambient language plays a large role in their segmentation of words from fluent speech.

In a seminal study, Jusczyk and Aslin (1995) investigated infant word segmentation. Using the head-turn preference procedure (see Figure 10.3), they familiarized 7.5-month-olds with two passages, each of which contained a target word six times. Then they presented infants with repetitions of four words—one word repeating during each trial. Two of the words were those that had occurred in the passages; the other two words did not. Infants attended longer to the words that were in the passages than to the other words, suggesting that they were able to segment words from fluent speech. Follow-up investigations have shown that English-learning 7.5-month-olds are not able to segment all words from fluent speech. They can segment ones that follow the predominant stress pattern of English (e.g., doctor, candle) but not ones that follow the less common stress pattern (guitar, surprise). These findings suggest that English-learning infants' sensitivity to the rhythm of their language influences their ability to segment words from fluent speech. Similar investigations have shown that English-learning infants' sensitivity to the orderings of phonemes in the ambient language also plays a role in segmentation (see Houston, 2005, for a review).

Table 10.2 Native language specialist (6–12 months). Toward the end of their first year, infants begin to exhibit skills that suggest they are specializing in their native language and figuring out how language works

Type of skill	Skill	Examples
Production/social skills	Reduplicated babbling	Repeat same speech sounds
	Follow a point	Look in direction of point
Distinguishing sounds	Speech contrasts	Can distinguish subtle phonemic differences
Segmentation	Stress detection	Segment words based on stress
	Statistical learning	Can use probability to determine if syllables go together
	Phonotactics	Familiar words 'pop out'

Language specialist summary

During the second half of the first year of life, infants become much more engaged with their caregivers and perhaps show a desire to communicate with language (Table 10.2). This is evidenced in two ways. One is that infants begin to produce sounds that sound more and more like the language they are hearing. Another is that they are encoding statistical properties of their language into memory, suggesting that, at least on some level, they are attending to the speech that is around them. These skills converge on an important ability for developing a vocabulary—the ability to segment words from fluent speech. Being able to segment and encode the sound patterns of words from fluent speech puts infants in a position to learn the meanings of those words.

Language learning sophisticate: 12–18 months

A child's second year of life is an exciting time. Along with the advent of their very first recognizable words, children transform into what Pinker (1994) referred to as 'vacuum cleaners' for words, acquiring up to nine new words per day. Not only do infants in this stage quadruple the size of their vocabulary, but also they begin to use words productively in a way that helps communicate their needs. For example, a 15-month-old might say 'cookie' to mean 'I want a cookie,' or 'no' to refuse a piece of broccoli. For parents, the advent of this single-word stage is a good thing, because it allows for a specificity of communication that was lacking at earlier stages. For infants, it is a time when they are truly beginning to grasp all the skills of learning to link sound to meaning: from social pragmatic abilities, to discovering appropriate constraints on word learning, and even to understanding the rudiments of grammar. In short, infants are becoming language learning sophisticates, with all the necessary abilities in place to 'explode' into language.

To see the complexity of this task, consider a mother trying to teach her child the word for pig. 'Hey, look at the big pig!' she says. The child must not only understand that labeling is what mom has in mind; then they must correctly identify the appropriate word to link in the speech stream (not 'the' or 'big'), and also somehow figure out that the label refers to the animal, not to its ears or the sound it is making. And then the infant needs to do this many hundreds more times in learning the names of objects, often in situations where mom doesn't explicitly label what she is talking about—perhaps even using the word when the referent isn't even present. This is the essence of the new language learning sophistication that infants exhibit as they enter the second year of life. This sophistication comes from a combination of social pragmatic understanding, an understanding of constraints on the possible meanings of words, and a new-found expertise with linguistic rules (called **grammar**).

Social pragmatic understanding

If the essence of language understanding is linked to understanding of communication (see Chapter 15), then this is the age at which infants first seem to 'get' what the caregiver is trying to talk about. They seem to have what MacNamara (1982) called a 'naming insight'; they ask their parents and practically anyone else: 'what's that?' It is as if they have discovered that they can use language to talk about the world and get what they want. Thus, infants at this age seem to reliably follow pointing and eye gaze, and they won't mislabel something that the experimenter didn't appear to intend to label. And most importantly, infants' ability to follow these cues is correlated with later linguistic competence (Carpenter *et al.*, 1998)

Social eye gaze

A variety of studies have noticed that infants begin to successfully follow social cues such as eye gaze between 12 and 18 months of age. For example, Scaife and Bruner (1975) found that 100% of 11- to 14-month-olds would spontaneously look in the same direction an experimenter was looking. Recent studies have shown that infants can use this ability to learn labels. For example, using the **intermodal preferential looking procedure**, Hollich *et al.* (2000) had experimenters label a boring object just using social eye gaze (see Figure 10.4). Even 12-month-olds would resist attaching the label to the most interesting object, and 19-month-olds successfully learned that the boring object was the object the speaker intended to label. These results imply that 12-month-olds will only learn a label if the speaker is looking at the object during labeling.

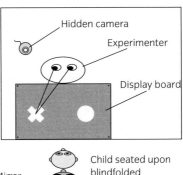

Figure 10.4 The interactive preferential looking procedure. In this version of preferential looking procedure, an experimenter labels an object on one side of a flip-board. During test trials, infants are tested on their ability to learn the label.

Sensitivity to referential intent

Eye gaze isn't the only thing that infants use to determine label meaning. In another clever series of studies, Tomasello *et al.* (1996) found that infants could infer meaning by watching the speaker for clues for **referential intent**, or what object they meant to label. In this study, the experimenter played a finding game with 18-month-old infants. The experimenter would say that they were looking for the 'gazzer.' Then they would look into first one box, then another. Upon opening the first and second boxes, the experimenter made a face and shook their head as if that wasn't what they were looking for. When they opened a third box, they smiled and nodded. When tested later, infants indicated they thought the label was for the object found in the third box. Likewise, Campbell and Namy (2003) found that infants would not misattach a label heard (over a baby monitor) while infants were looking at an object. This study, and others like it indicate that infants are not only cognizant of how to learn words, but they also understand when not to learn them. Indeed, Bloom (2000) has suggested that understanding social pragmatic intent is the primary skill that infants need to learn language, and the skill that separates humans from other animals.

Other constraints on word learning

Along with developing social understanding, infants appear to have picked up several other heuristics about possible **constraints** on meaning that help them quickly to narrow the range of hypotheses about the meaning of new words.

Whole-object bias

A majority of words in the vocabularies of infants are objects at the basic level of categorization (see Chapter 7): nouns such as **bike** or **bottle**, which highlight individual entities and their global shapes, rather than their constituent parts or accompanying actions. A child who assumes that novel words highlight (i.e., name) objects would be at a considerable advantage in the task of acquiring a lexicon, and there is considerable evidence for the existence of such a bias in older children. Woodward (1993), for example, presented 18-month-old children with a novel word and two possible referents. One referent was a visually attractive display representing an event (e.g., brightly colored dye diffusing through water); the other was a novel object in a static display. Despite a salience preference for the event, the children looked at the object more when asked to find the novel word.

Lexical contrast

One of the easiest ways for young infants and children to learn new words is in comparison to the words they already know. Specifically, Eve Clark (1987) suggested that in a case where infants knew one word, they might infer the meaning of an unknown word. This phenomenon has also been called **mutual exclusivity**, which refers to the idea that infants know that they can exclude objects that already have labels as possible candidates for new labels (Markman & Wachtel, 1988). For example, picture an infant in the fruit section of a supermarket. The mother might say 'here's an apple, and here's a mango!' Since the child knows what an apple is, learning the word for mango is easier. Indeed, even if the mother only said 'Here's a mango' (when it was beside some apples) the child could likely infer the meaning because they already know the word for apple, and can guess that 'mango' refers to the novel object.

Categorical induction

Children also understand something about how words referring to particular categories of objects get extended. That is, after learning a number of words, infants begin to make guesses about how words might be extended to other similar objects. This process, called **categorical induction**, is harder than it looks, because we have words to label all kinds of categories, from solid objects completely defined by shape (such as a chair) to substance terms where shape is irrelevant (such as rock, wood, or even toothpaste). Indeed, Samuelson (2002) found that children will extend a new word (for a C-shaped novel object made of wood) on the basis of shape, but only if the object labeled fits the category of a solid. However, if the researchers labeled an 'object' not well-defined by shape (e.g., a C-shaped object made of glitter), then infants ignored shape—especially if they had learned a few substance terms (such as frosting, Jell-O, lotion) beforehand. This suggests that even very young infants can use what they know about the categories they already know to extend new words.

Grammatical understanding

Recognizing parts of speech

Despite the large majority of first words being for concrete objects (which are likely easier to learn anyway), children learn words for things other than objects, and they seem to use language itself to help cue them when such learning is happening. This process has been called **syntactic bootstrapping** (Mintz & Gleitman, 2002), because infants are using grammar to discover possible meaning. Thus, for example, children assume that words proceeded by articles like 'a,' 'an,' or 'the' typically name objects, whereas words with adjective endings label properties (such as the 'fepish one'). In a dramatic example of this type of ability, Waxman and her colleagues (Waxman & Booth, 2001) have demonstrated that when 14-month-olds see a purple toy and are told that 'this one is blickish,' these infants will extend 'blickish' to other purple objects. In contrast, if told 'this one is a blicket,' 14-month-olds will extend the word blicket to other similarly-shaped toys. This sensitivity to **morphology** (the different forms that words can take) is one of the early signs that infants are grasping some aspects of grammar at this age and that they can use aspects of grammar in learning new words.

Understanding word order

Not only do infants know about parts of speech, but evidence also indicates that they understand something about how words combine to make meaning (a rule system called **syntax**), although these same children are not yet producing very many words in combination. In a seminal series of studies, Hirsh-Pasek and Golinkoff (1996) found that 19-month-olds would look at the correct picture when asked to 'See Big Bird and Cookie Monster bending!' vs. 'See Big Bird bending Cookie Monster!' Notice that it is not enough to know that Big Bird, Cookie Monster, and bending are involved. That is, infants must not only know something about the individual meanings of the words, but they must also know exactly how these words combine to create new meanings.

Question comprehension

Finally, in addition to knowing about parts of speech and word order, by 15 and 20 months of age infants know a little bit about how questions work. To demonstrate this, Seidl, Hollich, and Jusczyk (2003) tested infants' developing understanding of questions by familiarizing 15- and 20-month-olds with a scene of an apple hitting a flower and then asking not only a simple question, such as 'Where is the flower?', but also 'What hit the flower?' (a question that asks for the subject of the action), and 'What did the apple hit?' (a question that asks for the object). Notice that the answers to these 'subject' and 'object' questions depend on understanding the relationships among words and how questions that start with 'what' differ from questions that start with 'where.' Indeed, the answers to these questions are actually the opposite of the objects overtly mentioned in them. Thus, if infants were only pulling out the word 'flower' when asked 'what hit the **flower?**' the infants would look at the flower when they were supposed to look at the apple. Instead, both 15- and 20-month-olds looked significantly longer at the apple when asked 'What hit the flower?', and 20-month-olds even looked longer at the flower when asked 'What did the apple hit?' These results indicate that infants have a fairly sophisticated understanding of grammar including parts of speech, word order, and question construction, before they have reached their 24th month.

The wug test

Not only are infants aware of morphology, word order, and grammatical rules while learning new words, but if they are tested in just the right manner, some 18-month-olds can produce new word forms that correspond to the rules of their native language. In one of the earliest examples of this, Jean

Berko Gleason (1958) had children guess the plural form of a new word. Thus, an experimenter would introduce a new object and say, 'This is a wug, see the wug.' Then experimenter would introduce an identical object and say, 'Now there are two of them. There are two___?' Some children would inevitably complete this sentence with the word 'wugs,' even though they had never heard this plural before. These results show that infants, who are not yet combining words productively, still know something about how to make grammatically correct new words.

Language specialist summary

In the second year of life, as infants say their first recognizable words, their comprehension abilities indicate a sophisticated understanding of nearly all aspects of learning a language (Table 10.3). Infants can learn and extend a new word in as little as one repetition using social cues and cognitive constraints, such as the whole-object bias or lexical contrast (using known words to learn the meanings of new words). And although most of the words in their vocabulary are concrete nouns, they can learn and use words from all different classes, including social words such as 'bye-bye' and 'night-night'

Table 10.3 Language learning sophisticate (12–18 months). In the second year of life, infants not only begin to use their first words, but they demonstrate all of the skills necessary to expertly learn and use language

Type of skill	Skill	Examples
Production/social	First words	Use words to communicate interests, ideas, wants.
	Eye gaze	Follow eye gaze to 'correct' object.
	Pointing	Follow points to 'correct' label.
	Expression	Use expression to find 'correct' label.
Perceptual/cognitive	Whole object	Learn new words on the basis of whole objects.
	Contrast	Can use contrast to discover meaning of new words.
	Categorical induction	Extend new words on basis of experience with other similar words.
Linguistic	Part of speech	Nouns label shape, adjectives label color.
	Word order	Can tell Cookie Monster pushing Big Bird from Big Bird pushing Cookie Monster
	Question understanding	Know difference between 'Where is the apple?' and 'What hit the apple?'

and adjectives such as 'red' or 'wooden.' They accomplish this in part by using subtle grammatical distinctions in word endings (**morphology**) and ordering of the words (**syntax**) in complex questions. They even indicate that they understand the difference between a question like 'Where is the flower?' and 'What hit the flower?' Thus, even before infants have begun to combine words productively, the available evidence suggests that all the component parts are in place for rapid acquisition of their native language.

SUMMARY

Over the first 2 years of life, infants move from the primitive communication of crying to using specific words to get what they want. Along the way, they exhibit a threefold increase in sophistication in their social production skills, cognitive/perceptual skills, and linguistic skills. In the first 6 months of life, babies demonstrate sensitivity to nearly all the sounds found in all the world's languages. From 6 to 12 months of age, this sensitivity combines with a new-found skill of **segmentation**, and mapping frequent words to meaning, to allow infants to demonstrate their first comprehension of words (**semantics**). From 12 to 18 months, this comprehension has led infants to begin to express themselves with their first words and develop heuristics about how to use eye gaze and other social cues, along with other constraints to more quickly learn new words. They have even grasped the first rudiments of grammar. Together, these skills in phonology, semantics, and grammar put infants in the ideal position to quickly acquire their first language.

PART FOUR

Social Development

CHAPTER ELEVEN

How infants perceive and process faces

JENNIFER L. RAMSEY-RENNELS and JUDITH H. LANGLOIS

Introduction

Imagine going to a big party. You enter and find the room filled with people in lively conversation. Like most guests, unless you are really hungry, you will spend more time looking at people's faces than at the food on the hors d'oeuvres table. As you scan the faces in the room, you instantaneously and automatically determine the gender, race, age, and physical attractiveness of the other guests. You ascertain whether or not you recognize anyone's face as familiar. On the basis of their emotional expression, you guess what type of mood people are in. Also, you make a judgement about who is and isn't friendly, interesting, intelligent, and approachable on the basis of social cues you 'read' from faces.

Now imagine a newborn infant in the same room filled with people. Would the infant perceive the faces the same way as you did? What abilities are present at birth and what are acquired as a result of experience with faces? Seeking answers to these questions has interested researchers over the past four decades. This chapter summarizes much of the research in this area. We start with research investigating infants' interest in faces relative to other objects. Next, we discuss memory for faces and the development of face recognition. We then turn to the topics of whether or not young infants have preferences for certain types of faces, how infants perceive emotional expressions, and the role of faces for social development.

Before proceeding, however, let's briefly review the visual capabilities of infants in relation to face perception (for a more in-depth review, see Chapter 5). At birth, faces appear somewhat blurry to newborns even at fairly close range. Despite the fuzziness, however, there is still enough information available for newborns to see and perceive faces (Figure 11.1). During the next 6 months of development infants' visual acuity rapidly improves, and over the next 30 months, it gradually continues to improve until it becomes

Figure 11.1 What do newborns see? The picture on the left portrays an adult's view of Liz Taylor's face, whereas the picture on the right portrays a newborn's view.

similar to that of an adult. Even at birth, infants can perceive faces (albeit in a blurred fashion) and they rapidly become adult-like in their perception of faces.

Do infants like faces?

Infants need exposure to faces in order to recognize important people in their lives and learn about social and emotional cues. Therefore, it is not surprising that very young infants attend to and process faces at a variety of levels. In fact, faces attract infant interest as early as the first few months of life, but infants do not show a similar interest in the human body until 18 months of age (Slaughter, Heron & Sim, 2002). What is it about faces that attracts such interest in infants? To answer this question, we review the face-processing abilities present at birth and the proposed mechanisms driving newborns' interest in faces. Then, we discuss what changes in face processing occur during infancy and how experience may drive these changes.

Face-processing abilities at birth

Many studies show that newborns orient more toward schematic faces or photographs of real faces than to other objects or inverted and scrambled faces. In a seminal study, newborns tracked with their eyes and turned their heads further to follow a moving schematic face than a moving scrambled or blank face (Goren *et al.*, 1975). See Figure 11.2 for an example of these faces. Not all research, however, has replicated these findings. Although the research is generally in agreement that newborns show greater interest

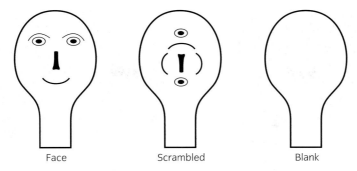

Figure 11.2 What do newborns prefer to look at? Several researchers have found that they prefer to look at the schematic face rather than the scrambled or blank face. Figure from 'Newborns' preferential tracking of face-like stimuli and its subsequent decline' by M. H. Johnson, S. Dziuawiec, H. Ellis, and J. Morton in *Cognition*, copyright © 1991 by Elsevier Science Publishers, reproduced by permission of the publisher.

in patterned than blank (nonpatterned) stimuli, some research finds that newborns show equal interest in both schematic and scrambled faces, despite being able to discriminate between the two types of faces (Easterbrook *et al.*, 1999). Faces have a clear advantage over nonpatterned objects and, in many cases, have an advantage over other patterned objects in eliciting newborns' attention. What mechanisms are responsible for this advantage? The question of why newborns may preferentially orient to faces has generated a substantial amount of research aimed at understanding this phenomenon which, in turn, has given rise to several theoretical accounts of the preference. Some of these accounts suggest that faces are appealing, not necessarily because they are face-like but because they display stimulus characteristics that are inherently appealing: they have areas of high contrast; they are 'top-heavy' in that there are more elements in the upper (e.g., the eyes) rather than lower portions (e.g., Cassia *et al.*, 2004), and they usually move and are dynamic. Other accounts suggest that infants may be born with an innate 'face-detecting' brain mechanism that directs their attention specifically toward face-like configurations (Morton & Johnson, 1991), or even that they are born with an innate representation of faces (Meltzoff, 2004).

Despite the disagreement as to what exactly causes newborns' preferential orienting to face-like stimuli, all possible mechanisms ensure that newborns attend to faces and this visual input helps a more sophisticated face-processing system to begin to develop (de Haan, Humphreys & Johnson, 2002).

Development of face processing during infancy

Shortly after the newborn period, infant preferences for faces briefly disappear between 1 and 2 months of age, much like other newborn reflexes, but then re-emerge between 2 and 3 months of age (Johnson *et al.*, 1991).

Thus, there is a very short period of time during infant development when infants show no preferences for faces. This lack of a preference for faces is mirrored in the way 1-month-olds scan faces. They rarely fixate a face and when they do, they usually look at its external features, such as the chin or hairline, rather than the internal features. Two-month-olds, however, spend a significant amount of time fixating internal features of faces, particularly the eyes and mouth (Maurer & Salapatek, 1976). See Figure 11.3. This change in scanning coincides with an increase in infants' sensitivity to contrast, thus enabling infants to better see the contrast between the eyes and mouth and the rest of the face. Because of the re-emergence of infant interest in faces and the changes in facial scanning at this age, it is likely that cortical regions of the brain are starting to become more specialized for face processing (Johnson & de Haan, 2001).

Indeed, from 3 months of age to the end of the first year, several changes are seen in infant brain and behavioral responses to faces, suggesting increasingly specialized response (e.g., Nelson, 2001). Also, by the time the infant is 3 months of age, most face perception researchers agree that infant interest in faces is now influenced by their experience with faces as a social stimulus,

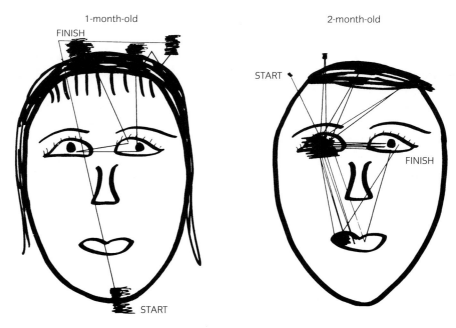

Figure 11.3 How do 1- and 2-month old infants scan the features of faces? One-month-olds tend to scan the external features of the face whereas 2-month-olds tend to scan the internal features. Figure from 'Basic visual processes' by P. Saltapek, in *Infant perception: from sensation to cognition*, edited by L. B. Cohen and P. Salatapek, copyright © 1975 by Academic Press, reproduced by permission of the publisher.

although there is disagreement as to the mechanism driving slightly older infants' interest in faces. Some researchers suggest that the same mechanism that is present at birth simply develops and gets more sophisticated (e.g., Bednar & Miikkulainen, 2003), whereas others posit that the face-processing mechanism used by infants 3 months and older is qualitatively different from the one used by newborns (e.g., Turati, Valenza, Leo & Simion, 2005). Some of the changes seen in infant brain development and behavioral responses during the first year can be interpreted to support either position.

With regard to changes in the brain, both the left and right visual fields and corresponding right and left hemispheres initially contribute to face processing. Starting around 4 months, however, infants start to show a left visual field, right hemisphere advantage in face processing (Nelson, 2001). At this point in development, cortical responses to faces become more localized (i.e., activated in a particular area).

Specific brain responses to faces also start to develop by 3 months of age (Halit, Csibra, Volein & Johnson, 2004). To illustrate, both infants and adults most commonly experience upright human faces, so changing the orientation or species of face can affect brain responding as measured by the **event-related potential (ERP)** component(s) most strongly linked to face processing. When adults see faces, a particular ERP component is activated, but the response tends to be more specific (i.e., the amplitude is smaller) when adults see faces of species they usually see (human vs. monkey) presented in the way they usually experience them (upright vs. inverted). Six-month-olds show two ERP components linked to face processing. One of these responds to type of face (larger amplitude for human than monkey faces), and the other responds to orientation of faces (larger amplitude for upright relative to inverted faces (de Haan *et al.*, 2002). Like adults, 6-month-olds respond to faces differently depending on the species and orientation of the face, but the ERP components and direction of effect in amplitude differences are not the same. This specialized response to upright human faces is in a rather rudimentary form during infancy and needs further development.

This specialized brain response to faces is mirrored in infant behavior. Like adults, infants approximately 3 months of age and older process and respond differently to inverted and upright faces (e.g., Fagan, 1972). For example, they have more trouble discriminating among facial movements produced by inverted vs. upright faces and have difficulty recognizing faces when they are inverted as opposed to upright (Stucki, Kaufmann-Hayoz & Kaufmann, 1987; Turati, Sangrigoli, Ruel & de Schonen, 2004). Additionally, 6-month-olds easily recognize both human and monkey faces, but 9-month-olds easily discriminate between human faces only and have difficulty discriminating between monkey faces (of the same species of monkey), suggesting their face-processing abilities become quite specialized toward the end of the first year (Pascalis, de Haan & Nelson, 2002).

The role of experience in infant face processing

Why might these brain and behavioral changes occur? In much the same way that speech perception gets more and more specialized based on the language to which the infant is exposed (see Chapter 10), face perception likely gets more and more specialized based on the faces to which the infant is exposed. Thus, the differential responses infants exhibit toward upright and inverted faces may occur because they have more experience with upright faces, and thus have more expertise in processing upright vs. inverted faces. Similarly, most infants have little or no experience with monkey faces, but a great deal of experience with human faces. Infants may be born with the ability to process and recognize any type of face, but over time, they become experts at processing commonly experienced faces and become less skilled at processing faces infrequently experienced (Nelson, 2001). This superiority in processing certain faces based on infant experience with faces is seen not only in the orientation and species of face, but the race and sex of faces to which the infant is most commonly exposed (Ramsey, Langlois & Marti, 2005; Sangrioli & de Schonen, 2004).

Experience with faces may cause infants to form a facial prototype (a composite representation of experienced faces) that infants use as a reference when processing faces). This ability to form a prototype is present in newborns (Walton & Bower, 1993), but not 1-month-olds (de Haan, Johnson, Maurer & Perrett, 2001), perhaps due to 1-month-olds' lack of interest in faces and poor visual scanning of internal features. Nevertheless, the ability re-emerges because 3-month-olds show evidence of forming facial prototypes (de Haan *et al.*, 2001). Facial prototypes may be linked to specialized processing because it should be easier for infants to process faces most similar to the prototype (Ramsey *et al.*, 2005) and more difficult to process faces that deviate from the prototype (e.g., monkey faces, inverted faces, other-race faces).

Conclusions regarding infant attraction to faces

Think back to our question at the beginning of this section regarding why faces may have special status in the world of the infant. Despite the disagreement regarding the mechanisms driving infant interest in and processing of faces during the newborn and later periods of infancy, there appears to be consensus that newborns orient more toward faces than toward other objects. This bias provides infants with experience with faces, which helps the brain develop localized areas for responding to faces and specialized ERP components. More evidence is needed to support the role of experience in facilitating specialization of infants' face processing, but the evidence is accumulating and it appears to be one of the more dominant theories influencing research in this area. This specialization helps infants learn about finer details of faces and recognize many faces in their environment, but it also hinders their ability to process and recognize faces that are not normally experienced, an issue we discuss further in the next section on infant face recognition.

Infant face recognition

Now that we have some background regarding infants' attraction to faces, the next question to ask is, 'When can infants recognize their parents and when can babies tell the difference among the faces of strangers?' This section differs from the previous section in that it focuses on infants' recognition of particular faces rather than infant recognition of 'faceness' (i.e., recognizing that a particular object is a face). Not only do these two abilities differ conceptually, but neurobehavioral evidence suggests that there are separate brain systems for processing representations of individual faces and 'faceness,' although there may be some overlap between the two systems (de Schonen & Deruelle, 1994).

Recognition of the mother's face

Because the mother tends to be the infant's primary caregiver and her face is one of the first faces the infant sees, it is the most important and most likely face for an infant to recognize early in development. Indeed, there is evidence that newborns can visually recognize their mothers shortly after birth. For example, 2-day-old newborns prefer to look longer at their mother than at a female stranger during a live presentation (Field, Cohen, Garcia & Greenberg, 1984). Even when the mother's and stranger's olfactory cues are masked with a strong air freshener, 2- to 4-day-olds still recognize their mother's face (Bushnell, Sai & Mullin, 1989; Pascalis et al., 1995). Newborns will also suck on a pacifier (dummy) at a rate necessary to control viewing a videotaped image of their mother relative to a videotaped image of a female stranger (Walton et al., 1992). This preference strengthens the more exposure newborns have to their mother's face, and develops after only 4–5.5 hours of viewing her face (Bushnell, 2001; Field et al., 1984).

Given newborn infants' remarkable ability to recognize their mother's face shortly after birth, some researchers have suggested that this ability is an evolutionarily adaptive process that ensures proximity between newborns and their mother (e.g., Field, 1985). Others have suggested infants may have a special system for recognizing their mother's face that differs from the system for recognizing other faces (de Schonen & Mancini, 1995; cited in de Haan & Nelson, 1999). Not all newborns easily recognize their mother's face, however. Newborns of depressed mothers take longer to habituate to her face and show no preferences for her face or a stranger's following habituation, suggesting early differences in mother recognition between this at-risk group and newborns of nondepressed mothers (Hernandez-Reif, Field, Diego & Largie, 2002).

Recognition of the mother's face is dependent on the newborn being able to see both the mother's external features, such as her hairline, and her internal features, such as her eyes and nose. When mothers and strangers cover either their external or internal features, newborns no longer recognize their mother. Sometime between 1.25 and 2 months, infants begin to recognize their mother's face when they see her internal features only. By 4 months, they recognize her via her external features only (Bartrip, Morton & de Schonen, 2001).

Not only do the cues infants use to recognize their mother's face change with age, their looking preferences also change. Around 1 month, infants look longer at a stranger's face than their mother's, at least when these faces are accompanied by their mother's or a stranger's speech (Burnham, 1993). If no speech accompanies the full face, the visual preference for the stranger is not evident until 5 months (Bartrip *et al.*, 2001). This developmental change in looking preferences does not mean that infants now prefer strangers to their mothers, but rather that babies are now very familiar with their mother's face and are interested in learning about other faces. Despite the decrease in looking time toward their mothers' face, infants still show more affect in their facial expressions when looking at their mother rather than a stranger (Burnham, 1993).

Interestingly, at 6 months, infants show no differences in looking time to their mother or a female stranger when pictures of the two women are paired together. Differences in ERPs, however, suggest that the brain reacts to the familiar face of the mother as different than the female stranger's face, regardless of whether this face is similar to the mother's face or not (de Haan & Nelson, 1997). These ERP responses remain strong for the mother's face up until 24 months of age, ensuring that the child establishes a good representation of the mother's face during the first 2 years. After 2 years of age, the child begins the transition to eventually showing stronger responses toward more novel faces (Carver *et al.*, 2003).

Recognition of the father's face

Given that infants are able to recognize their mother's face shortly after birth under certain circumstances, it seems likely that they would also learn their father's face early in development.

The minimal research that has been conducted to address this question, however, yields little evidence to support infant recognition of their father's face. No significant differences emerged in a small sample of newborns who sucked a pacifier (dummy) to view a videotape of either their father's or a male stranger's face (Walton *et al.*, 1992). Even at 4 months, infants show no visual preferences for their father's face over an unfamiliar male face when shown on videotape, although there is some evidence for differences in affective responsiveness (Ward, 1998). Clearly, more studies are needed to address this issue, but currently it appears that recognition of the father's face develops later than recognition of the mother's face and the recognition mechanisms may be qualitatively different from those for the mother's face.

Recognition of other faces

We discussed infant recognition of their parents' faces, but what about their ability to recognize other relatives, such as their grandparents, whom they may see only occasionally? Provided that infants have a sufficient amount of time to look at and learn about a face when first becoming familiar with it, infants as young as 2–3 months can later tell the difference between one female face and a very similar looking face. Much like the way they view their mother's face around 2 months of age, infants use both internal and external features, or internal features only, when encoding a stranger's face (Blass & Camp, 2004).

Similar to the way that an infant's brain responds differently to seeing their mother's face vs. a female stranger's face, the ERPs in infants as young as 3 months differ when they see a novel face vs. a face they saw previously (Pascalis, de Haan, Nelson & de Schonen, 1998). To find this difference in ERPs, young infants need sufficient exposure to a face they are seeing for the first time. By 8 months of age, however, infants' ERPs for novel faces and faces they have seen previously will differ even if the exposure to the face they saw previously was brief, suggesting they now need less time to process faces (Nelson & Collins, 1992).

The above studies tested infants' ability to recognize a face when the face viewed was oriented the same as the one initially presented, but when can infants recognize different facial views? Six-month-old boys and girls and 3-month-old boys recognized a frontal smiling view of a female face after seeing it in several other different views (e.g., a frontal neutral view, a smiling profile view) either 2 minutes or 24 hours earlier (Pascalis *et al.*, 1998). It appears to take a little longer to develop recognition of nonfrontal views, however. Whereas infants recognize a three-quarter view of a face after first seeing a frontal view at 7 months, they do not recognize a profile view of the face (Figure 11.4) until 12 months (Rose, Jankowski & Feldman, 2002b). At the end of the first year, infants also recognize faces after something has been added to or taken away from the face area, such as a scarf or hat (Lundy, 2000). Thus, infants' ability to recognize faces improves during the first year as they view people from different angles and with slight changes in appearance. If the person is engaged in an activity, however, the activity competes with the person's face for the infant's attention and infants did not show as good recognition memory than if they solely viewed the person's face (Bahrick, Gogate & Ruiz, 2002).

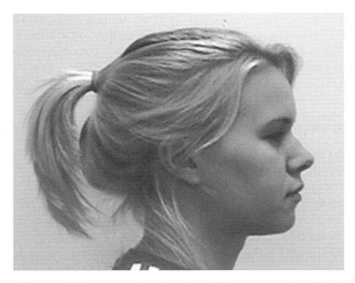

Figure 11.4 When can infants recognize a face from different orientations? By 6 months of age, infants can recognize the frontal view of a face after seeing only the profile view.

How do infants recognize faces and why do improvements in face recognition occur? Infants generally rely more on **configural**, rather than **featural**, information to process and recognize faces. Configural processing refers to infants' use of the spacing or relations among features (e.g., distance between eyes and nose), rather than features alone, to encode faces (Thompson, Madrid, Westbrook & Johnston, 2001). Having early experience with faces is important for this sophisticated face-processing ability to develop. Individuals who are deprived of this input as a result of vision problems in the left eye during the first few months of life rely more on featural, than configural, information to process faces (Le Grand, Mondloch, Maurer & Brent, 2003), a much less efficient method for recognizing faces. In contrast, infants who have regular visual experience with faces get more efficient at recognizing these faces during the first year because it takes them less time to process and recognize faces and they can more efficiently shift their gaze back and forth between two faces (Rose *et al.*, 2002b). Therefore, even though infants spend less time looking at faces overall as they develop, the number of fixations they make toward a face increases (Hunnius & Geuze, 2004). Preterm babies, however, are at a disadvantage in that they lag behind full-term infants in these processing abilities (Rose, Feldman & Jankowski, 2002a).

What mechanisms allow the infant to accomplish this difficult task? Maturation of both the visual system and the brain contribute to the acquisition of this ability. As infants' visual acuity improves, allowing them to more easily see individuals who are farther away, infants may begin using featural information, in addition to configural information, to encode faces (Rose *et al.*, 2002b). Also, as the infant's brain develops, **lateralization** begins, meaning that the left and right hemispheres begin to specialize. Starting around 4–5 months of age, infants use their right hemisphere more than their left hemisphere during face recognition, suggesting that, like adults, their right hemisphere has become specialized in recognizing faces, and it is possible that there may be a special system for recognizing faces (Deruelle & de Schonen, 1991). One other possibility, however, is that infants have greater expertise processing faces than other objects, and thus show a more specialized recognition response. Again, early visual input to the left eye (right hemisphere) appears important for such expertise to develop (Le Grand *et al.*, 2003). The type of visual input is also important—infants demonstrate better recognition of female than male faces (Quinn *et al.*, 2002), and of faces of their own race (Sangrigoli & de Schonen, 2004), types of faces with which they have more experience.

Recognition of their own face

While learning about other faces, it is not surprising that infants also begin to recognize their own face. By 4–5 months of age, infants discriminate between a videotaped **moving** image of themselves and another person or object with facial features (Figure 11.5) by attending more to the other person (Rochat & Striano, 2002). At 8 months, they also look longer at images of people other than themselves, even when the images shown are **static** images (Legerstee *et al.*, 1998). It is likely infants use simultaneity of actions and movement to learn about their faces, so discriminating between their face and another person during the static condition is more difficult than the moving condition (Legerstee *et al.*, 1998). This early discrimination between the self and other is not considered as advanced as recognition of the self in the mirror, which does not seem to emerge until 18–24 months of age (see Chapter 2). When **mirror self-recognition** first emerges, infants show greater interest in their own face than in another person's, but this interest is only temporary and is not maintained (Nielsen, Dissanayake & Kashima, 2003).

Conclusions about the development of face recognition

From this section, we can conclude that infants are able to recognize their mother's face shortly after birth, given some experience with her face. Infants appear to initially rely on both internal and external features and the relations among these features to process and recognize their mother's and unfamiliar people's faces. Development of the visual system, hemispheric lateralization, and experience with faces (including their own face) allow the infant to become better at recognizing faces from different angles, to process faces more easily, and to learn about them during briefer presentations.

Figure 11.5 Do infants recognize their own face (top left) when paired with an unfamiliar peer's face (top right) or an object with facial features (bottom left and right)? Between 5 and 8 months of age, infants show evidence that they can recognize themselves. Figure from 'Five- and eight-month-old infants recognize their faces and voices as familiar and social stimuli', by M. I. Legerstee, D. Anderson, and A. Schafer in *Child Development*, copyright © 1998 by the Society for Research in Child Development, reproduced by permission of the publisher.

Infant preferences for different types of faces

We just discussed how infants prefer their mother's face early in development and then prefer novel faces later in development. Infants do not respond to all novel faces in a similar manner, however. They look longer at some faces more than others. We will now describe what types of faces infants prefer, offer explanations for their preferences, and speculate about how these preferences may serve as rudiments of stereotyping based on facial appearance.

Infants' facial preferences

Infants' experience with their primary caregiver's face not only drives their attention toward that face, but toward other faces of the same gender. The majority of infants have a female primary caregiver, so they look longer at

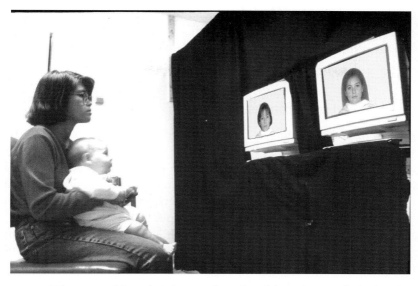

Figure 11.6 What types of faces do infants prefer? Like adults, infants prefer looking longer at the more attractive face on the right than the one on the left.

novel female than novel male faces when paired together. In contrast, a small percentage of infants have a male primary caregiver and they look longer at novel male than novel female faces when paired together (Quinn *et al.*, 2002). The sex of the primary caregiver appears to be an important cue for driving infant interest in novel faces.

Infants also respond differently if the novel faces vary in attractiveness (e.g., Langlois *et al.*, 1991). Even newborns, only a few days old, prefer attractive faces and look longer at faces adults rate as attractive than at faces adults rate as unattractive (Slater *et al.*, 1998; Figure 11.6). This preference for attractive faces is particularly robust for adult female faces (Langlois *et al.*, 1991) and has also been found for infant faces (Van Duuren, Kendell-Scott & Stark, 2003). Results suggesting infants prefer attractive male faces, however, are mixed—some studies have found that infants look longer at attractive male faces, whereas others have not (see Ramsey, 2003)—an issue we will discuss later.

By 12 months of age, infants not only look longer at attractive faces, but they play with and show more positive affect toward an attractive stranger than toward an unattractive one. Infants also avoid unattractive strangers more than attractive strangers (Langlois, Roggman & Rieser-Danner, 1990). These results demonstrate that facial attractiveness guides infants' looking during early infancy, and elicits differential social responses to strangers as the infant gets older.

Why does the gender of the primary caregiver guide infants' interest in faces? And why do infants show robust preferences for attractive female faces, but not attractive male faces? Given that most infants are not watching television or reading fashion magazines, attractiveness preferences are unlikely to result from socialization and the media. Another explanation is necessary.

Origins of facial preferences

Preferences for attractive female faces are based more on internal, rather than external, features of the face (Slater *et al.*, 2000a) In addition, faces need to be upright for newborns and older infants to demonstrate such preferences (Slater *et al.*, 2000b). Something about internal facial configurations rather than individual facial features elicits infant interest in faces. Research suggests individuals prefer **prototypes**, which are defined as the central tendency or mean of a population (e.g., Halberstadt & Rhodes, 2000). Facial configurations close to the average of the population should be considered attractive because they are more prototypical than configurations that deviate from the average of the population.

An averaged or prototypical face can be created by mathematically averaging together digitized images of faces (Figure 11.7). As predicted by prototype theory, adults rate averaged faces composed of 16 or more faces as more attractive than most of the individual faces used to create the averaged face (Figure 11.8; Langlois & Roggman, 1990). Infants also look longer at averaged female faces than at unattractive female faces, suggesting that, like adults, they prefer averaged faces. Thus, both adults and infants may visually

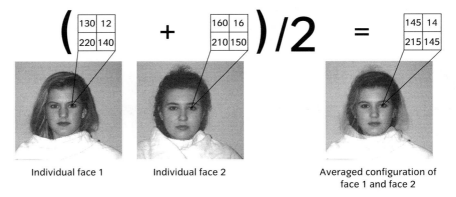

Individual face 1   Individual face 2   Averaged configuration of
                                                     face 1 and face 2

Figure 11.7 How are faces averaged together? Digitized images of faces are made up of small dots called pixels. Each of these pixels has a numerical value reflecting the darkness or lightness of that pixel. Thus, all the pixel values of two individual faces can be added together and then divided by two to create the pixel values comprising the 'averaged' face. Figure from 'What is average and what is not average about attractive faces?' by J. H. Langlois, L. A. Roggman, and L. Musselman in *Psychological Science*, copyright © 1994 by Blackwell Publishers, reproduced by permission of the publisher.

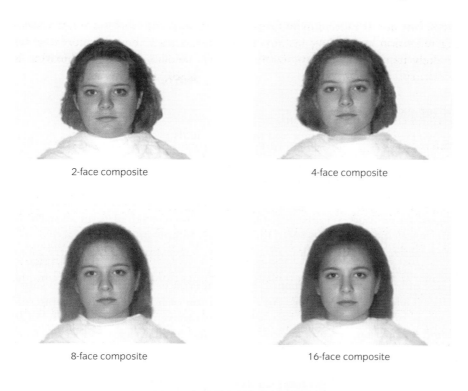

2-face composite

4-face composite

8-face composite

16-face composite

32-face composite

Figure 11.8 What makes a face attractive? As more and more faces are averaged together, the resulting composite face more closely resembles a facial configuration close to the population mean. Adults rate an 'averaged' face comprised of 16 or more faces as more attractive than the original faces used to create the composite, and infants look longer at the 'averaged' face than at less attractive faces.

prefer attractive female faces because their faces are close to the average facial configuration of the female face population.

This visual preference for averaged faces is dependent on the face with which it is paired. In one study, infants saw two versions of female faces, one made to be more average and one made to be less average, paired together. Although the more average faces were attractive, the less average faces were particularly odd-looking, and thus infants looked equally long at both faces. Their longest look, however, was to the less average than the more average face, perhaps because of its oddity (Rhodes, Geddes, Jeffery, Dziurawiec & Clark, 2002).

Other explanations

Some researchers have suggested that individuals prefer certain faces because of their symmetry, eye size, or feature height rather than their 'averageness.' None of these alternate explanations, however, can appropriately account for infants' and adults' preferences for certain faces. For example, infants who saw photographs of attractive and unattractive faces that were either altered to be more symmetrical or shown in their original form showed no differences in visual preferences for the faces. Infants preferred attractive over unattractive faces, regardless of symmetry, suggesting that symmetry alone cannot account for infants' attractiveness preferences (Samuels *et al.*, 1994). A test of how large eyes influence infants' interest in faces found only a subtle effect (Geldart *et al.*, 1999a). An investigation of how the height of internal features on an individual's face affected attractiveness ratings (Figure 11.9) found inconsistent results in how infants and adults responded to the faces (Geldart *et al.*, 1999b). Thus, 'averageness' currently is the best explanation for understanding infant interest in faces, but what mechanism is responsible for this preference for prototypicality?

How do preferences for 'averageness' develop?

The finding that the gender of an infant's primary caregiver affects infant interest in faces suggests that experience with faces affects development of

high height   medium height   low height

Figure 11.9 How does the height of internal facial features affect attractiveness ratings? Adults rate faces with their features at the low height (right picture) or medium height (middle picture) as more attractive than faces with their features at the high height (left picture), whereas infants prefer to look longer at faces with their features at the high height. Figure from 'Effects of the height of the internal features of faces on adults' aesthetic ratings and 5-month-olds' looking times' by S. Geldart, D. Maurer, and H. Henderson in *Perception*, copyright © 1999 by Pion Press, reproduced by permission of the publisher.

facial prototypes and visual preferences. Individuals may be born with a mechanism that allows them to average examples within a category, such as faces. Category members resembling the prototype should be more preferred than category members less like the prototype. Because facial prototypes are formed through experience with faces, this theory suggests experience with faces is necessary for developing attractiveness preferences. For this theory to be a viable explanation of infant interest in faces, infants must be able to average faces.

Do infants average across faces to form prototypes?

To investigate whether 6-month-olds can form prototypes of faces, Rubenstein *et al.* (1999) showed infants eight different, attractive female faces in order to familiarize them with the faces. They then tested whether a prototype created by averaging the eight female faces together seemed familiar to the infants. According to prototype theory, if babies have the ability to form prototypes by averaging together faces they have seen, the prototype face should seem familiar even though the baby has technically never seen it. The prototype face should seem even more familiar than any of the faces the baby saw because it is similar to each of the faces and is thus easily recognized by virtue of this similarity. Indeed, this is exactly what Rubenstein *et al.*'s (1999) study found. Prototype faces were more familiar to the infants than either a novel female face or the individual faces the infants originally saw. These results show that by 6 months of age infants have the ability to create prototypes of female faces. Three-month-olds, but not 1-month-olds, are also able to average female faces (de Haan *et al.*, 2001). Even newborns have the ability to form prototypes of faces (Walton & Bower, 1993). It may seem odd that newborns, but not 1-month-olds, can form facial prototypes, but remember from the section 'Infant Interest in Faces' that at birth there is a preference for 'faceness' that disappears around 1 month of age and does not re-emerge until 2–3 months of age. The ability to form prototypes may follow a similar trajectory.

Newborns between 14 and 151 hours old show attractiveness preferences (Slater *et al.*, 1998), suggesting experience with faces does not need to be substantial before the prototype forms, but some experience with faces is necessary because these preferences are not present in 15-minute-old newborns (Kalakanis, 1998). Because babies can average across faces and they prefer averaged faces, the cognitive prototyping mechanism is a plausible cause of infants' preferences for attractive female faces. Interestingly, however, young infants are unable to form prototypes of male faces, which may explain why infants do not demonstrate robust preferences for attractive male faces. The majority of infants have female primary caregivers and therefore their natural prototypical representation is likely very female-like, making it difficult for infants to form a male facial prototype, even within a controlled lab setting (Ramsey *et al.*, 2005).

Rudiments of a stereotype: 'beauty is good'

In addition to preferring attractive faces, adults and children also assign positive traits to attractive individuals and negative traits to unattractive individuals—the **beauty is good** stereotype. This stereotype may begin developing during infancy. Before infants begin associating positive or negative traits with attractive and unattractive faces, they must first categorize faces according to attractiveness, meaning they should group attractive faces together and unattractive faces together.

Indeed, by 6 months of age, infants can categorize female faces according to their attractiveness (Ramsey, Langlois, Hoss, Rubenstein & Griffin, 2004). After seeing a series of attractive female faces, 6-month-olds treated novel attractive female faces as familiar, but treated novel unattractive female faces as different. Conversely, after seeing a series of unattractive female faces, 6-month-olds treated novel unattractive female faces as familiar, but treated novel attractive female faces as different. These results suggest that infants categorized attractive female faces as one group and unattractive female faces as another group. Infants also demonstrated an ability to discriminate among the female faces within each category, suggesting that they recognized the invariant characteristics of the faces within each of the categories and were not simply treating the faces within the category as the same face.

Given that 6-month-olds categorize female faces according to attractiveness, when do infants begin associating positive traits with attractive female faces and negative traits with unattractive female faces? Twelve-month-olds look longer at attractive than unattractive female faces while a positive-sounding voice plays or a schematic smiley face is displayed. They also look longer at unattractive than attractive female faces while a negative-sounding voice plays or a schematic frowny face is displayed (Griffin, Hoss, Ramsey, Langlois & Rubenstein, 2004; Rubenstein, 2000). This matching of attractive faces with pleasant visual stimuli and voices and unattractive faces with nonpleasant visual stimuli and voices suggests that by the end of their first year of life, infants display some rudiments of stereotyping based on facial attractiveness.

Overview of the development of attractiveness preferences

Infants demonstrate reliable preferences for attractive female faces very early in development. Their preference for attractive female faces most likely results from infants' experience with faces, because we do not see the same robust preference for attractive male faces. As infants continue to develop, they show differential social responses to attractive and unattractive females, and they begin to associate positive traits with attractive female faces and negative traits with unattractive female faces. By the end of their first year, infants' preferential looking toward attractive female faces has transitioned to the rudiments of 'beauty is good' stereotyping.

Perceiving emotional expressions

Infants' differential social responses are elicited not only by facial attractiveness, but also by emotional expressions. As infants develop, they begin to look to their caregivers for cues about how to react during novel situations, such as whether to approach or to avoid a stranger. For example, mom's smiling face tells a young infant that they can safely approach a person or object, whereas mom's fearful face tells the baby to stay away (Striano & Rochat, 2000). This phenomenon is called **social referencing** and is one more reason why infants attend to faces more than other objects in the environment.

Recognizing and discriminating emotional expressions

Before infants understand facial expressions and what emotions they signify, babies must be able to recognize the featural or configural differences among facial expressions. Using live models, newborns as young as 1–2 days old can discriminate and imitate certain facial expressions, such as happy, sad, and surprised (Field *et al.*, 1983). By 3 months, infants can use pictures of faces to discriminate between their mother or a female stranger posing different facial expressions, such as smiling and frowning (Barrera & Maurer, 1981). Moreover, studies assessing 7-month-olds' ERP responses show distinct neural responses to happy and fearful expressions (Nelson & de Haan, 1996). To some extent, the infant's emotional environment (degree of maternal positive emotionality and depression) and the infant's familiarity with the person portraying the facial expression, affect the development of discrimination ability (e.g., de Haan, Belsky, Reid, Volein & Johnson, 2004). In addition, many studies report that infant girls are more advanced at processing emotional expression than infant boys (McClure, 2000).

Just because young infants recognize that one facial expression is different from another, does not mean that they actually understand the meaning of the emotions associated with different facial expressions. Rather, it is more likely that infants are responding to some change in features (e.g., teeth showing vs. not showing) and the ability to detect these featural changes allows them to later associate emotion with these different expressions in a meaningful way (Nelson, 1987).

Categorization of emotional expressions

It is important for infants to detect changes in facial expression for any individual with whom they interact, but it is also important for babies to recognize that similar facial expressions displayed by different individuals signify the same emotion. For example, infants need to recognize that smiling faces belong to the same category (happiness), regardless of the particular face displaying smiling happiness, regardless of whether or not teeth are showing, and regardless of whether or not the smile is intense or mild. Most researchers suggest infants can categorize some emotions between 4 and 7 months of age (see Chapter 12).

Infants do not learn all categories of facial expressions at the same point in development. For instance, Nelson and Dolgin (1985) found that 7-month-old infants categorize happy faces, but not fearful faces. Infants may categorize happy facial expressions before fearful facial expressions because, on average, they are more familiar with happy than with fearful facial expressions (Kotsoni, de Haan & Johnson, 2001). Infants categorize familiar emotions first and then categorize less familiar emotional expressions later in development. This developmental trend suggests that although some ability to recognize facial expressions may be innate, some experience with particular facial expressions, or perhaps faces in general, is necessary for infant categorization of facial expressions to develop (Ludemann & Nelson, 1988).

Infants 7 months of age and older can categorize across facial expressions even when they vary in intensity (Figure 11.10), meaning that they recognize

Figure 11.10 Can infants recognize faces varying in intensity of expression? By 7 months of age, infants can recognize these faces belong to the same category (i.e., happy expressions), even though they differ in intensity of smiling. Figure from 'Categorical representation of facial expressions by 7-month-old infants' by P. M. Ludemann and C. A. Nelson, in *Developmental Psychology*, copyright © 1998 by the American Psychological Association, reproduced by permission of the publisher.

that faces varying from mild to extreme happiness belong to the same category (Kotsoni et al., 2001). Facial expressions do need to be prototypical (i.e., a good example), however, for infants younger than 10 months to recognize that particular expressions belong to the same category. A facial expression is considered prototypical when most of the adults who view the face can accurately classify the emotion being portrayed (Ludemann, 1991). Infants younger than 10 months cannot categorize faces according to general affective tone; they do not group together different types of positive facial expressions nor do they group together different types of negative facial expressions. For example, infants younger than 10 months do not categorize happy and surprised faces as belonging together (positive emotions) or angry and fearful faces as belonging together (negative emotions). Rather, infants less than 10 months categorize according to specific facial expressions (e.g., happy faces), which suggests they require a high degree of featural consistency to recognize the similarities among different people displaying the same emotion (Ludemann, 1991).

This brings us to the question of how infants are able to categorize emotional expressions. Most infants under 8 months of age rely upon featural information (such as whether teeth are showing or not) to categorize facial expressions. By 8 months of age, however, infants use both featural and expressive aspects of the faces. To illustrate, Caron, Caron, and Myers (1985) found that 8- and 9.5-month-old infants attended to both the presence or absence of teeth as well as the type of expression (smiling vs. angry) when categorizing facial expressions. Kestenbaum and Nelson (1990) further investigated this phenomenon and found that 7-month-old infants will use configural information (i.e., the type of expression) to categorize emotions when this is the only information available. When changes in salient features, such as toothiness, are available, however, these features will override infants' use of expression when categorizing emotions. Although toothiness has been mentioned as the feature infants focus on while categorizing emotional expressions, they also use other features, such as the eye and brow areas. When the mouth is covered, 7-month-old infants can accurately categorize facial expressions by attending to changes in the eye and brow areas (Walker-Andrews, 1986). Thus, the actual facial features used to categorize particular expressions will differ according to the faces being seen and which features vary with the change in expression.

Understanding emotional expressions

We have discussed infants' abilities to discriminate and categorize particular emotional expressions, but displaying these abilities does not necessarily mean that infants understand the affective tone these expressions convey. Behavioral studies that assess infants' knowledge of the emotion or how the emotion affects the infant are necessary to investigate their understanding of emotion.

One way researchers have investigated infants' understanding of emotion is by testing their ability to match a facial expression with a sound or a voice depicting that particular emotion. For example, infants listened to a recording of a person speaking in an angry voice played through a speaker while they viewed two faces on either side of the speaker, a happy face and an angry face (Walker-Andrews, 1986). Seven-month-olds in these studies looked longer at a face displaying the same emotional expression as the voice being played than at a face displaying a different emotional expression. This matching of the face and voice, which is called **intermodal matching**, suggests that infants at this age may construe meaning from emotional expressions (Phillips *et al.*, 1990).

Another way researchers have assessed infants' understanding of emotion is by coding their behavioral responses to different facial expressions. Serrano *et al.* (1995) found that 4- to 6-month-olds showed more positive behaviors in response to happy facial expressions, more negative behaviors in response to angry facial expressions, and no difference between positive and negative behaviors in response to neutral expressions. These results suggest that even 4-month-olds have some understanding of the affective meaning of different facial expressions.

Overview of the development of the perception of facial expression

During the first 3 months of life, infants can detect changes in the facial expressions of individuals. Sometime between 4 and 7 months of age, they can categorize some facial expressions, meaning that they can recognize the same facial expression among different individuals. Infants first learn more familiar categories of emotional expressions and they rely upon simple featural information to categorize faces based on emotional expression. As they develop, they begin using configural information to categorize facial expressions, allowing them to recognize certain expressions regardless of slight variations among the features. Finally, as infants develop categorical knowledge of facial expressions, they also develop an understanding of what emotions some of these expressions signify starting sometime around 4–6 months of age. Research suggests infants may be born with an ability to detect differences in emotional expressions, but that they also require experience with faces to obtain categorical knowledge and meaning from these expressions.

Role of faces for social development

Understanding emotional expressions is not the only way infants learn to guide their social behavior. Social interactions also instruct them in the natural flow of 'give and take' during social exchange and regulate emotional arousal (e.g., Haley & Stansbury, 2003). Infants begin to expect caregivers to respond reciprocally and consistently with eye gaze and facial expressions during these interactions.

Eye contact and eye gaze

At 2 months, infants begin to look at faces much more frequently than previously, particularly within the eye region (Haith, Bergman & Moore, 1977), which suggests that infants now perceive the face (or at least the eyes) as something socially meaningful. The exchange of eye gaze between infants and their caregivers plays an important role in the development of their social bond. Support for this idea comes from evidence that infants look more at the eye region when an adult is talking, which encourages the adult to continue talking and participate in a social exchange because the infant is paying attention (Haith *et al.*, 1977).

Because infants look at the eyes of the person with whom they are interacting, it is important for the interacting person to maintain their gaze with the infant. When the interacting person shifts their direction of gaze away from the infant's eyes during an interaction, infants smile less and sometimes decrease their looking at the adult (Symons, Hains & Muir, 1998). These shifts in gaze do not need to be extremely large, but they do need to indicate a disruption of the social interaction. For example, small shifts in gaze by the adult from the infant's eyes to one of the infant's ears can cause the infant's behavior to change. Small shifts in gaze to the infant's head or chin, however, do not cause the infant's behavior to change because shifts to these areas of the face can help determine a person's emotional expression and may be perceived as a normal part of social interactions (Figure 11.11). Infants are particularly sensitive to small deviations in the interacting person's eye gaze and they seem to depend on this information for directing social interactions (Symons *et al.*, 1998).

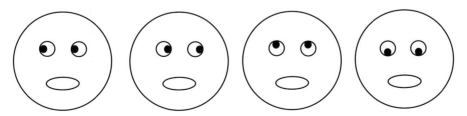

Figure 11.11 What happens if you stop looking directly at an infant's eyes while interacting with them? If a person interacting with an infant shifts their eye gaze to the right or left, as shown by the first two faces above, infants smile less and react to this change in eye gaze as a disruption of the social interaction. However, if a person interacting with an infant shifts their eye gaze up or down, as shown by the other two faces, infants do not react to this change.

Social expectations

Although breaking eye contact with infants alters how they behave within a social interaction, it does not produce as much negative impact as when a person's facial behavior unexpectedly changes during their interaction with the infant (Hains & Muir, 1996a). Early in development, infants depend upon their caretakers to structure their interactions. During these interactions, the caretaker and infant take turns gazing and smiling at each other's face. Based on their experience with these interactions, infants begin to form expectancies about social exchanges, and a violation of these expectancies affects the infant.

The most common way researchers investigate disruptions in social exchange is through a method known as the **still-face situation**, which was originally developed by Tronick, Als, Adamson, Wise, and Brazelton (1978). Generally, researchers investigate 1- to 6-month-olds in such situations and the sequence of events is as follows: the mother and infant play together for several minutes; the mother then poses with an expressionless face for several minutes; and this is followed by a 'reunion' session during which the mother and infant play again for several minutes to restore normal interactions. Infants' reactions to the still-face situation are of interest to face perception researchers because their reactions appear to be driven more by changes in the mother's facial expression than by changes in tactile or vocal expression (e.g., Adamson & Frick, 2003).

How exactly do infants respond to such situations? Most infants display positive affect and look at both their mothers and objects in the room during the first play session. During the still-face portion, however, most infants display neutral affect, although some infants respond with protest and negative affect (Mayes & Carter, 1990). They also look at their mothers very little and look around the room or focus on objects when their mothers are expressionless. Infants make pick-me-up gestures, twist and turn in their infant seat, and hiccup and spit up more during the still-face portion. Their heart rate also tends to increase during this episode. It appears that infants first start off with the goal of resuming normal interaction during this situation, but when they are unsuccessful, they withdraw from the interaction and look around the room. Finally, during the reunion play episode, infants display both positive and negative affect, greatly increase their looking to their mother's face, and show little interest in looking at objects in the room. At this point, most infants are happy to have their mothers resume normal interactions, but this happiness tends to be mixed with the emotions carried over from the still-face episode (Weinberg & Tronick, 1996).

Most studies have investigated the effects of the still-face situation using the mother in a live setting, but similar effects occur with the use of videos (Muir & Hains, 1993), with fathers (Braungart-Riker, Garwood, Powers & Notaro, 1998), and even with strangers (Hains & Muir, 1996b). As mentioned earlier, the still-face effect appears to be driven primarily by changes in facial expression, but these effects do not seem to occur simply due to the adult's face changing from dynamic to static. Rather, they occur because the initial play session with the adult set up expectancies in the infant concerning the quality of the interaction. The changes in infant affect and attention that occur during the still-face episode appear based on how infants perceived the person's facial expressions during that interaction compared to the previous one. This important skill of perceiving social interactions depends on the infant's basic abilities to perceive and understand faces.

SUMMARY

Now that you have finished reading this chapter, think back to the party discussed at the beginning and the question, 'How would a newborn perceive faces at the party?' As long as the faces are close enough to see, newborns will show much interest in the guests' faces. Aside from their mother, it is unlikely newborns will recognize anyone else in the room. Newborns may spend more time looking at the attractive guests if they can see several guests who differ in attractiveness. They most likely can detect changes in the guests' facial expressions, even though they probably do not know what these expressions signify. Last, newborns may be starting to form expectancies of facial behavior during social interactions. To review more, think about how you would answer the above question if the infant was 3, 6, 9, or 12 months of age. Consider what face-perception abilities change and how these develop. It is amazing what types of information babies get from looking at faces by the end of their first 2 years of life.

ACKNOWLEDGEMENTS

Preparation of this manuscript was supported by two grants from the National Institute of Child Health and Human Development, one granted to Jennifer Ramsey (HD48467) and one granted to Judith Langlois (HD21332).

CHAPTER TWELVE

Early emotional development

MICHAEL LEWIS

Introduction

If we observe newborn infants, we see a narrow range of emotional behavior. They cry and show distress when pained or lonely or in need of food and attention. They look attentive and focused on objects and people in their world. They listen to sounds, look at objects, and respond to being tickled. Moreover, they seem to show positive emotions, such as happiness and contentment. When fed, picked up, or changed, they show relaxed body posture, they smile, and they appear content. Although they show a wide range of postural and even facial expressions, the set of discrete emotions that they exhibit is limited. Yet, in a matter of months and, indeed, by the end of the third year of life, these same children display the full range of human emotions. For example, they show shame when they fail a task and pride when they succeed. Indeed, some have suggested that by this age, almost the full range of adult emotions can be said to exist (Lewis, 1992b). In 3 years, the display and range of human emotions goes from a few to the highly differentiated many.

In order to understand emotional development, we need to look at infant and toddler behavior in both the emotional and cognitive domains, for emotions and their developments are completely tied to cognitive developments. In fact, we often use emotions to infer cognitions and cognitions to infer emotions. For example, when young infants see a small adult (a dwarf) walking toward them, they show a face that can be scored as a surprise face. What are they surprised at? They are not surprised when they see a young child or an adult of normal height walking toward them, but they are when it is someone with the height of a young child but the face of an adult (Lewis & Brooks-Gunn, 1982). Surprise reveals to us who observe infants that the infant knows (has cognitions about) the relationship between facial configuration and body height. The discrepancy is what elicits surprise and informs us that the infant knows about the face–body relationship.

One particular cognition that is most important to the development of human emotions is that of self-knowledge or a **meta-representation** or idea that 'this is me' (Lewis, 1999). This idea of me is the same as **consciousness**. We measure it by observing whether infants/toddlers recognize themselves in mirrors. The emergence of self-knowledge or consciousness alters old emotions and gives rise to new ones. To understand emotional development, then, means that we have to understand cognitive changes and, in particular, the development of self.

In the discussion of emotional development, we can think of two broad types of emotions, those that we call **basic or primary emotions** and those that we call **self-conscious emotions**. The former are emotions that most likely are present in humans and other animals. The latter, self-conscious emotions, require elaborate cognitions including the central one having to do with consciousness; that is, the idea of 'me.' Charles Darwin in his famous work (1872/1965) was the first to make the distinction between these two types. He believed that a self was necessary in order for these later emotions to emerge. Moreover, he thought that they emerge around 3 years in the human child. He described blushing—a reddening of the facial skin—and suggested that blushing was a measure of these self-conscious emotions which for him involved elaborate cognitions involving 'the self thinking about others, thinking of us . . . which excites a blush' (p. 325).

A model of emotional development

Most of emotional life emerges over the first 3 years. Although not all emotions appear, the great majority are present in the 3-year-old. This is not to say that other emotions do not emerge after 3 years of age, or that the emotions that have emerged are not elaborated more fully. They do; however, the major framework exists by the age of 3. In our discussion of development, we will divide the chapter into three sections: (1) early or primary emotions; (2) the development of self-consciousness; and (3) self-conscious emotions. Figure 12.1 presents our model of emotional development. For example, we can see that in the first 6 months, the **primary emotions** appear and are the first to emerge. About the middle of the second year of life, consciousness emerges, which gives rise to the first set of self-conscious emotions. In the middle of the third year, or at about 2 1/2 years of age, the child acquires and is able to use societal standards and rules in order to evaluate their behavior. This second cognitive milestone, along with consciousness, gives rise to the second set of self-conscious emotions, those that are called **self-conscious evaluative emotions**.

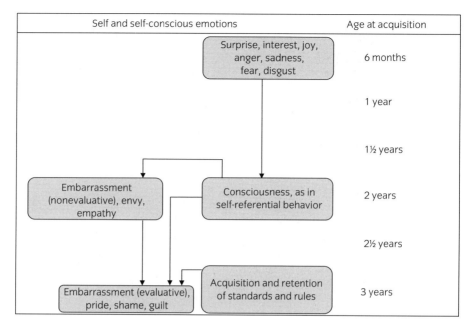

Self and self-conscious emotions	Age at acquisition
Surprise, interest, joy, anger, sadness, fear, disgust	6 months
	1 year
	1½ years
Embarrassment (nonevaluative), envy, empathy / Consciousness, as in self-referential behavior	2 years
	2½ years
Embarrassment (evaluative), pride, shame, guilt / Acquisition and retention of standards and rules	3 years

Figure 12.1 Behavioral experiments have led to a model of the emergence of self-conscious emotions. Some noncognitive, primary emotions are evident at birth; others emerge by the age of 6 months. Sometime in the middle of the second year, the child develops a sense of self, as evidenced by the emergence of self-referential behaviors. At this time emotions such as envy and empathy emerge. The child will also express self-conscious embarrassment when looked at, pointed at, or singled out in some way. Between the ages of 2½ and 3 years, the child starts to incorporate a set of standards, rules, and goals. The child also develops a sense of success and failure and the ability to determine whether they have lived up to expectations. At that point, between the ages of 2½ and 3 years, the child shows signs of complex self-conscious emotions. The child can express shame in its extreme forms and in its milder manifestation of embarrassment, as well as pride and guilt.

Early or primary emotions

These early emotions are present within the first 6 months or so of life. Following Bridges (1932), we assume that at birth the child shows a bipolar emotional life. On one hand, there is general **distress** marked by crying and irritability. On the other hand, there is **pleasure** marked by satiation, attention, and responsivity to the environment. Attention to the environment and interest in it appears from the beginning of life and we can place this either in the positive pole or, if we choose, we can separate this; thus, we suggest a tripartite division with pleasure at one end, distress at the other, and interest as a separate dimension (see Figure 12.1).

By 3 months, **joy** emerges (Figure 12.2). Infants start to smile and appear to show excitement/happiness when confronted with familiar events, such as

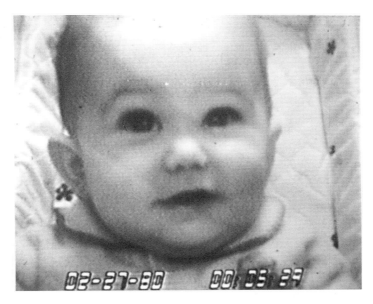

Figure 12.2 Joy face.

faces of people they know or even unfamiliar faces. Very early smiling to people and sounds appear to be reflective in nature. For example, sighted and blind infants do not differ in their smiling behavior in the first 3 months of life (Fraiberg, 1974). Later, however, smiling becomes more associated with pleasant events that the infant sees, such as the face of its mother, father, or older sibling. Smiling also now takes place when the infant is played with. Therefore, smiling after 2 months is not reflective and is related to the emotion of joy or happiness.

Also by 3 months, **sadness** emerges, especially around the withdrawal or loss of desired objects or actions (Figure 12.3). Three-month-old children show sadness when their mothers stop interacting with them. For example, when mothers sit opposite their 3-month-olds and play with them, smiling faces, even laughter, can be observed. However, this laughter and smiling turns to sadness and even anger when the infant's mother turns away from them. At this point, the child often becomes sad and in some cases even starts to cry. This sad expression disappears once the mother starts again to interact with the child.

Disgust also appears in its early form (Figure 12.4). Disgust is seen when infants spit out and try to get rid of unpleasant-tasting or -smelling objects placed in their mouths. This disgust face appears to be a defensive reflect designed to help get rid of food which does not smell or taste good to the infant. Given that there is little hand–mouth or grasping coordination, the infant's ability to spit out something unpleasant is an important adaptive response. As we will see, this early form of disgust becomes utilized later

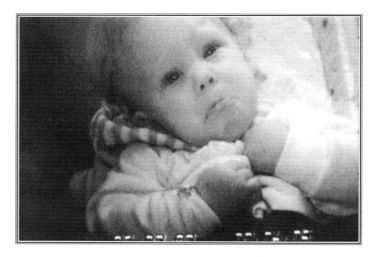

Figure 12.3 Sad face.

when it then reflects learned taste and smell aversion, such as specific food preferences. Thus, by 3 months, children are already showing interest, joy, sadness, anger, and disgust, and exhibit these expressions in appropriate contexts.

Anger has been reported to emerge between 4 and 6 months (Stenberg, Campos & Emde, 1983). Anger is seen on the face when children are frustrated, in particular when their hands and arms are pinned down and they are prevented from moving (Figure 12.5). However, Lewis, Alessandri, and Sullivan (1990) have shown anger in 2-month-old infants when a learned instrumental act was blocked. For example, a 2-month-old child can be taught that when they pull their arm, to which a string has been attached, a slide appears on the screen. Thus, every time the child pulls, a picture goes on. After only 3–5 minutes, most 2-month-olds learn the association between moving their arm and a picture appearing. Once they learn this, they show anger if we arrange it so that the picture does not come on. This study demonstrates the earliest known emergence of anger. Anger is a particularly interesting emotion since, from Darwin (1872/1965) on, it has been associated with unique cognitive capacities. Anger is thought to be both a set of facial and motor/body responses designed to overcome an obstacle. Notice that in this definition of anger, the organism has to have some knowledge about the relation between the arm pull and picture going on. For anger to be said to be adaptive it has to be a response whose function is to overcome a barrier blocking a goal. In some sense then, **means–ends knowledge** has to be available and the demonstration of anger at this early point in life reflects the child's early knowledge acquisition relative to this ability (Lewis, 1991).

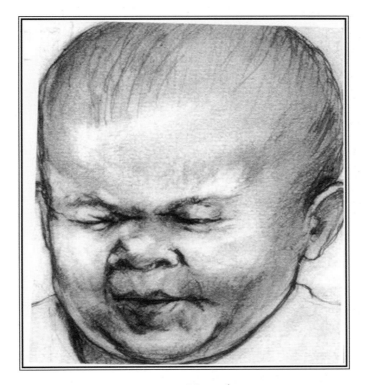

Figure 12.4 Disgust face.

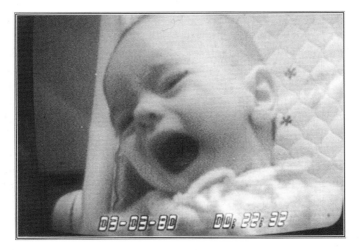

Figure 12.5 Anger face.

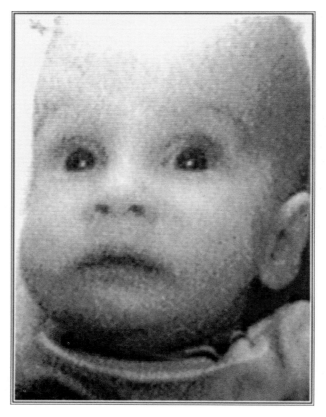

Figure 12.6 Fear face.

Fearfulness seems to emerge still later (Figure 12.6). Our best guess is that it is around 6–8 months, although it appears to reach its peak at 18 months, when measured as fearfulness at the approach of a stranger. Again, fearfulness reflects further cognitive development. For example, Schaffer (1974) has shown that in order for children to show fearfulness they have to be capable of comparing the event that causes them fearfulness with some other event. For example, in **stranger fear** the infant has to compare the face of the stranger coming toward it to that of its internal representation or memory of faces. Fear occurs when the approaching face is found to be discrepant or unfamiliar relative to all other faces that the child remembers. Children's ability to show fearfulness in these situations cannot emerge until a comparison ability appears. Children around 6–8 months of age begin to show this behavior, although it has been reported by some to occur even earlier, especially in children who seem to be precocious.

Surprise also appears in the first 6 months of life (Figure 12.7). Children show surprise when there are violations of expected events; for example,

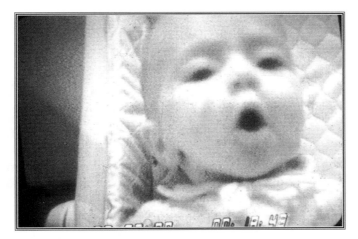

Figure 12.7 Surprise face.

when infants see a small adult walking toward them, they are reported to show interest and surprise rather than fear or joy (Lewis & Brooks-Gunn, 1978). Surprise can be seen when there is violation of what is expected or as a response to discovery as in an 'aha' experience. In the studies where children were taught to pull a string in order to turn on a picture, they showed surprise at the point when they discovered that the arm pull is what caused the picture to appear (Lewis, Sullivan & Michalson, 1984). Surprise here reflects insight.

In the first 6–8 months of life, children's emotional behavior reflects the emergence of the six early emotions, called by some primary emotions or basic emotions (see e.g., Izard, 1978; Tomkins, 1962). The cognitive processes that underlie these early emotions consist of perceptual abilities, including discrimination and short-term memory, and are representative abilities of some sort. Although these cognitive processes are necessary, it is likely that many species in the animal kingdom possess them. They do not require the elaborate cognitions that are involved in the next set of emotions. For example, anger is elicited in animals as well as infants when a learned response to obtain a goal is blocked. Infants show angry faces when the string pull does not produce the picture, and rats show angry behavior when the learned path to food is blocked.

Self-consciousness

As we have tried to indicate, the development of the early or primary emotions requires some cognition. One cognition that they do not have in the first 6 months, but do acquire in the middle of the second year, is the cognition related to self or what we have called **consciousness**. Infants younger than 8–9 months of age show all the basic emotions. The question is, do they experience them? If we think of facial expressions representing an internal emotional **state**, then we can say that infants have a happy state. However, before consciousness emerges, they may **have** the state, but do not **experience** the state. For example, emotional experience requires that the child knows it is having the emotional state. Consider that when we say 'I am frightened,' or 'I am happy,' the subject and object is the same, one's self. Thus, the statement, 'I am happy,' implies two things. First, it implies that I have an internal state called happiness, and second, that I perceive that internal state in myself. Until the child is capable of consciousness, the ability to experience the primary emotions does not exist. Consider this example:

Susan, a 7-month-old, sits in a chair watching a stranger move toward her. When the stranger reaches over to touch her hand, Susan pulls it away and begins to cry.

Susan's behavior, her crying, pushing away, and fearful face, suggests she is in a **state** of fear. However, if we ask whether she is **conscious** of being fearful, we would have to conclude that she is not. From a variety of studies we know that consciousness does not emerge until the second half of the second year. As such, we may say that, although Susan is in a state of fear, she is not aware of herself as being fearful. Thus, from a developmental perspective, it is reasonable to believe that Susan has a disassociation between the emotional state and her experience of that state. That state and experience of emotions can be disconnected is easily seen in adults who possess both state and consciousness.

Michelle is driving a car on a highway. As she is traveling at 65 mph, her left front tire blows. For the next 20 seconds, Michelle's attention is focused on getting the car to a safe spot off the road. Only when she has finally stopped the car does she **experience** her fearfulness.

We would hold that although Michelle was in a **state** of fear before stopping her car, she could not **experience** her fear (was not conscious of it) until she could focus her attention on herself. Thus, as in the case of the 7-month-old child, there is a dissociation between state and experience (Lewis & Michalson, 1983).

The idea of consciousness, our ability to experience ourselves, is best captured by looking at R. D. Laing's book *Knots* (1970). Laing argued for the importance and uniqueness of the human capacity for **self-reflexive behavior**. Such behavior can be observed in verb usage, for example, the difference when one makes reference to washing oneself as opposed to washing anything other than self. In French the verb structure would be *se laver* for washing oneself as opposed to *faire la vaisselle* for washing the dishes. Such reflexive behavior is seen as well in the social knots as described by Laing. Consider the example: 'I know my wife knows that I know that she knows that I bought a new tie.' Such an example of reflexive behavior implies that not only do I have knowledge of myself, but also I have knowledge of someone else's self having knowledge of myself. Such complex recursive behavior is what must be considered when we discuss consciousness or experience, especially from a developmental perspective. Consciousness, that is, thinking about the self, does not emerge until the second half of the second year of life. Moreover, we have been able to demonstrate that the emergence is dependent on a certain level of general mental maturity.

We study this by looking at infants' responses to mirrors. We place children in front of the mirror and look at what they do. For the most part, they look briefly and then turn away. After this initial exposure, we place a red dot on the child's nose and place the child back in front of the mirror (the 'rouge on the nose' test, mentioned in Chapter 1 and 2). At this point, the child has two possible responses; they can touch the mirror and the image or they can use the mirror to direct their fingers to touch their own noses. No child before the age of 15 months old touches their nose, while at 15 months approximately 20% do so. If the children are developing normally, 100% will touch their own noses by 24 months (Lewis & Brooks-Gunn, 1979). At the same time and in conjunction with this self-recognition, two additional features of their knowledge about themselves emerge. First, the development of personal pronouns such as 'me' and 'mine' and second, pretend play where the child pretends that the crayon is an airplane, even though they know it is not (Lewis & Ramsay, 2004)!

When consciousness emerges, and there is reason to believe that this is a maturational process common to all humans, the next set of emotions—the self-conscious emotions—start to appear.

Self-conscious emotions

Figure 12.1 shows the next step in emotional development. Once consciousness emerges, so do at least three new emotions: **empathy**, **jealousy**, and **exposure embarrassment**. These emotions require, at least, a sense of self. For example, empathy, by definition, involves the ability to put yourself in the role of another. So, for example, if I know that I am likely to feel unease in a strange social situation, I am able to utilize my own feeling to assume that you (another person) are also likely to feel unease. In one of the only studies to look at the association between self-recognition and empathy, Bischof-Kohler (1991) found that only after infants gain the ability to recognize themselves in mirrors were they able to show empathy, both on their faces (as in a sad expression), as well as in their actions (such as tapping the back of someone they imagine is sad). Likewise for jealousy. We need to have consciousness for jealousy, since jealousy is the emotion associated with wanting for the self what someone else has. Without a self or consciousness, it would not be possible to have jealousy.

Finally, the emotion of embarrassment is dependent on consciousness. We will discuss two kinds of embarrassment; the first one we call **exposure embarrassment** and the second one **evaluative embarrassment**. We will leave the evaluative embarrassment until later since it requires cognitions that only appear after 2 years of age.

In certain situations of exposure, people become embarrassed. It is not related to negative evaluation, as is shame. Perhaps the best example is the case of being complimented. The phenomenological experience of those who appear before audiences is that of embarrassment caused by the positive comments of the introduction. Consider the moment when the speaker is introduced: The person introducing the speaker extols his or her virtues. Surprisingly, praise, rather than displeasure or negative evaluation, elicits this type of embarrassment!

Another example of this type of embarrassment can be seen in our reactions to public display. When people observe someone looking at them, they are apt to become self-conscious, look away, or touch or adjust their bodies. When the observed person is a woman, she will often adjust or touch her hair; men are less likely to touch their hair, but may adjust their clothes or change their body posture. In few cases do the observed people look sad. If anything, they appear pleased by the attention. This combination—gaze turned away briefly, no frown, and nervous touching—looks like this first type of embarrassment.

A third example of embarrassment as exposure can be seen in the following experiment:

When I wish to demonstrate that embarrassment can be elicited just by exposure, I announce that I am going to point randomly at a student. I repeatedly mention that my pointing is random and that it does not reflect a judgment about the person. I close my eyes and point. My pointing invariably elicits embarrassment in the student pointed to. (Lewis, 2003)

In each of these examples, there is no negative evaluation of the self in regard to standards or rules. In these situations, it is difficult to imagine embarrassment as a less intense form of shame. Since praise cannot readily lead to an evaluation of failure, it is likely that embarrassment resulting from compliments, from being looked at, and from being pointed to has more to do with the exposure of the self than with evaluation. Situations other than praise come to mind in which a negative evaluation can be inferred, although it may not be the case. Take, for example, walking into a room before the speaker has started to talk. It is possible to arrive on time, only to find people already seated. When you are walking into the room, eyes turn toward you, and you may experience embarrassment. One could say that there is a negative self-evaluation: 'I should have been earlier; I should

Figure 12.8 Embarrassment figure.

not have made noise (I did not make noise).' I believe, however, that the embarrassment in this case may not be elicited by negative self-evaluation, but simply by public exposure. Figure 12.8 demonstrates the face and body posture associated with embarrassment.

These three emotions, at least, require the emergence of consciousness but do not require that the child be able to evaluate their behavior against some standard or rule which they have learned from the people around them. This occurs only later.

Self-conscious evaluative emotions

The self-conscious evaluative emotions depend on the development of a number of cognitive skills. First, children have to have absorbed a set of standards, rules, and goals. Second, they have to have a sense of self. And finally, they have to be able to evaluate the self with regard to those standards, rules, and goals and then make a determination of success and failure.

As a first step in self-evaluation, a child has to decide whether a particular event is the result of his own action. If, for example, an object breaks while the child is using it, he might blame himself for breaking it, or he might decide the object was faulty to begin with. If he places the blame on himself, he is making an **internal attribution**. If he does not blame himself, he is making an **external evaluation** and is not likely to go on to the next step of evaluation.

Whether a child is inclined to make an internal or an external attribution depends on the situation and on the child's own characteristics. Some people are likely to blame themselves no matter what happens. Dweck and Leggett (1988) studied children's attitudes toward their academic performance. They found that some children attributed their success or failure to external forces. Others were likely to evaluate success and failure in terms of their own actions. Interestingly, strong sex differences emerged: Boys are more apt to hold themselves responsible for their success and others for their failure, whereas girls are apt to do the opposite.

Psychologists still do not entirely understand how people decide what constitutes success or failure after they have assumed responsibility for an event. This aspect of self-evaluation is particularly important, because the same standards, rules, and goals can result in radically different emotions, depending on whether success or failure is attributed to oneself. Sometimes children assess their actions in ways that do not conform to the evaluation that others might give them. Many factors are involved in producing inaccurate or unique evaluations. These include early failures in the self system, leading to narcissistic disorders, harsh socialization experience, and high levels of reward for success or punishment for failure (Hoffman, 1988; Kohut, 1977; Morrison, 1986). The evaluation of one's own behavior in terms of success and failure plays a very important role in shaping an individual's goals and new plans.

In a final evaluation step, a child determines whether success or failure is global or specific. Global attributions come about when a child is inclined to focus on the total self (Abramson, Seligman & Teasdale, 1978). Some children, some of the time, attribute the success or failure of a particular action to the total self: They use such self-evaluative phrases as 'I am bad (or good).' On such occasions, the focus is not on the behavior but on the whole self. The self becomes embroiled in the self, because the self-evaluation is total. There is no way out. Using such global attribution results in thinking of nothing else but the self. During these times, especially when the global evaluation is negative, a child becomes confused and speechless. The child is unable to act and is driven away from action, wanting to hide or disappear (H. B. Lewis, 1971).

In some situations children make specific attributions, focusing on specific actions. Thus, it is not the total self that has done something wrong or good; instead, a particular behavior is judged. Consider the child who has not solved a puzzle in the set time period they were asked to do. At such times, children will use an evaluative phrase as, 'I forgot to look at all the pieces. Next time I'll look at them all.' Notice that the child's focus here is not on the totality of the self but on the specific behavior of the self in a specific situation. When they focus on specific features of their behavior, their attribution is specific not global.

The tendency to make **global or specific attributions** may be a personality style (Beck, 1979). Global attributions for negative events are generally uncorrelated with global attributions for positive events (Abramson *et al.*, 1978). It is only when positive or negative events are taken into account that relatively stable and consistent attributional patterns are observed (Kaslow,

Ream, Pollack & Siegel, 1988). Some children are likely to be stable in their global and specific evaluations under most conditions of success or failure. Such factors are thought to have important consequences for a variety of fixed personality patterns. For example, Beck (1979) and others have found that depressed people are likely to make stable, negative, global attributions, whereas nondepressed individuals are less likely to be stable in their global attributions.

Shame and guilt

Of all the self-conscious emotions, **shame**, until recently, has been the most undervalued in its power to motivate human behavior. Earlier theorists tended to attribute certain actions to guilt, but many psychologists now believe that shame is the more appropriate underlying emotion (Janoff-Bulman, 1979; Buss, 1980; H. B. Lewis, 1987; Lewis, 1992a,b).

Shame results when a child judges her actions as a failure in regard to her standards, rules, and goals and then makes a global attribution. The child experiencing shame wishes to hide, disappear, or die (H. B. Lewis, 1971; Lewis, 1992a,b). It is a highly negative and painful state that also disrupts ongoing behavior and causes confusion in thought and an inability to speak. The body of the shamed child seems to shrink, as if to disappear from the eye of the self or others (see Figure 12.9). Because of the intensity of this emotional state, and the global attack on the self-system, all that children can do when presented with such a state is to attempt to rid themselves of it.

Some children try to dissociate the shameful feelings from themselves. The most severe manifestation of this is in people with multiple personality disorder, where a child tries to create other selves to bear the shame (Ross,

Figure 12.9 Shame face.

1989). Often it is a child who has seriously traumatic incidents such as childhood sexual abuse who takes refuge in this way. It is not the sexual abuse that creates the disorder; it is the shame brought about by the abuse (Feiring, Taska & Lewis, 2002; Lewis, 1992a,b).

Shame is not produced by any specific situation, but rather by an individual's interpretation of an event. Even more important is the observation that shame is not necessarily related to whether the event is public or private. Failure attributed to the whole self can be public or private, and can center around moral as well as social action.

If shame arises from a global attribution of failure, **guilt** arises from a specific attribution (Ferguson, Stegge & Damhuis, 1991; Tangney & Dearing, 2002). Guilt and regret are produced when a child evaluates her behavior as a failure, but focuses on the specific features of the self that led to the failure. A guilty child is likely to consider actions and behaviors that are likely to repair the failure. Guilty individuals are pained by their evaluation of failure, but the pain is directed to the cause of the failure or the object of harm. Because the cognitive attributional process focuses on the action of the self rather than on the totality of self, the feeling produced is not as intensely negative as shame and does not lead to confusion and the loss of action. In fact, guilt almost always has associated with it a corrective action that the child can take (but does not necessarily do so) to repair the failure and prevent it from happening again (Barrett, 1995). In guilt, the self is differentiated from the object. The emotion is thus less intense and more capable of dissipation.

Guilt and shame have different physical manifestations as well. Whereas a shamed child hunches over in an attempt to hide or disappear, a guilty person moves in space as if trying to repair the action. The marked postural differences between guilt and shame are helpful both in distinguishing these emotions and in measuring individual differences.

Hubris

Self-consciousness is not entirely a negative thing. Self-evaluation can also lead to positive and even overly positive emotions. **Hubris**, defined as exaggerated pride or self-confidence, is an example of the latter. Hubris is the emotion elicited when success with regard to one's standards, rules, and goals is applied to a child's entire self. It is the global condition. Children inclined to be hubristic evaluate their actions positively and then say to themselves: 'I have succeeded. I am a success.' Often, hubris is considered an unlikeable trait that should be avoided.

Hubris is difficult to sustain because of its globality. The feeling is generated by a nonspecific action. Because such a feeling is alluring, yet transient, children prone to hubris ultimately derive little satisfaction from the emotion. Consequently, they seek out and invent situations likely to repeat this emotional state. According to Morrison (1989), this can be done either by altering their standards, rules, and goals or by reevaluating what constitutes success.

A child who considers himself globally successful may be viewed with disdain by others. Often the hubristic person is described as 'puffed up' or, in extreme cases, grandiose or narcissistic (Kohut, 1977; Morrison, 1986). The hubristic child may be perceived as insolent or contemptuous. Hubristic children have difficulty in interpersonal relations, since their hubris likely makes them insensitive to the wishes, needs, and desires of others, leading to interpersonal conflict. Moreover, given the contemptuousness associated with hubris, other children are likely to be shamed by the nature of the actions of the hubristic person. Narcissists often derive pleasure in shaming others by claiming their superiority.

Pride

If hubris is the global emotion that follows a positive assessment of an action, then **pride** is the specific emotion. A child experiencing pride feels joyful at the successful outcome of a particular action, thought, or feeling (Figure 12.10). Here the focus of pleasure is specific and related to a particular behavior. In pride, the self and object are separated, as in guilt, and unlike shame and hubris, where subject and object are fused. Heckhausen (1984, 1987) and Stipek, Recchia, and McClintic (1992) have made a particularly apt comparison between pride and achievement motivation, where succeeding at a particular goal motivates activity. Because the positive state engendered by pride is associated with a particular action, individuals have available

Figure 12.10 Pride figure.

to them the means for reproducing the emotion. Notice that pride's specific focus allows for action.

Embarrassment

Embarrassment as a consequence of evaluation of one's actions, called **evaluative embarrassment,** is closely related to shame. Embarrassment is distinguished in contrast to shame by the intensity of the latter. Whereas shame appears to be strong and disruptive, embarrassment is clearly less intense and does not involve disruption of thought and language. Furthermore, children who are embarrassed do not assume the posture of someone wishing to hide, disappear, or die. In fact, their bodies reflect an ambivalent approach and avoidance posture. An embarrassed person alternately looks at people and then looks away, smiling all the while (Edelman & Hampson, 1981). In contrast, the shamed child rarely smiles while averting her gaze. Thus, from a behavioral point of view, shame and embarrassment appear to be different.

The difference in intensity can probably be attributed to the nature of the failed standard, rule, or goal. Some standards are more or less associated with the core of self; for me, failure at driving a car is less important than is failure at helping a child. Failures associated with less important and less central standards, rules, and goals result in embarrassment rather than shame.

There are other types of evaluative self-conscious emotions, but these, pride, hubris, shame, guilt, and evaluative embarrassment, have been the ones most studied. The emergence of this class of emotions completes the major development of emotional life, creating in children both a wide array of different emotions, some more complex than others. It also includes the developmental shift from emotional **states** to emotional **experiences,** thus giving the human child the extra capacities both to have particular emotions and to be aware that they have them.

SUMMARY

By 3 years of age, the emotional life of a child has become highly differentiated. From the original tripartite set of emotions, the child comes within 3 years to possess an elaborate and complex emotional system. Although the emotional life of the 3-year-old will continue to be elaborated and will expand, the basic structures necessary for this expansion have already been formed. New experiences, additional meaning, and more elaborate cognitive capacities will all serve to enhance and elaborate the child's emotional life. However, by 3 years of age, the child already shows those emotions that Darwin (1872/1965) characterized as unique to our species—the emotions of self-consciousness. With these, the major developmental activity has been achieved.

CHAPTER THIRTEEN

Social development

MICHAEL LEWIS

Introduction

In order to understand social development, we need to remember that it is connected both to emotional and to cognitive development. For example, the nature of the infant's social life is highly dependent on those cognitions which allow for empathic behavior, since without empathic behavior the child's relationships to others cannot involve the same level of intimacy that is found when empathic behavior is present. Consider that a newborn infant will cry when she hears the cry of another child. This crying cannot be supported by empathic behavior since the newborn does not have the cognitive capacity for such a process. Rather, we say that the newborn's cry is produced by contagion; that is, an automatic response that has very little cognition associated with it. It is a well-known fact that contagion is a process to be found in all social creatures, not only in humans. Birds on a wire fly away when they see another bird flying away. Women who live together synchronize their menstrual periods. In the same way, newborns cry when they hear the cry of another infant. However, once empathy is established, somewhere around 2 years of age (see Chapter 12, 'Early Emotional Development'), the emotional response of another can produce an empathic response in the toddler. Thus, the child's sadness over the sadness of another child, and her attempt at comfort, is based not on contagion but on the toddler's being able to 'place herself in the role of the other.' This cognitive ability, associated with the emergence of consciousness and the idea of 'me,' leads to social behaviors not present until such cognitive capacities emerge.

Understanding social development also requires that we consider a child as embedded into a large network of people and activities and that we need to include not only the relationship of the child to its mother but also the other important relationships that the infant engages in from the beginning of its life. This embeddedness serves to provide the infant with many needs including protection, play, learning, and nurturance, as well as others. Part of our task is to understand the needs the young infant has. It is this network of different people and the collection of needs that the newborn child must adapt to and in which social development occurs.

In this chapter, we first address the nature of the entire social nexus in which the child is born, as well as going beyond the mother–child relationship and explore all the child's social relationships. Next, we map out how social relationships undergo developmental change and transformation as a consequence of the development of cognitive capacities; in particular, the development of consciousness. Finally, we discuss the social network and how we might understand the infant's social development.

Social nexus

By nature, humans are social animals. From the moment of birth the child is surrounded by other conspecifics, a small portion of which share the child's gene pool, a larger portion of which will influence and in turn be influenced by the child, and finally the largest portion, which forms the background in which these other interactions will take place. The smallest segment we call the family; the larger comprises lovers, friends, acquaintances, and even strangers; and the largest segment is the culture at large. Human newborns are surrounded by a large and diverse group of people, and it is within this array that the developmental processes of the child occur. Given that the major task of the newborn is the adaptation to this environment of people, it seems reasonable to assign to humans the feature of sociability. Not only must the newborn adapt to this world, but there is considerable evidence that many of the early sensory and cognitive abilities of young infants center around making sense of their social environment.

Social development is important as suggested by all the skills and biological structures that appear to be in its service. For example, much sensory processing seems keyed to social needs. Infants' discriminatory ability is greater for social than for nonsocial stimuli. By 12 weeks of age, English-speaking children can distinguish between social stimuli such as the speech sounds [pa] and [ba]. This discriminatory ability appears to be a function of social experience since infants who are not raised in an English-speaking environment are unable to distinguish these subtle differences. Nevertheless, the mechanisms which allow for this ability are not learned, but are part of the biological capacities the infant is born with. Moreover, although young infants are little interested in nonsocial stimuli, they are considerably more attentive—indexed by physiological processes—to social stimuli. Even brain structures appear more attuned to social than to nonsocial events. For instance, hemispheric differentiation for sound appears to be divided by social or speech sounds and nonsocial or all other sounds. Of equal importance to the social competence of children is the control of biological functions through social interactions. Important organizational processes, including the regulation of sleep–wake cycles, appear to result from the social interactions between caregivers and infants.

The amount of knowledge that children acquire about their social environment is incredibly vast, and the acquisition occurs rapidly. Lewis and Brooks-Gunn (1979) have shown that by the age of 9 months, infants already have some rudimentary knowledge about themselves. Moreover, children's knowledge about others also is highly developed. By 1 month, some infants and, by 3 months, most infants have some understanding of the intermodal connection between people's faces and voices. As early as 5 weeks of age, infants interact differentially with familiar persons and strangers (McGurk & Lewis, 1974). Some time between 3 and 6 months children acquire knowledge about human faces, and by 7 months they demonstrate discrimination of emotional expressions (Caron, Caron & Myers, 1982). By 3–4 months, infants begin to respond differently to children and adults, and by 6–8 months they show differential fear responses to people on the basis of gender and age. Also by 6–8 months, infants are surprised at the appearance of a small adult (i.e., a dwarf) and seem to understand that their height–facial feature integration is unusual (Lewis & Brooks, 1974). We have found that by 10 months, infants are using the facial expression and tonal quality of their mothers in their interactions with strangers. Infants are more friendly to strangers who are treated in a positive manner by their mothers (Feinman & Lewis, 1983).

People in the infant's life

Mothers are the primary focus in attachment theory, but children form important relationships and attachments with individuals other than their mothers. Some believe in a sequence; first, the relationship with their mothers, then with others. We believe that children are able to form parallel relationships with their mothers, siblings, and other caregivers at the same time. In this section we first discuss the relationship to mothers, but also consider others such as fathers, siblings, grandparents, and peers.

Mothers

Mothers play a primary role in the infant's life. The role of the mother was first clearly articulated by Sigmund Freud in his theory of socioemotional development. Psychoanalytic thought established the mother–infant bond as the primary social relationship of the child, although the conflict between the child and his mother and father, known as the Oedipus complex, also was seen as important. However, it was not until the object relation theorists, such as Melanie Klein (1930), W. R. D. Fairbairn (1952), D. W. Winnicott (1959), and Karen Horney (1939), that the idea of the mother–child dyad as the primary social relationship upon which all other social relationships were built became the central focus of study.

The relationship of the infant to its mother has been likened to a love affair and has been called **attachment**. John Bowlby (1969) described this relationship as an **affectional tie** and believed that this tie constitutes a model or representation of the child's social-affective relation with people after the first year of life. The initial representation of this attachment occurs in the first 3 months of life and has been called a dance-like interaction. During this time, the infant and its primary caregiver engage in a dance, learning how to interact with one another. The movement of this dance consists of the physical movements of each, gaze behavior, and affective attunement where the behavior of one leads to the response of the other. By the end of 9 months, the infant clearly discriminates between his mother and others and is often upset at the appearance of those he is not familiar with. This upset has been called **stranger anxiety** and is marked by attention toward the stranger, wariness, and in the extreme, fearfulness and upset when the stranger approaches. When stranger anxiety appears, the infant is now highly selective toward those she knows and those she does not.

The final phase of this attachment can be seen at 1 year of age when the infant shows a desire to be near his mother, is upset by her absence, and can use her as a secure base from which to explore his world. Bowlby, like Freud (1948), saw the infant's relationship to his mother as unique, without parallel, established unalterably for a whole lifetime as the first and strongest love object, and as the prototype of all later love relations.

Bowlby's work on attachment was further developed by Mary Ainsworth (1969) who created a paradigm for measuring attachment when the child is 1 year old. In this situation, known as the **Strange Situation**, the mother, child, and stranger are seen together in nine 3-minute episodes. The episodes where the child is left alone and then the mother returns are the two episodes used to measure the infant's attachment. The child's response to her mother's return, after she has left the infant alone in a strange room, is used to assess the type of attachment the child shows. Originally three types were described: (A) ambivalent, (B) secure, and (C) avoidant attachments. More recently, a fourth type, (D) disorganized attachment, has been added. Most work on attachment distinguishes between **secure** (B) and all others (A, C, D), which are called **insecure**.

The work on attachment in humans has its parallel in the work of Harry Harlow with monkeys (Harlow, 1969) and Jane Goodall with chimpanzees (Goodall, 1988). Harlow, in particular, showed that monkeys raised without their mothers turned out to have poor peer relationships when they were older and also made poor mothers (Harlow, 1969). This work has recently been criticized because Harlow not only raised his monkeys without their mothers, but kept them in social isolation without contact with anyone (Harlow & Harlow, 1965). Thus, not only were the babies without their mothers, they were also without any social contact, including peers. When baby monkeys are raised without mothers but in the companion of other babies, many of the problems that Harlow reported in terms of the child's subsequent social problems are not present. Most recent work reveals that although the early mother–infant relationship in the first year of life is important, it does not mark the child for life. In fact, Lewis (2004) has shown that the child's ongoing and often changing relationship with its mother and others, such as its father, siblings, peers, and teachers, contribute to the child's social development. Although the emphasis on the mother–infant relationship in the early years of life is important, without understanding the child's total social connectedness, it is not possible to completely understand the social development of the child.

Fathers

Twenty years ago, a visitor from Mars reading the developmental literature would hardly know that in American or westernized societies, babies usually had fathers living in the same household. The more recent research literature, although still dominated by studies of mother and child, has brought into focus some of the roles fathers play in children's lives. Four questions have been directed toward the father–child relationship.

- **Can fathers do what mothers do?** One important question raised about fathers is whether there is any biological difference between mother's and father's care for the very young. Perhaps mothers take care of infants better than fathers? Lamb's (2003) work with fathers and infants demonstrate that fathers' care, that is, the interaction patterns between fathers and children, is similar to mothers' care. Thus, one would say that fathers can care for their very young infants. Although fathers can care, it is apparent that, in general, they do not, especially in the case of the young infant under 9 months or so. Their daily contact remains low. In spite of the social milieu that makes contact acceptable, the sex-role-appropriate male behavior usually does not include the care of the very young. It has been demonstrated that even the increased multiple roles assumed by the mother (mother, worker-out-of-the-house, wife) have not led to much of an increase in fathers' involvement.

- **What do fathers do that is different from mothers?** Although fathers have been shown to be equally capable of caring for young children, there are differences that distinguish them from mothers. Mothers' behavior is likely to center around childcare activities, such as feeding, changing diapers and clothes, and bathing; fathers' interactions are more likely to include physical playful activities. Lamb (2003) has shown that fathers engage in more rough-and-tumble, bouncing, and tickling activities than mothers. Moreover, as the children become older, the father's role is likely to increase, mostly as a function of the declining need for caregiving activities and the increasing needs for exploration, play, and self-initiated action or efficacy in the context of the physical environment. In an important anthropological study, Mackey (1985) has shown that across many cultures, fathers interact more and are more likely to hold their infants and young children in public places (zoos, museums, public streets) than they do when they are at home.

- **What are the indirect effects of the father?** Fathers also affect their children's lives indirectly by affecting the lives of their wives (or partners). These indirect effects include emotional support of the mother. The interdependent nature of the child–parent and parent–parent subsystems has been amply demonstrated. A woman's successful adaptation to pregnancy is associated with the husband's support. Support can include other factors than emotional support. Studies have shown that mothers without husbands on a regular or temporary basis feel busier, more harassed, and more depressed as well as more oriented to immediate goals (Lynn, 1974).

- **Are the children attached to their fathers?** Surprisingly, this question is rarely asked. Perhaps because theory is oriented toward attachment to the mother, it took many years for the question to be asked at all. The answer is that of course, children are attached to their fathers. Children direct equal social behavior to each parent, the only difference being that fathers received somewhat less close-contact behavior.

Siblings

Thinking about Western myths pertaining to siblings, we come first to the story of Cain and Abel. This story is a prototype of the negative relationship, with competition, rivalry, and even hate between siblings as the prevailing moods. Indeed, there are many of these negative attributes associated with siblings. However, there are also many positive features, which tend to be downplayed. Siblings can affect the child's behavior and the child's relationship with other members of the family (Dunn, 1993). Even the child's view of itself is affected by siblings. Siblings play a variety of roles in relation to one another. They may protect and help one another. Many mothers note that when they are punishing one of their children the other will protect that child even if the punishment concerns a sibling conflict. Siblings help each other if their mother cannot help. For example, younger siblings depend on older siblings for help with homework or when they need an ally. Siblings provide important social models for each other. Children learn how to share, cooperate, help, and empathize by watching their siblings. Siblings spend their early lives sharing a variety of objects, experiences, and people. Thus, siblings share not only the same parents and grandparents and roughly the same genetic heritage but also possessions (toys, books, clothes, pets), space (sleep in the same room, use the same bathroom, live in the same space), people (mutual playmates, baby-sitters, teachers, doctors, etc.), and even the same life histories (go to the same camps, vacation together, experience disasters together, etc.). They often serve as playmates to one another and when they have friends often involve their siblings with their friends.

Moreover, and most important, siblings seem to form important and long-lasting attachments with each other, although it appears that younger siblings are more often attached to older siblings than the reverse. In a recent survey, we asked over 60 adults with siblings which sibling was more likely to call the other. More than 80% reported that the younger is more likely to initiate the call to the older, 10% said the older, and 10% said there was no difference. Infants appear upset by the loss of siblings, even when the siblings just stay away from home overnight or for weekends. Siblings show strong affective bonds, and these relationships show continuity over time.

Given these positive features, it is curious to note the negative view assigned to sibling relationships. In part, this may be due to an adult-parent perspective in which sibling rivalry is seen as a predominant factor, neglecting the positive features. Moreover, negative sibling behavior is likely to display itself under (or even be provoked by) the attention and focus of the parents; that is, siblings may be more likely to fight and quarrel in the company of their parents than when alone. In any event, it is clear that sibling aggression, competition, and rivalry do exist. Certainly they must compete for a limited resource, the most important of which is the parent. Although it is in the parents' interest that all children survive, it has been suggested by Trivers (1974) that sibling rivalry is unavoidable given that they must share the same parents and given that the attention of a parent increases one sibling's likelihood of survival while decreasing the likelihood for the other.

Grandparents

The failure to consider the possible role of the grandparents in children's development, like that for other social objects, is based on a particular view of social development. The neglect is surprising given the obvious facts that parents of parents exert strong influence on children's development, if for no other reason than that they influence the parents. Even the name 'grandparent' should make it obvious that such a role carries with it importance for both child and grandparent. Why have grandparents been neglected? In American households today, grandparents usually do not even live in the same home as the child, so how can we focus on only direct effects? It is clear that the lack of study of influence of grandparents on development reflects a culture that does not value age, that is highly age segregated, and in which intergenerational learning is not encouraged. In cultures such as that of Japan today, cultures where many grandparents, parents, and children live together, the role played by grandparents is more obvious.

In Western countries grandparents generally have contact with their adult children (the parents of the child) at least once a week. Hospital visits by grandparents at the time of the infant's birth are quite high: More than 90%

see the child on the first or second day, in spite of the geographic mobility of the child's family (Wilson & Tolson, 1983). Parents of mothers are seen more frequently than the parents of fathers. This reflects the well-documented point that in general mothers are the kin keepers; that is, that they arrange and maintain family contact. This role of 'kin keeper' also gives rise to the findings that the mothers' parents (maternal grandparents) are seen more often by infants than are the paternal grandparents (Hill, Foote, Aldous, Carlson & MacDonald, 1970). Grandmothers are more directly involved in the child's activities than grandfathers, reflecting sex-role differences as an intergenerational phenomenon.

Children can observe how their parents interact with their parents and thereby learn about how adult children behave. This effect does not involve the child directly. The other indirect effects of grandparents should mirror those of the father, except that the grandmother–daughter relationship may supply special support for children through affecting their mothers. Given the mother–daughter relationship and its unique role throughout the life cycle, it should be the case that grandmothers' approval and support have more importance for her daughter, the mother of the grandchild, than for her son, the father of the grandchild.

Aunts, uncles, and cousins

Simply stated, there is very little research literature on the role of aunts, uncles, or cousins in the development of the child. Within anthropology and animal behavior, the role of these others is well recognized. In many groups, lion prides for example, the social structure of the group includes the female relatives: mothers, aunts, daughters, and female cousins (if such terms can be used in this context). Moreover, the role of the father's brother and mother's brother has been recognized. In fact, Frazer (1915) points out that at the death of the father, the father's brother (uncle) becomes responsible for the family. Jocasta's brother Creon becomes king when Oedipus blinds himself. Hamlet's uncle Claudius becomes king and marries his brother's wife, Gertrude, when Hamlet's father dies. Thus, there is ample evidence for the role of uncles in the lives of families; the role of aunts is more unnoticed.

If aunts and uncles are in close contact, their children (cousins) also should be in close contact. In fact, for many children, their first peer contacts and long-lasting ones are with cousins. Thus, cousins are likely to play an influential role, and the social network data indicate considerable rate of cousin contact. Cousins are viewed as so close, at least genetically, that in many jurisdictions there exist laws against marriage between them. For aunts, uncles, and cousins, differences similar to those already reported for grandparents and siblings are likely to appear. Female cousins and aunts are more likely than uncles and male cousins to maintain contact, a sex-role difference that will appear throughout the social network structure. Moreover, the role of parents in the maintenance of adult sibling contact is probably important. That is, contact with aunts and uncles (and therefore the child's cousins) is more likely in some families than in others. The exact nature of the relationship that facilitates this is not well understood.

Peers

Beyond family members, there are any number of people who play an important role in children's development. Peers are surely the most important, for it is in peer relationships that most of adult social life exists. For this reason, of all people beside mothers, early peer relationships have been most studied. For a more complete review of peers, see Chapter 14 on infants at play.

The belief that young infants had no social or emotional interest in peers was due in part to the then prevailing view that the socio-emotional life of the child primarily revolved around their mothers; thus, early peer relationships either did not exist or were unimportant. The role of peers has been shown to be important if it is encouraged by the social structure. Cultural differences in peer contact is the primary factor affecting the degree and amount of socio-emotional involvement (Lewis & Rosenblum, 1975). In some cultures, peers are given more direct roles in childcare (Whiting & Whiting, 1975). On an Israeli kibbutz, or in China and Cuba, for example, we would expect more and earlier peer emotional-social interactions than where group childcare is not a part of the culture (e.g., Japan, although this is changing even now). Peers show interest, enjoyment, and emotional involvement from the earliest opportunities provided in the first year of life. Peer attachment has been shown to exist especially in the absence of adults (Freud & Dann, 1951; Gyomrai-Ludowyk, 1963).

Like siblings, peers perform both positive and negative functions. Peers, rather than adults, are good to play with and to model one's behavior on, since they share equal or nearly equal abilities with the child itself. Peers also are good at teaching, especially somewhat older peers, since their abilities do not differ too markedly from those of the child. Peers protect each other and, most importantly, peers are capable of forming attachments to each other.

The negative features of the peer relationship revolve around the lack of the adult perspective. Thus, for example, an adult may be able to give up a need for the sake of a child, but such behavior may be beyond the ability of young peers. Disputes are therefore often settled by power status variables such as strength, age, and gender rather than by true prosocial behavior. Aggressive behavior between peers represents another negative feature, with high physical interaction and direct aggression being two noticeable examples. Given that peer relationships themselves are embedded in the cultural rules, the study of peer behavior needs to be considered in the context of the entire social network. The absence of peer contact in a culture that does not promote contact cannot be taken as evidence for the unimportance of peers in early life.

Teachers, daycare personnel, and baby-sitters

Even during the first few months, infants are exposed to nonrelated adults who care for the child while the mother is at work, in school, or at play. Given the large number of mothers who work out of the home and the changing family structure, most infants and children are cared for daily by people other than relatives. There was some concern about infant daycare being harmful to the infant since they were without their mothers for a large portion of the day. Attachment theorists thought this would be harmful to the infant. Evidence from NICHD Daycare Studies indicates that young children are capable of forming important relationships with daycare personnel and that the relation with them does not negatively affect the child's social or emotional development (NICHD, 1994, 1996). In fact, daycare experiences with teachers, etc. may mitigate some of the difficulties created by the abusing or neglecting mother (Lewis & Schaeffer, 1981).

The failure to study children's attachment to other adult caregivers may rest on our general bias, which holds to the importance of a single adult attachment figure. Bowlby (1969) did not recognize the multiple-attachment capability of the human infant, and because of the emphasis on the mother, relatively little research with others has been done. Cross-cultural research, such as that of Konner (1975) and Greenbaum and Landau (1977), shows that even in the first few weeks, infants interact with many adults including nonrelatives to whom they may become attached. Given this possibility and the changing nature of childcare, it is necessary that we focus on the effects of multiple attachments and the child's relationship to adult caregivers other than parents and relatives.

From this review of the people in the infant's life, it is clear that the infant enters into a large social network in which the mother, as well as others, play important roles. The neglect of the other people reflects the bias we have which places the mother as the only and most important person in the child's social as well as emotional development. It is the attachment to the mother which has until recently limited the scope of understanding children's social development.

Types of relationships

Interestingly, for 1-year-olds only the attachment relationship to their mothers has been studied in detail, although friendship patterns have received some attention (see Chapter 14) in regard to play and peers. Given that there are many people in the infant's social world, it would be good to look at the type of possible relationships we adults have to give us some idea of what young children may be capable of. We need to keep in mind that it is toward these different types of relationships that the infant will move. Although some of these relationships may be more advanced than others, by 2 years of age the infant appears to possess most of them, the exception being the sexual aspects of relationships.

The social space of the child is made up of a potentially large number of social objects, including inanimate objects, such as security objects, plants, trees, and so on, and animate objects, including nonhumans, animals, and a wide range of people. So a first division is between objects and people. When considering people, we see the possibility of different types of social relationships. Figure 13.1 presents two-dimensional space, including sexuality and intimacy. although here the space is divided into eight cells, there is no clear separation between them and, in fact, movement between cells in either direction is possible.

Love relationships

First consider love relationships that take place within the family as well as outside it. Love relationships may be of two kinds: Those that are attachment relationships, that is, those that provide a secure base, and those that need not, for it is not clear that a secure base is a necessary part of all love relationships. For example, parents love their children, but children do not necessarily offer a secure base for parents. Love relationships also are divided by sexuality. In some love relationships, sexuality will play an important role, such as with a spouse, whereas in others, such as with mothers, fathers, and children, sexuality is absent. Thus, within love relationships the dimensions of secure base (attachment) and sexuality form a complex structure for a variety of different love relationships, all of which exist in our experience. The four cells within love relationships created by attachment and sexuality dimensions

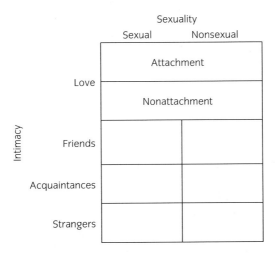

Figure 13.1 Types of relationships.

might contain: mates as an example of attached and sexual; parents as an example of attached, nonsexual; boy- or girlfriend as nonattached and sexual; and parent to child as nonattached and nonsexual. Whether such a complex set of love relationships exists for all children is unknown. However, older infants can and probably do have strong love relationships that both have and do not have an attachment dimension. For example, children love both their parents and their younger siblings, but they are probably attached to the former and not the latter.

Friendship relationships

Friendship relationships are different from love relationships, and although this may be difficult to describe, it is indicated by the language itself. Friendship relationships also vary along different dimensions and at times may merge with love relationships. Like love, friendship may or may not involve sexual behavior. Friendship relationships tend to vary with the age of the participants; thus, they may involve same-age peers or they may exist between older and younger persons, such as between a teacher and student. Like love, friendship relations can be enduring and can exist even without extended interactions.

Acquaintance relationships

Acquaintance relationships are those relationships that tend to be the least enduring and the most specific to the particular interactions that bring them into existence. They usually occur as a consequence of particular and highly structured social exchanges such as with a storekeeper or bank clerk. These relationships vary along a dimension of familiarity, from those in which the members recognize one another, know each others' names, and exchange information (such as between employers and employees or between a shop owner and a customer) to those less familiar interactions with the ticket collector on a train or with people whom we greet casually in passing on the street.

Although people do not have relationships with strangers, our analysis requires that this category of nonrelationships be included, especially since so much attention has been paid to children's social interactions with strangers. Strangers are by our definition those people with whom we have no relationship and who are unfamiliar to us. Yet even in this category of nonrelationships, there are variations that may be of some importance to our analysis. For example, strangers who possess particular characteristics may elicit different interactions than strangers without those characteristics. Thus, strangers of the same sex or racial background as the child are likely to evoke different interactions than strangers of the opposite sex or of another racial background (Lewis, 1980).

For any complete study of social development, it is necessary to recognize that infants do have relationships with people other than their parents and to trace the development of these relationships from the child's earliest social interactions. A complex array of relationships exists from infancy on.

The development of relationships

Infants certainly appear to form relationships early. They smile when their mother or father appears, they follow their older siblings around as soon as they are able to move around in the house, and they move away from and become wary of strangers when they are 8–9 months old. But are these relationships as we mean them when referring to adults or are they some primitive form of these, perhaps not too dissimilar from other mammals that interact with their young?

Robert Hinde, a biologist now retired from Cambridge University, wrote (1976) that relationships should be characterized as having goals, a diversity of different interactions, and reciprocity. The feature most important for our discussion is his belief that relationships require mental processes that allow members of an interaction to think of the other member as well as of themselves.

Notice that for Hinde, as for Lewis (1991), relationships require elaborate cognitions, cognitions which require a self and knowledge of other selves. These cognitions are not likely present until the end of the second year of life. We see social development dependent on the growth of particular cognitions which is present in Figure 13.2. In this model, what is commonly referred to as the mother–child relationship is really a set of social interactions. These interactions grow out of the basic capacities of the human genome; so for example, the baby is not taught how to smile, although his smiling behavior is very much influenced by his social environment. How and when people around the child smile will influence how and when the child will smile, but smiling itself is not learned from others.

These early social interactions—smiling mother–infant smiling, vocalizing infant–mother talking—are in place by the 3- to 6-month period. As attachment theorists indicate, these interactions constitute a kind of dance. However, unlike others who think this means a relationship, the model of Figure 13.2 suggests that they are not relationships. Because of the absence of sufficient cognitions, these complex interactions are the material for relationships once the concept of self or what we have called consciousness occurs.

Since the development of consciousness has been already described in Chapter 12, we will only say that somewhere between 15 and 24 months, infants indicate through the use of personal pronouns, 'me' or 'mine,' and

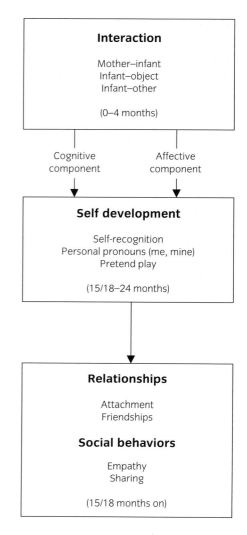

Figure 13.2 Transformational model of the development of relationships.

self-recognition in the mirror, that the self has emerged. With its emergence comes such capacities as empathy and sharing behaviors, behaviors absolutely necessary for the emergence of relationships.

Once the infant has formed a rudimentary concept of self and established particular habits, the next stage in the transformation is the utilization of these skills to form relationships. The mediating cognitive structures necessary for social relationships are: (1) a self-representation, and (2) from the self-representation, the development of two social affective skills, empathy and sharing. Having discussed the emergence of the self-representation (see Chapter 12), let us attend next to the emergence of empathy and sharing. One would agree that empathy (and sharing) is possible only through the recognition of the existence of two selves—one's self and another's self—each having a separate identity, a separate set of needs, different thoughts, and desires. Such an analysis requires that we understand both the development of a self-representation and the development of the understanding of the separate nature of selves. The process of growth by which children decenter, that is, do not consider that all people are exactly like them, has been widely discussed (Flavell 1999; Astington & Barriault 2001). It is now called a **theory of mind**. The timing of this decentering is still being questioned. Piaget (1952), for one, did not see this process as occurring much before 5 years, but others now see it as occurring earlier, indeed, as young as 3 years (Wellman, Cross & Watson, 2001).

With this in mind, the model of development of this ability gives rise to what we understand to be adult-like relationships. This adult-like ability, to take the other into account, is likely to occur in the latter part of the second year of life. Certainly by 2 years of age, the child's use of 'no' and the onset of the 'terrible twos' should alert us to the existence of two selves (child and parent) and the beginning of adult-like relationships based on the negotiation between them.

To reiterate, from an ontogenetic point of view, the mediating structure between interaction and relationships is the development of self. Even beyond its developmental role, the sense of self may play an important part in interactions and relationships. Relationships are based on interactions but require a sense of self and an integration of a self with others as in empathy to give them meaning. This is particularly true when we think of the recursive nature of thought. Not only can I think about how I behave toward you and how you behave toward me, but I can think about how I think you think I behave toward you, and you to me.

The social network

The attachment model argues that the earliest relationship with the mother is the single most important aspect for subsequent behavior. Social development is seen as a transformation of this earliest relationship into all other relationships. Peer interpersonal behavior is a consequence of present peer experiences and the secure attachment.

The notion of a **social network systems** model argues instead that the causes of social behavior and development are to be found in the structure of the social system itself and the past experience. An example of the interplay between an individual's behavior and a social network will underscore this difference between the two views. Rosenblum and Kaufman (1968) studied both bonnet and pigtail macaque monkeys. Bonnet macaques cluster together in matriarchal groups so that a mother, her sisters, her adult daughters, and their babies might all be found huddled in close proximity. Pigtail macaques, on the other hand, are much more isolate. There are no groups, just the adult female and her baby. In the former case, the baby is in close proximity to a large and varied number of others besides its mother. In the latter case, the baby and mother are alone. The bonnet baby interacts daily and forms relationships with mother, aunts, grandmother, and cousins while the pigtail baby only interacts and forms relationships with its mother, only later forming relationships with others.

When separated from its mother, the pigtail baby first shows marked distress, calling and moving about. This is followed by a state of deep depression. The bonnet baby shows a markedly different pattern. It too is distressed by the withdrawal of the mother; however, it soon recovers as it is 'adopted' and cared for by familiar others. This illuminates the effects of the social network. In a system where there is only the mother, her loss constitutes an enormously significant event, one from which the infant is not likely to recover. In Bowlby's (1951) attachment model, the loss of the mother is a life-threatening event. In a system where there are other people, the loss of the mother, although perhaps significant, no longer becomes a life-threatening event, and in fact, given the proper care from others, appears to cause relatively little subsequent disruption. Similar findings have been reported by Robertson and Robertson (1971), Rutter (1979), and Tizard and Tizard (1971), among others, when human infants are studied.

Likewise, in a system where there is only the mother as caregiver, the child's first (and only) relationship will be with her. Other relationships must be sequential (after this first one) and, in part, dependent on this first one. This sequential, deterministic feature (the hallmark of the attachment view) does not have to be a biological necessity for the species, as Bowlby has argued. There is little support for the notion that such a structure of mother as sole caregiver is necessary or indeed historically, culturally, or evolutionarily correct. For example, some cultures promote the use of multiple caregiving in the form of both mother and older female sibling or friend (Whiting & Whiting, 1975). In the United States today, most infants and children are in daycare settings with multiple adults and children. A social network systems approach appears as an important alternative to the attachment view.

Description and measurement of the social network

As an area of research, the study of social networks is about 50 years old. Bott's (1957) seminal work *The family and social network* is widely known to both sociologists and psychologists. Bott reported that—contrary to popular belief—middle-class couples did not live in isolation but formed coalitions with other middle-class couples in a network of social kinship. In interviews with couples, Bott discussed with both husbands and wives the type and frequency of contact with people in the categories of relatives, friends, neighbors, and organizations (e.g., school, clubs, unions, religious groups, etc.). Couples also kept diaries that helped the researchers determine the nature of the social networks. One interesting result from Bott's work involved the relationship between social network and family roles. Although networks have been examined in regard to adults, relatively little work has been done on networks, roles, and infants and children's development. An extensive literature exists that employs quantitative techniques for describing and specifying the characteristics of social networks. In addition, information about the needs satisfied by which members of the social network has been obtained and informs us about the relations between people in the child's network and the roles they serve.

Social matrix as a measure of the social network the relation between people and needs

We have seen that even in infancy and early childhood, children are likely to have multiple relationships. We also know that infants have many different needs; for example, needs like protection, love and attention, play, learning, etc. We need to develop a model that describes how these multiple people and needs interact.

In the model depicted in Figure 13.3, people form the Y axis and needs form the X axis. Together they form a matrix of objects and needs. In this figure, the set of people includes self, mother, father, peers, siblings, grandparents, aunts, plus any other people such as teachers, etc. to be considered. The

Social network model

		Functions					
		Care	Play	Protection	Nurturance (Love)	Education	Etc.
People	Mother						
	Father						
	Grandparents						
	Siblings						
	Younger						
	Older						
	Aunts, uncles						
	Cousins						
	Peers						
	Siblings' friends						
	Parents' friends						
	Etc.						

Figure 13.3 Social network model.

array of people is determined by a variety of factors. The needs consist of protection, caregiving, nurturance, and so forth. These are broad needs that can be broken down further. For example, under caregiving, feeding and changing could be included, while under nurturance, emotional behaviors such as kissing or sensitivity might be considered. The general form of this model provides a framework for considering the complete array of people and needs that describe the child's social network. By examining the matrix one can determine which people are present, which needs are being satisfied and, most important, which needs are achieved by what person. By examining the horizontal axis of the matrix, one can obtain an idea of what needs are characteristic of a particular person within this particular network. This axis will inform us whether mothers are predominantly concerned with caregiving and fathers with play. On the other hand, by examining the vertical axis of the matrix, one can study the different needs that characterize the network of a particular child. Although all of the listed needs are presumed to be important, it might be that for some children, caregiving, play, and learning are equally important. Likewise, a child whose network is predominantly concerned with protection will be quite different from one raised in a network concerned with nurturance. However, in order to determine the relationship of people to need, we must turn our attention to the individual cells of the matrix.

The matrix raises the general question of whether the satisfaction of a need by a particular person are more important for the child's development than others. For example, what is the consequence of having an older sibling as caregiver as well as the mother instead of just the mother? Or what is the consequence of having a caregiver as giver of care (as in daycare) in addition to the mother instead of just the mother?

In an attempt to determine whether the matrix is applicable to young children, Edwards and Lewis (1979) explored how young children perceive the distribution of needs and people (see also Dunn, 1993). Persons were represented by dolls of infants, peers, older children, and parent-aged adults. Social needs were created for the child in the form of a story. In the two studies to be discussed, children in the age range 3–5 years were asked to choose which person they wanted to interact with in a specific social activity. In all the studies, the functions were (1) being helped, (2) teaching about a toy, (3) sharing, and (4) play. For help, the adults were selected; for someone to play with, children chose adults and infants last and peers and older children first. For teaching, specifically, how to use a toy, older children were selected, but for sharing, there was no preference among social objects. In a second study, children were asked to point to photographs of infants, peers, older children, adults (parent-aged), and grandparents in response to the questions. For example, we asked the child to point to the photograph of whom you would go to for help, play with, or share a toy. The results indicated that older people were chosen for help. The teaching need result was like that in the first study since older children were preferred for teaching. There was no difference in the person chosen for sharing, a replication of the earlier findings. Interestingly, the data on grandparent-aged adults are most similar to those for parent-aged adults.

These specific people-by-need matrix exist by 1 year of age. At this age, infants play with peers more than with strange adult females or mothers, and mothers are sought after for protection and nurturance more than strange females and peers. Such findings suggest that the discrimination of persons and needs begins very early in life.

The construction of the people-by-need matrix provides us with a model for understanding the infant's social network. The variety of people and needs that comprise this network alters at least as a function of the child's age and culture. Until recently, the focus of most research has been restricted to examining particular cells of the matrix—such as the mother and caregiving needs. At the same time, certain needs and persons have been assumed to be synonymous. Moreover, by using the attachment model, researchers have assumed that the lack of a particular people by need relationship leads to harmful consequences. If we consider the entire matrix, however, it may be possible to determine whether there are specific people-by-need relationships; for example, whether 'mother' and 'mothering' are synonymous. In addition, it can be determined whether certain functions can be safely substituted for by others without harmful consequences, as, for example, whether a teacher or a peer can be substituted for a mother for the satisfaction of the needs of nurturance or teaching. Recent research indicates that this is the case (NICHD, 1997, 1998, 1999).

SUMMARY

The social network model may best characterize the infant's social world as well as reflecting ontogenetic cultural and idiographic differences. In the child's life there exists a variety of significant people. Which people constitute the important relationships for the infant depends on the structure and values of the particular culture. We view the social network as a system. The network is established by the culture for the transmission of cultural values. The composition of the network, the nature of the people, the needs they fulfill, and the relationship between people and needs are the parts of the vehicle through which the cultural values are determined. In fact, this structure may be as important as the specific information conveyed; indeed, it may constitute the information itself. Finally, we should be alerted to the dangers of assuming that the care of infants represents some unchanging and absolute process. The care of infants is the primary social activity of any society since it represents the single activity wherein the values of the society are preserved. Childcare must reflect the values of the culture at large; therefore, one should expect it to change as these values change. The issue of social values must be addressed in order for us to deal with the ideal relationship (if any) between people and the child's needs. The research tasks are to characterize various networks and to determine the outcome of various people by need relationships in regard to a set of goals and values rather than to argue for some ideal biological state.

CHAPTER FOURTEEN

Infants at play: development, functions, and partners

MARC H. BORNSTEIN and CATHERINE S. TAMIS-LEMONDA

Introduction

All humans and even nonhuman primates play. This observation has led developmental and evolutionary scientists to speculate that play is a distinct motivational/behavioral system that might serve diverse adaptive functions. Many theorists of play have focused on the functions of children's solitary play and play with peers or underscored the importance of adults and other social partners in supporting the development of children's thought during play. In this chapter we review the development and functions of infant play and the different roles that play partners serve during infants' first 2–3 years of life.

Development of infant play

Broadly speaking, play develops from exploration to pretense in infancy. In the first year of life, infants manipulate one object at a time and then move on to manipulating the parts of objects or juxtaposing objects to explore how objects fit together or relate. This form of concrete play, in which the infant's actions depend on the perceptual features of objects, is often termed **exploration**. A more advanced form of play is attained around the beginning of the second year of life. In this **symbolic play** or **pretense**, the child is no longer bound by the obvious characteristics of objects, but rather uses objects alone, in combinations, and in sequences to pretend about absent events or past experiences. Moreover, pretend play changes in three fundamental ways over early development: (1) play becomes distanced from self (e.g., as children move from pretending toward self to pretending toward others); (2) play becomes distanced from the observed properties of objects (e.g., as children move from pretending with literal replicas of objects to using substitutive objects); and (3) play becomes distanced from overt actions (e.g., as children move from enacting active themes to expressing emotive ones) (Tamis-LeMonda & Bornstein, 1996).

Table 14.1 identifies the two broad categories of play (exploratory and pretense) and further analyzes each category into four levels according to developmental changes in infants' play that have been observed across

Table 14.1 Play categories and levels

Play level	Definition	13 months	20 months
Exploratory play			
1. Unitary functional activity	Production of an effect that is unique to a single object	Throw or squeeze foam ball (25%)[a]	Dial telephone (21%)
2. Inappropriate combinatorial activity	Juxtaposition of two or more objects that do not naturally go together	Put ball in vehicle[b]	Put ball in vehicle[b]
3. Appropriate combinatorial activity	Juxtaposition of two or more objects that naturally go together	Put lid on teapot (44%)	Nest blocks (27%)
4. Transitional play	Approximate of pretense but without confirmatory evidence	Put telephone receiver to ear (without vocalization) (44%)	Put telephone receiver to ear (without vocalization) (57%)
Symbolic play			
5. Self-directed pretense	Clear pretense activity directed toward self	Eat from spoon or cup (39%)	Eat from spoon or cup (36%)
6. Other-directed pretense	Clear pretense activity directed toward other	Kiss or hug doll (41%)	Pretend vehicle makes sound (48%)
7. Sequential pretense	Link two or more pretense actions	Dial telephone and speak into receiver (30%)	Dial telephone and speak into receiver (45%)
8. Substitution pretense	Pretend activity involving one or more object substitutions	Pretend block is telephone and talk into it[b]	Pretend block is telephone and talk into it[b]

[a] Percentages in parentheses reflect the frequency of the example over the total frequency of play acts at that level.
[b] Because *any* inappropriate combination for level 2 or any object substitution for level 8 exemplifies that play level, none dominated.

the first 2 years. Definitions and examples are provided for each level, along with the relative frequencies of each level for infants aged 13 and 20 months. In this scheme, the four levels of exploratory play are: unitary functional activity (Figure 14.1 top), inappropriate combinatorial activity (Figure 14.1 bottom), appropriate combinatorial activity (Figure 14.2 top), and transitional play (Figure 14.2 bottom). The four levels of symbolic

Figure 14.1 Top: Unitary functional activity. Bottom: Inappropriate combinatorial activity.

Figure 14.2 Top: Appropriate combinatorial activity. Bottom: Transitional play.

Figure 14.3 Top: Self-directed pretense. Bottom: Other-directed pretense.

Figure 14.4 Top: Sequential pretense. Bottom: Substitution pretense.

play are: self-directed pretense (Figure 14.3 top), other-directed pretense (Figure 14.3 bottom), sequential pretense (Figure 14.4 top), and substitution pretense (Figure 14.4 bottom).

Figure 14.5 shows that, across the second year, infants decrease in level 1 play and increase in levels 3, 5, 6, 7, and 8 (they also increase in total symbolic play; Tamis-LeMonda & Bornstein, 1991). Although most infants follow this progression, infants of a given age vary greatly. For example, perhaps 15% of the total play of 13-month-olds is symbolic on average, but some infants

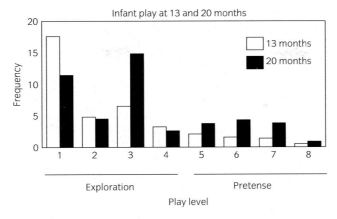

Figure 14.5 Infant play at 13 and 20 months.

never exhibit symbolic play, whereas in others as much as 51% of the play is symbolic. At 20 months, perhaps 30% of infants' total play is symbolic on average, but some babies engage in symbolic play only 2% of the time, whereas others display as much as 83% symbolic play (Tamis-LeMonda & Bornstein, 1990).

Functions of play

Play serves multiple functions in infant development:

- In the **intrapsychological domain,** play is a medium through which children regulate arousal and express emotions.
- In the **mastery domain,** play is associated with attention span and persistence in structured and unstructured tasks.
- In the **cognitive domain,** play enables children to acquire information and skills, engage in creative and divergent thinking, and advance in representational abilities.
- In the **social domain,** play serves as a context for the development of reciprocity, which provides a foundation for more mature forms of social understanding.
- In the **cultural domain,** play is a vehicle for transmitting social roles and cultural values.

Intrapsychological functions of play

Play affords a stage for infants to regulate arousal, express emotions, and resolve conflicts and traumas. Social play in the form of face-to-face exchanges with caregivers helps infants regulate their level of arousal. Infants bid and avert their gaze to initiate and terminate play, interactions thereby taking an active part in maintaining their level of arousal (Stern, 1985). Partners who respond appropriately to infants' need for more or less stimulation contribute to infants' self-regulation capacities. In turn, infants who are better able to regulate arousal are more apt to experience pleasure during play interactions and reduce negative states. Younger infants in particular rely on their play partners to interpret their signals, and mothers, for example, are more likely to respond contingently to 6- and 9-month-olds than are infants' older siblings or peers (Vandell & Wilson, 1987). In this way, play with parents provides stimulation that is tolerable and pleasurable for the infant. In the second year, play with adult caregivers continues to support children's self-regulation. Mothers who spend more time engaged in joint attention during play with their 2-year-olds have children who more effectively engage in self-soothing strategies when they become frustrated (Raver, 1996). Although this relation does not necessarily demonstrate a causal connection, it suggests that infants' acquisition of autonomous emotional regulation may be facilitated by their early play experiences.

In addition to helping to regulate arousal, play expands the range of emotions that infants express by enabling them to experience positive feelings, such as fun, excitement, and pleasure, as well as negative feelings of anger, sadness, and fear. Bruner (1972) contended that play also allows the young of the species to experiment with a full range of emotions by displaying behaviors that might not be safe in real or mature life as, for example, mock anger or aggression.

From the first days of life, mothers support their infants' experience of joy by playing with facial expressions, vocalizations, and touch, and by evoking gazing, smiling, and laughter from their infants. According to Stern (1985), mother–infant game rituals (e.g., peek-a-boo, tickling) boost infants to higher levels of joy than babies might achieve on their own. The infant's growing awareness of contingency in these interactions adds to feelings of pleasure, in addition to enabling greater tolerance for higher arousal states (Roggman, 1991). Mothers are more contingent with infants than are siblings or peers (Vandell & Wilson, 1987) suggesting that attuned adults best amplify and prolong the infant's experience of pleasure in the first months of life.

By the end of the first year, infants' positive emotional exchanges extend to peers. Between 10 and 24 months, play episodes with peers express positive emotions (Eckerman, Whatley & Kutz, 1975). At younger ages, positive feelings towards peers are expressed through smiling, vocalizing, and touching, whereas offering and accepting toys increased with age. At all ages, positive emotions in play outweigh negative emotions, as expressed through fussing and crying.

Play interactions between older infants and their siblings or peers allow for the expression of a wider range and greater intensity of emotions than play interactions with mothers. Specifically, toddlers spanning the ages of 17 months and 3 years laugh and smile more frequently with peers or siblings than with mothers (e.g., Farver & Wimbarti, 1995). Play with siblings is also more likely to incorporate exciting and frightening themes than is play with mothers, suggesting that siblings might engender a greater intensity of both positive and negative emotions.

Although infants' older siblings are capable of facilitating pretense, they are less likely than mothers to follow their younger siblings' lead (Dale, 1989). Thus, unless conflictual material or traumas are of mutual interest, older siblings may not allow younger ones enough independence to play out disturbing material. In the first years of life, therefore, adults support infants' ability to represent and resolve conflicts and traumas through play because of their combined support for infants' representational play skills and their ability to elaborate on and interpret infants' choices of play themes.

Mastery functions of play

The mastery functions of play are those that help children achieve a sense of self-efficacy and motivation to persist toward goals in both structured and unstructured settings.

Mastery motivation in structured tasks

In infancy, the concept of mastery motivation is captured by infants' curiosity about and exploration of objects. During this period, adults are more effective in focusing infants' attention to social and nonsocial stimuli than are peers or siblings (Vandell & Wilson, 1987). For example, mothers who encourage their 2-month-olds to orient to and explore objects in the environment have infants who explore objects more at 5 months, and parents' stimulation and responsiveness to infants at 6 months predicts infants' persistence on problem-solving tasks at 13 months (Yarrow, MacTurk, Vietze, McCarthy, Klein & McQuiston, 1984).

Between 1 and 2 years of age, children's goal-directed behaviors increase as they practice emerging skills and attempt multi-part tasks. During this period, adult play partners continue to foster infants' sense of efficacy and persistence on structured tasks. Mothers' early advantage in supporting infants' mastery motivation on structured tasks might be due to their responsiveness to infants' initiatives, accuracy in assessing infants' need for help, and/or the effectiveness of their assistance. Mothers are highly attuned and responsive to the level of their infants' play sophistication at both 13 and 21 months, which may serve to maximize infants' attention and interest during play (Bornstein, Haynes, Pascual, Painter & Galperin, 1999; Damast, Tamis-LeMonda & Bornstein, 1996; Tamis-LeMonda & Bornstein, 1991). Mothers prompt play at play levels that match or are slightly above their infants' own play, and rarely encourage their infants to engage in play below the level infants spontaneously exhibit. Vygotsky (1978) proposed that cognitive achievements are first experienced in the context of social interactions, with more advanced or expert partners (e.g., mother) raising the level of performance or competence of the less advanced or expert partner (the child). Vygotsky fostered a major conceptual shift in the study of play, regarding it to be not merely a solitary activity, but to be a formative activity that is largely shaped through the child's social interactions with significant others.

Mastery motivation in unstructured play

Although mothers support sustained attention for all forms of play during infancy, peers appear to be better suited to support sustained attention in unstructured, physically active play later. Peers are particularly adept at maintaining mutual interest and excitement in joint episodes of push–pull, chasing, climbing, sliding, and swinging and joint episodes of open-ended object exploration. During preschool, episodes of unstructured pretend play with peers are longer than those with mothers (Haight & Miller, 1992). It may be that after infancy the joint enthusiasm that characterizes peer play best supports continued engagement, as long as children can manage the cognitive and social demands of the task.

Cognitive functions of play

When infants are at play, more is going on than meets the eye. The cognitive functions of play are those that serve the acquisition of information and skills, divergent thinking and creativity, and representation.

Acquisition of information and skills

Throughout childhood, mother–child play partnerships serve a teaching function. Mothers play with sounds with their young babies, in ways that prepare their infants for future communication, and they also use play with objects to stimulate their infants' interest in objects and the environment. In the latter part of the first year, mothers support their infants' efforts to practice new skills.

Mothers' active participation in collaborative play is believed to raise the level of expression of symbolic sophistication in their children's play, making it richer or more diverse, or sustaining its duration. For example, Fiese (1990) showed that infants of 15–24 months spent a greater percentage of time in higher-level nonsymbolic and symbolic play, as opposed to lower-level exploratory play, during mother–child play compared to child-alone play. Toddlers engaged in higher levels of symbolic play following their mothers' modeling. Bornstein, Haynes, O'Reilly, and Painter (1996) likewise found that the degree to which mothers participated in and guided their infants' symbolic play affected the level of their infants' symbolic play. Infants engaged in more frequent symbolic play and for longer periods when in collaboration than when alone. Even when in collaborative play, the proportion of infant play that was symbolic was greater when mothers initiated play than when infants initiated play. Mothers have also been shown to respond frequently to infant play with play acts that are at a level equal to or just above the level of the preceding infant play act (Damast, Tamis-LeMonda & Bornstein, 1996). These responsive adjustments in mothers' play function to channel infant play toward greater sophistication. A mother might prompt her infant to pretend to talk on a toy telephone by handing the phone to her child and saying 'Daddy wants to talk. Say hello!'

Whereas mothers instruct infants about object use, set up models for infants to copy, and correct infants' behaviors while playing, siblings are less likely to display these teaching strategies (Farver & Wimbarti, 1995). Peers are less likely than parents and even less likely than siblings to take a teaching stance in play with age-mates, perhaps due to their own limited competence. Adult caregivers' more prominent role as teacher during play does not negate that role for peers and siblings, however. Towards the end of the first year, infants watch and imitate peers' actions with toys and are sometimes more prone to imitating other children than adults. Infants also use imitation to initiate pretend play with siblings 38% of the time, but never use this strategy to initiate pretense with mothers (Dunn & Dale, 1984).

Because imitation is an early learning strategy, peer and sibling play clearly helps infants acquire new skills after the first year. However, the skills emphasized by mothers are different from those generated in sibling and peer play. Mothers are more likely to convey information about the real world and encourage conventional object use and convergent thinking, for example. Mothers have been found to use pretend play to model a 'right' way of doing things, and to correct children's violations of reality, for example, protesting (seriously or playfully) when youngsters drink tea from the teapot instead of cup (Howes, 1992). Whereas mothers are prone to use play as a vehicle for learning, siblings and peers are motivated by play itself. Parent–child play has been linked to acquiring, refining, or extending a wide range of cognitive and social skills, including language competencies and creativity.

Divergent thinking and creativity

Bruner (1972) suggested that the opportunity to 'play' with learned behaviors outside of their real context allows the young of a species the freedom to combine actions and objects in novel ways, thereby engendering a flexible mindset. Play is correlated with success on divergent problem-solving tasks and measures of creativity. The opportunity to play freely with materials has been linked to innovative uses for objects, a flexible approach to problem-solving, and better performance on divergent-thinking tasks (Rubin, Fein & Vandenberg, 1983).

During the second year, peers and siblings support flexibility, creativity, and divergent thinking in both exploratory and pretend play. Siblings and peers often demonstrate novel actions in their play, perhaps because their play is less prescribed than that of adults. One study found that 17- to 20-month-olds engaged in more creative or unusual uses of objects during play with peers than during play with mothers (Rubenstein & Howes, 1976). Similarly, toddlers express more diverse themes when engaged in pretense with older siblings than with mothers (Dunn & Dale, 1984; Youngblade & Dunn, 1995). Two- and 3-year-olds' pretense with older siblings more often involved the creation of imaginary situations (superheroes), whereas pretense with mothers more often involved realistic situations (putting teddy to bed) (Dunn & Dale, 1984).

Representation

Both Piaget (1962) and Vygotsky (1967) emphasized the importance of play in the development of representational thinking. The capacity to simulate events out of their real context frees children from the here-and-now, and allows them to reflect on the past and anticipate the future. Symbolic gestures and the use of language are principal vehicles in these advances. This notion is supported by associations between children's pretend play and measures of language development, including vocabulary, verbal fluency, semantic diversity, and complexity of language structures.

Symbolic play

As noted, the second year of life is a time when children begin to re-enact activities in nonliteral ways (e.g., by pretending to drink from a cup or use a block as a telephone). Adults support these emerging abilities in infants' pretense. For example, a mother might respond, 'You're patting the baby!' as her child touches a doll. It is thus unsurprising that infants' symbolic play with mothers is more complex, diverse, and sustained than is their solitary symbolic play (Bornstein, Haynes, O'Reilly & Painter, 1996; Haight & Miller, 1992).

Moreover, variation in mothers' play sophistication is linked to variation in children's pretense abilities. Mothers who demonstrate and solicit more symbolic play with 13- and 20-month-olds have children who engage in more symbolic play. Moreover, these same general positive associations between mother and child play obtain in different cultures: Whether they are New Yorkers or from Tokyo or Buenos Aires Porteñas or Italians living in the north or south of their country, mothers who engage in more symbolic play with their children have children who engage in more symbolic play (Bornstein *et al.*, 1999). During the second year, mothers who increase in the frequency of their symbolic play have children who demonstrate more rapid gains in their symbolic play; mothers who show no change or decrease in their symbolic play have children who show no symbolic gain (Tamis-LeMonda & Bornstein, 1991).

During the same time, play with siblings is less supportive of infants' emerging pretense. Older siblings typically attempt to direct their younger siblings' play and elicit their compliance, and peers imitate one anothers' actions, but they are not yet capable of communicating pretense to each other. By 2–3 years of age, however, older siblings become supportive partners in infants' symbolic play, and pretend play with siblings increases in prevalence. One study reported that U.S. children engaged in pretend play more often with older siblings than with mothers by 33 months of age (Youngblade & Dunn, 1995). In Javanese families, pretend play has been found to be more frequent with siblings than with mothers at 18, 24, and 36 months old (Farver & Wimbarti, 1995).

On the one hand, mothers' tendency to focus on toy objects and their functions may provide better support for the emerging symbolic abilities of 2-year-olds. By 3 years of age, siblings' use of a combination of objects, pretend actions, and imaginary discourse may provide better support to children as they advance in representational abilities. Indeed, as the age of the older sibling increases, the frequency of role-play of 33-month-old younger siblings increases (Youngblade & Dunn, 1995). This suggests that most children still depend on a partner's expertise to foster role-play.

Language development

The representational abilities reflected in the emergence of symbolic play during the second year are also evidenced in concomitant language gains. As with symbolic play, adult caregivers hold a privileged status in fostering language development during this stage.

Mother–child play facilitates the use of more complex language than play with either siblings or peers (Perez-Granados & Callanan, 1997). Additionally, mothers' language during play is closely linked to infants' language gains. Mothers who are more verbally responsive during play with their 13- and 21-month-olds have toddlers with larger receptive and productive vocabularies at both ages and who express a greater range of meanings in their productive language at 21 months (Tamis-LeMonda & Bornstein, 1994). Mothers who respond to their 9- and 13-month-olds' language initiatives during free play, particularly by imitating/expanding on infant vocalizations and prompting symbolic play, have toddlers who imitate, express first words, achieve the vocabulary spurt, use sentences, and verbally express memories up to 6 months sooner in development than children of less responsive mothers (Tamis-LeMonda, Bornstein & Baumwell, 2001). Mothers who are attuned to their 9-month-olds' emotional expressions during play have children who achieve the same variety of language milestones earlier (Nicely, Tamis-LeMonda & Bornstein, 1999).

Similar to mothers, fathers' responsiveness during play also appears to greatly benefit children's language development. In one study of low-income fathers and their 2-year old children, fathers who were more responsive during play were approximately five times more likely to have children who performed within the normal range on the MDI in a population of low-income families. On the flip side, the likelihood of children with low-responsive fathers being in need of early intervention services for cognitive delays was 5 times that of children with highly responsive fathers (Shannon, Tamis-LeMonda, London & Cabrera, 2002). Moreover, fathers' play engagements with their children continue to predict children's outcomes after considering mothers' play behaviors in analyses. Specifically, in a recent longitudinal investigation of mothers and fathers at play with their 2- and 3-year old toddlers, sensitive and stimulating play (termed **supportiveness**) in both mothers and fathers was uniquely associated with children's language and cognitive development within and across the two ages (Tamis-LeMonda, Shannon, Cabrera & Lamb, 2004).

Towards the end of the preschool years, siblings and peers begin to support the development of symbolic play, and language is now the major medium for shared episodes of pretense among children. During this same period, adults continue to facilitate the growth of children's language abilities through their responsive engagements with toddlers during collaborative play. After the age of 3, children quickly develop communicative competence with a variety of partners. Thus, the cognitive benefits of mother–child play are salient early on and extend to later peer and sibling play.

Social functions of play

The social functions of play are those that foster children's understanding of others' feelings, intentions, and perspectives, thereby promoting more successful interactions and relationships. Early forms of mother–infant play are thought to build reciprocal patterns of communication and social understanding, both of which underpin and motivate later collaborative activity. Role-play, in particular, has been linked to the ability to understand feelings, mental states, and others' perspectives. Role-play is thought to enhance perspective-taking ability because the constant shifting between reality and pretense strengthens children's ability to consider multiple points of view. Here we examine how different partners support the two key social functions of communicative reciprocity and social understanding.

Communicative reciprocity

Communicative reciprocity involves conversational turn-taking and responding in a way that is topically related to a partner's prior communication. In infancy, play with adult caregivers is fundamental to the development of communicative reciprocity. For example, at 6 and 9 months, a greater number and longer durations of turn-taking exchanges characterize infants' play interactions with their mothers when compared to those with siblings or peers (Vandell & Wilson, 1987). Towards the end of the first year, games like 'peek-a-boo' reinforce reciprocal communication.

During the second year, adult caregivers continue to extend turn-taking exchanges during play by directing children's attention to their actions or linking their responses to children's own actions. Towards the end of the second year, peer communication during play becomes increasingly reciprocal, reflecting a growing awareness of peers' needs and intentions. The frequency of temporally related talk escalates when 20- and 24-months-olds play together, although responses related to the prior topic are still infrequent (Eckerman & Didow, 1996). By 29–38 months, peers are more likely to respond contingently to each other, although their responses are not necessarily verbal (Howes & Unger, 1992). As language increases, communications between peers become increasingly verbal, leading to greater understanding of feelings and intentions not bound to the immediate context of interaction or play.

Social understanding

Social understanding refers to children's ability to convey their own as well as seek understanding of others' thoughts and feelings. The origins of social understanding (termed **intersubjectivity**) are affective and are in evidence during the first months of life in early forms of communication (**protoconversations**) between mothers and infants. If either mother or infant fails to respond with appropriate emotional expression, play is disrupted. During later infancy, mother–infant play also involves teasing games and rituals that help the infant practice negotiation skills to build a deeper social understanding. Günçü (1993, p. 187) asserted that the 'intersubjectivity attained in mother–infant interactions prepares children to share meanings with peers' later on. Others have shown that both secure mother–infant attachments and secure teacher–toddler relationships shape current and future social competence and positive peer interactions in children up to 9 years of age (Howes, Hamilton & Phillipsen, 1998).

In older infants, pretend play with both mother and siblings supports the development of children's understanding of other people's feeling states, such as pain, distress, sleepiness, hunger, or sadness. Infants as young as 18–24 months are able to take on the perspective of a feeling state other than their own in pretend play with siblings. Research indicates that toddlers derive feelings of social support, trust, and intimacy from peers and will respond to the crying of another child if that child is a friend (Howes & Tonyan, 1999).

The emerging ability to engage in role-play with mothers and siblings also appears to support understanding others' mental states. Youngblade and Dunn (1995) found that children who engaged in more social pretense at 33 months performed better on a task measuring affective understanding at

40 months, whereas greater participation in role enactment predicted better performance on a task measuring children's understanding of false beliefs.

During later infancy, peers are not yet capable of joint pretense, but they do appear to enjoy simple collaborative play that enables them to practice communicating about common goals. Eckerman and Didow (1996) suggested that between 16 and 32 months age-mates use nonverbal imitation to create mutual understanding of the joint nature of activities. At the same time, Günçü (1993, p. 194) reported that children between 18 and 36 months communicate the idea of 'pretend' with 'exaggerated movements, facial gestures, and voice inflection, as well as brief verbal exchanges.'

In summary, adult caregivers build reciprocity and social understanding through early social play with infants. These abilities constitute the interpersonal building blocks of later successful social negotiations. In the second and third years, pretend play with peers, siblings, and mothers lays a foundation for understanding others' feelings and mental states, as reflected in the development of a theory of mind.

Cultural functions of play

Cultural functions of play refer to the ways in which play enhances children's understanding of the precepts and values of their culture. Expectations about the roles of different individuals within a society are communicated to infants and young children by virtue of who is deemed to be an appropriate play partner—parents, relatives, siblings, or peers. In some cultures, parents eschew play with children. Mexican mothers reputedly attach no particular value to play and likewise do not believe that it is important to play with their children (Farver & Howes, 1993). Guatemalan mothers reportedly laugh with embarrassment at the idea of playing with their children, as play is considered the territory of other children and occasionally grandparents (Rogoff, Mistry, Günçü & Mosier, 1993). Similar assertions have been made about Indonesian parents (Farver & Wimbarti, 1995).

In other cultures, parents consider play with children to be an important role of parenting and take an active part in children's play. Middle-class American parents think of themselves as play partners for their children and, consistent with such beliefs, promote and participate in pretend play with their young children (Bornstein *et al.*, 1996; Tamis-LeMonda, Bornstein, Cyphers & Toda, 1992).

Although many studies emphasize the cultural functions of play that are evidenced after infancy, research underscores the importance of interactions in infancy for cultural socialization. Parents' playful engagements with infants across a range of societies, including the United States, France, Argentina and Japan, communicate expectations about societal roles and cultural ideologies (Bornstein, Tamis-LeMonda, Tal, Ludemann, Toda, Rahn, Pêcheux, Azuma & Vardi, 1992; Bornstein, Toda, Azuma, Tamis-LeMonda & Ogino, 1990;

Bornstein, Haynes, Pascual, Painter & Galperín, 1999; Tamis-LeMonda & Bornstein, 1996). For example, cross-cultural research demonstrates that Argentine and Japanese mothers foster collectivist values whereas U.S. mothers foster individualist values in play with their young infants. When engaged in play with their infants, mothers in Japan more often encourage infants to attend to themselves, whereas mothers in the United States more often encourage infants to attend to objects in the environment. Japanese mothers also more often engage in 'other-directed' pretense play with their infants, for example prompting them to bow to or feed dolls; in contrast, U.S. mothers more often encourage their infants to engage in independent, concrete play (e.g., placing shapes in shape sorters), and they used the play setting as a forum for labeling and describing objects and events (Tamis-LeMonda *et al.*, 1992). In line with these differences in parental play, Japanese infants engaged more frequently in pretense play (particularly 'other-directed' pretense) and U.S. infants were more advanced in their receptive and productive vocabularies. These findings suggest that, during the period when infants' representational abilities are emerging, parents emphasize different modes of representation in their play, that preferred modes accord with traditional cultural values, and that they exert an early influence on children's developmental achievements.

After the second year, pretend play increasingly becomes a vehicle for transmitting information about cultural roles, routines, and conventions. Adult caregivers are critical conveyers of information about roles and routines as they help children elaborate their play ideas. For example, Miller and Garvey (1984) studied the development of the mother/baby role in children's play from 18 months to 3 years. In the earliest stages, mothers provided dolls and other props to their children (i.e., clothing, dishes, bottles) and gave a great deal of instruction about mothering behaviors. Similarly, Dunn and Dale (1984) found that mothers are far more likely to engage in play around nurturing themes and household activities with daughters than with sons, and much more likely to engage in action play with sons than with daughters. Play with toddlers may therefore be a particularly salient context for transmitting gender-typed information.

Like mothers, older siblings and peers are a source of information and modeling of social roles and conventions, particularly in the toddler and preschool years. In hunter–gatherer and agricultural societies, children rather than adults are primary playmates even for toddlers (Edwards & Whiting, 1993; Power, 2000).

In overview, the play partners of infants and toddlers vary across cultures, and these differences themselves communicate information about cultural norms concerning the roles of peers and adults as well as a child's social position in the larger group. In societies in which adults frequently engage in play with infants, social roles and cultural values are transmitted to infants from the first days of life. During infancy, peers are less likely to directly transmit specific social roles or values through role-play, both because of a lack of competence in coordinating social pretend and because of a lack of knowledge of social and cultural values. By using gender-typed behavior as one example of how cultural values are transmitted through play, adult caregivers reinforce gender-typed behavior most strongly during the toddler years, whereas peers become more influential during the preschool years.

SUMMARY

In the first year, play is predominantly characterized by basic manipulation of objects. As infants play they extract information about the perceivable qualities and concrete functions of objects. This form of play is exploratory because infants' play activities are tied to the tangible properties of objects. In the second year, infants' play takes on more of a nonliteral quality. Play is increasingly symbolic, representational and generative, as infants enact activities performed by self and others in simple scenarios—pretending to drink from empty teacups, to talk on toy telephones, and the like. The mastery, cognitive, social, and cultural functions of infant play are all significant and all supported by adult caregivers, siblings, and peers. Not surprisingly, the role of adult caregivers in supporting each of these play functions is paramount during early infancy. By 2–3 years of age, contributions of peers to certain play functions (e.g., divergent thinking, perspective taking) begin to outweigh those of either caregiver or sibling. Thus, it is safe to say that different play partners have unique characteristics that support different play functions at different developmental periods in the life course of the child.

Parent–child play holds a special place in infancy, in that it is a stage when the intrinsic pleasure and excitement of play predominates. During playful interactions, adult attunement and responsiveness to the infant's signals and needs are critical. For the infant, tactile, vocal, and visual theme-and-variation play with mothers supports the interrelated functions of regulation of arousal, expression of emotion, mastery motivation, and primary intersubjectivity. Over time, adults increasingly use play as a way to teach children object mastery and the pragmatics of communication with others. Mothers acting as teachers stimulate their children intellectually, as they prompt and support their children's cognitive achievements. As mothers transmit information to their children, they foster achievements in language, convergent and divergent thinking, and self-efficacy, while also communicating cultural expectations. Thus, by the time infants become toddlers, the pleasure caregivers derive from playing with their children has shifted from 'sheer delight' (Roggman, 1991) towards supporting cognitive and social competencies appropriate to the cultural context.

Mothers and fathers alike generally characterize pretend play as an enjoyable activity and facilitative of children's creativity and cognitive development. Although the bulk of the chapter focused on mothers, fathers also support their infants' play, and stylistic differences in fathers during play predict children's developmental achievements. There is both redundancy between parents (all parents like to play with their children), but also mothers and fathers have unique perspectives and contributions to offer, which suggests that they are not interchangeable but are complementary in their play with children.

Sibling–infant partnerships have certain characteristics that are similar to adult–child partnerships and others that are similar to peer–infant partnerships. Like adults, older siblings normally possess more expertise than their infant siblings and therefore are capable of modeling higher levels of play. Older siblings appear to play an important role in supporting symbolic play when their younger siblings are between 2 and 3 years of age. At this time, children are still too young to engage successfully in mutual pretense with peers, and therefore benefit from their older siblings' expertise and ability to share experiences. Moreover, when they pretend, older siblings engage in more role play than do parents, perhaps fostering representational abilities in their younger siblings. The shared experiences of older siblings, as well as their enhanced tendency to engage in role play, set the occasion for younger siblings to participate more effectively in pretend play about familiar routines. Because older siblings are more motivated by the sheer pleasure of play than by the desire to teach, play between siblings appears to be more pleasurable and affectively charged than infant–mother play.

Unlike caregivers or older siblings, peers are playmates who share similar developmental levels and relate to each other horizontally without an established hierarchy. Play partnerships between peers foster more sustained attention, pleasure, and excitement during joint episodes of physically active play than do mother–child partnerships. With each new form of play that is mastered, play with peers continues to be more engrossing and emotionally intense than mother–child play.

This integrative review underscores the changing nature of play functions and partners across infancy. It is simplistic to contend that certain play partners (e.g., mothers) support children's developmental achievements better than do others (e.g., peers). Rather, different social partners contribute in unique, and often complementary, ways to children's intrapsychological, mastery, cognitive, social, and cultural advances in play. The functions that are served in play, and the roles of different partners in supporting those functions, change in parallel with developments in children's cognitive, verbal, and socio-emotional competencies.

ACKNOWLEDGEMENTS

This chapter summarizes selected aspects of our research, and portions of the text have appeared in previous scientific publications cited here. We thank J. Katz and C. Varron for comments and assistance.

CHAPTER FIFTEEN

Learning to communicate

VIKRAM K. JASWAL and ANNE FERNALD

Introduction

The ability to communicate is essential for all animals living in social groups. Some social species such as ants and bees communicate through intricate but relatively inflexible behaviors that change little over the lifespan. In contrast, communication in primates changes fundamentally between infancy and adulthood. Young chimps and humans learn to convey information relevant to their needs through vocal, facial, and motor behaviors, and learn to monitor the behaviors of others in order to read their intentions and make sense of their actions, skills crucial for success in the complex social worlds in which they live. By the end of their first year, human infants move beyond the nonverbal behaviors shared with other primates, toward a medium of communication that is incalculably more powerful and flexible. This chapter focuses on how human infants learn to communicate, at first through voice, face, and gesture, and gradually through the use of language.

Infants are social creatures from the beginning, by virtue of being born into communities concerned for their survival. Caretakers in every culture tend to interpret babies' cries as a sign of discomfort and respond accordingly, although the cry of the newborn is certainly not an intentional communication. In his theory of attachment (see Chapter 12), John Bowlby pointed out that the cries and other reflexive behaviors of the young in many species serve an evolutionary function by alerting caregivers to the infant's needs. Such signals are particularly important in species where the young remain helpless for a prolonged period and need the parent to stay close by to provide food and protection. Infants in these **altricial** species can use species-specific social signals to draw attention to their needs: The gaping mouth of the herring gull chick elicits feeding behavior from the parent, and the ultrasonic distress cry of the rat pup inspires the mother to return to the nest and lick the pup, both examples of the complementary evolution of infant behaviors matched by appropriate parental behaviors. Bowlby extended these ethological observations to humans, the most altricial species of all, reasoning that the earliest social signals are cries, smiles, and other reflexive behaviors indicative of the infant's internal state. These communicative signals have evolved as the involuntary tactics of the helpless newborn for keeping the parent close at hand.

What is communication?

Although biologists, linguists, psychologists, and engineers still debate about how best to define communication, they generally agree that it occurs when a signal given by one organism is perceived by and influences the behavior of another organism. But what exactly is a signal? The uneven gait of an injured zebra reveals vulnerability to a hungry lion. Is this a social signal? Signals convey information, and the zebra's behavior is certainly informative. However, most ethologists (scientists interested in natural behavior) would agree that the wounded animal's gait is a direct consequence of a physical condition, not a signal specialized for communication. In contrast, the alarm call of a frantic monkey on seeing a predatory snake seems to more clearly qualify as an example of communication because it has evolved to convey information to conspecifics and because it is turned on and off in particular circumstances.

Even the monkey's alarm call seems different from human communication, however. Consider the following questions: Was the alarm call a deliberate warning to others in the troop informing them of potential danger? Did the monkey understand that the alarm call would cause the other animals to seek safety? Did the other monkeys understand that the caller had seen a snake? These questions get at whether the monkey's communicative signal was intentional, was perceived by others as intentional, and was motivated by assumptions about the intentions and future actions of others. In the case of a human shouting 'Watch out for the snake!' the answer to all these questions would be positive, but with monkey calls it is much less clear (Cheney & Seyfarth, 1990). This example makes the point that intentionality and an understanding of the mental states of others are critical in distinguishing human from animal communication.

In the first months of life, human infants' cries and smiles can influence the behaviors of their caretakers, but it is unlikely that infants as young as this understand why their cries have the effects they do. In the following sections, we briefly review research exploring infants' sensitivity to faces, voices, gestures, and the dynamics of social interaction, and discuss how this early sensitivity may serve as the starting point for building an understanding of other minds and ultimately for successful communication.

Listening to voices

The intonation of mother's voice, an auditory signal potentially rich in information, can be readily heard by the fetus (see Chapter 3). Infants only a few hours old prefer to listen to their own mother's voice rather than that of another woman, and even prefer to listen to the language they were exposed to prenatally rather than another.

After birth, the infant begins to experience voices in the context of increasingly rich forms of social stimulation. In many cultures, adults interacting with infants use a special form of speech that is more lively and musical than the speech typical of adult conversation. Figure 15.1 shows the vocal melodies of an American mother speaking to her 4-month-old child in the **infant-directed** (ID) speech style (sometimes called **motherese**), and also speaking to an acquaintance in the **adult-directed** (AD) speech style. Note how the intonation contours of ID speech are greatly expanded in pitch range. In a number of diverse languages, including English, German, Japanese, and Chinese, ID speech is typically higher in pitch with more exaggerated intonation contours, shorter utterances, and longer pauses than

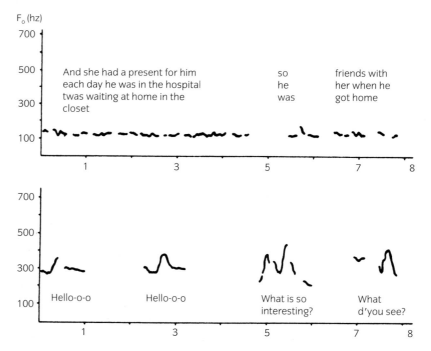

Figure 15.1 Intonation contours from the adult-directed (above) and infant-directed (below) speech of an American mother. Graph shows the movements in fundamental frequency (F_o), which corresponds to the pitch of the mother's voice.

in AD speech. When given the choice of listening to ID or AD speech in an auditory preference experiment, infants listen longer to ID speech and show more positive emotion when hearing it. Even newborns show this preference, suggesting that the vocal melodies of ID speech are appealing in themselves without extensive experience.

Through experience, however, these intonation patterns take on meaning for the infant because parents in different languages tend to use characteristic intonation patterns in particular interactional and emotional contexts. For example, the intonation contours used to praise an infant are typically wide in pitch range with a rise–fall pattern, quite different from the typical contours used for warning or prohibition which are shorter, more abrupt, and lower in pitch. Contrast how you might say 'What a good baby!' with how you would say 'No! That's not for you to play with!' By the age of 5 months, infants respond distinctively to these different contour types, even in a language they have never heard before. When English-learning infants heard 'praise' and 'prohibition' contours in German and Italian ID speech, they smiled more in response to the vocalizations that were positive in tone and looked wary in response to the negative vocalizations (Fernald, 1993). Since the words were unintelligible in any case and were spoken in an unfamiliar language, these findings show that certain culturally widespread features of ID intonation are effective in eliciting emotion in preverbal infants. However, even though 5-month-olds respond appropriately to intonation contours associated with communicative intentions such as praise and prohibition, we cannot conclude that they understand anything about the speaker's intentions at this age. In terms of communicative competence, these early selective responses based on intonation show an increasing sensitivity to emotion in the voice, but they are still not fundamentally different from the selective responses of monkeys to alarm calls.

Making sense of faces

Infants find faces as fascinating as voices from the beginning, and facial expressions provide another rich source of social information in human communication. Chapter 11 reviews research about how infants first process faces as visual stimuli and then gradually learn to interpret the emotional information available in facial expressions. Here, we consider another important question: How do infants begin to use their growing knowledge about faces in the process of communicating with other people?

By the age of 8 months infants can tell that happy faces are different from angry faces in terms of their visual features. Although this ability may be necessary for interpreting the emotional meaning of these expressions, it is far from sufficient. To interpret an expression in the flow of social interaction requires integrating information from multiple sources and making rapid inferences about what just happened and what will happen next. For example, when you see a big, sudden smile on your friend's face as she looks behind you, your response is not to conclude dispassionately 'Oh, the position of Sarah's mouth just changed' and leave it at that. Most likely you will make several automatic and instantaneous attributions, inferring that Sarah's expression indicates an internal state of pleasure, that she has seen something that caused the change in state, that whatever she has seen is something she regards positively, that she is more likely to approach than to flee from whatever it is she is looking at, and so on. As you make these rapid inferences you will probably also turn to follow her gaze so you can share her focus of attention. Without a word spoken and in a fraction of a second, you have processed several kinds of information from your friend's face that enabled you to make assumptions about aspects of the situation that you did not (and could never) experience directly, i.e., how Sarah is feeling, what made her feel that way and why, and what she might do in response. This kind of 'mind-reading' pervades human communication on every level, and by the end of the first year infants are well on their way to developing the complex mental abilities necessary for understanding other minds.

In the example above, at least three kinds of information could be extracted from what was happening on Sarah's face:

- the change in expression, marking the onset of the causal event
- the expression itself, indicating the nature and intensity of her internal emotional state
- the direction of her gaze, indicating attention to something presumably involved in the change of state.

Coordinating these different sources of information in the moment and initiating an appropriate response is a challenging task that demands much more than the ability to categorize static facial expressions. In their pioneering study of 'social referencing,' Campos and Stenberg (1981) explored how 12-month-old infants use these emerging mind-reading skills in action. Infants were placed on a 'visual cliff,' an apparatus originally developed for testing depth perception which gives the compelling illusion of a sudden drop (see Chapters 2 and 5). In fact the chasm is spanned by a sturdy plexiglass surface to support the infant, but most 12-month-olds stop at the brink and refuse to venture further. Positioned on the other side of the gap, the infant's mother was instructed to present one of two facial expressions—a big smile or an exaggerated fear face—when the infant stopped at the brink and looked across at her. If the mother smiled, most infants overcame their hesitation and proceeded across the chasm; however, if the mother displayed fear, all of the infants retreated from the edge and refused to cross. Campos and Stenberg concluded that in situations of uncertainty, infants check the mother's face to see her appraisal of the situation and then decide how to respond depending on the emotion she is displaying. This compelling phenomenon was dubbed **social referencing** because infants appeared to be referring to a social partner for nonverbal guidance, modifying their behavior based on the mother's positive or negative appraisal of a potentially dangerous situation.

Note that a potentially simpler alternative explanation of these results is also possible. The infant's avoidance response may result directly from discomfort at seeing the strange expression, or from past experience with fear faces followed by unpleasant events. This explanation does not presuppose any implicit reasoning about the mother's emotional state, i.e., that if the mother has this particular facial expression, she must be afraid of the chasm and thus it should be avoided. If simpler explanations can account for the infant's failure to cross the visual cliff, they imply no more (or less) mind-reading ability than monkeys use to flee in response to the alarm call of a conspecific.

We cannot resolve these complex questions here (but see Baldwin & Moses, 1996), but the example serves to make some important points. First, while the 3-month-old infant looks to the mother's face purely for the pleasure of interacting with her, the 12-month-old may look to the mother's face to seek information about something in the world beyond their interaction. Second, while the response of the 12-month-old may seem simple and straightforward, it represents an enormous advance in communicative competence, although the mental processes involved are complex and difficult to tease apart. And finally, our insights into the cognitive and emotional mechanisms underlying the development of communication over the first 2 years do not result from any one study or procedure; rather, they emerge slowly from many convergent studies of different behaviors which all reveal the infant's gradual progress in understanding other minds.

Following gaze and pointing gestures

Before the age of about 9 months, infants respond directly to salient sources of stimulation, crying in response to a loud noise or producing a charming smile in response to a game of peekaboo, without attempting to share their experiences with anyone else. Around 9 months, however, things begin to change, as infants try to communicate about things to other people For example, whereas a 6-month-old might smile in response to a wind-up toy, a 14-month-old would also be likely to look to his mother while smiling, as if to say 'Isn't this cool?' This is an important transition in a child's development, marking the beginning of intentional communication and an understanding of intentional communication by others. When older infants vocalize, these signals are often deliberate and may serve no other purpose than to gain the attention of their partner in interaction, quite unlike the cries and babbling of the younger infant. This section focuses on the development of two hallmarks of intentional communication: gaze-following and pointing.

Gaze-following

Following the gaze of another person is a deceptively simple activity. When you stare at an object, it is trivial for another adult to figure out what you have focused your attention on. Once both of you are looking at the same object and thus have established 'joint reference,' you can communicate about that object, talking about its features, whether each of you likes it, and so on. Before an infant reaches 8 months, the adult is the one responsible for following the gaze of the infant in order to establish joint reference. That is, when the infant chooses to focus on something, the adult then follows in, frequently labeling and/or commenting on the object of the infant's attention. If the adult looks at something different and tries to call attention to it, young infants will frequently look only at the adult's face, apparently unaware of the object of reference.

By about 12 months, however, infants have learned to follow an adult's gaze under most circumstances; if an adult across from the infant looks to the right or left, the infant will generally look in the appropriate direction. Interestingly, by 12 months, infants will also turn to follow the look of a decidedly nonhuman object, provided that the object provides cues to indicate that its actions might be intentional. To demonstrate this, Johnson, Slaughter, and Carey (1998) showed infants a round, fuzzy object that turned either to the left or to the right. The question was whether infants would follow the 'gaze' of this strange object. When the object had what could best be described as eyes, like the object on the right in Figure 15.2, infants did follow its gaze, turning to look in the same direction. Even when the object did not have eyes, like the object on the left in Figure 15.2, infants mirrored its turns, so long as it had earlier beeped in response to their vocalizations

Figure 15.2 Schematic drawing of the novel object with (right) and without (left) eyes. Infants always followed the gaze of the object with eyes, but only followed the gaze of the object without eyes if it had responded contingently to their behavior. From Johnson *et al.*, 1998; artwork by Kirsten O'Hearn.

and flashed attached lights in response to their movements. (Imagine the robot R2D2 from *Star Wars*.) However, in another condition where the object lacked eyes and also failed to respond contingently, the babies did not follow its 'gaze.' Thus, what drives infants to follow another's gaze seems to be cues related to that individual's intentionality—in this case, eyes and/or contingent responsiveness. By 12 months infants have learned that things with certain cues (i.e., ones human adults construe as intentional) are more likely to provide meaningful information about things in the environment than things without such cues.

Chimpanzees, our closest nonhuman relatives, can also follow the gaze of others, suggesting that they may be sensitive to the same cues signaling intentionality as human infants. However, we must bear in mind the caveat from the social referencing work described earlier: Infants and chimps alike may use intentional cues to attend to potentially meaningful things in the environment, but this does not necessarily mean that they are imputing anything like intentionality to the person (or object) emitting those cues. Eventually, humans do use intentionality to make inferences (e.g., why is she smiling? why is he looking in the wrong place?), but the picture is much less clear with chimpanzees. In fact, in experimental tests, chimps do not seem to understand the link between visual perception and knowledge at all: For example, they are as likely to request food from a human trainer wearing a blindfold over her eyes as a trainer wearing a blindfold over her mouth, as if they fail to infer that food would only come from the individual who could see the request (Reaux, Theall & Povinelli, 1999). Some scientists have argued that the ability to understand another's behavior as intentional—whether it be through eye gaze or some other action—is, in fact, what enabled human communication as we know it to emerge (Tomasello, 1999).

Pointing

Pointing gestures are another cue that adults frequently provide when directing a child's attention. As with gaze-following, the ability to interpret a point develops early in the second year of life. Before the age of about 12 months, infants tend to look at the pointer's hand rather than at the object being pointed to. As with gaze, interpreting a point is simpler in some situations than in others: For example, 9-month-olds may be able to follow a point as long as the target object is close to the end of the finger, and there are no intervening objects. However, infants are much more flexible by 14 months and can generally follow most pointing gestures. It is interesting to note that even for adults, pointing in a cluttered environment may not completely disambiguate an object of reference; however, pointing can be helpful in combination with words, which 14-month-olds are beginning to understand.

Figure 15.3 Infants begin to point as early as 9 months. Photo by Karen Thorpe.

Some infants begin to use pointing gestures themselves as early as 9 months (Figure 15.3), and most are regularly pointing by 14 months. Younger infants may point at things even when they are on their own and no social partner is present, suggesting that the earliest form of this behavior is actually noncommunicative. However, pointing clearly serves a communicative function a few months later, when the infant not only points but also looks to check that the adult is attending to the point. Bates (1979) has shown that early communicative pointing, where the infant checks with the adult for confirmation, correlates with a number of language measures of both comprehension and production. On the basis of these correlations, Bates argues that pointing is really a gestural form of naming and thus is closely related to the development of language skills.

Learning to communicate through language

First sounds

Long before infants produce recognizable words, they spend a good deal of time vocalizing, or babbling—an activity that provides them with valuable practice using the vocal modality. Indeed, the consonants that make up the first 50 words spoken by a child are typically created from sounds that occur frequently in babbling, suggesting that babbled sounds may provide the foundation for the production of a child's first words. The development of babbling unfolds in five stages (Oller, 1980), with transitions from one stage to another depending on the development of neural mechanisms and the vocal tract as well as the practice the child receives in each stage.

- In **Stage 1** (0–2 months), infants produce reflexive vocalizations, including crying, sneezing, and burping—sounds directly related to their physical state. These vocalizations account for about 90% of all vocalizations at 2 weeks, dropping to 50% by 8 weeks.

- In **Stage 2** (2–3 months), infants begin 'cooing,' so called because 'coo' is one of the few sounds infants first attempt to produce.

- In **Stage 3** (4–6 months), they start to experiment with the wide array of possible noises they can make with their vocal tract, resulting in a variety of vowel-like sounds as well as hoots and squeals.

- In **Stage 4** (6–7 months), babbling begins in earnest with the appearance of what are called **canonical syllables**. The term 'canonical' can mean 'true to life,' and canonical syllables are the first babbling sounds that sound like real words. These consist of a restricted set of alternating consonants and vowels, like the stereotypical 'gaga,' or 'mama' and 'dada.' Although 'mama' and 'dada' sound like the conventional names for parents in English (and many proud parents treat them as such), we would not call them true words until infants demonstrate an understanding of the correspondence between the sound and its meaning. This is an important caveat to keep in mind, and is related to our earlier discussion emphasizing intentionality as criterial for human communication. At 11–12 months reduplicated babbling ('gaga') gives way to variegated babbling, which involves stringing together different syllables ('bagoo').

- Finally, in **Stage 5** (12 months), infants begin a period of 'jargon' babbling, producing longer strings of consonant–vowel combinations with differing intonation and stress patterns. By this age the rate of babbling is already comparable to the rate of adult conversational speech. Infants typically produce their first words at around 12 months, just when they are also beginning to use jargon babbling. For several months, babbling and conventional words occur together, but beginning at about 19 months, as children's facility with conventional language increases, the amount of babbling drops off.

The restricted set of syllables in early babbling is fairly consistent across linguistic environments and is made up of sounds that occur frequently in the majority of languages. This suggests that the range of babbled sounds may be limited more by anatomical or physiological constraints than by environmental factors. However, the ambient language does influence the relative rate at which various sounds appear in babbling (de Boysson-Bardies *et al.*, 1992). For example, babies raised in languages that make frequent use of final consonants (e.g., English) tend to use final consonants in their babbling more than those raised in other languages (e.g., Japanese).

Deaf children also go through a period of vocal babbling, though they seem to be slightly delayed in the onset of reduplicated babbling, and to have a reduced repertoire of sounds. Deaf babies also go through a period of manual babbling, which shares many of the characteristics at the same ages as the vocal babbling of hearing infants (Petitto & Marentette, 1991). In particular, the manual babbling of deaf infants (but not of hearing infants) includes a restricted set of manual babbling gestures, reduplication, and even continuity between the forms used in manual babbling and the first symbolic signs.

First gestures

In addition to early vocal communication, hearing infants also communicate through a host of gestures like showing, giving, pointing, and ritual requests before they begin to speak their first words. These gestures are not symbolic because they are not used to 'stand for' something else. However, they can still be intentional and communicative if the infant demonstrates an awareness of the effect a particular gesture could have on a conversational partner and persists until the effect is obtained. For example, if a 12-month-old reaches up repeatedly for a favorite toy high on a bookshelf as her father watches, she might demonstrate intentional communication by looking back and forth between the father and the toy on the shelf, or by vocalizing until the desired goal is achieved. Many of infants' gestures meet these criteria by the age of 10 months. Even after infants begin producing words, they continue to support their linguistic communication with gestures, so gestural schemes are not simply replaced by verbal ones.

Just as babbling may be related to language development in that it provides practice with the communicative modality, regular production of some gestures may be related to language development in that it provides practice communicating via conventional signals. For example, as mentioned earlier, communicative pointing seems to be correlated with word comprehension at the beginning of the second year, perhaps because both pointing and word comprehension involve establishing joint reference to an external object (Bates, 1979).

Infants may also be able to communicate via symbolic gestures, or gestures that actually do stand for things. In fact, some researchers have suggested that infants can learn to produce symbolic gestures before producing words. One study showed that hearing infants exposed to American Sign Language (ASL) began producing signs around 8.6 months, 3 months before most children begin producing words (Bonvillian, Orlansky & Novack, 1983). The gestural modality may show this advantage for a number of reasons, including that motor control of the hands may develop more quickly than control of the articulatory system; signs might be more recognizable by parents than under-articulated words; and many early signs have a high degree of iconicity. By iconicity is meant that the sign might look like what it refers to, so that an early sign for 'I'm hungry' might be bringing the hand to the mouth. Before accepting a sign as a symbol, however, we must apply the same standards we require of an early word: It must be intentional and relatively context-independent. When these same standards are applied to the same group of children, the first symbolic signs and the first words both emerge around the age of 12 or 13 months.

For infants who are experiencing difficulty with vocal communication, Acredolo and her colleagues have argued that training them in sign may provide them with a useful communicative outlet (Acredolo & Goodwyn, 1990; Goodwyn & Acredolo, 1993). In one study, they trained mothers to make daily use of picture books and other materials in order to demonstrate target gestures (e.g., lip-smacking for 'fish,' arm-flapping for 'bird,' etc.) to their preverbal 11-month-olds. Biweekly interviews were conducted to collect information about the children's production and comprehension of these signs as well as the conventional words. On average, infants produced both gestures and words at about the same time, although there was substantial variability among children. In short, some children will progress faster with sign, some with speech, and some will produce words and signs at the same time.

Early comprehension

As you know from Chapter 10, infants have learned an enormous amount about the sounds of their language during the first year. By 8 months infants are attuned to the phonological (sound) system of the ambient or surrounding language, and can recognize recurrent patterns in sequences of speech sounds. These skills are all essential for recognizing words in fluent speech, which must be processed at a very rapid rate. However, identifying a sequence of syllables as familiar is just the first step in word recognition, which also requires learning an association between the sound sequence and a particular meaning. Moreover, this sound–meaning association must be more than just a conditioned response to a verbal routine to count as true comprehension.

The question of when comprehension begins has been debated since the earliest scholarly studies of language development 200 years ago. In a diary study published in 1877, Hippolyte Taine noted that when his 11-month-old daughter heard 'Where is Mama?', she always turned toward her mother. In fact, in a more recent experimental study, Tincoff and Jusczyk (1999) suggested that infants as young as 6 months of age may have already formed an association between a parent and their name. In this study, infants watched side-by-side videos of their parents and heard the word 'mommy' or 'daddy' several times. Results showed that they looked significantly longer at the video of the named parent than the video of the unnamed one. Another way of gathering data on early comprehension is to ask parents to fill out standardized checklists to keep track of which words their child appears to understand in daily interactions in the home. Figure 15.4 shows that, on one such checklist, infants understand an average of about 50 words by their first

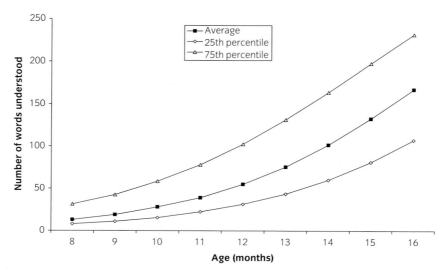

Figure 15.4 Receptive vocabulary size from 8 to 16 months. This figure shows the average number of words infants at various ages understand, and also includes the 25th and 75th percentile range in order to show the large amount of variability in early vocabulary size. Adapted from Fenson *et al.* (1994.)

birthday, and over 150 by the age of 16 months (Fenson, *et al.*, 1994). As the figure shows, however, there is considerable variability among children on these measures.

Although checklists give an estimate of changes in the size and extent of the child's receptive vocabulary over time, they don't reveal anything about important developments in the child's ability to recognize and understand familiar words in continuous speech. If a mother indicates on the checklist that her infant understands the word 'ball' at 12 months, she is likely to check the same box again at 15 months, although in the intervening months there have been dramatic changes in speech-processing efficiency that are not obvious in the child's spontaneous behavior. You are probably not aware of this, but as a fluent language user you typically process 15–30 different speech sounds every second in following a casual conversation! How do infants develop the skill to understand spoken language with such remarkable speed and efficiency?

The early development of competence in word recognition has been studied by tracking infants' eye movements as they listen to spoken sentences containing familiar words. Sitting on the parent's lap, infants are observed in a booth where they look at pictures while hearing speech naming one of the pictures, as shown in Figure 15.5. The infant's eye movements are videotaped during the test session, and then analyzed later in slow motion, frame by frame, to measure very precisely how quickly the infant's eyes moved to the named picture. By tracking infants' gaze patterns in the process of understanding,

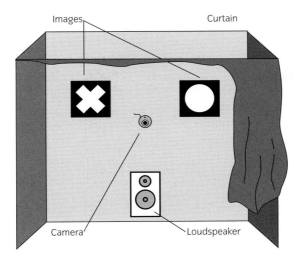

Figure 15.5 Experimental setup used by Fernald *et al.* (1998). Infants listen to speech naming one of the pictures. Does the infant look at the named picture?

it is possible to document impressive progress in the efficiency of spoken word recognition occurring over the second year of life (Fernald *et al.*, 1998). Figure 15.6 shows the average speed of response, or reaction time, for infants at 15, 18, and 24 months of age, as they orient to the appropriate picture in response to hearing the name of the picture. The bar graph in this figure is aligned with the waveform from one of the stimulus sentences, showing the time course of infants' responses in relation to the familiar target word 'baby.' Note that 15-month-olds shifted their eyes to the picture of the baby only after the target word was spoken. By 24 months, however, infants were several hundred milliseconds faster to respond, identifying the word 'baby' after hearing only the first syllable, before it was completely spoken. Other studies show that by 18 months infants are already becoming highly efficient in spoken language processing; like adults, they can recognize familiar words based on incomplete acoustic information, a skill which is essential for the rapid and reliable processing of fluent speech (Fernald, Swingley & Pinto, 2001).

Word learning and social understanding

Around their first birthday many infants begin to speak their first words, although some start a bit earlier and others don't talk for another several months. The first words spoken by most infants have a lot in common across different languages and cultures. These include words used in social routines such as **bye-bye** and **peekaboo,** names for family and pets such as **Mama** and **Fido,** lots of names for animals and common objects of interest to the child,

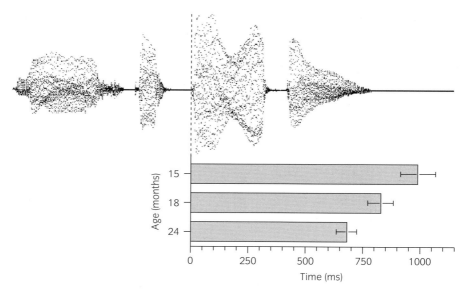

Figure 15.6 Mean reaction time to look at the named target picture when the infants were initially looking at the 'wrong' picture. 15-month-olds take about a second (1000 ms) and reaction time gets quicker with age.

such as **doggy, shoe,** and **train** (or **choo-choo**), along with a few action words such as **eat** and **push**. The infant's first utterances consist of single words, although some of these may be amalgams such as **gimmee** which the child treats as a single word.

One important question is how children figure out the meaning of new words. This might seem like a simple enough task: when the mother hands a new toy to the child and says 'This is a yo-yo', shouldn't it be obvious what **yo-yo** refers to? Actually it's not so obvious, because the new word could refer to many different features of the unfamiliar object. **Yo-yo** might mean **red,** or **round,** or **plastic,** or **string,** or **this-red-round-plastic-thing-with-a-string.** Questions about infants' cognitive strategies in guessing what new words refer to have been a research topic of considerable interest (e.g., Markman, 1989). But just as interesting (and in keeping with the theme of the present chapter) are questions about how infants use their emerging knowledge of other minds to help them learn new words, which we turn to in the next section.

Emerging knowledge that others have minds

We described earlier how children learn to follow the gaze of another person, and to understand that gaze can be indicative of that person's focus of attention. What role might gaze-following play in word learning? Considering the cluttered world most infants live in, adult gaze direction could be a valuable source of information to figure out what is being talked about. If an infant is playing with a fascinating toy car and hears his mother say 'Look at this yo-yo,' it would clearly be an error for the infant to assume that **yo-yo** referred to the car. Only by looking up to check and follow his mother's gaze could he make the correct association between the new word and the object it referred to. In fact, this is exactly what infants did in an experiment by Baldwin (1991). As the infant played with one toy, the adult said, 'It's a modi,' while looking at a second toy. At that point, most infants looked up to check the speaker's focus of attention. Later the children were shown both toys, the one they had been playing with and the one the speaker was looking at. When asked to choose the 'modi,' 18-month-olds chose the toy the speaker had been looking at, as if they understood that this was the one the speaker had intended to refer to.

As we have been stressing throughout, the ability to read the intentions of others has important implications for human communication. Someone who is unable to interpret social signals indicative of intent might therefore be expected to have difficulty learning to communicate. In fact, children with autism seem to have trouble making use of social signals like eye gaze. In an experimental situation like the Baldwin (1991) one described above, they tended to make just the kind of mapping errors that 18-month-olds without autism avoid (Baron-Cohen, Baldwin & Crowson, 1997).

Communication is very much a social skill, requiring the ability to interpret and understand the feelings, intentions, and mental states of others. Although infants can demonstrate an early understanding of some aspects of intentionality, it is worth emphasizing again that understanding intentionality is not an all-or-none ability. Carpenter, Nagell, and Tomasello (1998; see Table 15.1) argue that before about 12 months, infants begin to recognize only the idea that other people have intentions, although they are still unable to determine what those intentions are or how they come about. As a result, infants younger than 1 year can engage in activities where they share attention with another individual, but only as long as they do not have

Table 15.1 Average age at which infants first begin to demonstrate fundamental skills related to the emergence of communicative competence (from Carpenter, Nageli, and Tomasello, 1998)

Skill	Age (months)
Sharing of attentional focus with another person	9.0
Use of gestures to communicate	10.3
Following the attention of another person	11.5
Learning through imitation	11.9
Referential use of language	>15

to follow another's attention or provide purposeful cues to direct another's attention. Only later, around 12–13 months, do infants begin demonstrating an understanding of what other people's intentions are, which allows them both to follow another's attention and to consciously manipulate it. This new understanding enables word learning to begin in earnest, as infants can now treat a word uttered by another person as specifically intended to refer to a particular referent. Thus, in the Baldwin (1991) study described earlier, an 18-month-old can recognize that a speaker intended to refer to one object even though the infant's own attention was focused on a different object.

Another impressive example of young children's ability to use a speaker's intentions to learn new words is provided by Akhtar and Tomasello (1996). In their study, 2-year-olds participated in a finding game where they opened four containers and discovered an interesting object in each one. Importantly, these were objects that the children would not already have names for (e.g., a bike horn, a beanbag frisbee). After repeating this activity a few times, the children observed a speaker say 'Let's find the toma!' while unsuccessfully trying to remove one of the objects from a container that now appeared to be locked. Later, when the 2-year-olds were shown the four objects and asked to select the 'toma,' they tended to select the object that had been in the locked container. Even though they had never seen that object labeled directly with the word 'toma,' they inferred from the speaker's unsuccessful attempts to open the locked container that she intended to refer to that object.

SUMMARY

Human infants start out life capable only of involuntary signals closely tied to their physiological condition at the moment, not unlike other animals with a limited repertoire of inflexible social behaviors. From an evolutionary point of view, these primitive signaling behaviors serve a vital communicative function, because more mature and experienced humans are able to interpret them reliably as indices of the infant's needs and internal condition. But unlike other animals, the human infant's communicative skills expand and change continually from day to day, with experience and the development of new cognitive capacities that enable the child to extract socially relevant information from the voices, faces, and gestures of other people. By the end of the first year, the infant has moved well beyond the more limited capabilities of other primates. They have become able to communicate their own intentions through symbolic gestures and words and to read the intentions of others. During this period the young infant demonstrates increasing knowledge of other minds through continual transitions in many dimensions—the transition from looking into the mother's eyes with delight to following the direction of her gaze for information, the transition from smiling in response to the mother's voice to calling her attention with a smile to something unexpected, the transition from babbling single syllables to using words symbolically to influence the behavior of other people. Although a sophisticated understanding of others' thoughts, feelings, and intentions will still take several years to mature, the mind-reading ability that distinguishes humans from all other animals develops gradually over the first year, manifested first in nonverbal communication and then more clearly in the child's emerging ability to speak and understand language.

PART FIVE

Early Interventions, Culture, Nutrition, and Health

CHAPTER SIXTEEN

Early intervention research, services, and policies

ROBIN GAINES LANZI, CRAIG T. RAMEY,
and SHARON LANDESMAN RAMEY

Introduction

Early intervention offers an opportunity to improve the developmental trajectories of infants and young children who are identified as having developmental
disabilities or at risk for having developmental delay. New research on brain
development has shown the tremendous benefit of providing intensive, comprehensive, continual services, beginning early in life. The purpose of this
chapter is to present a context for understanding early intervention research,
services, and policies. We first begin with an overview of early intervention in
terms of what it involves, who is eligible, when it is conducted, and how it is
implemented. International beliefs, practices, and social policies are discussed
within this framework. Next, a review of the literature on early intervention
research is presented, including sections on the benefits of early intervention,
a brief overview of the origins of early intervention programs, and the scientific evidence of which programs are successful and why. Finally, a brief
synopsis of new early intervention resources including books, journals, and
websites is presented.

Overview of early intervention

In general, early intervention refers to a comprehensive set of individualized
services designed to meet the developmental needs of infants and young
children and their families (Ramey, Ramey & Lanzi, in press a). The variety
of early intervention programs and services is as varied as are the needs of the
individual infants and young children. Definitions of early intervention and
whether the label of 'early intervention' is used to define a program differ
across cultures and countries.

A fundamental principle of early intervention is that it should begin as
early in life as possible, and that it should be tailored to the specific needs
of the individual infants and young children. Early intervention programs

involve a broad array of services. These can include: educational and medical services for diagnosis, evaluation and support; health and nursing services; nutrition counseling; psychological services; occupational and physical therapy; audiological and vision services; and assistive technology devices and services. Additionally, services can support the family in terms of family training, counseling, home visits, service coordination, special instruction, transportation, and related costs. The development of individualized service coordination varies, depending on the specific needs of the infants and young children and their family situations. A case manager often oversees the planning and service coordination that involves a team of professionals including pediatricians, pediatric neurologists, developmental pediatricians, physical therapists, speech–language therapists, social workers, psychologists, special education teachers, occupational therapists, audiologists, optometrists and ophthalmologists, nurses, nutritionists, and specialists who have received interdisciplinary or multidisciplinary training (Ramey, Ramey & Lanzi, in press a; Ramey, Echols, Ramey & Newell, 2000).

In the United States, infants and young children enter early intervention programs from birth through 5 years of age. Some programs, however, begin working with pregnant women before the birth of their child. During the first 2 years of life, services are commonly provided in the home or childcare environment on a weekly basis. Once the child reaches 2 years of age the transition from home to school-based early intervention should begin, and be completed when the child reaches 3 years of age. The school-based early intervention program offers a broader set of services including early counseling services, early identification and assessment, parent counseling and training, recreation, rehabilitation counseling services, school health services, social work services in schools, and special education (Ramey, Ramey & Lanzi, in press; Ramey, Echols, Ramey & Newell, 2000).

In other developed industrialized countries, 'early intervention' as a concept is not widely used. However, services that Americans endorse as part of early intervention are widely implemented and funded in other industrialized countries. Britain is the only European country that focuses on 'children in need' or 'children at risk.' Implemented in 1991, the Children Act of 1989 addresses the need for targeted interventions on children with special needs in the UK. Interestingly, other countries that belong to the Organisation for Economic Cooperation and Development (i.e., democracies with a market economy) have implemented social policies for all children rather than 'at-risk,' 'special needs,' or 'vulnerable' children. Countries included in this pact include the western European countries, the Czech Republic, Hungary, Poland, Japan, and Korea, among others. Their focus is on encouraging development rather than limiting it to the prevention of problems. Further, compared to the United States, the intervention strategy in most industrialized Western countries includes three key elements: adequate family income, sufficient time for parenting, and supportive care and services.

In other countries, although not necessarily labeled as 'early intervention,' many services and activities are implemented with the same common goal of early intervention, but tailored to the specific cultural/traditional beliefs and practices of the community and family. In their book on international perspectives on early intervention, Odom, Hanson, Blackman, and Kaul (2003) present numerous examples of early intervention programs from around the world, including many developing countries. The authors note there are common themes among the cross-cultural early intervention programs, including developing programs that are culturally sensitive and relevant. Some examples include:

- Jamaican mothers and grandmothers have a special way holding and moving the baby after a bath consisting of 'stretching, tossing, molding, range-of-motion exercises' which may be important for babies with disabilities (Thorburn, 2003).

- Community workers in India use indigenous equipment and supplies found in the home to work with young children with cerebral palsy on their motor development.

- Operating through nongovernmental organizations in Ethiopia, community-based rehabilitation centers have begun 'door-to-door' home-based early intervention programs because most do not have access to early intervention. Further, in Ethiopia, raising awareness and acceptance of children's disabilities is important and is often done by community rehabilitation workers talking to mothers during community gatherings and ceremonies (Teferra, 2003).

Building on Feuerstein's theory of cognitive modifiability (see, e.g., Feuerstein, 1990), Israel has implemented a number of early intervention programs using the Mediational Intervention for Sensitizing Caregivers (MISC) model to support the development of children through mediated learning (Klein, 2003). Mediated learning refers to

learning that occurs in the presence of an adult who tries to mediate between the child and his or her environment to ensure that learning takes place. Intelligence is defined as the ability and the need to learn readily and easily from one's experiences. The MISC model is the process through which this goal is achieved. (Klein, 2003, p. 76)

This practice has been adopted and implemented in many other countries including Norway, Sweden, Belgium, Holland, Ethiopia, Sri Lanka, Indonesia, and the United States (Klein, 2003).

The service delivery of early intervention is to a large degree a function of the availability of trained professionals to provide the services. Many countries are advancing new and different models of service delivery (Odom, Hanson, Blackman, and Kaul, 2003). For instance, in Jamaica, individuals from the community are trained to conduct screenings and provide support in the home. Germany and Portugal have implemented 'team-based' models of training to maximize training efforts (Boavida & Carvalho, 2003). In Sweden, an interdisciplinary training program is conducted through distance education and in-service training (Bjürck-Åkesson & Granlund, 2003).

Social policies and legislation

In the United States, early intervention services are mandated through federal legislation. The Education for All Handicapped Children Act of 1975 initially mandated services for children with disabilities. The Education for All Handicapped Act Amendments of 1986 provided additional funding for children aged 3–5 and funded the creation of a system of early intervention for children from birth through their third birthday. Early intervention services are currently funded by Part C (birth to 3 years) of the Individuals with Disabilities Education Act (IDEA) Amendments of 1997. Although federal legislation mandates services and provides funding, not all services are fully funded by federal dollars, and are supplemented with additional state funds. Private insurance and Medicaid are often billed for services. State and local programs must work together to raise additional dollars to meet the operating costs (Ramey, Ramey & Lanzi, in press a; Ramey, Echols, Ramey & Newell, 2000).

Federal legislation dictates that states define which risk conditions qualify children to receive early intervention as well as which services will be provided for specific diagnoses. The majority of states have a Child Find program to identify infants at risk for disability. There are, however, no uniform definitions or criteria for determining eligibility. The criteria for the cut-off point for defining a child with a disability vary from state to state. Although determination of eligibility varies, almost all assessments involve tests or procedures to determine a child's mental development and performance in areas such as motor development, socio-emotional development, language, and cognition. An individualized family service plan (IFSP) is required to be developed before the receipt of services. Family members and health professionals work together to identify the primary needs of the child and family, and how these needs can be best met (Ramey, Ramey & Lanzi, in press a; Ramey, Echols, Ramey & Newell, 2000).

The United States is well known for advancing the field of early intervention in terms of theory and research. Unfortunately, comprehensive social policies that address the early intervention needs of infants and young children in the United States are somewhat lacking. Although the federal law dictates children aged 3–5 years with disabilities have access to early intervention services and provides monies to the states to support the services, not all children eligible for services receive them. European countries, on the other hand, have not necessarily emphasized early intervention theory and research as a concept but have established social policies that exemplify the concept, including progressive family policies concerning parental leave, childcare, home-health visiting and family support policies and programs. Additionally, the extensive European social policy infrastructure includes income transfers, health care, and housing assistance that provides a solid basis for supporting child and family services (Kamerman, 2000).

Increasingly, many countries are introducing legal changes to provide support and services for infants and young children. Examples of national laws include: South Korea's Promotion Law for Special Education; Egypt's National Strategy to Combat Handicaps; Sweden's establishment of a national social insurance system and the Child Health Services, with Child Rehabilitation Centers as part of the foundation for early intervention. Australia, on the other hand, does not have a national law; there grassroots efforts and a national professional organization have provided much-needed support. Nongovernmental organizations, funded from national and international sources, often provide early intervention services (Odom & Kaul, 2003).

Benefits of early intervention

Numerous comprehensive reports of early intervention research over the past four decades have shown that early intervention makes a difference in children's development (see reviews by Carnegie Task Force on Meeting the Needs of Young Children report, 1994; Guralnick, 1997; Haskins, 1989; Odom, Hanson, Blackman & Kaul, 2003; Ramey & Ramey 1998, 1999; Ramey, Ramey & Lanzi, in press b). The first 5 years of life is a critical time in the development of infants and young children, particularly for those with developmental disabilities. It is during this time that the brains of infants and young children have the greatest capacity to change, and the earlier intervention begins, the more opportunity the brain has to make changes and produce desired outcomes. Unfortunately, if children do not experience necessary stimulation during the early years, their brains may not be able to compensate for the critical loss (see Carnegie Task Force Report, 1994; Shore, 1997; Ramey & Ramey, 1998, 1999). The scientific findings are clearest for those children living in poverty, who are at risk for cognitive and language development delays, and for children who are biologically at risk due to low birthweight and premature birth (Ramey, Ramey & Cotton, 1998; Ramey, Ramey & Lanzi, in press b).

Traditional, religious, or cultural beliefs and practices are sometimes at cross-purposes with the scientific findings undergirding early intervention programs and services. For instance, some may believe that a child's disability is a function of a parent's action or behavior, or that the disability is due to an evil spirit or to supernatural forces. In these instances, parents may seek treatment for their children from a shaman or a healer prescribing traditional medicine. Of course, some treatments have positive effects for infants (e.g., physiotherapy with Ethiopian infants; Jamaican infant-handling routine after bathing babies); however, if traditional treatments are not helpful, effective early intervention services may be delayed or prohibited because of traditional beliefs (Odom and Kaul, 2003). A classic example of this was a Hmong family whose beliefs conflicted with the scientific medical community and whose daughter had severe disabilities. Unfortunately, the conflict resulted in tragic consequences for the daughter.

Odom and Kaul (2003) point out that conflict between traditional/religious/cultural beliefs and practices and scientific medical community occurs in the United States and other industrialized countries as well as in developing countries. For instance, some fundamentalist Christian beliefs dictate that a child's disability is a 'family burden from God' and that the family, rather than providers of early intervention services, should take care of their child. Interestingly, they note that what is scientifically acceptable or advanced as the appropriate treatment may not always prove to be correct. For example, in the 1960s Western science advocated that autism was a function of absence of emotional support from the mother, and the way to treat autism was to remove young children with autism from their families (Odom and Kaul, 2003).

Origins of early intervention programs

Examination of how early experiences and intervention might impact children's healthy development has been under way for about 70 years. A group of psychologists firmly grounded in learning theory, including Donald Hebb (1949), J. McVicker Hunt (1961), and Harry Harlow (1958), began to explore the role and consequences of early experiences on children's cognitive, social, and emotional development, and other psychologists followed with scientific experiments. In the 1930s and 1940s a series of notable studies focusing on infants and young children living in orphanages showed that the care provided to children in institutions was woefully inadequate when compared with the loving, attentive care typically provided by a family. The work of Bowlby, Dennis, Goldfarb, Skeels, Skodak, and Spitz, among others, raised concern about the lasting harm caused by the lack of care and stimulation found in institutions. The seminal work of Skeels and Dye (1939) proved that early experience had the power to alter the development of intelligence and the life course of institutionalized retarded children. Their work launched vigorous scientific examination of what children need in order to ensure healthy growth and development. A series of carefully controlled experiments using animal models were implemented that uniformly varied the type and timing of early experiences. The first set of findings from these studies revealed that deficits in social and sensory experiences produced aberrant social, emotional, and learning behavior in animals that were otherwise born healthy and with a good genetic foundation (Sackett *et al.*, 1999).

A second set of experiments sought to understand how children responded to nonoptimal environments and the extent to which stimulation could reverse or minimize the negative effects of early deprivation, including institutionalization (Landesman & Butterfield, 1987). The work from these studies showed that not all individuals respond in a similar way to the same environmental conditions. In social ecology, this principle is referred to as the **person × environment interaction**, which means the impacts of what occurs depends upon the person as well as the event (e.g., Bronfenbrenner, 1979). In other words, individual experiences, not just the mere exposure to environmental conditions, serve to mediate and moderate the effects of early deprivation. Factors such as biological and genetic differences, the age when a child first experiences deprivation, the child's own behavioral propensities theoretically can contribute to varying individual responses to similar environments.

In the early 1960s, a third line of investigation was a proactive effort to prevent suboptimal development and developmental delay in children living in poverty. The work of these studies was propelled by a national awareness of the devastating conditions of poverty in the United States, the inequality of educational opportunities for children living in poverty, and scientific findings from the fields of child development and mental retardation. Key findings included:

- Evidence that rates of mental retardation, most especially mild mental retardation with no identified biomedical cause, were elevated among very poor families (see Garber, 1988 for a review of epidemiological findings). It was also found that this form of mental retardation had a strong familial pattern (Zigler, 1967) and had a time-distributed onset with progressive mental retardation (Deutsch, 1967; Klaus & Gray, 1968).

- Strong associations between the quality of a child's home environment—as measured by the responsiveness and sensitivity of the mother to her child, the amount and level of language stimulation, and direct teaching—and the child's intellectual and problem-solving capabilities (e.g., McVicker Hunt, 1961; Vygotsky, 1962). This finding has been confirmed in hundreds of studies conducted in the last few decades (see review by Maccoby & Martin, 1983).

- Confirmation that very young infants are capable of learning, which disputed the once prevailing view that infants were passive and incapable of learning at such an early age (see Osofsky, 1979 for an early summary of these findings). These studies identified a multitude of ways infants could learn and how these experiences impacted their responses to subsequent learning experiences (C. T. Ramey & Ramey, 1999).

The findings from these studies prompted the creation of early enrichment programs, most notably the American national program, Head Start, based on a broad platform of empirical findings and theoretical support (C. T. Ramey & Ramey, 1998; C. T. Ramey & Ramey, 2001.) (The British equivalent of Head Start is Sure Start, and similar programs are to be found in most Western societies.) The original and continuing goal of these programs has been to discover the value of early educational intervention as an antidote for environmental deprivation (McVicker Hunt, 1964).

Early scientific studies

The first set of experiments testing the efficacy of providing enriched experiences for children at risk from impoverished homes was conducted in the late 1960s and early 1970s. Most took place in university child development centers, although they differed considerably in the amount and types of services provided, the age when children were enrolled, and the extent of risk among participants. Today, these programs are often labeled as compensatory in nature, in that they sought to offer elements found in many middle-class families, including responsive, educated caregiving; educational materials such as toys and games; nutritious meals; and a safe, stimulating environment where young children's thinking and problem-solving are actively encouraged. Although compensatory programs have sometimes been criticized because they implied a deficit model, in fact these programs appeared to be enacted with great care and concern for participants and were well received by the families. The Consortium for Longitudinal Studies was one such effort.

The Consortium for Longitudinal Studies

The Consortium represented a collaborative effort involving 11 systematic studies that used experimental or quasi-experimental designs to determine the efficacy of early intervention programs for children at risk, based on socio-demographic characteristics (Darlington *et al.*, 1980; Lazar *et al.*, 1982). Several key findings evolved from this study. The first finding reaffirmed earlier reports that children participating in these high-quality early intervention programs made significant gains in intellectual and cognitive performance. In addition, there were long-lasting effects in terms of their academic school competence; attitudes and values; and impact on the family. The second and more controversial finding was that IQ scores for children were highest at the end of the intervention and were maintained for 3 or 4 years, but began to decline over time. This phenomenon is widely referred to as the **fade-out effect**. It is somewhat disappointing that this second finding is often the only one cited, rather than an acknowledgement of the lasting benefits on children's real-world indicators, such as lower rates of grade retention (i.e., dropping back a grade or class) and decreased rates of placement in special education.

Longitudinal early intervention studies

In the 1970s, a number of model early intervention programs that were typically funded at higher levels and supervised more closely than large publicly funded programs were started. Five of these programs incorporated randomized trial research designs, which are considered the 'gold standard' of research. Randomized trials provide a more rigorous test of the impact of a new treatment by randomly assigning comparable types of children with treatment and control groups, thus eliminating potential selection bias factors. Randomized trials help researchers to be reasonably certain that there are no pre-existing and uncontrolled differences between the two groups. In addition, these five programs were relatively free of attrition (i.e., children withdrawing from the study) and gathered information on the children at least into the middle school year. These programs were the **Abecedarian Project** (C. T. Ramey & Campbell, 1984; Campbell & Ramey, 1994; C. T. Ramey *et al.*, 2000), the **Infant Health and Development Program** (IHDP, 1990; C. T. Ramey *et al.*, 1992), the **Milwaukee Project** (Garber, 1988), the **Perry Preschool Project** (Weikart *et al.*, 1978; Schweinhart *et al.*, 1993), and **Project Care** (Wasik *et al.*, 1990; C. T. Ramey *et al.*, 1995; Burchinal *et al.*, 1997). All of these programs were multi-pronged and provided at least one full year of intervention before the children were 5 years of age. The programs differed in their enrollment selection criteria, the age children entered the program, and the amount and nature of the services.

Factors for success

What factors determine the success of an early intervention program in preventing developmental delay, mental retardation, and poor school achievement? Four factors appear to make a critical difference: (1) timing and duration of the intervention; (2) intensity of services provided and received; (3) use of direct vs. indirect learning experiences; and (4) the provision of comprehensive services in addition to educational programming (Ramey, Ramey & Cotton, 2002; Ramey, Ramey & Lanzi, in press a and b).

Timing and duration

Most early intervention or 'school readiness' preschool programs for at-risk, low-income children begin at 4 years of age. The evidence shows, however, that the earlier an intervention is started and the longer it is maintained, the more likely it is to produce greater benefits for participants. Successful experimental model programs such as the Abecedarian Project (C. T. Ramey & Ramey, 2000), the Brookline Early Education Project (Hauser-Cram *et al.*, 1991), Project CARE (Wasik, *et al.*, 1990), and the Milwaukee Project (Garber, 1988), enrolled children in infancy and continued at least until they entered elementary school. All produced significant benefits for children's cognitive, academic, and/or language performance.

Intensity of services

Unfortunately, many early intervention programs do not demonstrate change in children's intellectual and academic performance. An examination of these programs show they are not intensive, as indicated by the hours per day, days per week, and weeks per year of educational services provided. The Utah State Early Intervention Research Institute conducted 16 randomized trials of early intervention programs for special needs children and found that none of the programs produced significant efforts on children's development. None of these 16 programs provided a full-day, 5-day per week program. Scarr and McCartney (1988) also failed to produce positive cognitive effects when they provided a parent-oriented, once-weekly intervention with economically impoverished families in Bermuda. Two home-visiting programs, however, showed that intense programs can make a difference. First, an early intervention home-visit program that provided services 3 days a week produced significant benefits, while the same program offered at a less intense level was not successful (Powell & Grantham-McGregor, 1989). Second, the Brookline Early Education Program (Hauser-Cram *et al.*, 1991) found that only the most intensive two-generation model they provided was adequate to benefit children at risk for school difficulties, while the lowest intensity program had no measurable consequences. The Infant Health and Development Program (1990) examined intensity at the individual level. It was found that the amount of services received had a strong positive relationship to the child's social and intellectual development at 36 months of age (C. T. Ramey *et al.*, 1992).

Direct vs. indirect services

Successful early interventions can be provided to children and/or families in a variety of forms. Some offer **direct services** to children in the form of classes in a child development center. Others may offer early intervention services to children by a more indirect method, most often a home-visiting program where trained personnel work with parents to inform them about how to promote children's development or where parenting classes (groups) are offered. Some programs provide a combination of these types of services.

The scientific literature examining the effects of these strategies are clear: indirect methods are far less powerful than direct approaches in terms of enhancing children's intellectual and social development for children from varying backgrounds (Madden *et al.*, 1976; Scarr & McCartney, 1988). Project CARE found that combining daily center-based intervention with weekly home visits produced significant gains in cognitive development, whereas the group that had regular home visits (indirect method) over a 5-year period had no documented benefits on children's cognitive and social development, parent attitudes or behavior, or the quality of the home environment. Although it is important to recognize and celebrate the role of parents in their children's development, careful consideration should be given to whether such programs actually produce adequate positive child benefits.

Comprehensiveness of services

Early interventions that adopt a broad multi-pronged approach to working with children and families in order to enhance children's development are more effective than those that have a more narrow focus. The Abecedarian Project, the Brookline Early Education Project, Project CARE, the Milwaukee Project, the Infant Health and Development Program, and the Mobil Unit for Child Health (Gutelius *et al.*, 1977) all provided comprehensive services for families and used multiple routes to enhance children's development. Interestingly, Romanian and American researchers have shown that Romanian children in orphanages who are at risk for developmental delay benefit greatly from a program introduced early in life that involves a broad spectrum of services including stable adult–child relationships, small group size, and a focus on enriched caregiving and educational activities (Sparling, Dragomir, Ramey & Florescu, 2005).

New early intervention resources

As we have described, early intervention research has been investigated for quite some time, and more and more countries are enacting programs and policies to address the developmental needs of infants and young children. Accordingly, new journals, books, and websites have been developed focusing on early intervention. Journals include the *Journal of Early Intervention*, *Infants and Young Children*, *Topics in Early Childhood Special Education*, *International Journal of Rehabilitation Research*, *Exceptional Children*, and the *Early Childhood Research Quarterly*. Examples of recent books are: *Early intervention: The essential readings* (Feldman, 2004); *Early childhood intervention: International perspectives, national initiatives, and regional practice* (Carpenter & Egerton, 2005); and *Early intervention practices around the world* (Odom, Hanson, Blackman & Kaul, 2003). The International Society on Early Intervention maintains a list of early intervention resources, including publications and useful websites; visit their site *<http://depts.washington.edu/isei/resources_links/links.html>* for details.

The Division for Early Childhood is one of 17 divisions of the Council for Exceptional Children, which is the 'largest international professional organization dedicated to improving educational outcomes for individuals with exceptionalities, students with disabilities, and/or the gifted.' The Division for Early Childhood has a particular focus on people who work with or for children with developmental concerns from birth through 8 years. They are dedicated to promoting programs and policies centered on supporting children and families. The Division of Early Childhood recently published a series of recommended practices (see Sopris West *<www.sopriswest.com/>* for publications).

CHAPTER SEVENTEEN

Culture and infancy

JAYANTHI MISTRY, ILA DESHMUKH,
and M. ANN EASTERBROOKS

Introduction

Consider two infants, born at the same moment in time, perhaps in the same hospital, or perhaps thousands of miles apart. Both of these infants will develop attachments to significant caregivers. Both will communicate with their families and learn the language(s) spoken around them. Both of them will develop cognitive competencies and intellectual skills. These are universals in development. But the cultural contexts and communities into which these infants are born and develop help to determine some of the interesting variations in infant development: which caregivers become attachment figures, how infants communicate with family members, and what kinds of cognitive skills are appropriated.

In this chapter, we use a cultural perspective as an organizing framework for exploring both what is universal and what is unique about infant development. We describe the major assumptions of this perspective and then use exemplars from core domains of infancy to illustrate how there are regularities in variation across cultural communities in the ways in which infant caregiving and learning is structured and how infant development is situated within these structures for infant caregiving and learning.

Cultural perspective: basic assumptions

There is widespread agreement that infants are born into a cultural world. Human infants experience a long period of immaturity during which they require extensive caregiving before they become capable of sustaining themselves. It is this universal characteristic of human infancy that requires us to understand human development as embedded within cultural processes. Rogoff (2003) emphasizes that humans are biologically cultural by pointing out that 'All humans have a great deal in common due to the biological and cultural heritage we share as a species: We all walk on two legs, communicate with language, need protection as infants, organize in groups, and use tools' (p. 64). The period of extended dependency provides ample opportunities for infants to learn the ways of their communities and become participants in the community; and it is through practices of these communities that aspects of cultural variation in infancy are revealed.

Three basic assumptions about the cultural nature of human development (Rogoff, 2003) serve as the foundation for this chapter (Table 17.1).

The first assumption about human development is the **inseparability of individual and culture.** Typically, the 'individual' and 'culture' are seen as separable—wherein the individual is assumed to have a set of basic, general characteristics and capabilities that are influenced by culture. Behavior is often seen as the 'outcome' of dynamic interaction between individual level characteristics and cultural influences that are external to the individual. In contrast, our assumption is that individual functioning and culture are mutually and integrally related and cannot be separated. In this view, culture

Table 17.1 Key assumptions, developmental tasks, and universals of infancy

Key assumptions of a cultural perspective	Key developmental tasks of infancy	Universals of the infant period
Individual and culture are inseparable	Physical and motor growth	The immaturity of the human infant requires extensive caregiving for their survival, and cultural communities develop systems of care to ensure thriving of the infant
Development occurs through participation in communities of practice	Sensorimotor growth	Throughout their infancy and childhood, children require opportunities to learn the mature ways of their communities to become capable of sustaining themselves
There are regularities in variation	Formation of attachment bonds between infants and caregivers	
	Appropriation of cognitive skills	
	Development of language	

is considered not as a categorical property, social address, or characteristic of an individual, but as configurations of routine ways of doing things in any community's approach to living. Individual development is situated and constituted through participation in ongoing, dynamic communities of practice. Further, communities are defined as 'groups of people who have some common and continuing organization, values, understanding, history, and practices' (Rogoff, 2003, p. 80). This means that individuals participate in multiple communities—e.g., those of home and community settings, school, work, marketplace and so on.

The difference in these two perspectives—i.e., culture as a 'social address' vs. culture as 'participation in communities of practice' (Rogoff, 2003) has important implications for understanding commonly used social address variables, such as social class. In the former perspective, cultural aspects of individual lives are represented by variables such as race, ethnicity, and social class, and thus are conceived of as static properties belonging to the individual. When behavior is viewed as the 'outcome' of interaction between individual level characteristics and cultural influences, then culture as a social address variable is implicitly interpreted as having explanatory value. According to a cultural perspective, social address variables are not, in and of themselves, explanatory. They must be 'unpacked' to define and clarify what comprises the constructs they represent and how these are linked to infant development.

Take the example of finding in the literature that maternal education consistently predicts developmental outcomes in infancy (e.g., as measured by developmental scales such as the Bayley) among most middle-class groups in the United States. However, maternal education may not represent the set of practices that facilitate developmental outcomes in other communities. In a study of adolescent Puerto Rican mothers, Garcia-Coll & Magnusson (1999) used an **emic** (insider) perspective to determine that the combination of having experience in taking care of young siblings and cousins, and access to a network of caregivers in the extended family, predicted maternally responsive practices among the young mothers. These researchers went beyond using a social address variable (maternal education as representing socio-economic status) to 'unpack' the configuration of individually lived experiences (having the experience of taking care of younger siblings, and access to caregiving help) that facilitated the appropriation of a set of maternal practices that in turn facilitated the infants' developmental outcomes.

The second assumption of **development as transformations in participation** extends from the first and describes the nature of developmental changes. We assume developmental changes reflect transformations in the nature of children's participation in communities of practice (Rogoff, 2003). Typically, developmental transitions are viewed as situated in the individual. For example, in the Piagetian perspective, an individual's understanding of the world happens from within, and progresses initially from sensorimotor schemas, to preoperational, then concrete-operational, and finally formal-operational schemas. In contrast, in the cultural perspective, Rogoff (2003) describes developmental changes as transitions in the individual's role in their community, or as situated in transformations in the individual's participation in communities. For example, among the Mayan community Gaskins (1996) observed that a baby's progress through phases of infancy is marked by changes from being a 'lap baby,' to a 'knee baby' and then a 'yard baby.' These labels represent changes in the infant's mobility—from no independent locomotion (needs to be held in arms or lap) to some independent mobility (but needs to be kept close to caregiver) to independent mobility (can move around within a limited space) and also represent changes in the infant's relation to the caregiving environment.

The third assumption of **regularities in variation** focuses on how cross-cultural variations of child-rearing practices are conceptualized (Rogoff, 2003). With research increasingly documenting a range of variations in cultural practices and traditions of caregiving, it is essential to articulate patterns of similarities and differences in cultural practices and child outcomes. Otherwise, existing cross-cultural literature can appear to be inundated with a seemingly infinite range of variations in practices. Rogoff (2003) argues that regularities in variations among cultural practices and circumstances exist because of two basic **universal features of human development**: (1) the immaturity of the human infant requires extensive caregiving for their survival, and adults develop systems of care to ensure infant thriving; and (2) children, throughout their infancy and childhood, require opportunities to learn the mature ways of their communities to become capable of sustaining themselves. According to Rogoff, cultural research suggests that these universals are the basis for cultural variations associated with infant mortality or survival; the availability of siblings and extended family; opportunities for children to engage widely in their community; and cultural prototypes for engaging as groups rather than in pairs (Rogoff, 2003). In the rest of the chapter, we use selected domains of development in infancy as exemplars to document these regularities in variations and to illustrate how cross-cultural variations in infant outcomes are situated and socially constituted within specific ways of structuring caregiving and learning experiences.

Exemplars of regularities in cultural variations in infant development

The domains of development included in this chapter are selected to represent major developmental tasks during infancy. Infancy is a period of origins—when an infant's capabilities, individuality, and first relationships begin to develop (Thompson, Easterbrooks & Padilla-Walker, 2003). Infants' major developmental tasks include establishing physiological and emotional regulation; developing motor and physical capacities and skills; forming relationships with individuals in their social world; learning and developing the use of language and communication; and learning to use objects, tools, symbols, and schemas in the process of participating in the physical and social world in which they are embedded. In the sensorimotor, socio-emotional, cognitive, and language/communication domains of development, extensive variations have been documented, along with varied interpretations of how differences arise. We use these selected domains and exemplars to suggest that focus on identifying regularities in variations enables a more coherent overview of specific domains of development than is possible when variations and differences are merely delineated. Exemplars of cultural variations in the development of sensorimotor skills; attachment relationships; learning and cognition; and the development of language and communication are discussed in the following sections to illustrate how these variations are situated in consistent patterns of similarities and differences in the ways in which caregiving and learning opportunities are structured.

Physical and motor growth: cross-cultural similarities and differences

Rapid physical and motor growth and development are perhaps the most obvious changes during the period of infancy. Although most aspects of development in these domains are common across cultures (e.g., birthweight triples and height doubles by 1 year of age), differences in physical and motor development do exist. Differences in rates of infant survival or mortality, average heights and weights, and milestones of motor development are often situated in varying features of the childcare-giving environment, including environmental resources and circumstances (e.g., nutrition, poverty, access to health care) that, in part, define social class, as well as socially and culturally embedded practices (e.g., breast-feeding, infant carrying and handling practices).

For example, indicators such as infant mortality and nutritional status (e.g., proportion of underweight children) are regularly tracked and studied in a number of countries and show clear country differences (for details see, e.g., UN Children's Fund <*www.unicef.org*>). Although differences between countries are often traced to poverty and circumstances related to income distribution, sometimes gains over time within a country are attributed to other aspects of the environmental context within which children are raised, such as the availability of targeted social programs. For example, in the United States, some of the gains in the nutritional status of children have been attributed to federal programs, such as school breakfast and lunch programs, and provision of nutritional supplements for those at risk (Gardiner & Kozmitski, 2005).

Similarly, although there are commonalities across cultures in the nature and sequence of sensorimotor development, cultural variations in motor development are also apparent. Researchers have noted differences in average age of walking and other motor skills. In Uganda, infants begin to walk at about 10 months, whereas in France 15 months is typical, and in the US the average age for walking is around 12 months (Gardiner & Kozmitski, 2005). Comparative studies of childcare-giving environments and practices suggest that such variations are the result of varying infant carrying and holding practices and availability of opportunities for practice and early stimulation of specific motor skills. For example, in many African and West Indian communities, members of the family, including the extended family, value and provide 'formal handling' experiences (such as stretching exercises and holding infants upright) that stimulate early sitting and walking (Hopkins & Westra, 1988; 1990).

Developing attachment: understanding the caregiving system across cultures

The development of attachment, a hallmark of socio-emotional development in infancy, can be used to illustrate both universals in development as well as regularities in variations across cultures (Table 17.2). The formation of bonds and attachment relationships is a universal accomplishment during the period of infancy and thereby an important domain of study in infancy. In taking a culturally inclusive view, we begin by noting universals, such as the need for caregiving systems that ensure infant survival, as well as variations in the caregiving systems and constructs humans have created to guide parenting activities. Systematic regularities in these variations appear to be situated in the extent to which infant mortality and survival is a critical concern and the availability of multiple caregivers for childcare and learning.

Ethological **attachment theory**, as conceptualized by John Bowlby (1969, 1973; see Chapter 12), states that human infants and their caregivers are biologically equipped with mechanisms that work to ensure the survival of the young. A dynamic developmental model outlines the ways in which infant behaviors, and caregiver behaviors, serve to signal the need for protection and care, bringing infants and their caregivers into close proximity. This physical proximity allows for physiological and emotional regulation (such as feeding, and strategies to minimize infant distress and crying). Thus, Bowlby outlined a case for the link between the infant attachment behavioral system and complementary behaviors of adults that work, in tandem, to promote infant survival. Although the attachment behavioral system is typically seen as universal and transcultural, because it is biologically 'hard-wired,' the specific ways in which attachment behaviors are expressed and interpreted take place in a cultural context.

Table 17.2 Development of infant–caregiver attachment relationships demonstrate both universal features and regularities in variation

Universal	Variation	Example
The formation of bonds and attachment relationships; need for caregiving systems that ensure infant survival	Likelihood of infant mortality or survival: The extent to which child survival is an immediate concern for parents	Among poor rural migrants in a shanty town in Brazil, where infant mortality rates were high, Scheper-Hughes (1985) observed mothers were 'detached' with infants they perceived as too weak to survive the harsh circumstances of their lives, whereas babies who seemed to be 'survivors'—i.e. active, playful, alert, and tough—were valued and nurtured
	The availability of multiple caregivers: The extent to which development in infancy is conceptualized as embedded in dyadic or group relationships	Among the Efe, a foraging community in the forests of Zaire, infants receive care from birth by many adults besides the mother, leading to strong connections and bonds with many people in the community (Morelli & Tronick, 1991; Tronick, Morelli & Winn, 1987)

The work of Mary Ainsworth and others (1967; 1977) focused on the contexts and consequences of individual differences in attachment patterns, highlighting the role that maternal sensitivity plays in the establishment of **secure** and **insecure** attachment bonds (De Wolff & van IJzendoorn, 1997). The assumption of this work is that 'sensitive, responsive maternal care will lead to the development of secure attachment relationships and subsequent socio-emotional competence' (Carlson & Harwood, 2003, p. 54). In middle- and upper-middle-class North American samples, researchers found that roughly 70% of infants seen in the Strange Situation paradigm used to assess individual differences in attachment behaved in ways that were consistent with secure attachment, while approximately 30% of them showed insecure (avoidant or ambivalent/resistant) attachment patterns. In other samples, where family circumstances were characterized by poverty or by maternal caregiving difficulties, the relative frequency of the secure pattern decreased, and another pattern of infant attachment, **disorganized/disoriented**, was found, demonstrating variations in response to caregiving contexts. As re-searchers used the Strange Situation methodology cross-culturally, finding different rates of secure and insecure attachment than in North American samples, the validity of this methodology was criticized as being grounded in 'western' ideals (Harwood, Miller & Irizarry, 1995; Rothbaum *et al.*, 2000).

In documenting variations across cultures in the nature and interpretation of attachment constructs, such as the security of infant attachment, cross-cultural, comparative research has raised questions about our assumptions regarding what mechanisms are basic. This research has sought to describe both what are considered to be **universal** ideas about infancy and parenting, as well as the cross-cultural variations embedded in these ideas (Harwood *et al.*, 1995; Honig, 2000). Much of this ongoing research is characterized by qualitative, ethnographic methods that seek to understand cultural **beliefs** and **practices** about infancy and parenting within a culture-specific or **emic** perspective (Kagitcibasi, 1996; LeVine *et al.*, 1994). Behavior is emic to the extent that it can only be understood within the cultural context in which it occurs; it is **etic** or universal in as much as it is common to human beings independent of their culture (Kagitcibasi, 1996).

These efforts to ground attachment behaviors within cultural meanings have lead to increasingly contextual understanding of the ways attachment develops in different cultural contexts, and in understanding different cultur-ally adaptive patterns. Although agreeing that a distinction must be made between basic human mechanisms that evidence suggests are universal, par-ticularly in infancy, and the cultural constructs that human beings have built in an attempt to understand those mechanisms, Harwood *et al.* (1995) caution that the very constructs used to describe these basic mechanisms are themselves culturally situated. Harwood claims that

> ... evidence suggests that it may be a human universal in later infancy for the subsystems of affiliation, wariness, exploration, and attachment to work together in coherent and recognizable patterns. It may even be that a sense of safety and emotional warmth underlies patterns of attachment behavior that are deemed desirable across a majority of cultures. However, these issues are separate from the cultural construct of security that we have created in U.S. psychology on the basis of these mechanisms. In particular, the concept of inner security, with its emphasis on the importance of self-sufficiency and inner resourcefulness for the autonomous, bounded individual, who is nonetheless capable of existing harmoniously and finding satisfaction in relationships with other autonomous, bounded individuals, is an ideal peculiar to dominant U.S. culture—a culturally constructed developmental endpoint that is not shared by much of the rest of the world. (Harwood *et al.*, 1995, pp. 36–37)

Regularities in cultural variations on the nature and meaning of attachment relationships during infancy appear to center on (1) the extent to which child survival is an immediate concern for parents and (2) the availability of siblings and extended kin for caregiving. Variations around these features of infants' caregiving environments can be linked to caregivers' goals, beliefs, and behavioral caregiving practices. For example, in the context of high infant mortality rates among the desperately poor rural migrants in a shanty town in Brazil, Scheper-Hughes (1985) observed maternal detachment and indifference towards infants who were judged to be too weak to survive the harsh circumstances of their lives. In this context, babies who have the characteristics of 'survivors'—i.e., active, playful, alert, and tough—are valued and nurtured, whereas selective neglect and maternal detachment are viewed as appropriate responses for infants who do not appear capable of survival.

Theory and research on attachment also can be used to illustrate the importance of considering cultural variations in the extent to which caregiving is shared by parents and extended family members such as grandparents, aunts, and siblings, illustrating regularities in variations around the availability of multiple caregivers. In the **attachment behavioral system**, infant behaviors serve to signal need for care (e.g., crying), to draw the infant and caregiver into closer proximity (e.g., reaching out, moving toward), and to maintain close proximity and contact (e.g., sucking, clinging). Adult behaviors (e.g., picking up the infant, holding, feeding, comforting) also serve to promote infant survival and thriving. However, the cultural arrangements of family life, and thereby the constitution of the primary caregiving system, vary across cultural communities. In some cultures, mothers or mother–father dyads make up the primary caregiving system for their children, and thus they become the primary, and perhaps only attachment figure; in other cultural contexts an extended group of caregivers constitute this caregiving system. Infants are capable of forming secure attachments to multiple caregivers including fathers, siblings, extended family members, and unrelated childcare providers (Howes, 1999).

Existing cross-cultural research suggests that consistent differences in patterns of caregiving and their outcomes for infant development can be linked to these variations in the availability of siblings and extended kin for caregiving, their culturally defined roles and responsibilities, and the underlying belief and goals for children's development. For example, among the Efe, a foraging community in the forests of Zaire, infants receive care from birth by many adults besides the mother, and this intense social contact leads to strong connections and bonds with many people in the community (Morelli & Tronick, 1991a,b; Tronick, Morelli & Winn, 1987). This cultural pattern of infant care not only ensures that young children are protected by accommodating to the wide-ranging foraging activities of men and women, but also incorporates diverse community members into infant care and socializes infants into the intrinsically interactive, cooperative features of community life (Thompson, Easterbrooks & Padilla-Walker, 2003).

Infant cognition and learning opportunities in cultural context

An infant's capacity for learning and intelligent action is an inherent aspect of infant development. Even for the preverbal infant, the first year is a period of intense cognitive engagement with the social and physical world. Further, this intense cognitive engagement, which supports development in all domains, occurs through the child's participation in caregiving systems that vary in structure, function, and nature across cultures.

While the capacity for intelligent action has deep biological roots and a discernible evolutionary history, the exercise of that capacity depends upon man appropriating to himself modes of acting and thinking that exist not in his genes but in his culture. (Bruner, 2001, p. 119)

In this section, we begin by describing universal features of the infant's engagement with the physical and social world, followed by examples of how these features, when situated within varying caregiving systems and contexts, give rise to varying infant outcomes. Further, we exemplify how the coherence of varying models and outcomes for development represent regularities in variations as delineated by Rogoff's (2003) tenets that form the basis for this chapter (Table 17.3).

Research on infant cognition has demonstrated that even within the first year of life, infants are able to learn new behaviors simply by watching others. They have a beginning sense of quantification, understand some properties of physical objects, they become attuned to causal relations between objects,

Table 17.3 Cognitive development in infancy demonstrates both universal features and regularities in variation

Universal	Variation	Example
Readiness for goal-directed, systematic learning	Likelihood of infant mortality or survival: Conditions and opportunities created for learning environments	More nonverbal means of infant–caregiver communication and more responsibility assumed by infant for learning through alert and active observation, rather than through structured learning activities, in communities where infant survival is a highly present issue
	The extent to which development in infancy is conceptualized as embedded in dyadic or group relationships: Underlying beliefs about valued cognitive abilities and intelligence	Intelligence that is more socially oriented is valued among many communities in Africa, while in the European and American contexts intelligence and cognitive abilities with a focus on verbal and analytic competencies are valued (Serpell, 1994)

and have some understanding of intentional actions (Chapter 8). In addition, infants are universally biologically 'wired to learn' and have an 'inborn motivation to develop competencies' (Shonkoff & Phillips, 2000, p. 148). With a focus on delineating universal features of the infant's engagement with the social and physical world, Bruner (2001) outlined four universal 'endowments' that provide foundations for learning, cognitive, and communicative development during the first years of life. These are defined below:

- **Means–end readiness**: The tendency to engage in goal-directed activity. Even in the earliest period of life, infants are active in seeking out regularities in the world around them.

- **Transactionality**: The social and communicative transactions with the social world within which the infant is embedded and that make up a high proportion of infant activity.

- **Systematicity**: The notion that much of early infant activity takes place in delimited, defined, and familiar situations, and infant actions show a high degree of order or systematicity.

- **Rule-governed actions**: That much of an infant's early actions and learning is governed by rules—even if the logic of the rules is incorrect.

It is these universal features of infant actions, and the inborn motivation to learn competencies, that enable infants to become participants in the practices and routines of the particular cultural groups within which they are embedded. However, since such universal readiness for learning and features of infant engagement and actions are situated in varying family and caregiving systems and contexts, there are accompanying variations in the outcomes and nature of infant learning and cognition. For instance, Gardiner and Kosmitzki (2005) describe a comparative study of infant cognitive development among English and Igbo infants, reported by Mundy-Castle and Okonji, in which the English infants' attention was more often focused on handling objects, whereas the Igbo infants' attention was more often directed to the social and emotional environment. Research suggests that these differences in early interactions are linked to differential assumptions about the nature of valued cognitive abilities; intelligence that is more socially oriented is valued among many communities in Africa, while in the European and American contexts intelligence and cognitive abilities with a focus on verbal and analytic competencies are highly valued (Serpell, 1994). In another example of differences in the salience of the object or the social world across cultures, Bornstein, Toda, Azuma, *et al.* (1990) observed that American mothers attended and responded more favorably to their babies' requests when the infants were playing with objects, whereas Japanese mothers were more responsive when their babies were engaged in play with them.

Although cross-cultural comparison of specific features of the interactive environment, or of specific competencies, is valuable in highlighting the range of cross-cultural variations, studies that have examined the coherence of relationships between child-rearing goals, practices, and infant outcomes in different cultural communities are more likely to illustrate regularities in variation on three of the tenets described earlier: (1) relevance of infant mortality/survival; (2) availability of siblings and extended kin for caregiving; and (3) extent of children's participation in mature community activities. Selected examples of such research are described in the following paragraphs.

LeVine and colleagues (LeVine, Dixon, LeVine, *et al.* 1994) provide a valuable example of contrasting cultural models of early childcare which illustrate interrelated regularities in variation. We describe these models at some length to illustrate the existence of equally valid alternate conceptualizations of parenting and children's development. These cultural models include assumptions and beliefs about normative and desired child rearing goals, the general strategy for attaining these goals, as well as the scripts for action in specific situations. LeVine and colleagues (1994) label the model of the Gusii people of Kenya **pediatric**, because its primary concern is with the survival, health, and physical growth of the infant, and the American model **pedagogic**, because its primary concern is with the behavioral and educational development of the infant. The adaptive and culturally coherent links between parenting goals, parenting strategies and scripts, and children's development in each model are briefly summarized from LeVine *et al.* (1994, pp. 248–270).

The primary goal in the pediatric model of the Gusii is to protect infants from life-threatening illnesses and environmental hazards, a goal that is particularly adaptive in the context of high mortality rates. Gusii mothers implicitly assume that infancy is a period of great danger to the child's life, requiring constant protection. Therefore, they keep their infants in physical proximity as a means of providing constant protection, and they focus primarily on soothing distress and keeping infants satisfied and calm. They assume that these states indicate that the baby is well and safe from harm. In contrast, the goals of the American **pedagogic** model are to promote the infant's alertness, curiosity, interest in surroundings, exploration, and communication with others. Survival and health are background concerns, perhaps because they are more likely assured in the context of modern medicine and comparatively lower infant mortality rates. In LeVine *et al.*'s construction of the pedagogic model, the American mother sees herself as a teacher, whose primary responsibility is to ensure the infant pupil's readiness for early education. Parenting strategies therefore focus on stimulation and proto-conversation aimed at facilitating engagement with the physical and social world.

This case study of infant care in the Gusii community goes beyond merely emphasizing the cultural relativity of childcare goals and practices. The different patterns of structuring of the childcare environment also represent alternative pathways to varying infant developmental outcomes. Although

Gusii toddlers did not experience the type of stimulation and support of cognitive and language skills common among American toddlers, the social experience of Gusii children with peer and community members after 30 months facilitated the development of these capacities that were not acquired earlier.

The Gusii case teaches us that the absence, during the first 2 to 3 years, of specific parental practices that promote cognitive, emotional, and language skills in Western contexts, does not necessarily constitute failure to provide what every child needs. Like many other peoples in Africa and elsewhere, the Gusii had socially organized ways of cultivating skill, virtue, and personal fulfillment that were not dependent on mothers after weaning and were not concluded until long after the third year of life; they involved learning through participation in established, hierarchical structures of interaction at home and in the larger community—a kind of apprenticeship learning, once widespread in the West, that we are only beginning to understand. (LeVine et al., 1994, p. 274)

Rogoff, Mistry, Goncü, and Mosier (1993) offer another example of contrasting, yet culturally coherent models of toddler–caregiver interaction that illustrate contrasting patterns of structuring learning opportunities for infants. The researchers selected four cultural communities (a Mayan peasant community in Guatemala, a tribal village in India, a middle-class community in Turkey, and a middle-class community in the U.S.) that represented variation in the extent to which children are segregated from adult activities. Observations of caregiver–toddler interaction revealed two patterns for learning that were consistent with variations in whether children were able to observe and participate in adult activities.

In communities where children were segregated from adult activities, adults took on the responsibility for organizing children's learning by managing their motivation, by instructing them verbally, and by treating them as peers in play and conversation. In contrast, in the communities in which children had the opportunity to observe and to participate in adult activities caregivers supported their toddlers' own efforts with responsive assistance. Toddlers appeared to take responsibility for learning by observing ongoing events and beginning to enter adult activity (Rogoff et al., 1993). Learning occurred through active observation and participation. Toddlers and caregivers often maintained simultaneous attention to several ongoing activities, and were responsive to each other often through nonverbal means. Thus, within each community there was a coherence of patterns linking cultural context in terms of the extent of segregation from adult activity, parental goals for children's development, differing assumptions about who takes responsibility for learning, and patterns of caregiver–toddler interaction.

The description by Gaskins (1996) of the pervasive social observation found even in young Mayan infants and toddlers, who can attend quietly to multiple events from which they are not segregated, yields another picture of strong engagement with the social world through focused observation. Through such active observation, Mayan toddlers learn to take into account what is already happening and to make judgements about whether and how to enter into ongoing interactions. Thus, variations in opportunities for learning not only reflect consistent variations across cultures, they also facilitate the development of different behaviors. In contrast to toddlers in the Mayan community, toddlers in Rogoff *et al.*'s (1993) U.S. community were more engaged in dyadic interactions and sought their caregiver's sole attention, rarely engaging in focused observations of multiple and competing events.

Developing communication and language in infancy

Just as readiness for goal-directed, systematic learning is a universal feature of infant learning, so also is readiness for communication (Table 17.4). Learning to communicate through language involves acquiring a set of phonological, syntactic, semantic, and pragmatic rules of the language community. Almost all children across the world acquire these rules and learn to talk

Table 17.4 Communication and language development in infancy demonstrate both universal features and regularities in variation

Universal	Variation	Example
Readiness for acquiring language	The extent to which development in infancy is conceptualized as embedded in dyadic or group relationships: Specific features of the world child is attuned to Likelihood of infant mortality or survival: Types of communication necessary for social interaction	Relative focus on 'object' versus 'social' world varies by culture; infants' vocabulary reflects expressive versus referential style
		In communities with high infant mortality, infants are kept in close proximity and carried or held extensively, and much of the infant–caregiver communication is nonverbal and physical, placing less emphasis on verbal means of communication

without explicit instruction by the age of 3 years (see Chapter 10). Further, the developmental trajectories of children learning different languages are remarkably similar across cultures. Bruner (2001) delineates infants' sensitivity to patterned sounds, to grammatical constraints, to referential requirements, and to communicative intentions as universal features underlying infants' readiness for language development. Further, this readiness for communication is situated in the process of fulfilling general, nonlinguistic functions or goal-directed actions that are universal, in that infants across all cultures are engaged in predicting and acting on the environment, interacting with the physical and social world, and enlisting the assistance of others in achieving goals.

Thus, the developmental tasks for infants the world over include mastering the conceptual structure of the social and physical world within which they are embedded, as well as the communicative and linguistic conventions through which their intentions can be relayed. However, these universal features of infant learning and communication, and universal developmental tasks, are situated in varying caregiving environments and contexts with accompanying variations in communicative and linguistic outcomes.

Though communicative competence develops through social interactions with communicative partners who highlight those features of the world to which the child is already attuned, the specific features of the world to which the child is attuned may vary across cultures. For example, middle-class Western contexts emphasize actions or agents acting on the **object** world, whereas many non-Western contexts emphasize agents and actions of the **social** world. Therefore, infants in the former contexts develop more **referential** early vocabularies (e.g., words that refer to objects and actions), foregrounding the physical world; conversely, infants in the latter contexts may learn more **expressive** words, foregrounding the social world.

Research on language-learning environments during infancy suggests that there are regularities in variations organized around the likelihood of infant mortality or survival, availability of siblings and extended family, opportunities for children to engage widely in their community, and cultural prototypes for engaging as groups rather than in pairs. In agrarian or nonindustrial communities, high infant mortality, availability of extended families, and extensive opportunities for children to engage in the mature activities of the community (because they are not segregated from adult activities) co-occur. In these contexts, infants are kept in close proximity and carried or held extensively, and much of the infant–caregiver communication is nonverbal and physical. The lack of need for communication at a distance places less emphasis on verbal means of communication and is usually supported by related beliefs that infants do not need to be spoken to directly.

Further, the constant presence of extended family and kin, and being embedded in ongoing community activities, also facilitate an implicit emphasis on the social world and on learning through active observation. For example, infants in Polynesia are held so that they face outward—implicitly emphasizing interaction with the social world. Infants are held in such a way as to enable them to both see and be seen by the individuals other than the mother or caregiver who is carrying them (Martini & Kirkpatrick, 1992; Schieffelin, 1991). Such caregiving environments give rise to accompanying variations in language-learning outcomes. Much of the communication between caregivers and infants in the early years takes place through nonverbal means, and infants may not produce their first words and sentences before they are 2 years old—though, like children across the world, children in these environments will also eventually talk by the age of 3. Similarly, differences in highlighting salience of the social over the physical world may result in differences in the infants' use of expressive vs. referential speech.

Once again, studies that focus on documenting multiple features of the caregiving systems and environments illustrate the coherence of regularities in variation. Heath's (1983) study of the language-learning environment of children in an African American community of mill workers is an excellent illustration of the coherent and interrelated nature of many features of the caregiving environment that co-vary systematically, with accompanying consequences for language learning and development. Heath describes the very communal environment within which infants in this community are embedded:

Encapsulated in an almost totally human world, Trackton babies are in the midst of nearly constant human communication, verbal and nonverbal. They literally feel the body signals of shifts in emotion of those who hold them; they are never excluded from verbal interactions. They are listeners and observers in a stream of communication that flows about them, but is not especially channeled or modified for them. (Heath, 1983, pages 74–75)

In this community babies are almost never alone, are more often than not embedded in groups, and very rarely are in the company of only one other person. They sleep with family members, and are held, carried, and cuddled not only by family members but by all residents of the community as well. Babies are often carried astride the hip or cradled in the arm, facing out away from the caregiver's body. In such caregiving environments toddlers do not produce verbal labels for objects and things in their environment. They are more likely to produce expressive rather than referential speech. Heath (1983) documents the richness of the expressive function in toddlers' speech in this caregiving environment.

SUMMARY

We began this chapter by considering two infants, each born and raised in distinct cultural communities, that come with their own distinct sets of beliefs and practices about child-rearing and caregiving. As they begin to develop, learn, and participate in their communities, these babies' development will occur within, rather than apart from, the particular ways in which their caregiving context is structured. The babies might grow at different rates; they might be cared for in different ways, and by different people in their lives; they might learn different ways of participating in their communities, based on the values of their communities; and they might learn to communicate differently from one another.

But regardless of the possible differences in their growth, the manner in which their caregivers' tend to them, their caregivers' beliefs about parenting, the kinds of things they learn, and how they communicate, these children will be similar in many ways. They will each have caregivers committed to ensuring their growth and survival, they will both, throughout their childhood, be given opportunities to learn and to participate in their cultural communities, they will both be born with the capacity for learning and intelligent action, and they will both be born with a readiness to communicate. Using a cultural perspective as an organizer, this chapter outlines the major assumptions of such a perspective and presents major exemplars from core domains of infancy to illustrate the regularities in variation across cultural communities—in the ways infant caregiving and learning is structured and how infant development is situated within these structures for caregiving and learning, to present a coherent framework for considering how universal features and those that vary are intricately entwined in the developmental process.

Health, nutrition, and atypical development

JOHN WOROBEY

Introduction

Every day, tens of thousands of infants are born into this world without incident. The vast majority of them are healthy, normal in functioning and appearance, and destined to grow and develop into happy children and, one day, productive citizens. Yet some—indeed, many—newborns are not at all well at birth. They are born too soon in some cases, so that their immature pulmonary and digestive systems impede their breathing or nutrient intake; or born at term but with a congenital deformity or illness that places them at perinatal risk. Still others, in an extrauterine environment that is less than supportive, may encounter problems in their first few years after birth that make their infancy a time of difficulty, where special care, early intervention, or remedial efforts will be necessary if they are to have any hope of normal development. In the chapters you have read so far, typical infant development has been described. In fact, one might argue that what has actually been described is optimal infant development, since the motor milestones, sensory capabilities, cognitive achievements, and socio-emotional characteristics that have been discussed so far portray a 'best-case' scenario. The intent of this chapter is not to portray a worst-case scenario. Rather, it is to illustrate the intertwining of nutrition and health in fostering normal development in infancy, and demonstrate how problems that impact these two factors, along with other circumstances, may instead move an infant toward atypical development.

Prenatal factors in infant health

As discussed in Chapter 3, a variety of factors exert an influence on the developing fetus during the prenatal period. Teratogens impact on the newborn's state of health at birth, with implications for its viability or chances of developing normally. As was shown in Table 3.1, a number of these factors are under the control of the mother. Although exposure to a disease like herpes simplex may be an unforeseen occurrence, it is nevertheless the result of some behavior by the mother, and in that sense may be considered preventable. On the other hand, a pre-existing condition like diabetes or a chronic stressor like malnutrition may be beyond her control, but as will be discussed later, might have reduced impact if a physician or other health-care worker can intervene early on. Despite the seriousness of these outcomes, it must be stressed that for the vast majority of infants, prenatal development progresses smoothly. The developing fetus is remarkably resilient, with not all infants being affected by exposure, nor exhibiting similar levels of effect.

Health

Immediately after delivery, a newborn infant is routinely assessed with a procedure called the Apgar (1953) scoring system. Ratings from 0 to 2 are made over five categories: skin color, heart rate, reflex irritability, muscle tone, and respiratory effort. The ratings are made at 1 minute and 5 minutes after birth. A rating of 7 or above indicates that the newborn is functioning satisfactorily, but a score of less than 4 at 5 minutes defines a newborn that is in critical condition and may require medical attention. Although the Apgar score is an index of the newborn's viability, it is extremely crude as an assessment device and should not be taken as a predictor of later developmental ability. If the gestational age of the newborn is in question, the attending nurse may administer the Dubowitz–Ballard scale (Allen, 2005), which estimates closeness to term by evaluating skin condition, foot creases, areola development, ear stiffness, genital maturity, and the absence of lanugo (fine bodily hair). A healthy full-term newborn of approximately 40 weeks has a heart rate of 120–160 beats/minute and a respiration rate of 30–60 breaths/minute.

To monitor and best ensure health throughout infancy, regular and frequent well-baby check-ups are recommended for all infants over their first 2 years. Table 18.1 lists the major genetic tests and physical measures that are done in the days after birth. The March of Dimes <*www.marchofdimes.com/pnhec/ 298_834.asp*> recommends that all newborns be screened for some 29 different disorders, including galactosemia—a disorder that prevents infants from converting milk sugar (galactose) to glucose for energy use, and can result in blindness, mental retardation, or even death. Determining that an inherited disorder such as PKU or sickle-cell anemia is present in the newborn can allow the caregiver and pediatrician to immediately consider preventive measures that will reduce later illness or symptoms (more will be said about PKU later in this chapter).

Table 18.1 Recommended screening and immunization schedule

	Age/frequency
Screening	
Hearing	Newborn
Phenylketonuria (PKU)	Newborn
Sickle cell anemia	Newborn
Hemoglobinopathies	Newborn
Hypothyroidism	Newborn
Head circumference	Birth–2 years
Length (height) and weight	Birth through childhood
Lead	1 year
Immunizations	
Hepatitis B	Birth–2 months
	1–4 months
	6–18 months
Polio	2 months
	4 months
	6–18 months (and 4–6 years)
Haemophilus influenza type B (Hib)	2 months
	4 months
	6 months
	12–15 months
Diptheria, tetanus, pertussis (DPT)	2 months
	4 months
	6 months
	15–18 months (and 4–6 years)
Measles, mumps, rubella (MMR)	12–15 months (and later in childhood)
Varicella (chickenpox)	As early as 1 year

Table 18.1 also provides an immunization schedule for the first 2 years. Despite some occasional news items that serve to frighten parents about the risks of vaccinating their infants, modern immunizations have an extremely low risk of causing the disease or other complications. For example, fewer than 1 in 1 million children have a serious allergic reaction to the mumps vaccine. Weighed against the 4000 cases of mumps per year in the U.S. today as compared to the 200 000 cases per year that were seen before the vaccine became available, it can be strongly asserted that the risks greatly

outweigh the benefits (*<http://cdc.gov/nip>*). In short, infants need their immunizations to protect against many serious diseases (Swanson, 2000a).

Common illnesses in infancy

Despite such precautions, most healthy babies suffer from occasional, but minor, illnesses. For example, infants may have as many as six colds in their first year of life, signaled by a congested or runny nose. Although breast milk offers some additional protection from cold-causing germs, infants should be offered water or juices between feeds to help reduce congestion. Fever is not a disease but a symptom that can accompany many childhood illnesses, especially infections. A **febrile seizure** is a convulsion that is caused by the infant's having a fever, without having a specific infection, such as meningitis, which can also cause symptomatic seizures. They commonly occur in about 4% of infants from 6 months and up, especially when they have a high fever that came on suddenly (NINDS, 1999). Fever symptoms should obviously trigger the seeking of advice from the baby's pediatrician.

Infections of the middle ear (**otitis media**) are common in infancy. Ear pain, fever, and irritability are telltale signs. Risk factors include exposure to large numbers of young children (as in daycare), and formula feeding with a propped bottle. Ear infections have traditionally been treated with antibiotics, although some may get better on their own. Unfortunately, as the bacteria that causes otitis media have begun to display greater resistance to antibiotics, physicians are finding that ear infections are becoming more difficult to treat (Dowell *et al.*, 1999).

Colic is also a common problem among infants, affecting perhaps one in four. Its most common symptoms are the sudden onset of screaming and crying that can last for 2–3 hours at a time, and appear to the caregiver as recurrent and inconsolable (Stifter & Spinrad, 1999). Colic may begin as early as 2 weeks after birth, peak at 6 weeks, and taper off by 4 months. Despite much research, its etiology is still unknown, but it is not thought to result from abdominal pain, gas, allergies, or the iron in infant formula (Barr *et al.*, 1999). Although difficult to live with while it occurs, the condition usually improves as the infant gets older.

Lead burden

Although it does not qualify as a disease, exposure to lead can assuredly result in illness. Although it is decades since lead was removed from house paint and gasoline, it continues to exert a negative impact on infant development.

In some cases, the fetus may have been exposed in the womb through its mother's cumulative exposures at her occupational workplace (Andrews, Savitz & Hertz-Picciotto, 1994). Research has demonstrated that infants exhibiting exposure at birth, as evidenced by lead in their umbilical cord blood, perform worse on developmental assessments such as the Bayley Scales of Infant Development (Bellinger & Needleman, 2003). However, the main route by which lead enters the bodies of toddlers, in particular, is through the 'hand to mouth' pathway while they are playing normally. The newly locomotive infant, pulling herself up to a window sill or engaged in play on the floor, who intermittently sucks her fingers or chews her toys, can ingest damaging levels of lead through the lead dust that may have come from household renovation or been tracked in from contaminated soil (Lanphear, Dietrich & Berger, 2003). Fortunately, interventions that instruct caregivers to wash their toddlers' hands, toys and play spaces, and to serve iron-rich meals, can counter some of the developmental delays that lead may have caused (Worobey, Pisuk & Decker, 2004).

Nutrition

Nutrition is an oft-neglected topic in textbooks on infancy. This is quite puzzling when one considers just how much of an infant's time is spent in being fed, and how critical the intake of nutrients is to ensure proper growth and development—indeed, even before birth. As a dramatic example of the importance of prenatal nutrition, recall from Chapter 3 the process by which the brain develops from the **neural plate.** Shortly after its formation, a fold appears that joins together in forming the **neural tube** (Moore, 1988). If the neural tube does not close properly, a number of possible anomalies can result. One is **anencephaly**, where the forebrain fails to develop correctly because the anterior portion of the neural tube does not close. A second is **spina bifida**, which results from the failure of the posterior portion of the neural tube to close. As it turns out, the likelihood of these neural tube defects occurring may be reduced through increased intake of folic acid (folate) in the mother's diet (Liptak, 2002). Recognizing the essentiality of folic acid to proper CNS development, the U.S. Food and Drug Administration made the addition of folic acid to enriched flour and other enriched cereal grain products mandatory as of January 1998, at a level of fortification that was estimated to increase the average daily intake of folic acid in women of childbearing age by about $100\,\mu$g. By 2002, this legislated 'fortification experiment' was credited with significantly decreasing the incidence of anencephaly and spina bifida, particularly among non-Hispanic white and Hispanic births, to approximately 3000 cases per year (Williams *et al.*, 2005).

Protein–energy malnutrition

Malnutrition, properly known as **protein–energy malnutrition** (PEM), refers to a state where the infant's diet is insufficient in both protein and overall energy intake. Although we usually associate PEM with conditions of poverty in the third world, recent reports have clearly demonstrated that modern societies, including the United States and the United Kingdom, are not immune to this problem. Among low-income populations in these developed societies, low birthweight, anemia, growth failure, weakened resistance to infection, increased susceptibility to lead poisoning, and so forth, are all associated with undernutrition in infancy, and unfortunately are not all that infrequent (James *et al.*, 1997).

There is not just one kind of malnutrition. Besides PEM, deficiencies in iron, iodine, and certain B vitamins may appear alone or in combination and contribute to the debilitating effects of each other (see Table 18.2). Iron deficiency, in fact, is the most common nutrient deficiency in the world (Gillespie *et al.*, 1991). But PEM is the most common form of malnutrition in the world, affecting an estimated 200 million children (UNICEF, 1997). Of the nearly 12 million children under the age of 5 who die each year in developing countries from preventable causes, the deaths of over

Table 18.2 Effects of nutrient deficiencies

Deficiency	Potential effect on infant
Protein–energy malnutrition	Apathy, fatigue, motor and cognitive delays
Vitamins	
B$_1$ (thiamin)	Infantile beriberi, heart failure
B$_6$ (pyridoxine)	Convulsions, reduced reactivity
B$_7$ (biotin, or vitamin H)	Retarded physical and mental growth
B$_9$ (folate)	Neural tube defects, e.g., spina bifida
B$_{12}$ (cobalamin)	Pernicious anemia
D (cholecalciferol)	Rickets
E (alpha-tocopherol)	Muscle weakness in premature infants
K (menadione)	Hemorrhagic disease of the newborn
Minerals	
Copper	Mental retardation (in males with mutant gene)
Iodine	Cretinism
Iron	Motor and cognitive delays
Selenium	Premature infants at risk (but consequences unknown)

6 million—more than half—are either directly or indirectly attributable to PEM, due to its association with diarrhea, malaria, measles, respiratory infections, and perinatal problems (Murray & Lopez, 1996). Adults may also suffer from hunger and starvation; however, PEM occurs most frequently, and also has its most devastating consequences, in infancy and early childhood.

Severe PEM in infants has traditionally been classified as either marasmus or kwashiorkor. **Marasmus** results from insufficient protein and energy intake, that is, an extremely low intake of both protein and energy. Marasmus is the form of PEM most commonly affecting infants aged 6–18 months, when they are weaned from breast milk to formula. In attempting to stretch her limited resources, the impoverished mother will dilute commercial formula, further contaminating it with dirty water, which in turn leads to bacterial infection. The infant then suffers from repeated episodes of diarrhea, dehydration, and anemia. In an attempt to cure the infant, the mother may even withhold food. Recurrent infections, coupled with little or no food, subsequently lead to marasmus. The marasmic infant is typically irritable, but may also appear to be weak and apathetic. The infant is also understandably hungry, but can seldom tolerate large amounts of food and will vomit easily (Torun & Viteri, 1988).

In contrast, **kwashiorkor** results from the insufficient intake of protein, with caloric needs usually satisfied. Typically developing when the toddler is 18–24 months of age, kwashiorkor results when a newborn sibling arrives, and the toddler is weaned from the breast and fed the high carbohydrate–low protein diet that the rest of the family subsists on. Although this diet may be adequate for the caregiver, it is insufficient for the rapidly growing toddler. Since the toddler of this age is beginning to explore the environment, the opportunity for exposure to bacteria and viruses can further exacerbate the consequences of the poor diet. However, one of the behavioral characteristics of kwashiorkor is a lessened interest in the environment, along with irritability, apathy, and frequently loss of appetite. Most notably, the toddler with kwashiorkor cries easily and often displays an expression of sadness and misery (Torun & Viteri, 1988).

PEM and early human development

If a malnourished woman becomes pregnant, she must face the challenge of supporting both the growth of her fetus and her own physical health with less than sufficient nutrient stores. There are, in fact, two mechanisms that serve to protect the fetus from inadequate nutrition: (1) the mother's intake of food provides a direct nutritional source; (2) the placenta transfers nutrients to the developing fetus which are stored by the mother. However, malnutrition before or around the time of conception can prevent the placenta from developing fully.

Severe PEM early in development will typically lead to a failure to maintain embryonic implantation, resulting in a spontaneous abortion (miscarriage). Moderate malnutrition throughout gestation will generally allow for the continued development of the fetus, but will also lead to changes in the growth of both placenta and fetus. If the placenta is poorly developed it cannot deliver proper nourishment to the fetus, and the infant may subsequently be born prematurely, small for gestational age, and with a reduced head circumference (Hay et al., 1997). In fact, a reduced head circumference may be the first indication that PEM, particularly during gestation and infancy, has resulted in permanent brain damage.

In recent years, there has been a veritable explosion of interest in malnutrition and the developing fetus. Recall the **fetal origins hypothesis** addressed in Chapter 3, which proposed that a significant number of adulthood diseases may trace their origins to undernutrition during fetal development (Barker, 2003). Despite some convincing epidemiological evidence for the hypothesis, the scientific and medical communities have not universally embraced this concept (Susser & Levin, 1999). However, a number of studies are currently under way that are testing this hypothesis (Langley-Evans, 2004). Future efforts to determine the effects of PEM on brain development will likely rely on the availability of magnetic resonance imaging (MRI), which can even be done on the fetus before birth. For example, research using the MRI procedure has already confirmed early reports that brain myelination is impaired in malnourished infants. Current research has also shown that fetal growth retardation appears to reduce the volume of gray brain matter more than white brain matter, although brain sparing may occur despite growth retardation (Gong et al., 1998).

Behavioral effects of severe malnutrition

Over the past 40 years, the relationship of PEM to behavioral development, particularly the development of intellectual competence, has been the subject of much research. A major question posed by investigators has been whether PEM of various degrees of severity, which typically leads to impaired brain development, will also cause impaired cognitive development (Pollitt, 1988; Ricciuti, 1993). Throughout the 1960s, the findings of reduced brain size and cell numbers in malnourished animals were supplemented with studies that reported lower IQ scores and school performance by impoverished children who experienced early clinical malnutrition.

On the basis of such findings, well-meaning policy-makers and scientists concluded that malnutrition in children was a direct cause of impaired mental development because of its effect on brain growth. In essence, a straightforward explanatory model was formulated, namely, malnutrition → brain damage → impaired behavior. A corollary to this model was that improving the dietary intake of children at risk for chronic PEM would produce a significant enhancement of their intellectual development (Ricciuti, 1993). It is now generally acknowledged that this model, despite its simplistic elegance, falls rather short in explaining how PEM compromises mental development (Gorman, 1995; Brown and Pollitt, 1996). Rather, a variety of adverse health and socio-environmental conditions are now seen as interacting with nutritional status to influence mental development, as well as other behavioral outcomes.

The ecology of early malnutrition

The primary cause of PEM is a lack of sufficient protein and energy intake, but the problem cannot be viewed in isolation from other social and environmental conditions (Wachs, 1995). Indeed, the environment of the malnourished infant is different in countless ways beyond the mere deficiencies of food intake. Grantham-MacGregor has cogently described the many disadvantages that the families of malnourished infants typically endure:

These include poor physical and economic resources, such as overcrowded homes with poor sanitation and water supply, few household possessions and low income. They also tend to have unstable family units, with large numbers of closely spaced children. Parental characteristics associated with infant malnutrition include poor health and nutritional status, poor obstetric history, extreme youth or age, low intelligence and educational levels, little media contact, few social contacts, traditional life styles, and low skilled occupations. The stimulation in the home is poor with few toys or books and little participation by the parents in play activities. (Grantham-McGregor, 1995, p. 2234S)

Instead of attributing cognitive deficiencies solely to brain damage from PEM, the model in Figure 18.1 displays the numerous factors that interact in reducing intellectual development. Of course, the brain may be directly affected as a consequence of PEM, but this model allows for a reversal if adequate nutrition is made available. Health may also be compromised, but illness itself can further reduce the infant's level of nutrient intake. From an ecological perspective, however, it is the reduced energy level, delayed motor behavior, minimal exploration of the environment, and lowered expectations by parents that may place the impoverished infant at greater risk for impaired cognitive development (Brown & Pollitt, 1996).

Effects in infants

A number of researchers have investigated the effects of malnutrition concurrent with infant cognitive development. Although tests of normative abilities are better at gauging performance relative to peers of the same age than in estimating actual intelligence, a number of instruments such as the Bayley scales have been used in studies of malnourished infants. Regardless of the

Classic theory

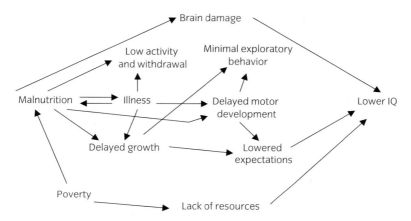

Current theory

Figure 18.1 Effect of malnutrition on cognitive development. Adapted from Brown & Pollitt (1996).

type of malnutrition, the development of infants and toddlers on such tests is significantly delayed (Grantham-MacGregor, 1995). PEM in infants has also been associated with abnormalities in cerebral functioning as measured by psychophysiological tests of arousal. For example, when an infant is presented with a novel stimulus, the heart rate is expected to decelerate. When the infant becomes accustomed to the stimulus, habituation then occurs. But it may be the case that this effect can only be seen with well-nourished infants. When malnourished infants viewed a novel stimulus, they displayed no deceleration in heart rate (Lester *et al.*, 1975). The infants' ability to integrate intrasensory information, that is, to know that a particular sound and image go together, is also delayed in malnourished infants (Cravioto & Arrieta, 1986). These data suggest that early PEM leads to a diminished responsiveness to environmental signals and, further, to a reduction in the infant's capacity for information processing. It is likely that these deficits in information processing will persist even after nutritional rehabilitation has been instituted.

As mentioned earlier, both marasmus and kwashiorkor are associated with distinctive compromises to the infant's behavior. Of all the behavioral symptoms associated with these two malnourished states, lethargy and reduced activity are the most commonly observed. In fact, it has been hypothesized that this reduction in motor activity may serve to isolate malnourished infants from their environment, resulting in limited opportunities for learning and thereby depressing mental development (Schurch & Scrimshaw, 1990).

Specifically, the **functional isolation** hypothesis proposes that the decreased activity, attention, and affect that characterize malnourished infants make them less likely to seek stimulation from their environment (Brown & Pollitt, 1996; Strupp & Levitsky, 1995). The same appears to be true for infants with iron deficiency (Lozoff *et al.*, 2003). In turn, the caregivers are less responsive to their infants and offer them less stimulation. Over time, this repeating cycle of less seeking and receiving of stimulation interferes with the infant's normal acquisition of information from the social and physical environment. Left unchecked, the infant's development is adversely affected (Pollitt *et al.*, 1993; Wachs, 1993). The functional isolation hypothesis may also explain the decreased responsiveness of infants who are iron deficient or anemic to their environments (Table 18.2). Thus, functional isolationism may be a common thread linking various types of nutritional insults to reduced motor and cognitive development in infants and toddlers.

Evidence that reduced activity from PEM compromises motor development is also provided by studies that have used supplementary feedings for malnourished infants. Regardless of the motor assessment employed, undernourished infants who received nutritional interventions in the form of high-energy feeding supplements show improved motor scores through 2 years of age (Husaini *et al.*, 1991; Pollitt *et al.*, 1993). Besides the reduction in motor activity that characterizes PEM, however, other noncognitive aspects of the malnourished infant's behavior may bear on the interaction between mother and infant, and further exacerbate the risk of lowered stimulation. Brazelton and his colleagues (1977) have shown that malnourished newborns are lower in social responsiveness and display poorer orienting to visual stimuli such as human faces. An infant who shows little social responsivity to his mother, and who persists in fussing or crying when awake, cannot be much fun to be around. With the mother likely to be malnourished herself, she has less energy to stimulate, rouse up, or play with her baby. Her caregiving efforts are likely to be minimal, and the infant's cognitive development is bound to suffer.

Such a cycle of depressed mother–infant interactions are sometimes seen in cases of **nonorganic failure to thrive**. Even in developed societies like the United States, some 1–5% percent of infants who by all accounts should be well nourished may nevertheless show deterioration in their rate of growth. Although some cases of failure to thrive are classified as organic in origin, the more common, nonorganic type consists of abnormal behavior and distorted caregiver–infant interactions, in association with slowed weight gain (Krugman & Dubowitz, 2003). Although apathy and reduced activity are characteristic of malnourished infants, many of the behaviors of infants failing to thrive cannot be attributed to PEM alone. Instead, the infants' irritability may discourage social interaction, which the mother may interpret as a personal rejection. In other cases, the mother may just not be very good at recognizing hunger signals. Alternately, the mother may recognize the signals, but because she is under heightened stress, or is frustrated with her unresponsive baby, she may be less likely to respond (Ricciuti, 1993).

Feeding in infancy

Ask a pediatrician, a nutritionist, or even a formula manufacturer about the best way to feed infants, and the answer you will almost certainly get is 'breast is best.' Indeed, breast milk is the ideal first food for the newborn and young infant. No substance is better suited to the needs of the growing infant, with scores of studies supporting its digestive superiority, better utilization of nutrients, immunological benefits, as well as promoting certain aspects of maternal physical health (Table 18.3). There are a few instances where breast-feeding may not be advisable, such as if the mother is on recreational or certain prescribed drugs, or if she is infected with HIV, since this virus can be transmitted to the newborn through breast-feeding (Rutstein *et al.*, 1997). But for most infants, most of the time, breast milk is quite close to the perfect food for the first 6 months of life. In recent years, the possibility that breast milk, through certain of its ingredients, may even promote infant cognitive development has been seriously examined.

Table 18.3 Benefits of breast-feeding

Nutritionally tailored to meet needs of infant
Readily available and always fresh
Provides immunity to viral and bacterial diseases
Decreases risk of respiratory and diarrheal diseases
Reduces risk of allergy
Promotes correct development of jaws and teeth
Decreases risk of sudden infant death syndrome (SIDS)
May reduce risk of childhood obesity
May promote infant intelligence
Promotes maternal physiological recovery from pregnancy
Can facilitate positive self-esteem in maternal role
Decreases risk of breast and ovarian cancers
Improves bone remineralization and reduces risk of hip fractures

Source: Adapted from Worthington-Roberts & Williams (2000).

Essential fatty acids and infant development

Studies on **polyunsaturated fatty acids** (PUFAs) represent one of the most rapidly growing areas of research in the study of early human development and functioning. Two major brain PUFAs are **docosohexaenoic acid** (DHA) and **arachidonic acid** (ARA), which are important components of membrane lipids and major constituents of the nervous system (Innis, 1991; Lucas, 1997). Since DHA is present in high concentrations in the retina it is likely that visual acuity is quite dependent on adequate DHA. In the brain, DHA is most abundant in membranes that are associated with synaptic function, and is accumulated in the CNS late in gestation and early in postnatal life. Studies that have manipulated DHA in the diets of both human infants and animals have shown results that support its role in brain functioning (McCann & Ames, 2005).

Breast milk contains DHA and ARA, but standard formulas in the United States traditionally did not. The United Kingdom and Canada began to make PUFA formulas available to consumers in the mid-1990s, and in late 2001 the United States also gave approval for them. This decision was made because of an emergent line of evidence that babies might fare more like breast-fed infants if given supplemented formulas.

One area in which such a comparison was made surrounds the frequent claim that breast-fed infants seem to be smarter as children than are formula-fed infants. In the latter part of the twentieth century, investigators began to look for differences in intelligence between breast- and formula-fed babies, and often found them, usually favoring the breast-fed infants (e.g., Johnson & Swank, 1996; Taylor & Wadsworth, 1984). From a scientific standpoint, however, breast-feeding was not the only factor that would seem to be favoring infants who are nursed, as numerous studies have also shown that breast-feeding is associated with higher socioeconomic status (Horwood & Fergusson, 1998; Worobey, 1992). Higher socioeconomic status is a marker for higher-level parenting, which usually translates into more attention being paid to the infant—whether through playing, reading, or all-around caregiving—which in turn will facilitate cognitive development in childhood. To address this important confound, efforts were made to control for socioeconomic status when evaluating the impact of breastfeeding on childhood intelligence. A recent meta-analysis concluded that children who were breast fed had IQ scores about 2–3 points higher than children who were formula fed (Anderson *et al.*, 1999), with another study reporting that the duration of breast-feeding displayed a dose–response effect on adult intelligence (Mortensen *et al.*, 2002). However, ongoing work still suggests that other family factors, like parental education and maternal IQ, may better account for higher childhood IQ scores than does breast-feeding (Jacobson *et al.*, 1999; Malloy & Berendes, 1998).

If we accept for the moment the premise that breast-feeding makes a positive difference in terms of childhood IQ, the question still remains as to why this may be the case. It should not be surprising that as researchers began to look for an explanation as to why early intelligence would be improved with breast-feeding, they would eventually target the substances that make up breast milk vs. formula. In fact, much of the impetus for analyzing the role of PUFAs was due to the recognition that a major difference between breast milk and standard formula was the absence of certain fatty acids in the latter, notably DHA. Does a substance so essential to nerve functioning make a difference in the unfolding of intelligence? Although those who investigate feeding differences in IQ or behavior have been quick to endorse this explanation (e.g., Anderson *et al.*, 1999; Lucas *et al.*, 1992; Mortensen *et al.*, 2002), their data are incomplete, as the composition of breast milk was not ascertained in their studies. For that matter, studies of breast- vs. formula-fed infants are not very useful in answering this question anyway, since DHA is but one of a very large number of substances that differ between these fluids. Instead, groups of infants who are fed formulas that differ in composition by only a single variable such as DHA should be used to best address this type of question (Shaw & McEachem, 1997). Fortunately, the results of studies that have looked at one fatty acid at a time and its effects on infant developmental outcomes are now available.

Since the retina is laden with DHA, a number of investigators have used the visual preference technique to assess visual acuity (see Chapter 5). Although some investigators using this approach found DHA formulas to result in better visual acuity than a standard formula (Birch *et al.*, 2005), particularly in preterm infants (Carlson *et al.*, 1992), a number of other investigations have not (Auestad *et al.*, 1997; Jorgensen *et al.*, 1998).

Using the Bayley scales with preterm infants, it was recently shown that supplementation of formula with DHA or DHA + ARA improved mental scores (Birch *et al.*, 2000). In fact, scores were highest for the DHA + ARA group, followed by the DHA group, which was followed by the control group. Some research suggests that measures of cognitive development such as object permanence may reveal even more robust effects (Helland *et al.*, 2003; Willatts *et al.*, 1998). However, recent studies with full-term infants have been convergent in showing no differences between DHA-supplemented and control groups on mental measures (Auestad *et al.*, 2001; Lucas *et al.* 1999; Makrides *et al.*, 2000). Given the complexity of brain–behavior relationships, it is likely that in the near future we will see reports of PUFA studies that look at aspects of infant behavior which go beyond visual acuity and cognition, such as language development, attention deficit, sleep patterns, and temperament (Richardson & Puri, 2002; Wachs, 2001).

Regardless of breast or bottle feeding, most infants will signal a desire for supplemental foods after only a few months of postpartum growth. Table 18.4 lists dietary guidelines for the feeding of infants. Although this is

Table 18.4 Dietary guidelines for infants

Build to a variety of foods

Listen to your baby's appetite to avoid overfeeding or underfeeding

Don't restrict fat and cholesterol too much

Don't overdo high-fiber foods

Sugar is OK, but in moderation

Sodium is OK, but in moderation

Babies need more iron, pound for pound, than adults

Source: Dietary Guidelines for Infants, Gerber Products Company, 1994.

adapted from early versions of guidelines for adults, it should be stressed that infants are not 'little adults.' For example, although skim or fat-free milk is currently prescribed for adults, infants should not be fed cow's milk before 1 year of age, nor should they be given fat-free milk before childhood. Both breast- and bottle-fed infants also require supplemental iron, through drops or its inclusion in formula.

Atypical development in infancy

As should be apparent from this chapter, a number of disabilities seen in infants may be traceable to deficiencies in micronutrients like folate or iron, or a general inadequacy of calories such as in PEM. Ironically, the recent upsurge in the incidence of child obesity in developed countries has led to the realization that overweight may be a more serious problem in these countries. Extended breast-feeding has been suggested as a possible deterrent to early obesity (Hediger *et al.* 2001), but simple overfeeding may prove to be the most parsimonious explanation for this problem in infancy. Since formula-fed infants begin to surpass breast-fed infants in terms of weight gained by 2–3 months, they may self-regulate their energy intake at a higher level than breast-fed infants (Dewey *et al.*, 1993). In addition to these conditions, problems such as allergies or inborn errors of metabolism are also related to nutrition, though they may be avoided through careful attention to the infant's diet. For example, **phenylketonuria** (PKU) is a genetic disorder that impairs the metabolism of an amino acid called phenylalanine. If undetected and left untreated, irreversible brain damage can result. Fortunately, the disorder can be screened for in the newborn period (Table 18.1), so that proper dietary precautions can be taken to avoid any impairments (Batshaw & Tuchman, 2002).

Aside from nutrition-related complications, there are numerous other conditions that affect many infants and comprise their normal development.

Space limitations prevent our considering all of the handicapping conditions that may define atypical development, but a few of the disabilities that require **early intervention** will be discussed here (see Chapter 16 for more details of early intervention programs). In the United States, a federal law known as the Individuals with Disabilities Education Act (IDEA) mandates that infants and toddlers with disabilities, and their families, receive special services through an early intervention system. Under IDEA, children from birth through age 2 are entitled to early intervention services if they are experiencing developmental delays, as measured by appropriate diagnostic instruments and procedures, in one or more of the following areas of development: cognitive, physical (including vision or hearing), communication, social or emotional, and adaptive (NICHCY, 2002).

Autism

Autism is a brain disorder that may affect as many as 1 in 1000 infants or children (NIMH, 1997). In contrast to detection by early screening or a standardized test, the parents are usually the first to notice something 'different' about their baby—perhaps an unresponsiveness to people or toys, or an unusual level of focus on a particular object. Whereas most infants are remarkably social beings, babies with autism show difficulties in social interaction by avoiding eye contact, resisting attention and affection, passively accepting cuddling, preferring to play alone, and appearing oblivious to the presence of others (Swanson, 2000b). Their interaction with the environment may be even more unusual, as they often fixate on objects, sniff or lick their toys, flap their hands, seem nonreactive to pain, and may even engage in self-mutilation. As might be expected, most parents find it terribly distressing to seemingly receive rejection instead of reinforcement from their infant.

Several other disorders may accompany autism, such as mental retardation (4 in 5 with autism), seizures (1 in 3 with autism), fragile X syndrome (1 in 10 with autism), and tuberous sclerosis (1 in 4 of these children are also autistic) (NIMH, 1997). It may be the case that these disorders all stem from a common underlying brain disorder. Although there is currently no cure for autism, infants and their families can be helped to live more normal lives through a combination of special education, family support, and in some cases, medication (Mauk *et al.*, 1997).

Cerebral palsy

Cerebral palsy is a condition caused by damage to the brain that affects the infant's ability to control his or her muscles, and is present in 1 in 350 children. Factors such as genetic conditions or problems with blood supply may affect how the brain develops while in the womb, and bacterial meningitis, bleeding in the brain, severe jaundice, or a head injury could cause the problem in infancy (Pellegrino, 2002). Indeed, events such as car crashes or child abuse have been determined to cause some cases of cerebral palsy after the neonatal period, along with meningitis and infantile strokes (CDCP, 1996).

Preventing head injuries is an important way to reduce the incidence of cerebral palsy in early childhood. However, another preventable cause is a condition called **kernicterus**, a type of brain damage that is due to a severe level of jaundice. In some newborns, the liver produces too much of a substance called **bilirubin** which turns the infant's skin yellow. If left untreated this may cause kernicterus which can lead to cerebral palsy, hearing loss, and mental retardation (CDCP, 2001). Fortunately, kernicterus can be prevented with the use of 'bili-lights' as a form of phototherapy (Newman & Maisels, 2000).

Down syndrome

Down syndrome is a genetic disorder in which an extra copy of chromosome 21 is present in the cells of the developing fetus. It is the most common cause of mental retardation, and is often associated with physical problems such as heart defects or difficulties in vision and hearing (Pace, 2001). Although it is not generally inherited, the influence of the mother is quite pronounced, as maternal age is a contributing factor in estimating the incidence of the syndrome. For example, at age 20, the incidence of Down syndrome is approximately 1 in 2000, while at age 47 it is about 1 in 20 (Frederickson & Wilkins-Haug, 1997).

When reaching childhood, most individuals with Down syndrome have intelligence scores in the mild to moderate range of retardation (Roizen, 2002). Infants with Down syndrome benefit greatly from early intervention services that provide a learning environment that can maximize their potential. The infant with Down syndrome may also be identified by numerous physical attributes which may or may not be present in every instance. Some physical characteristics are almond-shaped eyes, a single palmar crease on one or both hands, and small features such as ears, mouth, hands, and feet. A study of temperament in 3-month-old infants with Down syndrome revealed them to be more active, less intense, more distractible, and having a tendency to demonstrate more approach behaviors compared with normally developing infants, suggesting that infants with Down syndrome have some unique characteristics but are more like their normally developing peers than they are different (Zickler, Morrow & Bull, 1998).

SUMMARY

In the present chapter, factors that impact on the health and atypical development of the human infant were addressed. Genetic weaknesses, untreated illnesses, even unintentional exposures to toxins can all compromise health and well-being. Though achieving optimal development is assuredly a mix of genetic potential in a nurturing environment, the case was made that nutrition plays an important role in defining that environment. The early feeding regimen is increasingly believed to matter in terms of healthy infant outcomes—but it does not occur in a vacuum. For instance, it is abundantly clear that malnutrition in the form of PEM is just one component of an ecological framework that includes poverty, disease, illiteracy, inadequate parenting, and an absence of other support systems. With this complex a system in mind, it is safe to conclude that PEM has adverse behavioral consequences. Indeed, in the human infant, severe PEM can directly affect brain growth. But early irritability and inactivity can also depress mother–infant interactions. This will likely lead to a vicious circle of less attention paid to the developing infant, with less interest and attention in the environment displayed by the infant as well. Lowered intellectual abilities are the inevitable result, with reduced attention span, poor memory, and emotional instability also possible. The act of feeding thus provides nourishment for both the growing infant's body and mind.

References

Abel, E. L. (1989) *Fetal alcohol syndrome: Fetal alcohol effects*. New York: Plenum Press.

Abramson, L., Seligman, M. E. P. & Teasdale, J. (1978). Learned helplessness in humans. Critique and reformulation. *Journal of Abnormal Psychology, 87*, 49–74.

Acredolo, L. P. (1978). Development of spatial orientation in infancy. *Developmental Psychology, 14*, 224–234.

Acredolo, L. P. & Goodwyn, S. W. (1990). Sign language in babies: The significance of symbolic gesturing for understanding language development. In R. Vasta (Ed.), *Annals of child development* (Vol. 7, pp. 1–42). London: Jessica Kingsley.

Adamson, L. B. & Frick, J. E. (2003). The still face: A history of a shared experimental paradigm. *Infancy, 4*, 451–473.

Adolph, K. E. (1995). A psychophysical assessment of toddlers' ability to cope with slopes. *Journal of Experimental Psychology: Human Perception and Performance, 21*, 734–750.

Adolph, K. E. (1997). Learning in the development of infant locomotion. *Monographs of the Society for Research in Child Development, 62*(3), Serial No. 251.

Adolph, K. E. (2000). Specificity of learning: Why infants fall over a veritable cliff. *Psychological Science, 11*, 290–295.

Adolph, K. E. (2002). Learning to keep balance. In R. Kail (Ed.), *Advances in child development and behavior* (Vol. 30, pp. 1–30). Amsterdam: Elsevier Science.

Adolph, K. E. & Avolio, A. M. (2000). Walking infants adapt locomotion to changing body dimensions. *Journal of Experimental Psychology: Human Perception and Performance, 26*, 1148–1166.

Adolph, K. E. & Berger, S. E. (2005). Physical and motor development. In M. H. Bornstein & M. E. Lamb (Eds.), *Developmental science: An advanced textbook*, 5th ed. (pp. 223–281). Mahwah, NJ: Lawrence Erlbaum Associates.

Adolph, K. E. & Berger, S. E. (in press). Motor development. In D. Kuhn & R. S. Siegler (Eds.), *Handbook of child psychology*, 6th ed. (Vol. 2: *Cognition, perception, and language*). New York: John Wiley & Sons.

Adolph, K. E., Vereijken, B. & Denny, M. A. (1998). Learning to crawl. *Child Development, 69*, 1299–1312.

Adolph, K. E., Vereijken, B. & Shrout, P. E. (2003). What changes in infant walking and why. *Child Development, 74*, 474–497.

Agnetta, B. & Rochat, P. (2004). Imitative games by 9-, 14-, and 18-month-old infants. *Infancy, 6*, 1–36.

Ainsworth, M. D. S. (1967). *Infancy in Uganda*. Baltimore: Johns Hopkins University Press.

Ainsworth, M. D. S. (1969). Object relationships, dependency, and attachment: A theoretical review of the infant–mother relationship. *Child Development, 40*, 969–1026.

Ainsworth, M. D. S. (1977). Infant development and mother–infant interaction among Ganda and American families. In P. H. Leiderman, S. R. Tulkin & A. Rosenfeld (Eds.), *Culture and infancy* (pp. 49–68). New York: Academic Press.

Ainsworth, M. D. S., Blehar, Waters, E. & Wall. S. (1978). *Patterns of attachment: A psychological study of the strange situation.* Hillsdale, NJ: Lawrence Erlbaum Associates.

Akhtar, N. & Tomasello, M. (1996). Two-year-olds learn words for absent objects and actions. *British Journal of Developmental Psychology, 14*, 79–93.

Allen, M. C. (2005). Assessment of gestational age and maturation. *Mental Retardation and Developmental Disabilities, 11*, 21–33.

Alvarado, M. C. & Bachevalier, J. (2000). Revisiting the maturation of medial temporal lobe memory functions in primates. *Learning and Memory, 7*, 244–256.

Amiel-Tison, C. & Grenier, A. (1986). *Neurological assessment during the first year of life.* New York: Oxford University Press.

Anderson, J. W., Johnstone, B. M. & Remley, D. T. (1999). Breast-feeding and cognitive development: A meta-analysis. *American Journal of Clinical Nutrition, 70*, 525–535.

Andrews, K. W., Savitz, D. A. & Hertz-Picciotto, I. (1994). Prenatal lead exposure in relation to gestational age and birth weight: A review of epidemiological studies. *American Journal of Industrial Medicine, 26*, 13–32.

Anisfeld, M., Turkewitz, G., Rose, S. A., Rosenberg, F. R., Sheiber, F. J., Couturier, D. A., Ger, J. S. & Sommer, I. (2001). No compelling evidence that newborns imitate oral gestures. *Infancy, 2*, 111–122.

Apgar, V. (1953). A proposal for a new method of evaluation of the newborn infant. *Current Research in Anesthesia & Analgesia, 32*, 260–267.

Arterberry, M. E. & Bornstein, M. H. (2002). Infant perceptual and conceptual categorization: The roles of static and dynamic stimulus attributes. *Cognition, 86*, 1–24.

Aslin, R. N. (1981). Development of smooth pursuit in human infants. In D. F. Fischer, R. A. Monty & E. J. Senders (Eds.), *Eye movements: Cognition and visual development* (pp. 31–51). Hillsdale, NJ: Lawrence Erlbaum Associates.

Aslin, R. N. & Fiser, J. (2005). Methodological challenges for understanding cognitive development in infants. *Trends in Cognitive Sciences, 9*, 92–98.

Aslin, R. N. & McMurray, B. (2004). Automated corneal reflection and eye tracking in infancy: Methodological developments and applications to cognition. *Infancy, 6*, 155–163.

Astington, J. W. & Barriault, T. (2001). Children's theory of mind: How young children come to understand that people have thoughts and feelings. *Infants and Young Children, 13*, 1–12.

Auestad, N., Halter, R., Hall, R. T., Blatter, M. *et al.* (2001). Growth and development in term infants fed long-chain polyunsaturated fatty acids: A double-masked, randomized, parallel, prospective, multivariate study. *Pediatrics, 108*, 372–381.

Auestad, N., Montalto, M., Hall, R., Fitzgerald, K., Wheeler, R., Connor, W., Neuringer, M., Connor, S., Taylor, J. & Hartmann, E. (1997). Visual acuity, erythrocyte fatty acid composition, and growth in term infants fed formulas with long chain polyunsaturated fatty acids for one year. *Pediatric Research, 41*, 1–10.

Austin, M-P., Hadzi-Pavlovic, D., Leader, L., Saint, K. & Parker, G. (2005).

Maternal trait anxiety, depression and life stress events in pregnancy: Relationships with infant temperament. *Early Human Development, 81,* 183–190.

Bachevalier, J. & Vargha-Khardem, F. (2005). The primate hippocampus: Ontogeny, early insult and memory. *Current Opinion in Neurobiology, 15,* 168–174.

Bahrick, L. E. (2004). The development of perception in a multimodal environment. In G. Bremner & A. Slater (Eds.), *Theories of infant development* (pp. 90–120). Oxford: Blackwell Publishers.

Bahrick, L. & Pickens, J. (1995). Infant memory and object motion across a period of three months: Implications for a four-phase attention function. *Journal of Experimental Child Psychology, 59,* 343–371.

Bahrick, L. E., Gogate, L. J. & Ruiz, I. (2002). Attention and memory for faces and actions in infancy: The salience of actions over faces in dynamic events. *Child Development, 73,* 1629–1643.

Bai, D. L. & Bertenthal, B. I. (1992). Locomotor status and the development of spatial search skills. *Child Development, 63,* 215–226.

Baillargeon, R. (1986). Representing the existence and the location of hidden objects: Object permanence in 6- and 8-month-old infants. *Cognition, 23,* 21–41.

Baillargeon, R. (1993). The object concept revisited: New directions in the investigation of infants' physical knowledge. In C. Granrud (Ed.), *Visual perception and cognition in infancy.* Hillsdale, NJ: Lawrence Erlbaum Associates.

Baillargeon, R. (1994). How do infants learn about the physical world? *Current Directions in Psychological Science, 3,* 133–140.

Baillargeon, R. & DeVos, J. (1991). Object permanence in young infants: Further

evidence. *Child Development, 62,* 1227–1246.

Baillargeon, R. & Wang, S. (2002). Event categorization in infancy. *Trends in Cognitive Sciences, 6,* 85–93.

Baillargeon, R., Needham, A. & DeVos, J. (1992). The development of young infants' intuitions about support. *Early Development & Parenting, 1,* 69–78.

Baillargeon, R., Spelke, E. S. & Wasserman, S. (1985). Object permanence in five-month-old infants. *Cognition, 20,* 191–208.

Bakeman, R. & Gottman, J. (1989). *Observing interaction: An introduction to sequential analysis.* New York: Cambridge University Press.

Balaban, M. T. & Waxman, S. R. (1997). Do words facilitate object categorization in 9-month-old infants? *Journal of Experimental Child Psychology, 64,* 3–26.

Baldwin, D. A. (1991). Infants' contribution to the achievement of joint reference. *Child Development, 62,* 875–890.

Baldwin, D. A. & Moses, L. J. (1996). The ontogeny of social information gathering. *Child Development, 67,* 1915–1939.

Barela, J. A., Godoi, D., Freitas, P. B. & Polastri, P. F. (2000). Visual information and body sway coupling in infants during sitting acquisition. *Infant Behavior and Development, 23,* 285–297.

Barker, D. J. P. (2003). The fetal origins of obesity. In G. A. Bray & C. Bouchard (Eds.), *Handbook of obesity: Etiology and pathophysiology,* 2nd ed. (pp. 823–851). New York: Marcel Dekker.

Baron-Cohen, S., Baldwin, D. A. & Crowson, M. (1997). Do children with autism use the speaker's direction of gaze strategy to crack the code of language? *Child Development, 68,* 48–57.

Barr, R. G., Young, S. N., Wright, J. H., Gravel, R. & Alkawaf, R. (1999). Differential calming responses to sucrose taste in crying infants with and without colic. *Pediatrics, 103*(5), e68.

Barrera, M. E. & Maurer, D. (1981). The perception of facial expressions by the three-month-old. *Child Development, 52*, 203–206.

Barrett, K. (1995). A functionalist approach to shame and guilt. In J. Tangney & K. Fischer (Eds.), *Self-conscious emotions* (pp. 25–63). New York: Guilford Press.

Bartrip, J., Morton, J. & de Schonen, S. (2001). Responses to mother's face in 3-week to 5-month-old infants. *British Journal of Developmental Psychology, 19*, 219–232.

Bates, E. (1979). *The emergence of symbols: Cognition and communication in infancy*. New York: Academic Press.

Bates, E., Carlson-Luden, V. & Bretherton, I. (1980). Perceptual aspects of tool using in infancy. *Infant Behavior and Development, 3*, 127–140.

Bates, J. E., Bennett-Freeland, C. A. & Lounsburg, M. L. (1979). Measurement of infant difficulties. *Child Development, 50*, 794–803.

Batshaw, M. L. & Tuchman, M. (2002). PKU and other inborn errors of metabolism. In M. L. Batshaw (ed.), *Children with disabilities*, 5th ed. (pp. 389–404). Baltimore: Brookes.

Bauer, P. J. & Hertsgaard, L. A. (1993). Increasing steps in recall of events: Factors facilitating immediate and long-term memory in 13.5- and 16.5-month old infants. *Child Development, 64*, 1204–1223.

Bayley, N. (1993). *Bayley scales of infant development* (2nd ed.) New York: Psychological Corporation.

Bayley, N. (2005). *Bayley scales of infant development* (3rd ed.) Oxford: Harcourt Assessment.

Beck, A. T. (1979). *Cognitive therapy and the emotional disorders*. New York: Times Mirror.

Beckett, C., Bredenkamp, D., Castle, J., Groothues, C., O'Connor, T. G., Rutter, M. & the ERA Study Team (2002). Behavior patterns associated with institutional deprivation: A study of children adopted from Romania. *Journal of Developmental and Behavioral Pediatrics, 23*, 297–303.

Bednar, J. A. & Miikkulainen, R. (2003). Learning innate face preferences. *Neural Computation, 15*, 1525–1557.

Bellinger, D. C. & Needleman, H. L. (2003). Intellectual impairment and blood lead levels. *New England Journal of Medicine, 349*(5), 500–502.

Bendersky, M. & Lewis, M. (1986). The impact of birth order on mother–infant interactions in preterm and sick infants. *Journal of Development and Behavioral Pediatrics, 7*, 242–246.

Bendersky, M. & Lewis, M. (1998). Prenatal cocaine exposure and impulse control at 2 years. *Annals of the New York Academy of Sciences, 846*, 365–367.

Bennett, D. E., Bendersky, M. & Lewis, M. (2002). Facial expressivity at 4 months: A context by expression analysis. *Infancy, 2*, 97–114.

Berger, B., Alvaraz, C. & Goldman-Rakic, P. S. (1993). Neurochemical development of the hippocampal region in the fetal rhesus monkey. I. Early appearance of peptides, calcium-binding proteins, DARPP-32, and monoamine innervation in the entorhinal cortex during the first half of gestation (E47 to E90). *Hippocampus, 3*, 279–305.

Berger, S. E. & Adolph, K. E. (2003). Infants use handrails as tools in a locomotor task. *Developmental Psychology, 39*, 594–605.

Berger, S. E., Adolph, K. E. & Lobo, S. A. 2005. Out of the toolbox: Toddlers differentiate wobbly and wooden handrails. *Child Development, 76*, 1294–1307.

Berko Gleason, J. (1958). The child's learning of English morphology. *Word, 14*, 150–177.

Bertenthal, B. I. & Campos, J. J. (1984). A reexamination of fear and its determinants on the visual cliff. *Psychophysiology, 21,* 413–417.

Bertenthal, B. I. & Clifton, R. K. (1998). Perception and action. In D. Kuhn & R. S. Siegler (Eds.), *Handbook of child psychology,* 5th ed. (Vol. 2: *Cognition, perception, and language,* pp. 51–102). New York: John Wiley & Sons.

Bertenthal, B. I. & Fischer, K. W. (1978). Development of self-recognition in the infant. *Developmental Psychology, 14,* 44–50.

Bertenthal, B. I. & von Hofsten, C. (1998). Eye, head and trunk control: The foundation for manual development. *Neuroscience and Biobehavioral Review, 22*(4), 515–520.

Bertenthal, B. I., Campos, J. J. & Barrett, K. C. (1984). Self-produced locomotion: An organizer of emotional, cognitive, and social development in infancy. In R. N. Emde & R. J. Harmon (Eds.), *Continuities and discontinuities in development* (pp. 175–210). New York: Plenum Press.

Bertenthal, B. I., Rose, J. L. & Bai, D. L. (1997). Perception–action coupling in the development of visual control of posture. *Journal of Experimental Psychology: Human Perception and Performance, 23*(6), 1631–1643.

Berthier, N. E. & Keen, R. E. 2006. Development of reaching in infancy. *Experimental Brain Research, 169,* 507–518.

Best, C. T. (1994). Learning to perceive the sound patterns of English. In C. Rovee-Collier & L. P. Lipsitt (Eds.), *Advances in Infancy Research* (Vol. 9, pp. 217–304). Norwood, NJ: Ablex.

Bigelow, A. & DeCoste, C. (2003). Sensitivity to social contingency from mothers and strangers in 4- to 6-month-olds. *Infancy, 4,* 111–131.

Birch, E. E., Casteneda, Y., Wheaton, D. H., Birch, D. G., Uauy, R. D. & Hoffman, D. R. (2005). Visual maturation of term infants fed long-chain polyunsaturated fatty acid-supplemented or control formula for 12 mo. *American Journal of Clinical Nutrition, 81*(4), 871–879.

Birch, E. E., Garfield, S., Hoffman, D. R., Uauy, R. & Birch, D. G. (2000). A randomized controlled trial of early dietary supply of long-chain polyunsaturated fatty acids and mental development in term infants. *Developmental Medicine & Child Neurology, 42,* 174–181.

Bischof-Kohler, D. (1991). The development of empathy in infants. In M. E. Lamb & H. Keller (Eds.), *Infant development: Perspectives from German-speaking countries* (pp. 245–273). Hillsdale, NJ: Lawrence Erlbaum Associates.

Björck-Åkesson, E. & Granlund, M. (2003). Creating a team around the child through professionals' continuing education: Sweden. In S. L. Odom, M. J. Hanson, J. A. Blackman & S. Kaul (Eds.), *Early intervention practices around the world,* (pp. 171–190). Baltimore: Brookes.

Blakemore, C. & Cooper, G. F. (1970). Development of the brain depends on the visual environment. *Nature, 228,* 477–478.

Blass, E. M. & Camp, C. A. (2004). The ontogeny of face identity I. Eight- to 21-week-old infants use internal and external face features in identity. *Cognition, 92,* 305–327.

Bloom, P. (2000). *How children learn the meanings of words.* Cambridge, MA: MIT Press.

Bly, L. (1994). *Motor skills acquisition in the first year.* San Antonio, TX: Therapy Skill Builders.

Boavida, J. & Carvalho, L. (2003). A comprehensive early intervention training approach: Portugal. In S. L. Odom, M. J. Hanson, J. A. Blackman & S. Kaul (Eds.), *Early intervention practices around the world,* (pp. 213–249). Baltimore: Brookes.

Bonvillian, J., Orlansky, M. D. & Novack, L. L. (1983). Developmental milestones:

Sign language acquisition and motor development. *Child Development, 54,* 1435–1445.

Bornstein, M. H. (1984). A descriptive taxonomy of psychological categories used by infants. In C. Sophian (Ed.), *Origins of cognitive skills,* (pp. 313–338). Hillsdale, NJ: Lawrence Erlbaum Associates.

Bornstein, M. H. & Suess, P. E. (2000). Physiological self-regulation and information processing in infancy: Cardiac vagal tone and habituation. *Child Development, 71,* 273–287.

Bornstein, M. H., Arterberry, M. E. & Mash, C. (2004). Long-term memory for an emotional interpersonal interaction occurring at 5 months of age. *Infancy, 6,* 407–416.

Bornstein, M. H., Hahn, C-S., Bell, C., Haynes, O. M., Slater, A., Golding, J., Wolke, D. & the ALSPAC Study Team (2006). Stability in cognition across early childhood. *Psychological Science, 17,* 151–158.

Bornstein, M. H., Haynes, O. M., O'Reilly, A. W. & Painter, K. (1996). Solitary and collaborative pretense play in early childhood: Sources of individual variation in the development of representational competence. *Child Development, 67,* 2910–2929.

Bornstein, M. H., Haynes, O. M., Pascual, L., Painter, K. M. & Galperín, C. (1999). Play in two societies: Pervasiveness of process, specificity of structure. *Child Development, 70,* 317–331.

Bornstein, M. H., Tamis-LeMonda, C. S., Tal, J., Ludemann, P., Toda, S., Rahn, C. W., Pêcheux, M. G., Azuma, H. & Vardi, D. (1992). Maternal responsiveness to infants in three societies: The United States, France, and Japan. *Child Development, 63,* 808–821.

Bornstein, M. H., Toda, S., Azuma, H., Tamis-LeMonda, C. S. & Ogino, M. (1990a). Mothers and infant activity and interaction in Japan and the United States: II. A comparative microanalysis

of naturalistic interactions focused on the organization of infant attention. *International Journal of Behavioral Development, 13,* 289–308.

Bott, E. (1957). *Family and social networks.* London: Tavistock Institute of Human Relations.

Bourgeois, K. S., Khawar, A. W., Neal, S. A. & Lockman, J. J. (2005). Infant manual exploration of objects, surfaces, and their interrelations. *Infancy, 8,* 233–252.

Bower, T. G. R. (1966). The visual world of infants. *Scientific American, 215*(6), 2–10.

Bower, T. G. R. & Wishart, J. G. (1972). The effects of motor skill on object permanence. *Cognition, 1,* 165–172.

Bowlby, J. (1951). *Maternal care and mental health.* Geneva: World Health Organization.

Bowlby, J. (1969). *Attachment and loss: Vol. 1, Attachment.* New York: Basic Books.

Bowlby, J. (1973). *Attachment and loss: Vol. 2. Separation: Anxiety and anger.* New York: Basic Books.

Bowlby, J. (1982). *Attachment and loss: Vol. 1* (2nd ed.) New York: Basic Books.

Boysson-Bardies, B. de, Vihman, M. M., Rough-Hellichius, L., Duran, C., Landberg, I. & Arao, F. (1992). Material evidence of infant selection from the target language: A cross-linguistic phonetic study. In C. Ferguson, L. Menn & C. Stoel-Gammon (Eds.), *Phonological development: Models, research, implications* (pp. 369–391). Timonium, MD: York Press.

Braungart-Riker, J., Garwood, M. M., Powers, B. P. & Notaro, P. C. (1998). Infant affect and affect regulation during the still-face paradigm with mothers and fathers: The role of infant characteristics and parental sensitivity. *Developmental Psychology, 34,* 1428–1437.

Brazelton, T. B. (1984). *Neonatal behavioral assessment scale.* Philadelphia: Spastics International.

Brazelton, T. B., Tronick, E., Lechtig, A., Lasky, R. E. & Klein, R. E. (1977). The behavior of nutritionally deprived Guatemalan infants. *Developmental Medicine & Child Neurology, 19,* 364–372.

Bremner, J. G. (1978). Egocentric versus allocentric spatial coding in nine-month-old infants: Factors influencing the choice of code. *Developmental Psychology, 14,* 346–355.

Bremner, J. G. (2001). Cognitive development: Knowledge of the physical world. In J. G. Bremner & A. Fogel (Eds.), *Blackwell handbook of infant development.* Oxford: Blackwell Publishers.

Bremner, J. G. & Knowles, L. S. (1984). Piagetian stage IV errors with an object that is directly accessible both visually and manually. *Perception, 13,* 307–314.

Bremner, J. G., Johnson, S. P., Slater, A. M., Mason, U., Foster, K., Cheshire, A. & Spring, J. (2005). Conditions for young infants' perception of object trajectories. *Child Development, 74,* 1029–1043.

Bridges, K. M. B. (1932). Emotional development in early infancy. *Child Development, 3,* 324–334.

Bril, B. & Breniere, Y. (1989). Steady-state velocity and temporal structure of gait during the first six months of autonomous walking. *Human Movement Science, 8,* 99–122.

Bril, B. & Breniere, Y. (1993). Posture and independent locomotion in early childhood: Learning to walk or learning dynamic postural control? In G. J. P. Savelsbergh (Ed.), *The development of coordination in infancy* (pp. 337–358). Amsterdam: Elsevier/North-Holland.

Bronfenbrenner, U. (1979) The *ecology of human development.* Cambridge, MA: Harvard University Press.

Brooks-Gunn, J., Klebanov, P. K., Liaw, F-R. & Spiker, D. (1993). Enhancing the development of low-birthweight premature infants: Changes in cognition and behavior over the first three years. *Child Development, 64,* 736–753.

Brown, A. (1990). Domain specific principles affect learning and transfer in children. *Cognitive Science, 14,* 107–133.

Brown, J. L. & Pollitt, E. (1996). Malnutrition, poverty, and intellectual development. *Scientific American, 274*(2), 38–43.

Bruner, J. (1972). Nature and uses of immaturity. *American Psychologist, 27,* 687–708.

Bruner, J. (2001). From communicating to talking. In Gauvain, M. & Cole, M. (Eds.). *Readings on the development of children.* New York, NY: Worth Publishers.

Bruner, J. S., Goodnow, J. J. & Austin, G. A. (1956). *A study of thinking.* New York: John Wiley & Sons.

Bruner, J. S., Olver, R. R. & Greenfield, P. M. (1966). *Studies in cognitive growth.* New York: John Wiley & Sons.

Burchinal, M. R., Campbell, F. A., Bryant, D. M., Wasik, B. H. & Ramey, C. T. (1997). Early intervention and mediating processes in cognitive performance of children of low-income African American families. *Child Development, 68,* 935–954.

Burnham, D. (1993). Visual recognition of mother by young infants: Facilitation by speech. *Perception, 22,* 1133–1153.

Bushnell, I. W. R. (2001). Mother's face recognition in newborn infants: Learning and memory. *Infant and Child Development, 10,* 67–74.

Bushnell, I. W. R. (2003). Newborn face recognition. In O. Pascalis & A. Slater (Eds.), *The development of face processing in infancy and early childhood* (pp. 41–53). New York: NOVA Science.

Bushnell, I. W. R., Sai, F. & Mullin, J. T. (1989). Neonatal recognition of the mother's face. *British Journal of Developmental Psychology, 7,* 3–15.

Buss, A. H. (1980). *Self-consciousness and social anxiety*. San Francisco: W. H. Freeman.

Butterworth, G. (1974). The development of the object concept in human infants. Unpublished D.Phil. thesis, University of Oxford.

Butterworth, G. (1977). Object disappearance and error in Piaget's stage IV task. *Journal of Experimental Child Psychology, 23*, 391–401.

Calkins, S. D., Fox, N. A. & Marshall, T. R. (1996). Behavioral and physiological antecedents of inhibited and uninhibited behavior. *Child Development, 67*, 523–540.

Campbell, A. L. & Namy, L. L. (2003). The role of social referential cues in verbal and non-verbal symbol learning. *Child Development, 74*, 549–563.

Campbell, B. A. & Campbell, E. H. (1962). Retention and extinction of learned fear in infant and adult rats. *Journal of Comparative and Physiological Psychology, 55*, 1–8.

Campos, J. J. & Stenberg, C. R. (1981). Perception, appraisal, and emotion: The onset of social referencing. In: M. E. Lamb & L. R. Sherrod (Eds.), *Infant social cognition: Empirical and theoretical considerations* (pp. 273–314). Hillsdale, NJ: Lawrence Erlbaum Associates.

Campos, J. J., Anderson, D. I., Barbu-Roth, M. A., Hubbard, E. M., Hertenstein, M. J. & Witherington, D. C. (2000). Travel broadens the mind. *Infancy, 1*(2), 149–219.

Campos, J. J., Hiatt, S., Ramsay, D., Henderson, C. & Svejda, M. (1978). The emergence of fear on the visual cliff. In M. Lewis & L. Rosenblum (Eds.), *The development of affect* (pp. 149–182). New York: Plenum Press.

Campos, J. J., Svejda, M. J., Bertenthal, B., Benson, N. & Schmid, D. (1981). Self-produced locomotion and wariness of heights: New evidence from training studies. Paper presented at the meeting of the Society for Research in Child Development, Boston, MA.

Carey, S. (1978). The child as word learner. In M. Halle, J. Bresnan & G. A. Miller (Eds.), *Linguistic theory and psychological reality*. Cambridge, MA: MIT Press.

Carey, W. B. (1970). A simplified method for measuring infant temperament. *Journal of Pediatrics, 77*, 188–194.

Carlson, B. M. (1994) *Human embryology and developmental biology*. St Louis: Mosby.

Carlson, S. E., Cooke, R. J., Werkman, S. H. & Tolley, E. A. (1992). First year growth of pre-term infants fed standard compared to marine oil n-3 supplemental formula. *Lipids, 27*(11), 901–907.

Carlson, V. J. & Harwood, R. L. (2003). Attachment, culture, and the care-giving system: The cultural patterning of everyday experiences among Anglo and Puerto Rican mother–infant pairs. *Infant Mental Health Journal, 24*, 53–73.

Carnegie Task Force on Meeting the Needs of Young Children (1994). *Starting points: meeting the needs of our youngest children*. New York: Carnegie Corporation.

Caron, R. F., Caron, A. T. & Myers, R. S. (1982). Abstraction of invariant face expressions in infancy. *Child Development, 53*, 1008–1015.

Caron, R. F., Caron, A. T. & Myers, R. S. (1985). Do infants see emotional expressions in static faces? *Child Development, 56*, 1552–1560.

Carpenter, B. & Egerton, J. (2005) (Eds.). *Early childhood intervention: International perspectives, national initiatives, and regional practice*. Birmingham, UK: West Midlands SEN Regional Partnership.

Carpenter, M., Nagell, K. & Tomasello, M. (1998). Social cognition, joint attention, and communicative competence from 9 to 15 months of age. *Monographs of the Society for Research in Child Development, 64* (4, No. 255).

Carver, L. J., Dawson, G., Panagiotides, H., Meltzoff, A. N., McPartland, J., Gray, J. & Munson, J. (2003). Age-related differences in neural correlates of face recognition during the toddler and preschool years. *Developmental Psychobiology, 42,* 148–159.

Casasola, M. & Cohen, L. B. (2002). Infant categorization of containment, support, and tight-fit spatial relationships. *Developmental Science, 5,* 247–264.

Cassia, V. M., Turati, C. & Simion, F. (2004). Can a nonspecific bias toward top-heavy patterns explain newborns' face preference? *Psychological Science, 15,* 379–383.

Caviness, V. S., Kennedy, D. N., Bates, J. F. & Makris, N. (1996). The developing human brain: A morphometric profile. In: Thatcher, R. W., Lyon, G. R., Rumsey, J. & Krasnegor, N. (Eds.), *Developmental neuroimaging* (pp. 3–14). San Diego: Academic Press.

CDCP (1996). Postnatal causes of developmental disabilities in children aged 3–10 years—Atlanta Georgia, 1991. Centers for Disease Control and Prevention. *Morbidity and Mortality Weekly Report, 45,* 130–134.

CDCP (2001). Kernicterus in full-term infants—United States, 1994–1998. Centers for Disease Control and Prevention. *Morbidity and Mortality Weekly Report, 50,* 491–494.

Cernack, J. M. & Porter, R. H. (1985). Recognition of maternal axillary odors by infants. *Child Development, 56,* 1593–1598.

Chen, Z. & Siegler, R. S. (2000). Across the great divide: Bridging the gap between understanding of toddlers' and older children's thinking. *Monographs of the Society for Research in Child Development, 65*(2, Serial No. 261).

Cheney, D. L. & Seyfarth, R. M. (1990). *How monkeys see the world: Inside the mind of another species.* Chicago, IL: Chicago University Press.

Clark, E. V. (1987). The principle of contrast: A constraint on acquisition. In B. MacWhinney (Ed.), *Mechanisms of language acquisition: The 20th annual Carnegie symposium on cognition* (pp. 1–34). Hillsdale, NJ: Lawrence Erlbaum Associates.

Clifton, R. K., Muir, D. W., Ashmead, D. H. & Clarkson, M. G. (1993). Is visually guided reading in early infancy a myth? *Child Development, 64,* 1099–1110.

Cohen, L. B. & Amsel, G. (1998). Precursors to infants' perception of causality. *Infant Behavior and Development, 21,* 713–731.

Cohen, L. B. & Oakes, L. M. (1993). How infants perceive a simple causal event. *Developmental Psychology, 29,* 421–433.

Cohen, L. B., Chaput, H. H. & Cashon, C. H. (2002). A constructivist model of infant cognition. *Cognitive Development, 17,* 1323–1343.

Colombo, J. (2000). The development of visual attention in infancy. *Annual Review of Psychology, 52,* 337–367.

Colombo, J., Shaddy, D., Richman, W., Maikranz, J., Blaga, O. & Colombo, J. (2004). Developmental course of habituation in infancy and preschool outcome. *Infancy, 5,* 1–38.

Cravioto, J. & Arrieta, R. (1986). Nutrition, mental development, and learning. In F. Faulkner & J. M. Tanner (Eds.), *Human growth* (Vol. 3, pp. 501–536). New York: Plenum Press.

Dale, N. (1989). Pretend play with mothers and siblings: Relations between early performance and partners. *Journal of Child Psychiatry, 30,* 751–759.

Damast, A. M., Tamis-LeMonda, C. S. & Bornstein, M. H. (1996). Mother–child play: Sequential interactions and the relation between maternal beliefs and behaviors. *Child Development, 67,* 1752–1766.

Daniel, B. M. & Lee, D. N. (1990). Development of looking with head and eyes. *Journal of Experimental Child Psychology, 50,* 200–216.

Darlington, R. B., Royce, J. M., Snipper, A. S., Murray, H. W. & Lazaar, I. (1980). Preschool programs and later school competence of children from low-income families. *Science, 208,* 202–204.

Darwin, C. R. (1872/1965). *The expression of emotions in man and animals.* Chicago, IL: University of Chicago Press.

Darwin, C. R. (1877). A biographical sketch of an infant. In A. Slater & D. Muir (Eds.), *The Blackwell reader in developmental psychology* (pp. 17–26). Oxford: Blackwell Publishers.

de Haan, M. & Nelson, C. A. (1997). Recognition of the mother's face by six-month-old infants: A neurobehavioral study. *Child Development, 68,* 187–210.

de Haan, M. & Nelson, C. A. (1999). Brain activity differentiates face and object processing in 6-month-old infants. *Developmental Psychology, 35,* 1113–1121.

de Haan, M., Belsky, J., Reid, V., Volein, A. & Johnson, M. H. (2004). Maternal personality and infants' neural and visual responsivity to facial expressions of emotion. *Journal of Child Psychology and Psychiatry, 45,* 1209–1218.

de Haan, M., Humphreys, K. & Johnson, M. H. (2002). Developing a brain specialized for face perception: A converging methods approach. *Developmental Psychobiology, 40,* 200–212

de Haan, M., Johnson, M. H., Maurer, D. & Perrett, D. I. (2001). Recognition of individual faces and average face prototypes by 1- and 3-month-old infants. *Cognitive Development, 16,* 659–678.

de Schonen, S. & Deruelle, C. (1994). Pattern and face recognition in infancy: Do both hemispheres perceive objects in the same way? In A. Vyt, H. Bloch & M. H. Bornstein (Eds.), *Early child development in the French tradition:*

Contributions from current research (pp. 35–53). Hillsdale, NJ: Lawrence Erlbaum Associates.

de Villiers, J. G. & de Villiers, P. A. (1978). *Language acquisition.* Cambridge, MA: Harvard University Press.

de Vries, J. P. P., Visser, G. H. A. & Prechtl, H. F. R. (1985) The emergence of fetal behaviour. II. Quantitative aspects. *Early Human Development, 12,* 99–120.

De Wolff, M. & van IJzendoorn, M. H. (1997). Sensitivity and attachment: A meta-analysis on parental antecedents of infant attachment. *Child Development, 68*(4), 571–591.

DeCasper, A. J. & Fifer, W. P. (1980). Of human bonding: Newborns prefer their mothers' voices. *Science, 208,* 1174–1176.

DeCasper, A. J. & Spence, M. J. (1986). Prenatal maternal speech influences newborns' perception of speech sounds. *Infant Behavior and Development, 9,* 133–150.

Dehaene, S. (1997). *The number sense: How the mind creates mathematics.* New York: Oxford University Press.

Delorme, A., Frigon, J. Y. & Lagace, C. (1989). Infants' reactions to visual movement of the environment. *Perception, 18,* 667–673.

Deruelle, C. & de Schonen, S. (1991). Hemispheric asymmetry in visual pattern processing in infancy. *Brain and Cognition, 16,* 151–179.

des Portes, V., Pinard, J. M., Billuart, P., Vinet, M. C., Koulakoff, A., Carrie, A. *et al.* (1998). A novel CNS gene required for neuronal migration and involved in X-linked subcortical laminar heterotopia and lissencephaly syndrome. *Cell, 92,* 51–61.

Deutsch, M. (1967). *The disadvantaged child.* New York: Basic Books.

Dewey, K. G., Heinig, M. J., Nommsen, L. A., Peerson, J. M. & Lonnerdol, B. (1993). Breast fed infants are leaner than formula fed infants at 1 year of age: The

DARLING Study. *American Journal of Clinical Nutrition, 57*, 140–145.

Diamond, A. (1990). Rate of maturation of the hippocampus and the developmental progression of children's performance on the delayed non matching to sample and visual paired comparisons tasks. In A. Diamond (Ed.), *Annals of the New York Academy of Sciences: Vol. 608. The development of neural bases of higher cognitive functions* (pp. 394–426). New York: New York Academy of Sciences.

Dowell, S. F., Butler, J. C., Giebink, G. S., Jacobs, M. R., Jernigan, D., Musher, D. M., Rakowsky, A. & Schwartz, B. (1999). Acute otitis media: Management and surveillance in an era of pneumococcal resistance—a report from the Drug-Resistant Streptococcus Pneumonia Therapeutic Working Group. *Pediatric Infectious Disease Journal, 18*(1), 1–9.

Dunn, J. (1993). *Young children's close relationships beyond attachment.* Thousand Oaks, CA: Sage.

Dunn, J. & Dale, N. (1984). Collaboration in joint pretend. In I. Bretherton (Ed.), *Symbolic play: The development of understanding* (pp. 131–158). NY: Academics Press.

Dweck, C. S. & Leggett, E. L. (1988). A social cognitive approach to motivation and personality. *Psychological Review, 95*, 256–273.

Easterbrook, M. A., Kisilevsky, B. S., Muir, D. W. & Laplante, D. P. (1999). Newborns discriminate schematic faces from scrambled faces. *Canadian Journal of Experimental Psychology, 53*, 231–241.

Eckerman, C. O. & Didow, S. M. (1996). Nonverbal imitation and toddlers' mastery of verbal means of achieving coordinated action. *Developmental Psychology, 32*, 141–152.

Eckerman, C. O., Whatley, J. L. & Kutz, S. L. (1975). Growth of social play with peers during the second year of life. *Developmental Psychology, 11*, 42–49.

Edelman, R. J. & Hampson, S. E. (1981). The recognition of embarrassment. *Personality and Social Psychology Bulletin, 7*, 109–116.

Edwards, C. P. & Lewis, M. (1979). Young children's concepts of social relations: Social functions and social objects. In M. Lewis & L. Rosenblum (Eds.), *The child and its family: The genesis of behavior, 2* (pp. 245–266). New York: Plenum Press.

Edwards, C. P. & Whiting, B. B. (1993). 'Mother, older sibling, and me': The overlapping roles of caregivers and companions in the social world of two- and three-year-olds in Ngeca, Kenya. In K. MacDonald (Ed.), *Parent–child play: Descriptions and implications* (pp. 305–329). Albany, NY: State University of New York Press.

Eimas, P. D., Siqueland, E. R., Jusczyk, P. & Vigorito, J. (1971). Speech perception in infants. *Science, 171*(968), 303–306.

Ekman, P. & Friesen, W. V. (1978). *The Facial Action Coding System: A technique for the measurement of facial movement.* Palo Alto, CA: Consulting Psychologists Press.

Eppler, M. A. (1995). Development of manipulative skills and the deployment of attention. *Infant Behavior and Development, 18*, 391–405.

Eppler, M. A., Satterwhite, T., Wendt, J. & Bruce, K. (1997). Infants' responses to a visual cliff and other ground surfaces. In M. A. Schmuckler & J. M. Kennedy (Eds.), *Studies in perception and action IV* (pp. 219–222). Mahway, NJ: Lawrence Erlbaum Associates.

Fagan, J. F. III (1972). Infants' recognition memory for faces. *Journal of Experimental Child Psychology, 14*, 453–476.

Fairbairn, W. R. D. (1952). *An object-relations theory of the personality.* New York: Basic Books.

Fantz, R. L. (1958). Pattern vision in young infants. *Psychological Record, 8*, 43–47.

Fantz, R. L. (1964). Visual experience in infants: Decreased attention to familiar patterns relative to novel ones. *Science, 146*, 668–670.

Farah, M. J., Rabinowitz, C., Quinn, G. E. & Liu, G. T. (2000). Early commitment of neural structures for face recognition. *Cognitive Neuropsychology, 17*, 117–123.

Farroni, T., Massaccesi, S., Pividori, D., Johnson, M. H. & Farroni, T. (2004). Gaze following in newborns. *Infancy, 5*, 39–60.

Farver, J. M. & Howes, C. (1993). Cultural differences in American and Mexican mother–child pretend play. *Merrill-Palmer Quarterly, 39*, 344–358.

Farver, J. M. & Wimbarti, S. (1995). Indonesian children's play with their mothers and older siblings. *Child Development, 66*, 1493–1503.

Feinman, S. & Lewis, M. (1983). Social inferencing at ten months: A second-order effect on infants' responses to strangers. *Child Development, 34*, 878–887.

Feinman, S., Roberts, D., Hsieh, K., Sawyer, D. & Swanson, D. (1992) A critical review of social referencing in infancy. In S. Feinman (Ed.), *Social referencing and the social construction of reality in infancy* (pp. 15–54). New York: Plenum Press.

Feiring, C., Taska, L. & Lewis, M. (2002). Adjustment following sexual abuse discovery: The role of shame and attributional style. *Developmental Psychology, 38*(1), 79–92.

Feldman, M. A. (Ed.). (2004). *Early intervention: The essential readings.* Malden, MA: Blackwell Publishers.

Fenson, L., Dale, P. S., Reznick, J. S., Bates, E., Thal, D. J. & Pethicke, S. J. (1994). Variability in early communicative development. *Monographs of the Society for Research in Child Development, 59*, vol. 173.

Ferguson, T. J., Stegge, H. & Damhuis, I. (1991). Children's understanding of guilt and shame. *Child Development, 62*, 827–839.

Fernald, A. (1993). Approval and disapproval: Infant responsiveness to vocal affect in familiar and unfamiliar languages. *Child Development, 64*, 657–667.

Fernald, A., Pinto, J. P., Swingley, D., Weinberg, A. & McRoberts, G. W. (1998). Rapid gains in speed of verbal processing by infants in the second year. *Psychological Science, 9*, 72–75.

Fernald, A., Swingley, D. & Pinto, J. P. (2001). When half a word is enough: Infants can recognize spoken words using partial phonetic information. *Child Development, 72*, 1003–1015.

Fernandez, M., Hernandez-Reif, M., Field, T., Diego, M., Sanders, C. & Roca, A. (2004). EEG during lavender and rosemary exposure in infants of depressed and non-depressed mothers. *Infant Behavior and Development, 27*, 91–100.

Feuerstein, R. (1990). The theory of structural cognitive modifiability. In B. Z. Presseisen, R. J. Sternberg, K. W. Fischer, C. C. Knight, & R. Feuerstein (Eds.), *Learning and thinking styles: Classroom interaction* (pp. 32–59). Washington, DC: National Education Association.

Field, T. (1984). Early interactions between infants and their postpartum depressed mothers. *Infant Behavior and Development, 1*, 527–532.

Field, T. M. (1985). Neonatal perception of people: Maturational and individual differences. In T. M. Field & N. A. Fox (Eds.), *Social perception in young infants* (pp. 31–52). Norwood, NJ: Ablex Publishing.

Field, T. M., Cohen, D., Garcia, R. & Greenberg, R. (1984). Mother–stranger face discrimination by the newborn. *Infant Behavior and Development, 7*, 19–25.

Field, T. M., Woodson, R. W., Cohen, D., Greenberg, R., Garcia, R. & Collins, K. (1983). Discrimination and imitation of facial expressions by term and preterm neonates. *Infant Behavior and Development, 6*, 485–489.

Fiese, B. H. (1990). Playful relationships: A contextual analysis of mother–toddler interaction and symbolic play. *Child Development, 61*, 1648–1656.

Fifer, W. P. & Moon, C. (1989). Psychobiology of newborn auditory preferences. *Seminars in Perinatology, 13*, 430–433.

Fitzgerald, M. (1993). Development of pain pathways and mechanisms. In K. J. S. Anand & P. J. McGrath (Eds.), *Pain research and clinical management* (pp. 19–38). Amsterdam: Elsevier.

Fivush, R. & Hamond, N. R. (1990). Autobiographical memory across the preschool years. Towards reconceptualizing childhood amnesia. In R. Fivush & J. Hudon (Eds.), *Knowing and remembering in young children* (pp. 233–248). New York: Cambridge University Press.

Flavell, J. H. (1996). Piaget's legacy. *Psychological Science, 7*, 200–203.

Flavell, J. H. (1999). Cognitive development: Children's knowledge about the mind. *Annual Review of Psychology, 50*, 21–45.

Forman, D. R., O'Hara, M. W., Larsen, K., Coy, K. C., Gorman, L. L. & Stuart, D. (2003). Infant emotionality: Observational methods and the validity of maternal reports. *Infancy, 4*, 541–565.

Fox, N. A. & Porges, S. W. (1985). The relation between neonatal heart period patterns and developmental outcome. *Child Development, 56*, 28–37.

Fraiberg, S. (1974). Blind infants and their mothers: An examination of the sign system. In M. Lewis & L. A. Rosenblum (Eds.), *The effect of the infant on its caregiver* (pp. 215–232). New York: John Wiley & Sons.

Frankenburg, W. K. & Dodds, J. B. (1967). The denver developmental screening test. *Journal of Pediatrics, 71*, 181–191.

Frazer, J. (1915). *The golden bough*. New York: Macmillan.

Frederickson, H. L. & Wilkins-Haug, L. (1997). *OB/GYN secrets* (2nd ed.). Philadelphia: Hanley & Belfus.

French, R. M., Mareschal, D., Mermillod, M. & Quinn, P. C. (2004). The role of bottom-up processing in perceptual categorization by 3- to 4-month-old infants: Simulations and data. *Journal of Experimental Psychology: General, 133*, 382–397.

Freud, A. & Dann, S. (1951). An experiment in group upbringing. In R. Eissler, A. Freud, H. Hartmann & E. Kris (Eds.), *The psychoanalytic study of the child* (Vol. 6). New York: International Universities Press.

Freud, S. (1948). *The psychopathology of everyday life* (2nd ed.). London: Brenn.

Friederici, A. D. & Wessels, J. M. I. (1993). Phonotactic knowledge and its use in infant speech perception. *Perception & Psychophysics, 54*, 287–295.

Fullard, W., McDevitt, S. C. & Carey, W. B. (1984). Assessing temperament in one- to three-year-old children. *Journal of Pediatric Psychology, 9*, 205–217.

Gallup, G. G., Jr. (1977). Self-recognition in primates: A comparative approach to the bidirectional properties of consciousness. *American Psychologist, 32*, 329–338.

Garber, H. L. (1988). *The Milwaukee Project: Preventing mental retardation in children at-risk*. Washington, DC: American Association on Mental Retardation.

Garcia-Coll, C. & Magnusson, K. (1999) Cultural influences on child development: Are we ready for a paradigm shift? In A. Maasten (Ed.), *Cultural processes in child development: The Minnesota symposia on child psychology*. Vol. 29. (pp. 1–24). Hillsdale, NJ: Lawrence Erlbaum Associates.

Garciaguirre, J. S. & Adolph, K. E. (2006). Step-by-step: Infants' walking and falling experience. Manuscript in preparation.

Gardiner, H. W. & Kosmitzki, C. (2005). *Lives across cultures: Cross-cultural human development* (3rd ed.). Boston, MA: Allyn & Bacon.

Gaskins, S. (1996). How Mayan parental theories come into play. In S. Harkness & C. Super (Eds.), *Parents' cultural belief systems* (pp. 345–363). New York: Guilford Press.

Gauker, C. (2005). On the evidence for prelinguistic concepts. *Theoria, 20,* 287–297.

Geldart, S., Maurer, D. & Carney, K. (1999a). Effects of eye size on adults' aesthetic ratings of faces and 5-month-olds' looking times. *Perception, 28,* 361–374.

Geldart, S., Maurer, D. & Henderson, H. (1999b). Effects of the height of the internal features of faces on adults' aesthetic ratings and 5-month-olds' looking times. *Perception, 28,* 839–850.

Gesell, A. (1952). *Infant development: The embryology of early human behavior.* New York: Harper & Brothers.

Gibson, E. J. (1988). Exploratory behavior in the development of perceiving, acting and the acquiring of knowledge. *Annual Review of Psychology, 39,* 1–41.

Gibson, E. J. (1997). An ecological psychologist's prolegomena for perceptual development: A functional approach. In C. Dent-Read & P. Zukow-Goldring (Eds.), *Evolving explanations of development: Ecological approaches to organism-environment systems* (pp. 23–45). Washington, DC: American Psychological Association.

Gibson, E. J. & Pick, A. D. (2000). *An ecological approach to perceptual learning and development.* New York: Oxford University Press.

Gibson, E. J. & Schmuckler, M. A. (1989). Going somewhere: An ecological and experimental approach to development of mobility. *Ecological Psychology, 1,* 3–25.

Gibson, E. J. & Walk, R. D. (1960). The 'visual cliff.' *Scientific American, 202,* April, 64–71.

Gillespie, S., Mason, J. & Kevany, J. (Eds.). (1991). *Controlling iron deficiency* (Nutrition Policy Discussion Paper No. 9). Geneva: United Nations Administrative Committee on Coordination/Subcommittee on Nutrition.

Gluckman, P. & Hanson, M. (2005) *The fetal matrix. Evolution, development and disease.* Cambridge: Cambridge University Press.

Gold, E. M. (1967). Language identification in the limit. *Information and Control, 16,* 447–474.

Goldsmith, H. H. (1996). Studying temperament via construction of the Toddler Behavior Assessment Questionnaire. *Child Development, 67,* 218–235.

Göncü, A. (1993). Development of intersubjectivity in social pretend play. *Human Development, 36,* 185–198.

Gong, Q. Y., Roberts, N., Garden, A. S. & Whitehouse, G. H. (1998). Fetal and fetal brain volume estimation in the third trimester of human pregnancy using gradient echo MR imaging. *Magnetic Resonance Imaging, 16*(3), 235–240.

Goodall, J. (1988). *In the shadow of man.* San Diego, CA: San Diego State University Press.

Goodwyn, S. W. & Acredolo, L. P. (1993). Symbolic gesture versus word: Is there a modality advantage for onset of symbol use? *Child Development, 64,* 688–701.

Goren, C. C., Sarty, M. & Wu, P. Y. K. (1975). Visual following and pattern discrimination of face-like stimuli by newborn infants. *Pediatrics, 56,* 544–549.

Gorman, K. S. (1995). Malnutrition and cognitive development: Evidence from experimental/quasi-experimental studies among the mild-to-moderately malnourished. *Journal of Nutrition, 125,* 2239S–2244S.

Grantham-MacGregor, S. (1995). A review of studies of the effect of severe malnutrition on mental development. *Journal of Nutrition, 125*(8S), 2235S.

Grecco, C., Hayne, H. & Rovee-Collier, C. (1990). Roles of function, reminding, and variability in categorization by 3-month-old infants. *Journal of Experimental Psychology: Learning, Memory, and Cognition, 16*, 617–633.

Greenbaum, C. W. & Landau, R. (1977). Mothers' speech and the early development of vocal behavior. In P. H. Leiderman, S. R. Tulkin & A. Rosenfeld (Eds.), *Culture and infancy: Variations in the human experience*. New York: Academic Press.

Gregg, N. M. (1942). Congenital cataracts following German measles in the mother. *Transactions of the Ophthalmological Society of Australia, 3*, 35.

Griffin, A. M., Hoss, R. A., Ramsey, J. L., Langlois, J. H. & Rubenstein, A. (2004). Antecedents of the 'beauty is good' stereotype: Infants associate facial attractiveness with positive and negative valence. Presented at the biennial meeting of the International Conference on Infant Studies, Chicago, IL.

Gunnar, M. R. (1989). Studies of the human infants' adrenocortical response to potentially stressful events. In M. Lewis & J. Worobey (Eds.), *Infant stress and coping: New directions for child development* (Vol. 45, pp. 3–18). San Francisco: Jossey Bass.

Gunnar, M. R., Tout, K., De Haan, M., Pierce, S. & Stansbury, K. (1997). Temperament, social competence, and adrenocortical activity in preschoolers. *Developmental Psychobiology, 31*, 65–85.

Guralnick, M. J. (Ed.). (1997). *The effectiveness of early intervention*. Baltimore: Brookes Publishing.

Gusella, J. L., Muir, D. & Tronick, E. Z. (1988). The effect of manipulating maternal behavior during an interaction on three- and six-month-old's affect and attention. *Child Development, 59*, 1111–1124.

Gutelius, M. F., Kirsch, A. D., MacDonald, S., Brooks, M. R. & McErleand, T. (1977). Controlled study of child health supervision: Behavioral results. *Pediatrics, 60*, 294–304.

Gyomrai-Ludowyk, E. (1963). The analysis of a young concentration camp victim. *Psychoanalytic Study of the Child, 18*, 484–510.

Haight, W. & Miller, P. J. (1992). The development of everyday pretend play: A longitudinal study of mothers' participation. *Merrill-Palmer Quarterly, 38*, 331–349.

Hains, S. M. J. & Muir, D. W. (1996a). Infant sensitivity to adult eye direction. *Child Development, 67*, 1940–1951.

Hains, S. M. J. & Muir, D. W. (1996b). Effects of stimulus contingency in infant-adult interactions. *Infant Behavior and Development, 19*, 49–61.

Haith, M. M., Bergman, T. & Moore, M. J. (1977). Eye contact and face scanning in early infancy. *Science, 198*, 853–855.

Haith, M. M., Hazan, C. & Goodman, G. S. (1988). Expectations and anticipation of dynamic visual events by 3.5-month-old babies. *Child Development, 59*, 467–479.

Halberstadt, J. & Rhodes, G. (2000). The attractiveness of nonface averages: Implications for an evolutionary explanation of the attractiveness of average faces. *Psychological Science, 11*, 285–289.

Haley, D. W. & Stansbury, K. (2003). Infant stress and parent responsiveness: Regulation of physiology and behavior during still-face and reunion. *Child Development, 74*, 1534–1546.

Halit, H., Csibra, G., Volein, A. & Johnson, M. H. (2004). Face-sensitive cortical processing in early infancy. *Journal of Child Psychology and Psychiatry, 45*, 1228–1234.

Harlow, H. F. (1958). The nature of love. *American Psychologist, 13*, 673–685.

Harlow, H. F. (1969). Age-mate or peer affectional system. In D. S. Lehrman, R. A. Hinde & E. Shaw (Eds.), *Advances in the study of behavior* (Vol. 2, pp. 333–383). New York: Academic Press.

Harlow, H. & Harlow, M. K. (1965). The affectional systems. In A. M. Schrier, H. F. Harlow & F. Stollnitz (Eds.), *Behavior of nonhuman primates* (Vol. 2, pp. 287–334). New York: Academic Press.

Harris, G. (1997). Development of taste perception and appetite regulation. In G. Bremner, A. Slater & G. Butterworth (Eds.), *Infant development: Recent advances* (pp. 9–30). Hove: Psychology Press.

Harris, P. L. (1973) Perseverative errors in search by young infants. *Child Development, 44*, 28–33.

Hartshorn, K., Rovee-Collier, C., Gerhardstein, P. C., Bhatt, R. S., Wondoloski, T. L., Klein, P. J. *et al.* (1998). Ontogeny of long-term memory over the first year-and-a-half of life. *Developmental Psychobiology, 32*, 69–89.

Harwood, R. L., Miller, J. G. & Irizarry, N. L. (1995). *Culture and attachment: Perceptions of the child in context.* New York: Guilford Press.

Haskins, R. (1989) Beyond metaphor: The efficacy of early childhood education. *American Psychologist, 44*, 274–282.

Hatten, M. E. (1999). Central nervous system neuronal migration. *Annual Review of Neuroscience, 22*, 511–539

Hauser-Cram, P., Peirson, D. E., Walker, D. K. & Tivnan, T. (1991). *Early education in the public schools.* San Francisco: Jossey-Bass.

Hay, W. W., Catz, C. S., Grave, G. D. & Yaffe, S. J. (1997). Workshop Summary: Fetal growth: Its regulation and disorders. *Pediatrics, 99*, 585–591.

Hayes, R. A., Slater, A. & Brown, E. (2001). Infants' ability to categorise on the basis of rhyme. *Cognitive Development, 15*, 405–419.

Hayne, H. (2004). Infant memory development: Implications for childhood amnesia. *Developmental Review, 24*, 33–73.

Hayne, H., Boniface, J. & Barr, R. (2000). The development of declarative memory in human infants: Age-related changes in deferred imitation. *Behavioral Neuroscience, 114*, 77–83.

Hayne, H., Greco, C., Earley, L., Griesler, P. & Rovee-Collier, C. (1986). Ontogeny of early event memory: II. Encoding and retrieval by 2- and 3-month-olds. *Infant Behavior and Development, 9*, 461–472.

Hayne, H., Rovee-Collier, C. & Borza, M. (1991). Infant memory for place information. *Memory & Cognition, 19*, 378–386.

Heath, S. B. (1983). *Ways with words: Language, life, and work in communities and classrooms.* New York: Cambridge University Press.

Hebb, D. O. (1949). *Organization of behavior.* New York: John Wiley & Sons.

Heckhausen, H. (1984). Emergent achievement behavior: Some early developments. In J. Nicholl (Ed.), *The development of achievement motivation* (pp. 1–32). Greenwich, CT: JAI Press.

Heckhausen, H. (1987). Emotional components of action: Their ontogeny as reflected in achievement behavior. In D. Görlitz & J. F. Wohlwill (Eds.), *Curiosity, imagination, and play: On the development of spontaneous cognitive and motivational processes* (pp. 326–348). Hillsdale, NJ: Lawrence Erlbaum Associates.

Hediger, M. L., Overpeck, M. D., Kuczmarski, R. J & Ruan, W. J. (2001). Association between infant breastfeeding and overweight in young children. *JAMA, 285*(19), 2453–2460.

Held, R. & Hein, A. (1963). Movement produced stimulation in the development of visually guided behavior. *Journal of*

Comparative and Physiological Psychology, 56, 872–876.

Helland, I. B., Smith, L., Saarem, K., Saugstad, O. D. & Drevon, C. A. (2003). Maternal supplementation with very-long-chain n-3 fatty acids during pregnancy and lactation augments children's IQ at 4 years of age. *Pediatrics, 111*(1). <*www.pediatrics.org/cgi/content /full/111/1/e39*>.

Hepper, P. G. (1991) An examination of fetal learning before and after birth. *Irish Journal of Psychology, 12,* 95–107.

Hepper, P. G. (1992) Fetal psychology. an embryonic science. In J. G. Nijhuis (Ed.), *Fetal behaviour. Developmental and perinatal aspects* (pp. 129–156). Oxford: Oxford University Press.

Hepper, P. G. (1996). Fetal memory: Does it exist? What does it do? *Acta Paediatrica Supplement 416,* 16–20.

Hepper, P. G. & Leader, L. R. (1996) Fetal habituation. *Fetal and Maternal Medicine Review, 8,* 109–123.

Hepper, P. G. & Shahidullah, S. (1994) The development of fetal hearing. *Fetal and Maternal Medicine Review, 6,* 167–179.

Hepper, P. G., Dornan, J. C. & Little, J. F. (2005). Maternal alcohol consumption during pregnancy may delay the development of spontaneous fetal startle behaviour. *Physiology & Behavior, 83,* 711–714.

Herbert, J. & Hayne, H. (2000). The ontogeny of long-term retention during the second year of life. *Developmental Science, 3,* 50–56.

Herbert, J. S., Eckerman, C. O., Goldstein, R. F. & Stanton, M. E. (2004). Contrasts in infant classical eyeblink conditioning as a function of premature birth. *Infancy, 5,* 57–384.

Herbert, J., Gross, J. & Hayne, H. (2006). Age-related changes in deferred imitation between 6- and 9-months of age. *Infant Behavior and Development, 29,* 136–139.

Hernandez-Reif, M., Field, T. & Diego, M. (2004). Differential sucking by neonates of depressed versus non-depressed mothers. *Infant Behavior and Development, 27,* 465–476.

Hernandez-Reif, M., Field, T., Diego, M. & Largie, S. (2001). Weight perception by newborns of depressed versus non-depressed mothers. *Infant Behavior and Development, 24,* 305–316.

Hernandez-Reif, M., Field, T., Diego, M. & Largie, S. (2002). Depressed mothers' newborns show longer habituation and fail to show face/voice preference. *Infant Mental Health Journal, 23,* 643–653.

Hernandez-Reif, M., Field, T., Diego, M. & Largie, S. (2003). Haptic habituation to temperature is slower in newborns of depressed mothers. *Infancy, 3,* 47–63.

Hernandez-Reif, M., Field, T., del Pino, N. & Diego, M. (2000). Less exploring by mouth occurs in newborns of depressed mothers. *Infant Mental Health Journal, 21,* 204–210.

Hertsgaard, L., Gunnar, M., Erickson, M. F. & Nachmias, M. (1995). Adrenocortical responses to the Strange Situation with disorganized/disoriented attachment relationships. *Child Development, 66,* 1100–1106.

Higgins, C. I., Campos, J. J. & Kermoian, R. (1996). Effect of self-produced locomotion on infant postural compensation to optic flow. *Developmental Psychology, 32*(5), 836–841.

Hill, R., Foote N., Aldous, J., Carlson, R. & MacDonald, R. (1970). *Family development in three generations: A longitudinal study of changing family patterns of planning and achievement.* Cambridge, MA: Schenkman.

Hinde, R. A. (1976). Interactions, relationships, and social structure. *Man, II,* 1–17.

Hirsh-Pasek, K. & Golinkoff, R. M. (1996). *The origins of grammar: Evidence from early language comprehension.* Cambridge, MA: MIT Press.

Hoffman, M. L. (1988). Moral development. In M. Lamb & M. Bornstein (Eds.), *Developmental psychology: An advanced textbook* (2nd ed., pp. 497–548). Hillsdale, NJ: Lawrence Erlbaum Associates.

Hollich, G., Hirsh-Pasek, K. & Golinkoff, R. M. (2000). Breaking the language barrier: An emergentist coalition model for the origins of word learning. *Monographs of the Society for Research in Child Development, 65*(3, Serial No. 262).

Honig, A. S. (2000). Cross-cultural study of infants and toddlers. In A. L. Comunian & U. P. Gielen (Eds.), *International perspectives on human development* (pp. 275–308). Lengerich, Germany: Pabst Science Publishers.

Hood, B. M. (1995). Gravity rules for 2- to 4-year-olds? *Cognitive Development, 10*, 577–598.

Hood, B., Carey, S. & Prasada, S. (2000). Predicting the outcomes of physical events. *Child Development, 71*, 1540–1554.

Hooker, D. (1952) *The prenatal origin of behavior.* Lawrence, Kansas: University of Kansas Press.

Hopkins, B. & Westra, T. (1988). Maternal handling and motor development: An intracultural study. *Genetic, Social, and General Psychology Monographs, 114*(3), 377–408.

Hopkins, B. & Westra, T. (1990). Motor development, maternal expectations, and the role of handling. *Infant Behavior & Development, 13*(1), 117–122.

Horney, K. (1939). *New ways in psychoanalysis.* New York: Norton.

Horwood, I. J. & Fergusson, D. M. (1998). Breastfeeding and later cognitive and academic outcomes. *Pediatrics, 101*(1).<*www.pediatrics.org/cgi/content/full/101/1/e9*>.

Houston, D. M. (2005). Speech perception in infants. In D. B. Pisoni & R. R. Remez (Eds.), *Handbook of speech perception.*Cambridge, MA: Blackwell Publishers.

Howe, M. L. & Courage M. L. (1997). Independent paths in the development of infant learning and forgetting. *Journal of Experimental Child Psychology, 67*, 131–163.

Howes, C. & Tonyan, H. (1999). Peer relations. In L. Balter & C. S. Tamis-LeMonda (Eds.), *Child psychology: A handbook of contemporary issues* (pp. 143–157). Philadelphia: Psychology Press.

Howes, C. & Unger, O. (1992). Collaborative construction of social pretend play between toddler-age partners: Illustrative Study #2. In A. Pellegrini (Ed.), *The collaborative construction of pretend* (pp. 45–54). Albany, NY: State University of New York Press.

Howes, C. (1992). Mastery of the communication of meaning in social pretend play. In A. Pellegrini (Ed.), *The collaborative construction of pretend* (pp. 13–24). Albany, NY: State University of New York Press.

Howes, C. (1999). Attachment relationships in the context of multiple care-givers. In J. Cassidy & P. R. Shaver (Eds.), *Handbook of attachment: Theory, research, and clinical applications* (pp. 671–687). New York: Guilford Press.

Howes, C., Hamilton, C. E. & Phillipsen, L. (1998). Stability and continuity of child–caregiver and child–peer relationships. *Child Development, 69*, 418–426.

Huettel, S. A. & Needham, A. (2000). Effects of balance relations between objects on infants' object segregation. *Developmental Science, 3*, 415–427.

Hull, C. L. (1920). Quantitative aspects of the evolution of concepts. *Psychological Monographs* (Whole No. 123).

Hunnius, S. & Geuze, R. H. (2004). Developmental changes in visual scanning of dynamic faces and abstract stimuli in infants: A longitudinal study. *Infancy, 6*, 231–255.

Husaini, M., Karyadi, L., Husaini, Y. K., Sandjaja, Karyadi, D. & Pollitt, E.

(1991). Developmental effects of short-term supplementary feeding in nutritionally-at-risk Indonesian infants. *American Journal of Clinical Nutrition, 54*(4), 799–804.

IHDP (1990). The Infant Health and Development Program. Enhancing the outcomes of low-birth-weight, premature infants. *JAMA, 263*, 3035–3042.

Innis, S. M. (1991). Essential fatty acids in growth and development. *Progress in Lipid Research, 30*, 39–103.

Izard, C. E. (1978). Emotions and emotion–cognition relationships. In M. Lewis & L. A. Rosenblum (Eds.), *The development of affect* (pp. 389–413). New York: Plenum Press.

Izard, C. E. (1982). *Measuring emotions in infants and children*. London: Cambridge University Press.

Izard, C. E. (1983). *The maximally discriminate facial coding system (MAX)* (Revised). Newark, DE: University of Delaware, Instructional Resources Center.

Izard, C. E. (1995). *The maximally discriminative facial movement coding system* (3rd ed.). Newark, DE: Instructional Resources Center.

Jacklin, C.N, Snow, M. E. & Maccoby, E. E. (1981). Tactile sensitivity and muscle strength in newborn boys and girls. *Infant Behavior and Development, 4*, 261–268.

Jacobson, S. W., Chiodo, L. M. & Jacobson, J. L. (1999). Breastfeeding effects on intelligence quotient in 4- and 11-year-old children. *Pediatrics, 103*(5), 1–6.

James, D., Pillai, M. & Smoleniec, J. (1995) Neurobehavioral development in the human fetus. In J.-P. Lecanuet, W. P. Fifer, N. A. Krasnegor & W. P. Smotherman (Eds.), *Fetal development. A psychobiological perspective* (pp.101–128) Hillsdale, NJ: Lawrence Erlbaum Associates.

James, W. (1890). *The principles of psychology*. New York: Henry Holt.

James, W. P. T., Nelson, M., Ralph, A. & Leather, S. (1997). Socioeconomic determinants of health: The contribution of nutrition to inequalities of health. *BMJ, 314*, 1545.

Janoff-Bulman, R. (1979). Characterological versus behavioral self-blame: Inquiries into depression and rape. *Journal of Personality and Social Psychology, 37*, 1798–1809.

Joh, A. S. & Adolph, K. E. (2006). Learning from falling. *Child Development, 77*, 89–102.

Johnson, D. L. & Swank, P. R. (1996). Breast feeding and children's intelligence. *Psychological Reports, 79*, 1179–1185.

Johnson, M. H. & de Haan, M. (2001). Developing cortical specialization for visual–cognitive function: The case of face recognition. In J. L. McClelland & R. S. Siegler (Eds.), *Mechanisms of cognitive development: Behavioral and neural perspectives* (pp. 253–270). Mahwah, NJ: Lawrence Erlbaum Associates.

Johnson, M. H., Dziurawiec, S., Ellis, H. & Morton, J. (1991). Newborns' preferential tracking of face-like stimuli and its subsequent decline. *Cognition, 40*, 1–19.

Johnson, S. P. (2004). Development of perceptual completion in infancy. *Psychological Science, 15*, 769–775.

Johnson, S. P. & Aslin, R. N. (1995). Perception of object unity in 2-month-old infants. *Developmental Psychology, 31*, 739–745.

Johnson, S. P., Amso, D. & Slemner, J. A. (2003). Development of object concepts in infancy: Evidence for early learning in an eye tracking paradigm. *Proceedings of the National Academy of Sciences, 100*, 10568–10573.

Johnson, S. P., Bremner, J. G., Slater, A., Mason, U., Foster, K. & Cheshire, A. (2003). Infants' perception of object trajectories. *Child Development, 74*, 94–108.

Johnson, S. P., Slemmer, J. A. & Amso, D. (2004). Where infants look determines how they see: Eye movements and object perception performance in 3-month-olds. *Infancy, 6,* 185–201.

Johnson, S., Slaughter, V., Carey, S. (1998). Whose gaze will infants follow? The elicitation of gaze-following in 12-month-olds. *Developmental Science, 1,* 233–238.

Jorgensen, M., Holmer, G., Lund, P., Hernel, O. & Michaelsen, K. (1998). Effect of formula supplemented with docosahexaenoic acid and gamma linolenic acid on fatty acid status and visual acuity in term infants. *Journal of Pediatric Gastroenterology & Nutrition, 26,* 412–421.

Jusczyk, P. W. (1997). *The discovery of spoken language.* Cambridge, MA: MIT Press.

Jusczyk, P. W. & Aslin, R. N. (1995). Infants' detection of the sound patterns of words in fluent speech. *Cognitive Psychology, 29*(1), 1–23.

Jusczyk, P. W., Cutler, A. & Redanz, N. J. (1993). Infants' preference for the predominant stress patterns of English words. *Child Dev, 64*(3), 675–687.

Jusczyk, P. W., Luce, P. A. & Charles-Luce, J. (1994). Infants' sensitivity to phonotactic patterns in the native language. *Journal of Memory & Language, 33*(5), 630–645.

Kagan, J. & Lewis, M. (1965). Studies of attention in the human infant. *Merrill-Palmer Quarterly, 11,* 95–127.

Kagitcibasi, C. (1996). *Family and human development across cultures.* Mahwah, NJ: Lawrence Erlbaum Associates.

Kalakanis, L. E. (1998). *Newborns' preferences for attractive faces.* Doctoral dissertation: The University of Texas at Austin.

Kalter, H. (2003). Teratology in the 20th century. Environmental causes of congenital malformations in humans and how they were established.

Neurotoxicology and Teratology, 25, 131–282.

Kamerman, S. (2000). Early childhood intervention policies: An international perspective. In J. P. Shonkoff & S. J. Meisels (Eds.), *Handbook of early childhood intervention* (2nd ed., pp. 613–629). New York: Cambridge University Press.

Kant, I. (1787/1934). *Critique of pure reason* (J. M. D. Meikeljohn, Trans.). London: J. M. Dent & Sons.

Kaslow, N. J., Ream, L. P., Pollack, S. L. & Siegel, A. W. (1988). Attributional style and self-control behavior in depressed and nondepressed children and their parents. *Journal of Abnormal Child Psychology, 16(*2*),* 163–175.

Kavsek, M. (2004). Predicting later IQ from infant visual habituation and dishabituation: A meta-analysis. *Applied Developmental Psychology, 25,* 369–393.

Keating, M. B., McKenzie, B. E. & Day, R. H. (1986). Spatial localization in infancy: Position constancy in a square and circular room with and without a landmark. *Child Development, 57,* 115–124.

Keen, R. (2003). Representation of objects and events: Why do infants look so smart and toddlers look so dumb? *Current Directions in Psychological Science, 12,* 79–83.

Kellman, P. J. & Spelke, E. S. (1983). Perception of partly occluded objects in infancy. *Cognitive Psychology, 15,* 483–524.

Kelly, D. J., Liu, S., Liu, Q., Quinn, P. C., Slater, A. M., Lee, K. *et al.* (in press a). Cross-race preferences for same-race faces extend beyond the African versus Caucasian contrast. *Infancy.*

Kelly, D. J., Quinn, P. C., Slater, A. M., Lee, K. *et al.* (in press b). Three-month-olds, but not newborns, prefer own-race faces. *Developmental Science.*

Kestenbaum, R. & Nelson, C. A. (1990). The recognition and categorization of upright and inverted emotional expressions by 7-month-old infants. *Infant Behavior and Development, 13,* 497–511.

Klaus, R. A. & Gray, S. W. (1968). The Early Training Project for disadvantaged children: A report after five years. *Monographs of the Society for Research in Child Development, 33*(4, Serial No. 120).

Klein, M. (1930). The importance of symbol-formation in the development of the ego. In M. Klein (Ed.), *Contributions to psychoanalysis, 1921–1945.* New York: McGraw-Hill.

Klein, P. S. (2003). A mediational approach to early intervention: Israel. In S. L. Odom, M. J. Hanson, J. A. Blackman & S. Kaul (Eds.), *Early intervention practices around the world* (pp. 69–89). Baltimore: Brookes.

Köhler, W. (1925). *The mentality of apes* (E. Winter, Trans.). New York: Harcourt, Brace & World.

Kohut, H. (1977). *The restoration of the self.* New York: International Universities Press.

Konner, M. (1975). Relations among infants and juveniles in comparative perspective. In M. Lewis & L. Rosenblum (Eds.), *Friendship and peer relations: The origins of behavior, 4* (pp. 99–129). New York: John Wiley & Sons.

Kotsoni, E., de Haan, M. & Johnson, (2001). Categorical perception of facial expressions by 7-month-old infants. *Perception, 30,* 1115–1125.

Krugman, S. D & Dubowitz, H. (2003). Failure to thrive. *American Family Physician, 68,* 879–886.

Kuhl, P. K. & Meltzoff, A. N. (1982). The bimodal perception of speech in infancy. *Science, 218,* 1138–1141.

Kuhl, P. K. (1991). Human adults and human infants show a 'perceptual magnet effect' for the prototypes of

speech categories, monkeys do not. *Perception & Psychophysics, 50,* 93–107.

Laing, R. D. (1970). *Knots.* New York: Pantheon.

Lamb, M. E. (2003). *The role of the father in child development* (4th ed.). New York: John Wiley & Sons.

Landau, B. & Spelke, E. (1988). Geometric complexity and object search in infancy. *Developmental Psychology, 24,* 512–521.

Landers, W. F. (1971). The effect of differential experience on infants' performance in a Piagetian stage IV object concept task. *Developmental Psychology, 5,* 48–54.

Landesman, S. & Butterfield, E. C. (1987). Normalization and deinstitutionalization of mentally retarded individuals: Controversy and facts. *American Psychologist, 42,* 809–816.

Langley-Evans, S. C. (Ed). (2004). *Fetal nutrition and adult disease: Programming of chronic disease through fetal exposure to undernutrition.* Wallingford, UK: CABI Publishing.

Langlois, J. H. & Roggman, L. A. (1990). Attractive faces are only average. *Psychological Science, 1,* 115–121.

Langlois, J. H., Ritter, J. M., Roggman, L. A. & Vaughn, L. S. (1991). Facial diversity and infant preferences for attractive faces. *Developmental Psychology, 27,* 79–84.

Langlois, J. H., Roggman, L. A. & Rieser-Danner, L. A. (1990). Infants' differential social responses to attractive and unattractive faces. *Developmental Psychology, 26,* 153–159.

Lanphear, B. P., Dietrich, K. N. & Berger, O. (2003). Prevention of lead toxicity in US children. *Ambulatory Pediatrics, 3*(1), 27–36.

Lavenex, P., Banta Lavenex, P. & Amaral, D. G. (2004). Nonphosphorylated high-molecular-weight neurofilament expression suggests early maturation of the monkey subiculum. *Hippocampus,* *12,* 797–801.

Lazar, I., Darlington, R., Murray, H., Royce, J. & Snipper, A. (1982). Lasting effects of early education: A report from the Consortium of Longitudinal Studies. *Monographs of the Society for Research in Child Development, 47*(2–3, Serial No. 195).

Le Grand, R., Mondloch, C. J., Maurer, D. & Brent, H. P. (2003). Expert face processing requires visual input to the right hemisphere during infancy. *Nature Neuroscience, 6,* 1108–1112.

Leach, E. (1964). Anthropological aspects of language: Animal categories and verbal abuse. In E. H. Lenneberg (Ed.), *New directions in the study of language* (pp. 23–63). Cambridge, MA: MIT Press.

Lecanuet, J-P., Granier-Deferre, C., DeCasper, A. J., Maugeais, R., Andrieu, A-J. & Busnel, M-C. (1987). Perception et discrimination foetale de stimuli langagiers, mise en evidence àpartir de la réactivité cardiaque. Resultats preliminaires. *Compte-Rendus de l'Académie des Sciences de Paris.* Serie III, *305,* 161–164.

Lee, D. N. & Lishman, J. R. (1975). Visual proprioceptive control of stance. *Journal of Human Movement Studies, 1,* 87–95.

Leeuwen, L. v., Smitsman, A. & Leeuwen, C. v. (1994). Affordances, perceptual complexity, and the development of tool use. *Journal of Experimental Psychology: Human Perception and Performance, 20,* 174–191.

Legerstee, M., Anderson, D. & Schaffer, A. (1998). Five- and eight-month-old infants recognize their faces and voices as familiar and social stimuli. *Child Development, 68,* 37–50.

Leinbach, M. D. & Fagot, B. I. (1993). Categorical habituation to male and female faces: Gender schematic processing in infancy. *Infant Behavior and Development, 16,* 317–332.

Lester, B. M., Klein, R. E. & Martinez, S. J. (1975). The use of habituation in the study of the effects of infantile malnutrition. *Developmental Psychobiology, 8,* 541–546.

LeVine, R. A., Dixon, S., LeVine, S., Richman, A., Leiderman, P. H., Keefer, C. H. & Brazelton, T. B. (1994). *Child care and culture: Lessons from Africa.* New York: Cambridge University Press.

Lew, A. R., Bremner, J. G. & Lefkovitch, L. P. (2000). The development of relational landmark use in six- to twelve-month-old infants in a spatial orientation task. *Child Development, 71,* 1179–1190.

Lew, A. R., Foster, K. A., Crowther, H. L. & Green, M. (2004). Indirect landmark use at 6 months of age in a spatial orientation task. *Infant Behavior and Development, 27,* 81–90.

Lewis, H. B. (1971). *Shame and guilt in neurosis.* New York: International Universities Press.

Lewis, H. B. (1987). Shame: The 'sleeper' in psychopathology. In H. B. Lewis (Ed.), *The role of shame in symptom formation* (pp. 1–28). Hillsdale, NJ: Lawrence Erlbaum Associates.

Lewis, M. (1980). Issues in the development of fear. In I. L. Kutash & L. B. Schlesinger (Eds.), *Pressure point: Perspectives on stress and anxiety* (pp. 48–62). San Francisco: Jossey-Bass.

Lewis, M. (1991). Self-knowledge and social development in early life. In L. Pervin (Ed.), *Handbook of personality: Theory and research* (pp. 277–300). New York: Guilford Press.

Lewis, M. (1991). Ways of knowing: Objective self-awareness or consciousness. *Developmental Review (Special Issue), 11,* 231–243.

Lewis, M. (1992a). The self in self-conscious emotions. A commentary in D. Stipek, S. Recchia & S. McClintic (Eds.), Self-evaluation in young children. *Monographs of the Society for Research in Child Development, 57* (1, Serial No. 226).

Lewis, M. (1992b). *Shame, The exposed self*. New York: Free Press.

Lewis, M. (1997). *Altering fate: Why the past does not predict the future*. New York: Guilford Press.

Lewis, M. (1999). Social cognition and the self. In P. Rochat (Ed.), *Early social cognition* (pp. 81–98). Mahwah, NJ: Lawrence Erlbaum Associates.

Lewis, M. (2003). The emergence of consciousness and its role in human development. In J. LeDoux, J. Debiec & H. Moss (Eds.), *The self: From soul to brain* (Vol. 1001, pp. 1–29). New York: Annals of the New York Academy of Sciences <*www.annalsnyas.org*>.

Lewis, M. (2004). Emotional development: past, present and future. [Commentary on Rachel Conrad's paper 'As if she defied the world in her joyousness: Rereading Darwin on emotion and emotional development'.] *Human Development, 47*(1), 66–70.

Lewis, M. & Brooks, J. (1974). Self, other and fear: Infants' reactions to people. In M. Lewis & L. Rosenblum (Eds.), *The origins of fear: The origins of behavior, 2* (pp. 195–227). New York: John Wiley & Sons.

Lewis, M. & Brooks-Gunn, J. (1978). Self knowledge and emotional development. In M. Lewis & L. Rosenblum (Eds.), *The development of affect: The genesis of behavior, 1* (pp. 205–226). New York: Plenum Press.

Lewis, M. & Brooks-Gunn, J. (1979). *Social cognition and the acquisition of self*. New York: Plenum Press.

Lewis, M. & Brooks-Gunn, J. (1982). The self as social knowledge. In M. D. Lynch, A. Norem-Hebeisen & J. Gergen (Eds.), *Self-concept: Advances in theory and research* (pp. 101–118). Cambridge, MA: Ballinger.

Lewis, M. & Freedle, R. (1973). Mother–infant dyad. The cradle of meaning. In P. Pilner, L. Krames & T. Alloway (eds), *Communication and affect: Language and thought*

(pp. 127–155). New York: Academic Press.

Lewis, M. & Michalson, L. (1983). *Children's emotions and moods: Developmental theory and measurement*. New York: Plenum Press.

Lewis, M. & Ramsay, D. (1995). Developmental change in infants' response to stress. *Child Development, 66*, 657–670.

Lewis, M. & Ramsay, D. (1997). Stress reactivity and self-recognition. *Child Development, 68*, 621–629.

Lewis, M. & Ramsay, D. (2002). Cortisol response to embarrassment and shame. *Child Development, 73*, 1034–1045.

Lewis, M. & Ramsay, D. (2004). Development of self-recognition, personal pronoun use, and pretend play in the second year. *Child Development, 75*(6), 1821–1831.

Lewis, M. & Rosenblum, L. (Eds.). (1974). *The origins of fear: The origins of behavior, 2*. New York: John Wiley & Sons.

Lewis, M. & Rosenblum, L. (1975). Introduction. In M. Lewis & L. Rosenblum (Eds.), *Friendship and peer relations: The origins of behavior, 4* (pp. 1–9). New York: John Wiley & Sons.

Lewis, M. & Schaeffer, S. (1981). Peer behavior and mother–infant interaction in maltreated children. In M. Lewis & L. Rosenblum (Eds.), *The uncommon child: The genesis of behavior, 3* (pp. 193–223). New York: Plenum Press.

Lewis, M. & Sullivan, M. W. (1994). Developmental intervention in the lives of infants and parents. In C. B. Fisher & R. M. Lerner (Eds.), *Applied developmental psychology* (pp. 375–406). New York: McGraw-Hill.

Lewis, M. & Takahashi, K. (Eds.). (2005). *Human Development: Special Issue: Beyond the dyad: Conceptualization of social networks*. Switzerland: Karger.

Lewis, M., Alessandri, S. & Sullivan, M. W. (1990). Violation of expectancy, loss of control, and anger in young infants. *Developmental Psychology, 26,* 745–751.

Lewis, M., Goldberg, S. & Campbell, H. (1969). A developmental study of information processing within the first three years of life: Response decrement to a redundant signal. *Monographs of the Society for Research in Child Development, 34*(9, Serial No. 133).

Lewis, M., Hitchcock, D. & Sullivan, M. W. (2004). Physiological and emotional reactivity to learning and frustration. *Infancy, 6,* 121–144.

Lewis, M., Kagan, J. & Kalafat, J. (1966). Patterns of fixation in infants. *Child Development, 37,* 331–341.

Lewis, M., Kagan, J., Kalafat, J. & Campbell, H. (1966). The cardiac response as a correlate of attention in infants. *Child Development, 37,* 63–71.

Lewis, M., Meyers, W. J., Kagan, J. & Grossberg, R. (1963). Attention to visual patterns in infants. Paper presented at Symposium on Studies of attention in infants: Methodological problems and preliminary results, at Meeting of the American Psychological Association, Philadelphia, PA.

Lewis, M., Ramsay, D. S. & Kawakami, K. (1993). Differences between Japanese infants and Caucasian American infants in behavioral and cortisol response to inoculation. *Child Development, 64,* 1722–1731.

Lewis, M., Sullivan, M. W. & Michalson, L. (1984). The cognitive-emotional fugue. In C. E. Izard, J. Kagan & R. Zajonc (Eds.), *Emotion, cognition, and behavior* (pp. 264–288). New York: Cambridge University Press.

Lewis, M., Sullivan, M. W., Stanger, C. & Weiss, M. (1989). Self-development and self-conscious emotions. *Child Development, 60,* 146–156.

Liptak, G. S. (2002). Neural tube defects. In M. L. Batshaw (ed.), *Children with disabilities* (5th ed.) (pp. 529–552). Baltimore: Brookes.

Lishman, J. R. & Lee, D. N. (1973). The autonomy of visual kinaesthesis. *Perception, 2,* 287–294.

Lockman, J. J. (2000). A perception-action perspective on tool use development. *Child Development, 71,* 137–144.

Lozoff, B., DeAndraca, I, Castillo, M., Smith, J. B., Walter, T. & Pino, P. (2003). Behavioral and developmental effects of preventing iron-deficiency anemia in healthy full-term infants. *Pediatrics, 112*(4), 846–854.

Lucas, A. (1997). Long-chain polyunsaturated fatty acids, infant feeding and cognitive development. In J. Dobbing (Ed.), *Developing brain and behavior. The role of lipids in infant formula.* San Diego, CA: Academic Press.

Lucas, A., Morley, R., Cole, T. J., Lister, G. & Lesson-Payne, C. (1992). Breast milk and subsequent intelligence quotient in children born preterm. *Lancet, 339,* 261–264.

Lucas, A., Stafford, M., Morley, R., Abbott, R., Stephenson, T., MacFayden, U. *et al.* (1999). Efficacy and safety of long-chain polyunsaturated fatty acid supplementation of infant-formula milk: A randomised trial. *Lancet, 354,* 1948–1954.

Ludemann, P. M. (1991). Generalized discrimination of positive facial expressions by seven- and ten-month-old infants. *Child Development, 62,* 55–67.

Ludemann, P. M. & Nelson, C. A. (1988). Categorical representation of facial expressions by 7-month-old infants. *Developmental Psychology, 24,* 492–501.

Lundy, B. L. (2000). Face recognition performance in one-year-olds: A function of stimulus characteristics? *Infant Behavior & Development, 23,* 125–135.

Lynn, D. B. (1974). *The father: His role in child development.* Monterey, CA: Brooks/Cole.

Maccoby, E. & Martin, J. (1983). Socialization in the context of the family: Parent–child interaction. In P. H. Mussen (Series ed.) & E. M. Hetherington (Vol. ed.), *Handbook of child psychology*: Vol. 4. *Socialization, personality, and social development* (pp. 1–101). New York: John Wiley & Sons.

Mackey, W. C. (1985). *Fathering behaviors: The dynamics of the man–child bond*. New York: Plenum Press.

Macnamara, J. (1982). *Names for things*. Cambridge, MA: MIT Press.

MacNeilage, P. F., Davis, B. L., Kinney, A. & Matyear, C. L. (2000). The motor core of speech: A comparison of serial organization patterns in infants and languages. *Child Development, 71*, 153–163.

Madden, J., Levenstein, P. & Levenstein, S. (1976). Longitudinal IQ outcomes of the mother–child home program. *Child Development, 46*, 1015–1025.

Mai, J. K. & Ashwell, K. W. S. (2004) Fetal development of the central nervous system. In G. Paxinos & J. K. Mai (Eds.), *The human nervous system* (pp. 49–94). San Diego, CA: Elsevier.

Main, M. & Solomon, J. (1990). Procedures for identifying infants as disorganized/disoriented during the Ainsworth strange situation. In M. T. Greenberg, D. Cicchetti & E. M. Cummings (Eds.), *Attachment in the preschool years* (pp. 121–160). Chicago: University of Chicago Press.

Makrides, M., Neumann, M. A., Simmer, K. & Gibson, R. A. (2000). A critical appraisal of the role of dietary long-chain polyunsaturated fatty acids on neural indices of term infants: A randomized, controlled trial. *Pediatrics, 105*, 32–38.

Malloy, M. H. & Berendes, H. (1998). Does breast-feeding influence intelligence quotients at 9 and 10 years of age? *Early Human Development, 50*, 209–217.

Mandler, J. M. (1999). Seeing is not the same as thinking: Commentary on 'Making sense of infant categorization.' *Developmental Review, 19*, 297–306.

Mandler, J. M. (2004). *The foundations of mind: Origins of conceptual thought*. New York: Oxford University Press.

Mandler, J. M. & Bauer, P. J. (1988). The cradle of categorization: Is the basic level basic? *Cognitive Development, 3*, 247–264.

Mandler, J. M. & McDonough, L. (1998). On developing a knowledge base in infancy. *Developmental Psychology, 34*, 1274–1288.

Mandler, J. M., Bauer, P. J. & McDonough, L. (1991). Separating the sheep from the goats: Differentiating global categories. *Cognitive Psychology, 23*, 263–298.

Mandler, J. M., Fivush, R. & Reznick, J. S. (1987). The development of contextual categories. *Cognitive Development, 2*, 339–354.

Mareschal, D. & Quinn, P. C. (2001). Categorization in infancy. *Trends in Cognitive Sciences, 5*, 443–450.

Mareschal, D. (2002). Connectionist methods in infancy research. In J. W. Fagen & H. Hayne (Eds.), *Progress in infancy research* (vol. 2, pp. 71–119). Mahwah, NJ: Lawrence Erlbaum Associates.

Mareschal, D., French, R. M. & Quinn, P. C. (2000). A connectionist account of asymmetric category learning in early infancy. *Developmental Psychology, 36*, 635–645.

Markman, E. (1989). *Categorization and naming in children*. Cambridge, MA: MIT Press.

Markman, E. M. & Wachtel, G. A. (1988). Children's use of mutual exclusivity to constrain the meanings of words. *Cognitive Psychology, 20*, 120–157.

Martin, R. M. (1975). Effects of familiar and complex stimuli on infant attention. *Developmental Psychology, 11*, 178–185.

Martini, M. & Kirkpatrick, J. (1992). Parenting in Polynesia: A view from the Marquesas. In J. L. Roopnarine & D. B. Carter (Eds.), *Parent–child socialization in diverse cultures: Vol. 5. Annual advances in applied developmental psychology* (pp. 199–222). Norwood, NJ: Ablex.

Mastropieri, D. & Turkewicz, G. (1999). Prenatal experience and neonatal responsiveness to vocal expressions of emotion. *Developmental Psychobiology,35*, 204–214.

Mauk, J. E., Reber, M. & Batshaw, M. L. (1997). Autism and other pervasive disorders. In M. L. Batshaw (Ed.), *Children with disabilities* (4th ed.) (pp. 425–448). Baltimore: Brookes.

Maurer, D. & Salapatek, P. (1976). Developmental changes in the scanning of faces by young infants. *Child Development, 47*, 523–527.

Mayes, L. C. & Carter, A. S. (1990). Emerging social regulatory capacities as seen in the still-face situation. *Child Development, 61*, 754–763.

McCann, J. C. & Ames, B. N. (2005). Is docosahexaenoic acid, an n-3 long chain polyunsaturated fatty acid, required for development of normal brain function? An overview of evidence from cognitive and behavioral tests in humans and animals. *American Journal of Clinical Nutrition, 82*(2), 281–295.

McCarty, M. E., Clifton, R. K. & Collard, R. R. (1999). Problem solving in infancy: The emergence of an action plan. *Developmental Psychology, 35*(4), 1091–1101.

McCarty, M. E., Clifton, R. K. & Collard, R. R. (2001). The beginnings of tool use by infants and toddlers. *Infancy, 2*(2), 233–256.

McClure, E. B. (2000). A meta-analytic review of sex differences in facial expression processing and their development in infants, children, and adolescents. *Psychological Bulletin, 126*, 424–453.

McDonough, L. & Mandler, J. M. (1998). Inductive generalization in 9- and 11-month-olds. *Developmental Science, 1*, 227–232.

McDonough, L., Choi, S. & Mandler, J. (2003). Understanding spatial relations: Flexible infants, lexical adults. *Cognitive Psychology, 46*, 229–59.

McDonough, L., Mandler, J. M., McKee, R. D. & Squire, L. R. (1995). The deferred imitation task as a nonverbal measure of declarative memory. *Proceedings of the National Academy of Sciences of the USA, 92*, 7580–7584.

McGraw, M. B. (1935). *Growth: A study of Johnny and Jimmy.* New York: Appleton-Century.

McGurk, H. & Lewis, M. (1974). Space perception in early infancy: Perception within a common auditory-visual space? *Science, 186*(4164), 649–650.

McKenzie, B. E., Day, R. H. & Ihsen, E. (1984). Localisation of events in space: Young infants are not always egocentric. *British Journal of Developmental Psychology, 2*, 1–9.

McVicker Hunt, J. (1961). *Intelligence and experience.* New York: Ronald Press.

McVicker Hunt, J. (1964). The psychological basis for using preschool enrichment as an antidote for cultural deprivation. *Merrill-Palmer Quarterly, 10*, 209–248.

Mehler, J., Jusczyk, P. W., Lambertz, G., Halsted, N., Bertoncini, J. & Amiel-Tison, C. (1988). A precursor of language acquisition in young infants. *Cognition, 29*, 144–178.

Meltzoff, A. N. (1995). Infants' understanding of people and things: From body imitation to folk psychology. In J. L. Bermúdez, A. Marcel & N. Eilan (Eds.), *The body and the self* (pp. 43–69). Cambridge, MA: MIT Press.

Meltzoff, A. N. (2004). The case for developmental cognitive science: Theories of people and things. In G. Bremner & A. Slater (eds.), *Theories of infant development* (pp. 145–173). Oxford: Blackwell Publishers.

Meltzoff, A. N. & Moore, M. K. (1977). Imitation of facial and manual gestures by human neonates. *Science, 198,* 75–78.

Meltzoff, A. N. & Moore, M. K. (1983). Newborn infants imitate adult facial gestures. *Child Development, 54,* 702–709.

Meltzoff, A. N. & Moore, M. K. (2002). Imitation, memory, and the representation of persons. *Infant Behavior and Development, 25,* 39–61.

Melzack, R. & Scott, T. H. (1957). The effects of early experience on the response to pain. *Journal of Comparative and Physiological Psychology, 50,* 155–161.

Meuwissen, I. & McKenzie, B. E. (1987). Localization of an event by young infants: The effects of visual and body movement information. *British Journal of Developmental Psychology, 5,* 1–8.

Miller, P. & Garvey, C. (1984). Mother–baby role play: Its origins in social support. In I. Bretherton (Ed.), *Symbolic play: The development of understanding* (pp. 101–130). NY: Academic Press.

Mintz, T. & Gleitman, L. (2002). Adjectives really do modify nouns: The incremental and restricted nature of early adjective acquisition. *Cognition, 84,* 267–293.

Moessinger, A. C. (1988) Morphological consequences of depressed or impaired fetal activity. In W. P. Smotherman & S. R. Robinson (Eds.), *Behavior of the fetus* (pp. 163–173). Caldwell, NJ: Telford.

Moore, K. L. (1988). *The developing human: Clinically oriented embryology* (4th ed.) Philadelphia: Saunders.

Moore, K. L. & Persaud, T. V. N. (1998). *The developing human: Clinically oriented embryology* (6th ed.). Philadelphia: W. B. Saunders.

Moore, K. L. & Persaud, T. V. N. (2003). *The developing human* (7th ed.). Philadelphia: W. B. Saunders.

Morelli G. A. & Tronick E. Z. (1991a). Efe multiple caretaking and attachment. In J. Gewirtz & W. Kurtines (Eds.), *Interactions with attachment* (pp. 41–51). Hillsdale, NJ: Lawrence Erlbaum Associates.

Morelli, G. A. & Tronick, E. Z. (1991b). Parenting and child developments in the Efe foragers and Lese farmers of Zaire. In M. H. Bornstein (Ed.), *Cultural approaches to parenting* (pp. 91–114). Hillsdale, NJ: Lawrence Erlbaum Associates.

Morrison, A. P. (1986). The eye turned inward: Shame and the self. In O. L. Nathanson (Ed.), *The many faces of shame* (pp. 271–291). New York: Guilford Press.

Morrison, A. P. (1989). *Shame: The underside of narcissism.* Hillsdale, NJ: Analytic Press.

Mortensen, E. L., Michaelsen, K. F., Sanders, S. A. & Reinisch, J. M. (2002). The association between duration of breastfeeding and adult intelligence. *JAMA, 287*(18), 2365–2371.

Morton, J. & Johnson, (1991). CONSPEC and CONLERN: A two-process theory of infant face recognition. *Psychological Review, 98,* 164–181.

Muir, D. & Lee, K. (2003). The still-face effect: Methodological issues and new applications. *Infancy, 4,* 483–492.

Muir, D. W. & Hains, S. M. J. (1993). Infant sensitivity to perturbations in adult facial, vocal, tactile, and contingent stimulation during face-to-face interactions. In B. de Boysson-Bardies, S. de Schonen, P. Jusczyk, P. McNeilage & J. Morton (Eds.), *Developmental neurocognition: Speech and face processing in the first year of life* (pp. 171–185). Dordrecht: Kluwer Academic Publishers.

Muir, D. W., Humphrey, D. E. & Humphrey, G. K. (1999). Pattern and space perception in young infants. In A. Slater & D. Muir, *The Blackwell reader in developmental psychology* (pp. 116–142). Oxford: Blackwell Publishers.

Mullen, K. (1994). Earliest recollections of childhood demographic analysis. *Cognition, 52*, 55–79.

Müller, F & O'Rahilly, R. (2004). Embryonic development of the central nervous system. In G. Paxinos & J. K. Mai (Eds.), *The human nervous system* (pp. 22–48). San Diego, CA: Elsevier.

Munakata, Y., McClelland, J. L., Johnson, M. H. & Siegler, R. S. (1997). Rethinking infant knowledge: Toward an adaptive process account of successes and failures in object permanence tasks. *Psychological Review, 104*, 686–713.

Murphy, G. L. (2002). *The big book of concepts.* Cambridge, MA: MIT Press.

Murray, C. J. L. & Lopez, A. D. (1996). *The global burden of disease* (pp. 360–367). Cambridge: Harvard School of Public Health.

Nazzi, T., Bertoncini, J. & Mehler, J. (1998). Language discrimination by newborns: Toward an understanding of the role of rhythm. *Journal of Experimental Psychology: Human Perception and Performance, 24*(3), 756–766.

Needham, A., Barrett, T. & Peterman, K. (2002). A pick-me-up for infants' exploratory skills: Early simulated experiences reaching for objects using 'sticky mittens' enhances young infants' object exploration skills. *Infant Behavior and Development, 25*(3), 279–295.

Nelson, C. A. (1987). The recognition of facial expressions in the first two years of life: Mechanisms of development. *Child Development, 58*, 604–615.

Nelson, C. (1995). The ontogeny of human memory: A cognitive neuroscience perspective. *Developmental Psychology, 31*, 723–738.

Nelson, C. A. (2001). The development and neural bases of face recognition. *Infant and Child Development, 10*, 3–18.

Nelson, C. A. & Collins, P. F. (1992). Neural and behavioral correlates of visual recognition memory in 4- and 8-month-old infants. *Brain and Cognition, 19*, 105–121.

Nelson, C. A. & de Haan, M. (1996). Neural correlates of infants' visual responsiveness to facial expressions of emotion. *Developmental Psychology, 29*, 577–595.

Nelson, C. A. & Dolgin, K. G. (1985). The generalized discrimination of facial expressions by seven-month-old infants. *Child Development, 56*, 58–61.

Nelson, K. (1989). *Narratives from the crib.* Cambridge, MA: Harvard University Press.

Nelson, K. (1993). The psychological and social origins of autobiographical memory. *Psychological Science, 4*, 7–14.

Newell, K. M., Scully, D. M., McDonald, P. V. & Baillargeon, R. (1989). Task constraints and infant grip configurations. *Developmental Psychobiology, 22*, 817–831.

Newman, T. B. & Maisels, M. J. (2000). Less aggressive treatment of neonatal jaundice and reports of kernicterus: Lessons about practice guidelines. *Pediatrics, 105*, 242–245.

Nicely, P., Tamis-LeMonda, C. S. & Bornstein, M. H. (1999). Mothers' attuned responses to infant affect expressivity promote earlier achievement of language milestones. *Infant Behavior and Development, 22*, 557–568.

NICHCY (2002). National Information Center for Children and Youth with Disabilities. *Disabilities that qualify infants, toddlers, children and youth for services under IDEA.* Washington, DC: US Office of Special Education Programs.

NICHD Early Child Care Research Network (1994). Child care and child development: The NICHD Study of Early Child Care. In S. L. Friedman & H. C. Haywood (Eds.), *Developmental follow-up: Concepts, domains, and methods* (pp. 377–396). New York: Academic Press.

NICHD Early Child Care Research Network (1996). Characteristics of infant child care: Factors contributing to positive caregiving. *Early Childhood Research Quarterly, 11(3)*, 269–306.

NICHD Early Child Care Research Network (1997). The effects of infant child care on infant–mother attachment security: Results of the NICHD Study of Early Child Care. *Child Development, 68(5)*, 860–879.

NICHD Early Child Care Research Network (1998). Early child care and self-control, compliance and problem behavior at twenty-four and thirty-six months. *Child Development, 69(3)*, 1145–1170.

NICHD Early Child Care Research Network (1999). Child care and mother–child interaction in the first three years of life. *Developmental Psychology, 35(6)*, 1399–1413.

Nielsen, M., Dissanayake, C. & Kashima, Y. (2003). A longitudinal investigation of self–other discrimination and the emergence of mirror self-recognition. *Infant Behavior & Development, 26*, 213–226.

Nijhuis, J. G., Prechtl, H. F. R., Martin, C. B. & Bots, R. S. G. M. (1982) Are there behavioral states in the human fetus? *Early Human Development, 6*, 177–195.

Nilsson, J. G., Furuhjelm, M., Ingelman-Sundberg, A., Wirsén, C. & Forsblad, B. (1977). *A child is born*. London: Faber & Faber.

NIMH (1997). *Autism*. Bethesda, MD: National Institute of Mental Health.

NINDS (1999). *Febrile seizures*. Bethesda, MD: National Institute of Neurological Disorders and Stroke, National Institutes of Health.

Noirot, E. & Algeria, J. (1983). Neonate orientation towards human voice differs with type of feeding. *Behavior Processes, 8*, 65–71.

O'Connor, T., Heron, J., Golding, J., Glover, V. & the ALSPAC team (2003). Maternal antenatal anxiety and behavioural/emotional problems in children: A test of a programming hypothesis. *Journal of Child Psychology and Psychiatry, 44*, 1025–36.

O'Toole, A. J., Abdi, H., Deffenbacher, K. & Bartlett, J. (1991). Simulating the 'other-race effect' as a problem in perceptual learning. *Connection Science Journal of Neural Computing, Artificial Intelligence, and Cognition Research, 3*, 163–178.

Odom, S. L. & Kaul, S. (2003). Early intervention themes and variations from around the world: Summary. In S. L. Odom, M. J. Hanson, J. A. Blackman & S. Kaul (Eds.), *Early intervention practices around the world* (pp. 333–346). Baltimore: Brookes.

Odom, S. L., Hanson, M. J., Blackman, J. A. & Kaul, S. (Eds.). (2003). *Early intervention practices around the world*. Baltimore: Brookes.

Oller, D. K. (1980). The emergence of speech sounds in infancy. In G. H. Yeni-Komshian, C. A. Ferguson & J. Kavanagh (Eds.), *Child phonology: Production* (Vol. 1, pp. 93–112). New York: Academic Press.

Oppenheim, R. W. (1991) Cell death during development of the nervous system. *Annual Review of Neuroscience, 14*, 453–501.

Osofsky, J. D. (1979). *Handbook of infant development*. New York: John Wiley & Sons.

Pace, B. (2001). Down syndrome. *JAMA, 285*, 8, 1112.

Pascalis, O., de Haan, M. & Nelson, C. A. (2002). Is face processing species-specific in the first year of life? *Science, 296*, 1321–1323.

Pascalis, O., de Haan, M., Nelson, C. A. & de Schonen, S. (1998). Long-term recognition memory for faces assessed by visual paired comparison in 3- and 6-month-old infants. *Journal of Experimental Psychology: Learning, Memory, and Cognition, 24*, 249–260.

Pascalis, O., de Schonen, S., Morton, J., Deruelle, C. & Fabre-Grenet, M. (1995). Mother's face recognition by neonates: A replication and an extension. *Infant Behavior and Development, 18,* 79–85.

Patrick, J., Campbell, K., Carmichael, L., Natale, R. & Richardson, B. (1980). Patterns of human fetal breathing during the last 10 weeks of pregnancy. *Obstetrics and Gynecology, 56,* 24–30.

Pellegrino, L. (2002). Cerebral palsy. In M. L. Batshaw (ed.), *Children with disabilities* (5th ed.) (pp. 499–528). Baltimore: Brookes.

Perez-Granados, D. R. & Callanan, M. A. (1997). Conversations with mothers and siblings: Young children's semantic and conceptual development. *Developmental Psychology, 33,* 120–134.

Peterson, C., Grant, V. V. & Boland, L. D. (2005). Childhood amnesia in children and adolescents: Their earliest memories. *Memory, 13,* 622–637.

Petitto, L. A. & Marentette, P. F. (1991). Babbling in the manual mode: Evidence for the ontogeny of language. *Science, 251,* 1493–1496.

Petitto, L. A., Holowka, S., Sergio, L. E., Levy, B. & Ostry, D. J. (2004). Baby hands that move to the rhythm of language: Hearing babies acquiring sign languages babble silently on the hands. *Cognition, 93,* 43–73.

Phillips, J. O., Finoccio, D. V., Ong, L. & Fuchs, A. F. (1997). Smooth pursuit in 1–4-month-old human infants. *Vision Research, 37,* 3009–3020.

Phillips, R. D., Wagner, S. H., Fells, C. A. & Lynch, M. (1990). Do infants recognize emotion in facial expressions?: Categorical and 'metaphorical' evidence. *Infant Behavior and Development, 13,* 71–84.

Piaget, J. (1951). *Play, dreams, and imitation in childhood* (C. Gattegno & F. M. Hodgson, Trans.) New York: W. W. Norton.

Piaget, J. (1936/1952). *The origins of intelligence in children* (M. Cook, Trans.). New York: International Universities Press.

Piaget, J. (1953). *The origins of intelligence in the child.* London: Routledge & Kegan Paul.

Piaget, J. (1937/1954). *The construction of reality in the child* (M. Cook, Trans.). New York: Basic Books.

Piaget, J. (1962). *Play, dreams, and imagination in childhood.* New York: W. W. Norton.

Pinker, S. (1994). *The language instinct: How the mind creates language.* New York: William Morrow & Co.

Polka, L., Colantonio, C. & Sundara, M. (2001). A cross-language comparison of /d/–/ð/ perception: Evidence for a new developmental pattern. *Journal of the Acoustical Society of America, 109*(5), 2190–2201.

Pollitt, E. (1988). A critical review of three decades of research on the effects of chronic energy malnutrition on behavioral development. In B. Schurch & N. Scrimshaw (Eds.), *Chronic energy deficiency: Consequences and related issues.* Proceedings of the International Dietary Energy Consultative Group meeting held in Guatemala City, Guatemala. Lausanne, Switzerland: Nestlé Foundation.

Pollitt, E., Gorman, K. S., Engle, P. L., Martorell, R. & Rivera, J. (1993). Early supplemental feeding and cognition: Effects over two decades. *Monographs of the Society for Research in Child Development, 58*(7, Serial No. 235).

Porges, S. W., Doussard-Roosevelt, J., Portales, A. & Greenspan, S. (1996). Infant regulation of the vagal 'brake' predicts child behavior problems: A psychobiological model of social behavior. *Developmental Psychology, 29,* 691–712.

Porter, R. H. & Winberg, J. (1999) Unique salience of maternal breast odors for newborn infants. *Neuroscience and Biobehavioural Reviews, 23,* 439–449.

Poulson, C. L., Kymissis, E., Reeve, K. F. & Andreatos, M. (1991). Generalized vocal imitation in infants. *Journal of Experimental Child Psychology, 51*, 267–279.

Powell, C. & Grantham-McGregor, S. (1989). Home visiting of varying frequency and child development. *Pediatrics, 84*, 157–164.

Power, T. G. (2000). *Play and exploration in children and animals*. Mahwah, NJ: Lawrence Erlbaum Associates.

Prechtl, H. F. R. (1974). The behavioural states of the newborn infant (a review). *Brain Research, 76*, 1304–1311.

Prechtl, H. F. R. (1985). Ultrasound studies of human fetal behaviour. *Early Human Development, 12*, 91–98.

Prechtl, H. F. R. (1986). Prenatal motor development. In M. G. Wade & H. T. A. Whiting (Eds.), *Motor development in children: Aspects of coordination and control*. Dordrecht: Martinus Nijhoff.

Prechtl, H. F. R. (1988) Developmental neurology of the fetus. *Clinical Obstetrics & Gynaecology, 2*, 21–36.

Provence, S. & Lipton, R. C. (1962). *Infants in institutions*. London: Bailey & Swinfer.

Querleu, D., Renard, X., Boutteville, C. & Crepin, G. (1989). Hearing by the human fetus? *Seminars in Perinatology, 13*, 409–420.

Querleu, D., Renard, X., Versyp, F., Paris-Delrue, L. & Crepin, G. (1988). Fetal hearing. *European Journal of Obstetrics, Gynecology and Reproductive Biology, 29*, 191–212.

Quinn, P. C. (2002). Early categorization: A new synthesis. In U. Goswami (Ed.), *Blackwell handbook of childhood cognitive development* (pp. 84–101). Oxford: Blackwell Publishers.

Quinn, P. C. (2003a). Concepts are not just for objects: Categorization of spatial relation information by infants. In D. H. Rakison & L. M. Oakes (Eds.), *Early category and concept development: Making sense of the blooming, buzzing confusion* (pp. 50–76). Oxford: Oxford University Press.

Quinn, P. C. (2003b). Why do young infants prefer female faces? In M. S. Strauss (Organizer), *Development of facial expertise in infancy*. Symposium conducted at the meeting of the Society for Research in Child Development, Tampa, FL.

Quinn, P. C. (2004a). Development of subordinate-level categorization in 3- to 7-month-old infants. *Child Development, 75*, 886–899.

Quinn, P. C. (2004b). Is the asymmetry in young infants' categorization of humans versus nonhuman animals based on head, body, or global Gestalt information? *Psychonomic Bulletin & Review, 11*, 92–97.

Quinn, P. C. (2004c). Spatial representation by young infants: Categorization of spatial relations or sensitivity to a crossing primitive? *Memory & Cognition, 32*, 852–861.

Quinn, P. C. (2004d). Visual perception of orientation is categorical near vertical and continuous near horizontal. *Perception, 33*, 897–906.

Quinn, P. C. (2005). Young infants' categorization of humans versus nonhuman animals: Roles for knowledge access and perceptual process. In L. Gershkoff-Stowe & D. Rakison (Eds.), *Building object categories in developmental time: 32nd Carnegie symposium on cognition* (Vol. 32, pp. 107–130). Mahwah, NJ: Lawrence Erlbaum Associates.

Quinn, P. C. & Bomba, P. C. (1986). Evidence for a general category of oblique orientations in 4-month-old infants. *Journal of Experimental Child Psychology, 42*, 345–354.

Quinn, P. C. & Eimas, P. D. (1986). On categorization in early infancy. *Merrill-Palmer Quarterly, 32*, 331–363.

Quinn, P. C. & Eimas, P. D. (1996a). Perceptual cues that permit categorical differentiation of animal species by infants. *Journal of Experimental Child Psychology, 63*, 189–211.

Quinn, P. C. & Eimas, P. D. (1996b). Perceptual organization and categorization in young infants. In C. Rovee-Collier & L. P. Lipsitt (Eds.), *Advances in infancy research* (Vol. 10, pp. 1–36). Norwood, NJ: Ablex.

Quinn, P. C. & Eimas, P. D. (1997). A reexamination of the perceptual-to-conceptual shift in mental representations. *Review of General Psychology, 1*, 271–287.

Quinn, P. C. & Eimas, P. D. (1998). Evidence for a global categorical representation for humans by young infants. *Journal of Experimental Child Psychology, 69*, 151–174.

Quinn, P. C. & Eimas, P. D. (2000). The emergence of category representations during infancy: Are separate perceptual and conceptual processes required? *Journal of Cognition and Development, 1*, 55–61.

Quinn, P. C., Eimas, P. D. & Rosenkrantz, S. L. (1993). Evidence for representations of perceptually similar natural categories by 3-month-old and 4-month-old infants. *Perception, 22*, 463–475.

Quinn, P. C., Eimas, P. D. & Tarr, M. J. (2001). Perceptual categorization of cat and dog silhouettes by 3- to 4-month-old infants. *Journal of Experimental Child Psychology, 79*, 78–94.

Quinn, P. C., Yahr, J., Kuhn, A., Slater, A. M. & Pascalis, O. (2002). Representation of the gender of human faces by infants: A preference for female. *Perception, 31*, 1109–1121.

Rader, N., Bausano, M. & Richards, J. E. (1980). On the nature of the visual-cliff-avoidance response in human infants. *Child Development, 51*, 61–68.

Rakison, D. & Butterworth, G. (1998). Infants' use of object parts in early categorization. *Developmental Psychology, 34*, 49–62.

Ramey, C. T. & Ramey, S. L. (1998). Early intervention and early experience. *American Psychologist, 53*, 109–120.

Ramey, C. T. & Ramey, S. L. (1999). *Right from birth: Building your child's foundation for life.* New York: Goddard Press.

Ramey, C. T. & Ramey, S. L. (2000). Intelligence and public policy. In R. J. Sternberg (Ed.), *Handbook of intelligence* (pp. 534–548). New York: Cambridge University Press.

Ramey, C. T. & Ramey, S. L. (2001). Early educational interventions and intelligence. In E. Zigler & S. Styfco (Eds.), *The Head Start debates.* New Haven, CT: Yale University Press.

Ramey, C. T., Bryant, D. M, Wasik, B. H., Sparling, J. J., Fendt, K. H. & LaVange, L. M. (1992). Infant Health and Development Program for low birth weight, premature infants: Program elements, family participation, and child intelligence. *Pediatrics, 3*, 454–465.

Ramey, C. T., Ramey, S. L. & Cotton, J. (2002). Early interventions: Programmes, results, and differential response. In A. Slater & M. Lewis (Eds.), *Introduction to Infant Development* (pp. 317–336). Oxford: Oxford University Press.

Ramey, C. T., Ramey, S. L. & Lanzi, R. G. (in press a). Early intervention: Background, research findings, and future directions. In Jacobson (Ed.), *Mental retardation developmental disabilities handbook.*

Ramey, C. T., Ramey, S. L., & Lanzi, R. G. (in press b). Children's health and education. In I. Sigel & A. Renninger (Eds.), *The handbook of child psychology* (6th ed.), Vol. 4 *Child Psychology in Practice.* New York: John Wiley & Sons.

Ramey, C. T., Ramey, S. L., Gaines, R. & Blair, C. (1995). Two-generation early intervention programs: A child development perspective. In I. Sigel (Series Ed.) & S. Smith (Vol. Ed.), *Two-generation programs for families in*

poverty: A new intervention strategy.
Vol. 9 *Advances in Applied Developmental Psychology*
(pp. 199–228). Norwood, NJ: Ablex.

Ramey, C. T., Yeates, K. O. & Short, E. J. (1984). The plasticity of intellectual development: Insights from preventive intervention. *Child Development, 55,* 1913–1925.

Ramey, S. L., Echols, K., Ramey, C. T., Newell, W. (2000). Understanding early intervention. In M. L. Batshaw (Ed.), *When your child has a disability: The complete sourcebook of daily and medical care* (2nd ed) (pp. 73–84). Baltimore: Brookes.

Ramsay, D. & Lewis, M. (2003). Reactivity and regulation in cortisol and behavioral responses to stress. *Child Development, 74,* 456–464.

Ramsey, J. L. (2003). *Infant attention to male faces.* Doctoral dissertation: The University of Texas at Austin.

Ramsey, J. L., Langlois, J. H. & Marti, C. N. (2005). Infant categorization of faces: Ladies first. *Developmental Review, 25,* 212–246.

Ramsey, J. L., Langlois, J. H., Hoss, R. A., Rubenstein, A. J. & Griffin, A. M. (2004). Origins of a stereotype: Categorization of facial attractiveness by 6-month-old infants. *Developmental Science, 7,* 201–211.

Raver, C. C. (1996). Relations between social contingency in mother–child interaction and 2-year-olds' social competence. *Developmental Psychology, 32,* 850–859.

Reaux, J. E., Theall, L. A. & Povinelli, D. J. (1999). A longitudinal investigation of chimpanzees' understanding of visual perception. *Child Development, 70,* 275–290.

Reese, E., (2002). A model of the origins of autobiographical memory. In J. Fagen & H. Hayne (Eds.), *Progress in infancy research* (Vol. 2, pp. 215–260). Mahwah, NJ: Lawrence Erlbaum Associates.

Reissland, N. (1988). Neonatal imitation in the first hour of life—observations in rural Nepal. *Developmental Psychology, 24,* 464–469.

Rhodes, G., Geddes, K., Jeffery, L., Dziurawiec, S. & Clark, A. (2002). Are average and symmetric faces attractive to infants? Discrimination and looking preferences. *Perception, 31,* 315–321.

Ricciuti, H. (1993). Nutrition and mental development. *Current Directions in Psychological Science, 2,* 43–46.

Richards, J. E. & Holley, F. B. (1999). Infant attention and the development of smooth pursuit tracking. *Developmental Psychology, 35*(3), 856–867.

Richards, J. E. & Rader, N. (1981). Crawling-onset age predicts visual cliff avoidance in infants. *Journal of Experimental Psychology: Human Perception and Performance, 7,* 382–387.

Richardson, A. J. & Puri, B. K. (2002). A randomized double-blind, placebo-controlled study of the effects of supplementation with highly unsaturated fatty acids on ADHD-related symptoms in children with specific learning disabilities. *Progress in Neuro-Psychopharmacology & Biological Psychiatry, 26*(2), 233–239.

Robertson, J. & Robertson, J. (1971). Young children in brief separation: A fresh look. *Psychoanalytic Study of the Child, 26,* 264–315.

Robinson, A. J. & Pascalis, O. (2004). Development of flexible visual recognition memory in human infants. *Developmental Science, 7,* 527–533.

Rochat, P. (1989). Object manipulation and exploration in 2- to 5-month-old infants. *Developmental Psychology, 25,* 871–884.

Rochat, P. (1992). Self-sitting and reaching in 5- to 8-month-old infants: The impact of posture and its development on early eye–hand coordination. *Journal of Motor Behavior, 24*(2), 210–220.

Rochat, P. & Goubet, N. (1995). Development of sitting and reaching in 5- to 6-month-old infants. *Infant Behavior and Development, 18*, 53–68.

Rochat, P. & Striano, T. (2002). Who's in the mirror? Self–other discrimination in specular images by four- and nine-month-old infants. *Child Development, 73*, 35–46.

Roggman, L. A. (1991). Assessing social interactions of mothers and infants through play. In. C. E. Schaefer, K. Gitlin & A. Sandgrund (Eds.), *Play diagnosis and assessment* (pp. 427–462). New York: John Wiley & Sons.

Rogoff, B. (2003). *The cultural nature of human development*. Oxford: Oxford University Press.

Rogoff, B., Mistry, J., Goncü, A. & Mosier, C. (1993). Guided participation in cultural activity by toddlers and care-givers. *Monographs of the Society for Research in Child Development, Series-No. 236, 58*(8), 102–125.

Roizen, N. J. (2002). Down syndrome. In M. L. Batshaw (Ed.), *Children with disabilities* (5th ed.) (pp. 361–376). Baltimore: Brookes.

Rosander, K. & von Hofsten, C. (2000). Visual-vestibular interaction in early infancy. *Experimental Brain Research, 133*, 321–333.

Rosander, K. & von Hofsten, C. (2002). Development of gaze tracking of small and large objects. *Experimental Brain Research, 146*, 257–264.

Rosander, K. & von Hofsten, C. (2004). Infants' emerging ability to represent occluded object motion. *Cognition, 91*, 1–22.

Rosch, E. (1978). Principles of categorization. In E. Rosch & B. B. Lloyd (Eds.), *Cognition and categorization* (pp. 27–48). Hillsdale, NJ: Lawrence Erlbaum Associates.

Rosch, E., Mervis, C. B., Gray, W. D., Johnson, D. M. & Boyes-Braem, P. (1976). Basic objects in natural categories. *Cognitive Psychology, 8*, 382–439.

Rose, S. A., Feldman, J. F. & Jankowski, J. J. (2002a). Processing speed in the 1st year of life: A longitudinal study of preterm and full-term infants. *Developmental Psychology, 38*, 895–902.

Rose, S.A, Jankowski, J. J. & Feldman, J. F. (2002b). Speed of processing and face recognition at 7 and 12 months. *Infancy, 3*, 435–455.

Rosenblum, L. & Kaufman, I. C. (1968). Variations in infant development and response to maternal loss in monkeys. *American Journal of Orthopsychiatry, 38*, 418–426.

Rosenstein, D. & Oster, H. (1988). Differential facial responses to four basic tastes in newborns. *Child Development, 59*, 1555–1568.

Rosenstein, D. & Oster, H. (1997). Differential facial responses to four basic tastes in newborns. In P. Ekman, E. L. Rosenberg *et al.* (Eds.), *What the face reveals: Basic and applied studies of spontaneous expression using the Facial Action Coding System (FACS)* (pp. 302–327). New York: Oxford University Press.

Ross, C. A. (1989). *Multiple personality disorder: Diagnosis, clinical features, and treatment*. New York: John Wiley & Sons.

Rothbart, M. K. & Bates, J. E. (1998). Temperament. In N. Eisenberg & W. Damon (Eds.), *The handbook of child psychology* (5th ed.), *Vol. 3: Social, emotional, and personality development* (pp. 105–176). New York: John Wiley & Sons.

Rothbart, M. K. (1981). Measurement of temperament in infancy. *Child Development, 52*, 569–578.

Rothbaum, F., Weisz, J., Pott, M., Miyake, K. & Morelli, G. (2000). Attachment and culture: Security in the United States and Japan. *American Psychologist, 55*(10), 1093–1104.

Rovee-Collier, C., Hayne, H. & Colombo, M. (2000). Memory in infancy and early childhood. In E. Tulving & F. I. M. Craik (Eds.), *The Oxford handbook of memory* (pp. 267–282). New York: Oxford University Press.

Rubenstein, A. J. (2000). The ability to form stereotypic associations during infancy: A cognitive look at the basis of the 'beauty is good' stereotype. Doctoral dissertation: The University of Texas at Austin.

Rubenstein, A. J., Kalakanis, L. & Langlois, J. H. (1999). Infant preferences for attractive faces: A cognitive explanation. *Developmental Psychology, 35*, 848–855.

Rubenstein, J. L. & Howes, C. (1979). Caregiving and infant behaviour in day-care and in homes. *Developmental Psychology, 15*, 1–24.

Rubin, G. B., Fagen, J. W. & Carroll M. H. (1998). Olfactory context and memory retrieval in 3-month-old infants. *Infant Behavior and Development, 21*, 641–658.

Rubin, K. H., Fein, G. G. & Vandenberg, B. (1983). Play. In E. M. Hetherington (Ed.), P. H. Mussen (Series Ed.), *Handbook of child psychology: Vol. 4. Socialization, personality, and social development* (pp. 693–774). New York: John Wiley & Sons.

Rutstein, R. M., Conlon, C. J. & Batshaw, M. L. (1997). HIV and AIDS: From mother to child. In M. L. Batshaw (Ed.), *Children with disabilities* (4th ed.) (pp. 163–182). Baltimore: Brookes.

Rutter, M. (1979). Maternal deprivation, 1972–1978: New findings, new concepts, new approaches. *Child Development, 10*, 283–305.

Rutter, M. & the English Romanian Adoptees Study Team (1998). Developmental catch-up, and deficit, following adoption after severe global early privation. *Journal of Child Psychology and Psychiatry and Allied Disciplines, 39*, 465–476.

Sackett, G. P., Novak, M. F. S. X. & Droeker, R. (1999). Early experience effects on adaptive behavior: Theory revisited. *Mental Retardation and Developmental Disabilities Research Reviews*. New York: John Wiley & Sons.

Saffran, J. R., Aslin, R. N. & Newport, E. L. (1996). Statistical learning by 8-month-old infants. *Science, 274*, 1926–1928.

Sai, F. (2005). The role of mother's voice in developing mother's face preference: Evidence for intermodal perception at birth. *Infant and Child Development, 14*, 29–50.

Samuels, C. A., Butterworth, G., Roberts, T., Graupner, L. & Hole, G. (1994). Facial aesthetics: Babies prefer attractiveness to symmetry. *Perception, 23*, 823–831.

Samuelson, L. (2002). Statistical regularities in vocabulary guide language acquisition in 15- to 20-month-olds and connectionist models. *Developmental Psychology, 38*, 1016–1037.

Sangrigoli, S. & de Schonen, S. (2004). Recognition of own-race and other-race faces by three-month-old infants. *Journal of Child Psychology and Psychiatry, 45*, 1219–1227.

Sants, J. & Barnes, P. (1985). *Personality, development and learning: Unit 2, Childhood.* Milton Keynes: Open University Press.

Scaife, M. & Bruner, J. S. (1975). The capacity for joint visual attention in the infant. *Nature, 253*, 265–266.

Scarr, S. & McCartney K. (1988). Far from home: An experimental evaluation of the mother–child home program in Bermuda. *Child Development, 59*, 531–543.

Schaal, B, Hummel, T. & Soussignan, R. (2004). Olfaction in the fetal and premature infant: Functional status and clinical implications. *Clinics in Perinatology, 31*, 261–285.

Schacter, D. L. & Moscovitch, M. (1984). Infanta, amnesiacs, and dissociable memory systems. In M. Moscovitch (Ed.), *Advances in the study of communication and affect: Infant memory* (Vol. 9, pp. 173–216). New York: Plenum Press.

Schaffer, H. R. (1974). Cognitive components of the infant's response to strangeness. In M. Lewis & L. A. Rosenblum (Eds.), *The origins of fear* (pp. 11–24). New York: John Wiley & Sons.

Scheper-Hughes, N. (1985). Culture, scarcity, and maternal thinking: Maternal detachment and infant survival in a Brazilian shantytown. *Ethos, 13*(4), 291–317.

Schieffelin, B. B. (1991). *The give and take of everyday life: Language socialization of Kaluli children.* Cambridge: Cambridge University Press.

Schmidt, L. A., Fox, N. A., Rubin, K. H., Sternberg, E. M., Gold, P. W., Smith, C. C. & Schulkin, J. (1997). Behavioral and neuroendocrine responses in shy children. *Developmental Psychobiology, 30*, 127–140.

Schmuckler, M. A. (1997). Children's postural sway in response to low- and high-frequency visual information for oscillation. *Journal of Experimental Psychology: Human Perception and Performance, 23*, 528–545.

Schurch, B. & Scrimshaw, N. S., (Eds.). (1990). *Activity, energy expenditure and energy requirements of infants and children.* Lausanne, Switzerland: Nestlé Foundation.

Schwartz, A., Campos, J. & Baisel, E. (1973). The visual cliff: Cardiac and behavioral correlates on the deep and shallow sides at five and six months of age. *Journal of Experimental Child Psychology, 15*, 86–99.

Schweinhart, L. J., Barnes, H. V., Weikart, D. P., Barnett, W. S. & Epstein, A. S.

(1993). *Significant benefits: The High/Scope Perry Preschool Study through age 27.* Ypsilanti, MI: High/Scope Press.

Seidl, A., Hollich, G. & Jusczyk, P. W. (2003). Early understanding of subject and object Wh-questions. *Infancy, 4*, 423–436.

Sereno, M. I., Dale, A. M., Reppas, J. B., Kwong, K. K., Belliveau, J. W., Brady, T. J. *et al.* (1995). Borders of multiple visual areas in humans revealed by functional magnetic resonance imaging. *Science, 268*, 889–893.

Seress, L., Abraham, H., Tornoczky, T., Kosztolanyi, G. Y. (2001). Cell formation in the human hippocampal formation from mid-gestation to the late postnatal period. *Neuroscience, 105*, 831–843.

Serpell, R. (1994). The cultural construction of intelligence. In W. J. Lonner & R. Malpass (Eds.), *Psychology and Culture.* Boston: Allyn & Bacon.

Serrano, J. M., Iglesias, J. & Loeches, A. (1995). Infants' responses to adult static facial expressions. *Infant Behavior and Development, 18*, 477–482.

Shahidullah, S. & Hepper, P. G. (1993) The developmental origins of fetal responsiveness to an acoustic stimulus. *Journal of Reproductive and Infant Psychology, 11*, 135–142.

Shannon, J. D., Tamis-LeMonda, C. S., London, K. & Cabrera, N. (2002). Beyond rough and tumble: Low-income fathers' interactions and children's cognitive development at 24 months. *Parenting: Science and Practice, 2*(2), 77–104.

Shaw, C. A. & McEachem, J. C. (1997). The effects of early diet on synaptic function and behavior: pitfalls and potentials. In J. Dobbing (Ed.), *Developing brain and behavior: The role of lipids in infant formula.* San Diego, CA: Academic Press.

Shinskey, J. L., Bogartz, R. S. & Poirier, C. R. (2000). The effects of graded occlusion on manual search and visual attention in 5- to 8-month-old infants. *Infancy, 1*, 323–346.

Shonkoff, J. P. & Phillips, D. A. (2000). *From neurons to neighborhoods: The science of early child development.* Washington, DC: National Academy Press.

Shore, R. (1997). *Rethinking the brain: New insights into early development.* New York: Families and Work Institute.

Simcock, G. & Hayne, H. (2002). Breaking the barrier: Children do not translate their preverbal memories into language. *Psychological Science, 13*, 225–231.

Skeels, H. M. & Dye, H. A. (1939). A study of the effects of differential stimulation in mentally retarded children. *Proceedings of the American Association of Mental Deficiency, 44*, 114–136.

Slater, A. & Oates, J. (2005). Sensation to perception. In J. Oates, C. Wood & A. Grayson (Eds.), *Psychological development in early childhood.* Oxford: Blackwell Publishers.

Slater, A., Bremner, G., Johnson, S. P., Sherwood, P., Hayes, R. & Brown, E. (2000a). Newborn infants' preference for attractive faces: The role of internal and external facial features. *Infancy, 2*, 265–274.

Slater, A., Mattock, A. & Brown, E. (1990). Size constancy at birth: Newborn infants' responses to retinal and real size. *Journal of Experimental Child Psychology, 49*, 314–322.

Slater, A., Morison, V., Somers, M., Mattock, A., Brown, E. & Taylor, D. (1990). Newborn and older infants' perception of partly occluded objects. *Infant Behavior and Development, 13*, 33–49.

Slater, A., Quinn, P. C., Hayes, R. & Brown, E. (2000b). The role of facial orientation in newborn infants' preference for attractive faces. *Developmental Science, 3*, 181–185.

Slater, A., Quinn, P., Brown, E. & Hayes, R. (1999). Intermodal perception at

birth: Intersensory redundancy guides newborn infants' learning of arbitrary auditory–visual pairings. *Developmental Science, 2*, 333–338.

Slater, A., Quinn, P., Lewkowicz, D. J., Hayes, R. & Brookes, H. (2003). Learning of arbitrary adult voice–face pairings at three months of age. In O. Pascalis & A. Slater (Eds.), *The development of face processing in infancy and early childhood* (pp. 69–78). New York: NOVA Science.

Slater, A., Von der Schulenburg, C., Brown, E., Badenoch, M., Butterworth, G., Parsons, S. & Samuels, C. (1998). Newborn infants prefer attractive faces. *Infant Behavior and Development, 21*, 345–354.

Slaughter, V., Heron, M. & Sim, S. (2002). Development of preferences for the human body shape in infancy. *Cognition, 85*, B71–B81.

Sloutsky, V. M., Lo, Y. F. & Fisher, A. (2001). How much does a shared name make things similar? Linguistic labels, similarity, and the development of inductive inference. *Child Development, 72*, 1695–1709.

Sokolov, E. N. (1963). *Perception and the conditioned reflex.* New York: Macmillan.

Sorce, J. F., Emde, R. N., Campos, J. & Klinnert, M. D. (1985). Maternal emotional signaling: Its effect on the visual cliff behavior of one-year olds. *Developmental Psychology, 21*, 195–200.

Sparling, J. J., Dragomir, C., Ramey, S. L., Florescu, L. (2005). An educational intervention improves developmental progress of young children in a Romanian orphanage. *Infant Mental Health Journal, 26*(2), 127–142.

Sparling, J. W., van Tol, J. & Chescheir, N. C. (1999). Fetal and neonatal hand movement. *Physical Therapy, 79*(1), 24–39.

Spelke, E. R., Breinlinger, K., Macomber, J. & Jacobson, K. (1992). Origins of knowledge. *Psychological Review, 99*, 605–632.

Spelke, E. S., Kestenbaum, R., Simons, D. J. & Wein, D. (1995). Spatiotemporal continuity, smoothness of motion and object identity in infancy. *British Journal of Developmental Psychology, 13*, 113–142.

Spencer, J., Quinn, P. C., Johnson, M. H. & Karmiloff-Smith, A. (1997). Heads you win, tails you lose: Evidence for young infants categorizing mammals by head and facial attributes (Special Issue: Perceptual Development). *Early Development and Parenting, 6*, 113–126.

Spiker, C. C. (1956). Experiments with children on the hypothesis of acquired distinctiveness and equivalence of cues. *Child Development, 27*, 253–263.

Squire, L. R. (2004). Memory systems of the brain: A brief history and current perspective. *Neurobiology of Learning and Memory, 82*, 171–177

Steenbergen, B., van der Kamp, J., Smitsman, A. & Carson, R. G. (1997). Spoon-handling in two- to four-year-old children. *Ecological Psychology, 9*, 113–129.

Steiner, J. E. (1979). Human facial expressions in response to taste and smell stimulation. In H. W. Reese & L. P. Lipsitt (Eds.), *Advances in child development and behavior, 13*. New York: Academic Press.

Stenberg, C. R. & Campos, J. J. (1990). The development of anger expressions in infancy. In N. L. Stein, B. Leventhal & T. Trabasso (Eds.), *Psychological and biological approaches to emotion* (pp. 247–256). Hillsdale, NJ: Lawrence Erlbaum Associates.

Stenberg, C. R., Campos, J. J. & Emde, R. N. (1983). The facial expression of anger in seven-month-old infants. *Child Development, 54*, 178–184.

Stern, D. N. (1985). *The interpersonal world of the infant*. New York: Basic Books.

Stifter, C.A & Spinrad, T. L. (1999). Colic. In C. A. Smith (Ed.), *Encyclopedia of parenting theory and research* (pp. 73–74). New York: Greenwood/Plenum Press.

Stipek, D., Recchia, S. & McClintic, S. (1992). Self-evaluation in young children. *Monographs of the Society for Research in Child Development, 57*(1, Serial No. 226).

Stoffregen, T. A. (1986). The role of optical velocity in the control of stance. *Perception and Psychophysics, 39*, 355–360.

Stoffregen, T. A., Schmuckler, M. A. & Gibson, E. J. (1987). Use of central and peripheral optical flow in stance and locomotion in young walkers. *Perception, 16*, 113–119.

Streri, A. & Gentaz, E. (2004). Cross-modal recognition of shape from hand to eyes and handedness in human newborns. *Neuropsychologia, 42*, 1365–1369.

Striano, T. & Rochat, P. (2000). Emergence of selective social referencing. *Infancy, 1*, 253–264.

Strupp, B. J. & Levitsky, D. A. (1995). Enduring cognitive effects of early malnutrition: A theoretical reappraisal. *Journal of Nutrition, 125*(8S), 2221S–2232S.

Stucki, M., Kaufmann-Hayoz, R. & Kaufmann, F. (1987). Infants' recognition of a face revealed through motion: Contribution of internal facial movement and head movement. *Canadian Journal of Experimental Child Psychology, 44*, 80–91.

Sullivan, M. W., Lewis, M. & Alessandri, S. (1992). Cross-age stability in emotional expressions during learning and extinction. *Developmental Psychology, 28*, 58–63.

Susser, M. & Levin, B. (1999). Ordeals for the fetal programming hypothesis. *BMJ, 318*, 885–886.

Svejda, M. & Schmid, D. (1979). The role of self-produced locomotion in the onset of fear of heights on the visual cliff. Paper presented at the meeting of the Society for Research in Child Development, San Francisco.

Swanson, J. (2000a). Child health guide. In J. Swanson (Ed.). *Infant and toddler health sourcebook* (pp. 165–175). Detroit: Omnigraphics.

Swanson, J. (2000b). Autism. In J. Swanson (Ed.). *Infant and toddler health sourcebook* (pp. 287–311). Detroit: Omnigraphics.

Symons, L. A., Hains, S. M. J. & Muir, D. W. (1998). Look at me: Five-month-old infants' sensitivity to very small deviations in eye-gaze during social interactions. *Infant Behavior and Development, 21*, 531–536.

Taine, H. (1877). Acquisition of language by children. *Mind, 2*, 252–259.

Tamis-LeMonda, C. S. & Bornstein, M. H. (1990). Language, play, and attention at one year. *Infant Behavior and Development, 13*, 85–98.

Tamis-LeMonda, C. S. & Bornstein, M. H. (1991). Individual variation, correspondence, stability, and change in mother–toddler play. *Infant Behavior and Development, 14*, 143–162.

Tamis-LeMonda, C. S. & Bornstein, M. H. (1994). Specificity in mother–toddler language-play relations across the second year. *Developmental Psychology, 30*, 283–292.

Tamis-LeMonda, C. S. & Bornstein, M. H. (1996). Variation in children's exploratory, nonsymbolic, and symbolic play: An explanatory multidimensional framework. In C. Rovee-Collier & L. Lipsitt (Eds.), *Advances in infancy research* (pp. 37–78). Norwood, NJ: Ablex.

Tamis-LeMonda, C. S., Bornstein, M. H. & Baumwell, L. (2001). Maternal responsiveness and children's achievement of language milestones. *Child Development, 72*, 748–767.

Tamis-LeMonda, C. S., Bornstein, M. H., Cyphers, L. & Toda, S. (1992).

Language and play at one year: A comparison between Japan and the United States. *International Journal of Behavioral Development, 15*, 19–42.

Tamis-LeMonda, C. S., Shannon, J. D., Cabera, N. J. & Lamb, M. E. (2004). Fathers and mothers at play with their 2- and 3- year olds: Contributions to language and cognitive development. *Child Development, 75*(6), 1806–1820.

Tangney, J. P. & Dearing, R. L. (2002). *Shame and Guilt*. New York: Guilford Press.

Taylor, B. & Wadsworth, J. (1984). Breast feeding and child development at five years. *Developmental Medicine and Child Neurology, 26*, 73–80.

Teferra, T. (2003). Early intervention practices: Ethiopia. In S. L. Odom, M. J. Hanson, J. A. Blackman & S. Kaul (Eds.), *Early intervention practices around the world* (pp. 91–107). Baltimore: Brookes.

Teller, D. Y. (1979). The forced-choice preferential looking procedure: A psychophysical technique for use with human infants. *Infant Behavior and Development, 2*, 135–153.

Thelen, E. & Spencer, J. P. (1998). Postural control during reaching in young infants: A dynamic systems approach. *Neuroscience and Biobehavioral Reviews, 22*, 507–514.

Thelen, E. (1979). Rhythmical stereotypies in normal human infants. *Animal Behavior, 27*, 699–715.

Thomas, A., Birch, H. G., Chess, S., Hertzig, M. & Korn, S. (1963). *Behavior individuality in early childhood*. New York: New York University Press.

Thompson, L. A., Madrid, V., Westbrook, S. & Johnston, V. (2001). Infants attend to second-order relational properties of faces. *Psychonomic Bulletin & Review, 8*, 769–777.

Thompson, R. A., Easterbrooks, M. A., Padilla-Walker, L. M. (2003). Social and emotional development in infancy. In R. M. Lerner, M. A. Easterbrooks & J.

Mistry (Eds.), *Handbook of psychology: Developmental psychology, 6,* 91–112. Hoboken, NJ: John Wiley & Sons.

Thorburn, M. J. (2003). Paraprofessionals in low-cost early intervention programs: Jamaica. In S. L. Odom, M. J. Hanson, J. A. Blackman & S. Kaul, *Early intervention practices around the world* (pp. 191–208). Baltimore: Brookes.

Tincoff, R. & Jusczyk, P. W. (1999). Some beginnings of word comprehension in 6-month-olds. *Psychological Science, 10,* 172–175.

Tizard, J. & Tizard, B. (1971). The social development of two-year-old children in residential nurseries. In H. R. Schaffer (Ed.), *The origins of human social relations.* New York: Academic Press.

Tomasello, M. (1999). *The cultural origins of human cognition.* Cambridge, MA: Harvard Univeristy Press.

Tomasello, M., Strosberg, R. & Akhtar, N. (1996). Eighteen-month-old children learn words in non-ostensive contexts. *Journal of Child Language, 23, 157–176.*

Tomkins, S. S. (1962). *Affect, imagery, consciousness, Vol. 1: The positive affects.* New York: Springer.

Tomkins, S. S. (1963). *Affect, imagery, consciousness, Vol. 2: The negative affects.* New York: Springer.

Torun, B. & Viteri, F. E. (1988). Protein-energy malnutrition. In M. E. Shils & V. R. Young (Eds.), *Modern nutrition in health and disease* (pp. 746–773). Philadelphia: Lea & Febiger.

Trivers, R. L. (1974). Parent–offspring conflict. *American Zoologist, 14,* 249–264.

Tronick, E. Z. (2003). Things still to be done on the still-face effect. *Infancy, 4,* 475–482.

Tronick, E. Z., Als, H., Adamson, L., Wise, S. & Brazelton, T. B. (1978). The infant's response to entrapment between contradictory messages in face-to-face interaction. *American Academy of Child Psychiatry, 17,* 1–13.

Tronick, E. Z., Morelli, G. A. & Winn, S. (1987). Multiple caretaking of Efe (Pygmy) infants. *American Anthropologist, 89*(1), 96–106

Turati, C., Sangrigoli, S., Ruel, J. & de Schonen, S. (2004). Evidence of the face inversion effect in 4-month-old infants. *Infancy, 6,* 275–297.

Turati, C., Valenza, E., Leo, I. & Simion, F. (2005). Three-month-olds' visual preference for faces and its underlying visual processing mechanisms. *Journal of Experimental Child Psychology, 90,* 255–273.

UNICEF (1997). *The State of the World's Children 1998.* Oxford: Oxford University Press.

Van de Weijer, J. (1998). *Language input for word discovery.* Wageningen: Ponsen & Loijen, bv.

van der Meer, A. L. H., van der Weel, F. R. & Lee, D. (1994). Prospective control in catching by infants. *Perception, 23,* 287–302.

Van Duuren, M., Kendell-Scott, L. & Stark, N. (2003). Early aesthetic choices: Infant preferences for attractive premature infant faces. *International Journal of Behavioral Development, 27,* 212–219.

van Hof, P., van der Kamp, J., Caljouw, S. R. & Savelsbergh, G. J. P. (2005). The confluence of intrinsic and extrinsic constraints on 3- to 9-month-old infants' catching behavior. *Infant Behavior & Development, 28,* 179–193.

Vandell, D. L. & Wilson, K. S. (1987). Infants' interactions with mother, sibling, and peer: Contrasts and relations between interaction systems. *Child Development, 58,* 176–186.

Vaughan, A., Mundy, P., Block, J., Burnette, C., Delgado, C., Gomez, Y. *et al.* (2003). Child, caregiver, and temperament contributions to infant joint attention. *Infancy, 4,* 603–616.

von Hofsten, C. (1979). Development of visually directed reaching: The approach phase. *Journal of Human Movement Studies, 30,* 369–382.

von Hofsten, C. (1980). Predictive reaching for moving objects by human infants. *Journal of Experimental Child Psychology, 30*, 369–382.

von Hofsten, C. (1982). Eye–hand coordination in the newborn. *Developmental Psychology, 18*, 450–461.

von Hofsten, C. (1984). Developmental changes in the organization of prereaching movements. *Developmental Psychology, 20*, 378–388.

von Hofsten, C. (1991). Structuring of early reaching movements: A longitudinal study. *Journal of Motor Behavior, 23*(4), 280–292.

von Hofsten, C. (2004). An action perspective on motor development. *Trends in Cognitive Sciences, 8*(6), 266–272.

von Hofsten, C. & Ronnqvist, L. (1988). Preparation for grasping an object: A developmental study. *Journal of Experimental Psychology: Human Perception and Performance, 14*, 610–621.

von Hofsten, C. & Ronnqvist, L. (1993). The structuring of neonatal arm movements. *Child Development, 64*(4), 1046–1057.

von Hofsten, C. & Rosander, K. (1996). The development of gaze control and predictive tracking in young infants. *Vision Research, 36*(1), 81–96.

von Hofsten, C. & Rosander, K. (1997). Development of smooth pursuit tracking in young infants. *Vision Research, 37*, 1799–1810.

Vygotsky, L. S. (1962). *Thought and language* (E. Hanfmann & G. Vakar, Trans.). Cambridge, MA: MIT Press.

Vygotsky, L. S. (1967). Play and its role in the mental development of the child. *Soviet Psychology, 12*, 62–76.

Vygotsky, L. (1978). *Mind in society*. Cambridge, MA: Harvard University Press.

Wachs, T. D. (1993). Environment and the development of disadvantaged children. In R. J. Karp (Ed.), *Malnourished children in the United States caught in the cycle of poverty* (pp. 13–30). New York: Springer.

Wachs, T. D. (1995). Relation of mild-to-moderate malnutrition to human development: Correlational studies. *Journal of Nutrition, 125*, 2245S–2254S.

Wachs, T. D. (2001). Linking nutrition and temperament. In D. Molfese & T. Molfese (Eds.), *Temperament and personality development across the life span*. Hillsdale, NJ: Lawrence Erlbaum Associates.

Walker-Andrews, A. S. (1986). Intermodal perception of expressive behaviors: Relation of eye and voice? *Developmental Psychology, 22*, 373–377.

Wallace, D., Franklin, M. B. & Keegan, R. T. (1994). The observing eye: A century of baby diaries. *Human Development, 37*, 1–29

Walton, G. E. & Bower, T. G. (1993). Newborns form 'prototypes' in less than 1 minute. *Psychological Science, 4*, 203–205.

Walton, G. E., Bower, N. J. A. & Bower, T. G. R. (1992). Recognition of familiar faces by newborns. *Infant Behavior and Development, 15*, 265–269.

Wann, J. P., Mon-Williams, M. & Rushton, K. (1998). Postural control and co-ordination disorder: The swinging room revisited. *Human Movement Science, 17*, 491–513.

Ward, C. D. (1998). The role of multisensory information in infants' recognition of their fathers. Doctoral dissertation: Virginia Polytechnic Institute and State University.

Warren, W. H., Kay, B. A. & Yilmaz, E. H. (1996). Visual control of posture during walking: Functional specificity. *Journal of Experimental Psychology: Human Perception and Performance, 22*, 818–838.

Waxman, S. & Booth, A. E. (2001). Seeing pink elephants: Fourteen-month-olds' interpretations of novel nouns and adjectives. *Cognitive Psychology, 43,* 217–242.

Weikart, D. P., Bond, J. T. & McNeil, J. T. (1978). *The Ypsilanti Perry Preschool Project: Preschool years and longitudinal results through fourth grade.* Ypsilanti, MI: High/Scope Press.

Weinberg, M. K. & Tronick, E. Z. (1996). Infant affective reactions to the resumption of maternal interaction after the still-face. *Child Development, 67,* 905–914.

Wellman, H. M., Cross, D. & Watson, J. (2001). Meta-analysis of theory-of-mind development: The truth about false belief. *Child Development, 72(3),* 655–684.

Wentworth, N., Haith, M. M. & Karrer, R. (2001). Behavioral and cortical measures of infants' visual expectations. *Infancy, 2,* 175–196.

Werker, J. F. (1989). Becoming a native listener. *American Scientist, 77,* 54–59.

Wertheimer, (1961). Psychomotor coordination of auditory and visual space at birth. *Science, 134,* 1692.

Whiting, B. B. & Whiting, J. W. M. *(1975). Children of six cultures: A psychocultural analysis.* Cambridge, MA: Harvard University Press.

Wilcox, T., Nadel, L. & Rosser, R. (1996). Location memory in healthy preterm and full-term infants. *Infant Behavior & Development, 19,* 309–324.

Willatts, P. (1997). Beyond the 'couch potato' infant: How infants use their knowledge to regulate action, solve problems, and achieve goals. In G. Bremner, A. Slater & G. Butterworth (Eds.), *Infant development: Recent advances* (pp. 109–135). Hove: Psychology Press.

Willatts, P. (1999). Development of means–end behavior in young infants: Pulling a support to retrieve a distant object. *Developmental Psychology, 35(3),* 651–667.

Willatts, P., Forysyth, J. S., DiModugno, M. K., Varma, S. & Colvin, M. (1998). Effect of long-chain polyunsaturated fatty acids in infant formula on problem solving at 10 months of age. *Lancet, 352,* 688–691.

Williams, L. J., Rasmussen, S. A., Flores, A., Kirby, R. S. & Edmonds, L. D. (2005). Decline in the prevalence of spina bifida and anencephaly by race/ethnicity: 1995–2002. *Pediatrics, 116(3),* 580–586.

Wilson, N. & Tolson, S. H. (1983). An analysis of adult–child interaction patterns in three generational black families. Paper presented at the Society for Research in Child Development Symposium on Grandparents and Very Young Children.

Winnicott, D. W. (1959). Classification: Is there a psycho-analytic contribution to psychiatric classification. In *The maturational process and the facilitating environment.* New York: International University Press.

Witherington, D. C. (2005). The development of prospective grasping control between 5 and 7 months: A longitudinal study. *Infancy, 7,* 143–161.

Witherington, D. C., Campos, J. J., Anderson, D. I, Lejeune, L. & Seah, E. (2005). Avoidance of heights on the visual cliff in newly walking infants. *Infancy, 7,* 285–298.

Wittgenstein, L. (1953). *Philosophical investigations* (G. E. M. Anscombe, Trans.). Oxford: Blackwell Publishers.

Wolf, C. M. (1996). The development of behavioral response to pain in the human newborn. *Dissertation Abstracts International: Section B, 57,* 1472.

Wolf, S. & Wolff, H. G. (1947). *Human gastric function.* New York: Oxford University Press.

Woodward, A. (1993). The effect of labeling on children's attention to objects. In E. V. Clark (Ed.), *Proceedings* of the 24th Annual Child Language Research Forum (pp. 35–47). Stanford, CA: CSLI.

Worobey, J. (1992). Development milestones related to feeding status: Evidence from the Child Health Supplement to the 1981 National Health Interview Survey. *Journal of Human Nutrition and Dietetics, 5,* 545–552.

Worobey, J., Pisuk, J. & Decker, K. (2004). Diet and behavior in at-risk children: Evaluation of an early intervention program. *Public Health Nursing, 21*(2), 122–127.

Worthington-Roberts, B. & Williams, S. (2000). *Nutrition throughout the life cycle.* Boston: McGraw-Hill.

Xu, F. (2005). Labeling guides object individuation in 12-month-old infants. *Psychological Science, 16,* 372–377.

Yarrow, L. J. (1961). Maternal deprivation: Toward an empirical and conceptual re-evaluation. *Psychological Bulletin, 58,* 459–490.

Yarrow, L. J., MacTurk, R. H., Vietze, P. M., McCarthy, M. E., Klein, R. P. & McQuiston, S. (1984). Developmental course of parental stimulation and its relationship to mastery motivation during infancy. *Developmental Psychology, 20,* 492–503.

Yoshida, H. & Smith, L. B. (2005). Linguistic cues enhance the learning of perceptual cues. *Psychological Science, 16,* 90–95.

Youngblade, L. M. & Dunn, J. (1995). Individual differences in young children's pretend play with mother and sibling: Links to relationships and understanding of other people's feelings and beliefs. *Child Development, 66,* 1472–1492

Zickler, C. F., Morrow, J. D. & Bull, M. J. (1998). Infants with Down syndrome: A look at temperament. *Journal of Pediatric Health Care, 12*(3), 111–117.

Zigler, E. F. (1967). Familial mental retardation: A continuing dilemma. *Science, 155,* 292–298.

Index

THE
PRAYER
OF
JESUS

LIVING THE LORD'S PRAYER

KEN HEMPHILL

LifeWay Press®
Nashville, Tennessee

ISBN 0-6330-7624-4

Cover Photograph: Richard Nowitz

This book is a resource in the Prayer category of the Christian Growth Study Plan.
Course CG-0807

Dewey Decimal Classification: 248.32
Subject Heading: PRAYER\CHRISTIAN LIFE

Unless otherwise indicated, all Scripture quotations are from the NEW AMERICAN STANDARD BIBLE,
© Copyright The Lockman Foundation, 1960, 1962, 1963, 1968, 1971, 1972, 1973, 1975, 1977, 1995;
Used by permission.

Scripture quotations identified NIV are from the Holy Bible, *New International Version,*
copyright © 1973, 1978, 1984 by International Bible Society.

To order additional copies of this resource: WRITE LifeWay Church Resources Customer Service,
One LifeWay Plaza, Nashville, TN 37234-0113; FAX order to (615) 251-5933; PHONE 1-800-458-2772;
E-MAIL to *customerservice@lifeway.com*; ONLINE at *www.lifeway.com;*
or visit the LifeWay Christian Store serving you.

Printed in the United States of America

Leadership and Adult Publishing
LifeWay Church Resources
One LifeWay Plaza
Nashville, TN 37234-0175

CONTENTS

ABOUT THE AUTHOR

Dr. Ken Hemphill is National Strategist, Empowering Kingdom Growth; LifeWay Christian Resources and the SBC Executive Committee; Nashville Tennessee. Prior to accepting this position, he was President and Professor of Evangelism and Church Growth at Southwestern Baptist Theological Seminary in Fort Worth, Texas.

He came to Southwestern from Atlanta, Georgia, where he was director of the Southern Baptist Center for Church Growth from 1992-1994. Prior to that, he pastored several Baptist churches, including First Baptist Church, Norfolk, Virginia, which under his leadership grew from 800 to over 6,000 members.

Hemphill received his bachelor of arts from Wake Forest University, and both the master of divinity and doctor of ministry degrees from Southern Baptist Theological Seminary. He also holds a doctor of philosophy degree from Cambridge University.

He is the author of several books, including *The Names of God; Mirror, Mirror on the Wall; The Bonsai Theory of Church Growth; Revitalizing the Sunday Morning Dinosaur;* and *The Antioch Effect*. He and his wife, Paula, have three daughters, Kristina, Rachel, and Katherine.

The personal learning activities and leader guide were written by Dr. Daryl Eldridge, Dean of the School of Educational Ministries at Southwestern Baptist Theological Seminary. Eldridge is the editor of *The Teaching Ministry of the Church*, associate editor of *Evangelical Dictionary of Christian Education*, and has written numerous articles on leadership and church growth. He received the bachelor of arts degree from Drury College and both his master of religious education and doctor of philosophy degrees from Southwestern Baptist Seminary. He resides in Granbury, Texas, with his wife Carol. They have two grown children.

ABOUT THE STUDY

Welcome to the study of *The Prayer of Jesus: Living the Lord's Prayer*. This study makes a unique contribution to Christians who desire to live a "kingdom-focused" life. More than a book on how to pray, it offers insight on how to live the principles contained in Jesus' prayer in Matthew 6:9-13. Dr. Hemphill believes that following Jesus' pattern for praying could revolutionize families, churches, and our world. You will discover the answers to questions such as what is prayer, why should I pray if God already knows what I need, and why do my prayers seem so ineffective? In the introductory video, you will meet the author and hear his personal journey that led to the writing of this book.

The daily lessons in your member book, to be completed on your own during the week, should take no more than 20 minutes each. The personal learning activities will help you apply to your life what you learn. In the margins of each page you will find key statements and Bible passages. You will be asked to read some passages from your own Bible, so keep it close at hand.

In your group session each week, you will watch the video review while completing the viewer guide for the session. Following the video, you will have opportunity to discuss your week's reading and ask questions. The leader guide will assist the group leader in conducting each group session.

The basis for your prayer life is a personal relationship with God through His Son Jesus Christ. If you have not accepted Jesus as Savior and Lord of your life, turn to page 103 now and read how to become a Christian.

Accountability Questions

During this study, you will encounter seven "kingdom accountability" questions that will help you live the principles of Jesus' prayer. These questions can also be used in accountability groups following this study (see leader's guide):

1. What did you do today (this week) that "hallowed God's name"?
2. What words or deeds brought reproach on His name? How can you make amends?
3. What kingdom opportunity did you encounter? How did you respond?
4. How have you responded to God's will today (this week)? Share the victories of obedience and seek forgiveness for issues of disobedience.
5. How have you experienced God's daily provision?
6. How is your spiritual debt ledger? What do you need forgiveness for? Whom do you need to forgive? What actions are you prepared to take?
7. Have you avoided temptations and experienced spiritual victory?

THE
ℒORD'S PRAYER

Our Father who art in heaven,
Hallowed be Thy name.
Thy kingdom come.
Thy will be done,
On earth as it is in heaven.
Give us this day our daily bread.
And forgive us our debts,
as we also have forgiven our debtors.
And do not lead us into temptation,
but deliver us from evil.
For Thine is the kingdom, and the power,
and the glory, forever. Amen.

Matthew 6:9-13

An Answer to Prayer

The Promise of Living in the Lord's Prayer

Several years ago, the investment firm E. F. Hutton aired a series of commercials that shared a common thread. Amid the buzz of spectators at a tennis match, diners at an exclusive restaurant, or passengers near the luggage claim rack at the airport, someone would whisper, "My broker is E. F. Hutton, and E. F. Hutton says …" At that, everyone in the room would stop what they were doing, craning their necks or cupping their ears as the announcer's voice would matter-of-factly declare: "When E. F. Hutton talks, people listen."

The implication is obvious. Serious investors who want to maximize their earnings potential will listen with diligent attention and eagerness to their favorite financial experts. Those who dream of improving their skills at everything from making putts to puttering in the garden never tire of hearing a Tiger Woods or Martha Stewart explain the subtle nuances of their craft.

But how important are solid portfolios, a masterful short game, or lush azaleas when life gets hard and the usual answers can't dull the pain, when the suffering is serious and recreation no longer provides a viable escape? That's when all kinds of people with all kinds of interests find themselves wanting one thing more than just about any other. They want to know how to pray.

"I know," you might say, "but I've tried prayer, and it just doesn't work for me."

Have you ever said those words? Maybe they're not the kind of words you speak out loud, but they've probably run through your mind at some point in your life.

Truth is, it's a fair statement. And even those of us who profoundly disagree with the conclusion must honestly confess that it at least raises some good questions:

- What is prayer?
- Why doesn't it always work the way we think it should?
- Who knows the answers to questions like these anyway?

Have you struggled with any of these questions? Place a check beside questions you would like to have answered by this study.

My Own Struggle

I'll be the first to admit I've struggled over the years to have a consistent prayer life. But I can tell you this, and I imagine you can say the same thing: Desire hasn't been the problem. I have wanted to be close to God in prayer more than just about anything. But I could never seem to find that ... something ... that enabled me to find my way through the fog of an ineffective prayer life, to know that I was honestly communicating with my Creator and Father in a way that was pleasing to Him.

I've long known the biblical truths about prayer. I've taught and preached on the promises of God. I've quoted with great conviction those luminaries from the past who declared their confidence in prayer. But I have long had a passion to experience it myself on a daily basis.

Over the years I have tried numerous strategies to improve my own prayer life and to enable me to communicate to others how they, too, could approach God effectively. And some of those ideas have helped. But a few years ago I made a profound discovery—perhaps I should more rightly say that God opened my mind to something absolutely life-changing I had been missing—that has transformed my own prayer life and energized my daily walk with the Lord.

As a result I have gained new confidence and consistency in prayer. I have witnessed God doing incredible things in my heart and in my world. I have found that prayer has a purpose that goes far beyond answers, prayer lists, and quiet time in the morning.

I have seen what prayer can do and I have seen it work. But I'm certainly not the first one to learn this secret to effective praying. For that, you'd have to go back nearly two thousand years, sit down at the feet of the Master with His first-century followers, and see what Jesus Christ had to say about prayer.

TEACH US TO PRAY

That small group of disciples must have asked Him many questions over the course of His three years on earth. But the most significant request they ever made of Him was this:

> It came about that while [Jesus] was praying in a certain place, after He had finished, one of His disciples said to Him, "Lord, teach us to pray just as John also taught his disciples" (Luke 11:1).

Bear in mind that this request came from men who had seen Jesus heal the terminally sick, cast out legions of demons, and exercise amazing authority over nature. They had sensed firsthand the excitement of the crowds who flocked to hear Him teach. They had experienced the hubbub of being part of an exhilarating cause attracting wide attention.

Yet none of the disciples—as far as we know—asked Jesus to school them in any of the more visible ministry abilities like personal counseling, public speaking, or miracle working.

All they wanted to know was this: How do you pray like that?

How did you learn to pray?

Watching and hearing my parents Pray;

Would you like to be taught by the Master? (circle) Yes No

Somehow from observing Jesus, the disciples knew that prayer—or at least something that happened to Him in the process of prayer—was the key that gave Jesus the strength to do all the other miraculous things He did. Jesus knew a level of intimacy with His Heavenly Father that transformed prayer from ritual into raw, living, breathing power. He knew what prayer was, and His prayer connected!

These men who were asking Jesus for instructions weren't beginners when it came to prayer. They had been praying all their lives. Their

they prayed:
in the beginning of day
at " closing " "
Quoted the Shema De 6:4
3 times a day at fixed
times:
before meals, after meals
the Pharisees: I thank
thee:
Pray w/o ceasing
I Thess 5:17

Jewish heritage required them to be disciplined and consistent in the practice of prayer all the way back to their early childhood. At the beginning and ending of each day, for as long as they could remember, they had quoted the Shema, the Jewish confession of faith taken from Deuteronomy 6:4–5, along with other prayers and benedictions. They had also followed the custom of praying three times a day at fixed hours as well as before and after every meal. In fact, some historians say that the average Jew during the time of Jesus prayed three to four hours a day. Put it all together, multiply by their ages, and you could fill the Jordan River with the number of prayers they had showered toward heaven in their lifetimes.

I don't know about you, but I'm not at this level. If these men needed help with prayer, I know I need to hear what Jesus had to say.

Obviously, their request of Jesus wasn't about amounts and quantities, schedules and timetables. They had those kinds of details down to a science. Yet they knew something was missing, even with their habitual practice of prayer. They were dying to know what prayer was all about. They craved to experience the intimate communion Jesus had with God. They had seen it in His eyes, in His pace, in His calm. They just had to know.

So He told them, and like most of Jesus' answers it was simple and straightforward, concise yet comprehensive. We call His answer the Lord's Prayer.

LEARNING TOGETHER

Sadly, Christ's words have become merely commonplace—a whispered murmur that speaks in cold black and white what God intended as a way to color our lives with His vivid, personal presence.

So this is not a book that simply explains the Lord's Prayer, as others have capably done before. This is a guide to help you use this prayer as a pattern throughout your day—an ongoing prayer outline—enabling you to "pray without ceasing" as the Bible teaches, not just in the echoed halls of a Sunday church service.

This book is not to be read and discarded but read and practiced.

[handwritten: Saying the Rosary; Creating A Prayer!]

- Do you want to know what prayer is? *[handwritten: yes!]*
- Do you want to know how to ensure that it connects? *[handwritten: yes!]*
- Do you want to learn more about God the Father than you have ever known and more about yourself at the same time? *[handwritten: yes!]*
- Do you want to communicate more effectively with God who *[handwritten: yes!]* loved you so much that He sent His Son to die in your place?

Who do you know whose prayer life exhibits a deep intimacy with God? *[handwritten: not sure!]*

Why do you think this person has such a meaningful prayer life?

_____

_____

Living in the Lord's Prayer

I have often wondered how I could fulfill the command to pray without ceasing (1 Thess. 5:17). I instinctively knew that the Lord didn't intend for me to walk around mumbling meaningless, repetitious phrases or fingering worry beads. In fact, Jesus' instructions on prayer prohibit both meaningless repetition and anxiety.

So I have learned to begin my day with the prayer of Jesus and then hide this prayer in my heart, allowing the Holy Spirit to bring it to mind throughout the day. This has enabled me to carry on a daylong dialogue with my Father. And it has radically changed my life!

What a Difference a Prayer Makes

It is an everyday adventure to live in the power of the Lord's Prayer. Commit yourself to honor His name, ask Him to show you His activity, and immediately obey Him. Then you will see His daily provision, enjoy His full pardon, and walk daily in spiritual victory.

Your dialogue with the Father will enable you to receive constant prompting from your Father who is never surprised by your circumstances, who has the resources to provide for all you need in order to live victoriously, and who is completely trustworthy.

talking / listening

Say this in message

Talk to Him! Listen to Him! When you're struggling with a moment of temptation, talk to your Father. Run every decision through the threefold commitment: Would this act honor the Father's name? Further His kingdom? Be in obedience to His will?

I have discovered that throughout the day thoughts are constantly running through my head. Sometimes these thoughts are "self-talk" and sometimes "God-talk." Usually my self-talk is negative and defeating:

- *You dummy, why did you do that?*
- *Here we go again. I might as well give up.*
- *You'll never get all that work done.*
- *Nobody cares about me.*

Do any of those sound familiar? I'm sure you can add others to my list. I believe that our "self-talk" gives the adversary the opportunity to push us toward sin and spiritual defeat.

We need to train our hearts to listen for the Father's voice. He would never tell us such blatant lies. He will remind you that you are forgiven, you are beloved, you are strong, you can overcome evil, you can hallow His name, and you can participate in kingdom activity.

The prayer of Jesus provides a pattern for ongoing dialogue with our Dad. It provides us with the power for kingdom living.

Prayer Time

"Lord Jesus! Enroll my name among those who confess that they don't know how to pray as they should, and who especially ask You for a course of teaching in prayer. Lord! Teach me to be patient in Your school, so that You will have time to train me. I am ignorant of the wonderful privilege and power of prayer, of the need for the Holy Spirit to be the spirit of prayer. Lead me to forget my thoughts of what I think I know, and make me kneel before You in true teachableness and poverty of spirit. Fill me, Lord, with the confidence that with You for my Teacher, I will learn to pray. Amen."[1]

Signed: _____

---

[1] Andrew Murray, *With Christ in the School of Prayer* (Springdale, PA: Whitaker House, 1981), 15.

12

Viewer Guide
INTRODUCTORY SESSION

Five times in Matthew 6, Jesus tells us not to be _____.

Prayer really is about a _____ with our Father.

This is more a course on _____ change rather than _____ change.

His _____, His _____, His _____ is my passion.

Pray the prayer of Jesus anytime, _____, throughout the _____.

In those quiet moments of the day, we either participate in _____-talk

or _____-talk.

Prayer should be an ongoing, day-long _____ with your Dad
and a response from Him.

TILL YOU'RE BLUE
IN THE FACE

Three Reasons Prayer Doesn't Seem to Work

This Week's Verse
☙

While [Jesus] was praying in a certain place, after He had finished, one of His disciples said to Him, "Lord, teach us to pray just as John also taught his disciples."

—*Luke 11:1*

Remember the old joke about the guy who angrily brought his new chain saw back to the hardware store for a replacement? He stormed through the door and flung his purchase onto the front counter. It lay there, rocking slowly for a moment, bent and beat up, much of the paint chipped off and the teeth at all angles.

"I've been using this thing all day," he sputtered to the first face within shouting range, "and I haven't cut even a handful of firewood!"

The sales clerk, trying hard to remain cooperative, assured the man he'd be glad to take a look at it and do what he could. The saw was a mangled mess, all right. Trying to see if it might start in this condition seemed a foolish waste of time, but not knowing where else to begin, he took a chance and yanked hard one time on the rip cord. Sure enough, after several uncertain seconds of tired gasps and coughs, the motor somehow rattled its way to full throttle.

The red-faced customer suddenly went white, backing two full steps away from the counter in stunned confusion.

"So that's what that string was for!"

Do you ever feel your prayer life just isn't working? Check the statements that characterize your prayer life.
❑ **My prayers hit the ceiling and bounce back.**
❑ **I only pray when it's an emergency.**
❑ **I pray occasionally.**
❑ **I pray daily.**
❑ **I find it difficult to pray for a long time.**
❑ **I pray constantly.**
❑ **I want to take my prayer life to the next level.**

JOURNAL YOUR
THOUGHTS & PRAYERS

Use this thought to guide your prayers this week.

My goal is God Himself, not joy, nor peace,
Nor even blessing, but Himself, my God;
'Tis His to lead me there, not mine, but His—
"At any cost, dear Lord, by any road."[1]

Write what God is teaching you in His School of Prayer.

_____

_____

_____

_____

_____

_____

_____

_____

_____

_____

WHAT'S THE POINT OF PRAYER?

Here's the point: Before concluding that prayer doesn't "work," you need to ask yourself how you've been trying to use it.

- Have you been praying in the manner the Master taught?
- What have you been expecting prayer to do for you? And what would it look like to you if it were "working"?
- Is prayer actually supposed to "work" at all? Does it perhaps have a purpose far more significant than the shallow practicality we expect of a gas-powered lawn tool? Would it be asking far too little of prayer—and far too little of God—to demand that it, and He, perform just the way we want them to?

The answers to most of these questions are found in the sixth chapter of Matthew, in the middle of what we call the Sermon on the Mount. This teaching of Jesus, which covers three chapters of the Bible, contains instructions that are absolutely basic to understanding what it means to be a follower of Christ. Imbedded among them is a clear pattern of what God says prayer is supposed to be and do—the highest achievements that prayer is designed to fulfill.

Read Matthew 6:6 in the margin. This is how prayer works.

Check the promise contained in this verse.
❑ God likes to keep secrets. ❑ God rewards our prayers.
❑ God answers our prayers the way we want.

I have frequently heard people despair that their prayer wasn't answered. Perhaps someone they loved was sick, and they asked God for healing. Instead of getting better, the person died. They asked for one thing, but they got another. Therefore, their prayer didn't "work."

Don't misunderstand me. God does answer prayer. I know it from experience. Besides that, the Scripture is full of instances where God's people prayed, and He responded exactly as they had asked.

However, having our requests granted is not the primary goal of prayer. Prayer is not simply the process of giving God our wish list. Many times we ask for things that seem to be what we need, but we later recognize that, had we gotten them, they would have been far from our best interests. God does not exist merely to give us what we want.

> Before concluding that prayer doesn't "work," you need to ask yourself how you've been trying to use it.

> "When you pray, go into your inner room, and when you have shut your door, pray to your Father who is in secret, and your Father who sees in secret will repay you."
> —*Matthew 6:6*

16

Neither is prayer a way to alert God to our needs. As we'll see later in this Bible passage, God knows our needs even better than we do, and He needs no formal reminders about where we are and what we're up against. Prayer is in no way a squeaky wheel designed to manipulate God into remembering us.

One of the most primary purposes of prayer is to spend time in conversation with our Father. When this is our goal, we can pray at all times guaranteed that it will be rewarded.

Will it be answered the way we want? Maybe. Will it be rewarded by bringing us into the Father's presence? Absolutely.

You see, prayer is not about answers. Prayer is about reward.

I'm telling you, this understanding of the purpose of prayer will begin to revolutionize the way you approach God. It will cause you to marvel at the miraculous privilege of being able to engage in intimate conversation with the Creator of the universe. By His own grace and design, He has chosen to become our Father. He has opened the windows of heaven and allowed us to spend hours at a time in His awesome presence. In fact, as we'll continue to see throughout this book, this fellowship is hardly limited to what we usually consider our "prayer time" but is truly a constant, continuous, moment-by-moment relationship with God.

And you can enjoy His reward *every time you pray.*

> The reward of prayer is spending time in the Father's presence.

Check the best expression of the main purpose of prayer.
- ❏ **God granting our requests**
- ❏ **Making us feel better or more peaceful**
- ❏ **Spending time with our Heavenly Father**
- ❏ **Making sure God knows our needs**
- ❏ **Getting answers for our problems**

WHAT DID YOU BRING ME?

Before I accepted the presidency of Southwestern Seminary, I spent a great deal of time flying across America to lead church growth conferences. I felt all the usual guilt over leaving my family for several days each week. So like many frequent travelers, I got into the habit of always bringing home a small gift for my two girls who were still home at the time.

It happened almost without fail. As soon as my car would enter the driveway they would run from the house and greet me with the tender address, "Hi, Daddy. What did you bring us?"—their words and their hands coming out simultaneously. They would feel through my pockets, rifle through my briefcase, looking for the gift that they knew was hidden somewhere in my belongings.

After one particularly long and exhausting trip, I arrived home only to be greeted by the same predictable welcome: "What did you bring us, Daddy? What did you bring us?" But for some reason this time I just wasn't in the mood for giving presents. So instead I gave my girls a short but strong lecture.

I knew they wouldn't be able to relate entirely, but I explained how hard it was to be away from them and how tired I was every time I came home. I tried to help them imagine what it would feel like for them to be away from their family for days at a time. *Just once,* I expounded, it would mean so much to me if I knew they were simply glad to have Daddy home—not just glad to have a gift.

The following week I returned home after being out of town again, having forgotten about my lecture from the past weekend. As usual, my girls ran to meet me in the driveway. This time my youngest, Katie, leaped into my arms, gave me a big hug, and said in the sweetest voice, "I love you, Daddy. I'm so glad you're home."

Ahhhhh. My heart melted within me.

With her next breath she asked, "Now, what did you bring me?"

Well, at least it was a start. She was getting close. But my daughter's behavior made me realize that my own prayers to my heavenly Father often began like that, with little more than requests, requests, requests. I'm sure my words often sounded just like my girls' childish refrain: "What did you bring me, Daddy?"

When I finally comprehended the fact that prayer permitted me to come into the presence of my Father, to express my love for Him, to thank Him for His constant provision, and to give Him the honor He is due, I discovered a new passion for prayer.

Communicating with Him is reward enough.

Communicating with Him is reward enough. If that is the purpose, there is no such thing as an unanswered prayer.

Have you had a "What did you bring me, Daddy?" mentality in your prayer life? Circle one.

Yes   Sometimes   No

How do you feel when your loved ones treat you like an ATM machine? Circle one or more.

appreciated   used   grateful

disappointed   taken for granted   needed

other? _____

Prayer Time

Thank God for wanting a personal relationship with you. Do you need to apologize for being more concerned with what you need from Him than enjoying His presence?

_____

_____

_____

WHERE PRAYERS GO TO DIE

There *is,* however, such a thing as mistaken prayer—prayer that gets a different kind of reward.

Listen as Jesus describes three of the most common problems we often introduce into our prayer habits. They are misguided motives that ensure we'll become empty, discouraged, and spiritually out of sorts with God. And apparently these three conditions are universal across the generations, because they're just as prevalent now as they must have been in the days when Jesus first spoke these words.

The Phantom Prayer

"When you pray ...." (Matt. 6:5a)

The first reason prayer doesn't seem to connect people with God is so obvious I almost hesitate to mention it. In fact, I wouldn't bring it up at all except that it is so pervasive and widespread. You could ask just about any Christian believer if he had been guilty of it at some point in his life, and he would almost certainly confess that he had.

One of the main problems with our prayer life is we don't pray. Jesus spoke with the assumption that "when you pray" meant His followers would invest time and energy in prayer. "When you pray" says a lot more than "*if* you pray" or "whenever you *feel* like praying." But unfortunately, *"when you pray"* begins at a basic starting point that too many people rarely achieve.

A recent national survey conducted by a mainline Christian denomination indicated that 25 percent of its members admit that they *never* pray. Never! Add this to the number of people who'd be honest enough to tell you that their prayer life is sporadic or dull at best, and it doesn't take a genius to figure out that one glaring reason people are so dissatisfied with their prayer life is simple: They don't pray!

Why do you think many Christians fail to pray?
Check one or more.

❑ too busy ❑ too depressed
❑ too self-confident ❑ too guilty
❑ too comfortable ❑ too undisciplined

Is something keeping you from having a dynamic prayer life? If so, describe the problem.

_____

Think of the ridiculous analogies: A football team that never practices. An orchestra that never tunes its instruments. A farmer who never plants any crops. A sales rep who never calls on his clients. An artist who never buys herself any paint. Never to do something is the worst way to get any better at it.

But we're too busy, we say. Our schedules stay overlapped with nonstop activities that keep us about 2 days and 10 minutes behind all the time. Although our demands stressfully require us to keep the plates spinning constantly, somehow the power stays on, the bills get paid, and the dog gets fed whether we pray or not, so ... we don't. However, we still expect prayer to work on demand when the wheels come off or the kids get sick, when we resort to pleading with a God we largely ignore during the normal routine of life.

Prayerlessness makes absolutely no sense, yet just about all of us have been guilty of it and of foolishly putting the blame on God for not answering prayers we never pray.

Read the following Scriptures and draw lines to connect these important principles of prayerfulness.

Never to do something is the worst way to get any better at it.

Luke 6:12   Pray continually in all circumstances.
Acts 1:14   Pray for others.
Romans 1:9–10   Pray privately.
1 Thessalonians 5:16-17   Pray with others.

Prayer Time

Disciples of Jesus not only pray, they pray continuously. Listen for God's whisper to direct you in the things you should pray for throughout the day. Ask God to teach you how to "pray without ceasing" during this study.

_____

_____

_____

The Phony Prayer

Soon after I dedicated my life to the ministry, I was visiting my dad's church with my wife-to-be. During the service Dad called on me, his "preacher boy," to deliver the morning prayer. Suddenly feeling myself the focus of attention, I took a deep breath, intoned my best preacher's voice, and wowed the crowd with all the spiritual jargon and theological rhetoric I knew. After I finally reached the "amen" and took my seat, my fiancé, Paula, leaned over and whispered six sobering words in my ear: "Who were you trying to impress?" I got the message.

But isn't that the way we do it? We preachers may be the worst, using public prayer for everything from reinforcing the points of our sermon to communicating announcements. I shudder to think of how many times I've been complimented for saying a beautiful prayer and took it as a personal accomplishment, how many times I have been more concerned with the way I framed my words than with whether I was honestly communicating with my Father.

> "When you pray, you are not to be as the hypocrites; for they love to stand and pray in the synagogues and on the street corners, in order to be seen by men. Truly I say to you, they have their reward in full."
>
> —*Matthew 6:5*

When asked to pray in public, do you …(Check one or more.)
❑ **Feel self-conscious?**
❑ **Change your vocabulary or tone of voice?**
❑ **Seem concerned with what people will think of your prayer?**
❑ **Feel a desire to impress others?**
❑ **Struggle with what to say?**
❑ **Pray like you would in private?**

During the time Jesus was teaching, things were no different. To be asked to pray in the synagogue service in first-century Palestine was a mark of distinction. Though prayers were not normally practiced "on the street corners," as the verse says, people who were so inclined probably made a habit of observing their afternoon prayer in a public place—where they could be observed as well.

Whatever the case, their driving desire was certainly not to commune with God but to be seen and heard, admired and appreciated. They delighted at the sound of their own voices and the hearty approval of their colleagues.

But Jesus had a succinct response to such showboating—one little phrase that kind of says it all, that takes all the air out of phony praying. He said, "They have their reward."

If you want recognition, good. Take it.

If you want other people's approval, fine. Enjoy it.

If you want us to say you're wonderful, OK. You're wonderful.

Read the following Scriptures and identify what they tell us about Jesus' prayer life. Write your response on the line.

   Mark 1:35   Mark 6:46–47   Luke 5:15–16   Luke 9:18

Jesus _____

Prayer Time

If your prayers primarily have been said around the dinner table or at church, tell God that you desire times of prayer with Him alone in your private place.

_____

_____

_____

Notice the difference in rewards for those who prefer the inner room to the public square, who prefer the closed door to the open display. In the case of the hypocrites, their full reward comes from the crowd, from their friends, in some ways even from themselves—the kind of reward that feels good for a moment but is never enough to satisfy the endless demands of pride. For the humble and pure in heart, however, the reward of prayer comes from God Himself "who sees what is done in secret"—the precious reward of being in the glorious presence of the Father. His reward is always enough.

Does this mean we should never pray in public? Of course not. Jesus Himself prayed publicly when He blessed the five loaves and two fish before feeding more than five thousand people with them. In the Book of Acts the early church prayed in public on several occasions.

The problem is not public prayer but praying for effect. Whether in public or in private, we can and should pray with the singular desire of communicating with our Father and receiving the reward of His presence.

The Frivolous Prayer

To the first-century Greeks and Romans, prayer had both its formal and its magical sides. Since the pagan gods of their religious mythology each controlled some aspect of nature—but couldn't control their own behavior—prayer was the butter that greased the palms of the pantheon. In case the gods didn't hear or remember it the first time, these pagan worshipers would pray the same prayer again and again to make sure they had gotten some heavenly attention, to convince whichever god they wanted that this petition was worth rewarding.

This approach differs from the idea of *perseverance* in prayer, which Jesus later applauds and encourages. To these Gentiles, prayers carried their own magical power. Therefore, it was not merely an issue of repetition but one of repeating a precise formula or incantation that would gain the favor of a god. They thought the more frequently and fervently they spoke these words, the more powerful and effective their prayer became.

Today we would call this a mantra, like the New Age advocate's repeating of a certain phrase or the Muslim repetition of the Shahada. Jesus called it "meaningless repetition." The actual Greek word for this is *battalogeo.* If you try to pronounce it, you'll notice its similarity to the English term *babbling.* He may have used this term to underline the foolishness of praying in such a singsong manner.

Check the following questions that apply to you.

❏ Do you ever catch yourself daydreaming while you are in the middle of your prayer time?

❏ Do you ever pray with your mind in neutral, virtually unaware of the words you're thinking or speaking?

❏ Do you ever mouth the words of a hymn but think nothing of what you're singing?

❏ When you close a prayer "in Jesus' name," are you merely repeating a phrase or are you truly focusing on the One who has made a way for you to approach the throne?

> "When you are praying, do not use meaningless repetition, as the Gentiles do, for they suppose that they will be heard for their many words."
>
> —*Matthew 6:7*

Instead of frivolous prayers, God wants us to pray fervently, to cry out to Him in total dependence. An Old Testament story describes the difference between those who seek to get God's attention and those who seek God's heart.

First Kings 18 records the spiritual showdown between Elijah, the prophet of God, and 450 pagan prophets of the god Baal. The contest involved two altars—one piled high with wood and sacrifice and the other soaked with not one but 12 huge tubs of water until the runoff puddled up in a trench around the base. The question? Whose god would hear the prayers of his people and send down fire to lick up the waiting sacrifice?

The Baal worshipers went first, crying out from morning till noon, pleading, begging, running around, imploring their god to send even a spark to ignite this famine-dried tinderbox into a flame for his glory.

Elijah couldn't resist. He shouted above the din. "Either he is occupied or gone aside, or is on a journey, or perhaps he is asleep and needs to be awakened" (1 Kings 18:27).

Such coaching and encouragement from the other side simply heightened their frenzied passion, so they carried on till nearly dark—screaming, pounding the ground, cutting themselves to invoke the favor of their deity. Finally their songs and chants dissolved into silence. Flies buzzed around the now rotting carcass on the altar. They had prayed up a storm—you certainly couldn't question their zeal—but they had gotten nothing in return.

Slowly Elijah approached the waterlogged altar he had made and lifted a prayer to the one true God of heaven. In a flash, fire fell from the sky and not only consumed the dripping ox and firewood but even the rocks, the dirt, and every drop of water that had pooled underneath.

Why would God put a story like this in the Bible? It teaches us that long prayers, desperate pleading, and mechanical rantings are not required to request help from our Father. This One who treasures our intimate conversations with Him and knows what we need before we ask is not testing our faith with word counts and endurance records. Yes, there is a certain kind of shallow reward inherent in that, but (again) it's one that we give ourselves.

God's reward is reserved for those who seek His heart, not His attention.

God's reward is reserved for those who seek His heart, not His attention.

Read the Scriptures on the following page and describe the prayers that God desires. Write your response in the space provided.

Psalm 18:6   Micah 7:7   Luke 18:1-7   Luke 22:44

One evening when our oldest daughter, Kristina, was just a small child, I asked her to pray the blessing before dinner. Like most parents we had taught her several of the childhood prayers to be prayed at meals and at bedtime. But this particular night she got her memorized prayers mixed up and instead of "God is great, God is good," she bowed her head and began to pray, "Now I lay me down to sleep." Sheepishly, she cracked one eyelid open to see if anyone else was paying attention. When she noticed that I had looked up and was observing her with a curious stare, she grinned and said, "Oops!"

All words and no heart. Gets us nowhere every time.

Read the verses below and fill in the blank to describe the action that God wants from us.

2 Chronicles 15:2   Psalm 119:2   Luke 12:31   Hebrews 11:6

_____ **the Lord.**

Prayer is a precious privilege that allows us to have direct dialogue with the Father. We can never approach it with casual indifference or blank-check repetition and expect to get the reward He graciously offers. We must seek the Lord.

THE LORD'S PRAYER

While thousands of books, like this one, have been written on prayer, the Model Prayer of Jesus contains approximately 70 words. Perhaps no prayer has been more widely abused and mindlessly repeated than the Lord's Prayer. You hear it prayed at open assemblies where Christians and non-Christians alike are instructed to say or repeat it.

You hear it mumbled in a church service, usually with little understanding of what we're actually promising or asking of God. Even TV and movie characters have been known to resort to it when things look

bleak and personal charm has failed to solve their problems.
- Often it's prayed only in public (for effect).
- Often it's prayed without thinking (vain repetition).
- And more often, I suspect, it's not prayed at all (prayerlessness).

It is susceptible to all three mistakes of mishandled prayer.

In this book I want you to see the Lord's Prayer, not as a memorized mantra, but as a *pattern* you can use at all times and in all situations to express prayers to God that connect and communicate.

In your own Bible read the Model Prayer in Matthew 6:9-13. Keep this page open as you read the following outline.

Prayer is a precious privilege that allows us to have direct dialogue with the Father.

THE LORD'S PRAYER
MATTHEW 6:9-13

The Three-Part Address

Our	Stresses community
Father	Stresses relationship
Who is in heaven	Stresses authority

The Three-Part Commitment

Hallowed be Your name	Commitment to holiness
Your kingdom come	Commitment to participation
Your will be done	Commitment to obedience

The Three-Part Petition

Daily bread	Trust for physical provision
Forgiveness of debts	Trust for cleansing from sin
Deliverance from evil	Trust for power over temptation

The Three-Part Benediction

Yours is the kingdom	Focuses on His rule
The power	Focuses on His sufficiency
The glory	Focuses on His presence

Notice the obvious progression of the prayer—from praise, to promises, to petitions, to parting reminders. Jesus' prayer breaks into even series of three, making it easy to use and remember.

When we use this pattern, prayer becomes what Jesus intended it to be: a conscious, volitional opening of our lives to God as we invite Him to accomplish His purpose in and through us. It enables us to seek His resources unselfishly as we commit ourselves to the advancement of His kingdom.

The effectiveness of our prayer life does not depend on the amount of our faith. Such a misunderstanding subtly teaches that our works are a necessary, added ingredient to God's grace. Instead, the effectiveness of our prayer depends on God, who gives us faith in order to lead us to total dependence on Him. This faith helps us continually bear in mind both the promise and warning of Jesus in John 15:5.

The Lord's Prayer "works." It connects. It will literally change your life. That's why this study is subtitled "Living the Lord's Prayer."

Jesus taught the Model Prayer so that His disciples would not only know how to pray but would also be able to teach others to pray.

"I am the vine, you are the branches; he who abides in Me, and I in him, he bears much fruit; for apart from Me you can do nothing."
—*John 15:5*

Do you feel an obligation to help others around you learn to pray more effectively? (circle)   Yes   No

Who in your family could you teach this outline of the Lord's prayer?

_____   _____

_____   _____

To whom could you teach this outline at work? _____

Which of your friends could profit from learning how to

pray like Jesus? _____

Do you feel you would have to be an "expert" in prayer in order to share with someone else what you are learning about prayer? If so, rejoice that your author did not choose to wait! Sharing with others is a great reinforcement to your own learning.

Prayer Time

Tell God a new thought or action that you gleaned from your reading of the Lord's Prayer today. Ask Him to reveal the name of one or more persons with whom you can share that truth this week.

_____

_____

_____

READY TO GO?

One of my church members used to take me on short trips in his private plane. He was an accomplished, expert pilot. Yet every time before taxiing down the runway, he would always go through the same preflight checklist: Do a thorough walk around the plane to look for damage, drain the water from the fuel tank, turn the wheel to ensure good wing movement, check the rudder pedals, set the radios.

Once as we were preparing for takeoff, I remember asking him if—as flawless and professional as he was at flying—he always had to take the time to check off these most basic, nearly automatic requirements. I'll never forget his reply: "You'd better hope that I do." Even with all his experience, the only safe and practical way to begin flying an airplane was always, without fail, to work through his checklist.

Jesus has given us our checklist. No matter how many hours we've racked up behind the prayer wheel, we never outgrow our need to follow His commands. So take a seat with me. We're preparing to fly.

Traveling Mercies

In my job I travel a great deal. I have never been a patient person by nature, so for a long time I was one of those somewhat obnoxious and anxious travelers that you hate to stand behind in line. I wanted to know why the plane was late and when I might expect it to leave. But no matter how hard I complained, I almost always received one of those blank stares which indicated that the individual behind the desk knew no more about the problem with the plane than I did.

Truth was, it really didn't matter what was wrong with the plane; I couldn't fix it, and all of my anxiety was not going to advance the departure time a single minute. I also realized that my complaints and arguments were basically "me-centered" and not "God-centered."

God began to show me what my behavior was conveying. It communicated a lack of trust in His character. It assumed I knew more about the situation than He did. It never dawned on me that God in His omniscience already knew that the plane was going to be late before I even arrived at the airport. This was no surprise to Him! It had never crossed my mind that His plan for me might have included kingdom activity right there in the airport lobby.

Be anxious for nothing, but in everything by prayer and supplication with thanksgiving let your requests be made known to God.

—*Philippians 4:6*

I also realized that my rude behavior was inappropriate for one who bore His name. In truth my behavior profaned His name and negatively impacted my witness. After my rude and anxious response, it would have been next to impossible for me to effectively minister to anyone in the airport who had observed my behavior. Further, my anxiety directly disobeyed God's command in Philippians 4:6.

So among other things, the prayer of Jesus as an outline for dialogue with the Father is making me a more patient traveler. It is changing my life, and I believe it can change yours. When I walk into the airport today, I breathe a simple prayer. "Lord, don't let my behavior bring any harm to your name." Instantly my attitude changes and my blood pressure goes down. Sometimes I find myself smiling. I can hardly wait to see what God is about to reveal to me!

When I know that my plane is delayed, I remember that my Father knows my circumstances and that He cares for me. So I breathe the second part of the prayer. "Lord, help me see your kingdom activity here in the lobby while I wait for the next flight."

Then I make the final commitment—"Whatever you ask me to do the answer is 'yes.' "

Now I'm ready to fly.

---

[1] F. Brook, as quoted in Oswald Chambers, *Christian Disciplines* (Grand Rapids: Discovery House Publishers, 1995), 66.

Viewer Guide
SESSION ONE

The issue of prayer is not a laundry list of "me and mine" but rather

_____ and _____.

Three types of mistaken prayers mentioned in Matthew 5 and 6:

1. The _____ Prayer

_____

2. The _____ Prayer

_____

3. The _____ Prayer

_____

All of these prayers are inadequate because they ignore the _____ of prayer.

Prayer is about a relationship with our _____.

Outline of the prayer of Jesus

1. A _____

2. C _____

3. P _____

4. B _____

GOD AND THE FAMILY TREE

Three Realities from the Prayer of Jesus

This Week's Verse
♒

"Pray, then, in this way:
'Our Father who
art in heaven.'"
—*Matthew 6:9*

I'm the kind of person who likes to think out loud. Whenever I have an important decision to make, a sermon to preach, or a difficult discussion to conduct with someone, I usually prepare by talking myself through it—while I'm driving home in the car, sitting at my desk, or pacing in the living room. *How should I phrase this or that? What do I really want to say? Which things need to be stated right up front—right at the beginning?*

You've probably done that. Let's say you have an uncomfortable phone call to make—maybe to ask about a job you interviewed for two weeks ago but haven't heard a word from since. Perhaps a client is nearly six months late paying you, a fellow church member misunderstood something you said, or you've just learned that a dear friend who lives in another state has been diagnosed with cancer.

Before you make that call, because it's so important, you obviously will spend some time thinking about what you're going to say. And in particular you'll think about how you want to *begin* the conversation. Perhaps you've even picked up the phone a time or two, dialed half the number, then hung up because you just weren't ready yet.

The way you address someone matters. First things first. *Our Father in heaven ...*

JOURNAL YOUR
THOUGHTS & PRAYERS

Use these questions to guide your prayers this week:

• How did you pray for the larger community of believers this week?
• How did you address God in your prayers?

Write what God is teaching you in His School of Prayer.

_____

_____

_____

_____

_____

_____

_____

_____

_____

WHAT A PRIVILEGE IT IS TO BE HERE

Place an X on the scale to indicate the likelihood that the average person would have the opportunity to spend quality time with the President of the United States.

You've got to be kidding!   **I'm there!**

For most of us, the President is unapproachable. But if someone you knew had an "in" with the President, he could set up an appointment. I have a picture taken with George Bush, the father, and one with George Bush, the son. I am proud of both pictures. They are displayed in my den. Truth is, I don't actually "know" either of them, and they would have no reason to know me. I happened to be in the right place at the right time and they were gracious enough to allow me to have a picture taken.

Perhaps you have a picture of yourself with some celebrity. Have you ever stood in line to have your picture made with someone famous? Someone you admire? Perhaps we are inclined to think that our proximity or relationship with a powerful person gives us a certain measure of power or of access. We like to think we have access to powerful people.

Thanks to Christ, we can spend time with the Creator of the universe. Before we separate the first two words of the Lord's Prayer and look at each of them individually, let's first take a look at both of them together and experience the wonder of "Our Father." Prayer is the privilege of communication between a child and the Father. It's not a human right. Not a nonnegotiable demand. It's a privilege—a privilege made possible only by the redemptive work of Jesus Christ.

Read Hebrews 10:19-20. What has Christ done for us?

_____

_____

We have confidence to enter the Most Holy Place by the blood of Jesus, by a new and living way opened for us through the curtain, that is, his body.
—*Hebrews 10:19-20, NIV*

We should never go into the presence of God without remembering that we enter by virtue of Jesus' death on the cross, His resurrection from the grave, and His ascension into heaven.

That's why we pray "in Jesus' name." Those words *mean* something. They are not the equivalent of a stamp on a letter that guarantees delivery just because we happen to put it there. Our postage was paid at a demanding price before there was ever a "Dear God" at the top. We may not say the words *"in Jesus' name"* till the end of our prayer, but praying in His name should be the attitude of our heart from the beginning.

Yet there's even more to it than that. Jesus is not merely the doorkeeper. He is not an usher who points down the hallway and tells us it's OK to go in and see the Father—though that would be unbelievable enough. The Bible says that He actually goes in with us, praying for us (see Heb. 7:25).

The Holy Spirit also—the third member of the Trinity—joins us as we enter the presence of the Father (see Rom. 8:26).

You see, prayer is not something we naturally know how to do. That's why the disciples had to ask Jesus to teach them to pray. That's why all of us who have struggled with prayer continue to come back to Him, needing help, needing direction.

That's also why He has given us the example of the Lord's Prayer. That's why He has entered the holy place with the sacrifice of His perfect obedience and continues to stand at the right hand of the Father praying on our behalf. That's why the Holy Spirit Himself also intercedes for us, conforming our prayers to the flawless will of God.

Every time you pray "Our Father," you are praying a relational prayer that is absolutely assured of placing you in the holy, awesome, glorious presence of God. But you are also reminding yourself that this privilege of prayer is not a matter to be taken lightly. It cost Christ everything, and it has given us more than we could ever deserve.

> He is able also to save forever those who draw near to God through Him, since He always lives to make intercession for them.
> —*Hebrews 7:25*

> In the same way the Spirit also helps our weakness; for we do not know how to pray as we should, but the Spirit Himself intercedes for us with groanings too deep for words.
> —*Romans 8:26*

Have you been guilty of taking prayer lightly? Circle the words that describe how you feel when you think of the price Jesus paid for our privilege of prayer.

humbled   angry   ungrateful

unworthy   blessed   other?_____

The Community Context

Now, back to the first word—*"our."* Have you ever noticed that all of the first person pronouns in the Lord's Prayer are plural?

- *Our* Father
- *Our* daily bread
- *Our* debts and our debtors
- Lead *us* not into temptation
- Deliver *us* from evil

Isn't that something? I don't know what other conclusion to draw from that except this: According to Jesus, *prayer should always remind us that we are part of a larger community of believers.* Even though we do most of our praying alone, we should continually recognize that we live and function in a much bigger box than our prayer closets.

We may have a hard time thinking in those terms today, considering how isolated and individualistic our modern culture has become. But research has shown that even being allowed to recite the Lord's Prayer at all in the early church was a privilege reserved only for those who were fully recognized members. At their first communion following baptism, new believers were allowed for the first time to join in praying what was then known as the "disciple's prayer." And only then were they instructed to pray it daily—a mark that identified them as a part of the broader Christian community.[1] That generation understood the concept of community.

Think about how many times you say "I," "me" or "my" in your average prayer. If you replaced all those terms with "our," how would the change affect your prayers?

_____

_____

We're All in This Together

What does this idea of "community" mean today?

It means we should be praying for our Christian friends. Each of us knows certain individuals at church, in our Sunday school class, in our

> Prayer should always remind us that we are part of a larger community of believers.

family, in our neighborhood who are experiencing difficult situations in life. Marriage problems, health concerns, financial worries, job unrest. And we, as a part of the fellowship of Christian believers, should constantly pray for one another. This serves a twin objective: First, it enables us to care for other people, uniting with them in turning to God and God alone for help and healing, encouraging both them and us to maintain a humble perspective that lets us submit not just our dreams but even our sufferings into His divine plans. And second, it helps us take our minds off ourselves.

In fact, among the most noticeable changes you'll see in your prayer life as you begin using the Lord's Prayer as a pattern is this: You'll find yourself praying about others' needs *more* and your own needs less—and yet finding your personal needs met more fully than ever before. It's simply part of what happens when you begin thinking the way God thinks and seeking His kingdom above your own.

Even our personal needs become opportunities to intercede. As you pray in the context of community, even the personal requests and concerns you share with the Father can make you mindful of others who are enduring the same situations, "knowing that the same experiences of suffering are being accomplished by your brethren who are in the world" (1 Pet. 5:9). You're not the only one facing your present batch of troubles, temptations, and trials. And even though you may not know anyone by name who fits that current description, you can be sure that God knows someone, somewhere, who needs to know He cares. Consciously pray for them even as you pray for yourself.

> You'll find yourself praying about others' needs more and your own needs less.

List one of your current prayer concerns. _____
Do you know someone experiencing a similar difficulty?
❏ **Yes**   ❏ **No**   **If so, pause now and pray for that individual.**

Likewise, God's revealed truth to you should not become an end in itself. Many times God answers our prayers with a Bible verse, a passing thought, a moving message from a sermon, or a song. And often we tend to receive that word for ourselves without thinking how it might relate to others. God's truths, however, are usually more of an investment than a handout—timeless wisdom that is able not only to comfort or correct us but also to be communicated through us to others. When you rise up from prayer with a specific peace and empowerment from the Lord, don't keep it to yourself. Ask God to show you someone else who

> God's truths are usually more of an investment than a handout.

37

needs a similar encouragement, and be watching for Him to show you where to share it to keep His investment growing.

We should remember those who are being persecuted for their faith. For most of us, Christian faith costs little in terms of safety, freedom, and employment. But for millions today—literally millions around the globe—being a Christian comes at a staggeringly high price. According to current estimates from the U.S. State Department, Christians today suffer countless discriminations and atrocities in more than 60 countries—more than any other religious group in the world. These are our brothers and sisters in Christ, forced for no other reason than their faith to endure torture, imprisonment, harassment, and even death. By praying for them and their families to be spared such horrors and by asking God to preserve their bold witness for Christ without fear, we participate in their sufferings and experience the reward of walking in God's power ourselves. We also ask God to help them see their persecutions as blessings in disguise, "in the same way they persecuted the prophets who were before you" (Matt. 5:12).

We should pray for those in all areas of life and ministry. Professional ministers and missionaries are not the only people serving Christ with their life's work, though these people need and depend on God as He works through our prayers. We should also stay in prayer for those making an impact for God's kingdom outside the four walls of the church—in the statehouse and the schoolroom, on the court bench and at the car plant, in the home place and at the office park. All of these are viable mission fields where God is using real people to make a real difference every day, and your prayers can play a role in making them want to get up in the morning and meet the day head-on.

In the following Scriptures, identify on whose behalf each is praying.

Moses (Numbers 12:10-13) _____

Samuel (1 Samuel 7:5-6) _____

Man of God (1 Kings 13:6) _____

We are to pray not only for family members but also for governmental leaders and our nation. The Model Prayer teaches us to pray for others as well as pray for our own needs.

Prayer Time

Identify one person in each of the following categories and pray for their needs.

Christian leaders in government_____

Christian leaders in business _____

Christian leaders in public schools _____

Church leaders _____

Christians persecuted for their faith _____

When our prayers rarely escape the tight confines of our own homes, bills, and daily bread, then our prayers are too small. Why? Because we live, pray, and worship in the midst of an enormous band of believers— the ones we know by name and the millions more who share our Lord even if not our street address.

We pray for them because they need us. They pray for us because we need them. We grow larger each day by the company we keep in our prayer closets.

The Family Connection

On to the second word, *"Father."*

From our standpoint in history, from a culture that has replaced formality with chat rooms and casual day, we're not surprised to hear Jesus begin His prayer addressing the God of heaven by the name "Father." But to the Jews of Jesus' day, this intimate, personal way of approaching God was unheard of.

In the Old Testament, God is seldom spoken of as Father. Nonetheless, several references instruct us.

How do the following Old Testament writers speak of God?

Isaiah 63:16 _____

Jeremiah 3:19-20 _____

Malachi 1:6 _____

In the minds of the first–century Jews, there was more reverent fear and distance when they thought of God. They would not have dared to address Him with such an air of familiarity as "Father." Yet Jesus prayed like this regularly. In fact, every one of His prayers that are recorded in the Bible (except one)[2] begins with Him saying, "Father …"

Even a cursory reading of the Gospel of John will illustrate the significance of Jesus' use of the term "Father" and the reaction of His Jewish opponents. In John 5 we find the story of Jesus healing a man on the Sabbath. Jesus' simple response to their persecution—"My Father is working until now, and I Myself am working" (v. 17). Verse 18 includes a candid observation. "For this cause therefore the Jews were seeking all the more to kill Him, because He not only was breaking the Sabbath, but also was calling God His own Father, making Himself equal with God." Jesus' response was simple and direct. He indicated that He has done nothing of Himself, He had only participated in what He had seen His Father doing. Then He declared that the Father loves the Son and shows Him all that He is doing.

In John 6:32-33 Jesus declared that it was not their hero Moses who gave them bread from heaven (a reference to the manna). His Father gave them true bread. In John 8 we find His opponents boasting about their relationship to Abraham their father. Jesus responded, "I speak the things which I have seen with My Father …" (v. 38). I think you get the picture.

We see this relationship most clearly, perhaps, in Jesus' agonizing prayer from the garden of Gethsemane the night of His capture before the day of His death. His closest friends, unable to sense the gravity of the moment, had fallen asleep. Read Mark 14:35-36 in the margin.

"Abba! Father!" You probably know that many scholars believe the Aramaic word Abba equates to the affectionate name we know today as Daddy. Understand this as the radical statement it was—and is! I think that the uniqueness of addressing God as "Father" may not have

He went a little beyond them, and fell to the ground, and began to pray that if it were possible, the hour might pass Him by. And He was saying, "Abba! Father! All things are possible for Thee; remove this cup from Me; yet not what I will, but what Thou wilt."

—*Mark 14:35-36*

fully penetrated our consciousness. Can you imagine that the Creator of the entire universe has given you permission to address Him with the familiar and familial term, "Father"?

Jesus spoke to His Father the way we would speak to our dads—in the tender, trusting, respectful manner you know is good, even if it doesn't mirror your own personal experience with your earthly father. He talked to Him simply, openly, honestly, securely, without any reservation or hesitation.

And by teaching His disciples to pray in this way, Jesus was authorizing them to share His sonship, to relate to the sovereign God of the universe with the intimacy of a child climbing up in his daddy's lap, throwing his arms around his neck, and telling him, "I love You."

This is not irreverence; it is relationship. And to the first-century mind, it was absolutely revolutionary. The apostle Paul was astounded by it. He wrote about it to the church in Rome (see Rom. 8:15).

That prayer of Jesus had revolutionized Paul's praying. The same God who held sway over the course of history had given him permission to call Him "Daddy."

Has any so-called god ever shown such love?

> You have not received a spirit of slavery leading to fear again, but you have received a spirit of adoption as sons by which we cry out, "Abba! Father!"
> —*Romans 8:15*

Read Isaiah 64:8. Because God is our Father, how should we think of ourselves? Check one.
❑ **as a beautiful vase**
❑ **as clay ready to be molded**
❑ **as everyday dishes**

I am both humbled and encouraged by the thought that I can have daily and constant access to my Heavenly Father who is Creator and Sustainer of all things. Because of my personal relationship with His Son, I can address Him as "Abba, Father," and have constant access to Him. Further, He has promised to show me what He is doing because He loves me. This thought not only creates a sense of awe, it creates in me a desire to communicate with my "Dad" throughout the day.

We can hear the same sense of awe in Paul's voice. "For this reason, I bow my knees before the Father, from whom every family in heaven and on earth derives its name" (Eph. 3:14-15). I can pray to the Father of all, the Creator of the universe, the Lord of all, and I can call Him "Father."

> O Lord, Thou art
> our Father,
> We are the clay, and
> Thou our potter;
> And all of us are the
> work of Thy hand.
> —*Isaiah 64:8*

DADDY'S GIRLS

My girls are grown now. All three are off and married, but even now, when I think about them or hear one of their voices on the phone, I get a lump in my throat. I love them so much.

I can't imagine a time when I would be too busy to help them or would brush them off if they needed something from me. I rejoice in their accomplishments, support them in their dreams and endeavors, and take a hundred times more pleasure in their successes than in any of my own.

I keep their pictures in my wallet. I know their mailing addresses and phone numbers in my head. If you were to visit my office today, you would see a crayon-etched diploma inscribed to the "World's Best Dad" hanging right along with the official university diplomas and other awards I have received.

When my girls hurt, I feel their pain. When they cry, I weep right along with them. When they struggle, I lie awake at night thinking about them. Is there any doubt our Father will do any less? Doesn't this knowledge alone make you want to come into His presence and stay there throughout the day?

Prayer Time

Imagine that God has invited you to slip up into His lap. Feel His arms around you. What would you talk about?

_____

_____

_____

Talk to Him right now. Tell your Heavenly Father how much you love Him.

Daddy's Discipline

A father's love is not always a broad smile and an open hand. Sometimes—if his love is to be true love—it may be a knowing, penetrating look. It may be a stern tone of voice. Or it may be the disciplining finger of authority.

Yes, we should begin our prayers wrapped in the warm embrace of a Father who cares for us more deeply than anyone in this world, but we should also use the first moments of our prayer time to hear His words of warning.

We are sinners. We make many mistakes. Through our words, attitudes, and motives, we many times—even if unintentionally—bring dishonor on the very Christ we claim to worship. If our Father were unwilling to bring these matters to mind, we would rarely find a reason to correct them. And if He allowed us to continue on our wayward path, afraid He might offend us, we would find ourselves drifting further away from the blessed life He offers (see Heb. 12:7-10).

For each Scripture, identify the action that God honors in prayer.

James 4:10 _____

1 John 1:9 _____

1 John 3:22 _____

Being a child of God comes with both privileges and responsibilities—a sort of family accountability. To address Him as Father not only reminds us that we are welcome at His side but that we are also willing to receive His correction as one of the gifts fathers give to their kids.

Already at this early point in the prayer we find the need to confess our faults, open our hearts, and invite the revealing searchlight of His wisdom to show us where we are straying. It is here that we repent of our sins, not wanting to squander another moment of our lives resisting the touch of His hand upon our face or hoping He didn't see what we did last night when no one was looking.

God disciplines His children, but it is always in love. He is "our Father" and we are His children.

God deals with you as with sons; for what son is there whom his father does not discipline? But if you are without discipline, of which all have become partakers, then you are illegitimate children and not sons. Furthermore, we had earthly fathers to discipline us, and we respected them; shall we not much rather be subject to the Father of spirits, and live? For they disciplined us for a short time as seemed best to them, but He disciplines us for our good, that we may share His holiness.

—*Hebrews 12:7-10*

How would you describe your response to God's discipline?

❏ I'm not aware of God's discipline.

❏ I often experience God's discipline.

❏ Usually, God's discipline makes me angry.

❏ As a result of God's discipline, I grow as a Christian.

In the Koran, the sacred writings of Islam, there are 99 words for God but not one of them refers to God as Father or love. Islam rejects the idea that humanity can have a relationship with God. For Muslims, God is unknowable and impersonal. While they believe in an afterlife, people (predominately men) will be allowed to go to paradise, not heaven. Heaven is only for God and His angels. The life and teachings of Jesus describe God as a loving Father who desires an intimate relationship with us.

> When was the last time you called just to say, "I love you"?

When was the last time you called just to say, "I love you"?

THE SOVEREIGN PROVISION

> Our God is in the
> heavens;
> He does whatever
> He pleases.
> —*Psalm 115:3*

The final phrase of the three-part address—"Our Father *who art in heaven*"—focuses our attention on God's ability to know and care for every detail of our lives. The issue is not so much about His location as it is about His authority, not so much about where He lives as it is about what He can do.

So a fair question to ask at this point is: If God knows everything, and if God can do anything, and if, as the Scripture says, "your Father knows what you need, before you ask Him" (Matt. 6:8), then what's the point in praying at all?

Ask Away

First, God commands us to ask. Jesus told two parables that illustrate this point. One was about an unexpected guest who dropped in on a man and his family one night, catching them without enough food in the house to set before him. His host, though he knew the hour was late, crept out at midnight to the home of a friend, knocked on the door, and asked him for three loaves of bread. Roused from sleep, the neighbor at first showed reluctance to get out of bed, but—Jesus finishes the story—"even though he will not get up and give him anything because he is his friend, yet because of his persistence he will get up and give him as much as he needs" (Luke 11:8).

The second parable tells the story of a widow who repeatedly appealed to a local judge for legal protection against someone who was threatening her. For a good while the judge who did not fear God and did not respect man continued to put her off and dismiss her claim. But at last he relented. " ' "lest by continually coming she wear me out" ' " (Luke 18:5).

It's clear, then, that Jesus has instructed us not only to ask but to persist in asking (see Matt. 7:7-8).

The characters in Jesus' stories were in need, but they knew exactly where to go for help. Were it not for the humble task of asking, the man would have had to send his tired guest to bed hungry. Were it not for the courage of daily perseverance, the widow might have lost all her possessions to a ruthless opponent. They both exercised their dependence on one who had the power and authority to help them, and they both received as much as they needed from his hand.

Since we know that our Father gives good gifts to His children, we should continue to pray, even when we don't get an answer the first day, so that we are not tempted to try to get our needs met somewhere else.

> "Ask, and it shall be given to you; seek, and you shall find; knock, and it shall be opened to you. For everyone who asks receives, and he who seeks finds, and to him who knocks it shall be opened."
> —*Matthew 7:7-8*

What do these tell us about our Heavenly Father's nature or character?

1 Chronicles 29:10-13 _____

Psalm 100:5 _____

1 John 4:7-8_____

How does God's nature affect who or what you bring to Him in prayer?

_____

_____

Prayer Time

As you pray, use the following names for God to express your reverence and adoration of Him.

El Shaddai, pronounced El Sha-die, means *Almighty God.* We can accomplish nothing in our own strength, but He has abundant resources to enable us to do all that He requires.

Adonai, pronounced A-doe-nie, means *Lord.* He is Lord or master of the universe. You can know that He is sufficient. Therefore, you can freely surrender your life and your day to Him as your Lord.

Jehovah Shammah, pronounced, Ja-hoe-vah Sham-mah, means *the Lord is there.* When you feel alone and need to sense His presence, you can call upon Him as *Jehovah Shammah.*

_____

_____

_____

Maintain Your Focus

The second reason for praying to God—who already knows what we need before we ask Him—is to focus not on our *needs* but on our *Provider.* If you look carefully at the Lord's Prayer, you will notice that the overwhelming focus is always on the Father and His kingdom, not on me and mine.

In fact, all of the prayers of Jesus carry this unselfish tone and emphasis. As I began to evaluate my own prayer life under this lens, which totally reverses the way we commonly think and act, I made a painful discovery: Much of my praying had become *me-centered.*

Prayer must be *God-centered* and *kingdom-focused.* In order to approach God properly, we must be constantly looking at Him and not at our needs. We can spend so much time worrying about our own needs and wants and wishes that we rarely look beyond them to the One who has promised to provide all our needs "according to His riches in glory in Christ Jesus" (Phil. 4:19).

Unlike us human fathers, whose desire to give good gifts to our children is tempered by a limited amount of ability and resources, the Scripture teaches that our Father owns "the cattle on a thousand hills" (Ps. 50:10) and that He is "able to do exceeding abundantly beyond all that we ask or think" (Eph. 3:20). There is no shortage of supply that stops the love of God from showering us with everything we need in order to live as He wants us to.

This doesn't mean that we are not to ask and receive; it just means we are to seek *Him* instead of His *blessings*. Read about the miracle that happens in Matthew 6:32-33.

If our highest priority is to seek our Father and His righteousness, how does that affect how we:

Invest our time?_____

Invest our money?_____

Invest in relationships? _____

> "If you then, being evil, know how to give good gifts to your children, how much more shall your Father who is in heaven give what is good to those who ask Him!"
> —*Matthew 7:11*

> "Your heavenly Father knows that you need all these things. But seek first His kingdom and His righteousness; and all these things shall be added to you."
> —*Matthew 6:32-33*

When we focus on *our* kingdom—being as self-centered and short-sighted as we are—we still find ourselves distressed, incomplete, and unsatisfied. But when we focus on *God's* kingdom, He has promised to take care of our kingdom. That sounds like a pretty good deal to me.

> When we focus on God's kingdom, He has promised to take care of our kingdom.

Crossing the Line
My job in prayer is not to *inform* God; it is to *enjoy* God. As I approach the Father in this way, with all my attention on Him and His kingdom, I discover my focus is on Him, not me. My heart beats for others, not just myself. I feel at home in His presence. I don't avoid Him out of fear or boredom. I find that I love to pray and that I live to pray.

In Corrie Ten Boom's gripping autobiography, *The Hiding Place*, which tells of her family's efforts to shelter Jews from the Nazi forces in Holland during World War II, she describes in disturbing detail the conditions of the German concentration camp where she and her sister Betsie were interred for their role in the Resistance. It was a vicious labor camp. Whatever shred of human dignity wasn't stripped at the entry gate ended up in a pile of charred bones in the gas chamber.

Corrie walks us into the rancid dormitory where the smell of raw sewage and soiled bedding was so overpowering it took her breath. Narrow tiers of rotting bunk platforms were so hopelessly overcrowded that the prisoners had to sleep with others' feet in their faces and knees in their backs. And the fleas. Everywhere—biting, infested fleas.

She wailed to her sister, " 'How can we live in such a place!' " Betsie's reply came in short, wondering tones: " 'Show us. Show us how.' "

Corrie writes, "It was said so matter of factly it took me a second to realize she was praying. More and more the distinction between prayer and the rest of life seemed to be vanishing for Betsie."[3]

And so it does for those of us who approach our Father in heaven through His Son, on His terms, in His love. The fleas do not become the issue. Perhaps, like for Betsie, the fleas become a reason for renewed faith, but the issue becomes our faithful Father.

"Our Father in heaven."

The focus in our prayers should be on God, not us. Which of the following statements best characterizes your stage of spiritual development? Check one.

❏ **I desire a relationship with God, but I don't know how.**
❏ **I desire God, but I'm holding back in some areas.**
❏ **I want to know God with all of my being.**

If you do not have a personal relationship to God, turn to page 103 and read how to begin this relationship.

---

[1]These findings come from Joachim Jeremias, tr. John Reumann, *The Lord's Prayer* (Philadelphia: Fortress Press, 1964), 2-5.

[2]Jesus' prayer from the cross, "My God, My God, why hast thou forsaken me," does not begin with a reference to the Father because Jesus was quoting directly from an Old Testament source.

[3]Corrie Ten Boom and John and Elizabeth Sherrill, *The Hiding Place* (New York: Bantam Books, 1971), 197.

Viewer Guide
SESSION TWO

The threefold address in the prayer of Jesus:

"Our Father" is a privilege made possible by the _____ work of Jesus Christ.

The _____ _____ joins us as we enter the _____ of our Father.

"Our" means that I cannot pray selfishly for my bread without being

concerned for your _____.

The most radical word in this prayer is _____.

"Who art in heaven" refers to God's _____ and His sovereign _____.

Omniscient means God _____ _____.

Omnipresent means God is _____ _____ _____.

Omnipotent means God has _____ _____.

Omnibenevolent means God is all together _____ and _____.

When you say "Our Father, who is in heaven," you get the world's best _____.

ANYTIME, ANYWHERE

Three Responsibilities from the Prayer of Jesus

This Week's Verse

" 'Hallowed be
Thy name,
Thy kingdom come.
Thy will be done,
On earth as it is
in heaven.' "
—*Matthew 6:9-10*

For years I prayed the Lord's Prayer in a mechanical fashion, paying little attention to what I was actually saying.

- I would pray, "Hallowed be Your name," as if I were giving God my permission for His name to be declared holy.
- I would pray, "Your kingdom come," as if I were giving God my OK for Him to perform His sovereign work.
- I would pray, "Your will be done," as if His will were some generic concept totally disconnected from my own life.

Suddenly it dawned on me how naïve and foolish my praying had been.

- God's name is holy because God *by nature* is holy.
- God's kingdom will come whether *I* advance it or not.
- God can accomplish His will *with* me or *without* me.

So then, what do these clauses from Jesus' prayer really mean?

How would you answer this question? What do these clauses from Jesus' prayer really mean? At the end of week 3 you will be asked to review your answer.

_____

_____

_____

JOURNAL YOUR
THOUGHTS & PRAYERS

Use these questions to guide your prayers this week:

• What did you do this week that "hallowed God's name"?
• What actions, words, or deeds brought reproach on His name? What actions do you need to take in order to make amends?
• What kingdom opportunity did you encounter, and how did you respond?
• How have you responded to God's will today (this week)?

Write what God is teaching you in His School of Prayer.

_____

_____

_____

_____

_____

_____

_____

_____

_____

The Commitment Clause

I believe these three statements in the Lord's Prayer are best understood as personal *commitments* on our part to hallow God's name in our lives, to participate in the spread of His kingdom, and to become actively involved in doing His will.

"On earth as it is in heaven" modifies all three. This carries the meaning of *total commitment*. It's similar to Paul's appeal for us to present ourselves as "a living and holy sacrifice" to God (Rom. 12:1). This is normative Christian living and proper Christian praying.

It's pretty clear how we should respond: completely, immediately, and perfectly.

For example, as we pray about God's will, we should ask ourselves, "How is God's will accomplished in heaven?" The answer is simple: completely, immediately, and perfectly. So as He begins to reveal His will in our lives, it's pretty clear how we should respond: completely, immediately, and perfectly.

Prayer Time

As you begin this chapter, pray the following hymn.

All to Jesus, I surrender, All to him I freely give;
I will ever love and trust Him, In His presence daily live.
I surrender all. I surrender all.
All to Thee, my blessed Savior, I surrender all.[1]

Now, when we understand these statements not as requests but as responsibilities, several important things begin to happen:

First, we ask God to train us to look at the world from His point of view. It would be so pleasant to think that this world is filled with good, decent people who—with a little goal-setting practice and polishing up—could enjoy the multiplied blessings of the Christian life. But God teaches us through His Word that even some of the nice people who recycle their newspapers and keep their yards trimmed and volunteer to pick up litter by the roadside are held hostage by the power of evil. Even those of us who have been freed from Satan's grip by the grace of God must constantly fight the undertow of his lies and temptations. Everywhere—from the evening news to the grocery store aisle—we see the hideous hold the devil has on our culture.

Therefore, our desire for God to reveal His name on earth has a much bigger purpose than our devotional time and our church services. It has names and faces and family members and coworkers—people who desperately need to see God's name revealed as the answer for all their questions.

Read John 4:34-35. Jesus looked on the Samaritan town of Sychar and saw the spiritual needs of its inhabitants. Looking at your community from God's point of view, list specific needs.

Jesus said to them, "My food is to do the will of Him who sent Me, and to accomplish His work. Do you not say, 'There are yet four months, and then comes the harvest'? Behold, I say to you, lift up your eyes, and look on the fields, that they are white for harvest."

—*John 4:34-35*

_____

_____

_____

Second, despite the evil we witness around us, we know for a fact that God's promises are true and His victory is certain. How easy it would be to throw up our hands and surrender the battle. But God has promised to administer justice and to preserve His people who endure to the end. His kingdom is here and His kingdom is coming. No devil in hell can stop it.

Read these Scriptures and write the promises of God.

John 16:33 _____

Romans 8:35-37 _____

1 John 5:4-5_____

When you pray, are you confident in God's power to change the situation? Place an X on the scale to indicate your degree of confidence.

_____

Not confident   Very confident

Third, we acknowledge God's call on our lives to be His instruments. He could expand His kingdom and bring all things into submission to His will without using any of us, but God's delight and plan is to empower and enable us to be messengers of hope in our decaying world. The material things we see around us on this earth will not survive eternity, but the souls of those within range of our lunchroom conversations, our morning walks, and our compassionate touch bear the possibility of a glorious forever. When we commit our lives into God's service, He compensates us in eternal dividends. It's astounding what He chooses to do through us.

Name one thing God has done through your life that only He could

have accomplished. _____

Finally, we avoid asking for anything that would dishonor God's name, delay His kingdom, or thwart His will. In other words, we begin operating daily from a Christian worldview, letting God take care of our kingdoms while we concentrate our full attention on His. Again, it's "praying without ceasing," letting His presence permeate our thoughts and actions all day long—anytime, anywhere.

Prayer Time

Pray this prayer or say a prayer in your own words: *"Heavenly Father, help me see the world from Your point of view. Make me an instrument in accomplishing Your will. I don't want to ask for anything that will bring dishonor to Your name. May I sense Your presence all through the day and be sensitive to what You are doing in the lives of those around me. In the Name of Jesus, Amen."*

_____

_____

_____

HALLOWED BE YOUR NAME

Jesus turns our attention first to the Father's name—His hallowed name. The word literally means "to make holy" or "to treat as holy." In heaven this very hour, the angels are singing to the Father in joyous wonder: "Holy, holy, holy," extolling this One who is worthy of all praise and adoration. Not only is the *Father* holy; His *name* is holy.

> "Holy, holy, holy, is the Lord God, the Almighty, who was and who is and who is to come."
>
> —*Revelation 4:8*

One of the reasons I wrote the book *The Names of God* was to capture some of the awe and wonder expressed through the different titles ascribed to Him in Scripture. There are dozens of vivid, descriptive names that apply to every situation you face in life.

For example, when you or someone you love is ill, you can pray to Him knowing that He is *Jehovah-Rophe:* "The Lord heals." When you find yourself in the grip of temptation, you can sense His strength, victory, and protection by giving thanks to Him for being *Jehovah-Nissi:* "The Lord Our Banner." He is . . .

- *Jehovah-Shammah:* "The Lord Is There."
- *Jehovah-M'Kaddesh:* "The Lord Who Sanctifies."
- *El-Elyon:* "God Most High."

Prayer Time

Pray to our Heavenly Father. Use the following names for God to express your reverence and adoration of Him.

Jehovah, pronounced Ja-hoé-vah, means *I am.* God is absolutely self-existent. He is the same yesterday, today, and forever. He is faithful to fulfill His promises.

Jehovah Tsidkenu, pronounced S_d´-k_-new, means *the Lord is our righteousness.* God by nature is righteous, and therefore we commit to live by His righteous standards. He desires to be our righteousness as we pray for deliverance from evil.

Jehovah Shalom, pronounced Je-hoévah Sh_-loam, means *the Lord is peace.* Do interruptions in your schedule frustrate you? When you feel agitated, you can call on the Lord of Peace.

The Family Name

The day I left home for college to play football at Wake Forest University, I remember my dad walking me to the car to give me my "going off to college" lecture. You know the one.

My mom had decided to play it safe by staying behind on the porch. I could see her crying by the back door. As I turned to hear what Dad had to say, I braced myself for what I thought could be a pretty long speech.

Instead, his words were surprisingly brief. He said, "Son, I have only one piece of advice to give you. I want to remind you that you bear my name. Your great-grandfather was a church planter and preacher; your grandfather was a godly man, and I think you know I've tried to live faithfully before God. *The name Hemphill stands for something.* So don't take my name anywhere I wouldn't take it, and don't involve my name in anything I wouldn't do." With that the going-away speech was over.

Although I didn't grasp at the time how important his advice would become, that reminder helped me many times through the years to make difficult but appropriate decisions when there was no one around to tell me what to do or how to behave.

> Our family reputation was at stake. Our name would be judged by the things I did and the places I went.

You see, our family reputation was at stake. Our name would be judged by the things I did and the places I went. I didn't have to worry so much about the specifics of splitting hairs or skirting the gray areas. I just had to see Dad's face in my mind, and I always knew without a doubt what I was supposed to do.

In the same way, you and I bear the name of our Heavenly Father. Therefore, everywhere we go and everything we do casts a reflection on Him. Everywhere. Everything.

So in the morning when I get up and at frequent times throughout the day, I pray, "Father, hallowed be your name"—in *my* life, in your *people's* lives.

What does that do? How does that prayer connect?

- It's the kind of prayer I find rewarded when the cleaners have ruined one of my shirts and I'm tempted to take my anger out on the girl at the cash register. *Hallowed be Your name.* I don't want the stain of my bad witness to come off on Christ.
- It's the kind of prayer I find rewarded when the plane is delayed and I doubt there's any way I can make my connecting flight. *Hallowed be Your name.* I don't want to blow my chance right out of the gate to share Christ with the man sitting in the next seat.

- It's the kind of prayer I find rewarded when I'm away from home and anonymous in an airport magazine shop. *Hallowed be Your name.* I don't want my eyes to lead me astray or give me away.

Unfortunately, a lot of Christians have negatively impacted the gospel, not by deliberately blaspheming God's name but by not living up to their calling at the gym or the office or the Little League diamond. Hallowing God's name has anytime/anywhere implications.

Have you seen Christians bring dishonor to God's name and to the church? (circle)   Yes   No

What impact could the church have on the world if we daily lived, "Holy is your Name"? Place an X on the scale below.

No impact   Some impact   Much impact

What's in a Name?

I know how important this matter of reputation was to my father. But it is of even greater importance to our *Heavenly* Father.

In Ezekiel, chapter 36, the prophet rebuked Israel for their unrighteous behavior that has sullied the name of God and forced Him to punish them severely by banishing them into exile. Almost in the same breath (as he speaks the words of God), Ezekiel made a declaration. Read his words in Ezekiel 36:23.

Israel had profaned God's name, and the last thing they deserved was to be delivered from the captivity they had brought on themselves. Nevertheless, God promised to gather His people from the shackles of slavery and restore them to their homeland. Why? Because He was unwilling for the other nations to persist in mocking His name, to consider His arm too weak to save or His power no match for the armies of men. His name was at stake.

In Jesus' remarkable high-priestly prayer found in John 17, He summarized the most important aims of His earthly ministry: "I manifested Thy name to the men whom Thou gavest Me out of the world; ... I have made Thy name known to them, and will make it known; that the love wherewith Thou didst love Me may be in them, and I in them" (John 17:6, 26).

> "I will vindicate the holiness of My great name which has been profaned among the nations, which you have profaned in their midst. Then the nations will know that I am the Lord ... when I prove Myself holy among you in their sight."
> —*Ezekiel 36:23*

Jesus' ministry aim was to make His Father's name known among the nations. God calls us to join Him in that mission (Matt. 28:19-20). Write a personal statement that identifies how you are seeking to make God's name known (your mission statement).

_____

_____

_____

Of all the things Christ accomplished, He put a face on the name of God. And so do we—every time we keep our cool, maintain our integrity, and honor our commitment to hallow His name.

YOUR KINGDOM COME

My wife and I went to China recently with several other seminary presidents. We visited a number of seminaries and Bible colleges in China to see if we could assist them in theological training. Because we were escorted from appointment to appointment, we had little opportunity to interact with the Chinese people. But even if we had, the language presented a formidable barrier.

I assumed that the entire kingdom perspective of our visit would be lived out in the years ahead as we assisted men and women with their studies. But we took the trip from Nanjing to Shanghai by train, and we shared the ride with two young Chinese adults who were seated across the table from us. Paula soon discovered that the young woman spoke English very well. In fact, she was a communications major who enjoyed every opportunity to practice her English.

With the language barrier removed, we talked, laughed, shared, and asked questions. Near the end of our conversation, as we were exchanging email addresses and promising to keep in touch, I asked if I could give her a little booklet that explained our philosophy of life. *Yes! She'd be glad to receive it.* She enthusiastically took the *GotLife* tract[2] I had recently written, which communicates the truths about the abundant

Christian life. Once again, Paula and I discovered that the kingdom comes in unexpected ways and at unusual times—when we've made a commitment to look for it.

Coming Attractions

Simply stated, the kingdom of God is "His rule." Just as the king of a country has the total right and authority to govern his subjects, the coming of our Father's kingdom will bring about the full reign of God when it is ultimately consummated at the end of time. When we pray, "Your kingdom come," we are in part looking for—yes, *longing* for—that final establishment of God's rule over all His creation.

In a real sense the kingdom is already a present reality. John the Baptist warned the citizens of his day to " 'repent, for the kingdom of heaven is at hand' " (Matt. 3:2). With the commencement of Jesus' ministry on earth, the kingdom indeed began to grow and expand.

You can see both the present and the future in Christ's parable of the wheat and the tares (Matt. 13:24-30,36-43). It's the story of a man who planted his crops in the field, but during the night an enemy sneaked onto his land and randomly scattered some *other* kinds of seed across the hungry soil. As the weeks passed, the wheat began to grow—just as the farmer hoped it would—but signs of another harvest were also tangled throughout his field: the unwelcome invasion of weeds planted by a jealous neighbor.

Angry at the extra work involved in weeding a plant bed so knotted with wild grass, the laborers wanted to know how it happened and what they should do about it. The landowner wisely instructed them to "allow both to grow together until the harvest," not wanting to harm the good crops on account of the bad. Not until the final harvest would he pull up the weeds and burn them in their own pile, leaving the ripe, mature wheat crop to be gathered and stored.

Jesus explained that the good seeds represent the "sons of the kingdom"—present-day followers of Christ already growing in the world, as well as all who have lived before and all who will come to Christ in the days ahead. The kingdom concept is also seen in the future harvest time, when—with all the weeds removed—"the righteous will shine forth as the sun in the kingdom of their Father."

While God's kingdom is a coming event, it is also a present reality. So when we pray, "Thy kingdom come," we are at one moment recognizing the fact that God's ultimate rule is simply a matter of time, and

The kingdom comes in unexpected ways and at unusual times— when we've made a commitment to look for it.

While God's kingdom is a coming event, it is also a present reality.

we are also committing ourselves to participate in seeing it unfold before our eyes. That's what's really exciting!

Prayer Time

Praying "Your Kingdom Come"
   The church is God's instrument for sharing the gospel with the world. Pray for the church, the body of Christ.

Pray for your pastor and church staff.
Pray for God to send workers.
Pray for teachers and leaders.
Pray for mission activities in your church and denomination.
Pray for your involvement in the church's ministries.
Pray for God to provide financial resources for ministries.

Heaven in the Real World

This aspect of the Lord's Prayer continues to amaze me, not only because I missed the point for so long, but also because I now realize that it places me right on the cutting edge of kingdom living all day, every day. Again, just as the line between prayer and life begins to vanish through the "praying without ceasing" mentality of the Lord's Prayer, this kingdom focus dissolves the hard line between sacred and secular. If you take a good look at Jesus' life, you see that *all* of it was sacred. Every event and occurrence in His life, no matter how ordinary or offhand, had a kingdom priority to it.

> This kingdom focus dissolves the hard line between sacred and secular.

His *disciples* didn't always understand this. They would shoo the children away to keep Him on schedule and hustle the crowds along so they could get some rest. But Jesus saw everything through the lens of the Father's kingdom. Even with this sense of divine urgency, He never appeared rattled, stressed out, or in a hurry. He simply watched to see where the kingdom was working, and He moved toward it with eyes and arms wide open. And so can we.

Everywhere we go there are kingdom opportunities. And if our heart's desire is constantly trained to see His kingdom come, we'll be ready to share the hope of the gospel with anyone, anywhere.

- When you stop for gas on the way home, *Your kingdom come.* You're watching, looking, expecting an opportunity to hear something, to say something.
- When you take your family out to dinner, *Your kingdom come.* The waiter, the busboy, the hostess, the other people waiting for a table. Are they open to conversation? Has the Spirit placed the two of you here at this hour, in this particular circumstance?
- When you're running on the treadmill, *Your kingdom come.* When you finally stop to cool down and catch your breath, will someone be waiting? Someone worrying? Someone wanting to know that God is real and that He really cares?

Make a list of five people with whom you came in contact the past several days. Beside each name, check whether or not each person knows Jesus as Savior and Lord.

1. _____ ❑ Yes   ❑ No   ❑ I Don't Know

2. _____ ❑ Yes   ❑ No   ❑ I Don't Know

3. _____ ❑ Yes   ❑ No   ❑ I Don't Know

4. _____ ❑ Yes   ❑ No   ❑ I Don't Know

5. _____ ❑ Yes   ❑ No   ❑ I Don't Know

Am I suggesting that He wants to take all the fun out of your life, that never again can you simply go for a walk, or vacation at the beach, or kick back and relax without constantly feeling on call? Of course God understands your need for fun and rest. Remember the verse we looked at earlier, the one you probably know by heart, Matthew 6:32-33?

As you seek His kingdom, you can quit worrying about yours. If you'll focus on His thoughts and desires, *your Father* will make sure that you get enough sleep, that a skipped meal won't kill you, that you and your family will have all the time together you need. *You can't get in any better hands than His—not even your own!*

You are free to approach even your fun times as kingdom events:

- When you're away on vacation, let God use you to bring home a lot more than a well-read novel and a suntan. Bring home the

> "Your heavenly Father knows that you need all these things. But seek first His kingdom and His righteousness; and all these things shall be added to you."
> —*Matthew 6:32-33*

61

blessing of sharing Christ with someone you never would have had the chance to meet in your everyday routine.

- When your family gets together for a holiday, let God use you to interject hope and truth into conversations about world events and bear-market reports. See if it can't be the kind of homecoming for a lost relative or in-law that will make your family gathering the best one you've ever had.

Because the kingdom is here. Because the kingdom is coming. And you have suddenly become an active part of it.

Prayer Time

List places you will be or activities you will engage in this week.

_____   _____

_____   _____

_____   _____

Kingdom work is 24/7/365. God wants us to see all of our activities as opportunities to be engaged in His work. Pray for each activity. After each activity, say, "Your kingdom come." For example, "At the car wash—Your kingdom come."

YOUR WILL BE DONE

The third commitment is similar to the one before, except that—like the "hallowed be your name" pledge—it requires much more than your ears, your mind, and your mouth. It requires all of you, all the time.

When you pray, "Your will be done," throughout the day, you are committing yourself not only to His kingdom but also to the full accomplishment of His will in your life.

Now let me warn you right up front: *This will not be convenient.* These commitments demand that your own needs and emotions take a backseat to God's desires for your life. Does anything that is truly worthwhile require any less?

If you can be brave enough to look into the future and compare what your life will be like when you: (a) let God have control of your time and activities, or (b) waste it on your own self-interests, you will see that God's ways lead to a life of blessing, joy, and no regrets.

Which of the following activities reflect your commitment to the full accomplishment of His will? Check all that apply.
❑ **My calendar is controlled by God's priorities.**
❑ **My daily schedule includes time for God.**
❑ **My checkbook reflects Kingdom activities.**
❑ **I see my work as a ministry.**
❑ **My life goals are in line with God's will.**

This prayer makes every moment of every day an *adventure* with the Father. No two days of yours will ever be alike again! To the ordinary mind, this responsibility may seem like slavery. But I can assure you that it is the most freeing experience you will ever know. You get to enjoy it every day as you come to enjoy Him every moment.

> This prayer makes every moment of every day an *adventure* with the Father.

A Change in Plans

First, however, you need to see God's will in a much bigger perspective than the way most people usually think of it. Deciding which school to attend, choosing whom to marry, or considering God's call to the mission field are certainly decisions to be made in accordance with His will. But major milestones like these are not the *only* arenas where it's necessary to discern the plans of God. That could happen at any point of your day, every day of your life.

Let's say, for example, that around 2:00 one afternoon—in the midst of a long day at work—I start thinking that as soon as I leave the office in three or four hours, I'm going to go home, change clothes, and treat myself to some time at the driving range. Ah, my day is starting to pick up already. The rest of the afternoon and the whole way home, I can already feel the club in my hand, hear the whip of my swing, see the ball soaring long and straight and beyond the yardage markers.

Whose kingdom is going to win? Whose needs are going to get met? Whose will is going to prevail?

Imagine that when I get home, as I'm loosening my necktie and fumbling for a comfortable shirt, I find that my wife has also had a frustrating day. Things haven't gone well. A new problem has arisen. She needs to talk. She needs me to listen.

Whose kingdom is going to win? Whose needs are going to get met? Whose will is going to prevail? Mine or hers? What if God knows that what I *really* need this evening is not the pleasure of connecting with a golf ball but the responsibility of connecting with my wife?

Good questions, aren't they? Although we may think we know the right answers, we don't always quiet our growling appetites long enough to do the right thing.

Does this mean I never get to do what I want to do? Of course not. It simply means that I choose to put the full responsibility for that on God's shoulders because I trust Him to make sure I get all the recreation I need. Therefore, the right question to ask myself at 2:00 in the afternoon is not "Wonder if I can get to the driving range by 5:30?" but "Lord, will you keep me open to your will—whatever that is for this evening?" Because anywhere *in* the will of God is better than anywhere else *outside* of it.

Do interruptions bother you because they keep you from accomplishing things on your checklist? ❑ No   ❑ Sometimes   ❑ Yes

Busyness sometimes prevents us from seeing what God is doing around us. List messages you could give yourself that would encourage you to be more available for kingdom purposes.

A Full Day of Appointments

Let me show you how much fun this can be. At a preaching engagement in Florida, one of the staff members at the church began to share how God had used me to save his ministry. Several years before, I had been speaking at a conference in his state, and he had picked me up at the airport. Realizing we had a few hours before the conference began, I had suggested we stop somewhere and get a cup of coffee. For two hours that day he poured his heart out to me about his disappointments, his disillusionments, his discouragements. At that time he was serving at a church in bitter turmoil, but in those stolen moments in a little coffee shop, God had touched his heart and changed his focus. Instead of giving up, he had dug in. God had blessed his life and ministry with a new vision for reaching out and loving people.

If I had been plotting my schedule that day, those two hours would have fallen under the category "on the way to the conference." Instead, those were two divinely appointed hours that were just as important as the official business of the day. God used the "Your will be done" commitment to advance His kingdom and to honor His name. It happens like that all the time—on the way, in the process, while we wait.

Have you had a similar experience in which an interruption turned out to be a "God thing"? Describe the experience.

_____

_____

By the Way

Remember the day in Jesus' life when the ruler, Jairus, rushed up to Him and pleaded with Him to come to his sick daughter's bedside? We can identify with this father's sense of urgency. We too would have begged Jesus to *please, please come quickly!*

Somewhere along the way a woman who had suffered with internal bleeding for 12 years summoned the strength to work her way through the crowd and quietly touch the hem of His garment. She didn't want to bother Him or be embarrassed by suddenly becoming the center of attention.

Perhaps that's why she chose this moment, probably unaware of the crisis that caused the hurried pace of the Master. Isn't it interesting that the Master would slow His pace at a time like this to touch a woman with problems—when resurrection was on the calendar?

But He did stop. He did notice. His kingdom business had been current the moment Jairus skidded hard into the dust at His feet, but it would also be current at this moment, with this woman. God's name would be declared holy at both places that day—both *at* Jairus's house and *on the road* to Jairus's house.

"Your kingdom come, Your will be done." That's all that matters.

- When you're waiting somewhat impatiently in the doctor's office, *Your will be done.* What year-old magazine is worth missing the will of God?
- When you're wondering why you're wasting time at a social function you "had to attend," *Your kingdom come.* Your will be done. Hallowed be Your name. Right over the punch bowl.

You won't have more time later. It won't get any more convenient. It's now. It's here. It's not you. It's Him. And it's the most fun you'll ever have as a Christian—watching God turn your every day into an everyday adventure.

Review your answer to the learning activity on page 50. Would you change anything you said? If so, make the changes or add to your response in the margin.

Prayer Time

What decisions are you facing at work, school, with family, or with friends? Are you at the point that you can say, "Your kingdom come?" Write the decisions, the date God answered your prayers, and how God answered the prayers.

Decision	Date God answered	How God answered
_____	_____	_____
_____	_____	_____
_____	_____	_____

---

[1]Judson W. Van DeVenter, "I Surrender All," in *The Baptist Hymnal* (Nashville: Convention Press, 1991), 275.

[2]If you desire to witness but have never found a method that works well in the marketplace, I would recommend a tool called GotLife. It is simple but complete and comes with a comprehensive training CD. You can find the Action G.E.A.R. in your Christian bookstore, or you can order by calling 800-856-8886 or by logging on to *www.gotlife.org*.

Viewer Guide
SESSION THREE

The first three statements in the Lord's Prayer are _____ to God.

A. Hallowed be your name.
Psalm 72:17,19: "May His name endure forever; May His name increase as long as the sun shines; ... And blessed be His glorious name forever."

"Dad, help me _____ what your _____ stands for."

Praying this is a commitment to living in _____ to His name.

B. Your kingdom come.
The kingdom of God is the _____ of Christ in an individual's heart.

This prayer is our commitment to join our Father in His kingdom _____.

John 5:17-20 " 'My Father is working until now, and I Myself am working.' For this reason therefore the Jews were seeking all the more to kill Him, because He not only was breaking the Sabbath, but also was calling God His own Father, making Himself equal with God. Therefore Jesus answered and was saying to them, 'Truly, truly, I say to you, the Son can do nothing of Himself, unless it is something He sees the Father doing; for whatever the Father does, these things the Son also does in like manner. For the Father loves the Son, and shows Him all things that He Himself is doing; and the Father will show Him greater works than these, so that you will marvel.' "

C. Your will be done.
Two aspects of this commitment:

1. Trusting your Dad's _____ (Rom. 8:28).

2. We can _____ Him in His _____.

Jesus was constantly on _____ time.

I'VE GOT YOU COVERED

Three Requests from the Prayer of Jesus

Think back to the last time you tried breaking a bad habit or committing to a good one, and you'll agree that saying you'll do something and actually doing it are two different things. A genuine change in your focus or behavior takes a lot more than sheer guts and willpower. Success in a noble endeavor requires the joint forces of both heart and mind. And nowhere is that more evident than in the Christian's life.

A believer who is clinging to bitterness and unforgiveness, for example, cannot consistently achieve the goals of loving others unconditionally or being less judgmental. A person wanting to be more serious about prayer and Bible study but unwilling to give up a known habit of lust or laziness will invariably find that two desires going in opposite directions cannot coexist for long without the easiest one winning.

So when we, who have entrusted our lives into the hands of God, strive to make the kind of radical commitments we talked about in the last chapter, we need much more than a hearty zeal and a head of steam. We need help from God—help that goes right to the bone, to the soul, to the spirit. Our Father understands that. *Therefore, He has given us permission to ask Him to meet every possible need we will ever experience.*

That's because He knows that the needs we possess in one part of our lives will have an impact on another. A constantly worried mind will put a strain on our physical health. A frequently empty stomach will cloud our ability to think clearly. A brewing, angry temper will eventually show itself in acts of rage and aggression. All of these dampen our ability to seek His kingdom.

JOURNAL YOUR THOUGHTS & PRAYERS

As you journal your thoughts and prayers this week, ask yourself these questions:

- How have you experienced God's provision for your daily needs?
- How is your spiritual debt ledger? (What do you need forgiveness for, and who do you need to forgive? What practical actions are you prepared to take?)
- Have you avoided all issues of temptation and experienced spiritual victory this week?

Write what God is teaching you in His School of Prayer.

_____

_____

_____

_____

_____

_____

_____

_____

_____

STANDING IN THE NEED OF PRAYER

We need help to live the Christian life—the deep-down help that only God can give—and we need it now. So Jesus instructs us to ask ... for everything, for every dimension of our human existence.

- For our *bodies*—the sustenance of daily bread.
- For our *souls*—the peace of a clear conscience.
- For our *spirits*—the freedom to willfully obey.

Read the following Scriptures and summarize their teaching in the space provided.

Matthew 7:7-8   Mark 11:24   John 15:7   1 John 5:14-15

His Name, His Claim

I want to warn you not to confuse the bold petitions found in the Lord's Prayer with the false "name it and claim it" prosperity gospel that has pervaded the church in our day. Our requests for daily bread, forgiveness of sins, and deliverance from evil are not selfish demands; instead they are *understood requirements* for serving in His kingdom. They are not promises held over God's head to insist that He treat us to a certain level of lifestyle, but expressions of total dependence on Him for each day's provision.

We can agree that the Father loves us deeply, wants to bless us, and desires that we have everything in His storehouse that is intended for us. Furthermore, we can agree that we don't have to beg or whine like spoiled children to receive such favor; rather, it is His good pleasure to shower these blessings on us.

One of God's main purposes in supplying our human needs is to enable us to fulfill the kingdom commitments we've made. The commitments we've made enable us to focus our prayers and our lives on God, the giver, not on the size or specifics of His gifts. Remember—again: " 'Your heavenly Father knows that you need all these things. But seek first His kingdom and His righteousness; and all these things shall be added to you' " (Matt. 6:32-33).

> We don't have to beg or whine like spoiled children to receive such favor; rather, it is His good pleasure to shower these blessings on us.

We are not self-seeking when we ask the Father to meet our physical, emotional, and spiritual needs. We are merely asking for the strength needed to fulfill our kingdom responsibilities. We are kingdom-seeking.

In order to accomplish the kingdom commitments you've made, list your top three needs in each category.

Physical Needs	Emotional Needs	Spiritual Needs
1._____	1._____	1._____
2._____	2._____	2._____
3._____	3._____	3._____

Jesus promises that if we as His followers will focus on His kingdom, He will personally manage the affairs of our own kingdoms.

When we attempt to manage our own kingdom affairs, we become fretful and anxious because we have no power to control all the situations that come about or to alter our circumstances. Jesus understands this limitation. Read Matthew 6:27 in the margin.

In response He gives us an offer we should be unable to refuse: *You focus on My kingdom, and I in turn will manage your kingdom.*

What could possibly be more liberating than that?

> "Who of you by worrying can add a single hour to his life?"
> —*Matthew 6:27, NIV*

On Earth as It Is in Heaven

One day in the future, when God's kingdom has come in all its fullness, we will be free from all the conditions that require these requests.

- We will no longer need to ask for "our daily bread," because our physical needs will be met by being in His tangible presence.
- There will be no sin, no broken relationships that require Him to "forgive us our debts as we forgive our debtors."
- No desire to do wrong will even exist when God's heavenly reign is complete.

Despite the fact that we can only partially know this kind of freedom while we're here on earth, *Jesus allows us to pray that these kingdom realities will invade our daily living now!* By "praying without ceasing" and trusting Him for everything, we can progressively experience God's presence and provision in our daily lives right now—for His name, for His honor, for His glory! In a world where God seems remote, where sin enslaves, where hunger and thirst are everyday realities, His children can experience the current invasion of kingdom provision.

Prayer Time

The Prayer of Jesus acknowledges our desire for God's reign in Heaven to be fully accomplished on earth. Read Psalm 40:8 in the margin and paraphrase the verse as your personal prayer.

_____

_____

_____

Jesus taught us that in His kingdom, leaders serve. Givers receive. The last are first and the first are last. Those who mourn are comforted. Those who hunger are filled. Those who suffer persecution are blessed beyond measure. (See Matthew 5:1-12.)

Isn't it just like Jesus to continue the paradigm shift—not only to reverse our normal way of thinking but also to bend the constraints of time and space and transport the realities of the future into our present-day experience? That's what happens as we bring our requests to the Father. That's what happens as He meets our needs in His loving, powerful way. That's the exciting truth of this pattern of prayer.

Our Daily Bread

In order to think and pray this way, we must first shake off the false notion that life is separated into two distinct compartments—the secular and the sacred—and that the practical needs of everyday life occupy one place, while Christian faith and its responsibilities occupy another. The early church didn't see it that way. When you read Paul's words in 1 Corinthians 11:17-34, you get the idea that the first-century Christians combined their Lord's Supper observances with the enjoyment of a potluck dinner. The breaking of bread was a crucial part of their lives together, for it helped sustain many of the early believers who were living hand to mouth. Their gatherings had both *physical* and *spiritual* significance.

Paul's concern in the first part of that passage was not that they were eating supper at a time set aside for spiritual things. His problem was this: The wealthy were not sharing their abundance with those in need, "for in your eating each one takes his own supper first; and one is hungry and another is drunk" (v. 21). Since their fellowship meals intertwined the material with the spiritual, their lack of regard for others' physical needs brought reproach on the name of God. Even this meal, you see, was "the Lord's Supper" (v. 20).

Today we have lost much of this understanding—that all things fall under the category of *sacred* in the believer's life. For Jesus' followers in every generation, there should be no distinction between the two.

Daily bread and kingdom commitments don't live on separate streets. They live right in the middle of the intersection.

Read 1 Corinthians 10:31 and 1 Timothy 4:4. How can an ordinary meal turn into an opportunity to glorify God?

> Whether, then, you eat or drink or whatever you do, do all to the glory of God.
> —*1 Corinthians 10:31*

_____

_____

Father Nature

Your Father knows that you have a life. That life includes cereal on the breakfast table, diapers on the baby, a coat on your back, and a pair of decent shoes on your feet. It includes a roof over your head and the money to keep it there, a job to work and the opportunity to excel, a car that runs and a reliable mechanic to help it stay that way.

> Everything created by God is good, and nothing is to be rejected, if it is received with gratitude.
> —*1 Timothy 4:4*

To most people there is nothing spiritual about these things, nothing sacred about writing the check for this month's rent, eating a tuna sandwich, or fixing a leaky faucet. But for Christians, these routine matters provide ongoing evidence that a compassionate, loving God cares about the most ordinary matters in our lives.

"Look at the birds of the air, that they do not sow, neither to they reap, nor gather into barns, and yet your heavenly Father feeds them. Are you not worth much more than they? ... And why are you anxious about clothing? Observe how the lilies of the field grow; they do not toil nor do they spin, yet I say to you that not Solomon in all his glory did not cloth himself like one of these. But if God so arrays the grass of the field, which is alive today and tomorrow is thrown into the furnace, will He not much more do so for you, O men of little faith!"
—*Matthew 6:26,28-30*

Hard to believe? Jesus says to take a lesson from nature. Read Matthew 6:16,28-30 in the margin.

We are often guilty of asking the question, "What's in it for us?" But when we ask that question while intentionally focusing our attention on the kingdom of God, here's the incredible answer we receive: *"Everything!"* God delights in taking care of everything we need, as long as we realize that the things we receive from Him are *equipment*, not decorations. His provision gives us the security of being better prepared, not the cheap thrill of making a better impression.

Recently, how has God demonstrated that He cares about the most ordinary matters in your life?

_____

_____

Worry Free

Furthermore, by taking responsibility for our personal, physical needs, God actually declares a ban on worry. Jesus refers to *anxiety* five times in the short passage that follows closely after the Lord's Prayer (Matt. 6:25-34). In three of those occurrences He literally uses an imperative term that amounts to a *commandment* not to worry.

Place a slash (/) in each of the circles that bring you anxiety.
◯ Job　　◯ Finances　　◯ Relationships　　◯ Car/Transportation
◯ School　◯ Children　　◯ Parents　　　◯ Other

You have drawn the international *no* symbol. Look again at your list. Jesus said, "Do not be anxious" about these things.

This is not just a sweet, Sunday morning idea. He is serious. God has eliminated our need for worry. Have you ever noticed how small children do not exhibit anxiety like we adults do? They don't spend unnecessary time worrying about how they are going to pay for food. Food just appears "magically on the table" as far as the child is concerned. Children aren't anxious about their clothing or their bodies unless we adults project our anxiety onto them. They don't lie awake at night worrying about the mounting bills.

Don't you wish you could have a worry-free, child-like existence? Good news! That's what Jesus had in His child-like dependence with His Father and that is precisely what He invites us to experience as we join Him in praying, "Our Father." Is it any surprise that the section of Scripture immediately following this prayer includes a five-fold repetition of the imperative "do not be anxious!"?

Do you remember when the disciples asked Jesus about the greatest in the kingdom of heaven? He gave the disciples an object lesson they would never forget. He set a child before them and declared: " 'Truly I say to you, unless you are converted and become like children, you shall not enter the kingdom of heaven' " (Matt. 18:3). In verse 4 Jesus refers to the child's humility. The child is totally dependent on His father. He has no pretenses and no worries.

Because our focus is so often on ourselves, because our prayers are so *me-* and *mine-centered,* because we don't really believe that we can count on God to watch out for us if we turn our back on our own concerns to "seek first His kingdom," even our prayer lives can become worry central. Many times we are strangely more anxious *in* prayer than we are *out* of prayer.

It's human nature, of course. But God has chosen to have a relationship with us that transforms the natural. " 'Your heavenly Father knows that you need all these things' " (Matt. 6:32). This does not mean we shouldn't plan wisely, save money, and invest well. It does mean, however, that we cannot allow a reliance on our own income potential to replace our daily dependence on the Lord.

Jesus has invited us to live in such a dynamic relationship with our Father that we can ban anxiety. So we are instructed simply to ask Him for our daily bread.

Read Matthew 14:19. What did Jesus do before distributing the meal to the multitudes? _____

What should saying grace over a meal indicate about the person praying and those silently praying alongside?
❑ It's a customary tradition.
❑ They hope others will notice their piety and think well of them.
❑ They are grateful to God for His provision.

> Ordering the multitudes to recline on the grass, He took the five loaves and the two fish, and looking up toward heaven, He blessed the food, and breaking the loaves He gave them to the disciples, and the disciples gave to the multitudes.
> —*Matthew 14:19*

Jesus looked into heaven to acknowledge that God is the Creator of all things. He gave thanks for God's provisions.

As we ask Him for our daily bread ...

We are made aware that every meal we enjoy is eaten in His presence and provided by His hand. "He has satisfied the thirsty soul, and the hungry soul He has filled with what is good" (Ps. 107:9).

We are reminded that Jesus Himself is " 'the bread of life; he who comes to Me shall not hunger, and he who believes in Me shall never thirst' " (John 6:35).

We learn to trust God for each day's amount, just as Israel had to depend on God to provide manna from heaven to feed them during their wanderings in the wilderness. God warned them not to store their manna for the coming day—anything left overnight would be spoiled by morning—because He not only desired to provide for their nourishment but also to teach them that they could trust His daily provision sight unseen.

Read Exodus 16:11. What was God teaching the Israelites by giving them meat and bread? _____

What does God want to teach you about relying on His daily provision? _____

The Lord spoke to Moses, saying, "I have heard the grumblings of the sons of Israel; speak to them, saying, 'At twilight you shall eat meat, and in the morning you shall be filled with bread; and you shall know that I am the Lord your God.' "
—*Exodus 16:11*

We turn our back on the allure of riches, refusing to become dependent on our own resources—not just our money and our income-earning potential but also our family connections, our professional position, our personal charm. We depend on God alone for every aspect of our daily lives, trusting Him only for the things we need.

We recognize that the personal pronoun in this prayer is plural—that we are committed to sharing with those who do not have adequate provision. We know that God will provide us enough for the next day, so we are free to share our excess with anyone who may not have enough bread for this day.

Read Deuteronomy 15:7-11 in your Bible. Do you know of persons in your church family who could benefit from your sharing your excess with them? (check) ❏ Yes ❏ No ❏ I will look into it.

What would help you become more open-handed in giving to those in need? Check one or more.

❑ more trust that God will supply my needs
❑ more awareness of needs around me
❑ finding an appropriate way to help
❑ praying for compassion for others
❑ seeking forgiveness for selfishness and hoarding

Do you see the difference inherent in this kind of praying? Do you ever want to settle again for a prayer life that's always asking God for more stuff for you? Don't you hunger for a relationship with God that keeps you in the center of His will instead of just keeping you happy—one that keeps you fully fed while you're fully serving? Didn't Jesus Himself say, " 'Whoever wishes to save his life shall lose it; but whoever loses his life for My sake and the gospel's shall save it' " (Mark 8:35)?

All of life, you see, is a sacred trust. Daily bread is plenty when God is your portion. Get your Father's perspective on everything you experience. Ask Him how you can live to honor His name, advance His kingdom, and do His will. Then, relax in the knowledge that He will provide daily bread, forgiveness, and victory over evil.

Prayer Time

Jehovah Jireh, pronounced Jié-rah, means *the Lord provides.* Abraham experienced *Jehovah Jireh* when God provided a substitute sacrifice for his son, Isaac. (See Gen. 22:1-18.) Ask God to show Himself as Provider for your needs. Also, pray for others who need God's provisions for kingdom service.

_____

_____

_____

FORGIVE US OUR DEBTS

> "If therefore you are presenting your offering at the altar, and there remember that your brother has something against you, leave your offering there before the altar, and go your way; first be reconciled to your brother, and then come and present your offering."
>
> —*Matthew 5:23-24*

Debt is a concept we all understand. We know the extra hours that we work, the things we forego, the nights we labor over the budget trying to get the nagging monster of debt off our backs. It worries us even when we're not thinking about it. But when was the last time your *sin* kept you up at night? Not because you were ashamed of yourself, not because you didn't like the conflict it had created, but just because you realized that you were *in debt to God*—because you had grieved His Holy Spirit—because you had tarnished His hallowed name?

Sin is serious—*always* serious—because it drives a wedge between us and our Father. The time we spend in debt to God is time we spend away from Him. And the time we spend away from Him is time we waste forever. Clinging to sin and seeking His kingdom cannot happen at the same time.

Read the following Scriptures and match them with the effects of sin on our relationship with God.

Deuteronomy 31:18   He does not listen to us.
Psalm 66:18   He is separated from us.
Isaiah 59:2   He hides His face from us.

How does it make you feel to know that God will not listen if we continue in sin? Circle all that apply.

ashamed	sad	abandoned	depressed
lost	sorrowful	worried	scared

Debt Free

If we are going to fulfill the three commitments we have made to God, this petition to "forgive us our debts" must be given equal weight with our request for "daily bread." Yes, God wants us to have four good walls and grocery money. But for us to be useful instruments in His hand, we desperately need the freedom of a clear conscience. If we hide our sin or attempt to deny its existence, we will not experience the incredible joy of knowing God's forgiveness and the full privileges of sonship.

One evening years ago my older brother and I had a minor altercation at home that ended with a thrown basketball crashing into the mirror on our dresser. My dad quickly appeared on the scene. But by then the room was quiet except for two boys trying to look and sound as innocent as possible—and my brother holding the basketball. Leaping on this bit of leverage, I quickly blamed Philip for the whole affair and declared that I had nothing to do with it. So Dad took my brother out to punish him and left me alone to think about my involvement.

Well, you know how quiet that room felt. I struggled with my uneasy conscience for several hours, until finally I plucked up enough courage to walk into my father's bedroom and stutter out my confession. "Dad, I know you think Philip was responsible for the broken mirror, but I may have had something to do with it."

I'll never forget his response: "Son, I knew you were involved. I was just waiting for you to understand your guilt."

When we confess our sin to God, we don't reveal anything about us that He doesn't already know. We come before Him—this Father who loves us—with absolute honesty. We say the same thing He is already thinking, which is what the term *confession* literally means.

Confession is not a sweeping apology that makes us feel better on the outside while making no impact on our hearts. We must be specific as we pray this prayer throughout the day, personalizing the petition by allowing the Holy Spirit to bring areas of sinfulness to mind that are hindering our relationship with the Father and with others. When we are specific in confession—naming times and dates and details—God quickly overflows our sadness and brokenness with His overwhelming joy. We experience liberation from our debts and the restoration of intimacy that enables us to call God Father.

Anything less than full disclosure always brings less than full release.

> If we say that we have no sin, we are deceiving ourselves, and the truth is not in us. If we confess our sins, He is faithful and righteous to forgive us our sins and to cleanse us from all unrighteousness.
>
> —*1 John 1:8-9*

Explain the difference between an apology and true confession.

An apology is _____

but true confession is _____.

How would you know that you had expressed to God true

confession? _____

Come clean. Tell Him everything. He knows your need even before you agree with Him. Nothing that you can confess will surprise Him or exceed His desire and ability to forgive. Stay debt free through the day—moment-by-moment, at the slightest twinge from your conscience. Debt-free living enables you to hallow God's name, expand His kingdom, and do His will.

> *Prayer Time*
>
> **Read Psalm 51:1-2 in your Bible. If you need to ask God's forgiveness for a specific sin, pray these words as your prayer of confession.**

Moses made haste to bow low toward the earth and worship. And he said, "If now I have found favor in Thy sight, O Lord, I pray, let the Lord go along in our midst, even though the people are so obstinate; and do Thou pardon our iniquity and our sin, and take us as Thine own possession."
—*Exodus 34:8-9*

"Pardon, I pray, the iniquity of this people according to the greatness of Thy lovingkindness, just as Thou also hast forgiven this people, from Egypt even until now." So the Lord said, "I have pardoned them according to your word."
—*Numbers 14:19-20*

Share the Wealth

There is more to debt reduction than God's forgiveness for ourselves. We have the opportunity to be spiritual advocates for others who need His forgiveness. Disciples grieve at the sin in the world because they know its damaging effects. Jesus saw the city of Jerusalem and wept because the rebellious people did not recognize God's coming (Luke 19:41-42). We, too, should mourn at the sin we see in our world.

Read Exodus 34:8-9 and Numbers 14:19-20. What did Moses ask

God to do? _____

If you know of a sin that needs God's forgiveness in each of the following areas, ask God to forgive it. Check each one as you pray.

❑ Family   ❑ Sunday School class   ❑ Church members
❑ Church leaders   ❑ Community   ❑ Nation
❑ Others _____

The request for God to "forgive us our debts" also includes the adjoining phrase—"as we forgive our debtors." Now, this shouldn't be misunderstood to mean that offering forgiveness to others is a prerequisite to our receiving it. Not at all. The Bible is absolutely clear that we can do *nothing* to earn God's forgiveness (see Rom. 5:6-8 or Eph. 2:8-9). Grace flows from His very nature. It was made available to us even when we were dead in our trespasses and sins.

Those who are willing to forgive others show that they have been truly forgiven themselves. Jesus, using the terminology of *debt* as a vivid description of sin, told the story of a king who decided to settle some of his slaves' outstanding accounts (Matt. 18:21-35). Read this parable in your Bible.

The point of the parable is crystal clear. A true experience of grace makes us gracious toward others who have wronged us. When we remain unforgiving, we have not taken seriously the enormity of our own sin and the cost Christ incurred to provide our forgiveness. When we refuse to forgive, we are the ones held captive.

Read Colossians 3:13. Our motivation to forgive is because ...
❑ **People deserve our forgiveness.**   ❑ **Christ forgave us.**
❑ **People deserve a second chance.**   ❑ **God will punish them.**

... bearing with one another, and forgiving each other, whoever has a complaint against anyone; just as the Lord forgave you, so also should you.
—*Colossians 3:13*

None of us are worthy of forgiveness, it is a gift, an act of grace. None of us deserve a second chance—"The wages of sin is death." While God may choose to punish the person who wronged us, that's God's business, not ours. But we shouldn't want God's wrath to be spilled out on anyone. Our motivation to forgive is because Christ forgave us.

Prayer Time

Whom do you need to release from their debt of sin against you? What is keeping you from forgiving them? Ask God to give you a forgiving heart.

_____

_____

_____

DELIVER US FROM EVIL

Our sin problem would be bad enough if we only had to deal with the messes we've already made. But each day we dig the hole a little deeper. Each day we run the risk of making things even worse. But God—again—can be trusted to meet all of our needs. He knows that empty pantries devoid of "daily bread" can make us resentful, and strained relationships not mended by forgiving "our debtors" can make us bitter. Failing to live faithfully before Him robs us of both reward and reputation, of worship and witness, of courage and character.

We have a lot to lose by not obeying Him, and we don't have a prayer unless He helps us.

Nowhere Else to Hide

The quickest way to make this request a reality—not to lead us into temptation, but to deliver us from evil—is to realize that we can make no headway in holiness without God's constant provision. Not only are we no match for our adversary the devil, but we cannot even trust *ourselves* for help in keeping our lives clean.

According to James 1:13-14, which phrase best explains temptation?
❏ **The devil made me do it.**
❏ **God is trying to trip me up.**
❏ **Temptation is the pull of our own evil thoughts.**
❏ **Willpower is the key to overcoming temptation.**

While Scripture describes Satan as a deceiver and a tempter, we have no one to blame for temptation but ourselves. Temptation is the pull of our own lust, which leads to sin. As long as we are here on earth, we will have to contend with our enemy, with our environment, and even with ourselves in order to let God lead us to victory.

One day when His kingdom is fully revealed, we will escape even the presence of sin. Until that time comes, we must lean on Him every day—and at frequent points throughout the day—in order to escape the power of sin. We waste our time when we fight temptation with high goals and lofty reforms only, for God alone can give us strength to overcome our shortcomings. In the margin, read how David put it.

Let no one say when he is tempted, "I am being tempted by God"; for God cannot be tempted by evil, and He Himself does not tempt anyone. But each one is tempted when he is carried away and enticed by his own lust.
—*James 1:13-14*

He delivered me from
    my strong enemy,
And from those who
    hated me, for they
    were too mighty
    for me.
They confronted me
    in the day of my
    calamity,
But the Lord was
    my stay.
—*Psalm 18:17-18*

82

Help Me, Lord!

Look at both halves of this imperative petition, for it takes both to understand the full-service help the Lord provides.

When we pray for protection from temptation, we are asking God to spare us from exposure to situations that would severely test our vulnerability. He has said that He will never allow us to be tempted beyond what we are able to bear (1 Cor. 10:13). What a promise! Our Father has already measured the difficulty levels on all the temptations we're going to face, and none of them are able to defeat us unless we decide to let them. Even where sinning would be so easy and finding someone to understand would be no problem—*we can pray to be delivered from yielding to the temptation* and building another mountain of debt between us and our Heavenly Father.

As you start your day, ask God to keep you as far away from compromising situations as possible—the copy machine gossip, the lottery tickets, the wicked Web sites—wherever you're liable to lose sight of the kingdom. And as you pray throughout the day, ask Him for the strength to keep you from searching these places out yourself, especially when you're tired or discouraged, when you've unwittingly let your guard down. You know the sins that cause you the most trouble. You know the warning lights that flash when you're in the wrong place, around the wrong people, or under the influence of the wrong motive. Instead of letting them become stumbling blocks, make each one a trigger that reminds you to pray. When your hope for personal holiness is in Jesus Christ alone, you'll find you have muscles you never knew you had.

> Greater is He who is in you than he who is in the world.
> —*1 John 4:4*

When Jesus was tempted (Matt. 4:1-11), He quoted Scripture. What Scripture verses could you quote when dealing with specific temptations? (Clue: If you have a good concordance, look up the word and write one of the verses listed.)

Temptation   **Scripture Passage**

_____   _____

_____   _____

_____   _____

Need Anything Else?

Jesus' temptation was one of the most dramatic events in all the Bible. The devil met Him one-on-one in the wilderness—pure evil and pure righteousness squaring off for supremacy.

First, he made an appeal to His body. With Jesus physically starved from fasting, the devil tempted Him with a taste of bread.

Second, he made an appeal to His soul. High on top of the temple, with a mass of potential followers ready to swarm to the spectacle of a miracle-working Messiah, the devil made a power play for His pride.

Third, he made an appeal to His spirit. Up a notch from the temple to the mountaintops, the devil offered Him all the kingdoms in all the world ... if He would merely bow down and worship him.

But the Father supplied the Son with everything He needed—*body, soul, and spirit*—to withstand the onslaught of Satan's lies and deception.

And today God offers us—His children—the same provision.

- It covers our *past*—forgiveness for every sin we've ever committed.
- It covers our *present*—our daily need for daily bread.
- It covers our *future*—deliverance from each coming temptation.

We can live this day worry-free and with a clean conscience because our Father has us covered all the way around.

Prayer Time

Jehovah Mekadesh, pronounced Mek´-a-desh, means *the Lord who sanctifies you.* As you pray this name, ask God to keep you from sin and to allow you to be used to serve Him today. No matter your needs, God has them covered.

_____

_____

_____

Viewer Guide
SESSION FOUR

The three petitions: We are asking for everything we need to fulfill the three _____.

We are B_____, S_____, and S_____.

We are asking for b_____, f_____, and spiritual v_____.

A. Give us our daily bread.

The prayer reminds us there is no separation between the _____

and the _____.

Every meal is eaten in His _____ and _____ by His hand.

The key to worry-free living is in the command:_____

B. Forgive us our debts.

Forgiveness requires _____.

Requests for forgiveness enable and require us to _____.

When we refuse to forgive, we block our ability to believe and receive God's

forgiveness for our _____.

C. Deliver us from evil.

James 1:13-14 tells us God cannot _____ us to evil.

We ask God to keep us from _____ to temptation.

1 Corinthians 10:13: "No temptation has overtaken you but such as is common to man; and God is faithful, who will not allow you to be tempted beyond what you are able, but with the temptation will provide the way of escape also, so that you will be able to endure it."

When Jesus was tempted in the wilderness, He affirmed God's _____.

FEEL THE POWER

Three Reminders from the Prayer of Jesus

" '[Thine is the kingdom, and the power, and the glory, forever. Amen.]' "
—*Matthew 6:13*

Praying without ceasing shouldn't have an ending, and it doesn't. The prayer closes with a benediction reminiscent of 1 Chronicles 29:11 that again reveals a God-focused frame of mind, an eternal perspective that should run through all our prayers, all the time. " '[Thine] is the kingdom, and the power, and the glory forever. Amen' " (Matt. 6:13).

Oh, how quickly it rolls off our lips, how easy it is to withdraw from our memory banks. But encapsulated in this sacred sentence are all the confidence, assurance, and understanding you'll ever need in order to walk into your next meeting or appointment with your head up, to face the results of your latest lab work or job application, to walk through a difficult situation with your teenager, or to confront your spouse about a long-standing matter of concern.

Never fear: the kingdom will come.

His power will prevail.

He will cause His glory to shine.

All you have to do is trust Him. This Father who loves you beyond your ability to grasp it also has divine authority beyond life's ability to defeat you.

When you wrap your prayers in awe and worship—concentrating on the *Who* instead of the *whats, wheres, whys,* and *whens*—He rewards you with the knowledge that you are in the presence of complete provision.

Praise the Lord!

JOURNAL YOUR
THOUGHTS & PRAYERS

Use these questions to guide your prayers this week:

1. What did you learn this week about His kingdom, power, and glory?
2. How did you advance God's kingdom?
3. How did God demonstrate His strength and power in your life this week?
4. In what areas do you struggle to give God the glory due Him?

Write what God is teaching you in His School of Prayer.

_____

_____

_____

_____

_____

_____

_____

_____

_____

_____

POINT OF ORDER

Many times we quote this final passage from the Lord's Prayer in an almost singsong fashion. Let me make one suggestion that may help you break the cycle of rote memorization and force you to think about what you're praying. Place the emphasis on the word *Your.* Or for the more traditional among us, *Thine.*

The focus of prayer is always to be on God.

If we're going to pray the Lord's Prayer with the absolute abandon that Jesus prayed it, we must know our Father so that we fully trust Him. My prayer life has been greatly enhanced by understanding my Father's attributes. My Father knows everything. The Bible refers to this attribute as *omniscience.* I am moved by the truth that God not only knows everything but knows everything about me and still loves me. I can enjoy a sense of security throughout each day.

We've been discovering through this entire book that the focus of prayer is always to be on God. We've also seen that we humans are prone to worry more about *our* kingdoms, place undue trust in *our own* power, gravitate toward situations and positions where *we* get the glory.

Therefore, we need the discipline of making sure that we remember whose kingdom matters. We need the realization that we can do nothing by ourselves but that His power can turn any event toward His will and draw any person to repentance and salvation.

Jesus teaches that we are totally dependent upon Him for spiritual fruit. Explain John 15:5 in your own words.

_____

_____

> "I am the vine, you are the branches; he who abides in Me, and I in him, he bears much fruit; for apart from Me you can do nothing."
> —*John 15:5*

We need a constant check on our own pride and self-importance—a daily desire to do all things for His praise and glory.

Yours is the kingdom.

Yours is the power.

Yours is the glory.

Now and forever. Amen and amen.

As we keep coming back to this line from the Lord's Prayer throughout the day, we need to remind ourselves to look beyond the visible, the obvious, the natural, the immediate. We focus on this One " 'who made the world and all things in it,' " who is not " 'served by human hands, as though He needed anything, since He Himself gives to all life and breath and all things' " (Acts 17:24-25).

What difference would it make in your daily activities if you reminded yourself that everything should be done to advance God's kingdom in His power and for His glory?

---

0 degree difference   **180 degree difference**

When God fills up our scope of vision, we can't help but see things in a heavenly light.

> When God fills up our scope of vision, we can't help but see things in a heavenly light.

⌒

YOURS IS THE KINGDOM

The first part of this benediction reminds us that our greatest desire and privilege as children of God is to participate in the work of His kingdom. He is the King, and we gladly serve Him. He alone can grant us the resources we need for daily, victorious living. Therefore, all the

89

commitments and requests we make in prayer are placed in the context of the higher purposes of God, of His will, and of His eternal kingdom.

Jesus lived out His prayer. Match the following paraphrases with the Scripture passage.

"I don't seek my own glory."   Luke 22:42
"I do nothing on my own."   John 5:30
"Father, not my will, but Yours be done."   John 7:17-18
"My Father's will is for everyone to   John 6:38-40
  believe in His Son."

If we are to live the prayer of Jesus, we must submit to His divine will. Write the key thought in each of the following verses:

Psalm 40:8 _____

Psalm 143:10 _____

Ephesians 6:6 _____

James 4:15 _____

How teachable is your spirit when God's will contradicts human reasoning or interferes with your plans?
❑ Poor Student (Give me a D)
❑ Slow Learner (Give me a C)
❑ Good Student (Give me a B)
❑ Teacher's Pet (Give me an A)

Why? _____

_____

_____

As we saw before, this kingdom-focused living offers you an added bonus. When the driving desire of your life is to seek the advancement of His kingdom in the world that lies right in front of you—your home, your school, your workplace, even your weekly trip to the grocery—He removes all your reasons for worrying about the things you need. How foolish to " 'lay up for yourselves treasures upon earth, where moth and rust destroy, and where thieves break in and steal.' "

With God acknowledged as your total source of supply, you can " 'lay up for yourselves treasures in heaven, where neither moth nor rust destroys, and where thieves do not break in or steal; for where your treasure is, there will your heart be also' " (Matt. 6:19-21). "Be anxious for nothing, but in everything by prayer and supplication with thanksgiving let your requests be made known to God. And the peace of God, which surpasses all comprehension, shall guard your hearts and your minds in Christ Jesus" (Phil. 4:6-7).

If you had a "mood ring" that depicted your average stress level, what color would it be?
❑ Green: calm
❑ Blue: a little nervous
❑ Orange: concerned
❑ Pink: fretful
❑ Red: panicked

What is causing you the most stress in your life right now?

_____

_____

What does Philippians 4:6-7 suggest about how to reduce your stress? (The verse is printed in the above paragraph.)

_____

_____

Yesterday's prayer was for yesterday's needs. Tomorrow you'll need to recommit yourself to pursuing kingdom purposes. But for now there's just today—and a God more than able to meet your needs and enable you to meet His desires.

The kingdom comes first. The kingdom comes last. *The kingdom comes ... throughout the day.*

The kingdom comes first. The kingdom comes last. *The kingdom comes ...* throughout the day.

Much of our time and prayer life is devoted to praying for temporal things such as health and physical provisions. Read Matthew 6:19–21 in your Bible. What is the problem with focusing all of our time and energy on temporal things?

_____

What changes will you need to make in order to realign your time, energy, and resources to focus on eternal things?

time: _____

energy: _____

resources: _____

Prayer Time

We are called to join Jesus in accomplishing His mission (Matt. 28:19–20). Quietly reflect on the following question: Lord, how would you like to use me to advance your kingdom in my ...

home: _____

school (workplace): _____

community: _____

church: _____

As you pray, ask, "What would you have me do?"

YOURS IS THE POWER

On September 15, 2000, our seminary community was shaken by the slaughter of seven young people at Wedgewood Baptist Church in Fort Worth, Texas. Larry Ashcroft, a deluded outcast with contempt for all things religious, burst into a Wednesday night youth concert and ruthlessly, randomly began shooting. Three of the young adults killed included two students and a recent alumnus of our institution. Two other seminary students were seriously injured.

I remember the Lord bringing this passage to mind during those horrific few days of maddening questions and boiling disbelief: "We have this treasure in earthen vessels, that the surpassing greatness of the power will be of God and not from ourselves; we are afflicted in every way, but not crushed; perplexed, but not despairing; persecuted, but not forsaken; struck down, but not destroyed; always carrying about in the body the dying of Jesus, that the life of Jesus also may be manifested in our body. For we who live are constantly being delivered over to death for Jesus' sake, that the life of Jesus also may be manifested in our mortal flesh" (2 Cor. 4:7-11).

If ever there was a time when all of us felt totally powerless in ourselves to help these families deal with their crushing losses, this was it. If ever there was a time when innocent people felt powerless to defend themselves and their friends from the hellish rain of a wretched gunman's bullets, it was that mournful late summer evening at the corner of Whitman and Walton Streets.

What situations, circumstances, or events are you currently going through in which you feel powerless? Check all that apply.

❏ Parenting   ❏ Marriage

❏ Caring for parents   ❏ Health concerns

❏ Job   ❏ Catastrophic illness

❏ Finances   ❏ Death in the family

❏ Health   ❏ Other: _____

Read Genesis 50:20. What have you experienced that looked unfortunate but that God turned into something good? Write your response in the margin.

Joseph's words make clear that what life can dish out, God can transform into a spectacle of His glory, for *His* is the power. *All* power. *The* power. In the words of one of the ministers who prayed during the emotional memorial service following the Wedgewood tragedy, "We thank you, God, that you waste nothing."

And even on our more ordinary days, when we feel powerless to deal with a back-biting coworker, or to accomplish the mountain of tasks that lie between now and bedtime, or to make sense of an unfulfilling life that seems to be going nowhere, we can quit trying to respond in our own strength and rely instead on God's power.

Most of the struggles we have over daily provision, forgiveness, and temptation to sin—the three requests from the previous chapter that encircle every need in the human life—are the result of continuing to labor under the mistaken idea that we can live the Christian life out of our own resources. We must understand that we are spiritually *impotent,* but He is *omnipotent.*

We are without hope, but He is without limits.

We are weak, but He is strong.

We are without hope, but He is without limits. We are weak, but He is strong.

Through the centuries, people of faith have learned the importance of relying on God's power rather than their own. Read the following Scriptures and write the main thought.

2 Samuel 22:33 _____

Psalm 46:1 _____

Matthew 19:26 _____

2 Corinthians 12:9-10 _____

Which of the following best expresses your feelings about relying on God's strength? Check one or more.
❏ It is a crutch for weak people.
❏ I guess we all need God at some point.
❏ I fight my own battles, until I get into trouble.
❏ I rely on God for the big stuff.
❏ He is my strength in all things.
❏ Without Him I can do nothing.

If you have been able to make it in life on your own power, you have never experienced the thrill of being a part of something so big that only God could do it. Ask God for a vision that calls for His strength to complete. Then start your adventure in faith.

New Testament scholars have coined a phrase to capture this wonderful truth that we can experience God's eternal power in the present day. They call it "*eschatology becoming actualized*"—*eschatology* being a reference to final realities. When we declare "thine is the power," we are praising God for allowing us to experience in actual, real time the power of God that will last for all time.

Perhaps this benediction brings into sharper focus some of the great promises of Scripture, such as: "I can do all things through Him who strengthens me. ... My God shall supply all your needs according to His riches in glory in Christ Jesus" (Phil. 4:13,19).

As you read these familiar verses again, can't you just hear the echoing refrain? "Thine is the power." No matter what you're experiencing in your daily life, be confident that all power belongs to your King, and His power is available to you as you seek His kingdom.

Jesus affirms this attribute of omnipotence in His address when He declares "who art in heaven." There are many references to this truth throughout the Bible, but none any clearer than Psalm 115:3 where God is compared with the lifeless idols. "Our God is in the heavens; He does whatever He pleases."

Just think: we have a Heavenly Father who has all authority in heaven and on earth and who guides our every step. He knows no limitations for He has all power. I continue to be challenged by Jesus' assertions that he could do nothing apart from His Father. Yet He was fully confident that He could do everything His Father showed Him (John 5:19-20). Read these verses in the margin. Jesus models for us the sort of dependence and assurance our Father wants us to have throughout the day.

We can pray to our Father with absolute confidence. We know that He knows us, He cares for us, He is always with us, He has all power, and He is altogether good. Our Father invites us to spend our day in His presence. Prayer is a constant communion with our Dad.

Jesus therefore answered and was saying to them, "Truly, truly, I say to you, the Son can do nothing of Himself, unless it is something He sees the Father doing; for whatever the Father does, these things the Son also does in like manner. For the Father loves the Son, and shows Him all things that He Himself is doing; and greater works than these will He show Him, that you may marvel."

—*John 5:19-20*

Prayer Time

Call on the name of *El Elyon,* pronounced El El-yon, *God Most High.* God is the possessor of the heavens and the earth. He alone can provide for our needs. Ask God to provide you with the power and strength to accomplish His will. Claim the promise of Philippians 4:13 and 19, that *El Elyon* will provide for your needs according to His riches in glory.

_____

_____

_____

YOURS IS THE GLORY

Glory is a great Bible word. It refers to God's presence being made manifest on earth. In Old Testament times God's glory was seen in such spectacular expressions as the burning bush, the pillar of fire that guided the Hebrews by night, and the delivery of the Ten Commandments to Moses on Mount Sinai.

In the New Testament, of course, God is glorified through His Son, Jesus Christ—"glory as of the only begotten from the Father, full of grace and truth" (John 1:14). When He turned the water into wine at the wedding feast in Cana, we are told that this miracle "manifested His glory" (John 2:11). His raising of Lazarus from the dead was intended "for the glory of God, that the Son of God may be glorified by it" (John 11:4). And on the Mount of Transfiguration, His face, His hair, even the clothes on His back radiated with a glimpse of heavenly splendor that flung three tough, weather-worn disciples face down, flat on the ground, terrified at the awesome display of His holiness.

What do the following verses tell us about Jesus?

John 8:54-55 _____

John 11:4 _____

John 14:13 _____

John 17:26 _____

If we model our lives on Jesus' life, what do these Scriptures suggest about how we should live?

_____

_____

Such glory catches your breath, sends shivers up your spine, awakens you to realities uncommonly seen by eyes grown dim in this dingy, moth-eaten world. But nowhere was His glory more evident than when He approached the cross, praying in selfless abandon: " 'I glorified Thee on the earth, having accomplished the work which Thou hast given Me to do. And now, glorify Thou Me together with Thyself, Father, with the glory which I had with Thee before the world was' " (John 17:4-5).

He had done it all perfectly, just as His Father had told Him. He was within hours of completing His redemptive mission by shedding His blood for the sins of the world. Yet He had the vision to look beyond the splintery cross, the piercing nails, the heaving gasps for breath, out across the centuries to those He was sending into human history, just as His Father had sent Him into the world. " 'The glory which Thou hast given Me I have given to them; that they may be one, just as We are one. ... Father, I desire that they also, whom Thou hast given Me, be with Me where I am, in order that they may behold My glory, which Thou hast given Me; for Thou didst love Me before the foundation of the world' " (John 17:22,24).

For those who are in a saving relationship with Jesus Christ, there is something breathless even about daily, ordinary living, for "whom He called, these He also justified; and whom He justified, these He also glorified" (Rom. 8:30). The Scriptures tell us that in heaven "the city has no need of the sun or of the moon to shine upon it, for the glory of God has illumined it, and its lamp is the Lamb" (Rev. 21:23). Yet somehow, even here where pollutants contaminate our drinking water, industrial exhaust thickens the air, and seasonal allergens drive us to the medicine cabinet for relief, we can experience the glory of God "on earth as it is in heaven."

Reread John 17:22,24 and Romans 8:30 at the bottom of page 97. What does it mean that Christ has glorified us? Compare your response to the one given in the following paragraph.

_____

_____

_____

> "You are the light of the world. A city set on a hill cannot be hidden. Nor do men light a lamp, and put it under the peck-measure, but on the lampstand; and it gives light to all who are in the house. Let your light shine before men in such a way that they may see your good works, and glorify your Father who is in heaven."
> —*Matthew 5:14-16*

When we accept Jesus as our Savior, the Holy Spirit comes into our lives and dwells with us. This means God is with us, living inside us. We experience the glory of God, His light in our lives. This light enables us to make His presence known to the world. That is why Jesus said that we are not to keep our lights hidden.

When we acknowledge "Thine is ... the glory," we dare request in childlike faith that He reveal His glory in and through us. What a wonder that Almighty God would choose to express His awesome presence through our actions and deeds, lighting the corners of a world that is growing increasingly dark and spiritually bankrupt.

Read 1 Peter 4:11 in your Bible. How would it change your day if you consistently lived, "Thine is the glory"?

_____

_____

_____

> Whoever speaks, let him speak, as it were, the utterances of God; whoever serves, let him do so as by the strength which God supplies; so that in all things God may be glorified through Jesus Christ, to whom belongs the glory and dominion forever and ever. Amen.
> —*1 Peter 4:11*

If you would like to read related Scripture verses on this subject, check out Matthew 5:16, John 15:8, and 1 Corinthians 10:31.

Where God's people are, God's glory shines. The curtain that stands between earth and eternity parts for just a moment. And those smothering under the oppressive, suffocating deception of sin and its nasty side effects can open wide their weary arms and bathe in its liberating light.

Will you be an outpost of glory in your corner of the world? Then seek His kingdom, make your life a pure, available instrument for His power, and be willing to invade the darkness around you with anything He tells you to do and anything He tells you to say.

Glory be to God!

Where God's people are, God's glory shines.

Prayer Time

Address the Father as *Jehovah Nissi* **(pronounced Ja-hoe-vah Niss-e),** *the Lord is my banner,* **to be your banner of victory over the temptation to seek your own power and glory. He alone is worthy to be glorified.**

_____

_____

_____

_____

FINALLY

I hope that God will place this pattern of prayer into your heart and life. I hope you will pray it every morning and keep it on your mind throughout the day. God has done something marvelous in my heart by teaching me to use His prayer in this way, and I know He will do the same—and even greater—in your own life.

Today, when I walk around the seminary campus, I am constantly thinking, "Lord, your name is at stake here." When I respond to people who sometimes misunderstand or misuse me, I don't take it personally or try to defend myself. I just say, "Lord, the only issue I care about is this: Is your name being exalted in this decision I'm making, in this action I'm proposing, in this thing I'm about to do? If not, my mind is changed right now. But if so, I'll stand against any opposition in order to declare the name of the Lord." Not too many years from now, the name Hemphill may not mean a lot, but the name of the Lord Jesus Christ will stand forever. I want to make His name hallowed in and through my life.

When I wake up in the morning, I consider that whatever I will do for the kingdom is the most important business in front of me today. It may be something obvious or expected in my routine. But even during those times when I'm outside my official capacities or my church experience, I'm still seeking the kingdom because I know it can invade my life at any place, at any moment. Even the most mundane moments in my life have become electrified with meaning as God has shown me the kingdom realities that dwell within them.

When I consider the will of God for this day, I have decided that my answer is yes—no matter what the question is. Too many times I've waited to hear the question before I decided what I would answer. But as a Christian, I know that the only answer I can give to my Father is "yes, Lord." *Do you want me to serve you overseas?* The answer is yes. *Do you want me to share the gospel with my next-door neighbor?* The answer is yes. *Do you want me to go back to the person I spoke to harshly or apologize to the person I'm upset with?* Yes, yes, the answer is yes. I don't know what the question is; I don't even *care* what the question is. My answer is "yes, Lord, yes."

My prayer is that you will join me in making each moment a kingdom experience. We are here on assignment, and we've been given our orders. Let us pray that God will help us spend every minute in His presence and glorify His name with every inch of our being.

Why not start right now: *"Our Father who is in heaven …"*

Prayer Time

Repeat the following prayer or write your own below:

Father, remind us daily that Yours is the kingdom, Yours is the power, and Yours is the glory. We want to experience Your glory on earth, just as it is in heaven. Reveal Your glory through us. Express Your awesome presence through our words and actions—lighting the corners of our world that are dark because of sin. Make us instruments of Your power so that You may be glorified. Make us aware that each moment and every activity is an opportunity to make Your name holy. Help us to remember that kingdom business is more important than anything else we do. Whatever You want us to do today, our answer is yes. In the name of Jesus, Amen.

_____

_____

_____

_____

_____

Viewer Guide
SESSION FIVE

The prayer ends the way it begins with the focus on _____.

The prayer reminds us we are prone to worry about our _____,

to place undue trust in our _____, and to gravitate to situations

and positions where we get the _____.

A. Yours is the kingdom.
This is the key to _____ - free living: Seek first His _____.

B. Yours is the power.
Prayer is an affirmation of our _____."

Philippians 4:13: "I can do all things through _____"

Philippians 4:19: "My God shall supply _____"

C. Yours is the glory.
John 1:14: "And we saw His _____ as of the only
begotten of the Father."

We are _____ in the presence of God's awe and glory.

D. Four Challenges
1. Start _____ _____ this prayer.

2. Use a prayer _____.

3. Find an _____ _____.

4. Lead a _____ of *The Prayer of Jesus*.

HOW TO BECOME A CHRISTIAN

All of us want to love and be loved. That desire comes from God who is love (1 John 4:7). God wants us to love Him above anyone or anything else because loving Him puts everything else in life in perspective. In God we find the hope, peace, and joy that are possible only through a personal relationship with Him. When He lives in us, we can truly love others. We can develop a deep, enriching prayer life to communicate with the One who loved us so much that He sent His Son to die in our place.

John 3:16 says, " 'God so loved the world, that He gave His only begotten Son, that whoever believes in Him should not perish, but have eternal life.' " In order to live our earthly lives "abundantly" (see John 10:10), we must accept God's gift of love.

A relationship with God begins by admitting that we are sinners. Romans 3:23 says, "All have sinned and fall short of the glory of God." The price for these wrongdoings is separation from God. We deserve to pay the price for our sin. "The wages [or price] of sin is death, but the free gift of God is eternal life in Christ Jesus our Lord" (Rom. 6:23).

God's love comes to us right in the middle of our sin. "God demonstrates His own love toward us, in that while we were yet sinners, Christ died for us" (Rom. 5:8). He doesn't ask us to clean up our lives first—in fact, without His help, we are incapable of living by His standards. He wants us to come as we are.

Forgiveness begins when we admit our sin to God. When we do, He is faithful to forgive and restore our relationship with Him. "If we confess our sins, He is faithful and righteous to forgive us our sins and to cleanse us from all unrighteousness" (1 John 1:9).

Scripture confirms that this love gift and relationship with God is not just for a special few but for everyone. " 'Everyone who calls on the name of the Lord will be saved' " (Rom. 10:13, NIV). The way you begin this relationship is by simply asking Him. Pray this prayer:

Dear God, I know that I am imperfect and separated from You. Please forgive me of my sin and adopt me as Your child. Thank You for this gift of life through the sacrifice of Your Son. I will live my life for You. Amen.

In your Bible read 1 John 5:11–12. These verses assure you that if you accept God's Son, Jesus Christ, as your Savior and Lord, you have eternal life. You are a child of God!

Share your experience with your small-group facilitator, someone in your group, your pastor, or a trusted Christian friend. To grow in your new life in Christ, continue to cultivate this new relationship through reading the Bible, through a regular time of talking to God in prayer, and through fellowship with other Bible-believing Christians in a church near your home. Welcome to God's family!

LEADER GUIDE

by Daryl Eldridge

This leader guide will help you facilitate an introductory session and five group sessions for the study of *The Prayer of Jesus*. Group sessions are designed for 50 minutes to 1 hour in length.

If you feel led to introduce this prayer strategy in your church, and you are not a staff member, share the book with your pastor and secure his support.

Complete the activities listed under "Before the Session" for each week. After each session, evaluate the time together. Call members who were absent or need individual attention.

This is an excellent church-based small group study or groups can also be established at your home or at work. Ask God to give you ideas for ways to study this book with others.

Use in a Small Group

• Obtain a copy of *The Prayer of Jesus* for each participant. Your church might want to obtain several copies for those who cannot afford to buy a copy.

• Purchase *The Prayer of Jesus Leader Kit* which contains the videos for each session.

• Groups may study the material over a period of six weeks or in a retreat setting.

• During the study, form prayer partners or triplets that commit to meet on a regular basis, either in person or by phone. Prayer partners should usually be of the same sex, because prayer develops great intimacy. Exceptions would be a married couple or a parent and child. Even an engaged couple may want to consider teaming with another person or couple.

• When you meet for prayer, begin by reviewing your entries on your prayer journal sheet at the beginning of each week's study. It will take time to develop the intimacy required to share triumphs and failures. This will come as you develop trust in your prayer partner(s). Covenant together that things shared will be held in confidence unless permission is given to share them with a larger audience.

Use as a Family

Many families struggle with family devotions and prayer times because they don't have a consistent theme to give them structure. I would suggest that you use *The Prayer of Jesus* as a devotional study. Work through each of the five chapters. Explore various biblical themes such as what it means to call God "Father." Talk about God's attributes and how we can trust Him for our daily needs. Discuss what it means to participate in the kingdom of God, how to receive and give forgiveness, and how to experience victory over evil.

After you use the outline of the book for devotional study, use one of the kingdom accountability questions on page 5 to guide your prayer time each week.

Use in an Accountability Group

The Prayer of Jesus is designed as a small group study. When the study concludes, it can have an even greater impact when used as an accountability strategy. Remember that the pronouns used in this prayer are plural, reminding us of our relationship to other believers. If you form or continue as an accountability group, use the seven kingdom accountability questions on page 5 as a guide for discussion and prayer.

In addition, this study can be used by accountability partners. Participants will continue to use the journaling approach but now will have the opportunity to discuss their progress with an accountability partner.

Suggest that partners meet on a regular basis, preferably weekly. This can be accomplished over the phone or the Internet if the situation requires it, but a personal meeting is most effective. Partners may choose to use the accountability questions on page 5 as a guide for their time together.

INTRODUCTORY SESSION

Before the Session

1. Set up the room with a TV/VCR, chairs arranged in semicircles of 3-5 chairs or chairs around tables, and a markerboard in a place where all participants can see it.

2. Prepare a table with a sign-in sheet, pens and markers, blank paper, name tags, and copies of *The Prayer of Jesus* member workbook.

3. Watch the video and complete the viewer guide on page 13. Read the introduction and complete the activities (pages 7-11).

During the Session

1. As participants arrive, ask them to sign-in. Give participants a copy of *The Prayer of Jesus* workbook. Collect money if they are to pay for their books. Ask participants to fill out a name tag and wear it on their clothing.

2. Welcome participants to this study of *The Prayer of Jesus*. Introduce yourself, giving a brief testimony of your struggles with prayer and your desire to know how to pray more effectively. Open in prayer, asking God to teach you how to allow the prayer of Jesus to change your life.

3. Ask members to introduce themselves and share what interested them in this study.

4. Ask, *If you needed a car repair, would you like to go to a master mechanic? If you needed heart surgery, would you want the world's best surgeon to perform the operation?* Make the analogy to learning to pray effectively. *Would you like to be taught by the Master?* Explain that few Christians were taught how to pray when they became believers. Say, *You may not have grown up in a family that prayed regularly or had parents who modeled a dynamic prayer life. You may even feel uncomfortable about praying. This study will help you grow in your prayer life.*

5. Show the introductory video. Encourage members to take notes on the viewer guide on page 13 in their workbooks. If they are attending this first session to determine if they want to participate in the study, ask them not to write in their workbooks. Encourage them to take notes on the paper you provided on the entry table.

6. Ask volunteers to share what they wrote on their viewer guide. (Answers are given on the video.)

7. Ask, *From watching the video, what are some reasons for studying The Prayer of Jesus?* Write responses on the markerboard.

8. Form small groups of 3-5 members to answer these questions: (1) How did you learn to pray? (p. 9), (2) Who do you know whose prayer life exhibits a deep intimacy with God? (p. 11), and (3) Why do you think this person has such a meaningful prayer life? (p. 11).

9. When small groups have completed their assignment, ask them to read the introduction and week 1 for the next session. Remind participants to complete the learning activities. Encourage them to use each week's prayer journal page to record group and individual prayer requests as well as insights they are gaining from the study.

10. Close in prayer by reciting together the prayer by Andrew Murray found on the bottom of page 12. Ask participants to enroll in "The School of the Prayer of Jesus" by signing their names below the prayer in their workbooks.

WEEK ONE

Before the Session

1. Set up the room with a TV/VCR. Arrange chairs in semicircles of 3-5 chairs or chairs around tables for small group activities.

2. Prepare a table with a sign-in sheet, pens and markers, blank paper, name tags, and copies of *The Prayer of Jesus* member workbook for people who weren't present last week. Continue to collect money from participants for the books.

3. If using the alternate activities, secure videotapes of *Sister Act* and *The Amazing Adventures of Mr. Bean, Volume 1*. Cue each tape at the proper starting place.

4. Watch the video for this study and complete the viewer guide on page 31. Read week 1 and complete the learning activities.

During the Session

1. Welcome members and introduce newcomers to the group. Ask, *What does this expression mean: "You can talk till you're blue in the face"?* (Possible answer: you are talking, but you're not getting through.) Say, *Sometimes our prayer lives can feel like we're expending a lot of effort without much effect. The purpose of this study is not simply to understand the Prayer of Jesus but to learn how to pray in such a way that you will experience the presence of God.* Express your excitement about their participation. Open in prayer, asking the Lord to be your teacher during this session.

Alternate activity: Play the video clip from *Sister Act*. Use the segment in which Sister Mary Clarence (Whoopi Goldberg) says grace over her first meal with the nuns at the convent. Ask, *Have you ever had difficulty finding the right words to say in a prayer?* Ask volunteers to share an awkward public prayer experience. Point out that in today's

session, we will review the causes of ineffective prayer and how we can experience God through our prayers.

2. Show the session 1 video. Encourage members to take notes on the viewer guide on page 31. Then, ask volunteers to call out what they wrote on their viewer guides.

3. Ask, *What is the main purpose of prayer?* (to spend time with the Father.) Ask, *How does the Prayer of Jesus change your expectations of prayer?*

4. Explain that instead of phantom prayers, the Lord desires that we pray without ceasing. Invite volunteers to read the following Scriptures: Luke 6:12; Acts 1:14; Romans 1:9-10; and 1 Thessalonians 5:16-17.

5. Ask small groups to discuss these two questions: *Why do you think many Christians fail to pray? How can the Lord's Prayer become a continuous prayer in your life?*

6. Ask a volunteer to tell the opposite of phony prayer (powerful prayer). Ask, *What did you learn this week about Jesus' prayer life?* Refer them to the activity on p. 23.

7. Ask for the opposite of frivolous prayer (fervent prayer). Read Hebrews 11:6. Ask, *What is the action God wants from us?* (to seek the Lord).

Alternative activity: Show the video clip from *The Amazing Adventures of Mr. Bean, Volume 1*. Use the segment from "Mr. Bean Goes to Church." Select a portion of the church scene in which Mr. Bean falls asleep. Ask, *Can you identify with Mr. Bean?* Read Mark 14:37-41. Then say, *Even the first disciples, who trained at Jesus' feet, had a hard time staying awake while they prayed.*

8. Ask small groups to discuss the answers to the learning activities on page 28 and to pray for those persons with whom they could share the Lord's Prayer.

9. Remind the class to read and complete the activities in week 2 before next week's session.

WEEK TWO

Before the Session

1. Set up the room with a TV/VCR. Arrange chairs in semicircles of 3-5 chairs or chairs around tables for small group activities.

2. Obtain a recent version of a world globe.

3. Enlist a person to lead the group in singing the praise chorus, "Glorify Thy Name."

4. Watch the video and complete the viewer guide on page 49. Read week 2 and complete the learning activities.

During the Session

1. Welcome participants and introduce newcomers. Ask, *Has anyone traced your ancestry? How far back have you traced your roots? Where did your family come from?* Then say, *As believers in Christ, we all trace our spiritual heritage to the same Father. Today we will discover how our relationship as God's children can transform our prayer lives.*

2. Open in prayer.

3. Show the session 2 video. Encourage members to take notes on the viewer guide on page 49. Then, ask volunteers to call out what they wrote on their viewer guides.

4. Explain, *In our culture we value individualism. The first word in the Prayer of Jesus reminds us that we are part of a broader community of faith—the family of God. As we pray for our needs, we must include the needs of our brothers and sisters.* Call for one or more volunteers to come to the globe, spin it, and then place his or her finger on a part of the globe. After a country is identified, ask for a volunteer to pray for that country's people, government leaders, church leaders, and Christian witness.

Alternative activity: If your church has a weekly prayer ministry list, use it to pray for the needs of your church members. Obtain mission magazines from your church or denomination and identify in those resources prayer needs of Christians around the world.

5. Give an illustration from your personal experience of how your Heavenly Father has demonstrated His love for you. Ask for personal testimonies of how God has recently demonstrated His love as a Heavenly Father.

6. Ask small groups to discuss this question: *Imagine that God has invited you to sit in His lap. Feel His arms around you. How would you feel? What would you talk about?* (p. 42). After several minutes of discussion, ask groups to pray and thank their Heavenly Father for adopting them into His family and calling them His children.

7. Explain, *While our Heavenly Father desires an intimate relationship with us, we must also acknowledge that He is Lord of the universe. There is no one like God. He is Sovereign. He is Holy.* Ask participants to state names for God that are mentioned in the workbook such as *El Shaddai, Jehovah Shammah,* or *Adonai* (p. 46). Ask, *What did you learn this week about our Heavenly Father?*

8. Tell participants that if they do not have a personal relationship with God, you desire to share with them how they can know Him. Refer them to page 103, and invite them to talk to you after the session. Close in prayer or sing "Glorify Thy Name" as a prayer.

9. Remind the class to read and complete the activities in week 3 before next week's session.

WEEK THREE

Before the Session

1. Set up the room in the usual way.

2. On index cards or small pieces of paper make a copy of the following questions for every small group for the ice breaker activity: Were you ever a member of a team? Did you have uniforms? What was expected of the team in terms of your public behavior? How could the inappropriate actions of a few teammates bring dishonor to the entire team?

3. Cut slips of paper (approx. 1" x 4"). Prepare 1 or more slips for each member. Obtain a container such as a bowl or basket for each small group.

4. Enlist a person(s) to lead in singing, "Holy, Holy, Holy" and "I Surrender All."

5. Watch the video and complete the viewer guide on page 67. Read week 3 and complete the learning activities.

During the Session

1. Ask a volunteer how he or she uses the prayer journal page each week or to share a testimony about how God is using the study to deepen his or her prayer life. Open with prayer.

2. Hand each small group a copy of the ice breaker activity. After several minutes of sharing, say, *In a similar way our speech and actions can bring dishonor to God's name.*

3. Show the week 3 video. Encourage members to take notes on the viewer guide on page 67. Ask volunteers to share what they wrote.

4. Explain that the first commitment in Jesus' prayer is to make God's name holy. Discuss this question: *What are ways the church would impact the world if we daily lived, "Holy is your Name"?*

5. Invite participants to voice sentence prayers using the format: *Our Father, Your name is _____.* Ask members to fill in the blank with a characteristic of God or a word of praise. For example, "Your name is perfect." Then lead in singing (or call on the person enlisted to lead) "Holy, Holy, Holy."

6. Ask small groups to discuss the following questions from page 51: *What did you do this week that "hallowed God's name"? What actions, words, or deeds brought reproach on His name? What actions do you need to take in order to make amends?*

7. Say, *The second commitment in the prayer of Jesus is to participate in the advancement of God's kingdom.* Remind them as they pray to list their daily activities and end with the statement "Your kingdom come." For example, "While I'm in line at the bank—Your kingdom come."

8. Give each small group a stack of the slips of paper you prepared before the session as well as one of the containers you gathered. Ask them to write names of persons and ministries of the church on each slip of paper. Place the names in the container. Ask members to draw a slip of paper from the container and pray for the person or ministry listed during the coming week.

Alternate activity (for step 8): Conduct a prayer walk. Send small groups through the church. Ask them to stop outside various areas of the church and pray for the ministries of the church. Areas might include the church office; worship center; children, youth, and adult departments.

9. Say, *The third commitment in the prayer of Jesus is to do the Father's will.* Ask small groups to discuss the following questions: *Did you experience an interruption this week and you prayed, "Your will be done"? Are you facing a decision for which you need to pray for God's will to be revealed?* (p. 51).

10. Ask, *How could three commitments, "Holy is Your name, Your kingdom come, and Your will be done" make a difference in your life this week?* Conclude by reciting the Lord's Prayer or by singing "All to Jesus I Surrender."

11. Remind the class to read and complete the activities in week 4 before next week's session.

WEEK FOUR

Before the Session

1. Set up the room in the usual way.

2. Enlist someone to sing "Whiter than Snow."

3. Have available posterboard or newsprint.

4. Alternate activity: Obtain a CD player and a copy of "I've Got You Covered," by Christian artists Phillips, Craig & Dean on their CD *Restoration.*

5. Watch the video and complete the viewer guide on page 85. Read week 4 and complete the learning activities.

During the Session

1. Welcome participants. Open with prayer, thanking God for His provisions. Say, *In this session, we will discuss how we can approach God for all our physical, emotional, social, and spiritual needs.*

2. Show the session 4 video. Encourage members to take notes on the viewer guide on page 85. Ask volunteers to call out what they wrote on their viewer guides.

3. Explain, *The first request in the prayer of Jesus is for daily bread. God wants to provide for our physical needs.* Ask small groups to discuss the following questions: *What is God teaching you about relying on Him for daily provisions? How has God demonstrated recently that He cares about the most ordinary matters in your life?* (p. 74).

4. In small groups, ask members to list on posterboard or newsprint provisions they need from God this coming week. Allow groups to compare lists. Remind members that we are not to pray for our personal needs without remembering the needs of others. There are millions in our world who go to sleep hungry and others who are homeless. Lead a prayer for the needs of third world countries.

5. Explain, *The second request in the Lord's Prayer is for forgiveness.* Read Matthew 5:23-24. Ask, *How does this passage apply to forgiveness?* (Possible answer: Before we ask God to forgive us, we reconcile our relationship with others whom we have not forgiven.) Say, *Some translations of the Lord's Prayer read, "Forgive us our debts, as we have already forgiven our debtors."* Ask participants to silently name the person (or persons) they need to forgive (p. 81). Encourage them to take steps to express their forgiveness. Say, *Because of the grace that has been spilled out on us, we can forgive others.*

6. Ask, *How does sin affect your relationship with God and others?* (Possible answer: It creates an emotional, social, and spiritual break in our relationships.) Have a time of silent prayer, asking participants to confess their sins and to pray for God's forgiveness. After a few minutes, sing "Whiter than Snow."

7. Explain, *The third request in the Lord's Prayer concerns temptation.* Read James 1:13-15. Reinforce the idea that "Lead us not into temptation," is a cry for help from God. It is a request that God would keep us from places and situations in which we would be vulnerable. Read God's promise in 1 John 4:4.

8. Ask small groups participants to pray for leaders of your church who need God's protection from temptation. Pray that God will keep them close to Him and clean before His sight. Conclude by praying this same prayer for members of the group.

9. Alternate activity: Conclude by playing the song "I've Got You Covered." Say, *God provides for all our needs—body, soul, and spirit. God provides for our past—forgiveness of every sin we've committed. God provides for our present—our daily food. God provides for our future—deliverance from each coming temptation. We can live a worry-free life and have a clean conscience because our Father has us covered.*

10. Remind the class to read and complete the activities in week 5 before next week's session.

WEEK FIVE

Before the Session

1. Set up the room in the usual way.

2. Obtain a mirror and a flashlight.

3. Enlist someone to lead in praise choruses.

4. If using the alternative activity, obtain the videotape *Chariots of Fire* and cue up the scene described on page 110.

5. Watch the video and complete the viewer guide on page 102. Read week 5 and complete the learning activities.

During the Session

1. Welcome participants to this concluding session. Ask small groups to discuss this question: *What have you experienced in nature that made you awe-struck by the glory and power of the Creator?* (Example: Grand Canyon, mountains, ocean).

2. Say, *Let's pause and focus our attention on the God of the universe. Let's invite His presence and worship Him.* Lead in prayer. Praise God for His awesome power. Praise Him for being *Elohim,* Powerful God. Acknowledge His presence. Lead or ask for a volunteer to lead a worship chorus such as "Majesty," "Shout to the Lord," or "Blessed be the Lord God Almighty." Say, *In this session, we will examine the benediction of the Prayer of Jesus: God's kingdom, power, and glory.*

3. Show the session 5 video. Encourage members to take notes on the viewer guide on page 102. Ask volunteers to call out what they wrote on their viewer guide.

4. Ask small groups to discuss the following question: *What difference will it make in your daily activities if you remind yourself that everything should be done to advance God's kingdom, in His power, and for His glory?* (p. 89).

5. Read Matthew 6:19-21. Share, *When we acknowledge God as our total source of supply, we don't have to be anxious about our world. We can invest our time and energy in His kingdom knowing that God will take care of us.* Ask participants to discuss in small groups the following question: *What is God calling you to do to advance His kingdom?* (p. 92). Ask participants to pray for one another to allow God to use them to advance His kingdom. To bring the prayers to a close, lead in singing the chorus, "Seek Ye First the Kingdom of God."

6. Ask, *How did God demonstrate His strength and power in your life this week?* Call for testimonies.

7. Acknowledge that many of us are currently facing situations, circumstances, or events that require God's supernatural power. In pairs or triads, ask participants to share something they are experiencing in which they feel completely powerless, such as a loss of a job, finances, divorce, illness, or loss of a family member (p. 93). Ask them to call on the name of *El Elyon,* God Most High to provide them with the power to deal with these circumstances.

8. Give someone a strong flashlight. Hold a mirror. Ask the person with the flashlight to turn it on and point it at the mirror. Reflect the light to a wall. Ask, *How is this an example of our involvement in God's glory?* (Answer: We are to reflect God's glory to the world, and as we receive glory from others we should reflect it to God.)

9. Read 1 Corinthians 10:31. Ask, *How can ordinary things be done in such a way that they bring God glory?* Ask participants to select an activity they will complete in the coming week and discuss in their small groups how that activity could be done in such a way that God is glorified.

10. Alternative activity: Play the following scene from *Chariots of Fire*—Eric Liddell takes a walk with his sister, Jennie. Eric tells her he is going to China as a missionary, but first he must run in the Olympics. He says, "I believe that God made me for a purpose—for China. He also made me fast. And when I run I feel His pleasure. To give it up would be to hold Him in contempt. To win is to honor Him." Direct the participants to discuss the following questions in their small groups: *In what activity do you feel His pleasure?* and *What would you like to do to glorify Him?*

11. Ask, *How has this study changed your prayer life?* Ask members to share their testimonies.

12. Ask those who want to continue as a prayer or accountability group, or with a prayer or accountability partner(s) to contact you after the session.

13. Explain the use of this study for a family (see page 104).

14. Conclude by singing "The Lord's Prayer" or reciting it together.

After the Study

Follow up with those who want to continue learning to pray like Jesus with prayer or accountability partners. Use the suggestions on pages 104-105 for forming prayer and accountability relationships.